Geography of Travel & Tourism

Geography of Travel & Tourism

Third Edition

Lloyd E. Hudman
Richard H. Jackson

Delmar Publishers

an International Thomson Publishing company

Albany • Bonn • Boston • Cincinnati • Detroit • London • Madrid
Melbourne • Mexico City • New York • Pacific Grove • Paris • San Francisco
Singapore • Tokyo • Toronto • Washington

NOTICE TO THE READER

Publisher does not warrant or guarantee any of the products described herein or perform any independent analysis in connection with any of the product information contained herein. Publisher does not assume, and expressly disclaims, any obligation to obtain and include information other than that provided to it by the manufacturer.

The reader is expressly warned to consider and adopt all safety precautions that might be indicated by the activities described herein and to avoid all potential hazards. By following the instructions contained herein, the reader willingly assumes all risks in connection with such instructions.

The publisher makes no representations or warranties of any kind, including but not limited to, the warranties of fitness for a particular purpose or merchantability, nor are any such representations implied with respect to the material set forth herein, and the publisher takes no responsibility with respect to such material. The publisher shall not be liable for any special, consequential or exemplary damages resulting, in whole or in part, from the readers' use of, or reliance upon, this material.

Cover Design: Joseph Villanova

Delmar staff:
Publisher: Susan Simpfenderfer
Acquisitions Editor: Jeff Burnham
Acting Developmental Editor: Judy Roberts
Production Manager: Wendy Troeger
Production Editor: Elaine Scull
Marketing Manager: Katherine M. Hans

COPYRIGHT © 1999
By Delmar Publishers
an International Thomson Publishing company I(T)P®

The ITP logo is a trademark under license
Printed in the United States of America

For more information contact:

Delmar Publishers
3 Columbia Circle, Box 15015
Albany, New York 12212-5015

International Thomson Publishing Europe
Berkshire House
168-173 High Holborn
London, WC1V7AA
United Kingdom

Nelson ITP, Australia
102 Dodds Street
South Melbourne
Victoria, 3205 Australia

Nelson Canada
1120 Birchmont Road
Scarborough, Ontario
M1K 5G4, Canada

International Thomson Publishing France
Tour Maine-Montparnasse
33 Avenue du Maine
75755 Paris Cedex 15, France

International Thomson Editores
Seneca 53
Colonia Polanco
11560 Mexico D.F. Mexico

International Thomson Publishing GmbH
Königswinterer Strasße 418
53227 Bonn
Germany

International Thomson Publishing Asia
60 Albert Street
#15-01 Albert Complex
Singapore 189969

International Thomson Publishing Japan
Hirakawa-cho Kyowa Building, 3F
2-2-1 Hirakawa-cho, Chiyoda-ku
Tokyo 102, Japan

ITE Spain/Paraninfo
Calle Magallanes, 25
28015-Madrid, España

2 3 4 5 6 7 8 9 10 XXX 04 03 02 01 00 99 98

ISBN 0-7668-0371-6

Library of Congress Cataloging-in-Publication Data
Hudman, Lloyd E.
   Geography of travel and tourism / Lloyd E. Hudman, Richard H.
Jackson.—3rd e.
      p. cm.
Includes bibliographical references and index.
ISBN 0-7668-0371-6
1. Tourist trade. 2. Travel. 3. Geography. I. Jackson, Richard
H., 1941– . II. Title.
G155.A1H814 1998
   338.4′791—dc21
                                      98-20531
                                        CIP

Delmar Publishers is pleased to offer the following books on
HOSPITALITY, TRAVEL AND TOURISM

- **Catering & Convention Services**
  Ahmed Ismail

- **Conducting Tours, 2E**
  Marc Mancini

- **Destination: North America**
  Dawne M. Flammger

- **Dining Room and Banquet Management, 2E**
  Anthony Strianese

- **Domestic Ticketing and Airfare**
  Linda Hood

- **Geography of Travel & Tourism, 3E**
  Lloyd Hudman and Richard Jackson

- **Hospitality and Travel Marketing, 2E**
  Alastair Morrison

- **Hosting the Disabled: Crossing Communications Barriers Group Travel, 2E**
  Martha Sarbey deSouto

- **Hotel, Restaurant and Travel Law, 5E**
  Norman Cournoyer, Anthony G. Marshall, and Karen Morris

- **Hotel Sales & Operations**
  Ahmed Ismail

- **International Air Fares Construction and Ticketing**
  Helle Sorensen

- **International Travel and Tourism**
  Helle Sorensen

- **Introduction to Corporate Travel**
  Annette Reiff

- **Learning Apollo: Basic and Advanced Training**
  Talula Austine Gunter

- **Marketing & Selling the Travel Product, 2E**
  James Burke and Barry Resnick

- **Math Principles for Food Service Occupations, 3E**
  Robert Haines

- **Passport: An Introduction to Travel & Tourism, 2E**
  David Howell

- **Practical Food & Beverage Cost Control**
  Clement Ojugo

- **Practical Guide to Fares and Ticketing, 2E**
  Jeanne Semer-Purzycki

- **Sabre Reservations: Basic and Advanced Training**
  Gerald Capwell and Barry Resnick

- **Selling Destinations: Geography for the Travel Professional**
  Marc Mancini

- **Travel Agency Management**
  Gerald Fuller

- **Travel Perspectives: A Guide to Becoming a Travel Agent, 2E**
  Susan Rice and Ginger Todd

- **Welcome to Hospitality: An Introduction**
  Dr. Kye-Sung (Kaye) Chon and Dr. Ray Sparrowe

Delmar, At Your Service!

Delmar Publishers
an International Thomson Publishing company I(T)P®

Contents

Chapter 5   Geography and Tourism in South America   145

Chapter 6   Geography and Tourism in Western Europe   173

Chapter 7   Geography and Tourism in Northern Europe   207

Chapter 8   Geography and Tourism in Southern Europe   227

Chapter 9   Geography and Tourism in Central Europe and the Balkan States   253

Chapter 10   Geography and Tourism in Russia and the Countries of the Former Soviet Union   279

Chapter 11   Geography and Tourism in the Middle East and North Africa   323

Chapter 12   Geography and Tourism in Subsaharan Africa   357

Chapter 13   Geography and Tourism in East Asia   381

Chapter 14   Geography and Tourism in South and Southeast Asia   415

Chapter 15   Geography and Tourism in Australia, New Zealand, and the Islands of the South Pacific   457

Preface

Tourism is one of the leading industries in the world today. For some countries and regions, it is the primary economic activity. The traditional areas of tourist destinations, such as beaches, theme parks, winter ski areas, and cultural attractions, continue to attract millions of visitors. At the same time, new areas or nontraditional destinations are becoming important. One growth area is destinations involved in ecotourism. The primary factor that attracts tourists is geography. Whether it is the combination of climate and landforms as in sea-and-ski areas, such as the Alps or the Mediterranean, or cultural-historical geography as in Paris or China, the geographic factors that combine to give character to a place are what attracts the tourist. If the geography of the world were uniform, there would be no incentive to travel. Since each place on the face of the earth is different from all others, however, people will always have a desire to see what other places are like.

This text is designed to provide students and professionals of the field of tourism and interested readers a working knowledge of the geography of the world as it relates to tourism. The text provides a basic geographic overview of the world and each major geographic region to provide insights about the geographic character that comprises the setting for tourism to a specific region. All regions or countries have a brief overview of the cultural, physical, and tourism characteristics of the region or country. The cultural characteristics are in the form of cultural capsules pertaining to the people and some tips as to personal actions that are acceptable and others to be avoided. While it is difficult to provide geographic depth, readers should be able to obtain their own perception of each tourist destination region in terms of its geographic and tourism characteristics.

The text also provides a basic understanding of world travel patterns, including the origin, characteristics, numbers, and seasonality of travel to a particular region. The regional patterns illustrate how travel and tourism themselves contribute to the geography of each region. Understanding the characteristics of tourism to a specific region allows agents to inform clients about the trips and numbers of other tourists they can expect in the region. The general patterns of world and regional travel change only slowly, although dramatic events, such as wars, terrorism, and environmental disasters, can have a short-term impact. A basic understanding of the world and regional travel patterns combined with the travel updates available to professionals that indicate temporary fluctuations in those patterns will allow the travel professional to accurately counsel clients. The most comprehensive set of data is compiled by the World Tourism Organization, and the most recent edition of tourism statistics used was 1996, unless otherwise indicated. The data and discussion of the data illustrate trends and interconnections between origins and destinations.

FEATURES

The text also introduces and describes the major attractions in each area. The intention of this introduction is not to provide an encyclopedic or exhaustive listing, but to give an overview of the character of a tourist destination region. By understanding the major attractions of a destination, students and professionals will be able to develop their own mental map of destinations, a mental map sufficient to guide clients to the travel region of interest to them.

Readers will develop an understanding of the interrelationships between geography and tourism, including a comprehensive understanding of the character of major regions of the world.

Vignettes have been included to provide insights about the interrelationships between geography and tourism in each region. These vignettes describe the region from the tourist's view and further enhance the knowledge about each region.

Each chapter details a specific tourist region and concludes with an itinerary that provides further in-depth discussion of the attractions typically included in an itinerary to that region. The purpose of the itineraries is to provide additional knowledge of the region.

The key terms and words listed at the beginning of each chapter are terms and words important to understanding that region. While some are explained in the context of the chapter, others are used in a sentence assuming the reader understands the word. If the reader is unfamiliar with the term, all terms and words listed are defined in the glossary.

The increasing importance of the Internet in the travel industry has prompted inclusion of Internet addresses. These addresses include embassies, travel resources, geographic data on climate, population, and other web sites useful in the travel industry. Access to the Internet is not required, but is an additional tool that the user of this text will find useful.

An 8-page color atlas insert has been included for easy reference.

It is intended that any suggested activities and classroom assignments also use an atlas and other reference material to expand their use of resources and understanding of the various countries and regions of the world.

ACKNOWLEDGMENTS

We wish to express our appreciation to the staff of Delmar Publishers, who have provided guidance and assistance in the preparation of the manuscript, especially Judy Roberts, who also worked closely with us on this revision. The reviewer's critical comments were helpful and thoughtful.

Reviewers
David Schoenberg, Ph.D.
Fiorello H. LaGuardia Community College
Long Island City, N.Y.

Kathleen Swinney
Shelton State College
Tuscaloosa, Ala.

Elizabeth O'Donnell, CTC
Edmonds Community College
Lynnwood, Wash.

Beth Weatherford
Columbus Para-Professional Institute
Columbus, Ohio

Tim Becker, Ph.D.
Point Loma Nazarene College
San Diego, Calif.

John C. Kesler, Ph.D.
Lakeland Community College
Cleveland, Ohio

Sherry A. Hine, CTC, ACC
Mid-Florida Technical Institute
Orlando, Fla.

The cartography work was accomplished by Jeff Bird, the staff cartographer of the Department of Geography, Brigham Young University. Many of the individual country maps are from the *CIA World Fact Book*.

To these and all others who have been involved in the production of this volume, we express our gratitude.

Lloyd E. Hudman
Richard H. Jackson

About the Authors

Lloyd Hudman is the coordinator for the tourism program and a professor in the Department of Geography at Brigham Young University. He has taught classes in tourism and geography at Brigham Young for the past 25 years.

He received his B.S. degree from the University of Utah and his M.S. and Ph.D. degrees from the University of Kansas. He belongs to the International Association of Scientific Experts in Tourism, the Travel and Tourism Research Association, the Association of American Geographers, and the International Geographic Union Commission on Tourism and Recreation.

He has traveled extensively and has led university study-abroad programs to London, Madrid, Europe, and the Middle East. He is also the author of six books and numerous articles on tourism.

Richard H. Jackson is a professor of geography at Brigham Young University, where he teaches courses on geography and culture, Russia, Eastern Europe, and North America. He combines his background in geography with experience in living, studying, teaching, and travelling in many parts of the world. He has taught courses to students in the tourism major for nearly twenty-five years.

He received his Ph.D. degree from Clark University in Worcester, Massachusetts, in 1970. He is the author or co-author of several textbooks on geography and tourism and has written nearly one hundred scholarly articles and reports. He has led student study-abroad experiences in Europe and Russia, has lectured on cruise ships in the Baltic and Russia, and has developed lectures and student activities on tourism for North America, Europe, and the new countries created from the former Soviet Union.

GEOGRAPHY AND TOURISM:
The Attraction of Place

*For my part I travel not to go anywhere,
but to go. I travel for travel's sake.
   The great affair is to move.*
                              Robert Louis Stevenson

People have always traveled. Curiosity, a basic characteristic of humans, has led people of all eras to explore new environments, seek new places, discover the unknown, search for different and strange places, and enjoy other experiences. This suggests that one *place* is different from another place, or there would be no curiosity about other places. The *National Geographic* magazine, for example, is considered one of the truly fine magazines in the world today. It adorns many libraries, public and private. Its primary goal is to illustrate the differences that characterize the world's variety of places. Its popularity reflects people's curiosity about other places and cultures.

While people have always traveled, tourism as we know it today is a recent phenomenon. It has only been since World War II that tourism, particularly international tourism, has developed as a major activity in the world. Early travel and early tourism were reserved for the rich or the very brave. One important impetus for tourism was that World War II brought many people in contact with other people and places. People became more interested in the world. They realized that the events in one part of the world have an important impact on residents in another part of the world.

Growth and change in modes of *transportation* have also encouraged travel. Replacement of transatlantic ships by airplanes was followed by the jet age from the 1960s to today. Fast, cheap transportation has made world travel a possibility for millions of people.

There are well-developed links between tourism and geography, in that the uniqueness of a place (whether it be an Indian periodic market, a tremendous waterfall, a snowy mountain village, or a resort on a sunny, sandy coast) is the result of the geographic relationships at that place. *Geography* is the study of the earth as the home of humans. It is concerned with the combination of factors that makes each individual place on the face of the earth somehow unique. Study of geography represents an attempt to gain an understanding of what makes each place unique. Uniqueness results from the combination of the nat-

—*Courtesy Bermuda Department of Tourism*

Figure 1-1 Hamilton Beach, Bermuda

ural (or physical) setting of *climate, landforms,* and resources, and the cultural phenomena created by the residents of that place such as buildings, economy, dress styles, religion, and political or other cultural features. The combination of physical and cultural factors that make each place different is the stimulus for human curiosity about other places, which causes the growth and development of tourism.

The process of tourism itself also contributes to the uniqueness of place. Every place on the earth's surface changes over time. Changes in economy, political organizations, culture, population, and the physical *environment* constantly alter the texture and fabric of the complex mosaic that makes up a place. The impact of large numbers of visitors from another place for even a short period of time will affect the visited place, changing its uniqueness, and creating a new and different cultural, political, economic, and physical landscape. Thus, geography and tourism are interrelated in two ways. First, the uniqueness of place creates an attraction. Second, tourism is an agent of change, becoming an element in the uniqueness of place and an important variable in geographic studies.

THE ELEMENTS OF GEOGRAPHY

Location

A fundamental aspect of geography that directly affects tourism is the need for measuring and indicating exact *locations* on the earth. The grid of lines on a map represents the fundamental tool for describing location. The parallel lines extending east and west measure *latitude* north and south of the equator. Latitude is an indicator of how far north or south of the equator a given point is situated. Latitude is measured in degrees of arc from the equator (0 degrees) toward either pole, where the value reaches 90 degrees. All points north of the equator are in the northern *hemisphere* and are designated as north latitude. All points south of the equator are in the southern hemisphere and are designated as south latitude. These parallel lines (latitudes) are intersected by lines, called *meridians,* extending north and south. Meridians are not parallel, because each of them originates and terminates at the poles; therefore, they converge toward the poles and are most widely separated at the equator. Meridians measure *longitude.* One meridian was chosen as the base point

Figure 1-2 Rio de Janeiro

of reference, or the *prime meridian*. The prime meridian was established as the longitude of the Royal Observatory at Greenwich near London by the British. The British also developed the first accurate system for measuring longitude. *Longitude* is a measure of a point eastward or westward with respect to the prime meridian of Greenwich. Since the earth is circular, it has 360 degrees of longitude.

Any place can be identified by its latitude and longitude. For example, 40 degrees north latitude, 116 degrees east longitude identifies Beijing, China. The degrees are further subdivided into minutes and seconds for greater accuracy. Therefore, any location may be stated in degrees, minutes, and seconds east or west longitude and north or south latitude. This method makes it possible to identify a location to within a few yards.

The world can be divided into hemispheres (halves) in two ways: northern-southern and eastern-western. The northern-southern hemisphere divides the world at the equator, with all *parallels* of north latitude in the northern hemisphere and all parallels of south latitude in the southern hemisphere. The

eastern-western division originates from Greenwich. The eastern hemisphere includes all meridians of east longitude from 0 degrees to 180 degrees, while the western hemisphere includes all meridians of west longitude.

Time

World time is understood in relation to longitudinal location. East of Greenwich 180 degrees and west of Greenwich 180 degrees are, of course, the same thing. Here, another meridian separates east and west, marking the change in time from one day to another because of the rotation of the earth.

The meridian marking the change of date at 180 degrees is called the *international date line*. Traveling eastward from one *time zone* to another, clocks are advanced one hour in each time zone, until reaching the line of 180 degrees of longitude, where the day changes to the preceding day. Traveling westward, the opposite occurs; at 180 degrees west longitude, the date changes to the next day.

The surface of the earth is divided into twenty-four time zones (see the color insert). The time of the initial, or zero, zone begins at the prime meridian at Greenwich. Each succeeding zone is 15 degrees farther from Greenwich. Also, each zone is designated by a number representing the hours (+ or –) by which the zone differs from Greenwich. Therefore, if it is 12:00 N. (noon) in London, it is +5 hours (five hours earlier) in New York. When it is 12:00 N. in London, the time in New York is 7:00 A.M. It will be five more hours before the sun is at the midday location in New York. At the same 12:00 N. time in London, it is –3 hours (three hours later) in Moscow. It is 3 P.M. there when it is noon in London.

Because of the international date line, if it were Wednesday in Los Angeles, California, it would be Thursday in Sydney, Australia. Travelers flying from Sydney to Los Angeles find they arrive in Los Angeles the same day at an earlier local time than when they departed from Sydney (Sydney time) even after a thirteen-hour flight.

THEMES OF GEOGRAPHY

Geography focuses on four principal themes in explaining the world:

- Location
    absolute
    relative
    geographic
- Place and Space
    physical characteristics

climate
vegetation
landforms
human and cultural characteristics
language
food and clothing
political systems and religion
architectural styles
- Movement
- Region
  All are important in understanding tourism.

LOCATION: THE WHERE OF GEOGRAPHY

Absolute Location

Location of places on earth is of special concern to geographers, since location is one of the central elements that contributes to the uniqueness of place. The most obvious aspect is *absolute location*. (Where is it?) Absolute location (also referred to as *site*) identifies each location as a precise point on the earth's surface through use of the mathematical grid system that is measured in latitude and longitude. This locational system is used in orientation and measurement of distance.

Relative Location

Relative location (also referred to as *situation*) examines the location of places with respect to other places to understand interdependence at local, regional, national, and global scales. The relationship or *spatial interaction* between a place and the rest of the world depends on its relative location, its distance from other places, its *accessibility* or isolation, and its potential for contact. Places that have both a desired characteristic, such as a warm winter climate or access to good ocean beaches (known as *sun-sea-sand*), and important cultural attractions near large population centers are conducive to interaction with other places and development as a tourist center. Countries that have a poor location relative to the wealthy industrialized nations of Europe and North America, such as the interior of Africa, or are isolated by either physical or cultural phenomena, have few tourists even though they may have attractive physical or cultural relationships.

Location has been important in all forms of economic development for the various nations of the world. Nations such as Great Britain and Japan, which have excellent connectivity and site characteristics such as educated citizens and a good resource base, have developed a high standard of living. Countries that have a poor relative location from the rest of the world are apt to have a lower standard of living. Locations that are isolated by mountains, deserts, or cultural phenomena such as language have failed to benefit from the technological advances taking place in other areas of the world.

Countries such as Chad, Rwanda, and Burundi, which are located in the interior of Africa and are separated from contact with industrial Europe by physical distance, climate, landform, and culture, lack adequate transportation facilities to assist them in economic development in general or tourism development specifically.

Geographic Location

Geographic location is the combination of absolute location and relative location. Site (absolute location) is a description of the internal characteristics of a place, as opposed to situation (relative location), which looks at the external relationships of a place. Site also includes the absolute mathematical location of a place and the qualities or -attributes at that place. Site features include the number of people living at that place, their ethnic character, their income, and other attributes of their culture. Site also includes the physical characteristics such as landforms, climates, or resources. The word *place* is general and can refer to the site characteristics of a small area, town, city, county, state, region, or country.

The development of tourism at any specific geographic location depends on its site, its situation (reflecting the ease—usually expressed in time and money—with which a potential tourist can travel to that place), and its relationship to other attractions. More people visit Paris than Oslo because Paris is more accessible and because of the nature and extent of attractions in each city and in surrounding areas. Paris has a central location that facilitates visits to other European attractions such as London, while Oslo has a peripheral location in Europe. Isolated from the main populated and urban areas of Europe, Oslo is less accessible and has fewer attractions for tourists than Paris.

Another important element in the movement of visitors from one place to another is the *perception* by the potential tourist of other places. People have a tendency to react to the world not as it is, but as they think it is. In other words, the perceived and actual character may not be the same. Perception is formed in a cultural context of human behavior with a background steeped in the traditions, values, and goals of a person or group. The perception of an area can either enhance or deter tourism to that place. Travel advertisements may use the public perception of a place if it is positive, or attempt to create programs to change the perception of the place if it is negative. For example, New York is perceived by many as an unsafe place to visit. This negative view of the city carried over to the state. Realizing this perception, the state adopted the slogan "I Love New York." (This was the origin of all the "I Love ..." slogans that are expressed throughout the country.) The idea was to create positive images in the minds of potential tourists, with the hope that they would consider New York as a vacation destination. Tourism to New York increased following the introduction of this program, reflecting the success of this and other programs designed to develop a more favorable perception of the city and its attractions.

The perception of a place reflects the viewer's understanding of the characteristics that are imagined to represent a specific place. British Air has used America's perception of a typical Englishman to encourage travelers to take British Air when traveling to the United Kingdom. The Englishman used was a rather portly individual, in conservative dress with bowler hat and cane, who had a "dry" sense of humor. Filmed in various backgrounds throughout the United Kingdom familiar to Americans, the representative Briton related reasons to visit the United Kingdom via British Air. The advertising campaign resulted in a reported ten percent increase in travel via British Air.

PLACE AND SPACE: THE WHY OF GEOGRAPHY

All places on earth have distinctive tangible and intangible characteristics that give them meaning and character and distinguish them from other places. Geographers generally describe places by their physical or human characteristics. The physical characteristics are derived from the geological, hydrological, atmospheric, and biological processes that produce landforms, water bodies, climate, soils, natural vegetation, and animal life. Human ideas and actions shape the character of places. Places vary in their population composition as well as in their settlement patterns, architecture, kinds of economic and recreational activities, transportation, communication networks, ideologies, languages, and forms of economic, social, and political organization.

Physical Characteristics of Place

The nature of the physical environment in each place on the surface of the earth affects the ability of humans to live there and influences travel to each place. Three elements of the physical character of place important for tourism are climate, vegetation, and landforms.

Climate

Climate affects the sense of place that characterizes each individual place, regardless of scale, on the earth's surface and the actions of the human residents and visitors to that place. Climate is a major environmental factor that residents or visitors of any site on earth must consider. Whether it be the Eskimo's concern for temperatures and resultant snow quality, the ski resort operator's concern for quality and quantity of winter snow pack, or the farmer's interest in rainfall for crops, climate is involved in a large number of activities of the human population.

Climate is important for tourism for a number of reasons. First, in some cases, climate is an attraction. Locations with warm and sunny winters are in high demand by people from cold, snowy, northern locations. Climates attractive to tourists offer sunny days and weather conducive to enjoying the activity that attracted the tourists. For example, the Alps are a major ski area and naturally need an excellent snow pack, but too many snowy days may reduce the number of tourists. The Alps have many sunny days, which helps the visitors to enjoy skiing the snow-packed mountains.

Climate also affects what is known as an individual's comfort level. The comfort level is related to what geographers call *sensible temperature.* Sensible temperature refers to what our bodies sense the temperature and climate to be, rather than what the climatologist may say it is. Winds and humidity usually are key elements in the comfort level. For example, in winter destinations, windchill is an important consideration. The temperature can feel far below the recorded level if there is a high wind. The opposite is true in tropical areas. The combination of temperature and high humidity can make an area quite uncomfortable. A breeze or slight wind will make a place feel more comfortable. In the Caribbean, the *tropical* climate of many of the islands is moderated by the sea breezes blowing over the islands, creating a more comfortable place than the temperature and humidity would indicate.

The basic climatic controls consist of complex interrelationships between the amount of heat and precipitation received at a place, the landforms, prevailing winds, and land-water relationships. The central element of the climate of a place is caused by the amount of energy from the sun received at that location. The amount of solar energy is a function of the intensity of reflection and absorption of the sun's rays and the duration of time each day that the rays are striking the earth's surface. Consequently, places near the equator, where the sun's rays are concentrated and strike the earth most directly, receive

—*Courtesy Swiss National Tourist Office*

Figure 1-3 St. Moritz

greater solar energy and, therefore, have climates with warm temperatures year-round. In the middle latitudes (from about 30 to 60 degrees north and south of the equator) the amount of solar energy received varies with the seasons, resulting in distinct winter and summer. The high latitudes, north and south of approximately 60 degrees latitude, receive less solar energy and, therefore, have a cooler temperature throughout the year. Thus, latitude becomes one of the fundamental controls of the climate of a place. High latitudes are generally characterized as having cold winters and cool summers; low latitudes are warm to hot all year round; and the mid-latitudes have distinctive seasonal changes.

There are other elements besides latitude and related solar energy affecting climate. One important characteristic affecting climate is referred to as *continentality*. Land masses heat more rapidly in summer and cool more rapidly in winter than water. The climatic contrasts between locations near large bodies of water and those in the center of continents result in part from these different characteristics of land and water. Coastal areas, particularly those on the western side of the middle latitude areas, tend to have narrower

ranges of seasonal temperatures, whereas the interiors of continents in the middle and high latitudes are characterized by great variations in winter and summer temperatures. This is the continental effect, or continentality. This accounts, in part, for the moderate climate of Western Europe. It is surrounded by water, and the warm *current* of the North Atlantic Drift (also known as the Gulf Stream) causes both a narrower range of seasonal temperatures and warmer temperatures than interior locations even though it is near the northern border of the mid-latitudes. Places at the same latitude can have very different climates, depending on whether they have a continental or *maritime* (on the ocean) location. London, for example, is at the same latitude as Hudson's Bay of Canada. London has a winter climate that is generally rainy and cool, but Hudson's Bay has winters with heavy snow and subfreezing temperatures.

The impact of the differing nature of land and water on the climate of the earth is intensified by the earth's prevailing wind system. The middle latitudes, from 30 to 60 degrees north and south latitude, have a prevailing wind system blowing from west to east (the *Westerlies*). It carries air from the oceans eastward over land, creating the moderate climates, with less range of temperatures, on the west coasts of continents discussed previously. The same Westerlies cause the greater climate extremes found in the interior of continents to affect the eastern margins, creating greater seasonal extremes similar to those of interior locations than are found in west coast locations.

Another climatic variable is the amount, duration, and seasonal distribution of precipitation. Precipitation occurs when air that contains water vapor is cooled to the point that it cannot contain all of the moisture in the air. As air rises, it cools. Whether or not clouds and rain result from a rising air mass depends on the temperature and water vapor content of the air mass before it rises.

The amount of precipitation that a place receives depends on the air masses and the source region that influences the amount of water vapor content in the air mass. Air from the Gulf of Mexico is warm and moist, while air from Canada is dry and cold. Certain places on the earth have extremely heavy precipitation, while other large areas receive insufficient precipitation for most common human activities. The great deserts of the world, such as the Sahara, the Gobi, the Atacama, and Death Valley, represent regions in which human occupancy and tourism are handicapped by the high cost of obtaining adequate water supplies. Countries in desert regions can support large populations if they have access to water. For example, in Egypt, the Nile River brings water from a region with abundant moisture to a dry area. Conversely, tropical areas such as the Amazon region of Brazil receive so much rain that lush vegetation and disease have hindered development, including tourism.

A final climatic variable is associated with landforms. Landforms such as mountains may create unique climate characteristics in a place. Higher elevations in mountains have the same effect as higher latitudes, causing cooler climates. Thus, the Alps of France, Switzerland, and Austria have snow when the surrounding lowlands have only rain. Mountains may also prevent moist air from entering a place, causing drier conditions (rainshadow). The highlands of the Andes Mountains of Latin America, or those of Kenya in East Africa, for example, have cooler and less humid climates than are typically experienced in tropical regions.

The World's Climates

The climatic pattern of the world is a complex mosaic resulting from the *interaction* of the climatic variables discussed previously. Various classifications categorize these climates from the equator north and south to the poles. Equatorial areas have hot, humid climates, while polar regions have cold, dry climates. Between these two extremes are the humid climates of the middle latitudes, the desert climates of the world, and all the variations and combinations between.

The most common classification system used to describe the earth's climate is known as the Köppen system. The Köppen system recognizes five major climatic regions, with subdivisions creating eleven distinct climatic types. The major climate types follow:

Tropical Climates. Tropical climates are the humid climates that have no winter season. They are located near the equator. The temperatures are high and rainfall is heavy. The tropical climate is divided into two groups. The climate closest to the equator has rainfall all year (no month with less than two inches of rain) and is called the tropical rainforest. The other tropical climate is called the tropical savanna and has a distinct dry season. Popular tourist areas with tropical rainforest climates are the Hawaiian and other South Pacific islands. Popular tropical savanna destinations include much of the Caribbean; Acapulco, Mexico; Kenya, Africa; and Miami, Florida.

Dry Climates. The dry climates consist of the desert and steppe regions. Deserts are those areas that are very dry, with less than ten inches of rain per year. Steppes are semiarid climates, receiving from eight to sixteen inches of rain per year and having a greater amount of vegetation than the true desert. Some desert locations such as Palm Springs have developed outstanding winter sports. Arizona has become an outstanding winter destination for visitors from the cold, damp north.

Mesothermal Humid Climates. The mesothermal humid climates occupy the middle latitudes. These climates are usually found on the margins of continents in the middle latitudes where the temperatures are either warmer because of the latitude location, such as the southeast, or moderated by the water and winds on the west coasts of continents. Three mesothermal humid climates are recognized: the mediterranean and marine west coast on west coasts, and the humid subtropical on east coasts of the midlatitudes.

The mediterranean is found between 35 and 45 degrees of latitude. It has hot temperatures reaching 100 degrees in the summer, and mild winters, with temperatures rarely dropping below 32 degrees Fahrenheit. The mediterranean climate has dry summers and moist winters, making it an ideal summer tourist

—*Courtesy Finnish Tourist Board*

Figure 1-4   Lake Country, Finland

destination. Mediterranean climates in Southern California and Southern Europe help make them among the most popular tourist destinations in the world.

The marine west coast climate has relatively moderate temperatures all year, with no dry season. London, England; Paris, France; and Seattle, Washington typify the marine west coast climate.

The humid subtropical climate has hot (exceeding 90 degrees Fahrenheit) summers and mild (rarely reaching freezing) winters. It receives between twenty-five and fifty inches of rain yearly and is humid, which affects the comfort level for residents and tourists alike. The fall is the best time to visit places with such climates. The American South—Atlanta, Charleston, Orlando, and other Florida cities—characterize these climates and have an excellent tourist season.

Microthermal Humid Climates. Microthermal humid climates are also in the middle latitudes, but they have cooler winters than the mesothermal humid climates previously described. These are referred to and are more commonly known as the humid continental climates. They occupy the central and eastern portions of large land masses in the middle latitude. Cold, snowy winters alternate with warm (exceeding 80 degrees Fahrenheit), humid summer conditions. Chicago, Moscow, and Beijing are

examples of these climates. Spring and fall are ideal times to visit places in these climates, especially since they have vegetation characterized by mid-latitude forests. The autumn colors in New England typify the beauty of places with a humid continental climate.

Polar Climates. Polar climates include subarctic, tundra, and ice-cap climates. They are not used intensively by humans. Tourism is associated with hunting, fishing, camping, and naturalist-related activities like animal photography. The Arctic and Antarctica are examples of these climates. Tourism is limited and restricted to a very short season.

The climates of the world are illustrated in the color insert. The map is somewhat misleading as it shows distinct lines between regions of different climates. The change from one climate zone or region to another is one of transition, with the line representing the approximate boundary of temperature and precipitation that characterize the climate.

Vegetation

Patterns of vegetation broadly correlate with the patterns of climate. There are variations in vegetation in the broad zones, just as there are variations in climatic specifics from place to place within a climatic zone; but the general pattern of forested, grassland, and arid regions of the world follows the general pattern of temperature and precipitation and combines with landforms to create the character of the natural landscape of a place.

The forests of the earth can be divided into three broad categories. The tropical forests, which grow in areas with tropical rainforest climates, are the most diverse. The variety of species is enormous, and the thickness of the branches and leaves creates a canopy, which limits the amount of solar energy that reaches the surface of the ground. The tropical forest has no cool winter season, so trees grow year-round. This continuous growth creates the greatest amount of *biomass* (vegetative matter) of any region of the earth's surface. The same high temperatures and humid conditions foster the growth of disease organisms and parasites and generally result in health hazards for occupants and tourists of such regions. Animal life in the tropical rainforest is limited to smaller species such as monkeys, snakes, and a host of insects and parasites. The combination of heat, humidity, disease, and lack of attractions limits visitors to tropical rainforest climates to tropical islands or coasts where the climate is moderated by the water and water-related activities are available. The most

Travelers' Challenge: Compelling Antarctica

by Mike Kaplan

I had seen an ad for an Antarctic cruise in an issue of *American Museum of Natural History* magazine. One thing led to another, and I checked into the cruises of the area. The museum's trip appeared to be the best value.

The beauty I saw in South America was outstanding. Visiting Argentina was like being in Europe, and Uruguay is a neat little country; but the poverty in Peru and Paraguay was very discouraging to see.

I boarded ship at Ushuaia, Argentina. The southernmost city in the world, it is on the Beagle Channel. The eight-day cruise was on the M. V. Illiria, which is fully stabilized. . . .

Limited Tourism

We went ashore in zodiacs twice a day to visit abandoned whaling stations, penguins, science stations, and other sights.

Going ashore meant "don't smoke, don't drop anything and don't do anything to change the environment."

Antarctica World Treaty member countries are reviewing the treaty. I suspect there will be new rules about tourism, considering recent pollution.

I think the scientists would like to keep the area to themselves, and I can't blame them.

I visited Palmer, one of the three American stations, where scientific research is done. One project is to see how far and how deep penguins can dive. The station members gave us a tour and treated us to huge chocolate chip cookies.

This was the only place there was any shopping in Antarctica and the frantic shop-'till-we-drop folks loaded up on souvenirs.

Wildlife

I saw penguins—so many, you would not believe— mostly chinstraps, Adelie, and Gentoo. There were a few others.

The penguins were about two feet tall. They appeared very jealous of their nesting sites and I was not allowed to get any closer than about fifteen feet.

If I stood in their path and they approached me, then I could get closer. Thus, I got some good close-up pictures. I would not want to attempt to touch a penguin as they have very powerful beaks.

Other wildlife I saw included seals, sea lions, whales, and birds . . . and more birds. There was snow, ice, glaciers, icebergs, and mountains.

Conditions

I did not have any sunny days and was told that only one day in ten is clear in the Antarctic summer. I was informed that the best time to go is November to February when the average temperature is in the middle thirties. It was not bitterly cold, even with high winds.

What did I enjoy most? The whole experience, even the rough weather. I slept fore and aft and rolled from side to side all night. One night I fell out of bed into my suitcase.

I used the patches that are placed behind the ear to avoid seasickness. Most people wore them, and there were only a few passengers confined to their cabins. They all made it ashore on the zodiacs.

Many of the travelers were professional people, a few were scientific types, but most just wanted to visit the continent. My fellow one hundred nineteen passengers all were very gracious.

The museum staff and cruise line personnel were exceptional; the crew and waiters were well trained. The food was fabulous and the ship immaculate— you could eat off the engine-room floor. . . .

Would I go to Antarctica again? Sure, but I might take an oxygen mask.

Source: International Travel News. Jan. 1992, pp. 32–33.

famous example of a tropical rainforest is the Amazon region of South America.

The *coniferous* (cone-bearing) forests are located in the subarctic climates, marine west coast, and some of the cooler humid continental climates. Coniferous trees have needle-like leaves that generally do not fall in the winter. Major types include the pine, fir, spruce, and larch. Because they tend to occur in single-species stands, some of the major forest resources of the world are coniferous. Their use for tourism is limited. They do provide scenic views in the mountains and coastal areas of Northwestern United States and coastal areas of Alaska.

The *deciduous* forest, composed of such trees as oak, maple, chestnut, elm, or walnut, comprises the third forest type. Deciduous trees lose their leaves during the winter. These trees are highly useful, as many of them have a dense wood (hardwood) that is used in making furniture or other items of value. The New England area is an extremely popular tourist destination in the fall to observe the changing colors of the leaves of trees in these forests. Spring is equally beautiful as many flowering trees (wild cherry, chestnut, and so on) are found in the deciduous forest.

Grasslands are the dominant vegetation type in areas where there is insufficient moisture to support trees. Grassland types include steppes, savannas, and prairies. Steppes represent a transition between humid and arid climates. The typical vegetation of the steppe is short grass, which becomes sparser as one travels from the humid to the arid region. The grasses of the steppes are highly nutritious for grazing animals, and soils in the steppe lands are quite fertile. The steppes are home to nomadic peoples in Africa and Asia, people whose lifestyles are interesting to travelers. The steppes of Mongolia are a popular visit for tourists to China.

The grasslands of the tropical savanna are quite different from those of the steppe. Savannas have tall grasses and are less suited for most domestic animals. The savanna lands are home to the great animal herds of Africa. Zebra, antelope, wildebeest, and a host of others occupy the savannas. Safaris to observe and photograph the animals, Figure 1–5, are a common form of tourism in the savanna.

In areas that are too dry for grass to grow, vegetation that adapts to drought predominates. Drought-resistant (*xerophytic*) vegetation has thick bark, deep roots, water-storing capabilities, or spines to prevent damage to the surface of the plant. All xerophytic vegetation is found in the arid regions of the world in deserts and in the Mediterranean climate regions. Xerophytic vegetation is sparse; depending upon the amount of precipitation, it may range from scattered plants in the Sahara to other luxuriant shrub vegeta-

—*Courtesy South African Tourism Board*

Figure 1-5 Cheetah in Kruger National Park

tion in areas of mediterranean climate such as Southern California. The various forms of cacti are interesting and attractive to visitors to arid regions such as Arizona and Southern California.

In the tundra climatic zone, the temperatures limit growth. Tundra vegetation consists of low shrubs, willows, moss, lichens, and short grass. There is no vegetation in the ice-cap climate.

Landforms: The Character of the Earth

The surface features of a specific place are referred to as *landforms.* The characteristics and combination of landforms at a specific place give character to that place and affect the type of activities and tourism found there. The Alps of Switzerland, the Veldt of South Africa, the Serengeti Plain of Kenya, and the Andes Mountains of Peru are integral parts of the mental image that the name of each country conveys. The combination of landforms in a particular place is referred to as its topography. The seemingly infinite variety of the topography of the earth's surface is an important variable that contributes to the uniqueness of each locale.

Landforms also play an important role in the daily activities of the human residents and visitors to that place. In the past, the Himalayan Mountains of northern India and Tibet handicapped the development of Tibet by isolating this mountain kingdom from the rest of the world. The Himalayas have become an important destination for those desiring to climb and hike through and along the mountain range. By isolating certain regions, landforms such as mountains,

—*Courtesy South African Tourism Corporation*

Figure 1-6 Water buck in South Africa

deserts, and swamps affect economic development, including tourism. The existence of the Sahara served as an effective barrier to African contact with Europeans until late in the nineteenth century. The Sahara still draws few tourists except inveterate travelers who are interested in visiting the scattered oases of the desert or the nomadic people who use the desert for grazing animals (see Figure 1–6).

Mountain areas are often attractive as resorts for people from the crowded plains or lowland areas, which are hot in the summer. The relative location or situation of the mountains is important to the role of the mountains in affecting tourism in a place. The Poconos and the Catskills, which are small mountains, attract millions of vacationers from nearby New York and Philadelphia, while the spectacular Alaskan ranges attract few visitors because of their isolation. Tourists are drawn to those landforms that offer spectacular and unusual vistas.

Landforms are constantly changing. These changes may occur suddenly with catastrophic results, like an earthquake or volcanic eruption, or they may be a slow process, like erosion of the Great Plains of the United States. Catastrophic change can reduce tourism in an area if it is perceived as a threat. After the earthquake of 1985, tourists stayed away from Mexico City and surrounding areas for a long period after services and facilities were restored. Floods in Utah in 1983 were confined to a very localized area and channelled down only a major street in Salt Lake City, yet they had a serious impact on the numbers of visitors and tourism revenue. Other changes, such as volcanic activity in Hawaii or the eruption of Mount Saint Helens in Washington, may become tourist attractions in their own right. The existence of some types of erosional remnants has created

unique landscape features such as the Alps or the Grand Canyon, which are major destination places for tourists.

The physical landscape resulting from climate, vegetation, and landforms creates the major destinations for tourism. Within the tourism industry, places of high attractiveness are sometimes referred to as "nature's wonders." They range from the cold realms of a glacier bay in Alaska, Figure 1–7, to sand dunes in Colorado. They include diverse landforms ranging from volcanic craters to beautiful falls and bays. These wonders share a common combination of physical features that create a unique locale that is attractive to visitors.

Environment and Tourism

One of the most rapidly growing types of travel in the 1990s is referred to as *ecotourism*. Ecotourism is defined in a number of ways, including "travel that aims to preserve the natural world." As thus defined, travel related to ecotourism should leave a destination without destruction or change as a result of tourism unless it is an improvement of the natural environment of the area. A related term referring to travel that is concerned with maintaining the environment is sustainable development. The idea that tourism facilities and related travel to regions should be developed to minimize environmental damage in the destination area is the goal of both ecotourism and *sustainable development*. While ecotourism has been a major issue throughout the world, the travel industry also uses the idea as a way to sell tourism to individuals with an interest in the environment. Travel to environmentally unique or pleasing areas is a rapidly growing segment of travel and tourism, and ecotourism is a rather recent aspect of this growth.

—*Courtesy Alaska Division of Tourism*

Figure 1-7 Columbia Glacier

Historically the travel industry has been primarily a user of the environment rather than its protector. The environmental protection movement began in the industrialized countries in the last decades of the twentieth century, resulting in environmental regulation to protect some rare and scenic places that directly affected the travel industry. In the less industrialized countries the need for economic growth generally relegates environmental concerns to a very low priority in the development process. However, the travel industry has come to realize that even in less industrialized countries good environmental management may, in fact, be good for the development of the tourism industry in those areas. However, to date this has occurred in the more upscale or higher-cost resorts and developments. Now, ecotourism that emphasizes environmentally based management principles for all places has become an important part of the travel industry.

Travel related to unique and rare environments (such as Antarctica, or Mount Everest, the Serengeti Plain of Kenya, or other unique environments) is growing rapidly. The growth in concern for the environment is also rapid, and environmental awareness is becoming more of a reality among both travel professionals and tourists. Pressure for economic development continues to relegate ecotourism and sustainable development to a lower priority than sheer maximization of tourism revenues in some places, but growing awareness of the destructive impact of tourism that occurs without concern for the environment is growing. Countries that rely on tourism for a major part of economy development, such as Austria, are actively working to promote ecotourism in the less industrialized countries such as Indonesia, and the growing interest in ecotourism will continue as more and more people become concerned about protecting the environment.

Human and Cultural Characteristics of Place

The second component that makes a place unique is related to the differences among the people who occupy the earth. Each place has unique cultural and human characteristics that make it different from other places. These differences are referred to as the *cultural geography* of a place. The cultural geography that is associated with a place reflects both human changes in the physical environment and the cultural variables (language, religion, race, politics, economy) that differ from place to place.

An example of how people modify the physical environment can be illustrated by two groups in Indonesia. The *matrilineal* (family lineage traced through mother's family) tribes live in forested areas, and the *patrilineal* (lineage traced through father) live in grasslands. The climate is the same in the two locations. The grasslands would normally be a forested area, but the patrilineal group raises cattle. Since forested areas would not provide the food needed for the cattle, the tribe burns the land to kill the trees and maintain a grassland landscape. Thus, the grasslands are an obvious cultural landscape. The forests have also been modified, although to a lesser extent, so they too are a cultural landscape.

Much of the difference in places results from variations in culture. Culture is acquired behavior, the way of life held in common by a group of people. It is learned and provides people with similarities in speech, behavior, ideology, livelihood, technology, and language. Culture includes a sense of belonging to a distinct group of people. Cultural landscapes are a combination of the modification of the physical characteristics and the human features existing in a particular place. There are many elements of culture; they all either enhance or deter tourism. Language,

—*Courtesy Government of India Tourist Office*

Figure 1-8 Pooram Festival, India

food, clothing, political systems, religion, and architectural styles are the elements that affect cultural landscapes discussed here.

Language

Language is one of the most important aspects of culture, for it is the means by which ideas and concepts are transmitted within or between groups. It is one of the most important means of preserving a way of life from one generation to another. Several thousand languages and dialects are spoken in the world today (see the color insert). They can be grouped into nine language families: Indo-European, Ural-Altaic, Sino-Tibetan, Malayo-Polynesian, Papuan-Australian, Hematic-Semitic, Niger-Congo-Bantu, Amerindian, and Dravidian. These language families can be divided into thousands of dialects and linguistic cultural regions. For example, the Indo-European languages are divided into at least eleven subfamily groups, Table 1–1.

Further regionalization occurs in dialects. English in the United States is different from English spoken in the United Kingdom or Australia and New Zealand. Even in the United States, there are differences in English. While most of the people in the United States speak English, it is hardly uniform from place to place. The English heard in the inner city is considerably different from that heard in a rural village.

Languages are important for tourism in two ways. First, tourists often develop travel patterns visiting countries where people speak their language. For example, North Americans visit the United Kingdom; Germans visit Switzerland and Austria. The various islands in the Caribbean draw tourists from countries with similar languages in North America and Western Europe. The French visit Martinique and Guadeloupe; the English go to Trinidad, Barbados, Antigua, or the British Virgin Islands. North Americans travel to the Bahamas, the United States Virgin Islands, Jamaica, and other English-speaking island nations.

North Americans are comfortable in much of Western Europe because so many people (particularly those they come in contact with in the tourism industry) speak English. The desire to communicate and be understood is an important consideration for tourists. Also, the uniqueness of a language, even though it may be of the same family, affects tourism. Although English is spoken in the United States and the United Kingdom, part of the attractiveness of the United Kingdom for Americans is that in addition to being able to communicate, the English accent is distinctively different. The dialect creates a uniqueness of place that adds to the attractiveness of a place.

The second major element of language in travel is that it can act as a deterrent to tourists. Fear of being

Table 1-1 Major Indo-European Languages

Subfamily	Modern Language
Baltic	Latvian
	Lithuanian
Armenian	Armenian
Greek	Greek
Indic	Hindi
	Urdu
	Bengali
	Marathi
	Punjabi
Persian	Iranian
Romance	Italian
	Romanian
	Romansch
	Spanish
	Portuguese
	French
	Walloon
Celtic	Gaelic
	Welsh
	Breton
Germanic	Dutch
	English
	Flemish
	German
	Swedish
	Norwegian
	Danish
	Icelandic
Slavic	Russian
	Ukrainian
	Polish
	Czech
	Slovak
	Serb
	Croat
	Slovenian
Finno-Urgic	Finnish
	Estonian
	Hungarian
Basque	Basque

unable to communicate inhibits many potential tourists from traveling to a particular destination. Language barriers limit the movement and exploration of tourists in the new environment. Language is threatening in case of illness, for example, resulting in fear of being unable to communicate health problems in another language.

Food and Clothing

Food and clothing differences are other major elements in cultural differences between places that affect tourism. Foods that are eaten by various groups are chosen as a result of cultural attitudes and normal patterns of behavior toward food. Groups have strong feelings concerning food. The strong feelings develop from a variety of sources. Religion plays an important part in the prohibition of certain foods. Hindus in India, for example, eat no flesh, while across the Middle East and North Africa, pork is taboo. In other cases, certain members of a society may eat that which is forbidden to other members of the group.

Some groups avoid a certain combination of foods rather than a particular food. For example, meat and milk products are not eaten together by Jewish people and the Masai warriors of East Africa. The avoidance of certain kinds of foods developed as part of the cultural process of adapting to the environment. Part of the avoidance of the pig in the Middle East results from the unsuitability of the pig to the pastoral way of life of the nomads. The nomads saw the pig as a symbol of their antagonists, the people of the villages.

The more difficult types of strong feelings about food that affect tourism and the tourist industry are those that have developed implicitly for any number of reasons. It is common for family members to avoid eating animals they have raised. They become personally identified with them. An extension of this can develop in a group, thus defining what animals are acceptable to eat in some societies and what animals are not acceptable in other societies. The horse in North America is an excellent example. Horses in the American culture are pets, work animals, or used for recreational purposes. Although the taste is similar to beef, many Americans avoid eating horse. Many visitors to some European countries will enjoy horse meat until they learn what they are eating or have eaten.

Variations in foods provide further uniqueness of place. For example, the diet of India consists mainly of rice, pulses, chick peas, lentils, millet, wheat, and oils (peanut, coconut, sesame, and linseed). A typical Indian diet is lacking in meats and in dairy products, in part because of religious restrictions. In addition, most Indic dishes are heavily seasoned with a wide range of spices. The exotic flavors receive a mixed level of acceptance by visitors, even though the basic grains and oils are little different from what visitors eat at home.

While foods are part of the character of an area, they are generally not considered a major attraction in and of themselves. Tourists often select foods with which they are most familiar even when food is one of the attractions of a place. Certain places, such as France, are noted for their cuisine, and it does add to the country's attractiveness. While tourists like to explore and try new things, they like to take a bit of home with them. Food habits often go with them. The worldwide growth of fast food chains such as McDonalds®, Kentucky Fried Chicken®, and Burger King® results, in part, from tourism.

Clothing differences in the world are one of the more visible characteristics of place that tourists quickly observe. Dress adds character to a place. For example, periodic Indian markets in the mountains of Central America are popular destinations because of the atmosphere that is created by the dress of the Indians as they participate in the market. Individuals from different villages wear colorful clothing made from textiles whose design immediately identifies them to other Indians. Cloth can be purchased by tourists to take home and use, in the form of either a decoration or some item of clothing. Clothing and food, along with race and language, stimulate curiosity about a place that attracts people to visit and observe that uniqueness.

Political Systems and Religion

Political systems and religion are two forces that institutionalize the way of life of a group. Laws that describe what people can and cannot do are formed by political and religious institutions. Political systems and religion provide order to a place. The degree of interrelationship between religion, politics, and laws varies greatly in the world, ranging from China, where officially religion and political law are completely separated, to Iran, where church and state are based on Islamic law. However, separately or together, they contribute to the formation of the character of place.

The political character of a place is expressed in a number of ways. A formal political-cultural region is based upon matters of commonality. The most obvious political commonality is the legal system. The world can be divided into six broad regions based on *legal systems:*

1. Germanic law
2. Roman or Latin law
3. Socialist law
4. English common law
5. Islamic law
6. tribal and minor ethnic legal traditions

Legal systems directly impact tourists in a variety of ways, from currency regulations to entertainment activities, foods, and dress. In Europe, for example, only the tiny state of Monaco has legalized a full range of gambling. In the United States, female bathers are required to have tops on their swimming suits except at a few beaches. This is not required

—*Courtesy British Tourism Authority*

Figure 1-9   House of Parliament, London

in France. In Iran, Saudi Arabia, and other Islamic countries, alcohol and pork are unavailable, and wearing trousers or shorts may create problems for female tourists. Freedom of entry for tourists is directly regulated by legal requirements concerning visas, length of stay, and places that may be visited. Even photographs are regulated in some countries that make it illegal to photograph certain features.

Functional political regions reflect the organization of an area into some form of political unit such as country, state, and nation. These political organizations may contain a number of different cultural groups within their boundaries. However, in most political units, they have enough in common to be referred to as American, French, Thai, German, Idahoan, Californian, and so on, which creates a mental image of the people from that political unit.

Religion differs from one place to another. Religion or its absence has been an important trait in the character of place. It is reflected in some cases in the laws, personal interactions, dress, entertainment, leisure pursuits, and the cultural landscape. Religion has been important in tourism as both a motivator to travel and as an attractor. Faithful members travel to participate in meetings, to observe sacred places, and to be spiritually uplifted, as in the case of pilgrimages. People of other faiths are drawn to an area out of curiosity. Great religious centers, Figure 1–10, attract both the faithful and the curious. Rome is full of both Catholics and non-Catholics visiting the Vatican. Religious centers such as Mecca attract millions of faithful every year (see color insert).

Architectural Styles

One of the most visible aspects of the cultural landscape is the architectural style of that culture. Methods of construction and styles of buildings reflect different architectural styles that have become characteristic of various places. Even within the United States there is great variety, from New England white churches to large urban cathedrals, from southern mansions to frontier log cabins, from midwestern farms with their painted houses and barns and well-maintained farmyards to the unpainted barns and unkempt farmyards of parts of the rural West or South.

—*Courtesy Tourist Organization of Thailand*

Figure 1-10   Phra Pathom Chedi Shrine in Thailand

—*Courtesy Bahamas Ministry of Tourism*

Figure 1-11   Parliament Square, Bahamas

Epcot Center in Florida is one of the most innovative developments in tourism in the last two decades. A major emphasis of Epcot Center is to reflect the traditional architecture of various cultures of the world, emphasizing the importance of architecture to place. Architectural types vary from rural to urban in most areas of the world.

Cityscapes: The Focus of Human Activity. The world is undergoing an urban explosion with nearly one-half of the earth's residents living in cities. Cities are growing at an unprecedented rate, changing societies from rural to urban. In 1800, about three percent of the world's population lived in urban places of five thousand people or more. This had increased to thirteen percent by 1900 and had risen to nearly fifty percent by 1990. It is projected that by the turn of the century over half of the world's population will live in urban places.

Geographers have traditionally classified cities by their functions. The three major types are marketing, transportation, and specialized. *Market cities* are those that have developed to provide goods and services to the surrounding region, known as their trade area. Market sites are common and easily recognized in agricultural areas such as the Midwest of the United States. Farmers and others living in the trade area purchase goods and services in urban centers. These market towns provide a *central location* offering a variety of goods and services, including retail, wholesale, administrative, social, and financial. Marketplaces are located at points most accessible to the inhabitants of the surrounding trade area. Market sites are often very attractive to tourists because of their markets, handcrafts, and other items that are produced in an area, Figure 1-11.

Transportation or *transit cities* occur along land trade routes and at the interface of land and water transportation, Figure 1–12. Many cities developed where changes occurred in the transportation mode as materials or people changed from one mode of transportation to another or changed direction. Chicago's growth resulted from being a focal point for the railroads, canals, and the Great Lakes water routes. New York's growth resulted from its excellent protected harbor and central location to the population of the United States in the 1800s. Today, cities such as Frankfurt in Germany, Paris, Copenhagen, and Hong Kong typify transit cities where tourists change either direction or mode of transportation. Many tourists fly into Frankfurt and then begin a rail tour of Europe. Others fly into Copenhagen and then change carriers to visit other Scandinavian countries. Almost all tourists traveling from one region of France to another will change trains in Paris. Singapore's growth resulted from its location at the southernmost tip of the Malay Peninsula at a funnel point of the Straits of Singapore and Malacca through which world trade and commerce are channeled. Singapore has become a great center of commerce as one of the major port cities in Asia. Major transportation cities also attract tourists for reasons other than their role in transportation. These cities are generally among the largest and most important in a region and are tourist attractions in their own right.

There are also cities that have developed as a result of a specialized function such as recreation, mining, administration, and religion. Vail, Colorado,

—*Courtesy Irish Tourist Board*

Figure 1-12 Dublin, Ireland

and Park City, Utah, are winter resort towns that have capitalized on their locations in choice mountain areas. Brasilia in Brazil is almost exclusively an administrative center. It was developed for the sole purpose of moving the capital inland. Specialized cities such as Lourdes in France or Mecca in Saudi Arabia are based on religion. Whatever their origin, cities attract tourists.

Cities have not only provided the necessary facilities, services, and infrastructures for tourism in the form of hotels, restaurants, internal transportation, cultural events, sporting events, museums, or governmental and religious centers, but are distinctive in and of themselves, which further attracts visitors. In North America, cities such as Montreal, Quebec City, Vancouver, New Orleans, San Francisco, New York, and Boston are perceived as unique because of their distinctive nature. Worldclass cities such as Paris, London, Tokyo, Shanghai, Mexico City, Rio de Janeiro, New York, Hong Kong, and Rome have become household words for potential tourists. Each offers the amenities and infrastructure of large cities to support and attract tourists and serve as cultural centers for their various cultural regions.

One such city is Amman, Jordan. It is an Islamic city and as such it displays many characteristics that are unique. In the old city, tourists find the permanent central market (bazaar or *suq*), mosques, shrines, public baths, a citadel, and a walled older section unique and different from the non-Islamic

world. Islamic cities have two focal points—the *Friday mosque* and the market. The mosque is generally found along the main thoroughfare or at the crossroads of two main thoroughfares. Next to the mosque are the principal government buildings, including the palace. Near the mosque are the suppliers of the sanctuary, the stalls of the candle merchants, and the dealers in incense and other perfumes used in the mosque. The next set of stores is the booksellers and leather merchants, followed by the dealers in textiles, carpenters, locksmiths, and the producers of copper utensils. Near the gates of the cities are the makers of saddles and packsaddles. Outside the gates are the food vendors. On the edge of the town are industries that need space and those considered undesirable such as the dyers, the tanners, and the potters.

The compact nature of residences, open courtyard houses with windowless walls on streets and alleyways and a spatial organization entirely different from other cultures, make the old section of Amman, Cairo, and other predominantly Islamic cities exotic places for tourists. Within the residential quarters, there is hardly any open space. The Islamic house was oriented so that it received its light from an inner courtyard. The buildings were arranged to provide maximum privacy. For instance, doors on opposite sides of a street rarely faced each other, and many were set back in an L-shaped entrance. Amman provides a glimpse of Mideast life with the amenities of a Hilton or other major international hotel chain for the visitor.

As with Amman, it is in the older sections of world cities that the traditional cultural landscape is best observed. The methods of construction, styles of buildings, arrangements of streets and commercial and residential areas vary in different places within the city, reflecting the time when they were built.

Tourists desire three major elements that cities provide. First, they want to visit a unique place, representative of the area. Second, they want a few comforts of home (a clean bed, a good meal, and other amenities). Third, they want a variety of activities and leisure pursuits, from shopping, theaters, and museums to discos and sports activities.

Farm and Country: The Rural Landscape. It is in the rural areas of the world that much of the traditional cultural landscape and agricultural way of life is most expressed. In industrial societies, it is the countryside that offers an escape from the city and the routine of the workplace.

The world can be divided into agricultural regions, each as part of a unique culture. The general agricultural regions are shifting cultivation; plantation agriculture; paddy rice; peasant grain and livestock; Mediterranean; market gardening; commercial grain, livestock, or dairying; nomadic herding; and livestock ranching. These agricultural regions express the variation from reindeer herding in the northern lands to intensive garden farming around large cities and from seemingly endless wheat fields of Kansas with highly mechanized equipment to slash-and-burn agriculture utilizing digging sticks or hoes in the Amazon. To a visitor from the United States, the terraced agricultural landscape of the Philippines is fascinating and inspiring; to a visitor from Tokyo, the Central Valley with its large farms is unique and impressive.

A number of elements besides crop and livestock combinations are important in the variation of the agricultural landscapes around the world. One is the patterns of fields and properties created as people occupy the land for the purpose of farming. Field patterns vary in size of holdings, shape, and location. Farmers in Europe, Asia, and Africa, with the exception of the Communist countries, generally held their land in fragmented plots of small landholding, which were splintered and fragmented into many separate fields. In the Americas, Australia, New Zealand, and South Africa the land was held in large unit blocks of contiguous holdings.

Fencing material and style is another visible expression of rural regions. Different cultures have their unique methods and ways of enclosing land. Fences

—*Courtesy Israel Government Tourist Office*

Figure 1-13 Yichron Yaakov, Israel

in different places are made of substances as different as steel wire, logs, poles, split rails, brush, rock, and earth. A common landscape feature of Great Britain, Ireland, and Brittany and Normandy in France are the maze-like hedgerows.

Another element in the rural landscape is the different distribution and settlement patterns of rural areas. In many places in the world such as La Grande in France and Southern Italy, farming people group themselves together in clustered settlements called *nucleated settlements* or villages. Contained in these villages are the farmer's house, barn, sheds, pens, and garden; outside of the village are the fields, pastures, and meadows. This type of settlement is common in much of Europe, in parts of Latin America, in the densely settled farming regions of Asia, and among sedentary farming peoples of Africa and the Middle East. It was common with some cultural groups in the United States.

The opposite pattern is the dispersed rural settlement, with its isolated farmsteads. These are common in North America, Australia, and New Zealand and in some regions of Europe and South Africa. The development of dispersed rural settlements is a recent characteristic of farming, explaining its location in the newer countries settled by the Europeans. Thus, how people distribute themselves across the world is another visible expression of the cultural landscape, Figure 1-13.

Another element of the rural landscape is termed *folk culture.* A folk culture is a culture that has retained the traditional way of life. While folk culture can be an individual characteristic, some unique groups, such as the Amish, express a common folk culture.

Tourism to rural areas may involve something other than simple curiosity about farm life. It may reflect a desire to escape from city life and the workplace. Tourists often desire space, quiet, and the peace of nature for the renewal of body and soul. The pressures of modern city life may cause people to turn to the countryside for tranquility and rest. Much of this movement is not a result of the rural culture, however, although that might be a further attraction while enjoying the great outdoors.

In fact, the development of national parks and wilderness has resulted from the desire to preserve the natural environment without cultural impact. Wilderness designations have been particularly designed to preserve the environment with as little human impact as possible. While designated rural because they are not in cities, such natural environments attract tourists for entirely different reasons.

MOVEMENT WITHIN PLACES

Human beings are spread unevenly across the face of the earth. Some live on farms or in the country; others live in towns, villages, and cities. Yet, these people interact with each other; they travel from one place to another; they communicate with each other; and they rely upon products, information, and ideas that come from beyond their immediate environment. Increasing interaction among people as we near the end of the twentieth century is leading to *global interdependence.*

The most visible evidence of global interdependence and the interaction of places is the transportation and communication lines that link every part of the world. These demonstrate that many people interact with other places almost every day of their lives. This may involve nothing more than a Georgian eating apples grown in the state of Washington that have been shipped to Atlanta by rail or truck. On a larger scale, international trade demonstrates that no country is self-sufficient. Such interaction will continue to change as transportation and communication technologies change. An understanding of the changing technologies will help us to understand the changes taking place in the world in the future.

The uniqueness of place reflects the interaction of the physical and cultural elements at that place in addition to the degree and type of interaction with other places. Geographers are interested in spatial interaction, and tourism is one element in that interaction that affects the character of place. Three terms are important in understanding the interaction between places: *complementarity, intervening opportunity,* and *transferability* (accessibility).

Complementarity

The fact that places are different does not automatically ensure interaction between places. There must be a complementary relationship between two places. Northern Europe is a wealthy (by world standards) area with a damp, cool climate. Its inhabitants like to spend some time in the sunny, warm, sun-sea-sand environment offered by the Mediterranean nations of southern Europe. Thus, a complementary relationship generates interaction in the form of tourism as well as trade in agricultural products; for example, one may grow grapes and another potatoes, and then the two may trade. The two regions are complementary.

Intervening Opportunity

Intervening opportunity refers to the substitution of one place for another, as when growth of a suburban mall leads suburban residents to shop at it instead of going downtown. The mall becomes an intervening opportunity. In tourism, intervening opportunities are common as a nearer or less expensive (in terms of time or money) place is substituted for another. Residents of the Western United States might like a Pacific tropical vacation experience. They would be willing to substitute Acapulco, Mexico, for Tahiti or Fiji. The British can substitute coastal areas in France for the more distant locations in Spain, Italy, Greece, or the Caribbean.

Transferability

Transferability (or accessibility) is the ease (usually expressed in time and money) with which a person can go from one place to another. The greater the accessibility between complementary regions, the greater the interaction. For example, there was only a small degree of interaction by tourists between Europe and the United States before the advent of the jet plane. Travel to Europe across the Atlantic was reduced from three and one-half days by ship in 1950 to six hours by airplane in 1960.

Those destinations that are perceived as being too expensive in either time or money have little interaction, and tourists seek an alternative destination involving less time and expense. In general, this explains why domestic tourism has greater numbers of tourists than does international tourism. People can travel less expensively and more frequently to destinations within their own country. The next stage has more international tourists within their respective regions, such as Western Europe, North America, East Asia, North Africa, and Eastern Europe, than between regions. Interaction resulting from tourism on an international level occurs most between complementary regions such as between North America and Europe, which have strong cultural complementary characteristics.

Barrier to Travel: Tourist Safety

One of the major reasons visitors avoid a destination is concern over their safety. Articles in popular magazines and newspapers illustrate the concern with headlines that read "How to Survive a Holiday in the Florida Jungle" or "African Nations Take Steps to Improve Tourist Safety." Each time there is considerable news about problems in a destination region, tourism declines. The killing of tourists in Egypt in 1997 has frightened potential visitors.

Trips by Canadians, Germans, and English to Miami declined after a number of highly publicized slayings in 1992 and 1993. In Kenya reports of armed bandits along major paths to game reserves and mugging at popular beaches have given cause for concern to prospective visitors. Kings Cross in Sydney is noted for drug-pushers, prostitutes, and muggers; in Thailand tourists have been drugged and then robbed or even raped; in Italy individuals on motorscooters have been known to zoom up and snatch visitors' bags; in the United States in major cities it is perceived as unsafe to be on the streets alone at night. Tourism to Russia increased quickly following the fall of the U.S.S.R.; however, with reports of mugging, robberies, and other criminal activities tourism has not grown significantly recently.

In an effort to be helpful to American citizens the U.S. State Department issues a monthly list of warnings and the reasons for the warnings for citizens to consider when planning a trip to the various countries listed.

Since a lack of safety has serious impact on visitors and potential visitors, local, regional, and national governments establish measures to protect visitors. In Miami many problems were associated with the ability of local criminals to identify tourists either through rental cars or the visitor's obvious unfamiliarity with Miami. Most problems occurred in an area bounded by the airport and the hotel district. The measures officials instituted were offering free maps and providing better information at the airport; suggesting visitors rent automobiles at hotels; removing the easy identification of rental cars; posting clear directions around the airport and major expressways; and giving advice on what to do in situations such as being bumped from the rear (don't stop and investigate) and areas of the city to avoid.

REGIONS: ORGANIZING THE GEOGRAPHY OF TOURISM

The basic unit of geographic study is the *region*, an area that displays internal unity in terms of selected criteria. We are all familiar with regions showing the extent of political power such as nations, provinces, countries, or cities, yet there are almost countless ways to define meaningful regions depending on the problems being considered. Regions may be defined on the basis of cultural features such as language (a German-speaking region, for example) or a complex of features based on culture and environment, such as the Arab region. In any case, regions are used as a basis for helping us understand the world as an integrated system of places that we can comprehend as a planetary ecosystem. Events that occur in the world are located in regions, for example, the problems of the Middle East. Regions serve as a means of comprehending events in the world and simplifying a myriad of factual information. They are the basis for education in elementary, high school, and university settings in such diverse areas as history, fine arts, botany, or geology.

The division of the world into regions has been accomplished mostly in accordance with the purpose for the division. To divide the world into tourism regions is somewhat difficult. A central focus of geography is its attempt to provide a logical system for dividing the world into regions and supplying answers to the fundamental questions of science relating to these regions. Doing so for tourism is no simple task.

Distribution of Wealth

One popular way of dividing the world, which affects tourism, is the degree or distribution of wealth in the world. It has been popular to divide the world into three divisions based on economic development. The First World is historically defined as that of the wealthy, technologically industrial nations of the Western world. The Second World is defined as the centrally planned economies of the Soviet Union, China, Cuba, and others. The Third World consists of the poor countries of the world where the level of living is low, there is a relative lack of industry, and the majority of the people live in perennial conditions of near misery and mass poverty. In these Third World countries, the majority of the employed population is involved in farming or hunting activities and relies on human or animal power for energy. These countries are overpopulated in terms of the numbers of people who must be supported by the available cultivated land. This division is somewhat arbitrary since members of the so-called Second World are defined on the basis of politics (communism), not economic development. With the breakup of the Soviet Union and adoption of democratic governments and in Eastern Europe, the designation of "Second World" is rather meaningless.

Economic Development

A second method of division is based on the level of economic development without regard to political characteristics. In general, two broad regions are recognized: one rich, one poor. Further division can be made in these broad regions to include the newly industrialized countries of the world who are between the rich and the very poor. The newly industrialized countries of the world are those in which the cultural and economic climate has led to a rapid rate of industrialization and growth since the 1960s. These countries are in transition between the least industrialized countries of the world and the mature, industrialized economies of the developed world. They include such countries as Hong Kong, South Korea, Taiwan, and Singapore.

The wealthy nations with high per capita income, high levels of personal consumption, a large, well-developed middle class, a large number employed in manufacturing and service generally are the countries of Europe, North America, Japan, Australia, New Zealand, and Israel. It is from this group that most of the international tourists come. Also, most international tourist flows are between countries of this group.

The least developed, or poor, nations of the world comprise the majority of the nations and people of the world. In these countries, industry employs a minority, agriculture is the major occupation, and poverty is the rule. These countries have a mixed situation in tourism. Most international tourism involving these countries is that of destination travel. Destination travel occurs when international tourism is basically one way. These countries are destinations for tourists from wealthier regions but are not a major source of tourists. International tourism to the least developed nations varies with the individual country. Most international tourism to these countries relates to attractions such as the Taj Mahal of India or other cultural relics, unique physical attractions, or the culture itself. Total international tourism to the least developed countries is much less than to the developed industrial countries. There is a broad range of visitors to the least developed countries, from relatively large numbers in India and Kenya to few in Burma and interior African countries.

While the range from industrialized countries to least industrialized can also characterize the range of tourism, it is difficult to regionalize or generalize tourism patterns into this type of classification. While tourism follows economic patterns, this classification masks important differences because wealthy nations are both concentrated in North America and Europe and scattered throughout the other general regions such as Japan in Asia, Australia and New Zealand in the Pacific, and Israel in the Middle East.

The International Air Transportation Association

The *International Air Transportation Association (IATA)* has used a simple method of regionalizing world tourism, dividing the world into three zones with lines drawn from pole to pole (see color insert). Area one consists of the Americas and Greenland. Area two consists of Europe, the Middle East, and Africa. Area three consists of the Far East, Australia, New Zealand, and the Pacific Islands. This regionalization is for ease of marketing and control of air travel. It is less useful in explaining tourism since the broad regions include widely diverse cultures and physical and economic settings, making it difficult to understand the processes responsible for tourism. However, it can serve as an organization for this text to gain an understanding of the geography of tourism. Chapter 2 is concerned with the patterns and processes of world tourism. The remainder of this text is regional in nature. Chapter 3 starts in developed North America. Subsequent chapters follow the IATA regionalization around the world, ending in the Pacific.

This text is divided to provide ease of reading. For example, the countries of Europe are divided into a number of chapters, as one or two chapters on Europe would be unmanageable. In addition, the larger region of Europe does mask some regional patterns, hence the division of Europe into five economic, political, physical, and cultural regions of Western, Northern, Southern, Central, and Russia and its neighbors (the former Soviet Union). This division not only combines the various methods of regionalizing Europe, but assists in understanding the patterns within and without Europe. The same pattern holds true for the regional chapters. They are created in an effort to take into account economic, political, physical, and cultural characteristics of the major regions such as Africa, Asia, and Latin America.

REVIEW QUESTIONS

1. Why do people travel?
2. What is geography?
3. Describe the elements of geography.
4. Compare and contrast site and situation.
5. What makes a place an attraction for tourism?
6. What variables in the physical characteristics of places are important?
7. Discuss the impact that various climates have on tourism.
8. Identify several important landform types and state how they are important for tourism.
9. What are some factors that describe the cultural characteristics of place important to tourism?
10. How important are cities to tourism? Why?
11. Identify and describe several cities that have a distinctive nature for tourism.
12. Name some characteristics of the rural landscape that are of interest to tourists.
13. Define and state the significance of complementarity, intervening opportunity, and transferability.

GEOGRAPHY AND TOURISM:
Patterns and Processes of World Tourism

CHAPTER 2

In 1979, the famed futurist Herman Kahn predicted that tourism would be the world's largest industry by the year 2000. Seven years later, in 1986, according to Somerset Water, editor of *Travel World Yearbook: The Big Picture*, tourism had already become the world's largest industry. Total worldwide spending for domestic and international tourism in 1986 exceeded two trillion dollars, generating directly or indirectly, 64.3 million jobs (Waters, 1987). By 1996, total worldwide spending was more than 3.4 trillion dollars, and employment exceeded 200 million. Both continue to increase.

One of the characteristics of the modern world is the ease and degree of travel. Historically, people have always traveled, but much of that travel was not for pleasure, nor was it pleasurable. The terms "travel" and "tourism" are often used interchangeably and the terms may appear synonymous. However, in the past travel was generally undertaken for financial, military, or business reasons; tourism was travel for the sake of recreation and for the enjoyment of new and different places and people. While people have always traveled to some extent for the thrill of travel or curiosity about other places, mass tourism is a modern phenomenon. Until the last few decades, only a select few were able to travel for tourism.

Tourism has evolved from a time when travel was uncomfortable or inconvenient for both those who were forced to travel and the few who could travel due to curiosity or pleasure, to the present when people can and do travel by the millions. This evolution affects the world. A number of factors contributed to this change—societal changes that resulted from urbanization, the *Industrial Revolution*, technological advances in transportation and communication, two world wars (which brought large numbers of people into contact with other cultures), and a migration of large numbers of people (particularly Europeans) to other nations of the world.

DEFINING TOURISM

The definition of tourism includes three common elements:

1. Movement of people between two or more places (origin and destination)
2. Length of time of movement (temporary)
3. Purpose

The concept of tourism does not include normal activities of work and play, such as daily or weekly journeys to work. It does not include the availability of recreation and other *leisure* pursuits within a reasonable distance that can be reached in a same-day round trip after work or on a weekend day. Many official government tourism or economic divisions exclude trips within a fifty- or one hundred-mile distance when calculating total *tourists.*

Time involved in movement is divided into less than twenty-four hours and at least twenty-four hours. Periods away from home of less than twenty-four hours are not included as part of tourism. Migration, whether by migrant workers or other temporary workers, students, or permanent immigrants, is not part of tourism. At a conference on international travel and tourism in Rome in 1963, the United Nations divided visitors into two categories:

1. Tourists are temporary visitors staying over twenty-four hours in the country visited, whose journey falls in one of the following categories: leisure, recreation, *holiday,* sport, health, study, religion; or business, family, friends, mission, meetings.
2. *Excursionists* include temporary visitors staying less than twenty-four hours in the country visited, including cruise passengers.

The purpose for travel determines whether it is tourism by definition. Excluded purposes are: work (such as employment by public transportation, such as airlines, trains, buses, or journeying to place of work) or students traveling to and from school. Purposes included in tourism are business trips, visiting friends and relatives, and various forms of pleasure, such as entertainment, outdoor recreation, and so forth.

FACTORS INFLUENCING TOURISM

The growth in trips for tourism in the past quarter century reflects world changes that have made tourism an important part of many of the lives of the world's inhabitants, particularly those from the industrialized nations of the world. Three important factors had to coincide for tourism to become an important part of life: leisure time, *affluence,* and *mobility.*

Leisure Time

Leisure is important in that it increases the amount of time free from actual labor and the associated freedom to choose how time is spent in non-work situations. In 1850, the average workweek was seventy hours in industrial countries. Today it is slightly less than forty hours per week. In addition to the shortened week, paid vacations became the norm, rather than the exception, in industrialized nations. The rapid growth of labor unions just before and

following World War II increased the length of paid vacations to two to three weeks a year. When combined with eight to ten holidays (Easter, Christmas, and national holidays) per year, workers now have considerable opportunity to travel.

The sum of the total days of potential leisure time is quite impressive. A five-day workweek and a two-day weekend give 104 weekend days for potential leisure per year. Adding this to typical paid vacations of 10 to 20 days plus 10 days of holidays each year, we can conclude that Americans have about 125 to 140 days a year of potential leisure time for travel.

This means that more than one-third of the total days in a year could conceivably be used for an individual's leisure pursuits.

In addition, the age of retirement in the industrial world has been reduced significantly since World War II, while life expectancy has risen. The decreasing age of retirement and better health of the population continue to increase the amount of leisure time people can expect to enjoy. The economic trend in the industrial world as it changes from manufacturing employment to service industries and information processing in the computer era provides even more flexibility in leisure pursuits since work hours can be staggered or work can be done at home at the time of the individual's own choosing.

A second aspect of leisure important to the development of tourism is the attitude change that occurred with urbanization processes. The psychological prejudice against idle time began to crumble as Western Europe and North America changed from rural societies to urban. The Industrial Revolution not only increased the ability of the working person to produce more in less time but also forced people into a new social order, which recognized leisure as a justifiable characteristic of our society. Old habits die hard, though. We justify many of our current leisure pursuits, which keep us extremely busy, as being healthful and restful. There is still an underlying feeling that "idleness is the devil's workshop."

Affluence

The second element, affluence, refers to the majority of the population gaining a good standard of living. The transformation to an urban society brought about by technological advancement ultimately included another important factor affecting tourism. Henry Ford was a catalyst in raising the standard of living for the working person. When he began the mass production of automobiles, he set the wage rate at five dollars a day, which doubled the existing level. It was an unheard–of development. In the twentieth century, there has been a sharp increase in both real and disposable incomes. Combined with this increase in income has been the relative decrease in transportation costs. In 1926, airlines carried the first passenger from Los Angeles to Salt Lake City for $90. In 1997, the lowest price for the same trip was $49. Not only is the dollar value of the trip less today but also the average salary today is fifteen times higher than in 1927.

Mobility

The third factor is mobility. Henry Ford created the benchmark for increasing the general public's mobility. With the advent of mass production of the automobile, Henry Ford began a process in America that brought about the transformation of Western society and travel in one of the great revolutions in history. In 1900, there were 8,000 motor vehicles registered in the United States. This increased to a little over 5 million by 1917, 61.5 million in 1960, and 188 million by 1990. There were 2.9 trillion motor vehicles registered in the world by 1990.

In the United States and other industrialized countries, elaborate road systems provide for automobile travel. This vast network of roads and the mass production of the car at a price most citizens can afford has led to the development of a domestic tourist industry in the United States unmatched in the world. Motels, hotels, restaurants, service stations, curiosity shops, entertainment centers, and campgrounds support a phenomenal level of auto-oriented domestic travel.

The explosion in numbers of automobiles was followed by rapid improvements in air service. The most significant was the development of jet-powered passenger planes. In 1958, Pan American World Airways and BOAC (presently British Airways) began operating jet-plane passenger services across the Atlantic to London. The development of the Boeing 707 reduced flying time over long distances by 40 percent. The propeller-driven Douglas DC-7 was the best passenger aircraft at that time, with average speeds to 350 mph. With the introduction of the 707 (and shortly thereafter the DC-8), speeds advanced to 590 mph (Feldman, 1983).

Before this time, almost all transatlantic travel to Europe was via great ocean liners. However, by the end of 1958, only a little over a year later, airlines had captured 63 percent of the Atlantic passenger traffic. Yet tourism was still in its infancy, as only seven percent of the United States population had made a trip by air. The advent of jet aircraft in the 1950s set the stage for the international tourism boom of the post-1960s. The results of the *Jet Age* were lower

fares, a wider range of routes, reduced travel time, and longer distance travel.

HISTORICAL DEVELOPMENT OF TRAVEL AND TOURISM

Ancient Times

People did not travel much in ancient times. Travel was time consuming, expensive, and dangerous. Of the three elements important to the development of travel, transportation is the most important. The other two, money and ability to communicate, are also important, but are somewhat self-explanatory. Can you imagine how difficult it would be to travel under a barter system? In each time period, however, some form of currency was widely used. During the period that Greece was the center of Western civilization, for example, the money from Greek city-states came to be accepted as international currency. This gave the traveler more flexibility. Money, rather than goods, could be used for commerce. The problem of communicating with people speaking a different tongue is obvious. But the key to travel development has always been transportation.

The problems of travel by land were difficult and costly to overcome. Consequently, early travel was associated with the waterways. Ancient travel was associated with the growth of cities in ancient Mesopotamia, clustered along and between the Tigris and Euphrates rivers, and the Nile and the Mediterranean. This clustering of cities beside rivers and coastlines led to the commercial use of waterways for the carrying of goods and people. Records and legends of the ancient world outside of Western civilization mention some remarkable trips in Asia and the Pacific. The Pacific peoples performed prodigious feats of island hopping, and sea travel was of major importance to China and Japan well before the birth of Christ.

There are many records of early travel throughout the world. The early Polynesians, for example, traveled throughout Southeast Asia, Micronesia, and Polynesia. On some trips, they covered over two thousand miles at sea in outrigger canoes, navigating by stars at night and the sun by day.

Travel by land was limited. Consider, if the average person walks at a speed of two and one-half to three miles an hour, how long it would take to travel long distances. When Hammurabi, the Babylonian ruler between 1792 and 1750 B.C., dispatched a courier on a 120-mile trip, he was expected to travel night and day in order to reach the destination in two days. Thus, a trip from Washington to New York (about 240

Courtesy Egyptian Government Tourist Office

Figure 2–1   Luxor

miles) would take four days of day-and-night travel, or almost a week of twelve-hour-day walks.

With the advent of the wheel, little improvement in speed was realized at first. Paving was nonexistent in most places, and bridges were rare. When Alexander the Great visited India (no small journey in itself), he found a well-developed travel industry. There were carefully maintained roads lined with trees and dotted at intervals with wells, police houses, and rest stops. The Assyrians, from 900 to 612 B.C., developed a network to facilitate travel within the Assyrian Empire for military use. Roads leading to areas of economic, political, and military importance were paved, and stone bridges were constructed over strategic river crossings. Road markers were established to indicate the distance traveled. In addition, sentinel posts and wells were located every few miles for protection, communication, and water.

The Persians, following the Assyrians, contributed to travel mainly in the expansion of the empire and in improvement in the travel *infrastructure*. Roads that had been built by the Assyrians were expanded and refined, and new kinds of wagons were developed. These included classical four-wheeled, closed carriages for the wealthy and elite.

The Roman Era

The height of early tourism was reached during the *Roman Era*. The Romans' keen sense of military and administrative organization brought under control, politically and culturally, the greatest empire in Western civilization. The empire extended from the Scottish marshes in the north of Britain to the Euphrates River in Mesopotamia to the southeast. The Mediterranean was safe for travel and, for long periods, was free from strife. The Romans had the ability to build superior transportation networks, which shrank the known world for the Roman citizens. The building of roads also reached its apogee under the Romans, as they built all-weather roads designed to move an army and its equipment quickly. These roads became major thoroughfares from Rome to major tourist centers such as Naples and Pompeii and were much used by the new leisure class created by the increasing demand for goods and services of the vast empire.

Three other factors emerged during the Roman Era that were important contributors to tourism. Combined with the transport system, they allowed Rome to advance tourism to a level not reached again until modern times.

The factors that facilitated Roman tourism were a common coinage, language, and legal system. Roman coins were the only medium of exchange the traveler needed to carry since they were accepted throughout the empire. Greek and Latin were the principal official and business languages, enabling the traveler to communicate relatively easily in any part of the empire. The legal system provided protection from foreign courts and jurisdiction. These factors combined with the improved network of good roads and water routes to give travel during the Roman times some of the characteristics of modern tourism today in that more people traveled than at any time before or for centuries afterward. In addition to the common currency, language, and legal system, the Romans developed the concept of a leisure holiday that allowed Romans free time to travel.

Concurrent with the improvement in transportation, the concept of a holiday needed to develop. Originally the word was derived from two sources. The first source was, as the word suggests, "Holy Day": a day that was associated with religion and designated by religious orders, or clergy, as a day to recognize. Thus, in Christian Europe, certain days were set aside for fasting and prayer in remembrance of saints and important religious events. These days were initially celebrated by a limited number of the populace, the clergy, and religious leaders. Today a large number of days resulting from these early Holy

Days are observed in a number of countries as official national holidays.

The second source of development of the word "holiday" was Ancient Rome, in which there was a public holiday set aside for feasting and frolicking. This day was referred to as "Saturnalia." It was such an important occasion that even the slaves were allowed to participate in it.

In 1552, Edward VI established certain saints' days as holidays in order for civil servants to have a day of rest. On these days, public and semipublic offices were closed. However, it was not until the *impact* of the Industrial Revolution that general public holidays evolved for the masses. The modern concept of the word "holiday" is a product of the Industrial Revolution. The social changes that came about as a result of the change from a rural society to an urbanized one brought about an evolution from a religious day to a day of leisure and recreation.

EARLY INTERNATIONAL TOURISM

The growth of a middle class, combined with the achievements in art and thought of the Renaissance, established the forerunner of modern tourism—the *Grand Tour.* This tradition still exists today. The Grand Tour began with the ascension of Elizabeth to the English throne in the sixteenth century. The sons of the nobility and wealthy of England and France were sent for a period lasting almost three years to Germany, the Low Countries, France, and Florence, the focal point, where a traveler might spend the greater part of a year absorbing the culture and language of the Renaissance. Some destinations that have become popular today were avoided. Switzerland, with its Alps, was regarded as a barrier to travel, and the Riviera was a haven for pirates. Rome and some towns in Italy had overzealous local officials who the Protestants feared would involve them in the *Catholic Inquisition.*

To serve the wealthy aristocratic tourists and in some cases their tutors, marked improvements were made in the hospitality sector. Guidebooks, which covered diverse topics from items to take on a tour to books of observations and reflections of journeys taken, became popular. Until World War II, international tourism remained primarily an opportunity of the wealthy.

Late in the 1800s and early 1900s, seaside and mountain *resorts* became fashionable places for the wealthy. Many, such as Saratoga Springs in the United States and Bath in England, became showplaces for socialites, evolving into centers of amusement and entertainment. Throughout Europe, *spas* such as Davos, Baden-Baden, Karkov, St. Moritz, and

coastal areas in France and Britain became havens for the wealthy. Later, improved transportation and communication systems, particularly the railroads, changed the nature of the seaside resorts from wealthy playgrounds to large complexes for the masses, with expanded recreational facilities and amenities.

The Industrial Revolution brought about economic and social changes that completely altered lifestyles and the world. The changes brought about by the Industrial Revolution also increased the ability to travel. The following four factors associated with the Industrial Revolution were the basis for this change:

1. New machinery, which increased the ability to produce goods.
2. New kinds of power, which were being developed to facilitate productivity and move a greater number of people over greater distances at less expense.
3. New methods of extracting and using metals, providing a variety of new goods and construction materials.
4. The dramatic discoveries that would be used to provide new production, new occupations, and new goods, some of which would greatly affect tourism.

The resulting industrialization caused both population shifts and population increases. Population shifts to urban areas brought new lifestyles, with increasing leisure time and demand for recreational activities. This growing population, which occurred

Courtesy Turkish Cultural and Information Office

Figure 2–2 Ephesus, Turkey

at the same time as increases in industrial productivity and wealth, greatly increased the number of those wealthy enough to travel, which in turn stimulated the growth of resorts and tourism destination centers. The growth of labor unions during this period helped the worker obtain greater amounts of leisure time through paid vacations and a shorter workweek.

Tourism following the Industrial Revolution can be characterized as consisting of a growing middle class that flocked to resorts in the mountains and seaside close to their urban centers for short stays, while the wealthy traveled for extended periods to exotic places like the Riviera, Palm Beach, and so on.

EARLY NATIONAL PATTERNS IN THE UNITED STATES

One of the prime characteristics of the American experience has been, and still is, the "itchy foot" syndrome, which is the desire and willingness to travel, to be on the move looking for new experiences and at the same time reaching back to maintain ties with the past. This movement of Americans to new areas and new territories may not have involved tourists as we understand the term today, but these adventurers and pioneers started a trend for travel that has been passed down to us. Certainly, those who moved into the new territories became potential tourists to the areas of America they left behind. The great American dream was in part a result of the ability to travel, to roam, to seek new places and experiences.

In fact, the right to travel is guaranteed Americans by the Constitution. A 1958 Supreme Court decision indicated that the right to travel could not be denied without due process of law under the Fifth Amendment. This decision held that the secretary of state could not deny the right to travel abroad because of political views and associations. Two later rulings affirm this right in cases involving Communist-controlled organizations and groups going to Cuba in violation of passport regulations.

The settlement and expansion of entirely new and untouched country contributed to the unique nature of the American people. One mark of this was the extraordinarily rapid proliferation of roads. As the northeast seaboard began to fill with people, road building became important. The Philadelphia-Lancaster Turnpike opened in 1794 and was quickly followed by a series of roads. By 1820, roads were quite widespread throughout the eastern seaboard.

Once movement pushed inland, travel was facilitated by the country's network of rivers and streams that allowed access by steamboat to a broad expanse of the midsection of America after the 1820s. Besides their cargo capacities, steamboats quickly became very popular attractions for the potential traveler.

As with its European counterparts, tourism in the United States received real impetus from physicians encouraging people to bathe in health-giving waters at *spas* and the oceanside. Saratoga, New York, the Baden-Baden of America, was only one of a number of spas operating in the early 1800s. Although visits to spas were to improve one's health, spas that included other attractions as well were the most popular. The peak for spas was about the middle of the nineteenth century, but they continued operating into this century. Names such as Congress Spring, Saratoga, Putnam Spring, United States Spring, Eureka, Excelsior, and White Sulphur became well known. Travel even at this time remained limited to a select class of people. The impact of urbanization and unionization would not be felt for the majority of residents of the United States and other industrializing nations until after World War II.

The ocean, also originally attractive for its supposed health-sustaining qualities, increased in popularity in the nineteenth and twentieth centuries. By 1870, Long Beach (a resort on the shores of New Jersey, close to New York City and Atlantic City) became quite popular. Steamships were able to carry New Yorkers to Long Beach, Coney Island, and Manhattan Beach to take the curative water and enjoy sun and fun at the same time.

The railroad opened up additional attractions in the second half of the nineteenth century. Although Niagara Falls had previously been attractive to newlyweds and curiosity seekers, the completion of the Erie Railroad provided the catalyst for dynamic growth. By the 1870s, Niagara was offering magnificent rooms overlooking the falls.

In addition to railroad excursions to the ocean resorts, the vast river network of the interior opened new opportunities for the steamboat. Gambling throughout the Mississippi River valley, with New Orleans as the focal point, became a strong attraction for leisure and pleasure seekers.

New Orleans, noted not only for its gambling and entertainment but also for the Mardi Gras, became a major attraction for tourists. The pattern for the Mardi Gras was first established in 1795; but its golden era, with much the same characteristics that we know today, didn't start until the end of the Civil War.

The Industrial Revolution produced a growing class of wealthy Americans who had leisure time, making touring a popular activity. The Grand Tour of Europe attracted some Southerners, although most went north for an American-style Grand Tour. The

South was generally a rural society in which few had accumulated much wealth in the last half of the nineteenth century.

At the same time, the more urbanized northeastern United States was the major destination for both international and domestic tourists. New York, with its budding theater and opera, diverse population, and commerce was the focal point. Travelers were infatuated with New York. The cities of Philadelphia and Boston were also attractions because of the nation's history. In Philadelphia, travelers were drawn to the Mint, the Old State House (Independence Hall), and the Liberty Bell. In Boston, they saw the Commons, the Naval Yard, the State House, and Bunker Hill. These cities were also noted for their elegance and commerce, features that augmented the traveler's enjoyment of their historical sites.

In the late 1800s, the West attracted some people to explore scenic wonders, to see and possibly hunt buffalo, and to view the rugged life. Travel, regardless of type, was at best uncomfortable. Travel to and in America in the 1800s remained much like that in Europe: it was primarily for the wealthy.

Purposes for travel were varied. One purpose for travel in nineteenth-century America was for religious reasons. Foreign observers came to America to visit its various unique religious groups, such as the Amish, Quakers, and Shakers. The various groups were also attractions to some American travelers, and remain so today.

Foreign travelers, particularly the English, came to America to hunt buffalo, experience American culture, fulfill government missions, see the many different religious denominations, and view the American landscape. These are much the same reasons that tourists go to other countries or come to the United States today. Travelers from abroad often wrote many travel books about their experiences in America among slaves, Mormons, Indians, fur trappers, mining camps, or cities. By 1856, it took only nine days to cross the Atlantic, a time only improved on by four days until the advent of the airplane. By the late 1800s, people were traveling for the same basic reasons people travel today. Attractions in America that prompted tourism in the nineteenth century included:

- Resorts—leisure and health
- Cities—education, business, and historical interest
- Beaches—sun and fun
- Cultural landscapes
- Scenic beauty
- Religious interests
- Outdoor recreation
- Gambling
- Entertainment

Travel in the twentieth century prior to World War II was essentially an extension and intensification of the travel patterns that had developed during the latter part of the nineteenth century. The Industrial Revolution that was changing the nature of work and play in America produced new innovations in transportation after the two world wars which, when combined with changes in the work world, allowed American travel to expand after to a scale never before dreamed possible. Travel now has become as fundamental a part of American life as housing, food, and work.

CURRENT INTERNATIONAL PATTERNS OF TOURISM

International tourism has increased steadily since the end of World War II. In the 1960s, the number of world tourist arrivals more than doubled, reaching 183 million international arrivals by 1970 and nearly 600 million international arrivals by 1996. In the 1980s, the rate of growth in numbers of arrivals has been greatest in the less industrialized nations. Between 1981 and 1996, countries with less industrialized economies jumped from 10.8 million arrivals to 183.1 million, a seventeen-fold increase. The industrialized countries had a smaller percentage increase during this same time period. They had 178 million arrivals in 1981, which increased to 330 million in 1996, a 195 percent change. The increasing growth of tourism to less industrialized countries helps to improve their economies, and continued tourism growth is viewed as beneficial.

Two components of the patterns of tourism travel that are especially important in order to understand international patterns are the regional characteristics of origin and destination.

Destination Countries

Table 2–1 lists the top twelve tourist-drawing countries in order of rank. These twelve countries represent 58.98 percent of the total international tourist visits. European and North American countries dominate the list, indicating the strong attraction that the European region has for tourists. The large number of visitors to European countries can be accounted for by two factors. First, a large number of tourists are from other European nations. Consequently, they travel to other European countries that are close by in search of new experiences. Second, the historical ties of North America with Europe serve to stimulate

Table 2-1 Top Twelve Tourist-drawing Countries In 1996 (in millions)

Destination	Cumulative Number	Cumulative Percentage
1. France	61.5	—	10.39
2. United States	44.8	106.3	17.96
3. Spain	41.3	147.6	24.94
4. Italy	35.5	183.0	30.94
5. China	36.1	209.2	35.34
6. United Kingdom	25.8	235.0	39.70
7. Mexico	21.8	256.9	50.14
8. Hungary	20.7	277.5	46.86
9. Poland	19.4	296.9	50.14
10. Canada	17.3	314.2	53.07
11. Czech Republic	17.0	331.4	55.98
12. Austria	16.6	348.0	58.98

Courtesy Finnish Tourist Office

Figure 2–3 Pearl of Saimma, Eastern Lake, Finland

travel between these two major areas. In general, the Mediterranean countries receive the most tourists, reflecting cost advantages, Mediterranean climates, coastal locations with sun, sand, and sea, and cultural attractions from early civilizations. Italy, Spain, and Hungary attract far more tourists than leave these countries, making tourism a net income producer. Many travelers from Canada and the United States indicate only Europe as their destination, visiting several countries on one trip to reduce the cost of additional air fares on subsequent vacations. Interestingly, a number of Central European countries, headed by Hungary, have become important destinations with their recent change in governments. In 1986, China moved into the top twelve destination nations of the world for the first time, indicating growing interest in this socialist country. Since the opening of China in 1978 to international tourism, the increase in tourists to China has been rapid.

The United States, Mexico, and Canada benefit from large populations with easy access to each other. In addition, the cultural linkage between Anglo-America and Europe serves as an attraction for European travel to the region.

Table 2–2 shows international tourism arrivals by region. Europe dominates the international arrivals, accounting for 58.98 percent of tourist arrivals in 1990. The major reason Europe dominates in numbers of international arrivals is the high rate of intraregional travel occurring in Europe. Europe has the highest intraregional travel of all regions of the world. The relatively strong economies of Europe and the close proximity of many nations encourage considerable international travel.

However, there has been a shift in arrivals since 1977. In that time, Europe's percentage of total world arrivals has declined nearly 15 percent. Most of the shift has been to East Asia and the Pacific, which increased from 4.5 percent of the world arrivals in 1977 to 14.1 percent in 1994.

The opening of China and the political agreements between Israel and Egypt have had strong positive effects on tourism to these two regions. However, sociopolitical problems, terrorism, and the rise of Islamic fundamentalism in the Middle East and North Africa have resulted in very little growth for tourism in that region. In 1977, the area received 1.7 percent of all world arrivals; this figure had only risen 1 percent by 1996. In the Americas, the shift has been from Latin America to North America, which increased 2 percent, or over 10 million annual visitors.

The higher rates of growth for the less industrialized regions as well as a smaller intraregional dependency indicates that tourism has many of the characteristics of an income transfer. Tourists and their money flow from the wealthy industrialized

Table 2-2 International Tourism by Region (in millions)

Region	1977	Percent of World	1996	Percent of World
Africa	4.7	2.0	19.6	3.3
Americas	46.6	19.4	115.6	19.5
North America	31.3	13.1	84.1	14.2
Latin America and Caribbean	15.3	6.3	31.5	5.3
East Asia and the Pacific	10.8	4.5	89.8	15.0
Europe	171.7	71.6	347.3	58.9
Middle East	4.0	1.7	15.1	2.6
South Asia	2.0	0.8	4.5	0.7
Total	239.8		591.9	

Courtesy Barbados Board of Tourism

Figure 2–4 Submarine with glass sides for watching sea life in the Caribbean.

Table 2-3 Top Twelve Spending Countries of the World, 1996

Origin	Expenditures (millions of U.S. dollars)	Cumulative Number	Cumulative Percent
1. United States	52,563	——	12.5
2. Germany	49,887	102,450	24.2
3. Japan	37,040	139,490	33.0
4. United Kingdom	26,622	166,112	39.3
5. France	16,528	182,640	43.2
6. Italy	15,488	198,128	46.8
7. Netherlands	11,370	209,498	49.2
8. Canada	11,170	220,668	52.2
9. Austria	11,165	231,833	54.8
10. Belgium	9,338	241,171	57.0
11. Switzerland	7,479	248,650	58.8
12. Taiwan	6,493	255,143	60.3

nations of the world to the less industrialized nations of the world. This trend is also true even in the European nations. The southern nations of Spain, Portugal, Greece, Italy, and Cyprus have had the greatest growth and are more dependent upon travel receipts to sustain their economies.

Seasonality

The strongest seasonal fluctuations are Europe's. The number of arrivals in the region during the summer months almost triple those of the low season of the first quarter of the year. North Africa and North America have a seasonality, but it is not nearly as pronounced as Europe's. Latin America, the Caribbean, and South Asia have a peak for arrivals in the first or fourth quarter, coinciding with summer in the southern hemisphere. While there is a small difference in the other regions, seasonality is not as marked.

Purpose of Visit

Throughout the world, holidays are the major purpose for travel, accounting for approximately 70 percent of world arrivals. The Middle East and Africa have a high number of travelers visiting for business purposes, well above the average for business travel throughout the world.

Tourism-Generating Countries

The economic importance of Western Europe, North America, and Japan in tourism expenditures is impressive. Table 2–3 lists in order of rank the twelve largest spending countries in international tourism. European nations, particularly Western European nations, dominate this list. The three nations outside of Europe, the United States, Canada, and Japan, are all economically advanced nations. The United States accounts for the most expenditures with 12.5 percent of total expenditures. Germany, second, accounts for 11.7 percent of the total world expenditures. The economic strength and the location of the European countries allow quick, easy access to other countries.

Travel Patterns

Although major upheavals in politics or economics or environmental disasters such as a hurricane or earthquake affect tourist flows, there seems to be a stable pattern that has developed over many years. Certainly, a few bad experiences in any of the three categories will alter the opportunities of any given country to attract and keep the tourist trade, but they are somewhat stable. A few factors that account for travel patterns include the following:

- Proximity
- Presence or absence of international connectivity, including business, political, military, and other ties
- Type and degree of service offered
- General attractiveness of a country to tourists from another country or culture
- Cost of traveling
- Influence of intervening opportunities
- The national character of the source country
- The mental image of the target area held by potential visitors (Williams and Zelinsky, 1970)

Examining these factors indicates how they create travel patterns. The type and degree of services offered is important because tourists want to have an enjoyable experience. A number of British enclaves have been established in various locations along the Costa del Sol in Spain, for instance. This concentration of English allows them to communicate with each other. Many stores specialize by speaking English (due in part to the number of English in the area). Fish-and-chips and tea sales are high in these tourist towns, and bingo games are conducted for the public. Hotels can also be identified by groups such as the English, Dutch, Swedish, and German, who tend to cluster together. Transportation systems enforce these patterns. The increasing demand and the growth of charter fares and other low fares, in turn, draw additional tourists to an area, thereby perpetuating the travel-flow patterns.

These factors, then, are important once a pattern of connectivity is established. They tend to strengthen the existing patterns and encourage further travel until dramatic events, such as the Gulf War in the Middle East, change them. (The specific patterns for each region are discussed in the chapters pertaining to the individual regions of the world.)

THE INFLUENCE OF TOURISM

The three major impacts that tourism has on the host nation are economic, *social and cultural*, and environmental. Most positive comments about the impact of tourism are economic, although other benefits can and do occur from tourism. Most negative comments about the impact of tourism are social-cultural and environmental. Environmental negative impacts will occur unless good planning occurs.

Economic Impact

Tourism is a major factor in providing foreign exchange and tax revenues needed by many nations to raise the standard of living of their citizens. Mexico, Spain, Greece, and the Bahamas are examples of countries that need the assistance that the flow of tourist money provides. This transfer of funds is an important factor in tourism and serves to help a country's *balance of payments*. The balance of payments is an accounting of the flow of goods, services, and funds in and out of a country during a given period. If a country pays, or agrees to pay, more money than it receives, it has a deficit in the balance of payments. If it receives more money than it sends, or exports, it has a surplus in its balance of payments.

There are three types of payments and receipts in international accounts:

1. Visible balance of trade, which includes import and export goods
2. *Invisible trade*
3. *Capital transfers*

The visible balance of trade is most familiar, and we hear a great deal about it. The United States exports large quantities of agricultural products and manufactured items to other countries, and in turn imports such things as raw materials from South America, cars from Japan and Germany, and oil from the Middle East and South America as part of its visible balance of trade.

Tourism is part of the invisible trade in the balance of payments. In some countries, such as Spain, Austria, Greece, Ireland, and Mexico, it is an important source of income. Although they have large numbers of tourists, travel expenditures in countries such as the United States and West Germany are not a major part of their balance of payments. In recent years, however, the tourist account is becoming more important in the United States, helping to offset large deficits in the balance of trade account. In the highly industrialized countries, tourism has little impact on the balance of trade payments because the economies of these countries are very diversified and very large.

In an effort to control the flow of money out of the country through tourism, most countries, including Spain, Brazil, France, and England, have set limits on the amount of money that can be taken out by a traveling citizen. Most limitations on travel and the flow of money in the invisible account occur when the total balance of payments is extremely unfavorable and the country is undergoing serious financial stress. Tourism receipts help stabilize income flow to a country, thereby creating a greater dependency upon tourism receipts than other commodities in the balance of trade payments.

The income that a nation receives from tourism benefits that nation in several ways. The additional money flows into the economy and becomes part of the exchange of goods and services both within and outside of the country, affecting businesses and salaries throughout the country. Income is also generated for the governments in the form of *taxes*, some of which are paid as part of the general taxes of the country, such as sales tax, or specific tourism taxes that are levied because tourism exists, such as room taxes on hotel rooms or special user taxes on destination facilities, to assist in further development.

In addition to income, tourism creates employment. The tourist industry is a labor-intensive activity. It employs large numbers of people by providing

Courtesy Ministry of Tourism, Bahamas

Figure 2–5 Mardi Gras in the Caribbean

a wide range of jobs from the unskilled to the highly specialized. Employment ranges from semi-skilled jobs for maids, porters, gardeners, or custodians, to more skilled positions such as accountants, managers, or entertainers. Further employment is generated in that those hired for tourism jobs then have money to spend; therefore, grocery stores, clothing stores, gas stations, and so on hire additional workers to meet the increased demand. There is more employment generated in tourism in the less industrialized nations than in the industrialized nations, as tourism employs people from population groups that are generally the most severely impacted by unemployment (women and youth). Importantly, employment wages for those in tourism in less industrialized nations are generally higher than the country's wage average; while in the industrialized nations, tourism wages are lower than average wages.

Infrastructure (roads, airports, sewers, tourist facilities, and so on) developed to encourage tourism can also be used by the local residents to improve their quality of life. This is particularly true in less industrialized regions of the world.

There are some negative economic characteristics of tourism. Generally, tourism is seasonal. Thus, income and employment are not always constant.

Inflation results from increased demand by tourists, in some cases increasing the cost of living for the local residents. In the centrally planned economies, the demand for "hard currency" is so high that a strong black market has developed in spite of rigid controls by the authorities to keep such activities from occurring. These elements can be further magnified when a country becomes highly dependent upon tourism as the major source of its trade. Planning can partially offset this problem. In Majorca, Spain, for example, the government has imposed a tax on hotels that helps to support unemployed hotel workers during the low-tourist-flow season.

Social and Cultural Impact

One important aspect of tourism is the development of a cultural understanding that could help to reduce international mistrust and suspicion and build a better world. However, in this area there is considerable concern, and much has been written about the negative impact of tourism in the area of social and cultural contact. Titles of numerous books and articles reveal this concern. *The Golden Hordes, The Tourist Ghettos of Hawaii, Tourism: The Other Face,* and *Tourism as a Form of Imperialism* are just a few titles that illustrate the negative view of tourism.

Tourism may be important to the host country or area in preserving its history and folk culture. In many countries of the world, many traditional folk costumes and customs are continued or reestablished for the benefit of tourists, and folklore festivals are organized to attract visitors. The establishment of arts and crafts centers among Indian tribes such as the Cherokee and the Navajo have helped sustain interest in Indian crafts.

There are many arts and crafts centers throughout the world for the same purpose. Many countries have cultural centers such as the Polynesian Cultural Center in Hawaii, which provides guests with a chance to view some limited historical aspects of a lifestyle as it once was and provides the nation an opportunity to maintain its traditions. The growth of these "living museums" can reduce the pressure on local religion and popular beliefs where tourists can profane places of worship and objects of reverence. But they can also serve to prostitute the sacred elements of a people's culture, trivializing sacred rituals for tourist consumption.

Another benefit that can result from tourism is associated with the return to the country or area of their origin by immigrants or their descendants, which serves to bring them closer to their ancestral homeland. Probably the most hoped-for benefit of tourism is the bringing together of people of different views to help them understand each other. It is suggested that tourism can become a tool for effecting understanding among people and cultures by causing people to reconsider their traditional stereotypes of the different cultures.

The level of economic development of a country is an important factor in the degree of cultural stress between groups. Tourism between the more industrialized countries, with their similar societies and well-developed infrastructures, creates little stress, at least until tourism numbers become so great that they create competition for goods and services between residents and travelers. A good example of this is in England, where lower air fares have brought record numbers of tourists. Public transportation is crowded throughout the day and so full of tourists that, at times, there is hardly any room for local residents. Shops are full of travelers, forcing British people to change shopping patterns. Subways and streets are filled with visitors, slowing down traffic. Westminster Cathedral has so many tourists that it hardly seems like a church. There is a strong subjective feeling that tourism growth in London cannot continue to increase. Many believe there is a saturation level, at which point residents will declare that

enough tourists are enough. The notion of saturation and its impact was illustrated in the London *Sunday Times*, where the change that occurred to the Spanish town Lloret was reported:

> They say it used to be a fishing village . . . but the village itself has disappeared beneath an appalling welter of hotel blocks, fish-and-chips shops, pubs, souvenir shops, discotheques, and slot-machine arcades. In the height of summer Lloret is a quite dreadful place. . . . Perhaps the most obnoxious feature is the smell of cooking oil—the product of hamburgers, deep-fried chips, deep-fried fish, deep-fried chicken . . . (which) on hot summer nights drifts around the alleys and lanes, merging with other smells from broken sewers or spilt beer. The odd thing is so few people care. "Lloret is finished," says a Spanish waiter with a shrug . . . but thousands of tourists who pour into Lloret every summer from Britain, Germany, Holland, Scandinavia, and Belgium seem to disagree with that verdict. (*The Sunday Times*, 1972)

The same thing is happening in many other Spanish coastal cities. In fact, newspapers advertise for help, but add if an individual speaks only Spanish, he or she should not apply. In some of these cities very little, if any, Spanish is heard. An Australian lady moved from Marbella, on the Costa del Sol, to Malaga to learn Spanish. She was able to learn French or her native English from her interaction with the people on the streets in Marbella.

Alienation may be generated in the host area, leading to social unrest between the "haves" and "have nots." A number of factors account for this alienation. One results from the nature of the tourist, who is generally from an industrialized country and used to demanding service and receiving prompt attention, while in many host countries the pace of life may be slower and less hectic. Therefore, when a tourist demands service, he or she may become impatient with the different culture, creating resentment among the local people.

A second factor creating social conflict, particularly in countries or areas with serious economic problems, is tourist wealth. High-living tourists eat in fine restaurants and live in hotels among splendor in an area of hunger, unemployment, and little opportunity for jobs or education. This has led in some cases to militant revolutionary action. A third factor involved in alienation is the associated change that occurs in the local inhabitants of an area. In many cases, there are increases in male and female prostitution. Many young men, for example, flock to the coasts of Spain in hope of meeting young Swedish and

Time Zones of the World

The Western Hemisphere

0 _____ 5000 km
0 _____ 3000 miles

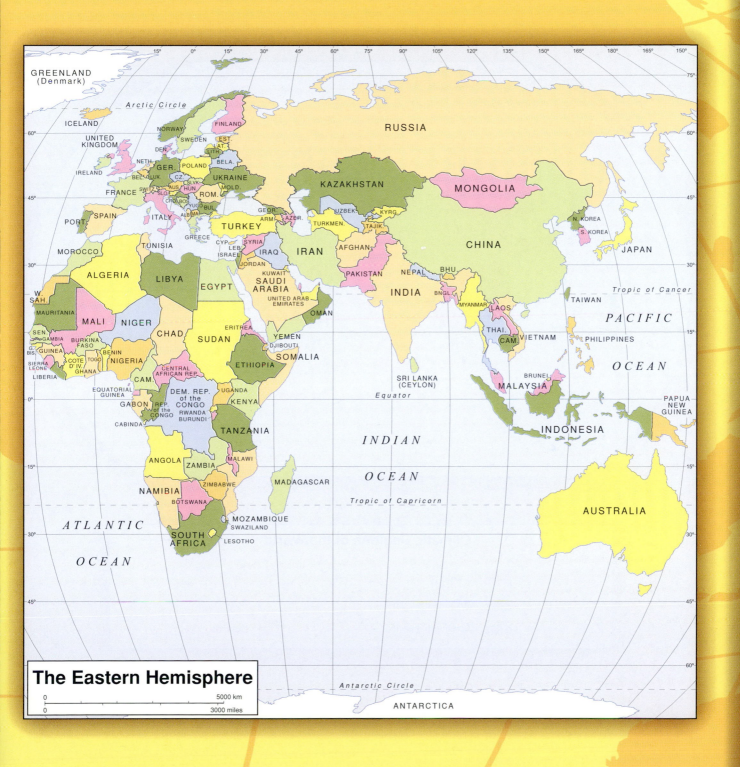

The Eastern Hemisphere

GREENLAND (Denmark)

Arctic Circle

ICELAND
NORWAY
SWEDEN
FINLAND
UNITED KINGDOM
DEN.
EST.
LAT.
LITH.
IRELAND
NETH.
GER.
POLAND
BELA.
BEL. LUX.
CZ.
UKRAINE
FRANCE
SWITZ.
AUS. SLOV.
HUN.
MOLD.
CRO. BOS.
ROM.
YUGO.
BUL.
SPAIN
ITALY
ALB. MAC.
GEOR.
PORT.
GREECE
ARM.
AZER.
MOROCCO
TUNISIA
CYP.
LEB.
SYRIA
TURKEY
TURKMEN.
ISRAEL
IRAQ
IRAN
JORDAN
ALGERIA
LIBYA
EGYPT
KUWAIT
SAUDI ARABIA
UZBEK.
KYRG.
TAJIK.
AFGHAN.
PAKISTAN
NEPAL
BHU.

RUSSIA

KAZAKHSTAN
MONGOLIA
N. KOREA
S. KOREA
CHINA
JAPAN

W. SAH.
MAURITANIA
MALI
NIGER
CHAD
SUDAN
ERITREA
YEMEN
DJIBOUTI
UNITED ARAB EMIRATES
OMAN
INDIA
BNGL.
MYANMAR
LAOS
TAIWAN
Tropic of Cancer

SEN.
GAMBIA
G. BIS.
GUINEA
BURKINA FASO
BENIN
TOGO
NIGERIA
GHANA
COTE D'IV.
SIERRA LEONE
LIBERIA
CENTRAL AFRICAN REP.
CAM.
ETHIOPIA
SOMALIA
THAI.
CAM.
VIETNAM
PHILIPPINES

PACIFIC

OCEAN

EQUATORIAL GUINEA
GABON
REP. of the CONGO
DEM. REP. of the CONGO
UGANDA
KENYA
RWANDA
BURUNDI
SRI LANKA (CEYLON)
Equator
BRUNEI
MALAYSIA
PAPUA NEW GUINEA

CABINDA
TANZANIA
INDONESIA

ANGOLA
ZAMBIA
MALAWI
INDIAN

NAMIBIA
ZIMBABWE
BOTSWANA
MADAGASCAR
OCEAN
Tropic of Capricorn

ATLANTIC

OCEAN
SOUTH AFRICA
MOZAMBIQUE
SWAZILAND
LESOTHO
AUSTRALIA

Antarctic Circle

ANTARCTICA

| 0 | | 5000 km |
| 0 | | 3000 miles |

Climatic Regions of the World

Tropical

Mesothermal Humid

Microthermal Humid

Dry

Polar

Uplands

Tourist Arrivals of the World:
Overnight Visitors (Thousands)

0 — 5,000 km
0 — 3,000 miles

- More than 10,000
- 1,001 to 10,000
- 101 to 1,000
- 10 to 100
- Less than 10
- Data missing or unavailable

Language Families of the World

Sino-Tibetan	Saharan	Japanese and Korean	Papuan and Australian
Indo-European	Khoisan	Dravidian	American Indian
Niger-Congo	Sudanic	Austro-Asiatic	Other
Afro-Asiatic	Ural-Altaic	Malay-Polynesian	Unpopulated Areas

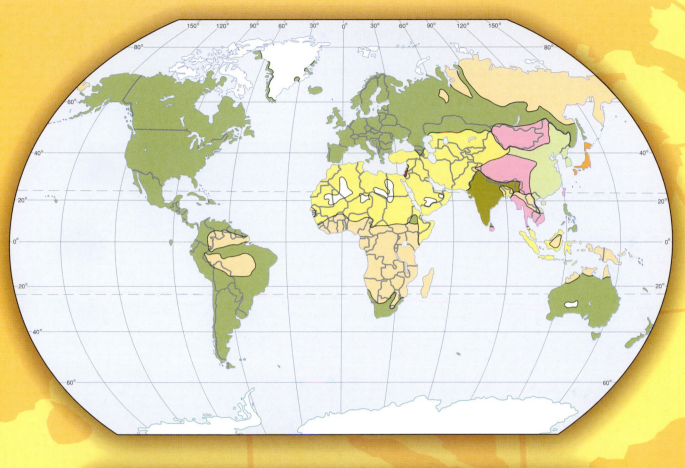

Major Religions of the World

0 ——————— 5,000 km
0 ——————— 3,000 miles

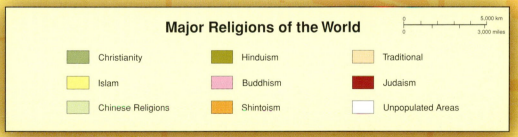

- Christianity
- Islam
- Chinese Religions
- Hinduism
- Buddhism
- Shintoism
- Traditional
- Judaism
- Unpopulated Areas

IATA Regions of the World

0 ————————— 5,000 km
0 ————————— 3,000 miles

AREA 1	AREA 2	AREA 3

AREA 1

North America
Latin America
South America

AREA 2

Europe
Middle East
Africa

AREA 3

Asia   New Zealand
Far East   Pacific Islands
Australia

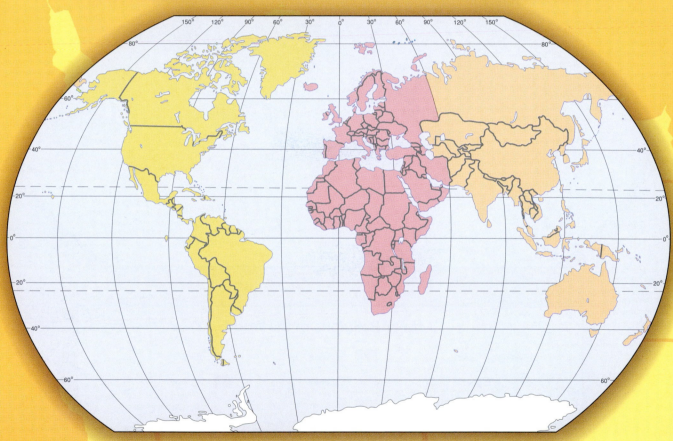

English girls for fun and profit. It is not an unfamiliar sight to see a young Spanish boy, with his shirt unbuttoned to the navel, passionately kissing a blond Swedish girl goodbye, swearing his undying love as she prepares to depart. Almost at the same time she is going through the portals of the airport, he is pursuing another Scandinavian beauty arriving on the same plane that the former friend is leaving on, swearing undying devotion and offering his services and companionship during her stay.

A fourth factor causing alienation occurs in some less industrialized countries that import foreign workers for the tourism industry. Many multinational corporations bring in workers from other countries who have experience at working in hotels and other tourist-related positions. They are placed in positions of management, giving the local residents a feeling of *economic colonialism* since the management positions are given to outsiders. The foreign workers generally fill the better–paying jobs and are in many cases supervisors of less-skilled citizens. Because they have the better-paying jobs, they can then compete more favorably for goods and services in the community and country.

Other changes that occur in many cultures as a result of tourism are in patterns of food consumption. Certainly very large numbers of tourists visit Kentucky Fried Chicken, McDonalds, Burger King, German beer halls, and English fish-and-chips parlors, depending upon the nationality of the tourist. The impact varies from place to place. In some areas, the importation of strange foods has small impact, while in other places a considerable change occurs.

In addition to changes in food, some areas of the world experience a continued westernization of the culture. For example, in the market town of Chichicastengo in Guatemala, the ability of tourists to outbid the local residents for the native clothing and material has created a shift to less-expensive western wear from the more colorful clothing of the areas. This, of course, changes the "local color" of the area and may in the future damage the ability to draw tourists to the market.

It is not an unfamiliar scene for a tourist to be met near an archaeological site by a native desiring to sell artifacts he "just discovered" (or made) that morning. In some cases, this allows important archaeological artifacts to leave the country, but it can be beneficial if properly controlled. The local residents can produce copies of relics or local jewelry to provide income and employment opportunities. Also, the tourists' interest may enhance the local awareness of the importance of such archaeological sites and develop their appreciation of native works of art and crafts.

The excerpt "Island Lifestyle" illustrates two cultures coming together to share an experience, which in the end neither enjoyed. Both cultural groups would have an unfavorable view of the other culture. However, it is the responsibility of the tourist to learn how to be a good visitor. Tourists from industrialized nations have come to expect travel experiences to provide them with the comforts of home. They look upon travel to many of the less industrialized nations as "quaint" experiences that will provide them with something to talk about when they go home.

Environmental Impact

It seems that some people, in their eagerness to capitalize on opportunities for immediate enjoyment or gratification, do not consider the future consequences of that enjoyment. This characteristic applies particularly in tourist areas where nature itself is the chief attraction. Tourists are attracted to scenic harbors, cascading waterfalls, and large lakes surrounded by high mountains or volcanoes. But in enjoying these attractions, tourists, being human, may threaten the natural beauty because they don't consider the long-term effect of increased tourist use. Increased visits to natural wonders has a tendency to destroy what we find attractive, unless effective plans to balance tourism and the *environment* are developed.

The term environment is used rather loosely, indicating both human and physical characteristics. Authors, speakers, and literature often refer to human environment, physical environment, or a combination of both. A term that can be introduced to describe the change that occurs in the character of an area is "pre-existing forms." Pre-existing forms characterize an area's human and physical environment before being "discovered" as a major tourist destination area. We use it simply to indicate what an area is like in its cultural and physical setting before tourism invades. The social and cultural impacts of tourism were discussed earlier, and in part deal with the human environment that occurs as a result of tourism.

An excellent example of changing pre-existing forms associated with both the human and physical environment is the development of coastal resorts and cities. In Spain, for example, several coastal villages have been changed rather dramatically in the past few years. Travel posters of the area usually highlight the area as it was before tourism. Yet, when visited by the tourist, the scattered villages of Torremolinos, Benidorm, Lloret del Mar, and other small villages are no longer recognizable.

A second factor of large tourist development has been the *pollution* of surrounding areas. Uncontrolled building on the coasts of southern Spain, the

Through Hosts' Eyes

The Island Lifestyle: Endangered Species

In one of our islands (Micronesia), arrangements were made for handling a luxury yacht with fifty passengers. The schedule called for an early morning arrival in the harbor and at 8:30, after breakfast on the yacht, two small buses would carry the visitors on a sightseeing tour across the island to a secluded beach where a barbecue lunch would be served "under swaying coconut palms, where the sparkling lagoon kisses the sandy shore." After lunch, the group would visit the rest of the island and stop at the handicraft shop for a look at the local offerings. The yacht was scheduled to "sail away on the outgoing tide, as the sun sets slowly in the west."

It sounded great. Even the local residents thought it would be fun. But let me tell you what really happened . . . as closely as I can recall the words of one of the tour escorts as he described the day's events some time later.

He said, "When the tourists came off the ship, they all had on white shoes. Nobody brought zoris (rubber slippers). All the men wore white pants. None of the tourists looked past the dock to see that it had rained all night and there was plenty of mud. Lots of local people came down to the dock to see the boat and the tourists took lots of pictures of them. Everybody was smiling. Almost everybody on the island was there. But missing was one of the two bus drivers. The night before was his birthday party and he had a hard time waking up and didn't get to the dock until nine o'clock, a half hour late. When the buses left after nine, the island people were still smiling but the tourists were not.

"When we reached the middle of the island, one of tourists on the bus looked at his watch and hollered, 'Hey, it's ten-thirty and the schedule says we're supposed to be at the village and we're not even halfway there yet. Let's go back to the ship.' Then everybody started arguing with each other. The bus driver and I didn't pay any attention but just drove on.

"After we reached the other side of the island and the tourists had their walk through the village, they came to the beach where the girls from the hotel were barbecuing spare ribs and chicken. We had a pickup truck set up with a bar because we know that tourists have to take a shot before they can eat. When the tourists reached the beach, they had mud on the outside and inside of their shoes and their clothes were real messy. When they saw the beach, they said it looked too dirty and they wanted to go back to the ship. They didn't like the place because there were palm branches and coconuts lying all around and they would have to sit on a coconut log to eat their lunch. So we took them back to the ship and finished cooking the lunch in the kitchen. After lunch, we gave them a ride around the other side of the island and stopped at the handicraft cooperative. But nobody bought anything. They wanted tapa, which we don't make. They wanted wooden story boards, which we don't make on our island. And they wanted a certain kind of purse that we don't make. And they said the prices were too high . . . they could get things cheaper in the Philippines.

"When the ship left late that afternoon, all of us standing on the dock felt mad. Then somebody said, 'Lucky they never stayed overnight,' and we all started to laugh. We were so happy because the tourists were leaving."

(Ashman, 1976)

Italian Riviera, the Vireggio Coast, and the Adriatic Sea has destroyed completely the natural character of those areas. Hundreds upon hundreds of miles of shoreline have been changed irreparably by the sprawl of hotels, restaurants, bars, and houses. Beaches have been partitioned by unsightly buildings, awash with noise from discos and jukeboxes, traffic fumes, and tremendous overpopulation during certain seasons of the year.

It can be expected that some change in pre-existing forms will be necessary to accommodate mass tourism. However, location and concentration of development can be controlled carefully by the government in order to take advantage of income and employment opportunities for tourism while reducing its social and cultural impact. Concentration limits the impact on both the social and natural environment.

A common concept used in discussing the environment (whether for tourism or any other use) is the *carrying capacity*. Carrying capacity is that level of tourism development that can occur in the destination or at an attraction that, when exceeded, will cre-

Figure 2-6 Elephants in game park in Africa

ate environmental degradation to the area that cannot be relieved with controls or other forms of tourism.

Ecotourism is becoming more and more important. Ecotourism is environmentally responsible travel to natural areas that helps to preserve the area being visited. It seeks to reduce the impact of tourism on sensitive areas and to protect the indigenous populations of a region by using tourism as a tool for conservation. Tourism has degradation potential for both the indigenous populations and the physical environment.

Elements of environmental degradation that take place as a result of tourism can be divided into a number of sub-elements.

Pollution

The use of automobiles, taxis, buses, and aircraft has resulted in a number of problems related to polluted air. Air pollution is probably less of a problem for the travel industry than for other industries, yet those locations with a number of conveyances to move people will suffer from some pollution. Two national parks, Yosemite and Shenandoah, among others, have had problems with congestion causing air pollution and hurting vegetation.

Most research and studies on pollution have focused on the discharge of untreated water from resorts or boats into seas, lakes, rivers, and the springs. The lack of an effective sewage system on Tarawa, an island in the South Pacific, for example, has led to the

widespread pollution of its inshore waters, making fish consumption inadvisable and swimming unhealthy. Mediterranean pollution, in part due to tourist development, is considered a threat to swimmers in some places. In addition, such diseases as cholera, typhoid, viral hepatitis, and dysentery can be traced to seafood from polluted waters.

Noise pollution is a third form of pollution associated with traffic congestion on land and in the air. Also, many recreational vehicles—motorcycles, motorboats, snowmobiles, and aircraft—cause excessive noise.

Vegetation

Destruction and degradation of vegetation in an area result from two factors: the large number of visitors that overwhelm an area and physical abuse to the vegetation, either by vandalism or collection. Loss of vegetation leads to soil erosion and further degradation of the environment.

Wildlife

Problems associated with wildlife changes result from the killing of animals or birds and the disruption of normal habits of feeding and breeding.

Natural Landscapes

Construction results in the encroachment of facilities or buildings upon open spaces, both natural and man-made, such as agricultural or pastoral lands. In some cases, the creation of suprastructures and infrastructures removes valuable natural sites from public access and reserves them only for the guests of resorts or hotels.

CONCLUSION

The general impact of tourism seems to be positive if the carrying capacity is not exceeded. Tourism has stimulated the rehabilitation of existing historic sites, buildings, and monuments. It has been an important impetus for converting natural resources into game parks as in Kenya and Tanzania. These parks were established in hopes of attracting tourists and resulted in preserving wild animals in many places throughout Africa. Recognition of the need for proper planning to conserve the environment for future generations has also resulted in tourism.

The economic and social impact on a poorer country can be very beneficial, and the greater awareness of life in other lands can lead to a better world. Examination of tourism in individual world regions helps to explain the impact of the ever-growing tourist industry on countries.

REVIEW QUESTIONS

1. Discuss the three common elements of the definition of tourism.
2. What are some reasons you might suggest to have a definition for visitors as tourists or excursionists?
3. Discuss three factors important for tourism.
4. Describe the Grand Tour.
5. Compare and contrast tourism during the Roman time with tourism today.
6. How did the Industrial Revolution contribute to an increase in tourism?
7. Describe the history of tourism in the United States.
8. What regions of the world generate the most tourists? Why?
9. Identify the positive and negative economic impacts of tourism.
10. What cultural and social problems occur as a result of tourism?
11. What are some environmental problems resulting from tourism?

GEOGRAPHY AND TOURISM IN
North America

CHAPTER 3

MAJOR GEOGRAPHIC CHARACTERISTICS

- Canada and the United States are characterized by urban and ethnically diverse populations.
- North America has a diversified resource base, including fertile soils that make it the major food-surplus region in the world.
- North America has a high total and per capita consumption of resources and consumer goods.
- The region is more dependent upon the automobile than any other region of the world.
- Canada and the United States are democratic federal states, but each has a unique political organization.

MAJOR TOURISM CHARACTERISTICS

- Tourism is an important element in the quality of life of residents of North America.
- The region is one of the largest origin regions for international tourism.
- The region is one of the largest international destination regions of the world.
- The automobile is the major form of travel for domestic tourism.
- The attractions in the region are extremely diversified.

MAJOR TOURIST DESTINATIONS

Canada
Toronto
Montréal
Edmonton
Québec
Ottawa-Hull
Calgary
Vancouver
London
Winnipeg
Halifax

United States
International Visitors
  New York City
  Washington, D.C.
  Las Vegas
  Miami
  San Francisco
  Los Angeles
  New Orleans
  Grand Canyon
Domestic
  Orlando, Florida
  Branson, Missouri
  Yellowstone National Park
  San Diego, California
  Lancaster, Pennsylvania
  Williamsburg, Virginia
  Oahu, Hawaii

KEY TERMS AND WORDS

AMTRAK
Canadian Shield
Civil War
Cultural Centers
Fall Line
Gaming
Hall of Fame
Historical Houses
Memorial
Middle Class

National Park
Piedmont
Province
St. Lawrence
State
Territories
Urban
Wealth
Wilderness

While geographically North America includes Mexico, the general perception of many North Americans is that the name refers to the United States and Canada. Since we have organized this book on a cultural basis, Mexico is included in Latin America. The discussion on North America focuses on what is commonly referred to in geography as Anglo-Amer-ica (Canada and the United States), Figure 3–1. The two countries are similar in that they have the same general ethnic origins and are the end products of the Industrial Revolution. They are *wealthy*, mobile, highly educated societies with an abundance of lei-sure time and consumer goods. Canada and the United States vie with the countries of Western Europe as a large travel region. Most European countries are close and small when compared to the United States and Canada. Consequently, they have a high proportion of their population involved in international travel. In spite of the great distances involved, the United States and Canada are world leaders in international (both as an origin and a destination) and domestic travel.

North America is one of the most urbanized societies in the world. The scale of urbanization exceeds that of any other region except Western Europe. The North American city is dominated by skyscrapers, even though these tall buildings occupy but a minor part of the total area occupied by the city. Regional and national cities dominated by impressive skylines and seemingly never-ending suburbs are a unique phenomenon. The ubiquitous automobile, found in America in numbers unmatched anywhere in the world, has allowed cities to sprawl across the landscape and is a dominant force in domestic tourism in both nations.

Although a few oil-producing countries, along with Sweden and Switzerland, have per capita gross national products that exceed those of Canada and the United States, these two nations combined represent the world's largest concentration of *middleclass* people. These middle classes enjoy a life of luxury compared to more than three-fourths of the world's people. They are middle class only because there exists an even wealthier elite in the two countries. These two countries together enjoy a standard of living that is only a dream for the world's hungry, illiterate, ill-housed, ill-fed, and underemployed majority. There are pockets of poverty and a low standard of living, particularly in African-American and Latino communities. However, the general wealth allows citizens of the two countries a degree of financial independence and free time to pursue travel-related experiences unmatched elsewhere. Since 1850, the workweek has been reduced from seventy hours a week to less than forty hours per week. Other benefits resulting from the efforts of labor unions include sick leave, paid vacations, and other fringe benefits, which allow the residents of these countries to spend approximately one-third of their time in leisure. The region is truly one in which leisure is one of the most important characteristics.

PHYSICAL CHARACTERISTICS

Landforms

The landforms of North America have been conducive to human use. The landforms of the region, Figure 3–2, include several that are common to both Canada and the United States. Major landforms are the *Canadian Shield*, the Atlantic Coastal Plain, the *Piedmont*, the Appalachian Mountains, the Central Lowlands, the Great Plains area, the Western mountains, and the Pacific Coastal Plain.

The Canadian Shield

The greater part of Canada consists of an old igneous rock mass that has been highly glaciated. Called the Canadian Shield, it is important because of its diverse and abundant mineral resources. Except for some relatively rugged hills in eastern Québec and Labrador, this is a gently rolling landscape with hundreds of thousands of water bodies, ranging in size from minute to large, connected by thousands of rivers and streams. The Shield was the center of continental glaciation in North America that leveled the land and created numerous lakes, marshes, and ponds.

The Atlantic Coastal Plain

The Atlantic Coastal Plain is a broad, easily accessible plain. There are two recognizable regions. The first is north of Cape Fear, North Carolina. It is an area of submerged coast, where the coast has sunk in the past, flooding the river mouths. The second is south of this point to the Mexican border. It is an emergent coastal plain, where the land is slowly rising. The submerged portion is the location of the flooded, or drowned, river mouths of the *St. Lawrence*, Hudson, Chesapeake, and Susquehanna rivers. These drowned river mouths are known as estuaries. They provide excellent harbors, allowing ocean-going vessels to travel some distance into the land area. The coastal plain is narrower in the area of the submerged coast, but the existence of the drowned river mouths allows access inland. The emergent coastal plain in the southeastern United States has poorly drained lands in which rivers are shallow and winding, and the sites for ports are few and less suitable.

POPULATION CHARACTERISTICS							
Country	Pop. (mil) 1997	Annual Growth Rate (percent)	Time to Double Pop. (yr)	Per Capita GNP	Life Exp (yr)	Calorie Intake (daily)	Percent Urban
Canada	30.1	0.5	127	19,380	78	3,482	77
United States	267.7	0.6	116	26,980	76	3,671	75

Figure 3–1 Map of Canada and the United States

The Piedmont

Between the Atlantic Coastal Plain and the Appalachian Mountains is the piedmont, a transition zone between mountains and plains. It is separated from the coastal plain by the *fall line*, the point at which streams descend from the high piedmont to the lower coastal plain. Rarely is the fall line an actual waterfall; it is normally a series of rapids and is the furthest point ships can travel upstream on the rivers. The fall line is the location for several important cities such as Washington, D.C.

The Appalachian Mountains

The Appalachians are a series of parallel mountains. Their elevations rarely exceed five thousand feet, but because of their north-south orientation, they have historically handicapped easy transporta-

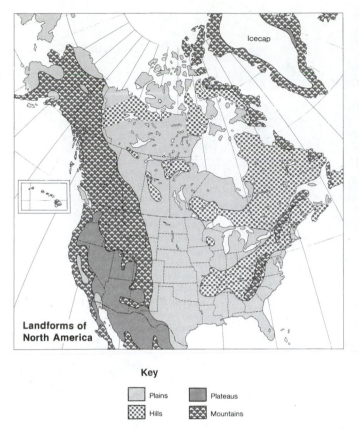

Key

Plains   Plateaus

Hills   Mountains

Figure 3–2 Map of landforms of Canada and the United States

tion from east to west in the United States. The Appalachians contain extensive deposits of high-grade coal in their sedimentary rocks.

The Central Lowlands

The Central Lowlands constitute the agricultural heart of the American continent. They are formed by the Ohio-Mississippi-Missouri drainage. In Canada these lowlands lie along the Great Lakes of Erie and Ontario, and the St. Lawrence River. This area is fertile, well-drained, and level, making it suitable for mechanized equipment.

The Great Plains

West of the Central Lowlands, the land rises and becomes the Great Plains of Canada and the United States. It stretches from San Antonio in the south to the edge of the Arctic Lowlands in the north. The plains rise from five hundred feet above sea level in the east to five thousand feet above sea level in the west. The combined area of the Great Plains and Central Lowlands in the United States constitutes more than one-half of the total landmass. This broad expanse of level, fertile land has provided a tremendous base for agricultural development. The Great Plains of Canada are interrupted far less frequently

by small hills or knolls than the Great Plains of the United States.

The Western Mountains

The Great Plains merge to the west into the north-south trending Rocky Mountains complex, which has elevations exceeding fifteen thousand feet. The mountains are important because of their impact on climate and transportation; their resources, as the source for many of the major rivers in the continent; as a recreational region; and as a barrier between the Great Plains and the West. The Canadian portion of the Rocky Mountains offers some of the most beautiful views in all the world. The area of Western Canada is known as the Western cordillera, which is an area of mountains and plateaus and valleys. The two main ranges are the Rocky Mountains and the Coast Mountains with peaks exceeding elevation of thirteen thousand feet. Between the ranges are other ranges of mountains, the Fraser River Plateau, and the Okanagan Valley. East of the Okanagan are ranges of the Rockies, such as the Caribou, Monashees, Selkirks, Purcells, and the Kootenays, and the Columbia ranges.

The Pacific Coastal Plains

In the United States the coastal ranges, the Sierra Nevada, and the Cascade Mountains are separated from the Rocky Mountains by a series of plateaus, block mountains, and basins, which is known as the Basin and Range region. The Basin and Range region in the United States is an arid region with internal drainage. An example is the Great Salt Lake.

The complex series of basins and plateaus comprising the Basin and Range is bordered on the west by the high mountains of the Sierra Nevada. West of the Sierra Nevada is the Central Valley of California, which is separated from the Pacific by the California coastal ranges. North of the Sierra Nevada, the Cascade Range of Oregon and Washington consists of volcanic mountains. With mountains in the west rising abruptly from the seashore, the coastal plain areas are limited.

Alaska includes the northern extension of the Rocky Mountains; the Brooks and McKenzie Ranges and the High Plateaus, which are dissected; the low volcanic mountains of the Alaskan Peninsula and Aleutian Islands; high coastal glaciated mountains; and the Alaska Range, which includes the highest peaks in North America in Denali National Park. Denali ranges over 20,000 feet in elevation. The northern extremes of Alaska and Canada consist of the Arctic Coastal Plain or Lowland.

Hawaii is an archipelago of more than 130 islands.

They are volcanic mountains in nature with a luxuriant tropical vegetation. Elevations reach 13,000 feet above sea level.

The River Systems

An important element of the physical character of North America is its natural transportation arteries. In the past, the river systems of the continent provided routes for expansion of settlement and fostered unification. Today the rivers provide major transportation for industrial and agricultural development. The most important river system is the St. Lawrence–Great Lakes, which can be navigated halfway across the continent.

The second major river system on the continent is the Mississippi and its tributaries, such as the Arkansas, Ohio, and Missouri. This system drains the entire central area of the continent. On a world scale, it is surpassed only by the Rhine River in importance for river transportation. It is navigable by locks as far upstream as Pittsburgh on the Ohio and Minneapolis-St. Paul on the Mississippi. It is tied to Lake Michigan by the Illinois-Michigan Barge Canal. Navigation on the Missouri is primarily from Omaha to its junction with the Mississippi. The Arkansas River is also navigable for barge traffic, and a massive canal-building project has made Tulsa, Oklahoma, a seaport. This river system provides low-cost transportation that makes New Orleans the largest port in the United States in terms of total tonnage.

In the West, two main river systems provide access to the interior. The Columbia River is navigable for barge traffic as far inland as Idaho. The Sacramento River is navigable to Sacramento. The Colorado, which is not important for transportation, provides water to the arid West. The importance of the water of the Colorado for agriculture, industry, and residential use in the arid American West makes it even more significant to the inhabitants of the lands through which it passes than the Mississippi is to the Central Lowlands. In addition, the Colorado is used for recreational activities by millions of people.

Climate Characteristics

There are a wide variety of climatic types in North America. The factors contributing to the continent's climatic pattern are:

- its great latitudinal extent
- its size
- the prevailing westerly winds
- the warm, moist air from the Gulf of Mexico
- the mountain ranges

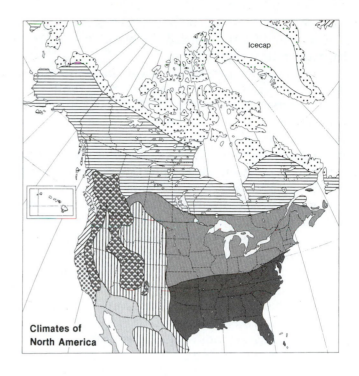

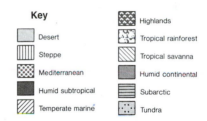

Figure 3–3 Map of climates of Canada and the United States

- the land and water relationships in and around the continent

North America has ten major climatic types, Figure 3–3. In the north is an area of tundra that is essentially uninhabited. Subarctic climate occupies much of Alaska and Canada and helps to explain the more limited economic development in Canada. The area is sparsely inhabited, except for localized settlements for mining, trapping, or other extractive economic activities. It is an area of coniferous forests.

The marine west coast climate extends from 60 degrees north latitude to approximately 40 degrees north latitude on the west coast of Canada and the United States. This area has relatively intensive settlement, particularly south of the 50th parallel starting with the city of Vancouver. North of Vancouver settlements become very scarce. The ocean bordering this area gives the region relatively cool summer temperatures and mild winters for its latitude, along with an abundance of precipitation to support coniferous forests. The moderate temperatures provide a long growing season. The region is less developed in Canada than in the United States because of more rugged landforms in Canada.

The southern part of California has a Mediterranean climate, with hot, dry summers and mild, wetter winters. This is one of the most important tourism areas in Anglo-America. The interior areas of Southern California have a desert climate, with low amounts of precipitation and isolated population settlements. Although precipitation ranges only from 6 to 25 inches per year, California is the most populous state in the United States, with more inhabitants than all of Canada.

The western mountainous region of the United States has desert and steppe climates. Some of the driest areas of the world are the interior deserts of California, Nevada, Arizona, and New Mexico. In Canada, cooler temperatures minimize the extent of the desert and steppe regions.

The eastern regions of the United States and Canada have humid continental climates. Both warm and cool summer types are found and are associated with some of the most fertile agricultural lands in the world.

Humid subtropical climate dominates the southeastern United States. Summers are hot and humid, and winters are typically moderate with long periods of subfreezing temperatures uncommon. The southern tip of Florida and the Florida Keys have a savanna climate with a hot, humid summer and a warm, drier winter, which has contributed to their development as a winter tourist center. Hawaii has a tropical rainforest climate with a trade wind that provides an excellent climate for tourism year-round.

The essentially north-south orientation of the mountains in North America results in important modifications of the humid continental and humid subtropical climates of the United States. The absence of any physical barrier across the central plains allows cold Canadian and Arctic air to move farther south in the United States than in any other continent. Consequently, the humid subtropical climate of the United States periodically experiences freezing temperatures, which damage citrus and vegetable crops in the deep South.

TOURISM CHARACTERISTICS

Tourism and the tourist industry are of major importance in Canada and the United States. North Ameri-

cans travel on a scale that is unequalled in the world for domestic and international travel combined. The versatility and variety of the industry, with its rich combination of public and private organizations, characterizes North American tourism.

Although it is considerably more isolated from international borders than the West European countries, international travel ranks high in the United States. The United States had the highest international and domestic expenditures and tourism receipts of all countries in the world in 1996, while Canada ranked eighth in tourism expenditures and eleventh in tourist receipts, Table 3–1. Another example of the health of the travel industry in North America can be seen in airport statistics. In 1996, of the top twenty airports in the world (ranked in terms of total number of passengers), only eight were outside North America. Of these eight, Heathrow Airport in London has the highest ranking, but it only ranks fifth in the world. Of the top fifty world airports, only twenty-two are located outside the North American market. Even Salt Lake City, with a relatively small metropolitan population of 1.2 million, ranks thirty-sixth in the world. This is even more impressive when considering that over 80 percent of trips taken in North America are by private automobile.

Table 3–1 World's Top International Tourism Dollars, 1996				
Country	Receipts (millions of US $)	Rank	Payments (millions of US $)	Rank
United States	64,373	1	52,563	1
Spain	28,428	2	4,921	16
France	28,241	3	16,528	5
Italy	27,349	4	15,488	6
United Kingdom	19,738	5	26,622	4
Austria	14,039	6	11,165	9
Germany	15,815	7	49,887	2
China	10,200	9	4,200	21
Switzerland	8,661	10	7,479	12
Singapore	7,916	11	6,104	18
Canada	8,813	12	11,170	8
Mexico	6,894	16	3,387	13
Poland	8,400	15	7,500	15
Netherlands	6,256	20	11,370	7
Belgium	5,893	19	9,338	10
Japan	4,069	25	37,040	3

Canada

PROVINCE PROFILE

Province	Capital	Square Miles	Population (1995)
Alberta	Edmonton	257,287	2,696,826
British Columbia	Victoria	365,948	3,724,500
Manitoba	Winnipeg	250,947	1,113,898
New Brunswick	Fredericton	28,355	738,133
Newfoundland and Labrador	St. John's	155,649	551,792
Northwest Territory	Yellowknife	1,322,910	64,402
Nova Scotia	Halifax	21,425	909,282
Ontario	Toronto	412,581	10,753,573
Prince Edward Island	Charlottetown	2,185	134,557
Québec	Québec City	594,860	7,138,795
Saskatchewan	Regina	251,866	990,237
Yukon	Whitehorse	186,661	30,766

Source: Statistics Canada, 1996

TRAVEL TIPS

Entry: United States citizens visiting Canada may be required to show proof of citizenship.

Time Zone: Time zones in Canada correspond to those in the United States with the exception of Atlantic time (one hour ahead of eastern standard time), which is observed in New Brunswick, Nova Scotia, and Prince Edward Island; and Newfoundland time (1 hour and 30 minutes ahead of eastern standard time), which is observed only in the Province of Newfoundland.

Transportation and Communications: Canadian telephone facilities are excellent, and direct dialing is possible between the United States and Canada. Public transportation in cities is excellent. Accessibility to the United States is excellent by both automobile and air service.

CULTURAL CAPSULE

Canadians tend to view their country less as a melting pot than as a cultural mosaic. Inuit, Indian Nations, French, English, and other immigrant groups have sought to maintain their unique cultural identities.

Cultural Hints:
- Do not compare Canada with the United States.
- Firm handshake and eye contact.
- Little or no casual touching.
- Offensive gestures are the same as in the United States.
- To signal a waiter, raise your hand.
- For the check, motion with one hand as if you are writing.
- In French-speaking Québec thumbs-down is offensive.
- Eating and food:
  In Québec do not eat on the street.

In Québec nod the head to beckon a waiter.
Tipping is 10 to 15 percent.
Dress appropriately for dinner.
Food is reflective of the region and ethnic character:
  French pastries and breads in Québec
  Potatoes, red meats, and breads
  Wild rice, smoked fish, beef, smoked salmon, and seafood

The infrastructure of the tourism industry in Canada is similar to that of the United States. Many of the hotels and restaurants belong to chains or are members of franchises based in the United States. Several United States airlines provide direct service to the larger Canadian cities. Air Canada has purchased a share of Continental Airlines and this should in the future integrate the whole North American market, creating greater interaction and better connectivity. Competition between government corporations and private industry is a tradition in Canada, evident in both airlines and railways. The Canadian equivalent of *AMTRAK* runs on both the government-owned Canadian National (CN) tracks and the privately owned Canadian Pacific (CP) tracks.

Private enterprise is more evident in bus service and in the travel trade. Canadian-owned firms predominate, although Greyhound Lines of Canada Limited is an associate of the American Greyhound system. Federal and provincial government tourism departments tend to have larger budgets than their counterparts in the United States. This reflects public acceptance of a higher profile for government in Canada than in the United States and also the fact that because of their smaller size, Canadian businesses have only limited resources for advertising and marketing research.

Agencies of government responsible for tourism development and marketing are found in every provincial and territorial government and at the federal level. These agencies endeavor to cooperate through a system of federal-provincial committees. Some federal financial assistance is provided for mutually agreed-upon projects.

In the private sector, the Tourism Industry Association of Canada (TIAC) has a role similar to that of the Travel Industry Association of America (TIAA). It represents the viewpoint of the industry to government. In Canada, there are also provincial tourism industry associations, which serve a similar purpose at the provincial level.

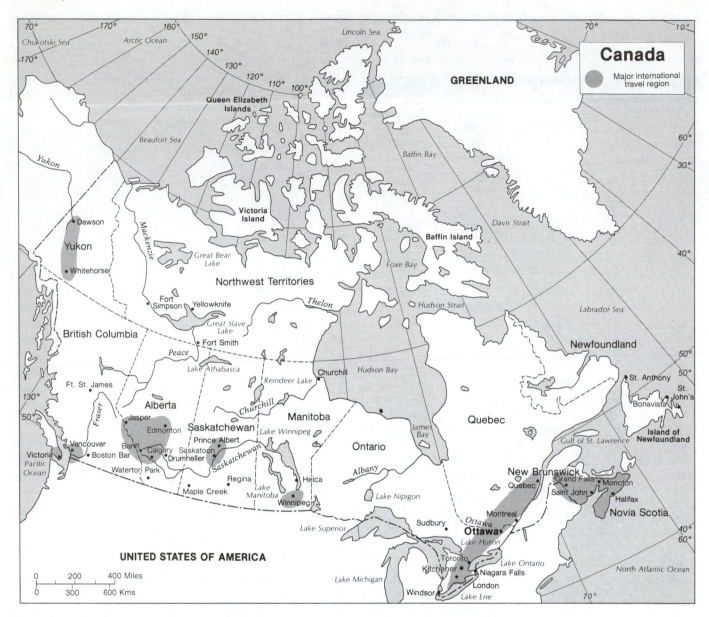

Figure 3–4 Canada

ONE COUNTRY, TWO PEOPLES: FRENCH SEPARATISM IN CANADA

Canada is a unique country, and one of the things that make it especially attractive to tourists is its heritage of both English and French settlement. Canada's total population is nearly thirty million, approximately one-fourth of which claim French as their first language. The French influence is most obvious in the Province of Quebec, because the largest percentages and numbers of French Canadians are located in this province. Language is only one of the cultural differences that distinguish the French in Canada, but it is the most easily recognizable to visitors. Eighty-two percent of Quebec's seven million people speak French, and less than ten percent claim English as their first language. The only other province with a large percentage of French speakers is New Brunswick, where one-third of the population claim French as their first language. No other province has even five percent of its population who are French Canadian, and the result is a French Canadian culture region concentrated along the lower St. Lawrence River Valley in Quebec and New Brunswick.

Visitors to this region will find evidence of the French culture everywhere, most obvious being the language, which is evident in the names of towns, newspapers, advertisements, and television and radio. Many names of places and people reflect the Roman Catholic Church, which was a central part of the French culture of early French settlers of the lower St. Lawrence River. Towns beginning with "Sainte" are common in the French culture region of Canada, such as Sainte Foy, Sainte Anne-de-Beaupre, or Sainte Therese-de-Blainville. Individual names in the French region reflect both the French and Catholic influence in French Canadian culture, such as Jean Paul or Marie. The Catholic Church was the focus of the French Canadian village and is still a prominent part of the French Canadian landscape. The distinctive characteristics of French Canada that appeal to visitors, however, do not reveal the political and cultural tension associated with the presence in Canada of two very different cultures of French and English that dominates the country.

The French were the first to settle Canada, but by 1763 the English had defeated the French in North America, and French settlement was confined primarily to the lower St. Lawrence River Valley. During and after the American Revolutionary War, British royalists settled in the Upper St. Lawrence River Valley, and in 1791 the United Kingdom created two political units in the Canadian Colony, Upper Canada (Ontario) and Lower Canada (Quebec and adjacent areas). Known as the Constitutional Act of 1791, this act legitimized the concept of two separate peoples in Canada, the French and English. The ensuing 200 years have seen the emergence of Canada as an independent country, and a series of legislative acts by either the United Kingdom or the Canadian parliament has maintained the importance of Canada as the home of two major cultures. When Canada formally unified as one country in 1867, the government was formed as a federation of distinct cultures, and Canada became one country in which French and English were both official languages. Since that time other migrant groups have come to Canada, but the two languages and cultures remain dominant. Later arrivals generally learned English, while the growth of the French-speaking population in Quebec and New Brunswick reflected mainly the natural increase of the people already residing there. The result was a gradual decline in the proportion of people speaking French in Canada in the last century.

The last half of the twentieth century has seen a remarkable change in the concept of "One Canada, two peoples." French Canadians, worried about the declining percentage of French in Canada, also believed that the French were not treated equally with the English in the country. The growth of Montreal's English-speaking peoples led to predictions that the French in Montreal would be a minority in their own city in the twenty-first century and gave impetus to growing French political activism. This culminated in the elections of 1960 in which the National Rally for Independence won control of the Quebec provincial government. From 1960 until today there has been a constant, if varying, demand for separatism from Canada among many French in Quebec.

Separatism, the division of Canada into two countries, raises the very real possibility that future tourists to Canada will need a separate visa to enter Quebec, but at the same time reinforces the French culture that makes Quebec so interesting to visit. Political demands for separatism led to the creation of the separatist Parti Québécois in 1968 and adoption of French-only requirements for the names of stores and businesses in Quebec. Concerned that French was being overwhelmed by English, the provincial government passed laws making it difficult for children to attend English-speaking schools, required new immigrants to Quebec to learn French, and mandated all government business be conducted in French. In 1980 a referendum was held to determine whether Quebec would remain in Canada or not, but the separatists lost by a 60-40 margin.

While the referendum failed to separate Canada into two countries, the result was to concentrate the French even more dramatically. Many large Canadian corporations who were headquartered in Montreal moved to Toronto with the English-speaking employees. Toronto replaced Montreal as the largest city, and Canada adopted the Constitution Act of 1982. This act officially removed the power of the British parliament to be involved in Canadian government, although still recognizing the Queen of England as the official head of the state. All of the provinces ratified the Constitution Act except Quebec, which insisted on more recognition of the unique place of French Canada in the country. Constitutional conventions attempting to modify the 1982 Constitution Act to do so failed, as the English majority refused to ratify the proposed changes. The separatists returned to power in Quebec in the 1990s with a new political party, the Bloc Québécois. A second referendum was held in 1995, and again the separatist movement was defeated in Quebec, leaving Quebec as an official part of Canada as of mid-1998.

How long Canada will remain one country is problematic, however. The separatists lost the referendum by less than one percent of the vote, making it clear that there is the very real possibility that a future referendum will be successful. The head of Quebec's government resigned after failing to win separation from the rest of Canada and was replaced at the end of 1995 by a new separatist leader, who has promised another election within a year. Many of the French in Canada believe that unless they become an independent country they will lose their unique French culture, and growing nationalism may well make a future referendum successful.

Domestic Tourism

Tourism in Canada is largely domestic, comprising eighty-four percent of all overnight travel in the country, Table 3–2. To ensure that increasing travel abroad did not draw away domestic tourists, Canadian tourism officials conducted a study in 1992 to determine what tourism-promotional programs would continue to encourage Canadians to remain home and travel. The study suggested that Canadian officials should emphasize the heritage and culture, parks, adventure, festivals and events, skiing, golf, water sports, and country resorts in Canada.

While the populations between the ages of 25 and 34 account for the largest numbers of overnight domestic travelers, the fastest-growing age group in the 1980s was over 65. Their overnight trip-taking rose 64 percent from 3 million in 1980 to 4.9 million trips in ten years. The greatest decline in trips from 1980 to 1992 was in the 15–24 age group. Family travel also declined in the 1980s, while there was an increase in one-person traveling. The numbers of couples traveling remained about the same, Figure 3–5.

The two major reasons for Canadians to travel are for pleasure (36 percent) and to visit friends and family (42 percent). However, business or convention accounted for the largest amount spent, 36 percent. The growth of travel to visit friends and relatives grew faster in the 1980s, with a 28 percent growth rate. Pleasure travel only grew 10 percent during the same period. Business travel increased the most, with 31 percent more overnight trips in 1990 than in 1980.

Intraprovincial travel for overnight visits is overwhelmingly greater than interprovincial travel. Only 14.5 million of about 84 million travelers left their *province* in 1992. The two most visited provinces were Ontario and Québec, dominating both intra- and interprovincial travel. The most popular destinations for Canadians were Toronto, Montréal, Edmonton, Québec, Ottawa-Hull, Calgary, and Vancouver, Table 3–3 (Statistics Canada, 1992).

The residents of the western provinces of Saskatchewan, Alberta, and Manitoba are the most fre-

Source: Touriscope International Travel, 1992. Statistics Canada

Figure 3–5   Size of Travel Party

quent travelers in Canada, while those living in the west coast province of British Columbia and the eastern island provinces of Newfoundland and Prince Edward Island are less inclined to travel. The greater distances between population centers and the official definition of a trip (minimum of 50 miles) are important factors in the higher propensity to travel by residents of the western provinces.

International Tourism

The most important characteristic of Canadian international travel is its linkage to the United States.

Table 3–2   Tourism in Canada

Overnight Travel in Canada by Origin	Share (Percent)	
	1980	1992
Canada	85	84
Intraprovincial	70	59.5
Interprovincial	15	14.5
United States	13	12
Other Countries	2	4

Source: Travel Log, Winter 1995. Statistics Canada.

Table 3–3   Total Travel—Leading CMAs of Destination, 1992

Census Metropolitan Areas of Destination	Total (000)	Business (000)	Leisure (000)
Toronto	13,349	4,813	8,536
Montréal	6,477	1,840	4,637
Edmonton	4,667	1,151	3,516
Québec	4,734	987	3,747
Ottawa-Hull	4,325	1,091	3,234
Calgary	3,354	934	2,420
Vancouver	3,548	1,049	2,499
London	2,776	718	2,058
Winnipeg	2,186	546	1,640
Kitchener	1,787	230	1,557
Halifax	1,875	347	1,528
Saskatoon	1,823	489	1,334
St. Catharines-Niagra	2,784	250	2,534
Hamilton	1,522	229	1,293
Regina	1,891	465	1,426
Victoria	1,347	212	1,135

Source: Touriscope: Domestic Travel, 1992. Statistics Canada.

Overnight Trips between Canada and
the United States, 1981,1985,1990, 1995

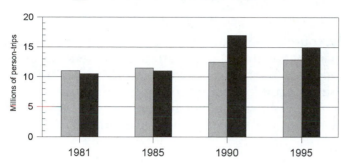

Source: *Touriscope International Travel, 1992.* Statistics Canada.

Figure 3–6 Trips between Canada and the United States

Table 3–4 International Visits to Canada 1994		
Trip Characteristics	**1977 (percent)**	**1994 (percent)**
Type of Transportation:		
Plane	21.0	19.2
Auto and Bus	79.0	74.8
Other		6.0
Season:		
Winter	11.5	11.5
Spring	27.3	26.4
Summer	45.1	45.7
Fall	16.1	16.4
Principal Country of Residence:		
Australia	0.7	0.8
Belgium/Luxembourg	0.2	0.2
France	1.7	2.4
Germany	1.7	2.2
Hong Kong	0.8	0.8
Israel	0.4	0.3
Italy	0.1	0.6
Japan	2.7	2.7
Mexico	0.4	0.5
Netherlands	0.6	0.6
Sweden	0.2	0.2
Switzerland	0.5	0.5
United Kingdom	3.6	3.7
United States	80.6	79.6
Other Countries	4.8	4.9
Purpose of Trip:		
Business, convention, employment	14.9	14.8
Visiting friends or relatives	23.3	20.4
Other pleasure, recreation, or holiday	54.9	56.2
Other, and combined	6.9	8.6
Sex:		
Male	48.1	46.2
Female	33.0	44.6
Not Stated	18.9	9.2

Over 30 million Canadians made a same-day trip to the United States in 1995, and 14.9 million stayed one or more nights. Eighty percent of Canadian departures for more than one-day visits are to the United States, Figure 3–6. The close proximity of the population centers of Canada to the United States border, combined with high taxes and trade agreements, encourages Canadians to shop in the United States. Also, winter encourages Canadians to visit the warm southeastern United States. Florida is a major destination for Canadians looking for sun-sea-sand vacations.

Approximately eighty percent of the international visitors to Canada are from the United States. Although it was stagnant in the early 1980s, international travel to Canada reached an all-time high in 1994 of 17.3 million. Over 13.5 million of these were residents of the United States, Table 3–4. The close proximity of large population centers in the United States to the Canadian border is a major factor in the dominance of tourists from the United States. The average length of stay of five days is another indication of the close major market of the United States. The second largest market is the United Kingdom, which accounts for only 3.7 percent of visitors. Visitors from the United Kingdom and other European countries reflect the cultural linkages existing between Europe and Canada (World Travel Organization, 1995).

There is a marked degree of seasonality in Canadian tourism, with almost 46 percent of visitors arriving in the summer. International travel by Canadians is also highly seasonal, with most traveling in the summer. The climate of Canada is in itself a major factor in summer travel. Much of the country experiences a northern continental climate with extremes of temperature that, in the area of the Great Lakes, are accompanied by high humidity in summer and abundant snowfall in winter.

The substantial ties between Canada and the United States and Europe are expressed in the fact that nearly 21 percent of foreign travelers listed visiting friends and relatives in Canada as the primary factor in their visit. Fifty-six percent of the arrivals were for the purpose of holiday or pleasure travel. Nearly 75 percent of foreign arrivals come by automobile, reflecting the proximity of the United States markets. Canada also benefits from this proximity as almost thirty-five million additional foreign visitors come for one-day visits.

Three provinces—Ontario, British Columbia, and Québec—receive the bulk (84 percent) of overseas expenditures. All are near large United States population centers. In 1990, residents of the East North Central region of the United States registered the most overnight trips to Canada. They recorded over 4 million trips, representing 27 percent of all one-or-more-nights travel to Canada by residents of the United States. The Middle Atlantic region (22.5 percent) followed by the Pacific region (17 percent) were the next two major contributors to Canada's tourism (Touriscope International, 1996).

Although the numbers of total international visitors have changed little, there has been an increase of overseas visitors. Asia has seen the most increase, while there has been a decline in visitors from the United States. Japan's share of international travel to Canada jumped from 0.6 percent in 1980 to 1.3 percent in 1994. Hong Kong has also increased significantly. The increase in Asian migration to Canada and the economic growth of the Pacific nations are important factors contributing to this tourism growth from Asia. Of the United States visitors, only 9 percent are first-time visitors, while for other nations 40 percent are first-time visitors.

TOURISM DESTINATIONS AND ATTRACTIONS

Ontario was historically the leading province in terms of numbers of overseas visitors. By 1994, however, British Columbia was first, ahead of Québec. The growth in the number of overseas visitors to British Columbia is related to the increasing numbers of Asians migrating to Vancouver, especially from Hong Kong.

Canada's most outstanding tourism destinations and attractions have historically been its cities and its scenic natural attractions. Canada has an outstanding *national park* system and vast expanses of virgin forest lands with innumerable rivers and lakes of extraordinary beauty. These attractions are particularly intriguing to visitors from the relatively affluent and crowded countries of Japan, Germany, and other Western European nations. Visitors from the United States have traditionally been attracted by the fishing and hunting opportunities offered by their neighbors to the north, and resort areas such as the Laurentians and the Muskokas are heavily used.

The Canadian government has focused efforts on changing its image to potential tourists in an effort to increase the numbers of visitors. Canada has historically been viewed as a costly vacation with limited historical and cultural scope and as a nation of moose, Mounties, and mountains. In an effort to alter this perception, the government reviewed its tourist product in 1983 and identified eight major categories that are important for international tourism.

Sporting/Adventure

An outdoor product that is found primarily in sparsely populated areas catering to extended visits and characterized by outdoor activities like hunting, fishing, camping, and canoeing. Similar to the types of products found in Northern Minnesota, Northern Manitoba, and salmon fishing in Scotland.

Wilderness/Expedition

The true *wilderness* product, characterized by inaccessibility, includes trophy hunting, fishing, safaris, rugged and unforgiving terrain, as in Canada's Arctic. Visitors generally require specialized equipment and qualified guides.

Leisure/Recreation

A leisure-oriented recreational product, easily accessed by local populations and suitable for day trips. These areas are characterized by numerous small-scale recreational and cultural products designed to cater to local populations, such as Southern Ontario.

Beach/Recreation

Recreational product built on beach resources. Similar to leisure/recreation, but with a more significant destination area character that encourages extended visits (such as Prince Edward Island or other beach areas of the world).

Heritage/Culture

Primary features of tourism region are based on either heritage or cultural travel generators and themes such as Québec City or Dawson City.

Urban

Significant urban experience. Cities evaluated as local urban product were not classified as tourist destinations.

Resort

Tourism product characterized by numerous activities and considerable accommodation plant, either contained in a central or major resort product or in groupings of more numerous, smaller products, such

Through Visitors' Eyes

Images of Canada Here

(Ranked in order of importance)

Country	Items important in selecting vacation destinations and attributed to Canada	Items important in selecting vacation destinations and not attributed to Canada
West Germany	Outstanding scenery	Interesting people
	Plenty of room to get away from crowds	Fascinating cities
	A quiet and unspoiled atmosphere	Historical and cultural interests
	A country easy to tour	Good beaches
	Simple entry formalities	Cheap travel to/from
United Kingdom	A quiet, unspoiled atmosphere	Good beaches
	Plenty of outdoor activities	Historical and cultural interest
	Stable political situation	Exotic and exciting
	Simple entry formalities	
Netherlands	Many forests and lakes	Different culture
	Plenty of room to avoid crowds	Good beaches
	Stable political situation	Historical and cultural interest
	Abundant outdoor activities	Cheap travel
	Exotic and exciting	Interesting people

Source: In-Depth Studies of Attitudes to Canada. Ottawa: Tourism Canada

as the Laurentians, the Poconos, and Majorca. For analysis of the Canadian product, this category distinguishes between four-season and seasonal resorts.

Scenic

An area characterized by an amalgam of small scenic, heritage, and cultural resources, without a destination travel generator, such as the Gaspé Peninsula and the Lake District.

TOURISM IN CANADA: PROVINCES AND TERRITORIES

Newfoundland and Labrador

The island of Newfoundland plus Labrador on the mainland create one province. The newest province of Canada, Newfoundland has fishing, scenic, cultural, and historical attractions. Newfoundland as a destination receives the second smallest number of visitors of all the Canadian Provinces, attracting only about 300,000 visitors a year. Also, tourism is most seasonal in the Atlantic provinces in general. Most visitors are from the neighboring provinces and visit during the relatively short summer season.

Since the arrival of the first significant group of British settlers in Newfoundland, the economy has been based upon the sea. In recent years the economy has suffered from overfishing and the closure of military bases. Newfoundland's unemployment is the highest in Canada. It has turned to oil and tourism in an effort to boost its economy, but tourism is limited because of its location. Newfoundland is noted for its village landscape with white, tall-spired churches and their adjacent cemeteries. The villages of Newfoundland differ from the New England villages in that they typically lack a village green; but many have covered bridges, which are common through all the maritime regions of Canada. Newfoundland and Labrador have more than 17,000 kilometers of coastline as well as two national parks and more than eighty provincial parks, providing numerous opportunities for sightseeing, camping, or wilderness adventures. A major focus of tourism is the St. John's area. St. John's is the capital and largest city. It is one of the oldest settlements in North America and is the eastern terminus of the Trans-Canada highway. It is named after John Cabot, who discovered Newfoundland on June 24, 1497. It was a contested area between the French and English until 1762, when the British defeated the French and recaptured St. John's. It has a number of national parks and museums that stress history and nature. Water Street in St. John's is the oldest business district on the continent, dating back to 1600. Gilbert Hill, where convicted criminals were executed, is another attraction. Fishing for cod and salmon is common in the area. Cabot Tower, located on Signal Hill, is where the first transatlantic wireless signal was received. Signal Hill National Historic Park is the site of the last battle of the French and English during the Seven Years' War in 1762. It also offers a spectacular view of the city, its harbor, and the adjacent coastline.

The tourist attractions in Newfoundland are associated with the early village and coastal life combined with beautiful coastal and mountain scenery. The Cape Spear Lighthouse is on the most easterly point of North America and is the oldest lighthouse in Newfoundland, serving as a marine beacon from 1836 to 1955. Cape Bonavista Lighthouse was built in 1843 and has been restored to the 1870 period. The Gros Morne National Park area has lakes, coves, fjords, and wildlife ranging from moose to black bear, volcanic sea stacks, caves, sand dunes, and scenic coastal overlooks. Whale watching at Trinity, a village dating back to 1500, is popular because the minke, humpback, and finback whales feed in Newfoundland's eastern fjords. The Hiscock House located in historic Trinity is restored to the 1910 period. At L'Anse-aux Meadows are a restored Viking settlement and a number of ancient Indian burial grounds, which remind visitors of the early history of the country dating back to 1000 A.D. In combination, Newfoundland's attractions led to the United Nations Educational, Scientific, and Cultural Organization (UNESCO) designating the area as a World Heritage Site in 1988.

Nova Scotia

Of the Atlantic provinces, Nova Scotia is the most popular tourist destination. Acadians established the first permanent European settlement north of Florida at Port Royal in Nova Scotia in 1605. During the next 100 years, Nova Scotia changed hands seven times. In 1713 England and France signed a peace treaty that gave mainland Nova Scotia to England and Cape Breton Island to France. The French built a fortress on Cape Breton Island, which was called Louisbourg. Many Acadians were scattered along the American coast in the British colonies, with a major settlement of Acadians (now called Cajuns in the United States) in the lower Mississippi River area, which was controlled then by France. After the defeat of the French in 1763, some Acadians returned to Nova Scotia and settled principally along the coast, relying on fishing for their livelihood.

Nova Scotia offers the visitor picturesque coastal seaside and fishing villages. Nova Scotia and Québec are Canada's top two honeymoon destinations. The Cabot Trail on Cape Breton is one of the most spectacular drives in North America and a major destination for visitors to Nova Scotia. It is named after John Cabot and has many lookout points and scenic villages on its route through Cape Breton Highlands National Park and along coastal waters and villages.

The Alexander Graham Bell Museum exhibits Bell's accomplishments near his family home in Beinn Bhreagh. Bell appreciated the beauty of Cape

Figure 3–7 Citadel Hill in Halifax

Breton, stating, "I have travelled around the globe. I have seen the Canadian and American Rockies, the Andes and the Alps, and the Highlands of Scotland; but for simple beauty, Cape Breton outrivals them all." Peggy's Cove is the most visited fishing village in the world. The cove's rugged beauty is part of a beautiful oceanside drive through villages, historic colonial towns, and long white–sand beaches.

Louisbourg is the largest historical reconstruction in North America. Life portrayed within the fortress is a re-enactment of military and social existence in 1744. For five decades in the eighteenth century, Cape Breton was called Ile Royale, serving as France's Atlantic bastion. Louisbourg was its capital. It was twice conquered by the English.

Halifax, the world's second largest natural harbor after Sydney, Australia, is considered one of North America's most beautiful cities, complete with a harbor boardwalk system. It ranks as one of the major destinations for both domestic and international visitors. It was the first English settlement in Canada and has numerous architectural attractions including historic churches, government, and public buildings. The Citadel Fortress at Halifax is Canada's most visited historic site.

Picturesque Lunenburg lies in southern Nova Scotia. Founded in 1753 by German, Swiss, and French Huguenot settlers, Lunenburg has long been known for its shipbuilding, seafaring expertise, and natural beauty.

Nova Scotia is noted for its unique cultural traditions. The Scottish influence is emphasized in annual festivals as people dress in traditional Scottish costumes, bagpipe bands perform, and Scottish games and food are enjoyed on festive days. Distinctive events reflecting the culture of the area include the Gathering of the Clans and Fishermen's Regatta in Pugwash, the Antigonish Highland Games, the Annual Scotia Gaelic Mod, and the Festival of the Tartans in New Glasgow, in conjunction with another Gathering of the Clans.

New Brunswick

New Brunswick is called the "picture province," and its scenery and natural phenomena are its most important attractions. New Brunswick is a forested region, with the notable exception of the Saint John River Valley, which is farmed intensively. The cities and villages of New Brunswick act as service centers for local areas of farming, fishing, and forestry.

St. John and its suburb Portland have developed serving two rich agricultural areas extending up the St. John and Kenebecasis rivers. Fredericton, a local service center and lumbering town, became the cap-

ital and center of higher education in New Brunswick. New Brunswick's most famous destination is the Bay of Fundy, with a tidal range that varies as much as fifty feet between low and high tide, the equivalent height of a four-story building. At Moncton, there is the tidal bore on the Petitrodiac River and Magnetic Hill, where drivers can stop their cars, set them in neutral, and seem to coast to the top of the hill. Near Moncton are the Hopewell Rocks, which Ripley describes as the world's largest flower pots. The rocks are huge, eerie, sandstone goblets sculpted by the tides over the years. They can be explored at low tide. Sixty miles south of Moncton is the Fundy National Park, and at St. John is the Reversing Falls. At low tide, the St. John River rushes into the bay, but at high tide the bay waters rise, seeming to send the river the other way.

St. John, the oldest incorporated city in the British Empire outside the British Isles, has many historical attractions, including the New Brunswick Museum, which is the oldest public museum in Canada, and Martello Tower, a fort from the War of 1812. The river road from St. John north is beautiful and very popular in the fall for its colorful autumn foliage. Near Fredericton, the architecture illustrates the life of the early English settlers. North is the Acadian Village, which illustrates the lifestyle of the Acadians, and the world's longest covered bridge.

Prince Edward Island

Prince Edward Island is mainly a rural area and has the lowest amount of travel of all the Canadian provinces. The capital city, Charlottetown, has a population of 31,000 people. In Charlottetown, the Province House is the historic site where the plan for a unified Canada was first discussed. While most islanders are descendants of early French, Scottish, English, and Irish settlers, the native Micmac people inhabited Prince Edward Island for a much longer period of time. The Micmac represent about 4 percent of the island's people. The island was discovered by the French explorer Jacques Cartier. The first white settlement was at Port-La-Jove, now Fort Amherst/Port-La-Jove National Historic Site, just across the harbor from Charlottetown. Later, the British occupied the island, deporting the Acadian settlers. Many ended up in southern Louisiana after stays in England and France. In the eighteenth century, it was noted for its shipbuilding around the town of Summershide. In the eighteenth and nineteenth centuries settlers came from Scotland and Ireland, adding to the cultural diversity of the island.

A number of attractions on the island are popular and worth visiting. The Green Gables House at Cav-

endish was the setting for *Anne of Green Gables*.
Lobster festivals and sandy beaches are the principal
attractions of the area. North Lake is famous for its
large bluefin tuna, which average 600 pounds. The
scenic drives on the island pass through picturesque
fishing villages, along white sand dunes, red cliffs,
and stunted fir and spruce trees.

Québec

Québec is the largest province in the area, accounts
for 25 percent of the population of Canada, and is the
center of French-speaking Canadians. At the time of
the establishment of the Canadian nation in 1867, the
French-Canada region was largely rural. Montréal
and Québec City were the only urban centers. Québec
province was largely French in language and custom.
The establishment of the federation of Canada guaranteed Québec use of Latin-based French law instead
of English common law; and it guaranteed religious
liberty. It also established French as one of two national languages. The issue of separatism based on
Québec's special constitutional provisions recognizing it as a "distinct society" in Canada remains important in Canadian politics.

The two major tourist destination centers are
Québec City and Montréal. Québec City was one of
the first French settlements in North America and,
in spite of two centuries of English rule, it is still
French. The French architecture and beautiful natural setting combine to make it one of the most beautiful cities in North America. Its rich history is
expressed in its older sections. With narrow, cobblestone streets and a citadel, it is the only walled city
in North America. The citadel is often referred to as
the "Gibraltar of America." The narrow streets twist
and turn from the Lower Town on the St. Lawrence
River upwards to the Upper Town. Its rich history is
expressed in the Basilica of Notre Dame Des
Victoires, which was built in 1688; the hotel Chateau
Frontenac; the Ursuline Convent; the Catholic Seminary; Parliament Buildings; the Provincial Museum;
and the Bois de Coulange. The wall between Lower
and Upper towns has been renovated into a wide
promenade overlooking the St. Lawrence River, Figure 3-8.

Ile d'Orleans, an island in the St. Lawrence River
below Québec City, is connected to the mainland by
a bridge. This picturesque island retains a great deal
of its eighteenth-century French-Canadian architectural influence. "Carnival" is Québec's famous winter festival. The Plains of Abraham is the site of the
Battle of Québec, which sealed the fate of New France
in 1759. Near Québec City is Sainte Anne De
Beaupré, a small village dominated by a large cathe-

Figure 3–8   St. Lawrence River at Québec City

dral. It is an internationally known religious shrine
and attracts millions of pilgrims seeking to be healed.
Just twenty-five minutes outside of Québec City is
the Mt. Sainte Anne ski resort.

Montréal, founded on an island in the St. Lawrence
River, is one of the largest and most cosmopolitan cities in Canada. It is the most culturally diverse city in
Québec and the second most popular destination for
tourists. The explorer Jacques Cartier discovered an
Indian fort and settlement on Montréal Island. A
French town grew on the site and became a strategic
fur and lumbering trading center. The large French
population makes it the second largest French-speaking city in the world. It is a cosmopolitan city with Old
World charm expressed in the older sections of the
city. Today Montréal is a large and modern city with
excellent urban and international transportation.

The principal attractions are the city's rich history, cultural events, museums, and gardens. The
Botanical Gardens are considered to be the third
largest botanical gardens in the world, featuring some
20,000 species of plant life. The Old Quarter has
sidewalk cafés and historic buildings, including
Notre Dame Church, opened in 1829; Place Jacques
Cartier, a cobblestoned square, which was once the
main marketplace; Chateau de Ramezay, a manor
built in 1705; and Notre Dame de Bonsecours Chapel,
the city's oldest church. Additional attractions are
the civic center, which was built around the theme
"Man and His World" on St. Helen's Island; Chinatown; the Dow Planetarium; Lafontaine Park; and the
Olympic park. A new popular attraction is a jet boat

Figure 3–9   Folk Housing in rural Québec, Canada

tour on the Lachine Rapids, which departs from the old port.

The Gaspe Peninsula in eastern Québec is a region of picturesque fishing villages, rolling hills, deep gorges, covered bridges, and rocky cliffs. The most impressive attraction is Perce Rock, a 400-million-ton landmark near the town of Perce. The rock juts some 300 feet out of the ocean. Just north of Montréal are the Laurentian Mountains, which have a number of popular resorts offering both winter and summer outdoor sports such as fishing, camping, hiking, and skiing.

Ontario

During the seventeenth and eighteenth centuries, large numbers of immigrants moved into what was then called Upper Canada, today's Southern Ontario. Many were former residents of the United States who were loyal to the King of England (Tories). They arrived because of the War of Independence. Other immigrants from the British Isles included Scots and Irish. The population grew rapidly, and Toronto became the largest city of the province. It is the largest metropolitan area in Canada today, with over three million residents. Ontario is the largest destination for tourists, and Toronto is the major destination city or area in all of Canada.

The population of Ontario is concentrated in the southeastern region of the province, located close to a number of United States cities that provide an abundance of visitors for short-term visits.

Ottawa's selection as the capital of Canada in 1858 ultimately transformed the former mill town into an important capital city of the world. The city is situated on a bluff overlooking the Ottawa River. Tourism's importance in the economy of Ottawa is only exceeded by government's. Ottawa-Hull ranks fourth in number of visitors in Canada.

The heart of Ottawa is the Parliament Buildings. They are a massive group of great stone Gothic buildings with copper roofs and spires. This area not only offers the best view of the area, but features one of Canada's outstanding summer attractions, the Changing of the Guard.

Ottawa has many important museums, including the Bytown Museum, illustrating the history of Ottawa; the Canadian Museum of Civilization; the Canadian Museum of Nature; the Canadian Ski Museum; the Canadian War Museum; the Lag Farm, a recreated farm of 1870; the Museum of Canadian Scouting; the National Aviation Museum; and the National Museum of Science and Technology.

The Rideau Canal in Ottawa, completed in 1832, is a commercial waterway and leisure center. In the wintertime it becomes a five-mile skating rink. Ottawa is the home of a number of festivals, notably the Canadian Tulip Festival in the spring and the Winterlude centered around the ice-bound Rideau Canal. Near Ottawa at Beachburg is the site of white-water rafting on the Ottawa River.

Toronto is one of the most ethnically diverse cities in Canada. It combines elements of the past with some of the most modern skyscraper landscapes of North America. The most outstanding tourist attraction is the world's tallest self-supporting structure, the CN Tower. In addition, the Metro Zoo, one of the finest in North America; winter sports; national museums and exhibits; and a number of ethnic neighborhoods are important attractions in Toronto. A visitor can take an ethnic tour through the various ethnic neighborhoods: Chinatown; Greek stores and restaurants; Little Italy; and Portuguese fish markets. The St. Lawrence Hall, Mackenzie House, and the Casa Loma, a castle built in 1911, are other important attractions.

The SkyDome hosts major sporting events and is home to the 1992 World Series Champions—the Toronto Blue Jays. The SkyDome is the world's only stadium with a fully retractable roof. It includes, in addition to a ball field and convention center, entertainment facilities such as movie theaters, health clubs, and restaurants.

Considerable effort has been made by Toronto citizens to develop a pleasing environment in an *urban* setting. Consequently, Toronto has a multitude of parks and wooded walks. The older buildings, such as the City Hall and Ontario Palace, blend in nicely with the modern buildings. Marineland, Game Farm, and Canada's Wonderland near Toronto offer live entertainment, rides, and various forms of family fun. Ontario Place, which is on the lake shore, has become a popular summer attraction, providing parks, lagoons, waterways, pubs, and restaurants. Toronto is the home of one of the world's top film festivals, the Festival of Festivals. Toronto also has other festivals in the summer, such as Caribana (the Caribbean festival) and Caravan (Toronto's multicultural festival).

The Toronto theater is appealing with "Broadway" shows such as Phantom of the Opera and Miss Saigon appearing regularly. Toronto has many theaters, and other cultural entertainment such as the ballet, opera, and the Toronto Symphony Orchestra.

Southwest of Toronto is the center of British culture and popular attractions. Common British names such as Windsor, Stratford, Chatham, London, Woodstock, Brantford, and the River Avon are scattered throughout the region. At Stratford one of the best Shakespearean Festivals in North America is held each summer.

The famed Niagara Falls is best seen from the Canadian side. Within the town of Niagara Falls sites include the Minolta Tower and aquarium; the Skylon Tower; Maple Leaf Village; and Marineland. Niagara-on-the-Lake is one of the best preserved nineteenth-century towns in North America. It was originally named Newark and was the first capital of Upper Canada (Ontario) from 1791 to 1796. The Shaw Festival features plays by Bernard Shaw, from May to October.

The area between Toronto and Ottawa has many attractions including the long, narrow farms along the banks of the St. Lawrence; numerous provincial parks; white sand bluffs at Picton standing over 30 yards high; Upper Canada Village, an authentic re-creation of an 1867 pioneer village; and Old Fort Henry at Kingston, a dramatic nineteenth-century fort where military displays include the thunder of cannon fire.

Fort William in Thunder Bay is a re-creation of the pioneer heritage and life of the late eighteenth century. The Agawa Canyon provides a scenic trip departing from Sault Ste. Marie along mountain ledges, through dark forests, over rivers and gorges, across a trestle bridge, and into fjord-like ravines. There is an underground tour of the old nickel mine in Sudbury. Historical sites of Sainte-Marie among the Hurons and the Huron Indian Village present a reconstructed sixteenth-century French mission and native community complete with longhouses and timber palisades. Across the road from this site is the Martyrs Shrine where martyred Jesuit missionaries are remembered.

Manitoba

Manitoba does not have a tourism industry comparable to that of Ontario and Québec. It was not settled until late in the 1800s. The major groups were Mennonite settlers from Czarist Ukraine, French Canadians from New England, English, Scots, and Irish. Winnipeg's favorable location on newly constructed rail lines brought additional immigrants to settle and work the land. More recent immigrants of Asian and Caribbean ancestry have added to the ethnic diversity of the region. Although it is a prairie province, its terrain is varied—from the tundra and boreal forest of the north to the rolling, wooded parkland of the central region and the grain-rich plains of the south.

Winnipeg, the capital of Manitoba, contains more than half of the population of the province. It is Manitoba's largest tourist destination, with its government buildings and Royal Canadian Mint. The Museum of Man and Nature in Winnipeg includes an exhibit of a full-scale replica of the Nonesuch, the first ship to bring furs from the New World to Europe. The Winnipeg Art Gallery has one of the world's finest collections of Inuit art. The Folklorama in Winnipeg is a major festival at which some forty pavilions illustrate Winnipeg's various ethnic groups with food, dance, and entertainment. The French quarter is the largest Francophone community west of Québec. Winnipeg is the only city between Toronto and Vancouver that is rated three-star by the *Michelin Guide of Canada.*

Outside of Winnipeg are other areas of interest, including Lower Fort Gary National Historical Park (the restored Hudson Bay Company supply center that dates back to the 1830s). Riding Mountain National Park provides typical camping experiences as well as the opportunity to watch buffalo. Thousands of lakes and woods offer excellent hunting and fishing opportunities. Far to the north is Churchill, Manitoba's northernmost settlement, on the shores of Hudson Bay. Churchill is a tourist center for observing the beluga whale, the polar bear migration, and the northern lights.

Saskatchewan

The development of the railroads in the late 1800s brought more and more settlers, largely second-generation immigrants, to the region in search of farming opportunities. The migrants created the rolling wheat fields of Saskatchewan, the bread basket of Canada.

The two leading tourist destinations are Regina and Saskatoon. At Regina, the capital of Saskatchewan, the Royal Canadian Mounted Police have a training center and museum. The museum displays

Industry, Science, and Technology Canada photo

Figure 3–10 Royal Mounted Police

old equipment, weapons, uniforms, and photos documenting history of the Royal Canadian Mounted Police. The farming industry is represented in the Western Development Museum, with its pioneer machinery, vintage cars, and indoor prairie village. One of the newest attractions in Regina is the Science Center with exhibits on the human body, the living planet, astronomy, and geology.

The Medel Art gallery in Saskatoon has works by Chagall, Picasso, and Lawrence Harris. The only national park in Saskatchewan is Prince Albert National Park, which is known for its lakes and fishing. There are a number of historical parks and Saskatchewan's famous Big Buddy Badlands.

Alberta

Alberta is the richest province in Canada and has a variety of spectacular scenery, from the flatlands of the east to the Rocky Mountains in the west. It is a showcase of the splendors of the Rockies. The two most famous attractions in Alberta are Banff and Jasper national parks. Both are well-known for their outstanding scenery, with hot springs and ice fields. The most famous of the latter is the Columbia ice field, which is the largest permanent body of ice between the Arctic and Antarctic. Between Lake Louise and Jasper is one of the most scenic drives in Canada. Snow-

capped peaks, wildlife, Peyto Lake, and the Athabasca Glacier are a few of the attractions along the trail. Two other attractive national parks in Alberta are Waterton Lakes and Wood Buffalo.

The two main destination cities of Alberta are Edmonton and Calgary. Edmonton ranks third in visitors for Canadian cities. The big carnival in Edmonton is Klondike Days, and the most famous festival in Canada is the Calgary Stampede Rodeo in early July. The Edmonton Mall was the world's largest shopping mall and indoor amusement park until the Mall of the Americas was completed in Minneapolis in 1992. The Edmonton Mall's Water Park is the length of five football fields and offers water skiing and body surfing on artificial waves. Its roller coaster is twelve stories high. The Edmonton Space Sciences Center is Canada's largest planetarium, featuring an IMAX theater, observatory, and science exhibits. Historic Fort Edmonton Park includes villages depicting Edmonton in 1885, 1905, and 1920 plus a replica of a fur-trading post.

Calgary, the gateway to the Rocky Mountains, ranks sixth in visitors for Canadian cities, receiving about two-thirds the number of visitors to Edmonton. Two popular sites in Calgary are Heritage Park and the Calgary Tower. Heritage Park is a 66–acre park depicting a prairie railroad town with over 100 exhibits including operative steam trains and a paddlewheel boat. Calgary Tower provides a view of the city and surrounding area from either an observation terrace or the revolving restaurant. The Calgary Zoo, the second largest in Canada with over 1,400 animals and birds, also features a Prehistoric Park with many life-size replicas of ancient dinosaurs. The most famous attraction for visitors is the Calgary Stampede every July. Just west of Calgary is the Canada Olympic Park, which was the site of the luge

Courtesy Province of British Columbia

Figure 3–11 Canadian Rocky Mountains near Banff

and bobsled events during the Olympic Winter Games of 1988.

An hour and a half's drive northeast of Calgary is a dinosaur land in the Red Deer River Valley. The Dinosaur Trail includes the Royal Tyrell Museum of Paleontology at Drumheller. The Drumheller Dinosaur and Fossil Museum features exhibits that explain the occupancy of the inland sea, petrified forests, coal formation, processes of fossilization, and many varieties of dinosaur remains found in the area.

British Columbia

The combination of the Pacific Ocean, beautiful wooded mountains, and a west coast marine climate makes British Columbia an outstanding destination for tourists. Culturally, its residents were mostly English with small groups of Russian, German, Japanese, and Chinese. The more recent heavy migration from Asia, particularly of Chinese, has created a new ethnic mix. British Columbia has nearly 17,000 miles of beautiful fjord-like coastlines, inland lakes, emerald forests of Douglas fir, and great rivers that breed more salmon than any place in the world. Both Vancouver Island and the entire region have wild and beautiful natural settings that do not fail to impress visitors. Settings for a variety of water sports are available, from well-kept, long, sandy beaches to fishing for salmon in the bays and fast–running rivers. Beautiful gardens and parks abound throughout the region. A short distance from the city of Vancouver are Vancouver Island and the provincial capital Victoria, which is a major destination for visitors. Vancouver Island also includes the world-famous Buchart Sunken Garden. Victoria claims to be more British than England, complete with big red double-decker buses. The center of historic buildings is the inner harbor with the Victorian-era Parliament Buildings, beautifully outlined at night with thousands of sparkling lights.

Vancouver, is a new city with modern architecture and the second largest Chinatown in North America. The University of British Columbia's Museum of Anthropology contains exceptional Northwest Indian art, including totem poles, ceremonial objects and other artifacts. The historic Gastown area was the original settlement and has buildings dating back to the 1800s. The thousand-acre Stanley Park borders the sea and provides a dazzling view of the city, port, and north-shore mountains. Just two hours north of Vancouver is the famous ski resort Whistler/Blackoomb.

Vancouver Island has sea caves, rain forests, mountain peaks, and a range of wildlife. Grey whales feed at Schooner Cove, and sea lions bask in the sun

Courtesy Province of British Columbia

Figure 3–12 Totem pole in Stanley Park

on the rocks. The interior of the province through the Caribou-Chilcotin range offers exciting views of deep canyons, impressive mountains, and the Indian villages of Ksan, Kispiox, Kitwanga, and Kitwancool with their totem poles.

The various areas of British Columbia also have tourist attractions related to the history and culture of the province. The Fort St. James National Historical Park illustrates the fur trade era of the 1880s in the Northwestern region. The Bakerville Historic Town takes visitors back to the gold rush dates of the 1860s and 1870s.

Northwest Territories

The Northwest *Territories* span four time zones with a population of only 64,000 people. The environment is important to the region for ecotourism and preservation. Four rivers are part of the Canadian Heritage River System, and four national parks (of which two are UNESCO World Heritage Sites) serve as examples of the region's commitment to preservation.

Tourism is important to this sparsely populated north land, home to the Inuit and Dene Indians. Total numbers of tourists are low, however, due to the isolation of the region. The land of the midnight sun, with its short summer and beautiful, picturesque flowers, has tremendous fishing opportunities, Figure 3–13. The primitive nature of the area is a unique attraction in itself. Opportunities abound to watch all types of creatures in their natural habitats. Visitors can observe great gatherings of sea mammals (beluga and bowhead whales, narwhals and tusked walruses, ringed and bearded seals) and land mammals (moose, mountain sheep, bearded muskoxen, grizzly bears, and polar bears).

From May through July the sun never sets. Golfers can tee off at midnight, which they do at the Western

Figure 3–13 Fishing in the Northwest Territories

Midnight Sun Golf Tournament at Yellowknife. It is an outdoor wonderland for active people. A visitor can hike the boreal forest in search of nesting birds and hardy wildflowers or rigorously climb amid the rock spires of Baffin Island's Auyuittuq National Park. Visitors may canoe or raft through the legendary Nahanni River and view the magnificent Virginia Falls (which are twice as high as Niagara Falls). Other attractions include fishing for fat Arctic char, kayaking the ice–floe edge where seals play, driving a dog team, hunting for polar bear using dog teams, or camping in igloos or tents on ice floes. Cultural attractions include meeting various native people and going to museums such as the Prince of Wales Northern Heritage Center, which traces the history of the Northwest Territories. Native artifacts, crafts, and paintings are also displayed in the Center. In the past decade, ecotourism to the Northern Rivers, exploration of the Arctic, Inuit village stays, whale watching, seal flow observations, and sea kayaking have become more popular. (Figure 3-13)

Yukon Territory

Many visitors combine travel to Alaska with visits to the Yukon, making tourism an important part of the economy. Many cruise ships and Alaskan ferries stop at Skagway, where passengers can take the train or motorcoach to Whitehorse over the historic White Pass on the Klondike Highway. Many visit Dawson from Alaska itself; thus, Dawson and Whitehorse are two heavily visited cities. Booming centers in gold rush days, both are now important tourist centers. Dawson City has Canada's only legal gambling casino, and there are many reminders of the glory days of the gold rush. Diamond Tooth Gertie's and the

Palace Grand Theater/Gaslight Follies provide gold rush–era entertainment.

Whitehorse is another city recreating the gold rush days, with the Frantic Follies Vaudeville Revue and the MacBride Museum. It also includes the important Yukon Gardens, Canada's only northern botanical gardens. Here, flora and vegetation of the territory and the Old Log Church Museum are found. Hikers who wish to recreate the gold rush era can follow the "Trail of '98," the Chilkoot Trail from Skakway, Alaska, to Bennet Lake.

THE UNITED STATES

The United States has a large and varied tourism industry, with a combination of public and private organizations. The United States is the world's largest market for international tourism, vying with Germany in number of international travelers. Residents of the United States spend more money abroad than any others. This is even more impressive considering that Germany has a unique position, bordering ten other countries. Americans spent $52 billion on foreign travel in 1996, but foreign tourism still created a surplus of $12.2 billion in the federal balance-of-payments ledger for tourism.

Almost all states have a state tourist agency of some form or another. The principal task of these agencies is to promote travel to and through their respective states. They accomplish this task by researching existing travel patterns in the state and by sponsoring promotional campaigns for state tourism.

There are a number of specific organizations serving the private sectors of the industry. The American Society of Travel Agents (ASTA) was created to provide service and information to travel agents and to establish an ethical code of conduct. The umbrella organization for the entire private industry is a nonprofit organization called Travel Industry Association of America. The United States Travel and Tourism Administration (USTTA), which was headed by an assistant secretary of tourism under the umbrella of the United States Department of Commerce, has been replaced by a public/private National Tourism Organization (NTO). The goal of the organization is to make the United States the premier travel destination in the world. A problem does exist in that there is no provision for federal funding.

In 1996 nearly 45 million international travelers visited the United States, Table 3–5. This was approximately 10 percent of total world travel. Canada's 15 million tourists and Mexico's 8.5 million account for approximately 53 percent of all international visitors to the United States. This is a decline from 1977, when they accounted for 75 percent of all arrivals. The high

Table 3–5 Tourism to the United States

Country of Residence	Arrivals (thousands)		
	1982	1984	1996
Canada	10,430	10,982	15,301
Mexico	2,475	2,518	8,530
Overseas	8,761	7,527	22,900
United Kingdom	1,298	928	3,105
Germany	668	545	1,972
France	426	331	990
Italy	234	218	552
Netherlands	191	134	434
Sweden	NA	NA	256
South America	1,278	771	2,550
Venezuela	550	170	456
Brazil	238	169	891
Caribbean	647	703	1,132
Central America	274	294	520
Asia/Middle East	2,284	2,294	7,623
Japan	1,447	1,415	5,047
South Korea	NA	NA	9,796
Oceania	385	338	631
Australia	NA	231	461
Africa	186	148	159
TOTAL	21,666	21,027	44,791

percentage of travelers from these two countries is due to their proximity, the higher standard of living, the major population centers of Canada near the United States border, and the language similarities.

Over the decade from 1965 to 1975, international travel to the United States increased nearly 10 percent a year, in contrast to the almost 7 percent at which the overall international travel market increased. In the five-year period from 1977 to 1982, it experienced an 18 percent increase. The increasing United States travel market is seen more dramatically in the growth rate for national income from tourism, in which the world increase in the decade from 1965 to 1975 was 12 percent and the United States increase ranged from 14 to 17.3 percent annually. From 1986 to 1993 tourism to the states doubled.

There has been a dramatic increase in tourism from overseas countries (defined as those not bordering the United States) between 1977 and 1997. In 1977, overseas countries represented less than one-fourth of all foreign arrivals, but by 1997 they represented nearly one–half of all international visitors. Other shifts in tourist arrivals include Japan replacing the United Kingdom as the number one overseas source of tourists to the United States. In 1965, Japan ranked sixth in overseas arrivals, with 44,385 arrivals. Since 1983, it has ranked first in overseas arrivals. In the future, Japan may even pass Mexico in the number of tourists to the United States. Japan's rapid tourism growth reflects its economic growth and the introduction of affordable package tours in the Japanese tourist industry.

Europe accounts for slightly more than 45 percent of all overseas tourist arrivals. This is due to its wealth, its longer vacation time, and its political and economic ties with the United States. Asia, especially Japan, is the second largest contributor to foreign tourism in America, with 26 percent of the overseas visitors. Asia is followed by South America, with 10.8 percent, and the Caribbean, with 3 percent of overseas visitors. The greatest growth of visitors, 1984-1994, has been from Korea.

The United States Travel and Tourism Administration's survey of potential visitors from eleven major world countries indicated the following destinations were the eight most popular: Grand Canyon; Los Angeles and Disneyland; Las Vegas; Miami; New Orleans; New York City; Orlando and Disneyworld; and San Francisco.

United States Travelers Abroad

In the 1990s over 40 million United States citizens traveled abroad each year, Table 3–6. Mexico has been the principal destination of United States tourists, accounting for nearly 35 percent of all United States visitors. Mexico's proximity, favorable costs, culture, archaeological ruins, and beautiful beaches all strongly attract the United States tourist. Canada comes in second, as the destination for slightly over 27 percent of all United States travelers.

The two major destinations of overseas trips are Europe (44 percent of trips) and the Caribbean (11.5 percent of trips). The historical ties of Europe to the United States combine with favorable air fares and charters to attract American travelers to Europe. The Caribbean has been the largest growth area in the 1980s and 1990s due to the increased attractiveness of air fares and increased demand for cruises.

Table 3–6 Travel from the United States

Country	1982 (000)	1993 (000)
Canada	10,974	11,998
Mexico	3,850	15,285
Overseas	8,510	17,102
Europe	4,144	7,610
Caribbean, Central and South America	529	5,729
Other	1,200	3,882
TOTAL	32,103	44,385

Sources: Yearbook of Tourism Statistics, World Tourism Organization, 1995. Statistical Abstract of the United States, 1995.

Domestic Tourism

The travel industry is the second largest industry in the United States. Americans spend $604 billion on trips of over 25 miles, generating 9.2 million travel industry jobs. In 1994, the automobile dominated, providing the means of transportation for 78 percent of pleasure trips. Air travel was proportionately greater for people traveling to attend conventions and conduct business, but still clearly second to the automobile. The heavy-use patterns of the automobile are simply an extension of the modern United States in which the auto is important in all private phases of life. The development of advanced freeway systems and relatively inexpensive gasoline have led to this high use of the automobile.

Tourist Destinations and Attractions

The attractions of the United States are diverse and multiple due to the size of the country, its culture, and economic development. The 1993 Outlook for Travel and Tourism identified the top destinations for auto travelers (in order) as: Orlando, Florida; Branson, Missouri; Yellowstone National Park; San Diego, California; Lancaster County, Pennsylvania; and Williamsburg, Virginia. They represent a variety of visitor experiences from cultural (Lancaster County's Amish people), to the national park experience (Yellowstone), to entertainment (Branson, Missouri's country music and Orlando's Disney World), to the historic (the recreated colonial Williamsburg).

Gambling (technically known as *gaming*) has been growing dramatically in the United States and has become a major part of the tourism industry. Connecticut has one of the largest and most attractive casinos (Foxwood). Every state with the exception of Hawaii and Utah has some form of legalized gaming. For many states, gambling includes Native American–owned establishments since they are able to offer gaming if there is any form of legal gambling in a state.

The Native American gaming started in Florida with the development of large bingo parlors by the Seminole tribe. Subsequently a number of tribes began casino gambling. One of the most successful has been the Foxwood Casino in Connecticut, because of its location in the populous northeastern United States. The upper Midwest has a number of Native American gaming centers, reflecting the presence of distinct tribes. The markets for these casinos are largely regional, such as the population centers of Chicago and Milwaukee for the Wisconsin Native American casino centers, but include international tourists. For example, Native American casinos in North Dakota attract Canadian visitors, who drive down for a day or two to visit the casinos.

Gambling continues to spread across the United States. Many states along the Mississippi River and Gulf Coast allow "River Boat," or tour ship gambling. Some of these "River Boats" are permanent buildings defined as *boats* only because some type of waterway, even if only a drainage ditch, separates them from the land. These have a largely regional market but also attract visitors from other regions driving through the area. Las Vegas is still the major destination for gaming in the United States, followed by Atlantic City, however. Both have major national and international markets that pre-date the growth of Indian gaming.

Nine travel regions in the United States have been identified by the United States Travel Data Center for the purpose of data gathering and analysis of travel in the country. The regions provide both a convenient geographic grouping for tourism analysis and readily available statistics to allow meaningful comparisons between regions.

New England

STATE PROFILE

State	Capital	Square Miles	Population (1995)
Connecticut	Hartford	5,009	3,275,000
Maine	Augusta	33,215	1,241,000
Massachusetts	Boston	8,257	6,074,000
New Hampshire	Concord	9,304	1,148,000
Rhode Island	Providence	1,214	990,000
Vermont	Montpelier	9,609	585,000

Source: U.S. Bureau of the Census, 1996.

With its coasts, mountains, forests, and rich colonial history, New England provides excellent opportunities for outdoor recreation, sightseeing, and entertainment. Winter sports and summer coastal activities are readily available to prospective tourists. Population in the summer resorts along the coast and on the small islands increases dramatically during the summer. The rich colonial history of the area is evident in restored villages and historical sites. The beauty of the fall season is nationally recognized, attracting people from all over to enjoy the colorful fall foliage of the season. These attributes, coupled with proximity to the

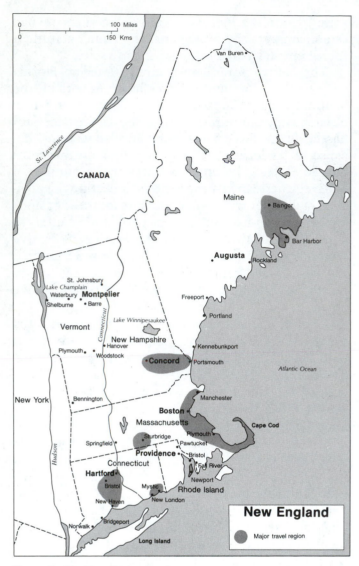

Figure 3–14   New England region

major attractions. A host of other cities provide glimpses of New England's past. Mystic, which was the center of early whaling and shipbuilding, has the nation's largest outdoor maritime museum. It has sailing ships, old-time shops, over sixty buildings, museums, and craftsmen demonstrations.

Maine

Maine is the home of Acadia National Park, New England's only national park. The park occupies nearly one-half of Mt. Desert Island and other smaller islands. It is a sea-lashed granite coastal area with forested valleys, lakes, and mountains. Bar Harbor is the entrance to Acadia National Park. Although there is no other national park, the Maine woods, filled with spruce, fir, cedar, birch, and maple are considered Thoreau country. The two major towns are Bangor and Portland. Bangor is the gateway to excursions in the Maine woods. The Rangeley Lakes, Baxter State Park, and Sebago are easily reached from Bangor. At Portland, the childhood home of the poet William Wadsworth Longfellow, which was built in 1785, exhibits the furnishings and personal belongings of the family Portland. Located on beautiful Casco Bay, it has stately old homes, historic churches, and charming streets.

Massachusetts

Massachusetts is the most populous New England state and has many important attractions. Boston is the capital of the state, but it is also a city whose history is an integral part of the entire United States. The Freedom Trail and the Boston Commons (the oldest public park in America) illustrate the history of the city and the nation. It was at the Boston Commons that the British troops assembled for their march on Lexington and Concord. Along the Freedom Trail is the Old North Church, from which the invasion of the British was signaled to Paul Revere, as well as other famous sites. These include Bunker Hill Monument, the ship the *U.S.S. Constitution* (Old Ironsides), and the Old Granary Burying Ground, with the headstones of John Hancock, Paul Revere, Samuel Adams, and others (including one for Mother Goose!). The modern city includes an array of important structures, including the Christian Science Center and a striking example of modern architecture, the John F. Kennedy Library. Across the river from Boston is Cambridge, which also has numerous historical sites including the location where Washington took command of the Continental Army in July 1775, the Longfellow National Historic Site, and Harvard University. At Lexington Green and Concord

populous Great Lakes region and New York, bring many tourists to New England to sightsee, participate in outdoor recreation, and enjoy the entertainment available in the urban centers.

TOURIST DESTINATIONS AND ATTRACTIONS

Connecticut

Connecticut's picturesque countryside is dotted with gracefully spired, white-frame churches and small cities. The two largest cities, Hartford and New Haven, are the two major visitor centers. In Hartford, the Mark Twain Memorial and the Connecticut State Library Museum are important attractions aside from the capital itself. At New Haven, the Yale University Art Gallery and the Peabody Museum of Natural History on the grounds of Yale University and the nearby Green and Grove Street Cemetery, where Noah Webster and Eli Whitney are buried, are the

Figure 3–15 Plymouth, where the Pilgrims landed

Bridge, visitors can reflect on the American Revolution at the Minute Man National Historical Park and the Minuteman Statue facing the replica of the Old North Bridge.

Near Boston is the Plymouth Plantation, Figure 3–15, a recreated historical village where the Pilgrims landed in 1620. Its exhibits illustrate housing, shops, and crafts of these early settlers of the United States. Cape Cod National Seashore is the home of New England's oldest and most popular resorts. Cape Cod has numerous museums, nature trails, beaches, wildlife sanctuaries, picnic grounds, fresh- and saltwater marshes, luxuriant forests, and migrating sand dunes.

Old Sturbridge Village between Boston and Springfield is a re-creation of an old New England farm community, complete with villagers in period dress demonstrating the crafts and trades of New England between 1790 and 1840. At Springfield is the National Basketball *Hall of Fame,* located in honor of Dr. James S. Naismith, who founded the sport here in 1891.

New Hampshire

New Hampshire contains less than one-tenth of the region's population. Mount Washington, the most famous mountain in New Hampshire, is a ski area and summer scenic region. The cog railway up Mount Washington provides a view into five states and Canada. Franconia Notch is a dramatic eight-mile gorge. Also part of the White Mountains is the Old Man of the Mountain, made famous by Nathaniel Hawthorne, which is a 40-foot-high naturally carved stone face on Mt. Cannon. The two major cities of New Hampshire are Manchester and Portsmouth. Portsmouth, the more popular of the two, is famous for its historical houses, including the John Paul Jones House. With its narrow streets, the older section around Market Square reminds the visitor of the merchant seamen who called Portsmouth home.

Rhode Island

Rhode Island's two major cities of Providence, the capital, and Newport are the chief tourist centers. Providence illustrates the architectural heritage of the pre-revolutionary period in many of its buildings. Roger Williams founded Providence while seeking religious freedom. Many of the streets in the city still bear names that Williams gave them such as Benefit, Benevolent, Friendship, and Hope. Slater Mill in nearby Pawtucket was built in 1793 and marked the beginning of the Industrial Revolution in America.

Newport is a center of water sports such as yachting and sailing and the world-famous Newport Jazz Festival. The Touro Synagogue, which was built in 1763, is the oldest synagogue in the United States. On the cliffs overlooking the ocean are many mansions, including the Breakers, a colonnaded four-story mansion overlooking Rhode Island Sound that was built for Cornelius Vanderbilt. Newport is also the home of the International Tennis Hall of Fame and Tennis Museum.

Vermont

Vermont advertises a green mountain landscape dotted with small towns and covered bridges. It is a popular ski area for the northeast, with world-class resorts such as Stowe, Sugarbush, Killington, Mount Snow, Smugglers Notch, and Bolton Valley. Vermont's granite rock is the basis for the world's largest granite quarry at Barre, from which comes granite used all across the United States. Like the other New England states, the fall foliage is one of the most important tourist attractions.

Mid Atlantic

STATE PROFILES

State	Capital	Square Miles	Population (1995)
New Jersey	Trenton	7,836	7,945,000
New York	Albany	49,576	18,136,000
Pennsylvania	Harrisburg	45,333	12,072,000

Source: U.S. Bureau of the Census, 1996.

This region is a major population center of the United States, including many of the country's largest cities. It receives many travelers for business reasons and offers a variety of attractions from gambling at Atlantic City, New Jersey, to the historic Liberty Bell in Philadelphia, to the mountain resorts of the Catskills in New York.

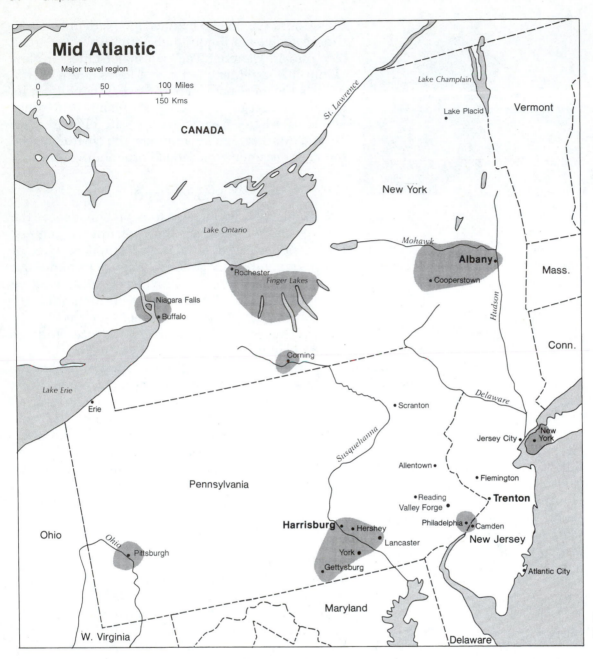

Figure 3–16
Mid Atlantic region

TOURIST DESTINATIONS AND ATTRACTIONS

New Jersey

Although New Jersey has the highest population density in the United States, it also offers a number of wooded, coastal, and historical attractions. The most famous attraction today is Atlantic City, with its famed boardwalk offering gambling, cabaret, nightclubs, shows, and entertainment. The coastal area has a variety of beach resorts. A sample of the many other attractions in New Jersey includes the historic town of Smithville, a recreation of a typical eighteenth-century New Jersey community; Edison National Historical Site, containing a workshop where Edison worked on the first motion picture camera, tinfoil phonograph, and other electrical items; and Morristown National Historical Park, which provided winter quarters for Washington and his men.

New York

Both the state of New York and the city of New York are major tourist attractions. The I-Love-New-York theme has been responsible for an increase in visitors to the city and state, but even without it the city is a major destination. It is the most important city in the world because of its combination of financial, manufacturing, and cultural roles.

The major attractions in the city are too numerous to list. Central Park, designed in the 1860s, remains the most important urban park in America, with over 800 acres of recreational attractions and cultural cen-

UN Photo 104 713 SAW LWIN

Figure 3–17 United Nations Building

France joined the colonies in their battle with England and is regarded as the turning point of the war. Saratoga Springs is a famous resort spa set in a scenic area with a number of operating springs and geysers. Lake George, at the foothills of the Adirondacks, serves as a center for winter and summer sports. Fort Ticonderoga is an authentically reconstructed eighteenth-century French fort, containing a large collection of artifacts from the French and Indian and Revolutionary wars.

In the center of the state at Cooperstown is the National Baseball Hall of Fame and Museum. The three major attractions in western New York are Niagara Falls, the Corning Glass Center, and the Finger Lakes region. Niagara Falls, near Buffalo, is one of the broadest and most spectacular falls in the world. *Maid of the Mist* cruises take visitors to the base of the falls. Corning Glass Center is a famous Steuben glassworks center. The Finger Lakes region is an area of lakes, waterfalls, steep gorges, and scenic vistas. In upstate New York, Rochester, which is the home of Eastman Kodak® Camera Company, has an international Museum of Photography, while Syracuse is home of the New York State Fair and the Salt Museum.

ters. Other major attractions include Fifth Avenue for shopping; the Lincoln Center for the Performing Arts; Rockefeller Center with Radio City Music Hall; the Empire State Building, the long-time symbol of New York City's skyscraper skyline; the United Nations Headquarters on the East River, Figure 3–17; Wall Street and the American and New York stock exchanges; and the Statue of Liberty National Monument, a gift from the French people to commemorate the Franco-American alliance of the Revolutionary War.

This list merely mentions some of New York City's most famous sights. The city also includes a host of other things to see and do, including cathedrals, museums, ethnic neighborhoods, plays both on and off Broadway, outstanding restaurants, and the beaches of the Atlantic Ocean.

The Hudson Valley, which is north of the city, is the home of the United States Military Academy at West Point. The Catskill Mountains are a major resort center with Ice Cave Mountain and the Catskill Game Farm. Albany, the capital, is the gateway to the Adirondacks and Saratoga National Historical Park, Saratoga Springs, Lake George, and Fort Ticonderoga. Saratoga National Historical Park is the site of the important Revolutionary battle where

Pennsylvania

Pennsylvania has some of the most important historical and cultural attractions in the United States. Philadelphia, the geographical center of the original thirteen colonies, was the site where the Declaration of Independence was signed and the Constitution of the United States was drafted. It was the first capital of the new nation. The attractions in Philadelphia include Independence Hall and Carpenters' Hall (two blocks from Independence Hall). Carpenter's Hall was the site of the first Continental Congress called to address the problem of taxation without representation. Christ Church was where George Washington, Ben Franklin, and other Founding Fathers worshipped. It contains the baptismal font used for William Penn's baptism in England. Other historic sites in the city include Congress Hall, America's first capital; the Betsy Ross House; and the Liberty Bell.

Not far from Philadelphia, in eastern Pennsylvania, are Hershey, Valley Forge, and the Pennsylvania Dutch Country. Hershey, the home of the Hershey® candy bar, has an eighty-one–acre theme and entertainment park in addition to the Hershey Factory. Valley Forge is the most famous site of Washington's Continental Army winter camps. Gettysburg National Military Park is the location of perhaps the most famous battle of the Civil War. A number of attractions in the area include the 300-foot-high National Gettysburg Battlefield Tower, National Civil War Museum, Hall of the Presidents, Gettysburg Battle Theater, Lincoln Room Museum, Gettysburg National Museum, and a cyclorama of the battlefield.

Pennsylvania Dutch Country is a unique area in America. The horse-drawn carriages of the Amish people, brightly colored hex signs on white barns, covered bridges, and rolling farms largely cultivated with horses are reminders of the Amish, Mennonites, Brethren, and other German religious sects who settled the region. A number of visitor centers and displays such as the Amish Farm and House, the Amish Homestead, the Pennsylvania Farm Museum, Kitchen Kettle shops, Intercourse, Ephrata Cloister in Ephrata, and the Plain and Fancy Farm and Dining Room all provide visitors with a view of the unique religious groups that settled in the area. To the west, Pittsburgh, the major city in western Pennsylvania, has undergone a renovation to provide a modern downtown cityscape. Once a gritty steel town, it is now a vibrant urban commercial center whose history is evident in attractions such as the Fort Pitt Blockhouse. The city's role as a center of entertainment and recreation in the region is typified by the Three Rivers Stadium for professional sports.

South Atlantic

STATE PROFILE

State	Capital	Square Miles	Population (1995)
Delaware	Dover	2,057	717,000
District of Columbia	Washington	67	554,000
Florida	Tallahassee	58,560	14,166,000
Georgia	Atlanta	58,876	7,201,000
Maryland	Annapolis	10,577	5,042,000
North Carolina	Raleigh	52,586	7,195,000
South Carolina	Columbia	31,055	3,673,000
Virginia	Richmond	40,817	6,618,000
West Virginia	Charleston	24,181	1,828,000

Source: U.S. Bureau of the Census, 1996

The South Atlantic region combines history and the nation's capital with the ocean to form a very popular travel region of the United States. The warmer environs extend the travel season in the northern states and the District of Columbia and provide year-round visits to the more southern locations in this region. There is a high degree of travel within the region since during the hot summer many from the southern part of the region move into North Carolina and Virginia for the summer, while in the winter the reverse is true.

TOURIST DESTINATIONS AND ATTRACTIONS

Delaware

Delaware, the second smallest state, has a number of summer resorts such as Rehoboth and Bethany beaches along the Atlantic Ocean shorelines. Wilmington, the largest city in the state, is the home of the Du Pont Company. The Winterthur Museum and Gardens, located six miles northwest of Wilmington, is a *historical house* with over 200 years of early American interior architecture and furnishings in more than 100 rooms. The Hagley Museum displays the history of American industry on a 185-acre complex. Old stone buildings and other buildings have been restored to display the early industries of the United States. The early history of Wilmington can be seen in the Holy Trinity (Old Swedes) Church; Hendrickson House, which is now a museum; Old Town Hall; and Fort Christina Monument, the site of the first Swedish settlement in Delaware. Near Dover is the John Dickinson Mansion, a restored colonial home of the author who wrote the first draft of the Articles of Confederation and who, with Thomas Jefferson, penned the "Declaration of the Causes and Necessity of Taking Up Arms."

District of Columbia

The District of Columbia, the nation's capital, can keep a visitor busy for a long period of time. The seat of government provides numerous attractions. The major ones are the Capitol with its marble rotunda, home of the House and Senate chambers, and the Old Supreme Court Chamber; the White House; the Library of Congress, which includes the Gutenberg Bible in its collections; the Bureau of Engraving and Printing, where the government designs, engraves, and prints United States coins, currency, bonds, and postage stamps; the National Archives, which displays a number of historical documents such as the original Declaration of Independence and the Bill of Rights; and a host of other government buildings such as the Department of Justice; Internal Revenue Building; Old Post Office Building; Interstate Commerce Commission; Health, Education, and Welfare

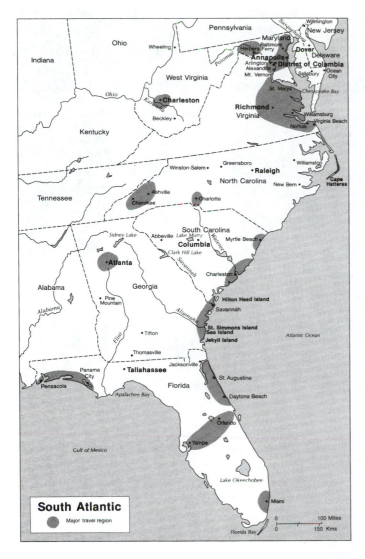

Figure 3–18 South Atlantic region

Air and Space Museum, Freer Gallery of Art, National Portrait Gallery, National Collection of Fine Arts, and the Renwick Gallery. A variety of other museums of interest are found in the city, but the most recent is a memorial of the Holocaust to remind visitors of the inhumanity some have practiced.

Florida

Florida is a major winter travel center boasting itself as the playground of America. The state receives more visitors by automobile than any other. South Florida's principal areas are the Florida Keys, Everglades National Park, and Miami. The Florida Keys extend some 135 miles south of the Florida peninsula. They contain marshes, coral reefs, grasslands, and palm trees. The John Pennekamp Coral Reef State Park, near Key Largo, is the first underwater park in the United States. The Ernest Hemingway Home and Museum at Key West was the location at which Hemingway wrote a number of his books. Reef cruises, fishing, boating, swimming, and wading areas are found in the Keys. South Miami Beach has revitalized its art deco architecture and has become a magnet for tourists.

The Everglades National Park is a subtropical wilderness of water, sawgrass, pines, palms, mangroves, alligators, manatees, and other birds and animals. Miami is the home port for many cruise vessels into the Caribbean and has more international travel by ship than any other city in the United States. Two of the city's most noted attractions are the Miami Beach strip of large modern hotels and Sea Aquarium, complete with viewing windows, jungle islands, and tidepools. Near Miami is Monkey Jungle, in which visitors in enclosed walkways can watch gorillas, orangutans, chimpanzees, and other primates. It is set in a re-creation of the Amazon rain forest.

Central Florida destinations include Tampa, Orlando, and the Kennedy Space Center. Orlando and the area surrounding it are becoming the heart of the travel industry in Florida. Walt Disney World Resort includes three major theme parks and three water parks: Magic Kingdom Park, Epcot, Disney-MGM Studios; Typhoon Lagoon, the new Blizzard Beach, and River County. In addition Disney's Animal Kingdom opened in 1998. This has a unique wildlife experience with a new kind of live-action adventure filled with the natural drama of life in the wild. Typhoon Lagoon is the world's largest water park; and Pleasure Island is a complex of restaurants, shops, and nightclubs built on a six-acre island at the Disney Village. A series of theme settings, such as the South Pacific, are being developed for hotels and restaurants. At the Disney-MGM Studio theme park, visi-

Building; Treasury Building; the Federal Reserve Building; and so on.

The John F. Kennedy Center for the Performing Arts, a modern memorial dedicated to the memory of John F. Kennedy, is the national center of performing arts. Other historical sites and *memorials* are Ford's Theater where John Wilkes Booth shot President Lincoln, the red-brick house where Lincoln died, and the famed Jefferson, Lincoln, and Washington monuments.

The centerpiece of museums in Washington is the Smithsonian Institute, which houses materials ranging from the original Star-Spangled Banner that flew over Fort McHenry to the Apollo 11 spacecraft. The Smithsonian is a series of museums, including the National Museum of National History, National Museum of History and Technology, Arts and Industries Building, Smithsonian Institution Building, National

Figure 3–19   St. Augustine, the oldest city in the continental United States

tors can walk through re-creations of palm-lined Hollywood Boulevard and Grumman's Chinese Theater, peek at movies under production, take a role in a television show, make their own music videos, and get a screen test. Universal Studios Florida is billed as the nation's largest working studio outside of Hollywood. Accessible from Orlando are the Florida Cypress Gardens with a water show and gardens; Seaworld; Master Gardens, which has a mosaic reproduction of Leonardo da Vinci's "Last Supper"; and Circus World, which includes a circus in which the audience also participates in certain acts. Also, Orlando has a wide variety of dinner shows and theme restaurants such as Rainforest Cafe, Hard Rock Cafe, and Race Rock.

The beaches on both coasts of Florida are world famous. East of Orlando on the Atlantic Coast is Cape Canaveral (Kennedy Space Center), which is open to the public and has a visitor information center. North of Cape Canaveral on the coast, Daytona Beach, home of the Daytona International Speedway, has long been a popular summer resort area. Daytona Beach has become the major destination for northern students on their annual spring break.

Tampa, on the Gulf of Mexico side of the peninsula, features Busch Gardens, where visitors wander through a re-creation of the Serengeti Plain of Tanzania to observe wildlife. Across the bay at St. Petersburg, MGM's Bounty Exhibit has a replica of the three-masted ship *Bounty* and a Tahitian setting with dioramas, outrigger canoes, and a longboat. Just north of Tampa is Weeki Wachee, where visitors can watch an underwater show in the clear spring waters. Visitors can also take a Wilderness River Cruise, stroll through tropical gardens and rain forest, and see bird shows.

St. Augustine, Figure 3–19, is the oldest permanent settlement on the mainland of the United States. It has been restored to illustrate elements of its original Spanish character. Ponce de Leon landed near St. Augustine in search of the Fountain of Youth. The most noted attraction is the Castillo de San Marcos National Monument, the old Spanish fort overlooking Matanzas Bay. Other attractions include the Mission of Nobre de Dios, the site of the first permanent Christian mission in the United States, and other reconstructed buildings and houses. St. George Street, where colonial houses have been reconstructed, contains houses and craft shops, including blacksmiths, candlemaking, leather, pottery, print, and a Spanish bakery.

Just east of Jacksonville stands Fort Carolina National Memorial, a reconstructed sod and timber fort that was first built by the French in 1564. The Gulf from Pensacola to Panama City features outstanding beaches, water sports, and resorts. The Naval Aviation Museum and Seville Square, a historic English and Spanish park, are located in Pensacola.

Georgia

The major attractions in Georgia are in and near the cities of Atlanta and Savannah. Old Savannah, a National Historic Landmark, is over 200 years old. Many of the buildings have been restored. Factor's Walk, a row of business houses, is accessible by a network of iron bridgeways over cobblestone ramps. South of Savannah near the Florida border is the Okefenokee Swamp, an important presence for alligators and other wildlife. The heart of the South is Atlanta, a modern city with its dynamic Omni International Center. The Omni is a sports and convention center that provides all forms of entertainment, shops, and arcades. Atlanta is the home of the James E. Carter Presidential Library. Near Atlanta are Stone Mountain Park, a granite dome with sculptures of the Confederate leaders Jefferson Davis, Stonewall Jackson, and Robert E. Lee; and the Martin Luther King Grave at Atlanta's Ebenezer Baptist Church. As in other large American cities and state capitals there are important museums, gardens, home and civic buildings, and amusement parks and other entertainment for visitors. Atlanta was the site of the 1996 Summer Olympics and several important structures were built to help host the games. In the northwest corner of Georgia is Chickamauga Battlefield, site of one of the bloodiest battles of the Civil War.

Maryland

The major attractions in Maryland are in Baltimore, at Annapolis, and around Washington, D.C. Baltimore is the home of Fort McHenry, where Francis Scott Key wrote the "Star Spangled Banner." Other unique attractions include the B&O Railroad Museum, the Edgar Allan Poe House, the Lexington Market, which has been in continuous operation since 1782, and numerous museums. Most famous is the National Aquarium located in the renovated Baltimore Inner Harbor. The Harbor itself is an excellent example of capitalizing on a unique geographic setting both to create a tourist attraction and revitalize a deteriorating inner-city area. The United States Naval Academy and the Maryland State House, which for a short period of time also served as the capital of the United States, are in Annapolis. Annapolis is one of the most scenic and visitor-friendly cities in the eastern United States. Near Washington, D.C., the Chesapeake and Ohio Canal National Historical Park along the Potomac River provides not only a museum and walking paths but also mule-drawn barge rides in a scenic setting.

North Carolina

Attractions are varied in North Carolina, ranging from the mountains through the flatlands to the coastal areas. One of the most beautiful scenic drives in America is the Blue Ridge Parkway. Asheville is the center for trips into the Great Smoky Mountains National Park from the North Carolina side. The Cherokee Indian Reservation has an eighteenth-century Oconaluftee Indian Village, where arts and crafts are demonstrated and the "Trail of Tears," which depicts Cherokee history, is performed.

The Biltmore House and Gardens at Asheville is a large French chateau country house set on an 11,000-acre estate. Nearby is Chimney Rock Park, a towering granite monolith in a beautiful mountain valley. Winston-Salem has Old Salem, a restored planned community, which the Moravians first built in 1766. Over thirty buildings have been restored, of which the Salem Academy and College are the most noted. In and near Charlotte are the World Golf Hall of Fame, the Mint Museum, Charlotte Nature Museum, the James K. Polk Memorial State Historical Site, and Carowinds, a family entertainment park built around an Old South theme.

The coastal area has outstanding beaches, most notable Cape Hatteras National Seashore; Cape Hatteras Lighthouse, the tallest lighthouse on the East Coast; and the Wright Brothers National Memorial, marking the spot where Orville and Wilbur Wright made their historic first flight. Cape Hatteras is a thin stretch of beach along the Outer Banks barrier islands.

South Carolina

The most dominant attraction in South Carolina is Charleston, one of the oldest cities in the country. Charleston's homes, historic shrines, old churches, lovely gardens, winding cobblestone streets, and intricate iron lace gateways are an outstanding example of historic preservation. A number of museums, such as the Charleston Museum, the Dock Street Theater, the first playhouse in the colonies (1736), and the aircraft carrier Yorktown in the Charleston Harbor all further increase the interest in the area. George Washington and Robert E. Lee attended services at St. Michael's Episcopal Church. Fort Sumter National Monument marks the site of the beginning of the Civil War. Just north of Charleston are the Magnolia Plantation and Gardens and Cypress Gardens with its giant cypresses, lagoons, azaleas, and subtropical flowers.

Along the coast are a number of resorts such as Hilton Head Island and Myrtle Beach, which provide all forms of sports and amusements. King's Mountain National Military Park, near the North Carolina bor-

Figure 3–20 Colonial Williamsburg, Virginia

der, reminds visitors of the southern campaign of the Revolutionary War where the British were defeated by mountain frontiersmen from Carolina, Georgia, and Virginia. A diorama and museum provide information about the battles and the war.

Virginia

Virginia's major attractions are concentrated in a triangle between Richmond, Norfolk, and Arlington. Many of Virginia's major attractions relate to the history and founding of the United States. Appomattox Court House National Historical Park, where General Robert E. Lee surrendered to Ulysses S. Grant to end the Civil War; the Virginia State Capital, where Aaron Burr stood trial for treason; Colonial Williamsburg, Figure 3–20, the nation's largest and most authentic privately funded restoration; and Monticello, the beautiful home of Jefferson, are notable examples of historic sites. Others include Jamestown National Historical Site, where Captain John Smith tried to found the first permanent English settlement in America; Cape Henry Memorial, both a popular seaside resort and the place where the first English settlers landed; Yorktown Battlefield, Figure 3–21, where Cornwallis surrendered his British Army to Washington and Rochambeau; and Mount Vernon, where Washington lived and died. Near Washington, D.C., is Arlington National Cemetery with the Tomb of the Unknown Soldier; the gravesites of John and

Robert Kennedy; and Arlington House, where Robert E. Lee courted and married Mary Ann Randolf.

West Virginia

West Virginia, a mountainous state, has three major attractions: Cass Scenic Railroad near Marlinton, Harpers Ferry National Historical Park, and the West Virginia State Capital. The Cass Scenic Railroad runs along the Leatherbark Creek and up a steep grade of over ten percent on logging train rails. Harpers Ferry is situated on a point where the Shenandoah and Potomac rivers meet. John Brown, an abolitionist, launched his famous abortive raid on the federal armory here. Remains of the arsenal, restored buildings, and exhibits recall the experience. The West Virginia State Capital, at Charleston, is one of the most beautiful state capitals in the United States. It was designed by Cass Gilbert in Italian Renaissance style with a golden dome and a huge Czechoslovakian chandelier. There are a number of resorts throughout West Virginia. Berkeley Springs is the most famous. It is the oldest spa in the nation and was made popular by George Washington. Its official name is Bath, named after a famous spa town in England.

The East South Central region combines the coastal Gulf states of Mississippi and Alabama with the mountainous environment of Kentucky and Tennessee, offering the visitor a rich variety of historic, environmental, and unique theme park attractions.

Figure 3–21 Battlefield at Yorktown

East South Central

State	Capital	Square Miles	Population (1995)
Alabama	Montgomery	51,609	4,253,000
Kentucky	Frankfort	40,395	3,860,000
Mississippi	Jackson	47,716	2,697,000
Tennessee	Nashville	42,244	5,256,000

Source: U.S. Bureau of the Census, 1996

TOURIST DESTINATIONS AND ATTRACTIONS

Alabama

Alabama contains the Confederacy's first capital (at Montgomery) and the space center at Huntsville. The Alabama State Capitol, a beautiful colonial-style building, is where Jefferson Davis was sworn in as president of the Confederacy. Across the street is the first Capitol building. Throughout the city are a number of museums and antebellum homes. The United States Space and Rocket Center at Huntsville has a hands-on type of exhibit where visitors can fire a rocket engine, guide spacecraft by computer, and feel the sensation of weightlessness. The town has a number of museums, including the Twichenham Historic District, a living museum of antebellum architecture.

Near Huntsville is Noccalula Falls at Gadsden, a ninety-five-foot cascade of white water dropping into a great emerald-green pool set in a scenic park. Near Mobile is one of the most beautiful gardens in North America, Bellingrath Gardens and Home. Surrounding a beautiful old brick and wrought-iron mansion are sixty-five acres of gardens, including huge live oaks covered with Spanish moss, giant Indica azaleas, rose bushes, camellias, chrysanthemums, poinsettias, and other flowers. The *U.S.S. Alabama* and a submarine in the Mobile harbor are open to visitors. Along the coast are a number of beaches such as the Gulf Shores Islands, which offer a complete range of water and fishing sports.

Kentucky

The mention of Kentucky elicits an image of horse racing and well-landscaped beautiful horse ranches. Churchill Downs in Louisville is the site of the world-famous Kentucky Derby, complete with race track and museum. The Man O'War Monument honors one of the great Thoroughbred horses in racing history. Lexington is the heart of many of the famous picturesque horse farms.

Fort Boonesborough State Park; Abraham Lincoln Birthplace National Historical Site; the Kentucky State Capitol; and My Old Kentucky Home, where Stephen Foster wrote the song by the same name, are found in the region of Lexington and Louisville. At the Kentucky State Capitol at Frankfort, the Governor's Mansion is a beautiful replica of Marie Antoinette's reception room at Versailles.

The most famous natural attractions in Kentucky are Cumberland Falls, Mammoth Cave National Park, and the Cumberland Gap. Cumberland Falls near Corbin are second in size in the country only to Niagara Falls. Nearby is Mammoth Cave National Park, which has the world's largest continuous underground passage. The Cumberland Gap National Historical Park, which is shared with Virginia and Tennessee, is the most famous natural pass through the Allegheny Mountains. Early explorers and settlers traveled west through the pass.

Mississippi

Some of the most important attractions in Mississippi are the Mississippi Petrified Forest, Natchez antebellum homes, Natchez Trace Parkway, and Vicksburg National Military Park. The Mississippi Petrified Forest, near Jackson, is a National Natural Landmark composed of a number of ancient giant stone logs in the only petrified forest in the eastern part of the United States. Vicksburg National Military Park commemorates an important Civil War battle. It was the site of a Union siege that lasted forty-seven days. The monuments, markers, and tablets include an exhibit modeled after the Roman Pantheon.

Natchez has one of the best collections of antebellum homes in the south. The Natchez Trace Parkway, a scenic parkway extending from Natchez to Tupelo, follows a trail used by Natchez, Choctaw, and Chickasaw Indians and early explorers and settlers. Markers along the parkway indicate archaeological, historical, and natural attractions. A resort center on the coast, Biloxi is considered the oldest town in Mississippi. It offers a number of museums and water activities associated with the Gulf.

Tennessee

Tennessee bills itself as the capital of country-and-western music. It capitalizes on its music fame and

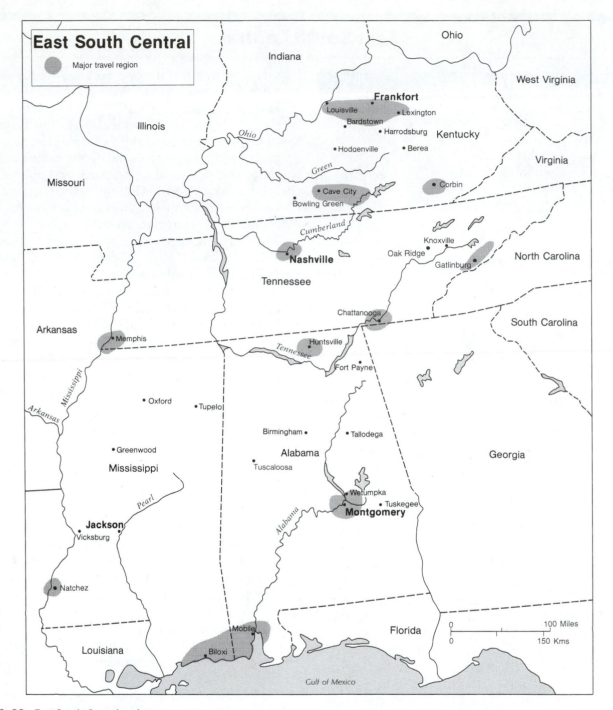

Figure 3–22 East South Central region

natural beauty to attract visitors. Opryland U.S.A. and the Grand Ole Opry provide country-and-western music lovers all forms of entertainment. The Parthenon, which is a replica of the Parthenon on the Acropolis in Athens, and the Hermitage, the home of Andrew Jackson, are also located in the Nashville area. The Hermitage consists of a tailor shop, two homes, and the burial place of President Andrew Jackson. Lookout Mountain at Chattanooga gives the visitor an excellent view of the surrounding Tennessee River Valley and an overlook of the battlefield

where a Confederate army surrendered to the Union Forces in November of 1863. Ruby Falls–Lookout Mountain Caverns offer beautiful falls and colorful caves. There are a number of other attractions in the Chattanooga area, including museums and a Confederama, which re-creates the drama of the battle of Chattanooga.

Tennessee also has part of the Great Smoky Mountain Natural Park, one of the most visited and scenic parks in America. The American Museum of Atomic Energy is located at Oak Ridge, where the first atomic bombs were manufactured during World War II. Although there are a number of other historical and scenic attractions, even a brief description of Tennessee would not be complete without recognizing Graceland, the home of Elvis Presley, and his gravesite in Memphis, an old Mississippi River town that is the commercial center of the state.

East North Central

STATE PROFILE

State	Capital	Square Miles	Population (1995)
Illinois	Springfield	56,400	11,830,000
Indiana	Indianapolis	36,291	5,803,000
Michigan	Lansing	58,216	9,549,000
Ohio	Columbus	41,222	11,151,000
Wisconsin	Madison	56,154	5,123,000

Source: U.S. Bureau of the Census, 1996

The East North Central Region is the heart of the industrial belt of the United States, often referred to today as the rust belt, since many of its old industries such as steel have declined in importance. The lakes and northern woods attract many to hunt, fish, and participate in water-related, hiking, or camping activities. Tourists to the area are also attracted by the large urban centers, with their rich variety of cities and industrial activities.

TOURIST DESTINATIONS AND ATTRACTIONS

Illinois

Chicago is the major tourist center of Illinois. The attractions in Chicago include the Lakeshore Drive with beaches, parks, and marinas; the Sears Tower, one of the world's tallest buildings; ethnic neighborhoods; John G. Shedd Aquarium, one of the largest in the world; the Adler Planetarium; the Art Institute of Chicago, which has the largest collection of French Impressionist paintings in the world; the Field Museum of National History, also one of the finest in the world; and the Museum of Science and Industry, a participation museum that includes a working coal mine and a German U-boat (submarine). In and near Springfield are the Lincoln Home National Historic Site, Lincoln Tomb Historical State Park, and Lincoln's New Salem State Park. The Old State Capitol in Springfield is the site of Lincoln's famous speech "House Divided."

Once the largest city in Illinois, Nauvoo has many buildings that have been restored and continues to add others. When the Mormons were driven out of Missouri, they moved to Nauvoo. Reminders of the Mormon history are expressed in the Nauvoo Restoration Visitor Center, which has a number of restored homes and the Joseph Smith Historic Center, which includes the graves of Joseph Smith and his wife Emma. The Old Carthage Jail near Nauvoo is a restored jail, where Joseph Smith and his brother died.

Indiana

Indiana's major attractions are scattered throughout the state. In the north on the shores of Lake Michigan between Gary and Michigan City, the Indiana Dunes National Lakeshore consists of rolling dunes, beaches, trees, shrubs, and bogs, which are centers for plant and animal life. In the middle of the state at Indianapolis is one of the most famous speedways in the world, the Indianapolis Motorway, affectionately known as the Brickyard. Other attractions in Indianapolis are the State Capitol, an impressive Corinthian structure of Indiana limestone with a copper dome; Soldiers and Sailors Monument, with a Civil War picture gallery; the World War Memorial Plaza, which is a five-block area dedicated to Indiana residents who lost their lives in the two world wars and the Korean and Vietnam conflicts; the renovated City Market; the Benjamin Harrison Memorial Home; the James Whitcomb Riley House; and the Scottish Rite Cathedral, a Tudor Gothic structure. Northeast of Indianapolis is the Tippecanoe Battlefield State Memorial, commemorating the American-Indian War.

There are a number of attractions in the south, including the Wyandotte Cave, a large five-level cavern over twenty miles long; the George Rogers Clark National Historic Park, commemorating the role of the man "who won the West" in the Revolutionary War; the Lincoln Boyhood National Memorial, gravesite of the president's mother; New Harmony, a utopian village; and the Spring Mill State Park, a restored early, nineteenth-century trading fort.

Michigan

The major tourist attractions in Michigan are in two general areas—the Detroit-Grand Rapids area and the northern area along the Great Lakes. In Detroit, the

Figure 3–23   East North Central region

Detroit Zoological Park is one of the largest and most attractive parks in North America. A number of automobile assembly plants such as Ford®are open to visitors. The Detroit Institute of Arts has an outstanding collection of seventeenth- and eighteenth-century Flemish and Dutch paintings. Greenfield Village and Henry Ford Museum in Dearborn provide an outdoor historical museum–entertainment park.

The Henry Ford Museum is a restored early-American village with shops, tradesmen, and demonstrations. The Civic Center in Detroit is a modern complex of buildings.

Grand Rapids is home to two important museums—the Grand Rapids Art Museum and the Grand Rapids Public Museum. Holland, which is near Grand Rapids, was settled by a group of Dutch people who were seeking religious freedom. Windmill Island provides a picturesque setting like that of Holland, complete with windmills, dikes, and flower gardens.

In the north, the attractions are mostly natural. They include Isle Royale National Park, Pictured Rocks National Lakeshore, and Sleeping Bear Dunes National Lakeshore. The three areas provide all types of outdoor experiences, including lakes, forests, dunes, sandstone cliffs, glacial sand, animals, and birds, in beautiful surroundings. Mackinac Island, the "Bermuda of the North," located in the straits between lakes Michigan and Huron, is very popular. No automobiles are allowed on the island. Bicycles or horse and carriage are the most common forms of transportation used to visit attractions such as the Old Fort and the Indian Dormitory.

Ohio

Ohio has many important attractions. Cleveland is the largest city. Located on Lake Erie, its history has been closely tied to trade and industry; but one important attraction is the Western Reserve Historical Center, with its turn-of-the-century village street and collection of Shaker artifacts. Kings Island is located in the south at Cincinnati, a historic river city that grew into a commercial and business center. It features a replica of the Eiffel Tower overlooking a number of theme parks such as Lion Country Safari, the Happy Land of Hanna-Barbera, Oktoberfest, Coney Island, and Rivertown. The *Delta Queen* and *Mississippi Queen* depart from Cincinnati for trips on the Ohio and Mississippi rivers. Cedar Point near Sandusky is a popular mile-long beach and amusement resort. The Aviation Hall of Fame at Damon traces manned flight from the Wright Brothers to space exploration. In the center of the state, Columbus has the Ohio Historical Center and the Ohio

Village, a museum of history, archaeology, and natural science set in a re-created Ohio village.

Roscoe Village, located between Columbus and Cleveland, is a restored Ohio and Erie canal town. The Schoenbrunn Village State Memorial, which was founded in 1772 by Moravian missionaries, has costumed guides who demonstrate old crafts and recount historical stories. The Football Hall of Fame at Canton houses professional football memorabilia and exhibits. Sea World has one of the few inland sea world exhibitions in existence. Perry's Victory and International Peace Memorial on the shore of Lake Erie reminds visitors of the victory in the Battle of Lake Erie during the War of 1812. Fishing, particularly in Lake Erie, is important in Ohio's tourism industry.

Wisconsin

Most of Wisconsin's major attractions are in the south. The north and center of the state have many lakes and forests for hunting, fishing, and other outdoor recreational opportunities. The Apostle Islands National Lakeshore was the center of French and Indian trade. In the south are the Wisconsin Dells, a natural scenic area where the river has carved the river banks into unique formations. There is a pioneer and entertainment park in the Dells. Other attractions are the Circus World Museum, complete with circus and circus paraphernalia from Ringling Brothers and Barnum and Bailey; Mid-Continent Railway Museum; Villa Louis, a mansion built in 1843 on the banks of the Mississippi River as a trading center; Cave of the Mounds, a colorful cavern of limestone and crystal; and the United States Forest Products Laboratory at Madison, which gives details on ways to use wood and wood products. Madison is the capital and the home of the University of Wisconsin.

West South Central

STATE PROFILES

State	Capital	Square Miles	Population (1995)
Arkansas	Little Rock	53,104	2,484,000
Louisiana	Baton Rouge	48,523	4,342,000
Oklahoma	Oklahoma City	69,919	3,278,000
Texas	Austin	267,338	18,724,000

Source: U.S. Bureau of the Census, 1996

The West South Central region has a variety of attractions, from coastal to wooded hill and spa resorts, that cut across a number of different cultures.

Tourism Destinations and Attractions

Arkansas

Arkansas is the home of the current president of the United States, Bill Clinton. Its tourist attractions include Bull Shoals Lake Area in the north part of the Ozark Mountains, which offers excellent trout fish-

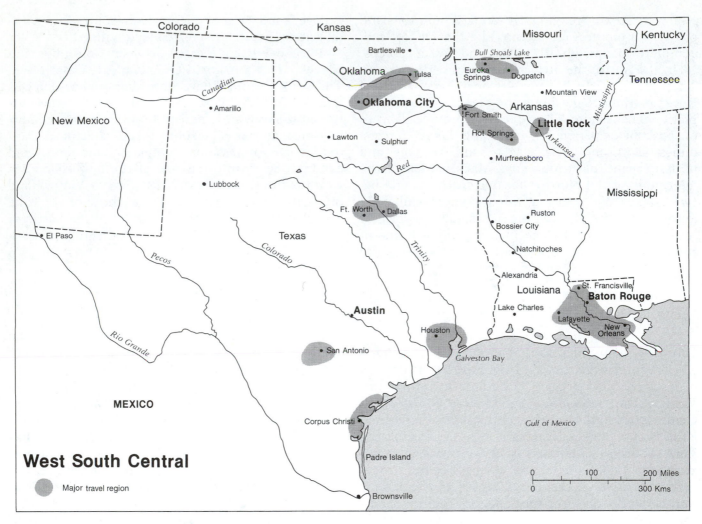

Figure 3–24 West South Central region

ing; Dogpatch U.S.A., a family amusement park located south of Harrison; the Ozark Folk Center, which features mountain music and crafts of the mountain people; Petit Jean State Park, which is full of natural wonders such as seventy-foot Cedar Falls, Bear Cave, Growing Rocks, Natural Bridge, and scenic drives. Next to the lake is the Winthrop Rockefeller collection of antique and classic vehicles and Winrock Farms, a prize cattle ranch.

In Little Rock, the state capital, the Arkansas Territorial Capital Restoration is an outstanding restoration project depicting life in the early nineteenth century. The capital itself is a smaller version of the nation's capital. One of the most noted attractions in Arkansas is the Hot Springs National Park and Hot Springs Resort. Hot Springs contains beautiful wooded hills, valleys, and lakes in addition to its forty-seven warm nonodorous hot springs. A variety of attractions (including Tiny Town, an indoor mechanical village) and Southern Artists Association Fine Arts Center are found in the area. The Crater of

Diamonds State Park at Murfreesboro is the only diamond-bearing field in North America. It can be explored by visitors, who can keep any diamonds they find.

Louisiana

The visitor attractions of Louisiana are concentrated in New Orleans and Baton Rouge. New Orleans combines a modern city with Southern and French culture to create one of the most interesting cities in North America. The French Quarter is the most important attraction. It is an exciting, colorful, and historic area in New Orleans. The annual Mardi Gras is the city's most famous festival, held each January. Around New Orleans, the visitor can enjoy the Natchez Steamboat, a replica of an 1887 sternwheeler; the Louisiana Superdome, near the French Quarter; Jackson Square, which was the political, social, and cultural center of the French Quarter; New Orleans City Park, a former plantation with lush lawns around lagoons, an old Spanish fort, and the New Orleans Museum of Art; International Trade Mart, which has an observation deck from which the visitor can see most of New Orleans; Lake Pontchartrain Causeway, the world's longest bridge; Chalmette National Historic Site, where Andrew Jackson won the Battle of New Orleans; and Acadian House Museum, a reminder of the French Canadians who settled in the region.

The Louisiana State Capitol at Baton Rouge is a beautifully designed marble statehouse. Nearby, the Rosedown Plantation and Gardens are a lavishly restored private mansion and gardens in the seventeenth-century French style. Between Baton Rouge and New Orleans is the old River Road paralleling the Mississippi, which passes numerous plantations.

Oklahoma

The history of Oklahoma is portrayed in a number of attractions such as the Will Roger's Memorial, with memorabilia and manuscripts from and about Will Rogers; the National Cowboy Hall of Fame and Western Heritage Center in Oklahoma City, illustrating life in the Wild West; Indian City, U.S.A., seven authentically restored Indian villages, complete with dance ceremonies, arts, and crafts; Fort Sill Military Reservation, displaying weapons from field guns to atomic artillery; the J. M. Davis Gun Museum; and the Thomas Gilcrease Institute of American History and Art in Tulsa, which displays the archaeology and history of the state. Chickasaw National Recreation Area offers mineral springs and nature viewing.

Texas

Texas is the largest state in the forty-eight continental states and is third after California and New York in population. In the Fort Worth–Dallas area one can visit the Amon G. Carter Museum of Western Art, containing many works of Charles Russell and Frederic Remington; the Dealey Plaza (now called the John F. Kennedy Plaza) in which John F. Kennedy was shot and killed, which contains the John F. Kennedy Museum; the Biblical Arts Center, with a 20-foot-high mural of the "Miracle of the Pentecost"; Six Flags Over Texas, a large popular theme park; Lion Country Safari for observing game; Will Rogers Memorial Center, containing a number of art museums, a planetarium, and the Museum of Science and History; and the State Fair park, which has a permanent exposition that is open year-round and contains a number of museums on science, art, and history.

Houston is the largest city. It is a center of sites related to the history of Texas, as well as the Astrodome, one of the first domed stadiums. Astroworld, a theme park; San Jacinto Battleground Park, where Sam Houston won independence for Texas; the NASA/Lyndon B. Johnson Space Center, which is open for visitors; and two historical parks, the Allen's Landing Park and Old Market Square, are other examples of Houston's attractions. The Alamo at San Antonio is the most famous battle site in Texas's fight for independence from Mexico. The area along the river in San Antonio has been restored and hosts a number of theaters, restaurants, and shops and the Hemisfair Plaza, a cultural and amusement center. The Lyndon B. Johnson National Historic Site in Johnson City near San Antonio is the restored boyhood home of President Johnson.

South on the Gulf Padre Island National Seashore is an 80-mile-long barrier island of shifting sand and grass that is very popular for fishing and swimming. West on the Rio Grande is Big Bend National Park, a wilderness home for the plants and animals of the desert Southwest. The Chamizal National Memorial at El Paso commemorates the settlement of a boundary dispute with Mexico. The Sierra de Cristo, with a figure of Christ on the Cross on the summit; an Aerial Tramway to Ranger Peak; and the Fort Bliss Replica Museum, expressing the history of the old Southwest, are also in El Paso. Many visitors travel across the border to Ciudad Juarez, Mexico, for shopping, bullfights, and other forms of entertainment.

West North Central

The wide open spaces and northern locations of the West North Central region have fewer visitors than other regions of the United States discussed to this point. Many tourists pass through Missouri, Nebraska, and Kansas on the interstate highway and some towns along it capitalize on their locations.

STATE PROFILE			
State	**Capital**	**Square Miles**	**Population (1995)**
Iowa	Des Moines	56,275	2,842,000
Kansas	Topeka	82,264	2,565,000
Minnesota	St. Paul	84,068	4,610,000
Missouri	Jefferson City	69,686	5,324,000
Nebraska	Lincoln	77,227	1,637,000
North Dakota	Bismark	70,665	641,000
South Dakota	Pierre	77,047	729,000

Source: U.S. Bureau of the Census, 1996

Tourism in the northern states is concentrated in the southern portion of each state.

TOURIST DESTINATIONS AND ATTRACTIONS

Iowa

Des Moines, the capital of Iowa, features an ornate capital building and a Living History Farms open-air museum. The Boione and Scenic Valley Railroad provides a ten-mile vintage train ride through the Des Moines River Valley. The Amana Colonies, which were settled in the 1840s by a religious group with members from Germany, France, and Switzerland, are located near Iowa City, site of the state's first capital. The oldest dwelling in Iowa is at Eagle Point Park. New Mellerary is one of four Trappist monasteries in the United States. Both are near Dubuque.

Kansas

Kansas's attractions include Dodge City, where the Wild West is relived along historic Front Street; Fort Leavenworth, which is the oldest army post in continuous existence west of the Mississippi and which has a museum of early history; and the Eisenhower Center near Abilene, including President Dwight Eisenhower's boyhood home and a museum. The eastern portion of Kansas has many lakes and rolling hills, providing regional visitors with fishing and water sports. A number of towns, such as Wichita and Topeka, offer some local attractions for those passing through or visiting friends and relatives in the region.

Minnesota

Minnesota has both unique cultural (ethnic settlement patterns) and natural (thousands of lakes) attractions. Around and in the twin cities of St. Paul (the capitol) and Minneapolis (the largest city) are the Minnehaha Falls, a very colorful waterfall on the Mississippi river that was made famous by William

Wadsworth Longfellow; Betty Crocker Kitchens at General Mills; the Guthrie Theater, a world-famous theater; Valleyfair, a family theme park; the Minneapolis Institute of Arts and the Walker Art Center, with a collection of both famous European artists and American Indian works; and the American Swedish Institute, a museum of Swedish arts, crafts, and pioneer relics. A recent attraction is the Mall of the Americas, completed in 1992 and reported to be the largest mall in North America (vying with the Edmonton Mall for that honor).

Two important destinations are found in the northern regions of Minnesota: Voyageurs National Park, which is noted for its fishing; and Grand Portage National Monument on Lake Superior, which has a restored stockade and a number of trails used by the early French and Indians.

The woods and lakes are well represented in numerous state parks. The lumber industry is remembered at Lumbertown U.S.A., a restored lumber town, and some early history dating back to the Vikings is found at the Runestone Museum.

Missouri

Missouri combines nature, history, and large urban areas to provide a number of excellent destinations. In the St. Louis area, the 630-foot-high Gateway Arch, one of the most creative architectural and engineering feats in North America, commemorates the role of the city as the gateway to the West. At its base is the Museum of Westward Expansion, with fascinating exhibits and memorabilia of the settling of the American West. Other attractions in St. Louis include Six Flags over Mid-America, another large family amusement park, and the Missouri Botanical Gardens, one of the largest in North America. All provide opportunity for a diverse visit. Kansas City and its surrounding area on the west have the William Rockhill Nelson Gallery of Art, one of the better art galleries in North America, and the Harry S. Truman Library, Museum, and gravesite. Near Kansas City at Hannibal is the Mark Twain Boyhood Home and Museum.

In the center of the state, the Missouri State Capitol has murals that depict the history, legends, and natural beauties of Missouri. To the south are found the Ozark National Scenic Riverways of Adventure in the Ozarks and Silver Dollar City, a recreated pioneer village with performers in authentic Ozark mountain costume who provide demonstrations of Ozark life. One of the most popular destinations in America today is Branson, Missouri, where country-and-western singers and other performers have built music halls and perform nightly.

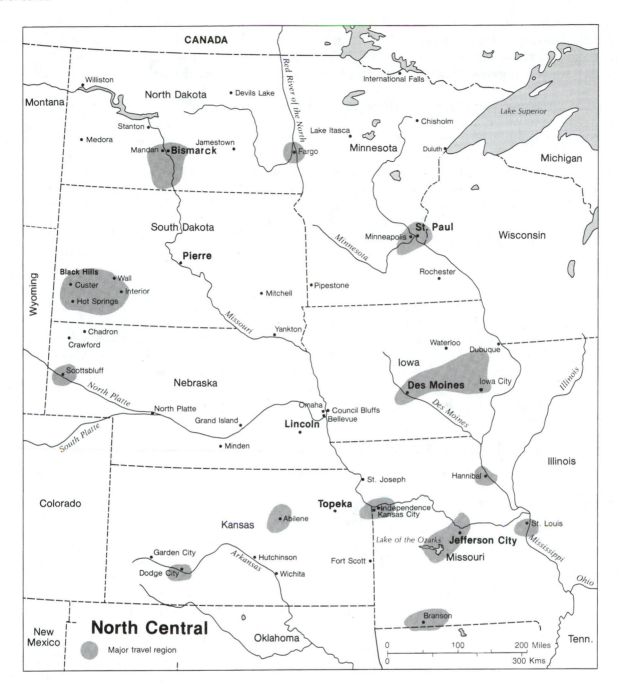

CANADA

Montana · Williston · North Dakota · Devils Lake

· Stanton · Jamestown
· Medora Mandan · **Bismarck**

· Chisholm · Lake Superior

International Falls

Lake Itasca

Minnesota · Duluth · Michigan · Fargo

South Dakota

Pierre · St. Paul · Wisconsin
Minneapolis ·
Black Hills · Wall · Rochester
· Custer · Interior
· Hot Springs · Mitchell · Pipestone

Wyoming

· Chadron · Yankton
Crawford · Waterloo · Dubuque
· Scottsbluff **Iowa** · Illinois
North Platte · **Des Moines** · Iowa City
Nebraska
North Platte · Omaha · Council Bluffs
· Grand Island **Lincoln** · Bellevue
· Minden

· St. Joseph · Hannibal · Illinois

Colorado · **Topeka** · Independence · St. Louis
· Abilene Kansas City
Kansas Lake of the Ozarks **Jefferson City**
· Garden City · Hutchinson **Missouri**
· Dodge City · Wichita Fort Scott ·

New Mexico **North Central** Oklahoma · Branson Tenn.

· Major travel region

0   100   200 Miles
0   300 Kms

Figure 3–25 North Central region

Nebraska

Nebraska's attractions illustrate its role in the settling of the West. Omaha is the largest city. Its attractions include the Joslyn Art Museum, the Union Pacific Museum, and refurbished Old Market area for shopping. The capitol of Lincoln is home to the University of Nebraska and the University of Nebraska State Museum, which has a large collection of fossils and life science exhibits. The Harold Warp Pioneer Village at Minden, which is an outdoor museum of authentic historical buildings, includes a sod hut, school, church, and railroad depot. The House of Yesteryear at Hastings exhibits a pioneer grocery store and other historical furnishings and artifacts. Scotts Bluff National Monument, in the scenic North Platte Valley, was an important stop along the Oregon and Mormon Trails. The museum has relics from both. The Museum of the Fur Trade at Chadron reflects the color and history of the fur trade and has a replica of the James Bordeaux trading post.

North Dakota

Most of North Dakota's attractions are in the southern half of the state. Theodore Roosevelt National

Memorial Park includes the dramatic badlands of colorful hills, buttes, and tablelands, a petrified forest, and a variety of animals such as deer, antelope, buffalo, and smaller animals. Near Bismarck is Fort Lincoln State Park, where Custer was stationed and left for his famous "Last Stand" at the Little Big Horn. There is also a restored Slant Indian Village on the site. At Fargo, in the east, is the Fort Abercrombie Historic Site, where the state's first U.S. Army post was established, and Bonanzaville U.S.A., a living museum of the bonanza farm of the nineteenth century. On the Canadian border is the International Peace Garden, which is shared with Canada and is dedicated to perpetual peace between America and Canada.

South Dakota

Most of South Dakota's attractions are in the west, combining natural attractions and history. The Badlands National Park is a uniquely colorful area of sharp ridges and deep gullies with a variety of wildlife from prairie dogs to mule deer. Wind Cave National Park is a beautiful cave of limestone labyrinth lined with calcite crystal formations on Elk Mountain. The Homestake Gold Mine provides visitors the opportunity to watch surface mining. Deadwood was made famous as the place where Wild Bill Hickok was shot. Today it has a museum, a melodramatic Centennial Theater and legalized casino gambling, which has become a major attraction. Mount Rushmore National Monument has impressive massive granite faces of Washington, Jefferson, Lincoln, and Theodore Roosevelt carved out of a 6,000-foot mountain. Floodlights are turned on at night and the national anthem is played, providing a moving experience for those in attendance. At Crazy Horse Monument near Mount Rushmore, sculptor Korczak Ziolkowski is creating a granite mountain monument to the Sioux chief Crazy Horse. In Sioux Falls is an impressive cathedral, while the area of farmland around the area is the center of fine pheasant hunting. West of Sioux Falls, the Corn Palace in Mitchell is decorated with pictures and designs formed by thousands of ears of natural-colored corn and grasses. The red rock gorge at Dell Rapids west of Sioux Falls is a picturesque drive.

Mountain

STATE PROFILES

State	Capital	Square Miles	Population (1995)
Arizona	Phoenix	113,909	4,218,000
Colorado	Denver	104,247	3,747,000
Idaho	Boise	83,557	1,163,000
Montana	Helena	147,138	870,000
Nevada	Carson City	110,540	1,530,000
New Mexico	Santa Fe	121,666	1,685,000
Utah	Salt Lake City	84,916	1,951,000
Wyoming	Cheyenne	97,914	480,000

Source: U.S. Bureau of the Census, 1996

The Mountain region is a popular outdoor, cultural, and entertainment travel region. It has a wide variety of physical and cultural phenomena to provide alternative activities and attractions for visitors and residents alike.

TOURIST DESTINATIONS AND ATTRACTIONS

Arizona

Arizona is one of the most important tourist states in this region. Its attractions are many and varied, from skiing in the mountains of the north to deserts in the south. In the north, nature has provided a number of outstanding attractions. Grand Canyon, Figure 3–27, one of the most impressive physical features in the world, was carved by the Colorado River. Most visitors observe the canyon from the south rim. Canyon de Chelly National Monument, also located in northern Arizona, provides a scenic Rim Drive overlooking sheer red sandstone cliffs, sandy canyon floors, Navajo hogans, and beautiful scenic cliff dwellings. Northern Arizona also has the Petrified Forest National Park, with its mineralized logs; Monument Valley Navajo Tribal Park, a beautiful red-hued landscape; and Meteor Crater, a huge crater, created by a meteor. Visitors can follow a trail to observe the crater, and there is a museum. Oak Creek Canyon, a scenic canyon that is excellent for fishing, and Sunset Crater National Monument, a volcanic crater and lava flow, are located near Flagstaff.

Phoenix is the largest city and a popular winter vacation area. The Heard Museum of Anthropology and Primitive Art, which has important holdings of Indian and Spanish arts and artifacts, is in Phoenix. A number of interesting attractions, such as the Phoenix Art Museum, the Phoenix Little Theater, and the Mineral Museum are found in the

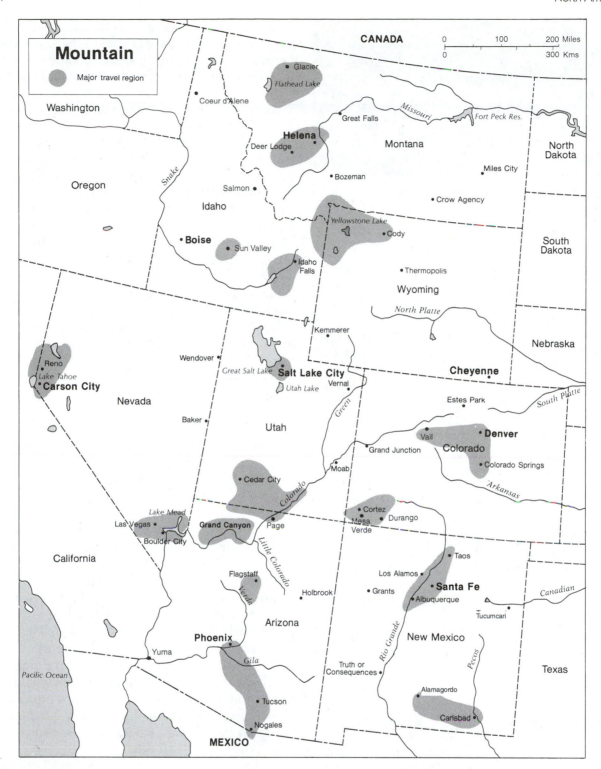

Figure 3-26 Mountain region

town. Phoenix also has professional basketball and football teams and Arizona State University. The Arizona State Museum at Tucson has many of the world's best Indian archaeological relics. Near Tucson are the Saguaro National Monument, which was established to protect the majestic saguaro cactus; the Arizona-Sonora Desert Museum, with all types of wildlife; and Old Tucson, a combination of an old town and family amusement park. Tumacacori National Monument, a monument to the Franciscan fathers and explorers to the region, and Tombstone, an authentic Wild West town that was famous for its gunfighters and boothill, are south of Tucson.

Figure 3–27 Canyonland overlooking the Colorado River

Colorado

Colorado is one of the most popular outdoor recreation states in the country with both outstanding skiing and summer outdoor resorts. Denver, the capital and largest city, has the U.S. Mint, and Larimer Square, a restored center of Old Denver that is full of boutiques, restaurants, art galleries, and gift shops. The Denver Art Museum is an impressive structure itself, and the Denver Museum of Natural History is well known for a number of well-presented dioramas of native birds and mammals in their natural settings. The State Capitol Complex, complete with its gold-leaf dome, the Colorado Heritage Center, and a Greek Theater are other Denver attractions.

Just south of Denver at Colorado Springs are the United States Air Force Academy and Pike's Peak, which can be climbed by an eighteen-mile-long road. Southeast of Denver in the plains is Bent's Old Fort National Historic Site, an important trading post built on the north bank of the Arkansas River. North of Denver, the Rocky Mountain National Park is a scenic glaciated park. Picturesque Estes Park serves as the gateway to Rocky Mountain National Park. A number of world–famous ski areas such as Vail, Winter Park, Aspen, and Snowmass are west of Denver.

The Great Sand Dunes National Monument near Alamosa is one of the most fascinating natural phenomena in the United States. The Mesa Verde National Park is home to the spectacular cliff dwellings of the Anasazi Indians; the Durango-Silverton Narrow Gauge Train through picturesque rugged mountains; and the Black Canyon of the Gunnison National Monument, a deep chasm and rushing stream, are found in the southwest part of the state. Colorado shares Dinosaur National Monument, which has an impressive visitor center and fascinating dinosaur quarry, with Utah.

Idaho

Idaho has a small population, but a great variety of natural attractions. In the north, Lake Coeur d'Alene is considered one of the most beautiful small lakes in the world. Nez Perce National Historical Park surrounds the Snake and Clearwater confluence. It is the site where the Nez Perce defeated the U.S. Army to begin the Nez Perce War.

Across the center of the state, the mountain scenery is impressive and rich. Set in the middle of the rugged peaks of Idaho's Rocky Mountains, Hells Canyon–Seven Devils scenic area is the deepest gorge on the continent. The Idaho Primitive Area, including the Salmon River, which is famous for river running, and one of the world's most famous ski resorts, Sun Valley, are in the center of Idaho. The Sawtooth Mountains in this central region are as impressive as the Alps. One of the most unusual monuments is the Craters of the Moon National Monument. It has trails through lava flows and an unusual landscape of cinder cones and craters. Throughout Idaho, outdoor sports such as hunting and fishing are extremely popular. Boise is the largest city and capital, and the Snake River plain is the center of potato production in America.

Montana

Montana tourism destinations combine the mountains and the plains. Its largest city is Billings, a regional business center. The scenic areas are best observed in Bob Marshall Wilderness Area and Glacier National Park, where the thick forests, scenic lakes, and precipitous peaks and ridges provide both a scenic view and homes for bighorn sheep, grizzly bears, and other wildlife. The Last Chance Gulch at Helena is the picturesque main street in this old mining town. South of Helena, the Lewis and Clark Caverns State Park is one of the largest limestone caves in the United States. Northeast of Helena is Old Fort Benton, a nineteenth-century center for the fur trade. South near the Idaho border, Virginia City is an Old West mining town complete with wooden boardwalks and a number of well-restored buildings. East of Billings on the Little Bighorn is Custer Battlefield National Monument, where the Sioux and Cheyenne destroyed Custer's troops.

Nevada

Nevada calls itself the entertainment capital of the United States. Las Vegas, with its famous hotel and casino strip, Reno, and Lake Tahoe are the entertainment centers, offering all forms of gambling and shows involving famous stars and acts. Las Vegas is the largest city and is currently undergoing tremendous changes as it tries to change its image from a gambling center to a family-oriented destination.

Three mega-resorts have been developed (Luxor, Treasure Island, and the MGM Grand) to lure the family market. All three include casinos, hotels, and theme parks. In addition, some existing casinos will evolve into resort complexes for the family. Virginia City, near Carson, and Rhyolite are two old mining towns. The Hoover Dam near Las Vegas is an impressive engineering feat. The newest national park in the United States is the Great Basin National Park in northeastern Nevada. Lehman Caves in the park is one of the more beautiful small caves in the United States. Reno provides Las Vegas attractions on a smaller scale and also has Harrah's National Automobile Museum, demonstrating the importance and evolution of the auto in America.

New Mexico

New Mexico combines a variety of outdoor and Southwest culture in a number of destinations. In the north, both nature and culture are displayed in Taos Pueblo, an artist community and one of the most picturesque towns in the world. The Bandelier National Monument, which has a scenic trail along Frijoles Canyon with pink and tan chasms, includes a plateau with ruins of cliff houses up to three stories high with unique cave rooms. Santa Fe is an old Spanish settlement with a picturesque central plaza surrounded by specialty shops. The Palace of the Governors in Santa Fe displays Indian jewelry and pottery. It is the oldest public building in America, erected in 1610 by the Spanish as a capitol. The Museum of New Mexico has an outstanding collection of contemporary American Indian paintings and is set in an impressive historic plaza. A visitor to Albuquerque, the state's largest city, can take a tramway to the top of the Sandia Peak for either skiing in the winter or nature trails in the summer. The old town is a combination of Spanish and Mexican historical buildings and shops.

The Acoma Pueblo near Albuquerque is a mesa-topped city high above the countryside. Further west, El Morro National Monument is famous for its "Inscription Rock," where Spanish conquistadors, early United States Army officers, Indian agents, and others carved their names into the 200-foot-high sandstone bluff.

Two destinations in the south are the White Sands National Monument, with its high dunes of shimmering white sand, the site of the first atomic bomb testing in 1945, and Carlsbad Caverns National Park, one of the most recognized caves in North America.

Utah

Utah combines a varied natural environment with a unique culture to create unusual attractions. It has five national parks, ranging from deep canyons such as Canyonland National Park to the unique erosional features of Bryce Canyon National Park to the sculpted stone mountains of Zion National Park. Erosion has created amazing natural arches in Arches National Park, the most famous being Rainbow Bridge National Monument. Rainbow Bridge National Monument is accessible via Lake Powell, a large man-made lake that is popular for houseboating, swimming, and fishing. The Great Salt Lake is noted around the world for its salty, buoyant waters. Golden Spike National Historic Site near Brigham City commemorates the meeting of the Central Pacific and the Union Pacific railroads, which gave the United States its first coast-to-coast link.

Salt Lake City is the capital, the largest city, and the center of Mormonism. The Temple Square is the most visited attraction in the state with over four million visitors annually. Temple Square includes the Temple, the Tabernacle, home of the famous Mormon Tabernacle Choir, and two large visitor centers. East of Salt Lake City, the Dinosaur National Monument is located on the border with Colorado. It is home to many different varieties of dinosaurs in addition to crocodiles and turtles. The Rocky Mountains and many lakes provide all forms of outdoor recreational opportunities for visitors to the state.

Wyoming

Wyoming's most impressive attractions are in the northwest corner. Yellowstone National Park, with entrances in both Montana and Wyoming, is the world's first national park established to preserve its unique natural features. Its hot-water geysers and vents are world renowned, and the abundant wildlife provide further attractions for the visitor. Grand Teton National Park and Jackson Hole are important outdoor centers, providing all forms of outdoor recreation such as hunting, fishing, river rafting, and so on. Skiing is popular at Jackson Hole, and the town is a major resort destination in winter and summer.

East of Jackson Hole at Cody is the Buffalo Bill Historical Center and the Whitney Gallery of Western Art, which has an impressive collection of Remington's and Russell's works. In the eastern part of the state, Fort Laramie National Historic Site allows visitors to experience what the early fort and trading center was like for travelers going west.

Pacific

STATE PROFILE

State	Capital	Square Miles	Population (1995)
Alaska	Juneau	586,412	604,000
California	Sacramento	158,693	31,589,000
Hawaii	Honolulu	6,450	1,187,00
Oregon	Salem	96,981	3,141,000
Washington	Olympia	68,192	5,431,000

Source: U.S. Bureau of the Census, 1996

The Pacific region is a popular tourist region that receives large numbers of tourists from all over the world.

Tourist Destination Attractions

Alaska

Alaska is noted for outdoor adventure. The natural features and scenery are immense, picturesque, and majestic from the Inside Passage in the south to Kotzebue and Nome in the north. The largest state, Alaska is sparsely occupied. Many tourists come via the Inside Passage in the southeast, either by cruise ship or ferries. It is a picturesque trip beneath snow-capped mountains, hurtling waterfalls, massive glaciers, and forests, past unique towns such as Ketchikan, Sitka, and Juneau. Juneau, the capital, provides visitors with historical and natural attractions. These include the Alaska State Museum, featuring Alaskan history, flora, and fauna; and the Russian Orthodox Church, which was built in 1894. The Mendenhall Glacier near Juneau can easily be reached by car or foot. Glacier Bay National Monument is a short air flight from Juneau. Ships take visitors to the edge of the glacier to watch and listen to the cracking and groaning as the ice crashes into the bay. Sitka was Czarist Russia's New World capital, and is Alaska's oldest town. The Russian church, St. Michael's Cathedral, and the Sitka National Monument, with its many totem poles, are attractions here. Ketchikan, a port on the Inside Passage, is a colorful town. It has a large collection of totem poles at Saxman Park.

With its international airport, Anchorage is the gateway for sightseeing and traveling to south central Alaska, the Kenai Peninsula, and the lower interior. The largest city, Anchorage is a rapidly growing town with an excellent historical museum and is close to the Alyeska resort area and Portage Glacier. Katmai

Courtesy Robert Angell

Figure 3–28   Caribou bull, Denali Park, Alaska

National Monument, some 250 miles south of Anchorage, was created in part by volcanic eruptions and flows. Included in the monument are the Valley of Ten Thousand Smokes and abundant wildlife. Beautiful Kodiak Island is a mecca for fishermen and big game hunters. North of Anchorage, the Denali National Park and Preserve has spectacular scenery, considerable wildlife, and Mount McKinley, the country's highest peak. (Figure 3-28)

Fairbanks, the second largest city in Alaska, was a gold-rush boomtown. Its attractions include old gold camps, sternwheel riverboat trips, and a pioneer theme park. The Indian villages of Circle and Yukon are nearby. For the visitor who wants a northerly visit, Nome, Kotzebue, and Prudhoe Bay fit the requirement. Nome, which was a gold-rush town, has preserved its frontier atmosphere. Kotzebue, north of the Arctic Circle, has the Living Museum of the

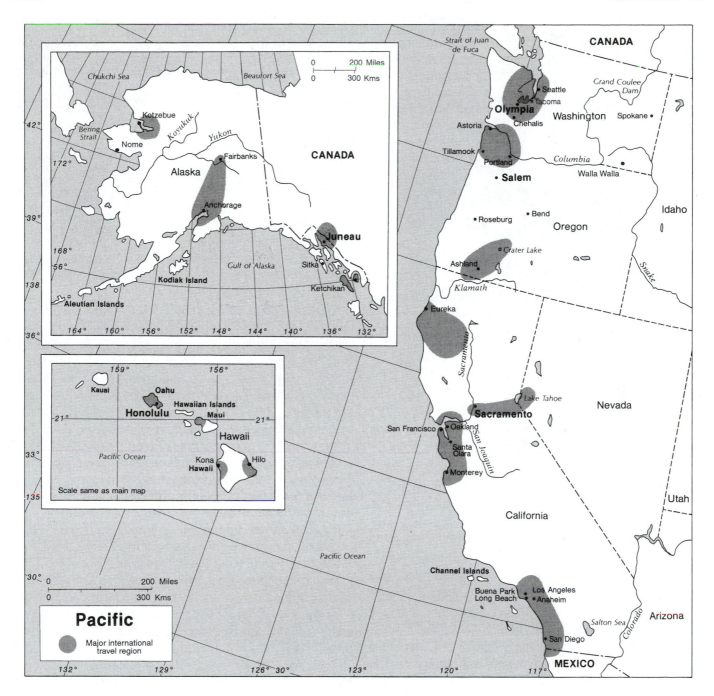

Figure 3–29 Pacific region

Arctic that features performances of the Inupiat (Eskimo) life and a diorama of arctic life. Prudhoe Bay and Point Barrow can be reached from Fairbanks by air. They have become better known with the development of the oil fields and pipeline.

California

California has more people and receives more visitors than any other state. It can be divided into three broad regions, the north, Los Angeles, and San Diego areas.

In the north, the Redwood National Park has trees that are twenty centuries old and the tallest in the world. The drive "Avenue of the Giants" illustrates the character of this park. Lassen Volcanic National Park, also located in the north, is a beautifully proportioned and visible peak set in a natural wonderland. The towns of Eureka and Crescent City are old mining and lumbering towns. Yosemite National Park on the slopes of the Sierra Nevada is one of the most visited parks in the United States. Its lofty granite domes, forests, thundering waterfalls, rushing

Courtesy Robert Angell

Figure 3–30 Brown bears at McNeil River

streams, meadows, and giant trees combine to attract large numbers of visitors.

California shares Lake Tahoe, a deep blue, cold lake and major summer and winter resort area, with Nevada. Just south of Tahoe, the Sequoia and Kings Canyon national parks have the largest trees and the highest peak in the lower forty-eight states. Sutter's Fort State Historic Park in Sacramento is where John Sutter discovered gold. The fort has been restored. There are many attractions around the San Francisco Bay area. They include Sonoma, where General Maiano Vellejo had his stronghold; Point Reyes National Seashore, where the crashing sea, the cliffs, and fir-forested ridges create beautiful scenery; Great America, a family-fun theme park in Santa Clara; and Marine World in Redwood City.

San Francisco itself has the Golden Gate State Park, a large and beautiful park and home of the Steinhart Aquarium and Morrison Planetarium. The San Francisco Cable Cars take visitors from Union Square to the North Beach or Ghirardelli Square and Fisherman's Wharf. The streets of San Francisco are unique because of their hilly scenic setting and their bustling and interesting activities. Alcatraz National Park, probably the most famous prison in America before its closure, and the Golden Gate Bridge, the world's second longest single-span suspension bridge, are equally noteworthy. The Palace of Fine Arts and Exploratorium has some four hundred touch-and-tinker exhibits in a Greco-Roman building. The California Palace of the Legion of Honor has an important art gallery of prints and paintings.

The coastal drive between San Francisco and San Diego is very scenic. The Monterey Peninsula has a picturesque rocky coastline and gnarled cypress trees. The cities of Monterey and the artists' colony town of Carmel center on the peninsula, which has white beaches, expansive golf courses, dramatic cypress groves, and large, well-landscaped estates. Just south of Monterey, the Big Sur Coast has a sandy beach and forested mountains. About halfway between San Francisco and Los Angeles, the Hearst Castle at San Simeon was built in the 1920s as a summer house for publishing tycoon William Randolph Hearst. It was one of the most fantastic and eclectic mansions in America. Within the one hundred–room Hispano-Moorish castle with its twin ivory towers are statuary, tapestries, and other art treasures collected from around the world. Located near Los Angeles, Santa Barbara has an excellent climate, pretty beaches and a lovely Spanish mission.

The Los Angeles area vies with Central Florida for the title of tourist capital of the United States. The area includes popular beaches such as Zuma Beach, Malibu, Santa Monica, Venice, Manhattan Beach, Hermosa, Redondo Beach, Huntington Beach, Newport Beach, and Laguna Beach. Theme parks such as Disneyland, Knott's Berry Farm, and Magic Mountain are large and well-planned to occupy the day of a visitor. Movieland Wax Museum, Universal Studios, NBC and Burbank studios, and Mann's Chinese Theater are for those interested in movies, movie making, and the stars. Each of the cities of Pasadena, Beverly Hills, Santa Monica, Hollywood, Long Beach, Burbank, and Anaheim has its own personality. History and culture are portrayed at Olvera Street, where Los Angeles was founded by Spaniards in 1781. The J. Paul Getty Museum, an authentic reconstruction of a Roman villa, and the Huntington Library, Art Gallery, and Botanical Gardens provide important attractions, as do the Rancho La Brea Tar Pits, with thousands of fossils. The Queen Mary is anchored in the harbor at Long Beach. Just offshore, Catalina Island is a resort center popular for its water sports and beaches. South of Los Angeles, the San Juan Capistrano Mission is famous for the swallows who are supposed to return each year on St. Joseph's Day.

San Diego is the third major tourist area of California. It has a world-famous zoo and Sea World. Other attractions include the San Diego Wild Animal Park, where a visitor can safari through Africa, Asia, Australia, and Central and South America; Old Town, a restored shopping center; and San Diego's mission. Balboa Park offers museums, art galleries, theaters, and sports facilities. Day trips across the border to Tijuana add to the attractiveness of the area. Inland, the Joshua Tree National Monument and Death Valley National Monument characterize the desert environment. Palm Springs, a world-famous winter resort center, has an aerial tramway from Chino Canyon to the top of Mt. San Jacinto.

Hawaii

Hawaii, the third major tourist region in the West, relies heavily on tourism and is a tourist destination worldwide. It includes twelve islands with their own distinct attractions in spite of general geographic similarities. The island of Oahu, the population and political center of the islands, attracts the most tourists. Honolulu, the largest city, is on this island. Honolulu includes Waikiki, probably the most recognized beach in the world, with its high-rise hotels and shopping area concentrated along the beach with its view of Diamond Head. Pearl Harbor serves as a reminder of December 7, 1941, with the impressive USS Arizona Memorial. Outside of Honolulu, major attractions on Oahu are the Iolani Palace, a restored royal palace; National Memorial Cemetery of the Pacific in the Punchbowl, a volcanic crater; and Bishop Museum, an outstanding museum of Hawaiian life and history. On the north side of the island, the Polynesian Cultural Center, Figure 3–31, has a number of recreated native buildings of the Pacific. The dances, arts, and crafts of the various island groups of the Pacific are demonstrated here. At Waimea Bay, famous for its surfing, surfers attract tourists. Waimea Falls is an area of beauty with an expansive valley that is home to tropical growth and exotic birds.

Maui, the Valley Isle, is the second–most-visited island of the group. High in the clouds, Haleakala National Park, over 10,000 feet in altitude, provides viewing and hiking trails through a volcanic landscape. Many resorts have developed on the coast from Lahaina and Kaanapali to Na Pai and from Kihei to Wailea. Lahaina is a preserved old port town that was once Hawaii's capital. It was also the center of Hawaii's whaling industry, which is represented in the whaling museum that is part of a large shopping center. Hana is somewhat remote from the major tourist resorts, but it is along a picturesque drive and still retains many of the old Hawaiian customs and pace of life. The Seven Pools, near Hana, is reported to be the bathing spots of the Hawaiian kings.

The Big Island (Hawaii) provides views of active volcanoes with the Hawaii Volcanoes National Park. There are a variety of landscapes, from the green lush jungle to the lava flows and streams. Hilo, the largest city on the island, has a number of points of special interest, such as the Rainbow Falls, the Hilo Florist Center, Lyman Memorial Museum (of ancient Hawaiian relics), and the Kalapana Black Sand Beach. Kona, on the leeward side, has become a resort center and is famous because Captain Cook was killed nearby. The City of Refuge south of Kailua is a National Historic Park.

Kauai, the fourth of the major islands, is referred to as the Garden Isle and is known for its lush greenery and deep valleys. Waimea Canyon, a "little Grand Canyon," provides spectacular views of multihued gorges that are nearly 4,000 feet deep. The Fern Grotto is attractive and noted as the setting for many weddings. The coastline is scenic, with beautiful beaches and good natural harbors.

Molokai, the Friendly Isle, is the last of the five major Hawaiian Islands attracting tourists. It is known for the leper colony that was founded there in the eighteenth century. Today it emphasizes sports activities such as hunting, fishing, golf, and swimming. The Kalaupapa Peninsula is a beautiful scenic area.

Figure 3–31 Polynesian Cultural Center

Oregon

Oregon's major attractions are located in the western half of the state. Portland is the largest city and is famous for its rose festival. Other attractions in and around Portland include the Astoria Column, an observation platform overlooking the Columbia River on the site of Lewis and Clark's visit; the Portland Gardens, home of the world-famous International Rose Test Gardens; the McLoughlin House National Historic Site in historic Oregon City; and Mt. Hood, some 60 miles east, with clear streams, blue lakes, and lush meadows. East of Astoria, the Fort Clatsop National Memorial is a log fort replica of the one built by Lewis and Clark. South is Crater Lake National Park, a deep water-filled caldera and lovely volcanic park. Jacksonville has nearly 80 historic buildings from the nineteenth century. During the summer, the town is quite active with Wells Fargo stagecoach tours and a number of historic buildings. The Rogue River National Forest has attractive forests of Douglas fir and Ponderosa pine along the Rouge River. One of the most popular and best-known Shakespearean festivals takes place at Ashland in the summer. Near the Rogue River National Forest is the Oregon Caves National Monument.

Washington

Washington has a number of important attractions that combine history, nature, climate, and culture. The physical environment is represented by Mount Rainier National Park, a scenic glacier-capped mountain, and Olympic National Park, with its beautiful midlatitude forests. Glacier-topped Mt. Olympus dominates the Olympic peninsula, and the rugged coastline provides a scenic drive. History is presented in the Fort Vancouver National Historic Site, a fur–trade center with a reconstructed fort. Whitman Mission National Historic Site, near Walla Walla, is the site where Cayuse Indians killed the Methodist missionary Whitman and his pioneer group. Cheney Cowles Memorial Museum in Spokane deals with Northwest history, and the Pacific Northwest Indian Center, which is also in Spokane, displays Indian history and artifacts.

The cosmopolitan metropolis, Seattle, is the largest city. It is dominated by the Seattle Space Needle, which has a revolving restaurant on top. The Seattle Center, around the Space Needle, has a variety of facilities such as an opera house, a repertory theater, an art museum, and the Pacific Science Center. Pioneer Square, Pike Place Market, and the Kingdome are important features in Seattle that add to the character of the city.

SOUTHEASTERN UNITED STATES

DAY 1   ATLANTA

Having arrived at Atlanta's Hartsfield Airport the night before, the tour will begin after breakfast at 8:30 A.M.

The Governor's Mansion: The beautiful Greek Revival home of Georgia's governors, including Jimmy Carter. Its furnishings are from the Federal Period, and it is landscaped with elaborate gardens.

The Swan House: One of the most famous of the lovely, historic mansions of Georgia. Restored by the Atlanta Historic Society. An example of Italian Palladian architecture.

Cyclorama: The world's largest painting in the round. It is the length of three football fields. It depicts the Civil War's Battle of Atlanta in 1864.

An hour lunch break from 12:30 to 1:30 P.M.

Martin Luther King, Jr., Historic District: Visit his birthplace, the church where he and his father preached, and finally the freedom hall complex that surrounds his tomb.

Westin Peachtree Plaza: The world's largest hotel, with seventy stories, a half-acre lake with floating cocktail bars, and beautifully landscaped grounds. Two more of the world's most spectacular hotels, the Hyatt Regency and the Ritz-Carlton, are also within this area. Then go shopping at the elegant shops in the surrounding downtown area.

Dinner at 6:30 P.M. at the revolving restaurant atop the Westin Peachtree Plaza, which has a gorgeous view of the city. The price is included in the tour package. Remember, it is best dress.

Stone Mountain: A night outing at 8:30 P.M. to the "Mount Rushmore of the South." The world's largest mass of exposed granite, carved with the monumental figures of Robert E. Lee, Stonewall Jackson, and Jefferson Davis, the president of the Confederacy. Also, visit the park and visitors' center, which are open late.

Back at the hotel by 10:30 P.M. for bed.

DAY 2   ATLANTA–BIRMINGHAM–MONTGOMERY

Leave for Birmingham, Alabama, at 8:00 A.M., arriving around 10:30 A.M.

Birmingham

Arlington Historic House and Gardens: A beautiful antebellum Greek Revival–style home. Built by slaves with handmade bricks and hand-hewn timbers. Furnished with authentic period furniture, a plantation kitchen with authentic utensils, and a museum and surrounded by beautiful gardens, shady lawns, and oak and magnolia trees.

Vulcan: Largest cast-iron figure ever made. Cast of Birmingham iron, it is a figure of the Roman god of fire and forge. It was made by Giuseppe Moretti for the Louisiana Purchase Exposition in St. Louis.

Lunch break from 1:00 to 2:00 P.M. and then leave for Montgomery. You will arrive in Montgomery around 3:30 P.M.

Montgomery

State Capitol Building: Here Jefferson Davis took his oath of office as the Confederate president.

First White House of the Confederacy: Across the street from the State Capitol Building, this was Jefferson Davis's home as Confederate president. It contains period furniture and personal belongings and paintings of Jefferson Davis and his family.

Dinner from 7:00 P.M. on, and then to bed.

DAY 3   NEW ORLEANS

Leave at 8:00 A.M. for New Orleans and arrive in the early afternoon.

Lake Pontchartrain Causeway: On your way into New Orleans, you will drive across Lake Pontchartrain on the world's largest causeway. Upon arriving in New Orleans, you will have a two-hour lunch and rest break until 3:30 P.M.

Garden District: Once the social center of New Orleans aristocracy, the Garden District is comprised of fancy old mansions and homes. Most have lacy ironwork and Corinthian columns. Some homes are bright pink, blue, or green and are surrounded by oaks and magnolias.

continued

Old French Quarter

This area is known for its Dixieland jazz and Creole cuisine. This historic district looks a lot like it did two hundred fifty years ago. It is made up of narrow streets, buildings with ornate, wrought-iron balconies and railings, and patios and courtyards filled with flowers.

Royal Street: Shopping and browsing in the shops, many of which are filled with antiques and open onto lovely courtyards.

French Market: You can get the real flavor of the old city here where they sell fish, meats, fruits, vegetables, and so on.

Dinner at 7:00 P.M. at Antoines, one of the most famous restaurants in the Old French Quarter. Here you can try Creole cuisine or even some of the dishes such as Oysters Rockefeller or a gumbo for which New Orleans is famous.

Bourbon Street: At 9:30 P.M. you will visit Bourbon Street, famous for its "honky-tonk" nightclubs full of Dixieland jazz.

DAY 4   NEW ORLEANS–VICKSBURG

Touring of New Orleans will continue at 8:00 A.M.

Jackson Square

Located in the heart of the French Quarter is Andrew Jackson Square, with a statue of him. The square is full of mimes, musicians, and artists. Jackson Square contains the Pontalba Apartments, St. Louis Cathedral, and the Cabildo, the old Spanish Government building, which now houses the Louisiana State Museum.

St. Louis Cathedral: The oldest cathedral in the United States.

Pontalba Apartments: The first apartment houses in the United States.

After a short lunch break at 11:00 A.M., you will leave at 11:30 for Vicksburg. You will pass through flat lands full of many green broadleaf trees, needleleaf trees, and some cypress trees. You will arrive in Vicksburg around 3:30 P.M.

Vicksburg, Mississippi: Vicksburg National Military Park: A park on the site of the battle of Vicksburg. Confederate and Union avenues wind through the park, following the defensive or offensive lines of both armies. There is a pictorial display at the visitors' center of the forty-seven-day battle that ended with the Confederate surrender. The park is full of historical tablets, markers, and commemorative monuments. Go on a Spirit of Vicksburg cruise on an authentic paddlewheel boat.

You will leave Vicksburg at 6:30 P.M. and arrive in Jackson by 7:00 P.M. for dinner and then to bed.

DAY 5   VICKSBURG–MEMPHIS–NASHVILLE

Leave for Memphis, Tennessee, at 8:00 A.M. The landscape will be much like that between New Orleans and Vicksburg. You will arrive in Memphis around 11:30 A.M. There will be a lunch break until 12:30 P.M.

Memphis

Graceland: You will take a one-and-one-half–hour tour of Elvis Presley's home and see his personal belongings, gold records, and so on.

Beale Street: The birthplace of the blues. You can walk down the street or even go into one of the clubs and hear some genuine "blues" music.

At 3:30 P.M. depart from Memphis and go to Nashville. You will arrive in Nashville at 7:00 P.M. and have a quick dinner until 8:30 P.M.

Nashville

Often called the Athens of the South because of its Greek–style architecture, Nashville is known as the capital of country music.

Grand Ole Opry: The original downtown building is closed, but country music is still thriving at Opryland U.S.A. You will watch the music radio program "Grand Ole Opry" be presented.

DAY 6   NASHVILLE–GATLINBURG

Up and ready at 9:00 A.M. to see Nashville.

Country Music Hall of Fame: A museum of music. People such as Elvis, Eddy Arnold, and Al Hirt recorded hits here. You can see Elvis's "solid-gold" Cadillac® and country music memorabilia.

Lunch break from 11:30 A.M. to 12:30 P.M.

Recording Studio of America: Since Nashville also is the home for many big record companies, why not record your hit record? You can here if you have enough courage and $9.95 (price not included in tour package).

continues

continued

Centennial Park: A beautiful park with a replica of the Parthenon that is a must see!

At 3:30 P.M. you will leave for Gatlinburg, the entrance city to the Smoky Mountains. There will be a stop for dinner at Knoxville from 6:30 P.M. to 7:30 P.M. From Knoxville, you'll begin traveling over some of the Achain Mountains.

You'll arrive in Gatlinburg at 8:30 P.M. and have the remainder of the evening free.

DAY 7   GATLINBURG—COLUMBIA

The day will begin at 8:00 A.M.

The Smoky Mountains: These mountains have some of the highest peaks east of the Rockies. There are huge, barely touched forests and tons of wild flowers. There are many wild animals, so watch and be careful of bears. You will visit the three "musts" of the park: Newfoundland Gap; Clingman's Dome; and Cades Cave, a mock settlement where life is as it was in the early settlers' days. If there is enough time, you can even take a train ride that is held up by Indians (not for real, of course).

At 4:00 P.M. you will leave for Columbia, South Carolina, passing through mountainous areas for some time and then gradual hilly areas, with both broadleaf and needleleaf trees. During the last hour of the journey the land will become much flatter, but it will still be full of trees and greenery. You will arrive in Columbia around 7:00 P.M. for dinner, and then you will be free to do as you please.

DAY 8   COLUMBIA—ATLANTA

Leave Columbia at 8:00 A.M. to travel to Atlanta and fly home.

REVIEW QUESTIONS

1. What are the major landforms of North America? Which is most important for tourism? Why?
2. Compare and contrast the east and west coastal plains in North America.
3. Discuss the importance of the river systems in North America.
4. Why is American agriculture so productive?
5. What is Canada's major tourism market? Why?
6. Which region outside of North America is the most important source of international tourists to Canada? Why?
7. What is the United States' major tourism market? Why?
8. Are residents of the United States the greatest travelers of the world? Why or why not?
9. Describe and discuss the general divisions of tourism attractions in Canada.
10. Compare and contrast the attractions of California and Florida. Which state has the best set of geographic relationships for tourism? Why?

GEOGRAPHY AND TOURISM IN
Mexico, Central America, and the Caribbean

CHAPTER 4

MAJOR GEOGRAPHIC CHARACTERISTICS

- Highly diverse physical and cultural environment
- Accessible to major markets in North America and Europe
- Important colonial influence on the region
- Continued dependency upon plantation agriculture
- Distinct climate zones that reflect topography
- Marked contrasts between rich and poor

MAJOR TOURISM CHARACTERISTICS

- The major attraction of the region is sun-sea-sand.
- The region includes major archaeological sites of early American civilizations.
- With the exception of Mexico, tourism is highly seasonal.
- This is the major cruise region of the world.
- Visitors perceive the Caribbean region as a tropical environment, but have little specific knowledge of individual islands.

MAJOR TOURIST DESTINATIONS

- Capital cities of each country
- Colonial towns
- Resorts of the Caribbean islands
- Archaeological sites in Mexico, Guatemala, Honduras
- Beach resort towns of Cancún, Mazatlán, Acapulco, Ixtapa, Puerto Vallarta
- Border towns on the United States–Mexican border
- Bahamas, Jamaica, Puerto Rico, United States and British Virgin Islands, Dominican Republic, St. Maarten

KEY TERMS AND WORDS

ABC Islands	Hurricanes
African	Ibero-European
Anthropology	Karst
Arawaks	Leeward
Barrios	Maquiladoras
Border Towns	Mayan World Circuit
Calderas	Mesa Central
Calypso	Mesa del Norte
Caribbean	Mestizos
Caribs	Middle America
Cathedrals	NAFTA
Central America	Playa Lakes
Cinder Cones	Pyramids
Colonial Territories	Rain forest
Creole	Sinkhole
Cruise Ships	Tourist Patrol
Cultural Links	

INTRODUCTION

Mexico, *Central America*, and the *Caribbean* are some of the world's most important tourism destinations, Figure 4–1. The proximity of the region to the two major industrial countries of North America—the United States and Canada—as well as historic colonial ties with Europe, are major factors in the region's ability to attract a high number of visitors. The continued growth in the region is due to its mild climate, clear blue waters, and cultural attractions. However, while the Caribbean, Mexico, and Central America are in some ways similar, their respective tourist industries differ markedly in size and income generated. Factors such as location, political stability, and concern for personal safety help explain these differences. The political situation in much of *Middle America*, for example, has seriously hurt tourism trade to the countries in that part of the region.

The region consists of the countries from Mexico to Panama and the Caribbean, which in this text is considered to be the islands or nations with frontage on the Caribbean Sea plus the Bahamas and Bermuda in the Atlantic just north of the Caribbean Sea. The islands of the Caribbean are sometimes referred to as the West Indies or Antilles. The continental region is less easy to define, typically being referred to as Mexico and Central America. In many regional geographical references, however, Mexico is included as part of North America; but in others it is included in a region called Middle America with the countries from Guatemala to Panama. In this text we will refer to all of the continental countries from the United States border to South America as Mexico and Central America to make it clear Mexico is included.

Mexico, Central America, and the Caribbean were the first areas where the Spanish imposed their colonial rule and began the process of developing an exploitative economy. There are major differences in the countries of the region, particularly between Mexico and the other seven countries.

Mexico is the third largest independent state in Latin America and has the second largest population. It receives more tourists than any other country or island in the region and is one of the major generators of tourism receipts. Geographically, Mexico is complex, ranging from the arid and semiarid north to the moderate highland climates of central Mexico (where the majority of the population lives) to the tropical southern and eastern lowlands. More than one-half of the population is concentrated in the valleys and basins of central Mexico, particularly around Mexico City proper.

The poorest Mexicans are those who are classified as Indian, not necessarily according to their ethnic background, but according to their culture. Indians speak a native language (even though they may also speak Spanish), emphasize Indian rather than Euro-

POPULATION CHARACTERISTICS, 1997

Country	Population (millions)	Annual Growth Rate (percent)	Time to Double Pop. (years)	Per Capita GNP	Life Exp. (years)	Daily Calorie Supply	Percent Urban
CENTRAL AMERICA							
Belize	0.2	3.3	21	2,630	69	2,662	48
Costa Rica	3.5	2.0	35	2,610	76	2,808	44
El Salvador	5.9	2.6	27	1,610	68	2,317	45
Guatemala	11.2	3.0	23	1,340	65	2,235	39
Honduras	5.8	3.2	22	600	68	2,247	47
Mexico	95.7	2.2	32	3,320	72	3,052	71
Nicaragua	4.4	3.1	23	380	66	2,265	63
Panama	2.7	1.9	37	2,750	73	2,539	55
CARIBBEAN							
Antigua and Barbuda	0.1	1.2	58	N/A	73	2,458	36
Barbados	0.3	0.3	204	6,560	75	3,207	38
Cuba	11.1	0.7	102	N/A	75	2,833	74
Dominica	0.1	1.4	48	2,990	77	2,778	N/A
Dominican Republic	8.2	2.1	32	1,460	70	2,359	61
Grenada	0.1	2.4	29	2,980,	71	2,402	32
Guadeloupe	0.4	1.2	60	N/A	75	2,682	99
Haiti	6.6	1.8	39	250	50	2,013	32
Jamaica	2.6	1.7	41	1,510	74	2,609	50
Martinique	0.4	1.0	71	N/A	76	2,829	81
Netherlands Antilles	0.2	1.2	59	N/A	75	2,587	90
Puerto Rico	3.8	1.0	71	N/A	74	N/A	73
St. Kitts-Nevis	1.2	1.2	56	5,170	68	2,419	43
Saint Lucia	1.9	1.9	36	3,370	72	2,588	48
St. Vincent and the Grenadines	0.1	1.6	44	2,280	73	2,347	25
Trinidad and Tobago	1.3	0.9	79	3,770	71	2,853	65
Bahamas	0.3	1.7	42	11,940	72	2,624	86
Bermuda	0.1	0.7	91	N/A	N/A	2,679	N/A
Turks and Caicos	0.1	2.7	26	2,020	N/A	N/A	N/A

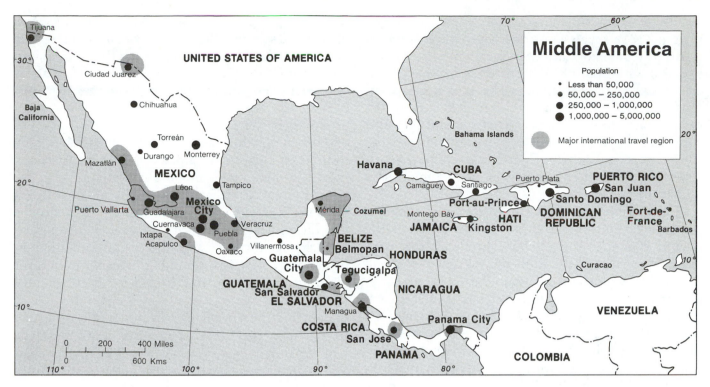

Figure 4–1 Middle America and the Caribbean

pean customs, and are primarily involved in agriculture. Approximately ten percent of Mexicans remain illiterate, and nearly one-third live in poverty. In rural areas, Indians practice their traditional agriculture on even the steepest slopes in the highland valleys. Production of corn, beans, squash, and other traditional crops remains important for this sector of the agricultural economy.

In the cities, major industries include textiles, steel, automobiles, electrical products, and food processing. The dominant manufacturing center is the Valley of Mexico, where more than 75 percent of the country's industry is concentrated. In the past few years *border towns* have become the focal point for industries and rapid population growth. Through trade agreements with the United States a large number of assembly plants have located along the border. Imports from these plants (known as *maquiladoras*) have lower tariffs on their exports to the United States.

Mexico joined the United States and Canada in an economic union called the North American Free Trade Association (*NAFTA*) in the early 1990s. NAFTA has resulted in increased economic growth in Mexico and, greater movement of Mexicans to the United States and vice versa.

The concentration of industrial activity in the Valley of Mexico and along the United States border has created urban problems on a scale rivaled in only

one or two other cities of the world. Mexico City is the world's largest city, with some twenty million people in the metropolitan area. Urban problems range from lack of housing and jobs to massive air pollution and vast slum areas (*barrios*) inhabited by migrants from rural areas. Mexico has significant oil reserves, but its tourism industry has developed to such a level that tourism ranks second to oil as a major earner of income for the country.

The seven other countries of Central America consist of the nations of Guatemala, Belize, El Salvador, Honduras, Nicaragua, Costa Rica, and Panama to the south of Mexico. This region is the least traveled area of Mexico, Central America, and the Caribbean. In part this results from political instability and conflict. Notable recent examples are found in El Salvador, Nicaragua, and Guatemala. Even the stable countries of the region are often perceived as unsafe by potential tourists because of past violence in the others.

The seven countries of Central America have many similarities. Their physical geography is dominated by complex mountain systems. The mountains include spectacular volcanic mountains with *cinder cones, calderas,* and other volcanic features, and sedimentary mountains composed primarily of limestone. The climate is generally tropical or subtropical and is characterized by heavy rains during the hot summers and by decreased rainfall in the winter.

But there is no truly dry season anywhere in the region. These seven countries typify the less industrialized regions of Latin America, relying on a few exports, with high illiteracy rates and great disparities between rich and poor. The economies of all these countries rely heavily on tropical agricultural exports, especially bananas and coffee, but they also have been based largely on foreign capital. In general, these countries lack good communication systems, capital for investments to develop more rapidly, and political stability.

The Caribbean, one of the world's most popular tourist destinations, is an arc of islands extending about 1,700 miles from offshore Florida to the coast of South America. The Caribbean was discovered and claimed by Columbus for Spain during his four voyages in search of a route to the riches of the Far East. The most densely populated region of the Americas, the Caribbean, is also one in which there are great differences between the rich and poor. Although it is a region with a low per capita income for many of its people, abject poverty is the exception apart from Haiti. Haiti has little industry or tourism, relies on agriculture that has resulted in erosion and small farms as the population has increased dramatically, and has an unstable government. Some countries are exceptions to the lower standard of living found in some of the Caribbean countries, particularly Puerto Rico (which is a commonwealth of the United States); the British Virgin Islands, a British dependency; and some small islands, such as the United States Virgin Islands, an unincorporated territory of the United States. All three receive high revenues from tourism and economic assistance from Britain or the United States.

The Caribbean region is a tropical, lowland environment with most of its 35 plus million people living at elevations below 1,000 feet. With a diversity of environmental characteristics, it can be divided into three major regions: the Greater Antilles, the Lesser Antilles, and the Continental Islands.

THE PHYSICAL ENVIRONMENT

Landforms

The Caribbean

The Greater Antilles. The Greater Antilles include the four large islands of Cuba, Hispaniola (Haiti and the Dominican Republic), Jamaica, and Puerto Rico. These four islands have 90 percent of the total land area and population of the Caribbean. They also have a diversity of environmental conditions.

The largest island, Cuba, is 800 miles long. Most of its 4,000 square miles consists of either flat terrain or gently rolling hills, with three small mountainous areas rising to elevations of 3,000 to 6,000 feet above sea level. The subtropical, rainy climate of Cuba enables the island to be one of the world's major producers of sugar cane.

Hispaniola, the second largest island in the Caribbean, is far more mountainous than Cuba. It is dominated by four major mountain systems, with the population clustered along the coast and on strips of lowland between the parallel ranges. Climate and vegetation, which vary with altitude and exposure, have created a complex of microenvironments now occupied by the Hispanic and European people of the Dominican Republic and the black African population of Haiti.

Jamaica, the third largest island in this group, is a heavily dissected limestone plateau, a very marginal land inhabited by peasant farmers. The inward coast and lowland areas have been carved into sugar plantations, and bauxite is mined on a large scale.

Puerto Rico, the smallest and most easterly of the Greater Antilles, is a large dissected plateau like Jamaica, with a mountain core. It, too, has sugar plantations in the wet coastal lowlands.

The Lesser Antilles. The Lesser Antilles are a 700-mile concave band of islands that cross the Caribbean from Puerto Rico in the north to the coast of Venezuela in the south. These islands are the peaks of a double line of submerged volcanoes. They consist of an outer ring of low islands composed of old volcanoes and limestone banks (referred to as the Leeward Islands) and an inner ring of higher volcanic peaks (the Windward Islands). There are two types of islands in the Lesser Antilles: those that are relatively low and include considerable areas of fairly level limestone reefs, such as Anguilla, Barbuda, and Antigua; and those that are more mountainous, and volcanic. Some of the more noted islands within the mountain chain are St. Kitts, Montserrat, Guadeloupe, Martinique, St. Lucia, and Grenada. The largest of the low-lying Leeward Islands are Guadeloupe and Antigua.

The principal economic activity in the Lesser Antilles is the production of sugar cane on large estates. On the higher or Windward Islands, agriculture is more varied despite their similar terrain and tropical environment. Forested mountain spines of between 3,000 and 4,000 feet with rich volcanic soil, little level land, and abundant rainfall characterize this island group. St. Vincent produces arrowroot, a

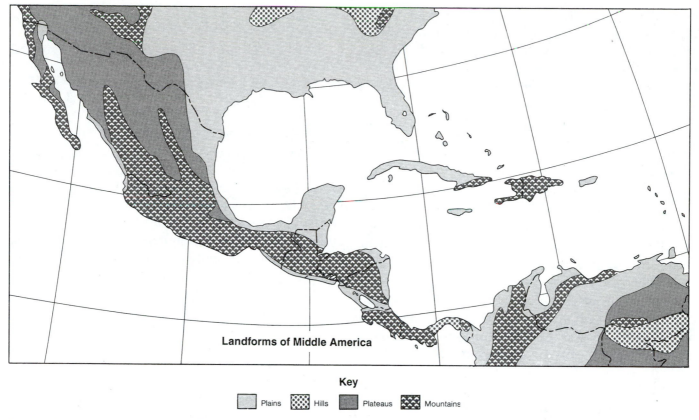

Key

☐ Plains   ▦ Hills   ▪ Plateaus   ▨ Mountains

Figure 4–2 Landforms of Mexico and Central America

starchy tuber; Dominica, banana, coconuts, and copra; Anguilla, fishing, banking, and tourism; Grenada, cocoa and nutmeg; Martinique and St. Kitts, sugar; St. Lucia, bananas; and Nevis, cotton. On small islands like Grenada, small landholdings dominate. On Martinique and St. Lucia, much land is taken up by large commercial estates.

The Continental Islands. Near the South American coast, the Lesser Antilles merge with a line of islands defined as "continental" because they have many characteristics of the nearby Latin American continent. The continental islands are similar in surface characteristics and important to tourism. They are a series of over 700 islands generally characterized by low flat patches of porous limestone and coral. The shallowness of the reefs and cays, with rocks close to the water's surface, makes the area an outstanding area for snorkeling and related water activities.

The most important continental islands are Trinidad and Tobago, and two larger islands of the Netherlands Antilles, Aruba and Curacao. Sugar and rum have historically been the major agricultural exports, but Trinidad relies heavily on petroleum production and refining, and Aruba and Curacao are transshipment points for refined petroleum products. Tourism and international banking are important in the econ-

omies of the continental islands, with Aruba and Curacao being particularly important destinations.

Mexico and Central America

Diversity best describes the physical characteristics of Mexico and Central America. In short distances, there are great variations in landform, climate, soils, and vegetation. The physical landscape, Figure 4–2, can be divided into the following categories.

The Mexican Plateau. This high plateau of Northern Mexico extends from just south of Mexico City to the United States–Mexico border. The plateau is one of the largest landforms of Middle America and one of the most significant for human settlement in Mexico. The northern half of the plateau, the *Mesa del Norte,* is extremely dry and is characterized by basins separated by low mountains. The eastern section of these ranges consists of limestone and shale. The western side is volcanic. There is little water in the area, with *playa lakes,* resulting from interior drainage, containing water only after the rare heavy showers.

The southern half of the plateau, the *Mesa Central,* is a geologically active volcanic area. The volcanic landscape is characterized by low cinder cones, crater lakes, lava flows, and volcanic craters within the mountainous area. The Mesa Central receives much more precipitation than the northern half. The increased moisture creates rivers and lakes, which combine with the fertile volcanic soils to support a dense population. Mexico obtains much of its food supply from basins in the plateau, including the valleys of Mexico, Huamantla, Puebla, Toluca, Morelia, and Guadalajara.

The steep escarpments that flank the Mexican Plateau on the east, west, and south are spectacular features of the plateau. The eastern edge of the plateau is bordered by the Sierra Madre Oriental Mountain Range, a series of elongated limestone ranges, which are oriented north-south and act as a barrier to the plateau from the coastal lowland. The western edge of the Mexican plateau is the Sierra Madre Occidental Mountain Range, which also acts as a barrier to the coastal lowlands, but is made of volcanic rather than limestone materials.

The Balsas Depression.   To the south of the Mexican plateau are the high volcanic mountains of Central Mexico, which are interspersed with basins and river floodplains.

Located immediately south of the Mexican Plateau, the Balsas Depression is a low, hot, dry area with low hills bisected by the Balsas River. The Balsas Depression is less densely settled than the basins of the Central Plateau because of the hot climate and limited water supply. The Balsas Depression typifies much of the region south of the Central Plateau.

The High Mountain Range of Southern Mexico and Central America.   Extending from Southern Mexico, except for a slight break at the Isthmus of Tehuantepec, Southern Mexico and Central America are characterized by rugged mountains, escarpments, and hills. This series of ranges is extremely rugged, with high mountains, both volcanic and nonvolcanic, and peaks over 10,000 feet (3,000 meters) above sea level. Part of the nonvolcanic mountain ranges in northern Guatemala and southern Mexico continue into the Caribbean to form the mountain islands of the Greater Antilles. Further south, the volcanic mountains of Central America extend into the Caribbean, creating the Lesser Antilles. The Pacific side of Central America has a series of volcanoes from southern Mexico to Costa Rica. This is the longest and most spectacular mountain range in Middle America. As in Mexico, the fertile volcanic soils in the tropical highland basins have attracted and support the highest population densities in Central America.

The islands closer to South America (Trinidad, Tobago, and the Dutch islands of Bonaire, Curacao, and Aruba) are an extension of South American mountain ranges.

Plains of the Yucatán Peninsula.   The plains of the Yucatán Peninsula are characterized by *karst* topography. Karst topography occurs in limestone as water dissolves the rock to create underground passages. The surface lacks surface streams and has related erosional features such as *sinkholes*, caves, subterranean stream channels, and red terra rosa soils. The southern portion of the Yucatán is divided between Mexico and the Petén of northern Guatemala. It consists of low elongated limestone hills interrupting extensive plains. There are surface streams and some lakes in this southern region.

Coastal Plains.   The coastal plains are the widest on the eastern side of Central America and Mexico and relatively narrow on the western side. This eastern side is characterized by low hills, coastal lowlands, and alluvial activity, which in Mexico and Costa Rica has created productive agricultural areas.

Climate Characteristics

Central America and Mexico

The diversity of the climate, Figure 4–3, in Central America and Mexico results from latitudinal location, altitude influence, and land-water relationships. Northern Mexico's climate is controlled by its mid-latitude location, which combines with the high plateau to create an arid environment on the plateau and the western coastal areas of Mexico. The southern two-thirds of Mexico is influenced by tropical location and altitude. Altitude affects climate in the same ways latitude does. An increase in elevation is associated with cooler temperatures. Increased elevation creates altitudinal zones of climate in the mountainous areas of the region. There are three major climate zones recognized in this region. The tierra caliente, or hot land, is the lowest zone, extending up to approximately 3,000 feet (900 meters). This has all the characteristics of a tropical *rain forest* climate, and population densities are low. The economy is based on plantation agriculture, bananas, sugar cane, rice, cocoa, and nutmeg for export. The second zone is the tierra templada, or temperate land. This zone has a cooler climate with conditions similar to the

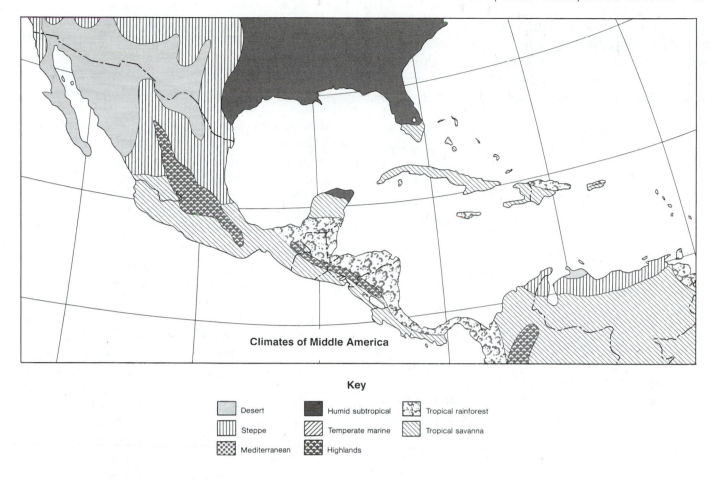

Climates of Middle America

Key

Desert		Humid subtropical	Tropical rainforest
Steppe		Temperate marine	Tropical savanna
Mediterranean		Highlands	

Figure 4–3 Climates of Mexico and CentralAmerica

humid subtropical climates. The Europeans settled here. A major activity is coffee production. The third zone, the tierra fria, or cold climate, is above about 6,000 feet. It is the home of much of the Indian population of Central America, who practice a subsistence agriculture with corn, squash, and small grains as dominant crops. The largest concentration of tierra fria in the region is in Mexico and Guatemala, which are among the most densely populated areas of Middle America.

The eastern shores of Central America and Mexico are influenced by the warm currents of the Caribbean Sea and the Gulf of Mexico, creating either a humid subtropical climate along the east coast of Mexico or a true tropical climate southward into South America. Many of the popular tourist locations such as the Yucatán are in an area of tropical savanna, or tropical monsoon-type climate with tropical *hurricanes* from July through October. The hurricanes in both these locations and the Caribbean make tourism to both regions high seasonal. During the hurricane season, tourism is dramatically reduced. Warm ocean currents also affect the western coasts of much of

Central America and southern Mexico. However, northern Mexico's west coast is affected by the cold water of the California current, which brings cool, pleasant, year-round temperatures along the coast.

Caribbean

Although they are located in a tropical environment, the Caribbean islands are considered temperate. The islands are swept by the easterly trade winds, which moderate the hot tropical climate. The major attraction of the Caribbean as a tourist area is its beautiful year-round warm temperature. It can be expected that temperatures in the Caribbean will range from daytime highs of up to about 85 degrees Fahrenheit to lows of 70 degrees Fahrenheit. This is not a particularly high temperature, but the feeling of warmth reflects the effect of heat plus relative humidity. Therefore, fluctuations in rainfall are as important as the temperatures in attracting tourists.

There is a tremendous increase in rainfall from early summer into late November. This increases the humidity and adds an additional five to ten degrees to the apparent temperature. Therefore, the atmosphere in the Caribbean from late April until the first part of December seems more muggy and uncomfortable than during the winter and early spring months. The humidity is modified somewhat by the offshore breezes that constantly blow throughout much of the Caribbean, especially at locations near the water. In addition, in some islands (like Haiti with its higher mountains), wind movement up the hills combines with the cooler temperatures at higher elevations to create a much more comfortable environment. The hurricane season is from August through October, which adds to the discomfort during the summer and early fall.

Discomfort caused by high temperatures and increased humidity takes its toll on the tourist industry. The rainy season seriously interferes with enjoyment of the beaches. The best time to travel in the Caribbean is from December through April. The industry tries to stimulate demand in the slow season by offering bargain rates during the months from May through the early part of December.

The Caribbean Tourism Association has called the April through December 15th period "the season of sweet savings." During that period, nearly half of the Caribbean Tourism Association members reduce their rates from 10 to 30 percent on shopping, travel, and lodging. But, of course, the bargain-hunting tourist is gambling on the weather.

The Caribbean has frequent hurricanes, which pose problems on given years for the tourism industry. For example, in 1995 hurricanes Louise and Marilyn struck St. Thomas and eleven other islands, leaving some 160,000 hotel rooms damaged, air service suspended, and tour companies unable to accept bookings for some of the most affected islands. When service was re-established, tourists still avoided the region. Other Caribbean islands such as Aruba, Jamaica, and Grand Cayman increased in numbers. The Virgin Islands were just recovering from these hurricanes when they were struck again in July of 1996. Puerto Rico was struck by Hurricane Hortense in September of 1996, with extensive flooding. This again will divert visitors to other islands or other regions of the world.

Bargain packages are given catchy titles to lure unwary tourists. For example, the French West Indies have established a package entitled "Fete Francaise Tours," which offers a choice of accommodations on the French islands in a variety of hotels. Haiti's program, called the "Summer Spellbinders," offers three- and seven-day packages at tempting rates.

CULTURAL CHARACTERISTICS

The cultures of the region, like the physical characteristics, are diverse. Mexico, Central America, and the Caribbean include a variety of ethnic, social, political, and economic patterns unmatched in the world in an area of comparable size. There are three major languages—Spanish, English, and French—plus numerous Indian tongues. Within these languages, there are a number of complex, local dialects.

The region was an Indian world before the arrival of the Europeans and Africans. The Southern Central Plateau of Mexico, the Yucatán, and the highlands and coastal lowlands of Central America were inhabited by technologically advanced Indians with high population densities, large cities, and an intensive agricultural base. The remnants of these early civilizations, the Mayas of Guatemala and Yucatán and the Aztecs of Central Mexico, have become centers of attraction for a modern tourism industry. In the Caribbean and the arid portions of Mexico, the Indian population was smaller and less technologically advanced. The *Caribs* and *Arawaks*, both originally from South America, settled in the Caribbean. They practiced primitive agricultural techniques, hunted, and fished. The Carib, the more warlike and primitive of the two, reportedly practiced cannibalism and relied more on food gathering, hunting, and fishing than agriculture.

The conquest and settlement of Middle America and the Caribbean by the Europeans after the voyage of Columbus changed the cultural map. The Spanish, English, French, Dutch, Danes, Portuguese, and eventually Americans contributed to the present ethnic makeup of the region. Spain was by far the most dominant force in Mexico and Central America, imposing its language, religion, and customs upon the new colonial empire. Colonial activity by English, French, Dutch, and Danes added to the European impact in the Caribbean. Wars and battles changed some of the *colonial territories*. Jamaica, for example, was seized from the Spanish by the British. The French gained possession of Haiti, and the French, Dutch, and Danes obtained the various islands of the Lesser Antilles. Plantation crops were introduced, requiring additional African slaves, and Africans soon outnumbered their European masters by a wide margin. Indians from India were later imported to some Caribbean islands, further complicating the cultural ways. All of the groups interacted with one another to a greater or lesser extent, creating cultural groups distinct from European, *African*, Indian, or Asian. The present cultural land-

Table 4–1 International Tourism to Middle America

Country	Number of Visitors (thousands) 1986	1996 Receipts (millions of US $) 1996	1996 Receipts (millions of US $)	1996 Average Expenses per Visit (millions of US $)
Belize	94	143	75	524
Costa Rica	261	781	654	837
El Salvador	134	283	76	268
Guatemala	287	520	284	546
Honduras	126	257	81	315
Mexico	4,625	21,428	6,894	321
Nicaragua	44	303	58	191
Panama	308	362	343	948

scape can be divided into Euro-African, Euro-Asian, Euro-Indian, and Mestizo groups.

Descendants of African, European-African, or Indian-African intermarriages are concentrated in the coastal lowlands of Central America (where plantation agriculture was practiced), Cuba, Puerto Rico, the Dominican Republic, Haiti, the Netherlands Antilles, British West Indies, Martinique, Guadaloupe, St. Lucia, and Grenada. The appearance of each of these groups varies, reflecting intermarriage with specific groups (such as the French in Haiti, the Spanish in Puerto Rico or Cuba) or specific North European groups (as in British West Indies or the Netherlands Antilles). In each country, there is generally a group that classifies itself as of "pure" European ancestry, but they often reflect only the group with the greatest social or economic prestige rather than a distinct ethnic origin.

The mainland areas of Mexico and Central America are generally inhabited by descendants of Indians and Europeans. Indian influence is most dominant in the southern basins of Mexico, the Yucatán Peninsula, southern Mexico's highlands and Guatemala, and western Honduras and western Nicaragua. Descendants of intermarriage between Europeans and Indian, (mestizos) dominate in Central Mexico, El Salvador, Honduras, Nicaragua, and Panama. Europeans are concentrated in Costa Rica and northern Mexico, although each area has representatives of all three groups. Asians (Indians from India primarily) are found in Antigua, Jamaica, and Trinidad and To-

bago, which have the largest concentration of East Asians.

Thus, the cultural groups in Middle America include the remnants of the original Indian inhabitants, the descendants of mixed marriages between Indians and Europeans (mestizos), the black population descended from slaves in the Caribbean or European-African intermixing, and descendants of mixtures of European-mestizo-African combinations.

TOURISM

Tourism to the region is dominated by Mexico and the Caribbean, largely because of their proximity to Canada and the United States. Distances, intervening opportunities represented by Mexico and the Caribbean, and political conditions in the region south of Mexico have led to a smaller travel industry in that region. Mexico and the Caribbean compete with Hawaii for the same market. The average length of stay in Mexico is nine days per visitor, above the eight-day average for the region. The lower averages in the Caribbean result from two factors. First, the Caribbean is a leading cruise region of the world and cruise ships generally stay slightly less than one day per island. Second, the airlines in the past have used an unlimited type of airfare, making it not only easy but desirable to visit several islands during a one- or two-week trip. Today, the inclusive tours concept, which began in Jamaica, has spread through the Caribbean, creating an excellent bargain for North American tourists.

MIDDLE AMERICA

Mexico

1000 km

Tijuana
Ciudad Juárez
Chihuaha
Monterrey
Matamoros
La Paz
Durango
Gulf of Mexico
Guadalajara
Mérida
MEXICO ★
Veracruz
North Pacific Ocean
Oaxaca
Acapulco

Capital: Mexico City
Government: Federal republic operating under a centralized government
Size: 761,605 square miles (about three times the size of Texas)
Language: Spanish
Ethnic Division: 60% Mestizo, 30% Amerindian, 9% Spanish, 1% other
Religion: 89% Roman Catholic, 6% Protestant
Tourist Season: April through September; Coastal: November through April
Peak Tourist Seasons: March (11%) and December (10%)
Currency: Peso

 TRAVEL TIPS

Entry: No requirements for day trips across border. Tourist Card obtained at travel agencies, airlines, and Mexican government tourism offices. Need proof of citizenship.
Transportation: Excellent air and road connectivity to and from Mexico. Transportation between cities in Mexico is available by bus, plane or good roads. Mexico City has a good subway system and bus. Public transportation is inexpensive and provides good service in Mexico City and other tourist destinations. Travel by automobile is better during the daylight hours. For those driving, automobile insurance is available at the border and is required.
Health: Some areas require malaria suppressants.
Language: While Spanish is the official language, English is understood widely in urban areas that have significant numbers of tourists.
Shopping: Typical items are silver, copperware, blown glass, onyx, pottery, handwoven fabrics such as rugs and serapes, embroidery, and Indian arts. Reproductions of artifacts of ancient civilizations are available near archaeological sites.

CULTURAL CAPSULE

Sixty percent of the people of Mexico are mestizo (mixed Spanish and Indian). Thirty percent are pure Indian, descendants of the Mayans and Aztecs. Nine percent are European. While Spanish is the official language, there are nearly one hundred Indian languages spoken in parts of Mexico.

Cultural Hints:
- Greet by a soft handshake or a nod of the head.
- Let women make the first move toward the handshake.
- Mexicans stand close when talking to each other.
- Mexicans like to touch others as a sign of friendliness.
- Hand items to another person rather than tossing them.
- Be patient when encountering delays.
- Obscene gestures common in the United States are understood in Mexico.
- Dress conservatively (no shorts or tank tops) when visiting religious sites.
- Eating and food:
  Call a waiter with a "psst-psst" sound.
  To ask for the check, get the waiter's attention and pretend writing in the palm of your hand.
  Keep both hands above the table.
  On the street eat food at the stand, rather than eating and walking.
  Food basics are corn, beans, and chili. Typical foods are corn tortillas, frijoles refritos (refried beans), tortas (hollow roll stuffed with meat or cheese), quesadillas (tortilla baked with cheese), moles (spicy sauce on many food items), and tacos (folded tortilla filled with meat, cheese, and onions). Regional variations exist.

Physical Characteristics

Mexico has mostly high, rugged mountains, many of which are extinct volcanos, with low coastal plains and high plateaus. Much of the north is hot and dry. The central plateau, including Mexico City, is bounded by two mountain ranges, the Sierra Madre Oriental on the east and the Sierra Madre Occidental on the west. The climate varies by region from desert in the north to tropical in the south and along some coastal areas.

Tourism Characteristics

The Mexican government is very active in tourism development. Next to oil, tourism is the largest earner of foreign exchange for the country. Although an increasing number of manufacturing assembly plants (maquiladoras) in border towns along the United States–Mexico border have created a booming economy, tourism is important even in these towns.

The government has been involved in large-scale development and planning projects, with economic assistance through Fondo Nacional De Fomento al Turismo (FONATUR), and has also actively pursued attracting more tourists through innovating highly visible policies. One such policy is Mexico's *Tourist Patrol* service, which provides free emergency assistance to motoring tourists in case of highway problems. It is operated by the Mexican government's Ministry of Tourism, which hires English-speaking men who patrol the heavily traveled tourist routes in green patrol cars with emergency supplies of gas and first-aid equipment. These cars pass check points twice a day every day of the year.

FONATUR has fifteen mega-tourism projects in various stages of development throughout Mexico. Upgrading some of the existing resorts is included. Acapulco underwent a massive upgrading and renovation capped by the construction of a motorway from Mexico City. Two of the new projects are Huatulco and Baja California. The government has been working cooperatively with Belize, Guatemala, El Salvador, and Honduras to develop and market jointly a Mayan World Circuit (el Circuito Mundo Maya) tourist itinerary including some of the most impressive archeological sites in the world.

Although Mexico has had a high rate of inflation, the continued devaluation of the peso and partial deregulation of Mexico's airlines have effectively reduced airfares, creating one of the greatest travel bargains in the world. Also, the all-inclusive packages that have become popular from the United States and Europe have generated increasing numbers of visitors to Mexico. By 1996 tourism had reached more than 21 million visitors. The United States is the dominant source of tourists who enter Mexico for longer than one day. Nearly 84 percent of the tourists to Mexico are from the United States. Recognizing its high dependency upon the United States, the government has increased advertising and marketing in Europe, emphasizing Germany and France. Europe's market share increased from 2.5 percent in 1989 to 6 percent in 1995, surpassing Canada. Europeans stay longer and spend more money, and Europe accounts for 9 percent of total tourist receipts.

An additional 65 million day visitors, mostly from along the United States–Mexican border, enter border towns in Mexico for a quick visit. The largest number travel from San Diego to Tijuana. The government has plans for two large Epcot-type theme parks in Tijuana

and Cíudad Juarez (World Tourism Organization, 1992, and International Tourism Reports, 1993).

Mexico has a strong tourist trade year-round, although the winter has the largest number of visitors. Coastal areas and the Yucatán have their peak tourist season in the winter months, since the weather is better here at this time of the year and worse in the United States and Canada. Tourism in the inland areas, such as Mexico City and Merida, peaks in the summer during the normal school vacation months of the industrial countries.

Tourist Destinations and Attractions

While tourism is strong throughout Mexico, the dominance of United States trade can be seen in the northwest zone of Guadalajara and the coastal regions of Mazatlán and Puerto Vallarta, which receive over 30 percent of the visitors to Mexico. The central zone of Guanajuato, Mexico City, and San Miguel Allende receives 23 percent of all visitors to Mexico. The four leading destinations are Cancún, Acapulco, Mexico City, and Guadalajara.

The major tourist regions of Mexico are as follows:

Border Towns. The border towns of Tijuana, Cíudad Juarez, Nuevo Laredo, Reynosa, and Matamoros attract millions of day trippers, mainly for shopping.

Baja California. Ecotourism and the newly developing coastal resorts are important to Baja. Coastal towns include Ensenada on lovely Bahía de Todos los Santos, Bahía de los Angeles on the Sea of Cortez, and La Paz, capital of Baja California Sur. Guerrero Negro is one of the better places in the world for whale watching, as the California gray whales head for Scammon's Lagoon from November through February to breed and train their young. The high desert of the Baja in the winter provides a kaleidoscope of desert colors for those interested in ecotourism. The new development taking place in the southern tip of Baja when complete will rival the other west coast resorts and towns of Puerto Vallarta and Mazatlán. The Los Cabos area in this region is one of the fastest growing destinations in Mexico.

Northwest Region. The northwest region includes Guadalajara and the coastal towns of Mazatlán, Guaymas, and Puerto Vallarta. Guadalajara is the second largest city in Mexico. It has an impressive town square focused on the Cathedral and Palace de Gobierno (Palace of the Governor). The church of

Santa Mónica, which is intricately carved in the Churrigueresque style, was completed about 1720. The churches of San Francisco and Aranzazu both face the shady Jardín de San Francisco. The church of San Francisco has a most impressive exterior. The Hospicio Cabañas represents the best work of muralist Orozco, whose paintings decorate the chapel. To provide ease of viewing the ceiling, benches are available to lie on. The State Museum, which is located near the central plaza, contains art galleries and exhibits covering history, zoology, and archaeology. Across the street from the park and the flower market, the State Library exhibits contemporary art, including the great three-dimensional mural by Gabriel Flores on the ceiling of the auditorium dome.

A number of small villages surround Guadalajara. These include Tiaquepaque, noted for its pottery; Ajijic, with its lovely embroidery and hand-loomed cotton and wool fabrics; and Zapopán, which is famous for its Huichoes Indian handicrafts, Figure 4-4. This region, which includes Lake Chapala, draws many North American retirees visiting to escape the cold, damp North American winter. The coastal resorts centered in Guaymas, Mazatlán, and Puerto Vallarta are within easy access of the western United States and provide year-round resorts focused on the Pacific. All of the resorts offer a variety of water sports, such as surfing, deep-sea diving, waterskiing, and some of the best fishing in the world. Puerto Vallarta is the most unspoiled of these west coast resorts. Puerto Vallarta was made famous as the site for the movie *The Night of the Iguana*, starring Elizabeth Taylor and Richard Burton. It is a highly picturesque town with flaming bougainvillea and blue jacaranda bushes hugging stucco walls. An important ecotourism attraction is Copper Canyon. The canyons are located in the Tarahumara Range of the Sierra Madre. This formidable landscape possesses the world's largest proliferation of major canyons confined to a relatively small area. It is deeper and larger than the Grand Canyon in the United States. It is located between Chihuahua and Los Mochis on the coast.

An important ecotourism attraction is Copper Canyon. The canyons are located in the Tarahumara Range of the Sierra Madre. This formidable landscape possesses the world's largest proliferation of major canyons confined to a relatively small area. It is deeper and larger than the Grand Canyon in the United States. It is located between Chihuahua and Los Mochis on the coast.

Central Highlands. The central highlands area is centered around Mexico City and the old city of

Figure 4–4 Girl in local dress in Highlands

Puebla. Mexico City, Mexico's capital, is the oldest city in North America. Pre-dating European settlement, Mexico City is located on the site of the Aztec capital, Tenochtitlán, in the Valley of Mexico. It is surrounded by volcanic mountains. It has fourteenth-century Aztec ruins, sixteenth-century colonial buildings, and modern skyscrapers. It is the second largest city in the world. With the tremendous industrial development and heavy migration of people, air pollution and poverty are major problems. Many of its residents live in rather poor conditions, many as squatters on the edge of the city. Nezahualcoyotl, on the east side, is an immense squatter settlement with over two million poor residents. While great effort is made by the government, the size of the population migration to the city overwhelms their efforts.

The city boasts a number of outstanding museums. There are native cultural events, such as concerts with marimbas, mariachis, singers, and dancers, which can be seen in Mexico City and in other Mexican cities and towns. Chapultepec Park is a cultural and recreational center. It is home to one of the most impressive museums in the world. With its 168-ton figure of Tlaloc, the rain god, the National Museum of *Anthropology* within it is an impressive architectural building in its own right. Its collections and displays are equally as impressive as the building. Three more of the country's finest museums—the Museum of Modern Art, Chapultepec Castle, and the Museum of Natural History—three lakes with boating facilities, a variety of playground equipment, an amusement park, complete with a large roller coaster ride, and a number of flower gardens, fountains, and sculptures are also located in the park.

The seat of government and religion for the country is the Zocalo. Two municipal palaces—the Supreme Court building, the National Palace where the Palace of Montezuma once stood, and the magnificent Metropolitan Cathedral—are on the Zocalo. Leading away from the Zocalo, the Avenida Madero, renamed to honor the leader of the Revolution of 1910, has a number of excellent reminders of the history of Mexico. The Church of La Profesa was built by the Jesuits in the sixteenth century; the Palace of Iturbide, constructed in 1779, has a private dwelling built by the Count of San Mateo; the Church and Monastery of San Francisco was a dominant force in the spiritual and social life of the people from 1524 until 1850; the House of Tiles was built in 1708 as the town house of the Counts of Orizaba; and the Numismatic Museum has a collection dating back before the European Conquest.

There are many notable attractions within a one hundred-mile radius in Mexico. They include the floating gardens of Xochimilco, including a colorful market and park; Cuernavaca, a Spanish colonial city; Xochicalco, an archaeological site near the Pyramid of Teopanzalso; Taxco, a hillside silver-mining town with cobblestone streets, flower-decked shops, and colorful houses; Tula, the capital of the ancient Toltec civilization; the spectacular Pyramids of Teotihuacan, the once holy site of the Toltec civilization; and Puebla, an ancient colonial city that was founded in 1521.

Central Coastal Resort Towns. The central coastal resort towns include Acapulco, Zihuatanejo, and Ixtapa. Acapulco, the oldest of the towns, has historically been the fashionable resort of Mexico, with its famous cliff divers and a large well-developed tourist infrastructure along its coastal areas, Figure 4–5. Acapulco is set at the base of mountains on a partly enclosed bay. The three resort towns are in a more tropical environment than the northwest coastal areas, thus the waters are much warmer. The town of Zihuatanejo is the support center for the beach resort development of Ixtapa with its sixteen-mile-long white sand beach, which is an excellent example of state planning and development of tourism. It was the first of FONATUR's developments that used modern technology to build a quality tourism environment in an outstanding setting while preserving the Mexican culture.

East Coastal Towns. The main east coastal towns are Tampico and Vera Cruz. These are old colonial towns on the Gulf of Mexico. They exhibit

Figure 4–5   Cliff diving in Acapulco

the planning that the Spanish used in establishing their cities in the New World. Both are in the hot tropical coastal zone. Tampico is particularly good for fishing and hunting. Vera Cruz is the main port on the east coast of Mexico, Figure 4–6. Cortez landed in the harbor and founded the city in 1519. Activity centers on the waterfront with fish and food markets, arcades, and curio shops. Vera Cruz is also excellent for fishing.

The Yucatán. The Yucatán combines outstanding archaeological sites and Caribbean resorts. Palenque features temples in a picturesque setting, Figure 4–7. Chichen Itza and Uxmal are religious centers of the Mayan culture that are adorned with pyramids, temples, arches, vaults, and beautifully carved friezes. Cozumel is one of the top scuba diving areas of the world, while Cancún is a planned destination

Figure 4–6   Fortress Castillo, Vera Cruz, Mexico

Figure 4–7 Temple of The Cross, Palenque, Yucatán, Mexico

reserves, and the karst topography offers a unique physical environment for the visitor. The major attractions in Merida are the fortress-type cathedral; the Montejo mansion, which was built by the Spanish conqueror and founder Francisco de Montejo; and the Museum of Archaeology, which displays Mayan artifacts.

The Southwest. Tourism in the Southwest centers around Oaxaca. Oaxaca represents the Indian culture of Mexico and still has a local periodic market. It is a colorful city where the Indian population still wears clothing that identifies them as being from a specific village. Oaxaca is known for its crafts of pottery, gold and silver jewelry, skirts, blouses, men's shirts, tablecloths, and knives. Near Oaxaca, Monte Alban is an impressive archaeological site high on a mountain. Monte Alban is composed of a huge central plaza and several tombs. Another impressive architectural wonder, the ancient town of Mitia, is also near Oaxaca. Mitia was a Zapotec-Mixtec ceremonial center. Particularly impressive is the intricately carved stone fretwork on the facades of the temples. A number of small Indian villages around Oaxaca are interesting to tourists. These include Azompa, which is known for its pottery; Santo Tomás, which specializes in weaving of sashes using the backstrap loom; Ocotlán, which offers baskets and embroidered and pleated blouses; and Teotitlán del Valle, which produces sarapes found in the markets in the region.

In the Gulf of Tehuantepec at Huatulco, the Mexican government is developing a new coastal resort. Computer models are being used once again to create the resort of the future. The first phase opened in 1988, and it already has the largest Club Mediterranée in the Western Hemisphere and over 1,500 beds. Plans are to have nearly 50,000 beds by 2018, making it one of the largest in all of Mexico.

resort and Mexico's most popular coastal resort. Cancún was developed by FONATUR using a computer-generated development plan. Although it is an excellent location, the sand had to be brought in to create the white sandy beaches. The crystal-clear Caribbean waters and the abundance of fresh seafood, fruit, and vegetables make both Cancún and Cozumel ideal Caribbean playgrounds that are easily accessible to the United States and Canada. Merida, the capital of Yucatán, combines old colonial buildings and modern homes with thatched Indian huts, presenting a unique setting. In 1988 Merida hosted an ecotourism conference. The region has a number of wildlife

Belize

Physical Characteristics

The terrain is mostly a flat, swampy coastal plain with low mountains in the south. The climate is tropical—very hot and humid. The rainy season extends from May to February.

Tourism Characteristics

Belize is just beginning to be discovered as an excellent ecotourism destination. Although tourist arrivals increased from 94,000 in 1986 to 220,000 in 1990, they fell to 134,000 in 1996. The government does not want to expand too rapidly, but continued managed growth would be beneficial to the country. The joint marketing of the *Mayan World Circuit*, its ecotourism potential, its long barrier reef, its pristine beaches, and the fact that it is English-speaking should certainly encourage future growth.

Capital: Belmopan
Government: Parliamentary democracy
Size: 8,800 square miles (slightly larger than Massachusetts)
Language: English (official). Spanish, Maya, Marifuna (Carib)
Ethnic Divisions: 30% Creole, 44% Mestizo, 11% Maya, 7% Garifuna, 2.1% East Indian
Religion: 62% Roman Catholic, 30% Protestant
Peak Tourist Season: December through March
Currency: Belizean dollar

CULTURAL CAPSULE

Belize is one of the most sparsely populated countries in Central America. Most Belizeans are of multiracial mixture. More than 45 percent are of African ancestry. A little more than 25 percent are mestizo. Another one-fifth is Carib, Mayan, and other Amerindian ethnic groups. The remainder includes Europeans, East Indians, Chinese, and Lebanese. Over the past few years the population has increased significantly from an inflow of Central American refugees, mostly from El Salvador and Guatemala.

English is the official language and is spoken by almost all of the population except recently arrived refugees. Spanish is the native tongue for about half of the people and is spoken as a second language by another 20 percent. The various Indian groups still speak their original language. An English-Creole dialect similar to that of the English-speaking people of the Caribbean islands is also used. About half of the people are Roman Catholic, while the Anglican Church and Protestant Christian groups make up most of the rest.

Cultural Hints:
- Greet with a handshake.
- Most North American gestures are understood.
- Keep hands above table when eating.
- Eating and foods:
  The best restaurants are in the hotels.
  Foods include seafood, beef and chicken, and rice and beans.
  National dishes are rice, beans, and lobsters.

TRAVEL TIPS

Entry: No visa is required for visits of less than thirty days. Evidence of sufficient funds is required and proof of travel out of country.
Transportation: Belize is served by one United States and several Central American airlines with connections to Mexico and the United States. Buses, taxis, light aircraft, and boats provide internal transportation. Buses and taxis are available in Belize City, and shopping areas are close to hotels.
Health: Check for malaria, yellow fever, and cholera before visit.
Shopping: Good buys are wooden handicrafts. Care must be taken buying Mayan arts and tortoise shell crafts. They may be restricted or not allowed in the United States.

Tourist Destinations and Attractions

The capital was moved from Belize City to Belmopan, a safer upland area than the coastal location of Belize City, which was devastated by Hurricane Hattie in 1961. Belize City still remains the major tourist destination. It has the oldest Anglican cathedral in Central America—St. John's Cathedral—built in 1857. The Government House,

the residence of the British governor, was built in 1814. The remnants of former slave quarters are still evident along Regent Street. The Supreme Court building, overlooking Central Park, continues elements of the British colonial style.

The coastal area has excellent beaches. A mosaic of islands off the barrier reef, one of the largest in the world, provides outstanding scuba diving and game fishing. Jacques Cousteau explored the waters of Belize in the 1970s. His exploration of a five hundred-foot-deep *karst sinkhole* now known as the "Blue Hole" transformed this area into a remarkable recreational paradise for divers. Belize has a wealth of Mayan ruins. Major sites are at Altún Ha, a small rich ruin, 30 miles northwest of Belize City and Xunantunich, 80 miles southwest of Belize City. At Lamanai stand 700 ceremonial structures in which 75,000 Mayans once lived.

The country is developing its ecotourism. The Mountain Pine Ridge is famed for its orchids and wildlife. There are some 450 varieties of birds. The Cayo district contains a jaguar reserve, a baboon sanctuary, numerous wildlife and marine reserves, national parks, and an active Audubon Society.

Through Visitors' Eyes

Wilderness and Wildlife Appreciation at the Heart of Belize

by John and Jane Greverus Perry

Belize has much to teach the rest of the world! So said our first day's tour guide. Ten days later, we agreed.

Belize Backgrounder

Belize is a delight. Its 170,000 people are a mix of African, Creole, Mayan, Carib, mestizo, Asian, and European, with no aristocracy of race or color.

Because it was British Honduras until 1981, the official tongue is English; but the street language is largely Creole. Also, Spanish seeps in from neighboring countries.

Conservation efforts have been assisted by World Wildlife Fund, Program for Belize, Wildlife Conservation International, The Nature Conservancy, and others. The Belize Audubon Society is influential and assists in operating the national parks.

Environmental laws are strict and strictly enforced. Industries that would pollute or damage the environment aren't welcome. Most hunting is prohibited. Gun ownership is regulated. A fisherman who takes lobster out of season may forfeit his boat.

It's not all laws and regulations. The Community Baboon Sanctuary is a voluntary compact signed by seventy-two local farmers. (Howler monkeys are baboons.) Each farmer has agreed to preserve his part of the riverside forest and other essential baboon habitats.

One can withdraw from the pact, but no one has. Indeed, the baboons have become a matter of local pride. The farmers have built overhead runways for baboons to cross the road safely.

On our first day, we toured Altún Ha (a major Mayan archaeological site), Guanacaste National Park, the Baboon Sanctuary, the new Belize Zoo, and many intermediate points. Maurice doesn't watch the clock; we left early, returned late.

Wilderness Lodge

Tom and Josie Harding, proprietors of Chan Chich Lodge, had arranged with Javier Air to fly us to the airstrip at Gallon Jug. John sat in the copilot seat. The seat beside Jane was occupied by five dozen eggs. The little Cessna® flew most of the way at 500 feet—fine for jungle sightseeing.

Gallon Jug is headquarters of a handsome private farm; the owner has bought 125,000 acres of rain forest to preserve it. United States-based Program for Belize has bought an adjoining 150,000 acres. Chan Chich Lodge is at the heart of this huge wilderness.

Tom designed and built the thatch-roof lodge and twelve spacious cabins with local materials. The grounds resemble a Mayan plaza surrounded by temple mounds. Each cabin has two queen-size beds, electricity, and a deck on all four sides with chairs and hammocks.

The lodge, also surrounded by a deck, has a dining room, bar, lounge, and shop. Grounds are landscaped with flowering plants. Flocks of colorful ocellated turkeys stroll about. The hardworking staff was friendly and efficient. The lawns were raked each morning.

Radiating from the plaza into the rain forest are miles of well-maintained trails. Guides lead morning, afternoon, and night walks.

We walked alone, using the sixty-four-page guide to the amazing array of orchids, bromeliads, fungi, vines, palms, figs, and towering trees. Muddy patches make nonskid shoes or boots advisable. Many guests are bird-watchers. They can add to their life lists while sitting on the lodge deck. Tom, Josie, and Josie's brother Norman usually are nearby to spot bat falcons, roadside hawks, and guans. Visitors also can swim, canoe, or go horseback riding.

Belize City

Back in Belize City, we enjoyed another day with Maurice, visiting more parks and preserves. Wherever we stopped he was greeted as a friend. He's an active member of the Belize Audubon Society.

continues

continued

We had expected to be back at the hotel by 5 P.M., but Maurice insisted on giving us a tour of the city, including a stop at his home.

Many tourists transfer immediately from the Belize International Airport to San Pedro or one of the other cayes for swimming, scuba diving, and fishing.

The coral reefs are among the world's best. We flew over the island chain, admiring the deep-blue water. Next time, perhaps.

Source: International Travel News, May 1993, pp. 10–11.

Guatemala

Capital: Guatemala City
Government: Republic
Size: 42,042 square miles (about the size of Tennessee)
Language: Spanish; 40% speak an Indian dialect, including Quiche, Cakchiquel, Kekchi
Ethnic Division: 56% Mestizo, 44% Indian
Religion: Predominantly Roman Catholic, some Protestant, traditional Mayan
Tourist Season: Year-round
Peak Tourist Season: None
Currency: Quetzal

 ## TRAVEL TIPS

Entry: Visas or tourist cards are required. Passports must be carried at all times. Tourist cards can be purchased at the airport en route to Guatemala.
Transportation: Direct connections from North America are available to Guatemala City. There is bus service between cities. Roads between major cities are paved, but the rest are unimproved. Public transportation in Guatemala City is by bus and is inexpensive. It is better to use taxis and tour buses.
Caution: At various times, the State Department has advised caution when traveling in certain areas because of conflict and crime. Tour-group travel is probably the best option in the country. Check with the State Department before visiting.
Health: Food should be cooked (no raw meat or fish) and hot. Drink boiled or bottled water. At times visitors need protection for malaria, cholera, and yellow fever. Consult with health officials or your physician before travel.
Shopping: Popular items are Indian handicrafts including antique embroidery, handwoven fabrics, silver jewelry, handwoven bags, basketwork, and *huipiles* (Indian blouses).

CULTURAL CAPSULE

Over half of the population are descendants of Maya Indians, most living in the mountain area. Ladinos—Westernized Mayans and mestizos (Spanish-Indian)—live in a crescent-shaped area running from the northern border on the Pacific, along the coastal plains, and up through Guatemala City to the Caribbean. The dominant religion is Roman Catholicism, which many Indians have superimposed onto their traditional forms of worship. While Spanish is the official language, there are some thirty Indian dialects. Some Indians do not understand Spanish.

Cultural Hints:
- Greet with a handshake.
- Good eye contact during greetings and talking.
- Ask permission to take photographs of people.
- Making a fist and pushing the thumb between the index and middle fingers is a very rude gesture.
- North American gestures are understood and should be avoided, particularly the "OK" signal.
- Eating and food:
  Keep arms above the table.
  It is polite to finish all the food on your plate.
  To attract the waiter, raise your hand.
  For the bill, raise your hand and then make a writing motion on your hand.
  Common foods are tortillas, black beans, rice, tamales, meats (beef, pork, and chicken), and fried platanos (bananas). Papaya and breadfruit are also common.

Physical Characteristics

Guatemala is mountainous with a narrow coastal plain and the Petén, which is a rolling limestone plateau. The lowlands are tropical, hot, humid, and wet. The highlands are cooler with chilly nights.

Tourism Characteristics

Guatemala's tourist industry has suffered in the 1980s because of the political instability of the region. It is easily accessible from the southeastern United States, and if the government becomes more stable, tourism will likely increase more rapidly. Tourism has begun to increase, but the half million

Figure 4–8 Lake Atitlan, Guatemala

most beautiful lakes in the world. The lake is ringed by a number of villages, each with its Indian tribe with distinctive colorful costume and periodic markets for the Indians. Chichicastenango and other mountain market towns are another attraction. Chichicastenango has become one of the outstanding Mayan market towns in all of Latin America. In addition to the market, a number of religious ceremonies are performed on the steps and inside the church of Santo Tomás. It is a picturesque mountain village of cobbled streets, red-tiled roofs, and whitewashed houses. The colonial city of Antigua was the capital until it was devastated by earthquakes. It has fascinating colonial buildings and ruins. The Tikal Mayan ruins are one of the most extraordinary archaeological sites in Latin American or, indeed, the entire world. The mutual marketing of Tikal as part of the Mayan World Circuit would be an additional growth factor for the country. Tikal sits in 222 square miles of dense rain forest. The city sprawls for some 50 square miles. Five imposing temples and thousands of stately structures emit an aura of power. Until recently, most visits were by air for a day trip. However, now there is a new 150-room hotel with plans for further development. One of the advantages of tourism in Guatemala is that all these destinations, with the exception of Tikal, are relatively close to each other and are located in the high elevations with pleasant climates.

tourists who visited in 1996 were the same number that were visiting Guatemala in the early 1970s. Other Latin American countries account for most of the total visitors. The United States accounts for 25 percent and has the potential to increase its share once stability returns to the region and country. Europe, led by Germany, accounts for 16 percent of its visitors.

Tourist Destinations and Attractions

There are currently five principal destinations of interest to tourists. Guatemala City, the capital, has museums and buildings that remind the visitor of Mayan Indian history and the city's role as a colonial capital. Lake Atitlán, (Figure 4-8) a volcano-surrounded lake, is considered by many to be one of the

---

Through Visitors' Eyes

Tracing Mayan Culture

Guatemala is one of the most diverse trips available within a short range of the United States. After arriving in Guatemala City, we left on a two-day trip over primitive roads into Honduras to see Copán, one of the finest of Mayan ruins. A great plaza with monumental stelae (standing stone pillars or blocks carved with pictures and hieroglyphs) is the main restored section of Copán.

The museum in the small village is being redone, but a preview allowed us to see the excellent displays and artwork being prepared.

The Highlands and Lowlands

After a day in Guatemala City, we again left by bus for Lake Atitlán. In the most scenic section of

the country, this seven–thousand-foot-high lake is surrounded by the cones of volcanoes. On the edge of the lake is Hotel Atitlán, an old Spanish, style building set in grounds full of flowering plants.

Many of the highland natives we saw still were wearing traditional clothing. Each village has a woven costume with its own typical pattern; some even resembled those seen on the Mayan stelae of one thousand years ago.

A few tourists go to the traditional markets, but they still are held, primarily for the Indians to exchange their goods. The market at Solola, high on the mountain above the lake, is more natural than the larger, more famous one at Chichicastenango where tourists are more frequent.

continues

continued

We saw more minor sets of ruins on the way to Atitlán and on the way back. We also stopped at Antigua, the early capital of Guatemala before an earthquake destroyed it in the 1700s. The town is preserved in the fashion of two hundred years ago.

We flew to Tikal in the Petén lowlands. Tikal is the largest of all explored Mayan sites, with temples up to two hundred feet high. There are hundreds of mounds representing unexplored buildings as well as the dozen or more that have been reconstructed.

From climbable temples, I could see for miles over the lowland jungle; other temples rose above the trees.

Source: *International Travel News.*
September 1986, pp. 20–21.

Honduras

150 km

Swan islands

Caribbean Sea

Islas de la Bahía

Puerta Cortés

San Pedro Sula

Puerto Lempira

Santa Rosa
de Copán

Justicalpa

TEGUCIGALPA
★

Choluteca

Golfo de
Fonseca

*Boundary representation is
not necessarily authoritative.*

Capital: Tegucigalpa
Government: Republic
Size: 32,277 square miles (slightly larger than Tennessee)
Language: Spanish, Indian dialects
Ethnic Division: 90% Mestizo, 7% Indian, 2% Black, 1% European
Religion: 97% Roman Catholic, Protestant minority
Tourist Season: Highland, year-around; Coastal, January through April
Peak Tourist Season: None
Currency: Lempira

 ## TRAVEL TIPS

Entry: Valid passport. No visa required for short stay.
Transportation: Direct flights from North America, Mexico, and other Central American countries to Tegucigalpa. There is good road connectivity from Guatemala to Honduras. Major cities are accessible by airplane. Rural areas are isolated with poor transportation and communications.
Health: Water must be boiled and filtered. Fruits and vegetables must be cleaned carefully and meats cooked well. Protection for malaria, typhoid fever, and cholera is advised. Check with health officials or physician before travel.
Shopping: Wooden carvings, Panama hats, woven straw items, and pottery are popular items.

CULTURAL CAPSULE

The population of Honduras is 90 percent mestizo with small minorities of European, African, Oriental, and American Indian ancestry. Most Hondurans are Roman Catholic. Spanish is the predominant language, although some English is spoken along the northern coast and on the Caribbean Bay islands. Native Indian dialects and Garifuna are also spoken. Honduras is one of the poorest countries in the Western Hemisphere. Its economy is rural, exporting bananas, coffee, sugar, cotton, timber, and some metals.

Cultural Hints:
- Greeting is a warm, gentle handshake.
- Hondurans have close personal space, standing near to converse.
- Hondurans recognize North American gestures.
- Waving the index finger is used to say no.
- Touching the finger below the eye warns caution.
- The hand in a fist with the thumb between the index and middle fingers is an obscene gesture.
- Eating and foods:
  Keep both hands above the table.
  Foods include beans, corn, tortillas, rice, and fruit. Typical dishes are tapado (a stew of beef, vegetables, and coconut milk), mondongo (tripe and beef), and nacatamales (pork).

Physical Characteristics

Honduras is mostly mountainous with a narrow coastal plain. The climate is subtropical in the lowlands and temperate in the mountain regions.

Tourism Characteristics

Like the other Central American nations, Honduras feels tourism is important but has not yet developed a substantial tourist infrastructure. Its development is retarded by its position between Guatemala and Nicaragua. Since the end of the civil war in Nicaragua and El Salvador, its tourism industry has grown. It increased from 126,000 in 1986 to 257,000 in 1996.

Treasures of Honduras

by Patricia Arrigoni

Fantasy Island

North Americans are just beginning to discover what the worldwide scuba-diving community has known for years. The great reef that runs along the coast of Honduras is one of the largest and most pure in the world. It is considered second in size only to the Great Barrier Reef of Australia.

People snorkeling can see abundant coral formations through crystal-clear water. The brightly colored tropical fish are everywhere, especially around the Bay Islands, which are located in the Caribbean about forty miles north of the Honduras mainland.

I stayed at Fantasy Island Beach Resort on Roatán, the largest of the Bay Islands, some thirty miles long and four miles wide. There is no pollution in the water around this island, nor has the coral been picked over by previous divers. Even the precious black coral still is growing just offshore.

The resort has built a short causeway that leads to a picturesque "Beach Dive Gazebo." From there you climb down a ladder and find yourself right over part of the reef. With a snorkeling mask you can see hundreds of tropical fish, colorful sponges, and different kinds of coral. There are plentiful elkhorn, pillar, star lettuce, and brain corals around these islands plus swaying sea fans.

I also snorkeled off a boat on the island's West End at a place called Half Moon Bay Wall. The diver who took us out was Jandero "Alejo" Monterroso, who operates a dive shop in Half Moon Bay.

Besides the schools of bright tropical fish and the coral, we saw a hawksbill turtle swimming below us.

Planning a Visit

The best time to visit the Bay Islands is between January and August; it rains during the rest of the year. Avoid June also; the Paya Indians slash and burn at this time–causing smoke to cover much of Central America.

English is spoken in the Bay Islands, as they used to be under British rule.

The islands also were used by pirates who hid there while raiding the rich Spanish galleons. The native population of the islands was happy to have these freebooters plunder and sink the hated Spanish treasure-and-slave ships.

Botanical Gardens

We visited several places on Roatán, including the town of Coxen's Hole (the capital of the islands) and the Carambola Gardens.

These botanical gardens were started by a young man, Bill Brady, who came to Honduras with the United States Peace Corps. Two and a half acres have been developed out of a twenty-five-acre parcel owned by Bill's Honduran wife, Irma.

The gardens, which opened in 1989, were delightful with their hummingbirds, yellow-head parrots, woodpeckers, crows, and iguanas.

Among familiar plants and trees were mahogany, sandalwood, the cacao or chocolate tree, and traveler's palm.

The hike entry fee was $1, or $2.50 to hike the jungle or rain forest trails.

On to Copán

After three days of Roatán Island, we flew to the bustling city of San Pedro Sula to take some other tours. Our first was an overnight to the famous Mayan ruins at Copán on the west side of Honduras.

The bus ride to Copán took about three hours through lush green fields silhouetted with purple mountains. Ever so often we would pass wooden carts pulled by oxen or red tractors.

One was filled with tobacco leaves on which two little boys were perched. They waved to us shyly and grinned widely—typical of the friendly people in Honduras.

The archaeological zone in the Copán Valley 100 miles west of San Pedro Sula contains some 3,500 ruins, all important remnants of the Mayan civilization.

The origins of Copán may date back to 2000 B.C. It is thought that the city was active until around 800 A.D., with its classic age spanning the last 350 years.

continues

continued

The ruins today include fabulous pyramids and temples built of carved stones plus hieroglyphics, intricately carved stelae, ball courts, altars, a magnificent hieroglyphic stairway, and tombs.

The excavations cover some 15 square miles, showing the remainsof a busy city that grew to around 15,000 residents.

The Museum of Copán located in the small adjoining town of Copán Ruinas contained selections of carved stone with hieroglyphs and pottery. There also were samples of jewelry, a reconstructed tomb, and a skull with jade filling in a tooth.

Source: International Travel News,
December 1992; pp. 43–45.

Honduras will also benefit from political stability and increased tourism to Guatemala as its major Mayan site is close to the border between the two countries.

Tourist Destinations and Attractions

The most famous attraction in Honduras is Copán, an ancient religious and cultural center for the Mayan Indians. It is considered to be an outstanding example of ancient Mayan civilization and is included in the Mayan World Circuit promotion and marketing with other Central American countries. Structures such as stone temples, courts, and an amphitheater have been restored. Comayaguela, a remarkably well-preserved sixteenth-century town, is a major attraction. The capital, Tegucigalpa, is a picturesque city with winding cobblestone streets. Honduras has sandy beaches on both the Pacific and Caribbean coastal areas. This combined with the Bay Islands in the Caribbean with their pristine beaches and coves provide a potential base for the development of a tourism industry, but it has yet to be realized.

El Salvador

75 km

Boundary representation is not necessarily authoritative.

Chalatenango
Santa Ana
★ **SAN SALVADOR**
Acajutla   San Vicente
La Libertad   San Miguel
                  La Unión

North Pacific Ocean

 TRAVEL TIPS

Entry: A visa is required and cannot be obtained at the border.
Transportation: Airline access is good from North America, Mexico, and other Central American countries. Highway access with neighbors (Guatemala and Honduras). Public transportation in San Salvador is an inexpensive bus.
Health: Precautions for malaria, yellow fever, and cholera advised. Check with local health officials before trip.
Caution: Although the war has ended, check with State Department on present status.
Shopping: Gold, ceramics, wood carvings, dolls, leather goods, and textiles are popular.

Capital: San Salvador
Government: Republic
Size: 8,124 square miles (about the same as Massachusetts)
Language: Spanish, Nahua among some Indians
Ethnic Division: 94% Mestizo, 5% Indian, 1% European
Religion: 75% Roman Catholic, balance mainly Protestant
Tourist Season: Year-round
Peak Tourist Seasons: November (10%) and December (12%)
Currency: Colón

CULTURAL CAPSULE

The people of El Salvador are very homogeneous (90 percent mixed Indian and Spanish). There are a few Indians who have retained their old customs and traditions, while the vast majority have adopted the Spanish language and culture.

Cultural Hints:
• Handshake is the common greeting. Some people only nod.

- Eye contact is important.
- It is impolite to point with finger or feet.
- Eating and food:
  Men stand when women leave the table.
  Food includes black beans, refried beans, tortillas, rice, eggs, meat, and fruit. Food is less spicy than in other Latin American countries.

Physical Characteristics

El Salvador is mountainous with a narrow coastal plain and a central plateau. The climate is tropical with a rainy season from May to October and a dry season from November to April.

Tourism Characteristics

In the past El Salvador, like Guatemala, had a reasonably strong tourist trade even though it was the smallest country in Central America. It is the most densely populated and most industrialized of the Central American countries. Today, tourism is insignificant because of the political situation. Of the few yearly tourists (300,000) they receive, nearly 25 percent are from the United States. Currently, the majority of their visitors are from other Central and South American countries. If the political situation stabilizes, they will be able to increase tourism rather rapidly as they have good accommodations and other tourist facilities that are currently under-used.

Tourism Destinations and Attractions

El Salvador has some very scenic mountains, volcanoes, and lakes. Surrounding the lakes are unique Indian villages where the inhabitants still wear traditional dress and use traditional markets. El Salvador also has excellent beaches along its Pacific coastline. There are a number of pre-Columbian ruins near Taxumal and San Andreas. The capital, San Salvador, is a modern city. The culture and art of the country are expressed in the museums and palaces of San Salvador. One of El Salvador's most impressive sites is Joya de Cerem, a village buried by a volcano 1,400 years ago. Due to the swift eruption, the village was left largely intact and quite well preserved.

Nicaragua

Capital: Managua
Government: Republic
Size: 50,193 square miles (about the size of Iowa)
Language: Spanish, English, and Indian-speaking minorities
Ethnic Division: 69% Mestizo, 17% European, 9% Black, 5% Indian
Religion: 95% Roman Catholic
Tourist Season: Year-round
Peak TouristSeason: December and January
Currency: Cordoba

TRAVEL TIPS

Entry: A visa is required and proof of sufficient funds and evidence of onward transportation.
Transportation: Nicaragua is served by international airlines with frequent connections to the rest of Central America. Rental cars, taxis, and an extensive bus service are available in Managua.
Health: Precaution advised for malaria, yellow fever, and cholera. Check with local health officials before travel. Food and water in better restaurants is generally safe.
Shopping: Brass, leather goods, wood carvings, masks, jewelry, and handwoven fabrics are common items purchased.

CULTURAL CAPSULE

Most Nicaraguans are mestizo. The Indians of the Caribbean coast remain ethnically distinct and retain tribal customs and dialects. A large African minority (of Jamaican origin) is concentrated on the Caribbean coast. Nicaraguan culture follows the lines of its *Ibero-European* ancestry with the Spanish influence prevailing. Roman Catholicism is the major religion, but Evangelical Protestant sects have increased recently. Spanish is the official language with English spoken on the Caribbean coast.

Cultural Hints:
- Greet with a warm, friendly handshake.

- Smiles are important.
- Nicaraguans have close personal space, standing closely in conversations.
- Eye contact is important.
- Most American gestures are understood and used.
- A fist with the thumb between the index and middle finger is obscene.
- Eating and food:

  Keep both hands above the table.

  Food staples are beans and rice. Typical dishes are tortillas, enchiladas, nacatamales (meat and vegetables), mondongo (tripe and beef knuckles), baho

Physical Characteristics

Extensive coastal plains surround a mountainous region. The climate is tropical in the lowlands and cooler in the highlands.

Tourism Characteristics

Nicaragua's visitors include more politically motivated rather than pleasure travelers than other Central American countries. Its similarity to other Central American countries and its political problems have been factors in its small tourist industry. Nicaragua has a growing industry, expanding from 44,000 tourists in 1986 to 257,000 in 1996. The Nicaraguan government has encouraged tourism and tourism-related projects in the 1990s as part of its attempt to restore the country's economy. A luxurious new resort has opened on the seaside estate of Anastasio Somoza, with the private airport being converted into an international airport. On Corn Island, sixty miles off Nicaragua's Atlantic coast, additional development is occurring. If the political situation continues to improve and stabilize, growth in tourism will continue.

Tourism Destinations and Attractions

Nicaragua's attractions include its Indian heritage; ancient Spanish cities such as Grenada, the oldest Spanish city in Nicaragua; Leon, near the scores of excellent sandy beaches that dot the coastline from the Gulf of Fonsceca to the Costa Rican border; beautiful lakes and volcanos; and the old English colonial town of Bluefield, with its houses built on stilts and surrounded by coconut palms. In addition, Nicaragua has coastal resorts on both the Pacific (Masachapa and Pochomil) and the Caribbean, which are undergoing development for tourists. Fifty miles offshore from Bluefield are two small, beautiful, peaceful, unspoiled islands, with white sand beaches bordered by coconut trees and clear turquoise water—the Corn Islands. Development is now taking place to provide access for international visitors to the wonderful snorkeling, horseback riding, and hiking on the islands.

Costa Rica

100 km

Capital: San José
Nicoya
Puntarenas
★ **SAN JOSÉ**
Cabo Gracias a Dios
Liberia

Caribbean Sea

Puerto Limón

San Isidro

North Pacific Ocean

Golfito

Isla del coco is not shown.

Capital: San José
Government: Democratic republic
Size: 19,730 square miles (just smaller than West Virginia)

Language: Spanish, some Jamaican dialect of English
Ethnic Division: 96% European, 2% Black, 1% Indian, 1% Chinese
Religion: 95% Roman Catholic
Tourist Season: Year-round
Peak Tourist Season: None
Currency: Colón

✴ TRAVEL TIPS

Entry: No visa is required for stays of less than ninety days. Tourists card issued upon arrival. Also, visitors need evidence of transportation to leave Costa Rica.
Transportation: Costa Rica has good international connections between San José and North America and other Latin American countries. Transportation between cities is by bus. San José has excellent bus public transportation.
Health: Some areas have cholera. Check with local health officials.
Shopping: Items include carved wood (mahogany), native dolls and costumes, leather, and embroidery.

CULTURAL CAPSULE

Costa Ricans are largely European (Spanish ancestry), with a few Africans, descendants of Jamaican immigrant workers. There are about one percent native American Indians and another one percent ethnic Chinese. Spanish is the official language, with English widely understood. Creole English is spoken by the black population, and Bribri is spoken by Indians. About 95 percent of the population is Roman Catholic. Costa Rica has the most politically stable government in Central America.

Cultural Hints:
- Men smile and shake hands.
- People waiting for public transportation line up in an orderly manner.
- Most American gestures are understood.
- A fist with the thumb between the index and middle finger is obscene.
- Eye contact is important.
- Chewing gum while speaking is impolite.
- Eating and foods:
  Keep both hands above the table.
  It is impolite to talk with food in your mouth.

Physical Characteristics

Costa Rica has a rugged mountain interior with coastal plains on the Caribbean and the Pacific. The climate is tropical, with the rainy season from May to November and the dry season from December to April.

Tourism Characteristics

Costa Rica is more economically advanced than the other Central American countries, and it is one of the most stable countries of Central America. In 1985, recognizing tourism potential, the government began a tourism-development program that resulted in the development of a number of new hotels and an increase in marketing to the North American market. Although most of its tourists are from other Latin American countries, the United States is a significant and growing market, as it accounts for some 35 percent of all the visitors to Costa Rica. Costa Rica is seeking ways to increase the visitors from North American countries.

Tourism to Costa Rica has become the most dynamic in Central America, largely based on ecotourism. The number of visitors tripled from 261,000 in 1986 to 781,000 in 1996. In an area the size of West Virginia, it has a rain forest, high mountain cloud forests, coral beaches, and 29 parks set aside to protect their natural ecology. The parks contain more than 850 species of birds, 1,200 varieties of orchids, and a number of other fauna and flora. Costa Rica now protects some 20 percent of the country's territory. In 1990, Costa Rica raised the tourism department to a cabinet status and appointed a new minister of tourism, using room and airport tax to provide revenue for this office.

Tourism Destinations and Attractions

The country's most noted attractions are its volcanic scenery, national parks, and oceans. The capital, San José, has some excellent museums and is a good representative of Costa Rican culture. The national parks exhibit a variety of flora and fauna with a remarkable collection of birds, flowers, mammals, and fish.

The Central Highlands contain the majority of the population, virtually all of the colonial town's *cathedrals*, and the majority of the country's most dramatic natural beauties, such as the great steaming volcanoes, the luxuriant misty cloud forests, the rocky gorges, waterfalls, and rushing streams.

A short day's trip from San José is Puerto Limon. Puerto Limon is the only deep-water port on Costa Rica's Caribbean coast. The coast south of the port is lined with superb beaches. One of the best and most popular in Central America is Cahuita, with its white and black sand beaches, coral reefs, and transparent waters. Great diving, swimming, sunning, and beachcombing are available.

The stability of the government, the moderate climate, and the variety of attractions from beaches to rich national parks provide a resource for expanding its tourism industry.

Panama

Physical Characteristics

There are steep, rugged mountains and dissected upland plains in the interior. The coastal areas are largely plains and rolling hills. The climate is tropi-cal, hot, and humid during the rainy season from May to January. January to May is a short, dry season.

Caribbean Sea

North Pacific Ocean

Capital: Panama City
Government: Centralized republic
Size: 29,762 square miles (a little larger than West Virginia)
Language: 86% Spanish, 14% English, many bilingual
Ethnic Division: 70% Mestizo, 14% West Indian, 10% European, 6% Indian
Religion: 85% Roman Catholic, 15% Protestant
Tourist Season: Year-round
Peak Tourist Season: January through April
Currency: Balboa

Tourist Characteristics

Panama was a relatively stable country until 1988, but tourists traditionally stayed only for a short time. Most of its visitors were in transit, either from *cruise ships* traveling through the Panama Canal or international flights between South America and North America. The number of visitors has risen slightly, from 308,000 in 1986 to 362,000 in 1996. This is partly due to the United States government, who appropriated $30 million to improve tourist facilities and related employment in Panama. Panama's currency, the balboa, has been tied to the United States dollar, which is attractive to tourists and helps account for the increase of visitors from the United States.

Panama's strategic location has allowed the development of a tourist industry. Although the United States and Panama's neighbors are the most important contributors to its tourist industry, Panama attracts tourists from a much greater diversity of nations than do other Central American countries because of ships passing through the Panama Canal.

Tourism Destinations and Attractions

The tourist industry centers on Panama City and its duty-free shopping, nightlife, and treasures from its

TRAVEL TIPS

Entry: Tourist card with proof of citizenship (a passport is best) from airline serving Panama. Also, need evidence of continued transportation out of Panama.
Transportation: Panama is served by several international airlines from North America and Latin America. It is known as the bridge of the world. The Inter-American Highway connects Panama to the other Central American countries and the United States. Public transportation in Panama City is by bus service, which is crowded.
Health: Concern for malaria, yellow fever, and cholera. Check with local health officials before travel.
Shopping: Panama is a duty-free country for goods from around the world. Local handicrafts such as embroidery, beaded beaded collars, leather, straw, and wooden goods are typical of the country.

CULTURAL CAPSULE

The people of Panama are predominantly Caribbean Spanish. Ethnically, the majority are mestizo, or mixed Spanish, Indian, and West Indian. A number of minorities exist such as elements of the West Indians and indigenous Indian groups. Spanish is the official language; however, English is a common second language.

Cultural Hints:
- A nod or handshake are common greetings.
- Women should dress conservatively.
- American gestures are known and understood.
- Eye contact is important.
- Eating and food:
  Hands should be kept above the table.
  Typical foods are kidney beans, rice, plantains, corn, fish, beef, chicken, pork, and tropical fruits.

history of colonialism and piracy. The Altar of Gold in the Church of San José is an important attraction. Panama is trying to emphasize other attractions such as its beaches and offshore islands, which offer fishing, watersports, and other resort amenities, in an effort to increase the length of stay of tourists.

Naturally, Panama's single, most important attraction is the Canal and locks. For observing the Canal, Cristóbal and Colón on the Atlantic and Balboa on the Pacific are major points of interest. A short flight from Panama City, San Blas Island is the home of the Cuna Indians who have maintained their unique language and customs for thousands of years.

CARIBBEAN

One of the most popular tourist destinations in the world today, the Caribbean is the most densely populated region of the Americas. It is a region of extreme wealth and extreme poverty. The economy of the region has long been associated with one major crop or resource. Sugar has been the chief source of income and at one time brought in much wealth. After an initial era of prosperity, however, the sugar economy collapsed. Since that time, many of the Caribbean people have struggled to obtain a livelihood. Tourism has offered some relief and will continue to grow in importance to the economy of the region. Millions have migrated, especially to the United States, with the Caribbean being the third largest source of immigrants to the United States in the last decade.

For most of the people in this area, life is deficient due to the lack of arable land and the uncertainties of an agriculture-based economy. Years of drought, cold weather, and hurricanes have spelled disaster for many families.

With a limited economic base, the Caribbean nations have seen tourism as a way to improve their standard of living. Tourism is not only a capital investment but a labor-intensive industry that employs many individuals, both skilled and unskilled. Despite the serious problems and drawbacks that are part of tourism in this area, it has become a leading moneymaker for many Caribbean nations; and its future looks hopeful, promising steady growth.

Tourism has become the region's leading industry despite damage from hurricanes, civil unrest, bankrupt tour operators, and volcano eruptions. Direct scheduled air service from the American market reaches a number of islands. The Caribbean is the largest cruise destination in the world. However, while the cruise industry continues to grow, the longer-stay tourist market has declined with competition from Florida and Cancún in Mexico.

In the past, the flow of wealthy visitors to this region sometimes led to hostility among some local residents. They resented the free-spending and raucous tourists whose demands that the native hosts adapt to their tastes and attitudes debased the island culture. Tourism, then, is a mixed blessing in the Caribbean, but it endures because it provides much-needed income to the residents.

Travel Patterns

The Caribbean region is dominated by tourists from North America, (Table 4–2). Some 61 percent of its visitors are from the United States and Canada.

The nearness of the United States with its large population along the eastern seaboard and the lack of warm winter weather in Canada are two reasons for this influx of visitors from North America. The two major forms of transportation to the Caribbean are ship and airplane. There are well over two hundred cruise departures a year from ports along the North American coasts, such as Miami, New York, Port Everglades, and San Juan, and within the Caribbean islands themselves. Cruise ships visit between four and six islands, depending upon the length of the cruise. While many of the Caribbean islands are not part of the major cruise itineraries, airlines (American®, Delta®, and Island® airline companies) offer all-inclusive programs for North American customers that have both enhanced the opportunities of the small islands and brought many tourists from the western United States as well. In addition, there are flights and connections from European cities such as London, Paris, and Amsterdam to their former Caribbean colonial islands. The European share of tourists has increased to over 15 percent, aided by the greater number of air charter packages available in Europe.

Table 4–2 Caribbean Tourist Arrivals by Region of Origin (Percentage)						
Region	1982	1983	1984	1985	1987	1994
United States	58.9	62.4	62.0	62.4	61.8	51.5
Canada	6.3	5.9	6.2	7.1	6.3	5.5
Europe	10.8	9.8	8.9	8.7	10.4	17.7
Caribbean	9.4	9.2	9.4	8.8	7.6	8.8
Other/Unspecified	14.6	12.7	13.5	13.0	13.9	16.5

Source: Tourism Statistical Report 1994. Christ Church Barbados, Caribbean Tourism Research and Development Centre; 1994, p. 21.

The two largest receivers of Americans are the Bahamas and Puerto Rico. Together they receive almost half of the total visitors from the United States. The Canadians' major destinations are the Dominican Republic, Jamaica, and the Bahamas. These three destinations account for about 48 percent of the Canadian arrivals in the Caribbean. Cuba also receives a significant number from Canada each year. The Europeans' major destinations are Martinique, Barbados, Puerto Rico, St. Maarten, and Jamaica.

The three largest cruise destinations in the Caribbean are the Bahamas, the U.S. Virgin Islands, and Puerto Rico. They account for over 50 percent of the arrivals by cruise ships in the Caribbean.

Cultural links with European nations have added to the attractiveness of these islands for Europeans. The three major European groups of tourists to the Caribbean are English, French, and German. England and France have developed strong patterns of tourism from their long colonial ties, and Germany has a prosperous population looking for exotic places to spend money in the sun. This European linkage is observed in Guadeloupe, with 70 percent of its visitors from France, and Martinique, with 72 percent of its visitors French, and in the high number of Europeans who visit the British Virgin Islands, Barbados, Antigua, Barbuda, and Curacao.

Table 4–3 indicates the number of visitors to the Caribbean region. While not geographically part of the Caribbean, Bermuda, the Bahamas, and Turks and Caicos are included because most international organizations include them in the Caribbean for statistical purposes even though they are technically Atlantic islands.

The most visited islands are Puerto Rico, the Bahamas, the Dominican Republic, Jamaica, and the United States Virgin Islands. All of these islands are close to the United States, and the use of English, except in the Dominican Republic, is common. The average length of stay varies from approximately three days in Puerto Rico to sixteen days in Trinidad and Tobago. The two major income beneficiaries are the Bahamas and Puerto Rico, accounting for about 26 percent of the region's total visitor receipts. Montserrat was decimated by volcanic action in 1997, and it is doubtful that any significant economic activity, including tourism, will be viable for a considerable length of time.

The varied cultural backgrounds of the inhabitants of this area have produced a unique pattern of life that is expressed in the language, music, dance, art, architecture, and foods of the region. Basic languages include French, English, Spanish, and combi-

Table 4–3   Tourism to the Caribbean

	1982 (000)	1994 (000)	Length of Stay (1994)
Bahamas	1,101.1	1,561.1	5.8
Bermuda	416.6	416.0	6.2
OECS Countries			
Anguilla	6.7	43.7	9.4
Antigua and Barbuda	87.0	262.9	(1985) 7.0
Dominica	19.0	56.5	7.8
Grenada	23.2	109.0	7.2
Montserrat	15.0	21.3	(1985) 10.6
St. Kitts-Nevis	34.5	94.2	9.4
St. Lucia	70.2	218.6	9.6
St. Vincent and the Grenadines	37.1	55.0	(1985) 9.0
Other Commonwealth	1,318.5		
Barbados	303.8	425.6	11.3
British Virgin Islands	113.7	240.4	(1993) 7.0
Cayman Islands	121.2	341.5	(1991) 4.9
Jamaica	467.8	976.6	10.7
Trinidad & Tobago	190.0	265.6	(1985) 16.0
Turks & Caicos	13.3	70.9	7.4
Netherlands Antilles			
Aruba	220.2	582.1	7.3
Bonaire	30.3	55.8	7.6
Curacao	174.4	226.1	7.9
Saba	6.0	29.6	4.6
St. Eustatius	4.9	10.7	5.4
St. Maarten	213.4	585.7	(1987) 4.8
French West Indies	365.4	331.3	
Guadeloupe	189.4	475.0	5.7
Martinique	176.2	419.0	(1988) 5.2
United States Territories	1,903.7	2,042.4	
Puerto Rico	1,563.7	3,042.4	2.8
U.S. Virgin Islands	340.0	540.0	4.4
Other Countries			
Cuba	139.3	617.3	9.3
Dominican Republic	480.0	1,766.9	2.6
Haiti	135.0	120.0	N/A

Source: *Caribbean Tourism Statistical Report 1994*. Christ Church Barabdos, Caribbean Tourism Research and Development Center, 1994, pp. 5, 57. *World Tourism Yearbook of Tourism Statistics*, 1992, p. 78.

nations of words from two or more languages to create a distinctive language known as Creole. English is the official language spoken in former British possessions, French in the former French possessions, French Creole in Haiti, and Spanish in Cuba and the Dominican Republic. Both Spanish and English are official languages accepted in Puerto Rico, but most business is conducted in English. In the Netherlands Antilles, Dutch is the official language, but English is spoken in the northern islands. In the southern islands, most of the people speak Papiamento, a Creole language that mixes Dutch, Spanish, Portuguese, English, and African words. To the African-modified forms of English and French heard in the Caribbean, there can be added several imported languages, with Hindi especially strong in Trinidad.

Catholicism dominates religion on most of the islands, with the exception of the former British islands where Protestant denominations, particularly the Anglican Church, dominate. On most islands, religious tolerance is the norm.

The Caribbean area also has an important legacy from Africa. In places, it strongly resembles western equatorial Africa in the construction of village dwellings, the operation of open markets, the role of women in rural life, the preparation of certain foods, the methods of cultivation, and artistic expression. The mixture of blacks with whites varies from 90 percent black in Haiti to 15 percent black in the Dominican Republic. This composition is further complicated by the presence of Asians from India and China and other small populations from other countries.

During the nineteenth century, the emancipation of slaves and the later importation of laborers brought some far-reaching changes. For example, 100,000 indentured Chinese laborers were brought in to work in the sugar fields. In Jamaica, Trinidad, Guadeloupe, and Martinique, a quarter of a million East Indians arrived for the same purpose. This helps to explain the ethnic and cultural variety of Caribbean America.

A combination of the African, European, and Asian led to a unique and lively style of music and dance. The Caribbean has long been known for its *calypso* music and steel bands, with calypso flourishing especially in Trinidad. African rhythms and European dances are combined for a wealth of festive sound to delight tourists. Carnivals held throughout the Caribbean, such as the pre-Lenten carnival in Trinidad and the annual June meringue festival in the Dominican Republic, are popular tourist attractions. People come from all parts of the world to enjoy the rhythms and activities associated with them. Dance is as varied throughout the Caribbean as the language.

Art is also an expression of the Caribbean's rich history. The art of the original people of the Caribbean, the Arawak and the Carib, in addition to the primitive art of Africa and the variety of European traditions, offers travelers a rich opportunity to enjoy a variety of styles no matter which nation they visit.

The varied architecture of the Caribbean instantly captures the visitor's eye, providing the backdrop for music, dance, and art. Most buildings feature the distinctive patterns of the colonizing nations modified by climate and the changes wrought by history. The former Spanish West Indies, which are now the United States Virgin Islands, are marked by Danish influence, particularly the town of Christiansted on St. Croix. Those islands formerly under Dutch rule in the Caribbean echo the architecture of Holland, with Willemstad, Curacao, as the best example. Spanish architecture can be seen in Puerto Rico and the Dominican Republic. Victorian English details have been transplanted to the islands that were under British control, particularly in Frederiksted, St. Croix.

As might be expected, a wide variety of food is available, with various specialties from each culture throughout the islands. This variety results from the adaptation of European foods to the region, the incorporation of cuisines from the various settlers, the creation of specialties of the islands, and the availability of seafood. The variety of foods and cuisines has helped the Caribbean to attract tourists.

The cultural heritage of diversity in language, food, music, and dance has led to a special effort by many Caribbean countries to preserve the traditions of the past in institutes, theaters, and organizations of performing artists. These, along with the traditional carnivals and festivals, have saved the tremendous cultural variety of the people. While entertaining to the tourists who visit the Caribbean, it is important to remember that it is part of the life of the people of the region.

GREATER ANTILLES

The Greater Antilles are Cuba, the Caymans, Dominican Republic, Haiti, Jamaica, and Puerto Rico.

Cuba

Capital: Havana
Government: Communist
Size: 42,804 square miles (slightly smaller than Pennsylvania)
Language: Spanish
Ethnic Division: 51% Mulatto, 37% European, 11% Black, 1% Chinese
Religion: 85% nominally Roman Catholic
Tourist Season: December to April
Peak Tourist Season: none
Currency: Cuban peso (CUP)

 ## TRAVEL TIPS

Entry: United States citizens need a Treasury Department license. United States citizens cannot transact financial trade in any form to support tourism to Cuba. It has to be paid by other sources.
Transportation: There are direct flights from North America, Europe, and Latin America to Havana.
Health: No requirements.

CULTURAL CAPSULE

Cuba is a multiracial society with a population mostly of Spanish and African ancestry. The organized religion is Roman Catholic.

Physical Characteristics

Cuba has relatively large flat and rolling plains with some hills and mountains. The climate is tropical, but it is moderated by trade winds. The rainy season is from May to November and the dry season is from November to April.

Tourism Characteristics

Tourism to Cuba from the United States is restricted, which handicaps Cuban industry considerably. Travel to Cuba has increased each year. The number of tourists is increasing, reaching 600,000 in 1996. They arrive on European, Russian, Cuban, Czech, and Slovakian airlines. Cuba also has connections to Canada, Mexico, and other Latin American countries. Some Latin American countries, however, will not admit anyone carrying a passport with a Cuban stamp on it.

Major new Cuban development has been taking place outside of Havana with the help of European investors from Germany, Italy, Spain, and Austria. Cuba's hosting of the Pan American Games in 1991 was a boost for its tourism image. In 1992 Cuba became a member of the Caribbean Tourism Organization, which helps in marketing Cuba as part of the Caribbean outside of the United States.

Tourist Destinations and Attractions

Havana, the capital, has become somewhat run-down, but the old town near the docks is still the focal area for visitors. The city was founded in 1515, and many of the ancient palaces, plazas, colonnades, churches, and monasteries are still part of the landscape. Around the old town, there are narrow and picturesque streets. The presidential palace now holds the museum of the Revolution. Near Havana is Guanabacoa, a well-preserved, small colonial town with a historical museum containing a voodoo collection located in the former slave quarters.

Cuba has some excellent beaches and deep bays that are good for snorkeling and other water sports. Santiago de Cuba on the east side of the island is home to a number of museums, the most noted of which is the Colonial Museum located in the Diego Velasquez house.

Cayman Islands

Physical Characteristics

The Caymans include three islands: Grand Cayman, which is the largest; Cayman Brac; and Little Cayman. They consist of a low-lying limestone base surrounded by coral reefs, which provide exciting underwater scenery and shipwrecks. The climate is

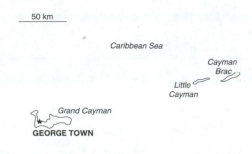

Figure 4–9 Pirate Week in Cayman Islands

Capital: George Town
Government: British-dependent territory
Size: 100 square miles (slightly less than twice the size of Washington, D.C.)
Language: English
Ethnic Division: 40% Mixed, 20% European, 20% Black, 20% expatriates
Religion: United Church (Presbyterian and Congregational), Anglican, Baptist, Roman Catholic, Church of God, and other
Tourist Season: November through March
Peak Tourist Season: March and December
Currency: Cayman Island dollar (CI$)

 TRAVEL TIPS

Entry: Proof of citizenship and outgoing transportation.
Transportation: Access to the Cayman Islands by air from Miami and Puerto Rico. Local transportation by taxi, bicycle, motorcycle, and car.
Shopping: Grand Cayman has duty, free goods and no sales tax, which is beneficial to visitors. Jewelry from black coral (an environmental concern), wood carvings, lacework, and local crafts are popular items.

CULTURAL CAPSULE

The Cayman Islands are inhabited by an English-speaking population. The food specialties are turtle soup, turtle steak, oyster, conch pie, snapper, and barracuda.

---

generally good year-round because of the trade winds. Most rain falls between May and October, but even then it is generally only in the form of short showers.

Tourism Characteristics

The Caymans were first sighted by Columbus on his last voyage in 1503 and he named them Las Tortugas,

the island of turtles. Over 77 percent of the 340,000 annual visitors in the Caymans are from the United States. However, visitors from Northern Europe increased 162 percent from 1990 to 1994. The only two island industries are tourism and international banking. They offer a wide range of accommodations and eating establishments.

Tourist Destinations and Attractions

The Cayman Islands beaches are among the best in the Caribbean. The Seven Mile Beach, with its dazzling white sand and tall Australian pines, is the most famous. The reef and the many shipwrecks attract all kinds of underwater tropical fish and both snorkelers and scuba divers. In addition to great beaches, the coastline provides other water-related experiences such as blowholes and unusual rock formations. The Cayman Turtle Farm on Grand Cayman is the only commercial turtle farm in the world. Cayman Brac and Little Cayman provide visitors with a more relaxing lifestyle, as both have small populations of warm and friendly people.

Dominican Republic

Physical Characteristics

The Dominican Republic is composed of rugged highlands and mountains with a fertile plain in the north and east, which contains most of the population. The Dominican Republic occupies two-thirds of Hispaniola, and Haiti occupies the other third. The climate is tropical maritime, with little seasonal temperature variation. The rainy months are May and June, and September to November.

Capital: Santo Domingo
Government: Republic
Size: 18,704 square miles (equal to New Hampshire and Vermont)
Language: Spanish
Ethnic Division: 73% Mixed, 16% European, 11% Black
Religion: 95% Roman Catholic
Tourist Season: December through April
Currency: Peso

Tourism Characteristics

The Dominican Republic is trying to increase its tourist trade and has many attractions that can be used to generate tourism. Tourism is by far the largest earner of income in their international trade. Tourism arrivals tripled between 1987 and 1994, with over 1.7 million visitors in 1994. The Dominican Republic has become one of the major destination countries of the Caribbean. The fastest growth in arrivals is from Europe. There are large numbers of charters from the European countries of the United Kingdom, Germany, Spain, Switzerland, and France as well as an increase from Canada.

Tourist Destinations and Attractions

The capital and major seaport, Santo Domingo, is the center of the tourism industry to the Dominican Republic. It was founded by Bartholomew, the brother of Christopher Columbus. The city was the base for the Spanish exploration and conquest of the American continent. Today there are many colonial buildings that have been restored as major tourist attractions. The Cathedral of Santa Maria La Menor is the oldest cathedral in the New World, and the remains of Christopher Columbus were buried there. In 1992, the remains were moved to a new monument at Playa Dorado where an eleven-story lighthouse in the shape of a cross was completed for the five-hun-

TRAVEL TIPS

Entry: Tourist card with proof of citizenship. Currency restrictions and/or exchange requirements. Arrival and departure tax.
Transportation: Santo Domingo is accessible by international airlines from North America, Europe, and other Caribbean islands. There are both rail and road connections within the Dominican Republic.
Health: Cholera. Check with local health officials before visit.
Shopping: Amber jewelry is the most noted item. Devil masks, cigars, and ceramic lime figurines that symbolize the Dominican culture are valued by visitors.

CULTURAL CAPSULE

The Dominican Republic was originally occupied by a branch of the Arawak people from South America. After the discovery by Columbus, the native population was reduced. The Spanish began bringing African slaves to the island in 1503. During the 1600s, the French settlers occupied the western end of the island, which is now Haiti. The population today is mixed with a sizeable European minority. Baseball is the national pastime and provides many major league players to the professional leagues in the United States.

Cultural Hints:
- The handshake is a common greeting.
- Most American gestures are understood.
- Eating and foods:
  Keep both hands above the table.
  The basic cooking is Spanish with a number of foreign ethnic restaurants such as Italian, Chinese, and French. Typical foods are sancocho (thick, heavy soup-cum-stew of pork, yams, sausages, onions, tomatoes), arroz con pollo (chicken and rice), pastelitos (small pastries filled with chicken or other meat), empanadas (meat patties), and fritos (assorted fritters).

dredth anniversary of Columbus's discovery of the New World. Other impressive buildings are the Torre del Homenaje, which was built in 1503–1507 and is the oldest fortress in America; the Museo De las Casas Reales, a reconstructed early sixteenth-century building; the Alcazar de Colon, which was built by Diego Colon (Columbus's son) and was the seat of the Spanish Crown in the New World; and the ruins of the Monasterio de San Francisco, the first monastery in America. The region along the coast from Santo Domingo contains a number of popular resorts, towns, and beaches. Boca Chica, eighteen miles east of Santo Domingo, is the most popular resort. It has a reef-protected shallow lagoon and good beaches.

With its rugged landscape, the interior provides the scenery for hill resorts. The town of Jarabacao and the Constanza region have many beautiful pine forests, rivers, waterfalls, and impressive peaks, of which the Pico Duarte is the highest in the Caribbean.

The majority of international visitors interested in sun-sea-sand enter the country at Puerto Plata, which was founded by Columbus. It is here at Playa Dorado that the Columbus memorial referred to was built. It is also a major stop for many cruise companies. In both directions from Puerto Plata along the Atlantic coast, there are excellent beach resorts, providing diving and water sports.

Haiti

CULTURAL CAPSULE

Haiti is one of the world's most densely populated countries. Its population is almost 95 percent of African ancestry. The remainder are mixed African-Caucasian (mulattoes). Language is French based, with Creole the most common. Roman Catholic is the dominant religion, but voodoo practices are widespread.

Cultural Hints:
- Greet with a friendly handshake.
- Many residents offer to be guides.
  Food is based on French cuisine creating Creole specialties, combining French, tropical, and African ingredients. Typical dishes are guinea hen, tassot de dinde (dried turkey), grillot (fried island pork), diri et djondjon (rice and black mushrooms), riz et poils (rice and kidney beans), lobster, pork chops, and various sauces.

Capital: Port-au-Prince
Government: Republic (frequent coups)
Size: About the size of Maryland
Language: 10% French, Creole 90%, many bilingual
Ethnic Division: 95% Black, 5% Mulatto and European
Religion: 75–80% Roman Catholic (most practice voodoo), 10% Protestant, 10% other
Tourist Season: December through March
Peak Tourist Season: December (12%) and July (12%)
Currency: Gourde (GQU)

TRAVEL TIPS

Entry: Proof of citizenship (passport is best). Arrival and departure tax.
Transportation: International airlines provide access from North America, France, and other Caribbean countries. Local buses are overcrowded. Taxis are best in cities.
Health: Concern for malaria and yellow fever. Check local health officials before travel.
Shopping: Best buys are wooden statuettes, inlaid boxes and trays, embroidered clothes, copper jewelry, heavy bedspreads and draperies, and paintings by local artists.

Physical Characteristics

Haiti, which occupies the west one-third of the island of Hispaniola, is a rough mountainous country. The climate is tropical, but semiarid where the mountains block the moisture from the east. The offshore breeze in the mornings and at night cools the temperature.

Tourism Characteristics

Tourism to Haiti has suffered due to political problems since the ending of the Duvalier dictatorship in 1986. Until stability returns to the country, the tourist industry will continue to suffer. In fact, Haiti saw a 51 percent decrease in tourist numbers from 1990 to 1994. Haiti desires to have tourists and the people have been very friendly towards visitors. In the past, nearly 85 percent of the visitors were from the United States and Canada (73 and 12 percent) (World Tourism Organization, 1992). It has had excellent connectivity with a number of carriers providing air service and Port-au-Prince was a major port stop for cruise lines from the United States. However, political unrest in the past few years has left the tourist industry in disarray.

Tourist Destinations and Attractions

Haiti offers tourists at least four important attractions: its culture, including African voodoo and associated African music; shopping, especially in the Iron Market; the unique scenery; and outstanding beach resorts.

Port-au-Prince, the capital and port city, is located on a beautiful deep bay with high mountains in the background. The houses are colorful and unique in architectural style. A short distance up the mountains at Pétionville, the cooler mountain environs were the primary location of the Europeans. The Iron Market in the center of town is crowded with people (both inside and outside) buying and selling their wares, Figure 4–10.

A number of museums display Haitian art, relics, costumes, paintings, and historical documents. There are superb beaches near Port-au-Prince. Sandy City is reported to have one of the better coral reefs in the world. A second major area of interest centers on Cap Haitian, which is the second largest city in Haiti. The coastal area around Cap Haitian has a number of excellent beaches and locations providing good access to the coral reefs.

One of the most important attractions in the area near Milot is the Citadelle, a large ruined fortress built for King Henri Christophe in the 1800s. The Haitians regard it as the eighth wonder of the world. It is on top of a mountain accessible by either a two-hour walk or a horseback ride. The ruins of the Sans Souci Palace, which was built in the early nine-

Figure 4–10 Iron Market, Haiti

teenth century as a rival to Versailles, are also located at Milot.

Jacmel, a port city on the south coast, is an area of many beaches, some with black sand and others with white. The area provides some scenic steep and rocky mountains with waterfalls and bays.

Jamaica

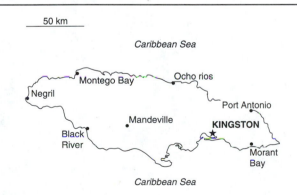

Caribbean Sea

Caribbean Sea

Capital: Kingston
Government: Independent state within Commonwealth
Size: Slightly smaller than Connecticut
Language: English, Creole
Ethnic Division: 76.3% African, 15.1% Afro-European, 3.1% East Indian and Afro-East Indian, 3.2% European, 1.2% Chinese and Afro-Chinese, 1.2% other

Religion: Dominantly Protestant, some Roman Catholic, and some spiritualist cults
Tourist Season: December through April
Peak Tourist Season: January through March
Currency: Jamaican dollar

 ## TRAVEL TIPS

Entry: Tourist cards are issued on arrival with proof of citizenship. Return tickets and sufficient funds are required. Arrival and/or departure tax is collected.
Transportation: International and Jamaican airlines provide good access to North America, Britain, and other Caribbean markets. Local buses are overcrowded but provide fairly regular service. Taxis are available. Main roads are paved. The mountain roads are narrow and winding.
Health: Concern for yellow fever and cholera.
Shopping: Local items are Jamaican cigars, rum, calypso music boxes, shells, carvings, pottery, clothing, fabrics, and straw work.

CULTURAL CAPSULE

The population of Jamaica is primarily of African origin. Minorities are Afro-Europeans (15 percent), Afro-East Indians and East Indians (3 percent), Caucasians of European descent (3 percent), and some Chinese and other groups. The Anglican Church is the largest of the established churches, followed by many Baptist sects, the Roman Catholic, and the Methodist. Jamaica has several Muslim and Hindu groups, along with a small Jewish community. Rastafarians, who see former Ethiopian Emperor Haile Selassie as the embodiment of God (Jah), are also found here.

Cultural Hints:
- Greetings are a nod, bow, or handshake.
- To call attention make the "psst" sound.
- Abundant hand gestures are common when talking.
- Eating and food:
  Keep hands above the table.
  Meals are relaxed and sociable.
  Foods are spicy. Typical dishes are ackee and saltfish, rice,

Physical Characteristics

Jamaica is the third largest island in the Caribbean. It is an outcrop of a submerged mountain range with a series of spurs and forested gullies running north and south. The island's most notable feature is the mountain range that begins with foothills in the west and runs through the center of the island to the high eastern peaks. The Blue Mountains are higher than any other in the eastern half of North America. The mountainous terrain of this beautifully rich country accounts for Jamaica's stunning waterfalls and striking rocky coastline. The climate varies from tropical and humid at sea level to temperate in the mountains. Rainfall is seasonal, May to November, with marked variations.

Tourism Characteristics

Tourism started in Jamaica in 1905 at Port Antonio. Many of the early tourists were English visiting the beautiful tropical resort. The continued growth in tourism has been important as Jamaica's other industries have declined. North America dominates tourism trade to Jamaica, accounting for 75 percent of all arrivals, with the United States alone accounting for 64.2 percent. Tourism from the United Kingdom is growing and becoming more important. This is reflected in the increased number of flights from London by British Airways. The Ministry of Mining, Energy, and Tourism has not been successful in developing new source markets due to the lack of direct air service to major markets such as Japan, Scandinavia, and Latin America. Jamaica's

principle ports of Ocho Rios and Montego Bay are popular cruise ship stops. Today tourism is the largest earner of foreign exchange and the island's major employer.

Tourist Destinations and Attractions

An important attraction in Jamaican trade has been the development of the all-inclusive resorts modeled after the Club Med style, where one price includes the entire cost of the holiday from food and accommodations to water sports and drinks.

The Montego Bay–Negril region is Jamaica's principle tourist center and has an international airport. Around Montego Bay, there are beautiful coastlines of white sand beaches and deep blue water, which provide for all types of water activities year-round. The majority of its hotel and motel rooms are in this area. The second major resort area is Ocho Rios, which is on a sheltered bay. It claims some of the best beaches on the islands and is a popular stop for cruise ships. Near Ocho Rios are the beautiful Fern Gully and two falls, Roaring River Falls and Dunn's River Falls, where visitors can be seen climbing through the waterfalls enjoying the cool fresh water, Figure 4–11.

Courtesy Danielle Hayes

Figure 4–11 Dunn's River Falls in Jamaica

The third area is around Port Antonio, cradled between the Blue Mountains and the shores of the Caribbean Sea. It is the home of actor Errol Flynn. He was reported to have said that Port Antonio was among the most beautiful places known. West of the town near Buff Bay is Crystal Springs, a nature reserve home to 23,000 orchids and hundreds of tropical birds. It is the island's oldest tourist area, and its beaches are less crowded than the two more popular resorts at Montego Bay and Ocho Rios. It also has good fishing. However, one of the major attractions is in the mountains, where visitors ride two-person bamboo rafts down the rapids of the Rio Grande to a

point on the coast near Port Antonio. Southeast of town is Nonsuch Caves at Athenry Gardens, with lovely stalagmites, stalactites, and fossilized sponges.

Kingston, the capital and largest city, is located on the southern coast. It receives few tourists, but does have some museums with historical relics of the Arawak culture. A number of old homes and villages throughout the island are open to visitors. These include Spanish Town, the former capital, with historical reminders of the English and the Spanish. Rose Hall and Greenwood, two great houses, are near Montego Bay.

Puerto Rico

Capital: San Juan
Government: Commonwealth of the United States
Size: 2,515 square miles (about half the size of New Jersey)
Language: Spanish and English
Ethnic Division: Hispanic
Religion: 85% Roman Catholic, 15% Protestant and other
Tourist Season: Year-round
Peak Tourist Season: December to May
Currency: United States dollar

 TRAVEL TIPS

Entry: No visa or passport required for United States citizens.
Transportation: Excellent airline connections to and from Puerto Rico. Puerto Rico is the Caribbean hub for American Airlines®. Public transportation by bus is available and provides good service in all major towns. Públicos (non-scheduled, five-passenger cars) serve much of the island.
Shopping: Local items of hand-carved wooden religious figures, tortoiseshell, embroidery, jewelry, ceramics, woven hammocks, and fine cigars. Also a musical instrument similar to a 12-string guitar called a *cuatros* and hand–screened fabrics are popular items.

CULTURAL CAPSULE

The population of Puerto Rico is over 95 percent Hispanic. The official languages are Spanish and English with Spanish the most heavily used. Eighty-five percent of the population are Roman Catholics, and Catholic traditions and customs prev

Cultural Hints:
- Handshake when greeting.
- Improper to beckon with palm facing up. Turn palm down.
- Do not toss or throw objects at another person. Hand them.
- American gestures are recognized and used.
- Eating and foods:
  Both hands should remain above the table.
  Summon waiters with a "psst" sound.
  Puerto Rican food dishes are Spanish in character. Common foods are rice and beans, arroz con pollo (chicken and rice), paella (includes shrimp, mussels, lobster, and other seafood), suckling pig roasted on a spit, fish, and chicken barbecue.

Physical Characteristics

The interior of Puerto Rico consists of old volcanic mountains. The northern part is a karst area, which has resulted in a series of small steep hills and deep holes. The mountains are surrounded by coastal plains, which are cooled on the Atlantic side by winds. The climate is warm and sunny with some rain each month.

Tourism Characteristics

Puerto Rico has a strong tourist industry because of its political ties, and accessibility, to the United States. It receives more visitors than any other island in the Caribbean. Almost 70 percent of its visitors are from the United States. Europe accounts for only 3.3 percent of the market. A large number of former Puerto Ricans residing in the United States return to visit friends and relatives. The excellent airline connections (it is the major hub for American Airlines in the Caribbean), the common use of English, and the climate are also important factors to the large number of visitors. It also has become a major cruise center ranking fourth in cruise passenger arrivals in 1994.

Tourist Destinations and Attractions

San Juan, the oldest city under the United States flag, is both the capital and the principal tourist center in Puerto Rico. Its main attraction is its Spanish culture. San Juan is one of the oldest cities in the Western Hemisphere, with narrow, shaded streets, Spanish-style architecture, and beautiful patios and gardens. Many of the old houses have been restored and now serve as museums. Others have been whitewashed and decorated with an intricate lacing of black wrought iron to provide tourists with a view of the area when it was the commercial, governmental, and major residential area in its early history. All of these cluster around the large fortress to offer the traveler days of great scenic enjoyment. Two of the most dominant features of San Juan are the two forts of El Morro and San Cristóbal. El Morro, completed in 1785, is an impressive fortress guarding the entrance to the harbor, Figure 4–12. Fort San Cristóbal was begun in the seventeenth century to protect San Juan from land attacks. It is larger than El Morro and provides magnificent views from its ramparts and gun emplacements. La Fortaleza, the Governor's Palace, was built between 1533 and 1540 as a fortress and later expanded. The Institute of Culture restores and renovates all buildings. There are a number of excellent museums of art and history.

Puerto Rico has a number of excellent resorts, such as Luquilla Beach and the Dorado area, which have outstanding facilities and excellent water. All types of sports, including horseback riding, swim-

Figure 4–12 Fort El Morro, Puerto Rico

ming, fishing, and snorkeling, are found in abundance on and around the island. Combined with the water sports Puerto Rico has been a golfing mecca with world-famous courses.

El Yunque National Forest is a tropical rain forest complete with a large species of birds and varieties of trees. It is one of the most luxuriant rain forests in the world, with giant ferns, exotic trees, wild orchids, green vines, brilliantly colored parrots, and scenic waterfalls.

Ponce, the second largest city, has a fine art museum, and its ancient firehouse (Parque de Bombas), is the most photographed site in Puerto Rico. Near Ponce is Phosphorescent Bay, where the slightest movement sets the water sparkling. San Germán, the second oldest town (1573) on the island, still has preserved its Spanish colonial atmosphere.

LESSER ANTILLES

The Lesser Antilles are the United States Virgin Islands, British Virgin Islands, Anguilla, Antigua, Barbuda, St. Kitts-Nevis, French Antilles, Martinique, Guadeloupe, Netherlands Antilles, Windward Islands, Dominica, St. Lucia, St. Vincent and the Grenadines, and Grenada.

United States Virgin Islands

Physical Characteristics

The Virgin Islands are a group of small islands between Puerto Rico and the *Leeward* islands. The terrain is mostly mountainous, with many beaches

and bays. The climate is subtropical, tempered by easterly trade winds. There is little seasonal temperature variation, with the rainy season from May to November.

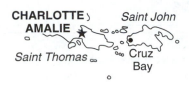

20 km

North Atlantic Ocean

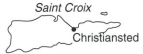

Caribbean Sea

Saint Croix

Christiansted

TRAVEL TIPS

Entry: No visa or passport required.
Transportation: Excellent airline access to North America and other Caribbean nations. Inter-island connections can be made by both air and water.
Shopping: Popular items are liquor, linens, imported china, crystal, jewelry, hand–painted batik, and hook bracelets.

CULTURAL CAPSULE

The majority of the population is a mixture of West Indian (74 percent born in the Virgin Islands and elsewhere in the West Indies). Minorities are Puerto Ricans and United States mainland people who have moved to the Virgin Islands. English is the official language, but Spanish and Creole are widely spoken. In 1992, the islands celebrated the seventy-fifth anniversary of their transfer from Denmark to the United States for $25 million.

Cultural Hints:
- Greeting is a handshake and smile.
- American gestures are understood.
- Eating and foods:
  Keep both hands above the table.
  Typical dishes are fish soups, fungi (spiced cornmeal paste), turtle, kalaloo (a spinach-type soup), gundy (herring balls), and soursop (a local fruit and cream).

Capital Charlotte Amalie, St. Thomas
Government: United States Territory
Size: 133 square miles (about twice the size of Washington, D.C.)
Language: English, Spanish, Creole
Ethnic Division: 80% Black, 15% United States mainland, 5% other.
Religion: 42% Baptist, 34% Roman Catholic, 17% Episcopalian
Tourist Season: Year-round
Peak Tourist Season: January through March
Currency: United States dollar

Tourism Characteristics

Tourism is very important to the Virgin Islands as almost all of their income comes from tourism. They have a strong tourist industry with excellent airline and cruise connections to the United States. The number of cruise visitors to the Virgin Islands is exceeded only by the Bahamas, averaging 5 million in the 1990s. There is a well-developed infrastructure to provide all services required by visitors. Visitors from the United States represent nearly 84 percent of all tourists. The Virgin Islands were damaged by hurricanes in 1995 and 1996.

Tourist Destinations and Attractions

The duty-free shops (rum, jewelry, and cigarettes are popular items) in Charlotte Amalie on St. Thomas can be crowded, especially when more than two cruise ships are in port at one time, which is common. The town was built by Danes, and visitors can see old Danish houses, picturesque churches, and one of the oldest synagogues in the western hemisphere. The well-known beaches of Magens Bay and Sapphire are active and noisy at times. However, the real St. Thomas is secluded beaches, endless vistas, and restaurants ensconced in Danish manor homes. It's a world of water sports, tennis (at least eight hotels have their own courts), and golf.

St. John, five miles east of St. Thomas, is, in part, a United States National Park. It has a number of hiking trails. The pace is much slower than at St. Thomas. St. John has a unique water snorkeling trail that is maintained by the national park. St. Croix, which is thirty-five miles south of St. John, has a number of restored sugar mills and museums that remind the visitor of the Danish rule. The two major towns are Christiansted, which is the old Danish capital, and Frederiksted. The focal point in Christiansted is the old town square and waterfront area, with its shops and restaurants. The red-roofed pastel houses found throughout Christiansted are reminders of the Danes. Seventeen miles from Christiansted, Frederiksted is best noted for its charming gingerbread architecture.

British Virgin Islands

Anegada

North Atlantic Ocean

Jost Van Dyke

ROAD TOWN ★

Tortola

Virgin Gorda

Caribbean Sea

Capital: Road Town
Government: British dependent territory
Size: 59 square miles (about the same as Washington, D.C.)
Language: English
Ethnic Division: 90% African ancestry
Religion: Majority Methodist
Tourist Season: December through March
Peak Tourist Season: December through March
Currency: United States dollar

 TRAVEL TIPS

Entry: No visa required for visits up to three months. Proof of citizenship, sufficient funds, and evidence of onward transportation are required.
Transportation: Connections with North America through San Juan and other Caribbean nations. Direct flights from London. There is both air and water service between islands. Taxis and car rentals are available.
Shopping: The best items are art, jewelry, and clothing.

CULTURAL CAPSULE

The population is dominantly black (90 percent) with minorities of Asian and white. Language is English, and there is a mixture of religious groups, mostly Protestant (86 percent).

Cultural Hints:
- Greeting with a handshake.
- American gestures are understood.
- Do not use the V for victory with palm facing you.
- Eating and food:
  Keep hands above table.
  Typical dishes are seafood and local West Indian dishes.

Physical Characteristics

The British Virgin Islands are a chain of lush, mountainous coral and volcanic islands with beaches, coral reefs, grottos, and caverns. The climate is warm to hot tropical, year round. However, it is tempered by trade winds from November through April.

Tourism Characteristics

Sixty-six percent of all visitors come from North America, with the United States accounting for nearly 63 percent. The British Virgin Islands have good connections with other Caribbean islands. They have a small number of cruise visitors compared to the United States Virgin Islands.

Tourist Destinations and Attractions

Of the approximately 60 islands in the British Virgin Islands, the population and tourism are concentrated on Tortola and Virgin Gorda along with the groups of Anegada and Jost Van Dyke. Tortola has a rain forest with superb walking tours. The Baths on Virgin Gorda is a coastal area where boulders as big as houses have fallen together to form grottoes, caverns, and pools. The British Virgin Islands have some excellent snorkeling, diving, and cruising.

Anguilla, Antigua, Barbuda, and St. Kitts-Nevis

Physical Characteristics

The climate is tropical with little seasonal variation. The rainy season is from May to November. Frequent hurricanes occur from July to October. The tropical heat is moderated by the trade winds. The terrain is mostly low-lying limestone and coral islands with some higher volcanic areas on Antigua and Barbuda. The islands of St. Kitts and Nevis are volcanic with mountainous interiors. Anguilla is a low, flat coral island.

Barbuda

Caribbean Sea

SAINT JOHN'S ★   *Antigua*

Redonda

Anguilla

Capital: The Valley
Government: Dependent Territory of United Kingdom
Size: 35 square miles (1/2 the size of Washington, D.C.)
Language: English
Ethnic Division: African
Religion: Protestant Methodist
Tourist Season: December through April
Peak Tourist Season: December through March
Currency: East Caribbean dollar

Antigua and Barbuda

Capital: St. John's
Government: Parliamentary Democracy
Size: 170 square miles (2.5 times the size of Washington, D.C.)
Language: English
Ethnic Division: African
Religion: Anglican
Tourist Season: December through April
Peak Tourist Season: December through March
Currency: East Caribbean dollar

St. Kitts-Nevis

Capital: Basseterre
Government: Constitutional Monarchy
Size: 104 square miles (1.5 times the size of Washington, D.C.)
Language: English
Ethnic Division: African
Religion: Anglican
Tourist Season: December through April
Peak Tourist Season: December through March
Currency: East Caribbean dollar

 ## TRAVEL TIPS

Entry: Proof of citizenship. Evidence of onward ticket.
Transportation: Direct from London and Frankfurt, Germany and connections through San Juan and the U.S. Virgin Islands. Taxis are the best transport on the islands. Car rentals available.
Health: Concern for yellow fever.
Shopping: Local items of interest are straw hats, baskets, batik, pottery, and hand-printed cotton clothing.

CULTURAL CAPSULE

The peoples of the Leeward Islands are dominantly African with a small minority of British and Portuguese in Antigua and Barbuda. All speak English and are Protestant, mainly Anglican.

Cultural Hints:
- Shake hands when greeting.
- American gestures are recognized.
- Eating and food:
  Wave hand to call waiter.
  Keep hands above table.
  Seafoods are the main dishes. Lobster and some West Indian curry are common specialties.

Tourism Characteristics

Anguilla, Antigua and Barbuda, and St. Kitts Nevis are all part of the Leeward Islands. They have a common English-speaking background and are all well-endowed with beaches and water sports. Anguilla has quite unspoiled and nearly deserted dazzling white beaches, clear turquoise water, and colorful undersea gardens. Recently it is becoming the playground for the royalty and wealth of Britain.

The United States is the largest single generator of visitors, accounting for 34 percent of visitors. The peak season accounts for approximately 45 percent of all visitors from December to March. Concern is being expressed because of the fragile ecosystems of the sandy beaches. The lack of adequate development controls allows many new accommodation projects to be built on the beachfront.

Travel Destinations and Attractions

Antigua also has white sandy beaches and the Restored Nelson's Dockyard at English Harbor where Admiral Lord Nelson dropped anchor. Antigua is more lively than Anguilla in that it has gambling casinos and luxurious resorts. Barbuda, a small island forty miles to the north, is a coral island with sandy beaches but little tourism development.

The two-island nation of St. Kitts-Nevis is located west of Antigua. It is a member of the West Indies Associated States and the British Commonwealth. St. Kitts is a mountainous island with both black and white sand beaches. Nevis offers golden-sand beaches and snorkeling on the coral reef. Both St. Kitts and Nevis are trying to expand their tourism and have encouraged cruise ships to add the island to their ports of call with little success.

FRENCH ANTILLES

The French Caribbean Islands consist of Martinique and Guadeloupe and its offshore islands of Marie Galante, Les Saintes, La Desirade, Saint Barthelemy, and St. Martin. These islands are represented by officials in the French Parliament. The tourism industry to the French Caribbean is dominated by visitors from France because of cultural ties.

TRAVEL TIPS

Entry: Passport and onward or return transportation ticket.
Transportation: Airline connections through San Juan and direct from Paris.
Shopping: Local handcraft items such as wood carvings, madras table linens, island dolls, finely woven straw baskets and hats, salako hats made of split bamboo, Creole gold jewelry, tapestries, and slave bracelets are popular.

CULTURAL CAPSULE

The people are dominantly African, African-Caucasian-Indian mixture, East Indian, Caucasian, and some Chinese. The language is French and Creole. Religion is overwhelmingly Roman Catholic.

Culture Hints:
- Greeting by a handshake.
- Eating and food:
  Keep both hands above the table.
  Eating is a combination of French and Creole especially with seafood. Stuffed baby crabs, sea urchins, baby clams, langoustines (prawns), calalou (a green herb soup), and colombo (a spicy meat and rice dish).

Physical Characteristics

The terrain is mountainous with indented coastline. The climate is tropical, with the rainy season occurring between June and October.

Tourist Destinations and Attractions

Fort-de-France is a major port of call for cruise vessels in the Caribbean. It is similar in character to New Orleans and boasts of being the birthplace of Napoleon's wife, the Empress Josephine. The Martinique Museum contains material found from the Arawak and Carib period. It has a colorful market and a popular artisan center that visitors from the cruise ships enjoy.

Martinique

Capital: Fort-de-France
Government: Overseas Department of France
Size: 425 square miles (slightly smaller than Rhode Island)
Language: French, Creole
Ethnic Division: 90% African and African-Caucasian-Indian mixture, 5% European, less than 5% East Indian, Lebanese, and Chinese
Religion: 95% Roman Catholic, 5% Hindu and pagan African
Tourist Season: Year-round
Peak Tourist Season: December (10%)
Currency: French franc

Guadeloupe

St Martin and St. Barthélemy are not shown.

Capital: Basse-Terre
Government: Overseas Department of France
Size: 687 square miles (about half the size of Rhode Island)
Language: French, Creole
Ethnic Division: 90% Black or Mulatto, 5% European, less than 5% East Indian, Lebanese, and Chinese

Religion: 95% Roman Catholic, 5% Hindu and pagan African
Tourist Season: Year-round
Peak Tourist Season: December
Currency: French franc

Physical Characteristics

Guadeloupe is volcanic, but landforms include low limestone formations. Guadeloupe is surrounded by the small islands La Desirade, Marie Galante, and Les Saintes. The climate is subtropical tempered by trade winds, but is still relatively humid.

Tourist Destinations and Attractions

Pointe-à-Pitre is the major port and commercial center. It has a picturesque harbor with a colorful central marketplace. On Grande-Terre, away from Pointe-à-Pitre, the most important attractions are the ruins of the eighteenth-century fortress, Fort Fleur d'Epee; Gosier, the resort center; and Sainte-Anne, a popular beach resort.

Basse-Terre is a port town of narrow streets and well-planned squares with palm and tamarind trees offering a picturesque setting between the sea and the high volcano. It has a seventeenth-century cathedral and the ruins of Fort St. Charles.

The outer islands of Guadeloupe are some of the prettiest in the West Indies. They have a number of excellent beaches and unique fishing villages such as those of the Breton fisherman.

Netherlands Antilles

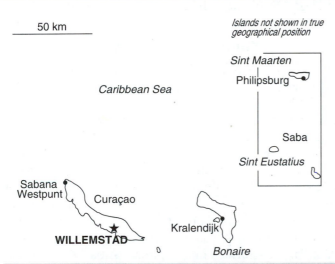

Capital: Willemstad
Government: Parliamentary Federal Democracy (In 1986, Aruba was granted separate status. It will be fully independent in 1996.)
Size: 309 square miles (six small islands)
Language: Dutch, French, Spanish, English
Ethnic Division: 85% mixed African ancestry; others include European, Latin, and Oriental
Religion: Predominantly Roman Catholic
Tourist Season: Year-round
Peak Tourist Season: December through March
Currency: Antillean guilder (Aruba: Aruban florins)

Physical Characteristics

The Netherlands Antilles are the islands of Aruba, Bonaire, and Curacao (*the ABC Islands*), St. Eustatius, Saba, and the southern part of St. Maarten. The ABC Islands are off the coast of Venezuela and are considered part of the Leeward Islands, while the other three are part of the Windward Islands.

The ABC Islands are mostly flat with some hills. Saba is an extinct volcano. The climate of the ABC Islands is tropical marine with little seasonal temperature variation. The three Windward Islands have tropical climates moderated by the trade winds of the Atlantic.

TRAVEL TIPS

Entry: Visas not required for stays up to fourteen days. May be extended to three months. Proof of citizenship and onward or return ticket. May ask for evidence of sufficient funds for stay.
Transportation: Airline connections are available from San Juan, Caracas, and other Caribbean countries. There is a tax on arrival or departure.
Shopping: Most items are imported and are an excellent buy.

CULTURAL CAPSULE

The population on Aruba is mixed European/Caribbean Indian, while Bonaire and Curacao are mainly African with minorities of Carib Indian, European, Latin, and Oriental. Some 40 nationalities are represented in the Netherlands Antilles and Aruba, but the mixture varies from island to island. Dutch is the official language, but Papiamento, a Spanish-Portuguese-Dutch-English Creole dialect predominates. English is widely spoken.

Tourism Characteristics

Aruba, Curacao, and St. Maarten have the most tourists and the best-developed tourist industry. The other three are more relaxed and offer a slower pace. Constant sunshine combined with unique scenic surprises give the islands considerable tourist potential. However, growth will be somewhat limited because of the location of the islands off the coast of Venezuela. Tourism competes with oil refining as the major generator of foreign income. There are several oil refineries scattered through the islands, taking advantage of the oil production in Venezuela.

Aruba was originally named "Oro Uba" by the Spanish conquistadors. To help solve the high unemployment problem, which is compounded by crop failures, the government of Aruba has developed an aggressive tourism promotion program. It focuses on the North American market.

Tourist Destinations and Attractions

Aruba has two locations considered to be both picturesque and good for surfers at Andicouri and Dos Playas. Palm Beach is a broad, white beach. The countryside is picturesque, with cactus fences, Aruban cottages, bougainvillea, oleanders, flamboyant hibiscus, and other tropical plants. Oranjestad, the capital of Aruba, is a free-port town, with some Dutch character expressed in a few of the homes.

On Curacao, Willemstad, which has an outstanding harbor, provides many examples of Dutch architecture in pastel colors, rococo gables, arcades, and bulging columns on homes, shops, and government buildings. The Dutch colony house of Willemstad is a prime example of this unique Dutch architecture. Other buildings of interest are the Mikve Israel Emanuel synagogue, probably the oldest in the Western Hemisphere; an eighteenth-century Protestant church; the Governor's Palace; and the Curacao Museum. The Floating Market is a unique market comprised of Venezuelan, Colombian, and other schooners in the small canal leading to the Waaigat.

Bonaire (Flamingo Island), one of the most beautiful islands in the Caribbean, is only beginning to awaken to its potential as a tourist center. The coral reefs surrounding Bonaire rank it just behind the Caymans and Cozumel for diving and snorkeling. The beaches and water sports are the main attractions. The capital, Kralendijk, has little to offer the tourist other than a folklore museum.

St. Maarten's slogan "Two for the price of one" stresses the two cultures of the island, French (Saint Martin) and Dutch (Sint Maarten), complete with architecture and cuisine, set amid white beaches and tropical blossoms. The international airport and most of the tourist development is on the Dutch side of the island. St. Maarten, a historical townhouse in Philipsburg and the capital of the Dutch side, is a popular shopping area for visitors from cruise ships.

The island of Saba is unique in that it has no beaches, but rises 2,900 feet from the ocean to its large volcanic mountain top. The principal population center and capital, The Bottom, is inside the crater of the volcano. In spite of the lack of beaches, Saba is a major attraction with its scuba diving, cool climate, and beautiful environment of flowers and trees.

St. Eustatius (Statia) is quiet and mostly visited on day trips from St. Maarten. It has a few historical sites, including a Jewish synagogue, a Reformed Church, and Fort Oranje, which is the seat of the government.

Other Windward Islands

The rest of the Windward Islands are small and have had English connections. All have their major tourist season between January and March, with February being the peak tourist season. From April to December, the climate is hotter than in the Leeward Islands. However, the climate is somewhat moderated by the trade winds. The weather between June and October is particularly unpredictable. The terrain is generally mountainous, with a considerable portion volcanic. The Windward Islands are small, ranging from slightly larger than Washington, D.C., to considerably smaller than Rhode Island. The people are mostly of African ancestry, and the Roman Catholic religion dominates although there are some Anglican, Methodist, and Seventh-Day Adventist groups. English is the official language, with some French spoken throughout the islands. All the islands use the East Caribbean dollar. They are all dependent upon tourism and continue seeking methods to increase visitor numbers.

Dominica

Tourist Destinations and Attractions

Dominica, the largest of the Windward Islands, has one of the least developed tourist industries in the region. It is mountainous and rugged, with a tropical jungle and few settlements to support tourism. Dominica is popular with day trippers from Guadeloupe and Martinique. As the largest and most mountainous

Windward Island, it has a number of hiking trails, dramatic scenery, lush forests, waterfalls, orchids, and other wild plants. The remnants of the original inhabitants live on the Carib Reserve. Other attractions are the market in Roseau, the capital, and the ruins of the eighteenth-century Fort Shirley near Portsmouth. Straw goods are popular in Dominica.

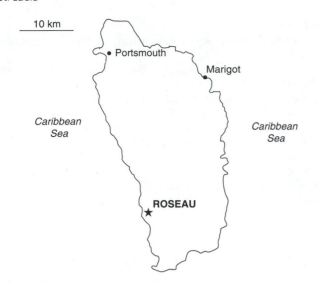

Capital: Roseau
Government: Independent Member of the British Commonwealth
Size: 290 square miles (about four times the size of Washington, D.C.)
Language: English (official), French patois widely spoken
Ethnic Division: Mostly African ancestry with some Caribs
Religion: 77% Roman Catholic, 15% Protestant
Tourist Season: December through April
Peak Tourist Season: December through March
Currency: East Caribbean dollar

St. Lucia

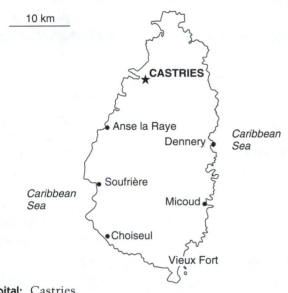

Language: English (official), French patois widely used
Ethnic Division: 90% African ancestry, 3.8% East Indian
Religion: 90% Roman Catholic, 10% Protestant
Tourist Season: December through April
Peak Tourist Season: December through March
Currency: East Caribbean dollars

Tourist Destinations and Attractions

St. Lucia combines outstanding water sports utilizing great beaches and warm sea and sunshine with some of the best mountain scenery in the Caribbean islands. The twin peaks of Piton are beautiful and scaled by experienced climbers. A volcano provides a visitor with views of pools of boiling water, sulfur baths, and steam venting from the volcano. Castries, the capital, was rebuilt after a fire in 1948. It is on a natural harbor with beautiful mountains in the background. It has an excellent market and an old fortress. The beach resorts are near Castries.

Capital: Castries
Government: Independent Member of the British Commonwealth
Size: 240 square miles (slightly less than 3.5 times the size of Washington, D.C.)

St. Vincent and the Grenadines

Tourist Destinations and Attractions

St. Vincent, known as the "Breadfruit Island," is a picturesque island with fishing villages, coconut groves, and fields of arrowroot. Kingstown, the capital, is on a sheltered bay and has the famous Botanical Gardens with the first breadfruit tree, which was planted by Captain Bligh of the *Bounty*.

St. Vincent has some excellent beaches, most of which have the black sand that is common around volcanic islands. The mountains provide scenic drives with lush valleys and sea views.

The Grenadines (some are administered by Grenada and some by St. Vincent) are composed of over one hundred islands and are particularly good for yachting, fishing, and snorkeling. Carriacou and Petit

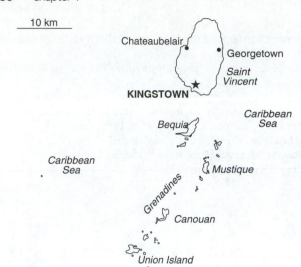

Capital: Kingstown
Government: Independent State within British Commonwealth
Size: 132 square miles (slightly less than twice the size of Washington, D.C.)
Language: English with some French patois
Ethnic Division: African ancestry with some Caucasian, East Indian, and Carib Indian
Religion: Anglican, Methodist, Roman Catholic, Seventh-Day Adventist
Tourist Season: December through April
Peak Tourist Season: December through March
Currency: East Caribbean dollars

Martinique are the part of the Grenadines that are administered by Grenada. They are attractive sandy islands with good underwater reefs. Bequia and Mustique are the largest of the St. Vincent dependencies and receive the most tourists.

Grenada

Tourist Destinations and Attractions

St. George's, the capital, is one of the most picturesque towns of the Caribbean with terraces of pale, color-washed houses with red roofs. It blends the character of the French in typical eighteenth-century provincial houses with English Georgian architecture.

Grenada has some of the best beaches in the world. Grand Anse, a two-mile stretch of white sand beach, is considered one of the best in the world.

Capital: St. George's
Government: Independent State
Size: 1,323 square miles (slightly less than twice the size of Washington, D.C.)
Language: English with some French patois
Ethnic Division: African ancestry
Religion: Roman Catholic, some Anglican
Tourist Season: December through April
Peak Tourist Season: December through March
Currency: East Caribbean dollar

OTHER ISLANDS OF THE CARIBBEAN

Barbados

5 km

North Atlantic Ocean

• Speightstown

• Bathsheba

Caribbean Sea   ★ **BRIDGETOWN**   • The Crane

Capital: Bridgetown
Government: Independent State within the Commonwealth
Size: 166 square miles (about twice the size of Washington, D.C.)
Language: English
Ethnic Division: 80% African ancestry, 16% mixed, 4% European
Religion: 67% Protestant, 4% Roman Catholic, 29% other
Tourist Season: December through March
Peak Tourist Season: December and March
Currency: Barbados dollar

 TRAVEL TIPS

Entry: No visa required for up to three months. Proof of citizenship and onward or round-trip ticket.
Transportation: Airline connections through San Juan and London. There is either an arrival or a departure tax. Public transportation is good and consists of buses and taxis.
Shopping: Local goods including straw mats, custom-made clothing, coral jewelry, wood carvings, basket work, pottery, woven goods, and Barbados rum. Duty-free goods (particularly British woolens) are abundant.

CULTURAL CAPSULE

The original peoples of Barbados were Arawak and Carib Indians. The British settled in the 1600s and brought African slaves to the island. Today Africans dominate, with 80 percent of the population. The official language is English. Bajan, descendants of African slaves, also use a dialect that can be understood by English speakers. Seventy percent of the people are Anglican and a mixture of other religions.

Cultural Hints:
• Handshake and smile is a common greeting.
• Taxis and buses are called by waving the hand.

• Eating and food:
 Keep hands above table.
 Typical dishes are seafood (flying fish, lobster, shrimp, dorado, red snapper, turtle, tuna, and kingfish), cou cou (okra and corn meal), white sea urchin eggs, tropical fruits, pepperpot (a spicy stew), and jug-jug (Guinea corn and green peas).

Physical Characteristics

The island is relatively flat with a gentle rise to a central highland area. The climate is tropical, with the rainy season from June to November. It is the most easterly of the West Indies islands.

Tourism Characteristics

Barbados has one of the best-developed tourist industries and receives the largest number of tourists in the eastern Caribbean. The connectivity with the United Kingdom is strong, with a number of international flights between Barbados and London. Barbados is highly dependent upon tourism.

Tourist Destinations and Attractions

Barbados is probably the most typical English island, Figure 4–13. Standing near Trafalgar Square or on Bond Street in Bridgetown, you get the feeling that you are in London—but in a London with no fog, only sunshine. Bridgetown, the capital and center of tourism, has a number of excellent tourist attractions. The old part of town with wooden houses contrasts with the modern part of town. Other attractions are Broad Street, Independence Square, Nelson's statue, the Cathedral, and the Straw Market. There are some excellent beaches on the south and west coasts, where most of the tourism of the island is located.

Courtesy Peter Rothholz Associates

Figure 4–13 Sunbury Plantation, Barbados

Trinidad and Tobago

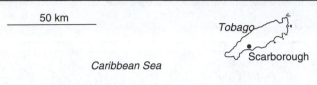

Foods are mixture of English, American French, Indian, or Chinese.
Some popular Creole dishes are callaloo soup, stewed tatoo (armadillo), crab backs, fried iguanas or tum tum (mashed green plantains), and cascadura (freshwater fish).

Capital: Port of Spain
Government: Parliamentary Democracy
Size: 1,980 square miles (about the same as Delaware)
Language: English
Ethnic Division: 43% African ancestry, 40% East Indian, 14% Mixed, 1% White, 1% Chinese, 1% other Religion: 32.2% Roman Catholic, 24.3% Hindu, 14.4% Anglican, 14% Protestant, 6% Muslim, 9.1% unknown
Tourist Season: December through March
Peak Tourist Season: February (12%)
Currency: Trinidad and Tobago dollar

TRAVEL TIPS

Entry: Visas not required for stays up to two months. Proof of citizenship.
Transportation: Airline connections are through San Juan and Barbados. Public transportation is by bus and taxi.
Health: Concern for yellow fever. Check with local health officials. Do not drink water from an unknown source.
Shopping: Good buys are Asian and East Indian silks and cottons. Local crafts from straw and cane are also popular.

CULTURAL CAPSULE

The peoples of Trinidad and Tobago are mainly African or East Indian. Almost all speak English, ranging from standard British English to local dialects. Some speak Hindi, French patois, and several other dialects. The two major folk traditions are Creole (a mixture of African influenced by Spanish, French, and English culture) and East Indian.

Cultural Hints:
* Handshake is a common greeting.
* American gestures are understood.
* Eating and food:
  Keep hands above the table.

Physical Characteristics

The terrain is mostly plains with some hills and low mountains. The climate is tropical, with the rainy season occurring from June to December.

Tourism Characteristics

While Trinidad and Tobago have a well-established tourism industry, tourism is not as important to them as it is to other Caribbean islands because they have a stronger industrial base, including oil production and refining. Trinidad and Tobago had a total of nearly 265,000 arrivals in 1994. The United States accounts for some 37 percent of the arrivals. Canada ranks second, accounting for 12 percent. Seventeen percent visit for the purpose of business, indicating the importance of oil production and refining (Yearbook of Tourism Statistics, 1994).

Tourist Destinations and Attractions

Reflecting the Hindu culture that was imported with Indian laborers in the last century, Trinidad and Tobago surprise the eye with Hindu temples and Indian saris. The architectural mixture of English and Indian creates a unique landscape. Trinidad is the birthplace of the calypso, and the steel drum was first developed there. Carnival in February is one of the great festivals of the year and accounts for the large number of tourists visiting the island in that month, Figure 4–14.

Port of Spain, the capital, has a mixture of old wooden houses dotting the modern landscape. Important buildings of interest are the Red House, the Anglican Cathedral, Church of Holy Trinity, the Roman Catholic Cathedral, and a Hindu temple. A principal tourist site outside Port of Spain is Pitch Lake, which is about 110 acres of black tar. The beaches are not as good as on the other islands.

Tobago claims to be the island of Robinson Crusoe. The tradition and the beautiful setting of the island make it an interesting notion. It has a number

Courtesy Trinidad and Tobago Tourist Board

Figure 4–14 Las Cuevas Bay, Trinidad

of excellent beaches and fine snorkeling and swimming. Throughout the island, exotic tropical birds such as brown pelicans can be observed.

THE ATLANTIC ISLANDS

Although the island groups discussed here, particularly the Turks and Caicos Islands, the Bahamas, and Bermuda are physically part of the Atlantic, they are often included in programs and itineraries with the Caribbean.

Turks and Caicos Islands

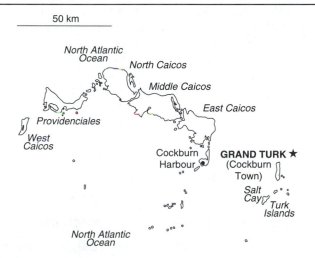

Capital: Grand Turk (Cockburn Town)
Government: British Dependent Territory
Size: 166 square miles (about two and one-half times the size of Washington, D.C.)
Language: English
Ethnic Division: Majority of African descent
Religion: Anglican, Baptist, Methodist, Seventh-Day Adventist, and others
Tourist Season: December through April
Peak Tourist Season: February (10%) and March (13%)
Currency: United States dollar

 TRAVEL TIPS

Entry: Proof of citizenship.
Transportation: Airlines access through Puerto Rico, the Bahamas, and British Virgin Islands. Local transportation is by bus and taxi.
Shopping: Baskets woven from local grasses and small metal products are the only native crafts available.

CULTURAL CAPSULE

The people of Turks and Caicos islands are mainly African who speak English. Religion is dominated by a Protestant mixture of Baptist, Methodists, Anglican, and Seventh-Day Adventists.

Eating is mostly in hotels, and specialties are mostly seafood.

Physical Characteristics

The Turks and Caicos Islands are located at the southeast end of the Bahamas about 575 miles from Florida. They consist of about thirty low-lying islands of which only eight are populated. Two of the populated islands, Grand Turk and Salt Cay, are part of the smaller Turks, while the other six are part of the larger Caicos group. They are South Caicos, Middle Caicos, North Caicos, East Caicos, West Caicos, and Providenciales. The terrain is low, with marshes and mangrove swamps on limestone rock. The climate is tropical, moderated by the trade winds.

Tourism Characteristics

Tourism and fishing for conch and crayfish are the major sources of income for the islands. However, they do not receive large numbers of visitors. Almost 80 percent of their visitors are from North America, with the United States accounting for some 68 percent of all visitors. They are reasonably accessible, with airline connections to Florida and the Bahamas and charter services to Europe.

Tourist Destinations and Attractions

Grand Turk is principally a resort island. A second international airport has been developed at Provo (East Caicos), and the government is developing that island as a resort center. It already has attracted such famous names as Club Med. In addition to the usual water sports, the area has some outstanding bonefishing waters.

The Bahamas

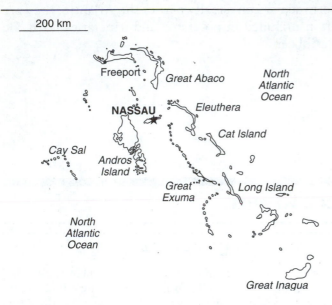

Capital: Nassau
Government: Independent Commonwealth of the United Kingdom
Size: 5,382 square miles (about the size of Connecticut)
Language: English, some Creole
Ethnic Division: 85% African ancestry, 15% White
Religion: 32% Baptist, 20% Anglican, 19% Roman Catholic, 24% other Protestant, 5% other
Tourist Season: November through August
Peak Tourist Season: March (12%)
Currency: Bahamian dollar

 TRAVEL TIPS

Entry: No visa required for visits up to 3 months. Proof of citizenship required. Evidence of onward or return transportation required.
Transportation: Excellent airline connections from North America. Also a major cruise destination. Public transportation is by bus and taxi.
Shopping: Local items include basketwork, conch-shell, and tortoiseshell souvenirs.

CULTURAL CAPSULES

The people of the Bahamas are of African ancestry who speak English and some Creole. The most distinctive food dishes are from the sea such as the conch (a shelled mollusk), boiled crawfish, green turtle pie (turtle meat baked in a shell with vegetables), and desserts of coconut and guava duff.

Physical Characteristics

The Bahamas consist of some 700 low-lying coral islands and two thousand cays. Only fifteen have been developed. The terrain consists of long, flat coral formations with some low, rounded hills. The climate is tropical marine, and the islands are bathed by the warm waters of the Gulf Stream.

Tourism Characteristics

The Bahamas have one of the strongest tourist industries in the region. It is close to Florida (only 60 miles from Miami) and has many cruise ships that either focus on the Bahamas or make stops as a major part of their program. The Bahamas receive by far the greatest number (nearly 2 million in the 1990s) of cruise passenger arrivals in the Caribbean region. Some 89 percent of the visitors are from North America, with the United States accounting for 82 percent of the total. Tourism and banking are the major sources of income for the Bahamas. Tourism now accounts for nearly 60 percent of the jobs on the islands.

Tourist Destinations and Attractions

The Bahamas, flamboyant next-door neighbors to the United States and a former British colony, boast a glorious year-round climate with brilliant sky and sea, lush vegetation, bright-feathered birds, vivid fish, and multicolored coral. The pomp and ceremony remaining from years as an English colony combine with the other attractions to draw many visitors to the islands.

The two major islands are New Providence and the Grand Bahamas. Nassau, the capital, and Paradise Island provide the visitor with all types of watersports, including fishing, skin diving, skiing, and boating. It has some attractive local architecture of white and pink houses, and houses built of limestone with wide wooden verandas. A fine aquarium near the unique Ardasta Gardens is the home of the famous trained flamingoes. On the harbor front is the Straw Market, Figure 4–15, which is constantly full of cruise passengers.

Courtesy Ministry of Tourism, Bahamas

Figure 4–15 Straw Market at Nassau

The Grand Bahamas is the nearest to the United States, and its casinos make it an attractive place to visit for a short stay for gaming. It has some of the best beaches in the Bahamas, as they face south and are protected from the northerly winds. Freeport is the major city and international airport. It has a number of attractions. Like Nassau, Freeport has an International Bazaar for duty-free shopping, a Museum of Underwater Exploration, and a central location for access to a number of fine beaches.

Bermuda

Capital: Hamilton
Government: British Dependent Territory
Size: 21 square miles (about one-third the size of Washington, D.C.)
Language: English
Ethnic Division: 61% Black, 39% European
Religion: 37% Anglican, 14% Roman Catholic, 10% African Methodist Episcopal (Zion), 6% Methodist, 5% Seventh-Day Adventist, 28% other
Tourist Season: March through October
Peak Tourist Season: May through August
Currency: Bermuda dollar

TRAVEL TIPS

Entry: Passport is required.
Transportation: Direct flights between Bermuda and New York and London. Cruise ships operate from April to November. Public transportation is by bus, which is usually crowded. Taxi service is available. A ferry service connects Hamilton with points across the harbor.
Shopping: In addition to British goods, local items include wood carvings, shell jewelry, copper enamel, basketwork, ceramic tiles, pottery, antiques, and angelfish and seahorse souvenirs.

CULTURAL CAPSULE

Nearly two-thirds of the Bermudians are of African descent. There are both Americans and Britons living in Bermuda. The language is English with a distinctive Bermudian accent. The Church of England predominates, though many other sects are represented. Most of Bermuda's food is imported, but there are local tropical fruits and vegetables. The specialty dish is cassava pie (pork and chicken in a pie crust made from the grated root of the cassava plant). Bermuda is quite expensive and formal. Formal attire for restaurants is a must.

Physical Characteristics

Bermuda is a group of some 150 islands and islets in the Western Atlantic about 600 miles east of Cape Hatteras, North Carolina. The main islands are connected by bridges. The terrain consists of low hills

Courtesy Bermuda Department of Tourism

Figure 4–16 Bermuda Roofs. The only source of drinking water on-island is rainwater. It is collected via stepped roofs constructed of quarried limestone.

Courtesy Bermuda Department of Tourism

Figure 4–17 St. George Alleyway. St. George is Bermuda's first capital.

separated by fertile depressions. The climate is subtropical. It is mild and humid in the summer, with strong winds and gales common in the winter.

Tourism Characteristics

Bermuda receives most of its income from tourism. It has developed excellent services and good airline connectivity. It also receives a number of cruise ships. Most of its visitors are from North America, accounting for 90.6 percent of all visitors, with the United States accounting for 81 percent of the total. Because it limits the number of automobiles, mopeds and motorbikes are quite popular.

Tourist Destinations and Attractions

The two major towns, St. George and Hamilton, are picturesque harbor towns in an English setting with a very quiet lifestyle. They are the center of tourism for Bermuda. Hamilton, the capital and major commercial center, houses the world's second oldest parliament and has a historical museum and the Flatts aquarium. There are excellent coastal sites nearby with deep tidal pools and a variety of wildlife. St. George, Figure 4–17, the capital from 1612 to 1815, is an interesting old-world town. St. Peter's Church is the oldest Anglican church in the Western Hemisphere. It also has a number of museums of interest.

WESTERN EXPLORER

Copper Canyon

1st DAY   ARRIVE LOS MOCHIS / EL FUERTE

On arrival at the Los Mochis airport, you will be transferred to the picturesque sixteenth-century colonial town of El Fuerte and the historic Villa del Pescador (or El Fuerte Lodge or Posada Hidalgo with fewer meals) for 2 nights. Dinner this evening will be served in your lodge's lush tropical courtyard.

2nd DAY   EL FUERTE–CEROCAHUI

Early morning transfer to the Chihuahua al Pacifico train depot for the dramatic 8,000 ft ascent up the Pacific Palisades (7:30 A.M.-12:15 P.M.). View the most spectacular segment of the railway in optimum daylight on this odyssey into the Sierra Madre, featuring fantastic bridges, tunnels, and switchbacks. On arrival, transfer to the Paradiso Del Oso Wilderness Lodge for 2 nights. Afternoon trek to Cueva de las Cruces, an Indian burial cave reached by a gradual uphill walk through a fertile valley that was an ancient agricultural site with the remains of stone trincheras used for terrace-style farming. All sightseeing with our native Cerocahui guide. 3 meals.

3rd DAY   CEROCAHUI

Morning departure on the Cerro del Gallego rim tour. Look down over 1 mile into the grandiose Urique Canyon, largest and deepest of the canyons in this mystical region, on an expedition that takes you past high mountain vistas and remote ranchos and includes a stop to visit cave-dwelling Tarahumara Indians. Also visit the seventeenth-century gold-domed Jesuit mission church and the Tarahumara school in Cerocahui. For the able-bodied, hike to a beautiful, secluded canyon waterfall. Optional Urique Canyon descent (extension of Gallego tour) and horseback riding available directly from lodge. 3 meals.

4th DAY   CEROCAHUI–DIVISADERO

Morning nature walk along a creek behind the lodge for a glimpse of the unique birds and flora native to this northern Mexico habitat. Afternoon train (12:20 P.M.-1:25 P.M.) to Divisadero. On arrival, transfer to the Mansion Tarahumara (or Posada Mirador—add $60 per person) for 2 nights. Embark on an orientation canyon rim walk viewing the breathtaking vistas of Copper and Taraecua canyons from the lodge's pristine setting. All sightseeing with our resident guide. 3 meals.

5th DAY   DIVISADERO

Enjoy a canyon rim drive (Mansion only) allowing you an opportunity to view and photograph the canyons from a variety of natural panoramic overlooks. For the able-bodied, hike into the canyon depths. Optional Creel/Cusarare tour and horseback riding available directly from lodge. 3 meals.

6th DAY   DIVISADERO–CHIHUAHUA CITY (or Los Mochis)

Trek to an inhabited Tarahumara Indian Cave before early afternoon transfer to depot for train to Chihuahua City (1:35 P.M.-8:50 P.M.). On arrival, transfer to Holiday Inn Suites or Hotel San Francisco. Breakfast and lunch.

7th DAY   DEPART CHIHUAHUA CITY (or Los Mochis)

Morning Chihuahua City tour (time permitting) including Pancho Villa's home/museum and other sites of interest. Afternoon transfer to airport. Optional executive-class motorcoach with transfer to El Paso also available. Breakfast.

Used by permission of Travel Columbus

REVIEW QUESTIONS

1. Discuss the climatic zones associated with altitude and their importance in terms of crops and population characteristics in Middle America.
2. What impact does climate have on tourism to the Caribbean? What aspect is most important? Why?
3. Describe the major cultures of the Middle American region and explain how they came to be.
4. What factors account for Mexico dominating travel to Middle America?
5. Describe the seven major tourist regions of Mexico. Which is the most important? Why?
6. Describe the life of Middle American Indians and their contributions to tourism in the area.
7. Which of the Middle American countries below Mexico has the greatest potential for tourism? Why?
8. Discuss three major factors for the low level of tourism to Middle America other than Mexico.
9. Why is tourism so important to the economies of the Caribbean countries?
10. Discuss four factors that account for the high number of tourists to the Caribbean.

GEOGRAPHY AND TOURISM IN
South America

CHAPTER 5

INTRODUCTION

Although South America has a great variety of tourist attractions, it attracts less than two percent of world tourists, Table 5–1. Only Africa south of the Sahara Desert receives less. Tourists to South America also stay for a short amount of time, averaging only 4.2 days. Visitors to many South American countries are more often visiting for business than visitors to other regions in the world.

The region has only a small number of visitors in spite of the fact that it has magnificent scenery, outstanding beaches, excellent skiing, picturesque towns, cities of great cultural diversity, and *archaeological* sites as impressive as any in the world.

There are several factors that account for South America's failure to attract tourists. First, the tourism industry is largely underdeveloped. Second, it is far from the main tourist-generating countries of the world, North America and Europe. Third, there are a number of countries that are both closer to Canada and the United States and less expensive to visit than South America. These other countries offer some of the same general attractions as South America and are located between North and South America (*intervening opportunities*). Fourth, potential tourists may perceive the service in South America as poor and many areas as unsafe. This has become more of concern today with the problems of drugs and drug wars in Colombia and guerilla movements in Perú. Indi-

Figure 5–1   South America

Table 5–1 International Tourism to South America

Country	Number of Visitors (thousands)		1996 Receipts (millions of US $)	1996 Average Expenses per Visit (US $)
	1986	1996		
Argentina	1,600	4,286	4,572	1,067
Bolivia	133	375	160	427
Brazil	1,934	2,210	2,273	1,028
Chile	547	1,450	889	613
Colombia	732	1,450	864	596
Ecuador	306	500	281	562
French Guiana	N/A	N/A	N/A	N/A
Guyana	67	102	46	451
Paraguay	371	418	236	565
Perú	303	515	535	1,039
Suriname	20	21	14	666
Uruguay	1,168	2,152	599	278
Venezuela	317	621	846	1,362

viduals traveling alone are cautioned to be careful as they may be suspected of being involved in drug movement in addition to being caught in the middle of drug raids. With political problems in a number of countries such as Perú, travelers are reluctant to travel in and to South America.

Although most travelers to the countries of South America come from the other countries of South America, many still come from outside the region. The United States is the single most important tourist source country outside of South America. There are also some important European linkages that account for foreign tourists, such as linkages between Germany and Bolivia, Paraguay and Brazil, the Dutch and Suriname, and Italy and Argentina.

LANDFORMS

The physical landscape of South America can be broadly described as one dominated by three mountain or plateau regions and three river basins, Figure 5–2.

The Cordillera of the Andes

The *Andes* is one of the greatest mountain chains in the world, stretching from Venezuela to the southernmost regions of Argentina and Chile. In places in Bolivia the range is over 200 miles in width, and many mountains exceed 20,000 feet in elevation. Mixed in the folded and faulted mountains are three active

POPULATION CHARACTERISTICS, 1997

Country	Population (millions)	Annual Growth Rate (percent)	Time To Double Pop. (years)	Per Capita GNP	Life Exp. (years)	Daily Calorie Supply	Percent Urban
Argentina	35.6	1.2	56	8,030	72	3,113	87
Bolivia	7.8	2.6	27	800	60	1,916	58
Brazil	160.3	1.4	48	3,640	67	2,751	76
Chile	14.6	1.5	46	4,160	72	2,581	86
Colombia	37.4	2.1	33	1,910	70	2,598	70
Ecuador	12.0	2.3	30	1,390	69	2,531	59
French Guiana	0.2	2.5	27	N/A	76	2,900	N/A
Guyana	0.8	1.7	40	590	63	2,384	31
Paraguay	5.1	2.8	25	1,690	69	2,757	50
Perú	24.4	2.2	32	2,310	67	2,186	70
Suriname	0.4	2.0	35	880	70	2,547	49
Uruguay	3.2	0.8	85	5,170	72	2,653	90
Venezuela	22.6	2.1	33	3,020	72	2,582	85

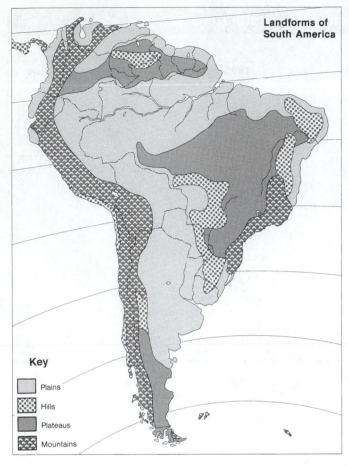

Figure 5–2 Landforms of South America

volcano groups—in southern Colombia and Ecuador, in middle and southern Perú and along the border of Bolivia and Chile, and in southern central Chile.

The Plateaus of Brazil and Guiana

Northern Brazil and Guiana are dominated by old, crystalline plateaus that have been elevated and then eroded. The surface is very irregular, making transportation difficult. The elevations are still sufficient to modify the tropical climate, making them more attractive to human settlement.

The third region is in southern Brazil, a broad plateau composed of a lava flow, which is more resistant to erosion. Some of the outstanding waterfalls of South America are in this region where the water plunges over the edge of the steep lava formations.

The River Lowlands

Three large river systems drain eastward to the Atlantic. They are the Orinoco in the north, the *Amazon* basin in northern Brazil, and the Parana in south Brazil. The Parana is called the Río de Plata in Paraguay, Uruguay, and Argentina; but it is the same river.

CLIMATIC PATTERNS

Climatic patterns in South America are diverse and complex, Figure 5–3. The dominant climate feature is the tropical nature of the continent. A belt of tropical rain forest extends across the Amazon Basin. Savanna climates are found north and south of this tropical rain forest, while subtropical climates are located in the southern portions of Brazil and in Argentina. They are characterized by high temperatures throughout the year, with only the subtropical area of southern Brazil and northern Argentina having very rare periods of frost. None of the subtropical, tropical rain forest, or savanna climates experiences the extreme winter temperatures found in North America.

Figure 5–3 Climates of South America

The other climatic types of South America consist of a small area of Mediterranean climate in central Chile, a small area of marine west coast climate in southern Chile, and dry steppe and desert climates in Argentina, Paraguay, Northern Chile, and Perú. These dry climates, especially in Argentina, are important for livestock ranching, which was introduced by Europeans.

Climates in the Andes are modified by elevation, which geographers identify as distinct *altitudinal zonation*. The *tierra caliente* (hot land) is the lowest zone, extending to about three thousand feet elevation; the *tierra templada* (temperate lands) occupy a zone from about three to six thousand feet elevation; while the *tierra fría* (cold lands) are above six or seven thousand feet. Each zone is characterized by distinctive crops and human activity.

DIVISIONS OF SOUTH AMERICAN TOURISM

South America can be divided into three distinct physical and cultural regions that influence tourism: the Andes countries, including Venezuela, Colombia, Ecuador, Perú, Bolivia, and Chile; the middle-latitude countries of Argentina, Uruguay, and Paraguay; and Brazil, which by both its size and cultural distinctiveness is a region by itself.

The Andes Countries

The Andes countries are one of the most important tourist regions in South America because of their unique historical and cultural attractions. The people of the Andes differ in each climatic zone. The Indian and mestizo (mixed Indian and European ancestry) peoples are concentrated in the tierra fría (high altitudes), the European population is more highly concentrated in the moderate valleys and basins of the tierra templada zone, and a combination of Indians, mestizos, and descendants of African workers who were imported to exploit mineral and agricultural potential live in the tierra caliente of the lowlands. Ecuador, Perú, and Bolivia are less industrialized countries and share the major economic problems of other countries in Latin America. They have predominantly *Indian* populations, concentrated mostly in the highlands and engaged in farming. Social and economic problems, especially land ownership, have led to revolutions in all three countries. The richest country of the Andes is Venezuela. Its wealth primarily comes from oil deposits in the Lake Maracaibo region.

Venezuela

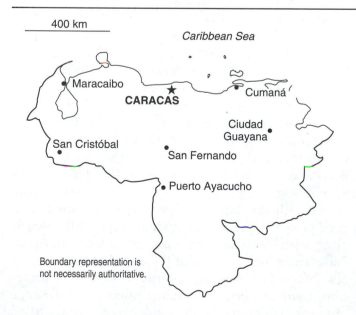

400 km

Caribbean Sea

Maracaibo

CARACAS

Cumaná

San Cristóbal

Ciudad Guayana

San Fernando

Puerto Ayacucho

Boundary representation is not necessarily authoritative.

Capital: Caracas
Government: Republic
Size: 352,142 square miles (twice the size of California)
Language: Spanish, Indian dialects in remote interior
Ethnic Division: 67% Mestizo, 21% European, 10% Black, 2% Indian
Religion: 96% Roman Catholic, 2% Protestant
Tourist Season: Year-round
Peak Tourist Season: February and March
Currency: Bolívar (VBO)

 TRAVEL TIPS

Entry: Passports and visas or tourist cards are required. Tourist cards can be obtained from airlines serving Venezuela.
Transportation: There is good access to Caracas from North America, Europe, and Trinidad and Tobago. Within the country transportation is by bus, taxi, or domestic air service. Caracas and other major cities have both buses and taxi-like automobiles that travel a regular route picking up and letting off passengers at any point.
Health: Concern for malaria, yellow fever, and cholera. Check with local health officials before travel.
Shopping: Best buys include Indian wall hangings, hammocks, hand-woven blankets, heavy wooden furniture, leather work, gold trinkets, wood carvings, and masks.

CULTURAL CAPSULE

Over 80 percent of the people of Venezuela live in urban areas. The majority of the population is mestizo (67 percent). In the coastal regions, there is a concentration of either Europeans (Spanish and Italian) or mulattoes (mixed European and Black). Some 10 percent of the population is Black and 2 percent is Indians. Although the people are mostly Roman Catholic, the church is somewhat less important than in other Latin American countries. Spanish is the official language, but English is required as a second language. It is not uncommon to hear Portuguese as well as a number of native languages.

Simón Bolívar, the South American liberator, was a Venezuelan. Consequently, most cities have a Plaza Bolívar near the city center. It is rude to behave disrespectfully in the plaza.

Cultural Hints:
- Greet and depart with a handshake.
- People stand close, and it is not polite to back away.
- Maintain good eye contact.
- Keep feet on floor when seated.
- Pointing with index finger is rude.
- Eating and food:
  Wait for all to be served before eating.
  It is not appropriate to eat on the street.
  Restaurants add a service charge, but an additional tip is expected.
  When finished eating, place utensils parallel and diagonally across your plate.
  Typical dishes are hot foods, casseroles, meat pies, stews, corn, rice, and pasta. Some specialties are arepa (a deep-fried, thick pancake filled with butter, meat, and cheese), punta-trasera (tender steak), and pabellón criollo (black beans, rice, shredded meat, and plantain).

Physical Characteristics

Venezuela can be divided into four distinct regions: the highlands of the Andes mountains along the Colombian border; the Maracaibo Lowlands around the fresh-water Lake Maracaibo; the central plains in the Llanos region; and the Guayana Highlands over the southeastern half of the country. The climate is hot and humid tropical in the lowland areas and more moderate in the highlands.

Tourism Characteristics

The government of Venezuela recognizes the importance of tourism. Since the world recession affected its oil sales by reducing revenue, tourism is considered a means of bringing in badly needed foreign exchange. To help do this, the government is encouraging the development of new hotels and resorts. The number of tourists is increasing, reaching 600,000 in 1996.

Good airline connections to the United States and Europe have resulted in the majority of visitors coming from these two areas. The United States, Canada, and Europe account for over three-quarters of all arrivals (World Tourism Organization, 1995). Some cruise ships stop in Venezuela also. Location on the Caribbean and the proximity to Trinidad and Tobago and the ABC Islands are reasons for the high number of American tourists.

Tourist Destinations and Attractions

The country's main attractions are its superb beaches surrounded by backgrounds of beautiful mountains and forests. Caracas, one important tourist center, is a modern city with botanical gardens, museums, parks, and a cable-car trip to the top of Mount Avila that offers a breathtaking view. Because of rapid growth, *colonial* buildings have been replaced by modern buildings, many of which are quite impressive. These include the University City, the twin towers of the Parque Central, the Centro Simón Bolívar, and the Círculo Militar. Two important national monuments are the Pantheon Nacional, where the remains of Simón Bolívar lie, and the Capitolio Nacional. There are a number of other museums in Caracas, such as Casa Natal del Libertador, a reconstructed house where Bolívar was born.

In addition to the beaches around Caracas, the Los Roques Islands (requiring an overnight trip) provide beautiful islands with long stretches of white beaches and an excellent coral reef. Venezuela is an important destination for ecotourism. Environmental protection has been effectively implemented, and now national parks or monuments represent nearly 22 percent of the country's territory.

Bolívar, another delightful city, is noted for its handicrafts in gold. It is an active town with river craft bringing all forms of items to the city for trade. Bolívar is popular for shoppers. It also serves as an excellent starting place for tourist excursions into the Indian villages. Bolívar, along with Canaima, is a good place to see the magnificent Angel Falls, which along with Devil Mountain is a scenic wonder. Angel Falls is the highest falls in the world with a drop of 2,937 feet. In Canaima, another Venezuelan attraction, tourists sleep in thatched cabanas on the edge of a pink lagoon that is surrounded by an orchid-filled *jungle*. The muffled roar of the La Hacha waterfalls serves as background to the panorama—the Río Currao tumbling over the several falls and the pink lagoon with its soft beige beach.

Colombia

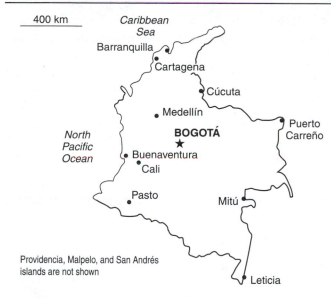

400 km

Caribbean Sea

Barranquilla

• Cartagena

• Cúcuta

• Medellín

North Pacific Ocean

BOGOTÁ
★

• Buenaventura

• Cali

Puerto Carreño

• Pasto

Mitú

Leticia

Providencia, Malpelo, and San Andrés islands are not shown

Capital: Bogotá
Government: Republic
Size: 439,733 square miles (about the size of Texas and California combined)
Language: Spanish
Ethnic Division: 58% Mestizo, 20% European, 14% Mulatto, 4% Black, 3% mixed Black-Indian, 1% Indian
Religion: 95% Roman Catholic
Tourist Season: Year-round
Peak Tourist Season: No peaks; however, North Americans prefer February and March
Currency: Peso (COP)

 TRAVEL TIPS

Entry: Passport and proof of onward or round-trip transportation for stays up to ninety days.
Transportation: There is good access to Bogotá, Barranquilla, Cali, Medellín, and Cartagena from North America, Europe, and other Latin American nations. Between cities both bus and air service is good. Public transportation within cities includes buses and taxis. Tourists should use only taxis with green and off-white paint.
Health: Concern for malaria, yellow fever, and cholera. Check with local health officials before travel. The tap water is not always safe. Food should be prepared carefully.
Caution: Because of sporadic drug and guerilla activity, travel in certain areas may be hazardous. Check with your Department of State before travel.
Shopping: Preferred items include emeralds, brightly colored woolen ponchos, silver work, leather goods, and pottery.

CULTURAL CAPSULE

Colombia is the fourth most populous country in Latin America. There has been a large migration from rural to urban areas. The urban population of the country is now over 70 percent. There is a diversity of ethnic origins resulting from the intermixture of indigenous Indians and Spanish (58% mestizo) and African (15% mulatto) colonists. Today, only about one percent of the people can be identified as fully Indian on the basis of language and customs. The official language is Spanish; however, English is widely understood in the cities and required as a second language in school. There are some forty different Indian languages throughout the country. The state religion is Roman Catholic (95 percent of the population).

Cultural Hints
- Use a warm, friendly handshake as a greeting and upon departure.
- Yawning in public is impolite.
- Do not eat on streets.
- To show height of people the flat palm is held sideways rather than facing down.
- To show length by using the index fingers spread apart is rude.
- Eating and food:
  Overeating is impolite.
  The tip is usually included in bill.
  When finished with your meal, place your knife and fork horizontally across the plate.
  Typical foods are fruit, eggs, soup, rice, meat, potatoes, salad, and beans. A common dish is arroz con pollo (chicken with rice).

Physical Characteristics

Colombia has extensive mountainous and highland areas, but it also has flat coastal lowlands and plains in the east. The climate is tropical along the coast and eastern plains, but cooler in the mountains.

Tourism Characteristics

The government of Colombia recognizes that tourism is important and tries to attract tourists to the country. Colombia's role in illegal drug production and related violence handicaps attempts to increase visitor numbers. The location of Colombia does provide it many resorts along both the Caribbean Sea and the Pacific Ocean. Most of the visitors are from other South American countries. Of the 1.4 million visitors in 1996 the United States only accounted for about 12 percent.

Tourist Destinations and Attractions

The Andean ranges, interspersed with green valleys and dense jungles, offer a spectacular tourist environment. In addition, as with other Latin American countries, there are some interesting archaeological attractions.

Bogotá, the capital, is on a high *plateau* with a mixture of colonial and modern buildings. The Palace of San Carlos where Simón Bolívar once lived, the Cathedral, La Toma de Agua, the Muséo de Oro with more than 15,000 pieces of pre-Columbian gold, the *National Museum*, the Planetarium, and the Museum of Natural History are some interesting places to visit. A funicular railway takes visitors to the top of Monserrate for a good view of Bogotá. Around the Plaza Bolívar, the old quarter of the city has barred windows, carved doorways, brown-tiled roofs, and sheltering eaves.

North of Bogotá, tourists can visit the salt mine of Zipaquirá, which has an underground cathedral that

was carved by the Chibcha Indians. It holds about ten thousand people. Cartagena is one of the major attractions of South America. Founded by Pedro de Heredia in 1533, the "Heroic City" was built as a Spanish base for the conquest of the continent—an impregnable port with a heavily armed garrison to protect the gold routes and slave trade. Surrounded by the Caribbean Sea, the Bay of Cartegena, and lakes and lagoons, the old walled city has many forts and other reminders of the early Spanish era, such as parade grounds, colonial baroque architecture with typical balconies, cloisters, patios, stone entrances, and wood doors.

Ecuador

Capital: Quito
Government: Republic
Size: 109,482 square miles (about the size of Colorado)
Language: Spanish and various Indian languages
Ethnic Division: 55% Mestizo, 25% Indian, 10% Spanish, 10% Black
Religion: 95% Roman Catholic
Tourist Season: Year-round
Peak Tourist Seasons: January, July, and December
Currency: Sucre (SUC)

TRAVEL TIPS

Entry: Passport and proof of onward or return transportation is needed. Departure-by-air tax is collected.
Transportation: There is international access to North America, Europe, and other Latin American countries. Between major cities within the country, bus and air travel connections are the major systems. Public transportation is by buses, taxis, and colectivos (small minibuses that are more comfortable and faster than buses).

Health: Concern for malaria, yellow fever, and cholera. Check with local health officials before travel. Altitude sickness is common in Quito.
Shopping: Purchases of Panama hats, handwoven rugs and ponchos, wood carvings from native wood, pottery, basketwork *tsantas* (goatskin replicas of Jivaro headhunter shrunken heads), gold, and silver are common.

CULTURAL CAPSULE

The population of Ecuador is ethnically mixed, combining mestizo, African, Spanish, and other European strains. The dominant pre-European group was the Inca. In the fifteenth century, the Inca Empire spread from Perú into what is now Ecuador. Spaniards later took advantage of Inca weakness and tribal resentment to subdue Quito. The people in the Amazon region are mostly Indians and are culturally distinct from others. Ecuadorians maintain their own traditions even in the cities. Spanish is the official language, with Quechua (the Indian language) spoken in the highlands. English is understood by business and tourism officials.

Cultural Hints:
- A firm handshake is the common greeting.
- Touching and closeness are common.
- Fidgeting with hands and feet is impolite.
- Pointing is impolite.
- Eating and food:
  Common foods are corn, potatoes, rice, beans, fish, soup, and fruit. Typical dishes are arroz con pollo (fried chicken with rice), locro (soup of potatoes, cheese, meat, and avocados), llapingachos (cheese and potato cakes), ceviche (raw seafood marinated in lime and served with onions, tomatoes, and other spices), fritada (fried pork), and empanadas (pastries filled with meat or cheese).

Physical Characteristics

The country has coastal plains and flat-to-rolling eastern jungle surrounding the Andes Mountains and

Through Visitors' Eyes

Exploring Ecuador
and the Galápagos Islands

by Nancy Adcox Esposito

Guayaquil is the most important port city in Ecuador and also the most populated. Allow one day to visit the Malecon or waterfront area. Along your stroll you will find many monuments including one for the United Nations and La Rotonda, a Moorish-style clocktower. Interesting churches include Santa Domingo and the Church of San Francisco, which was built in 1548, making it the oldest church in Ecuador. Parque Bolívar, directly adjacent to Church of San Francisco, is the home to many land iguanas. At first, you may notice only the ornamental gardens; but look closer. The trees are filled with these prehistoric-looking reptiles. If you are lucky, some will be only a few feet away lunching on the greenery.

Expeditions into Ecuador's Amazon Basin will enthrall your senses. Waterfalls, piranha, jaguar, parrots, toucans, and orchids await your observation. Animals here are not as accessible as in the Galápagos, and you will need patience. . . .

Quito is the capital and third largest city in Ecuador, and is a personal favorite. At an altitude of 9,500 feet, this picturesque city and its surrounding areas have much to offer. Located in the Andes Mountain region, the cool climate warms up as the day progresses, never getting too hot or humid. Items of interest in Quito are Muséo del Banco Central (an archaeological museum) and the Muséo del Ciencias Naturales (natural history museum). The monastery of San Francisco has exquisite original tile work and baroque wood-carved ceilings and walls, while La Companía de Jesus is said to have used seven tons of gold to gild this ornate structure.

On Panecillo Hill is a glorious panoramic view of Quito and the enormous statue of the Virgin of Quito. La Companía, a sixteenth-century baroque church, and La Plaza de la Independencia are also worth visiting. A wonderful day trip to Saquisili market is advised. Here you will find everything for sale, from animals to furniture to handicrafts.

The Galápagos Islands, described by Darwin as "a separate center of creation" and inspiration for his origin of the species theory, remains a naturalist's wonderland. This archipelago, consisting of forty-eight islands and rock formations, was created over three million years ago by volcanic eruptions. An hour-and-a-half from Guayaquil, the Galápagos's first documented discovery occurred in 1535 when the Bishop of Panama, Tomás de Belanga, sailed off course on his way back to Panama from Perú. Prior to 1959, when Ecuador declared the Galápagos islands a National Park, these islands were used by pirates, whalers, and as penal colonies. The near-extinction of the Galapagos giant tortoise was caused by their confiscation as a food source (they can survive without water and food for almost a year), and by misdirected early twentieth-century research. With only five of the islands colonized and two of these containing fresh water supplies, animals and plants have had to evolve to survive. Existing on the islands are goats that drink sea water and iguanas that have glands above their noses that "spit out" excess salt from their diet.

Our first wet landing was at Darwin Bay on the island of Genovesa. Here we walked along the mounds of black lava rocks to within inches at times of nesting frigate birds, red-footed boobies, and masked boobies. Looking over the edge of a cliff, we saw five very large sharks swimming in the bay. According to our guide, Patricio, there are three types of sharks that live in and around the islands. The Galápagos, white-tipped reef, and hammerhead sharks have to date never attacked humans in the Galápagos Reserve. Given the abundant food sources available, it makes sense that they would not look elsewhere for food that is not on their natural diet. (At least this is what I told myself as I donned snorkeling gear and dove in looking for a close encounter.) As I floated around with the colorful tropical fish and a very playful sea lion, I watched . . . in search of sharks. My close encounter was witnessed by other snorkelers. As three of us headed up to complain about not seeing any sharks, three

continues

continued

of them swam right between us. Close, but not on Kodak® this time. As I returned to shore slightly disappointed, I saw a baby sea lion napping in the sand. He playfully lifted his head, looked around at all the people passing him by, dropped his head and continued to wallow in the hot sun. (In my next life, I want to come back as a sea lion in the Galápagos.) While the land iguanas are so abundant that you almost step on them, the marine iguanas tend to be more difficult to locate because their habitat is rocky, wet cliffs. We later located these elusive amphibians on the other side of the island.

Santa Cruz is home to the Charles Darwin Research Center where you can visit the breeding pens of the giant tortoises and land iguanas. Here, you will be able to visit Lonesome George, the last tortoise of his specific genetic make-up. (There are at least a dozen different tortoise species in the Galápagos).

San Salvador's lava-created water pools allow you to swim with the fur seals, while Bartólome Island is home to the curious and playful endemic Galápagos penguin. Sea turtles, storm petrels, waved albatross, and more mockingbirds and finches than I could name will cross your path on these islands. With over 800 species of plants, 250 being endemic, the Galápagos Islands are a phenomenal experience.

Source: Jax Fax Travel Marketing Magazine.
May 1993, pp. 80–82.

central highlands. The climate is tropical along the coastal area and in the jungle lowland. It is cooler in the highland and mountain areas.

Tourism Characteristics

The tourist industry in Ecuador is small but growing. Tourism revenue ranks seventh in revenue earned, behind oil, bananas, shrimp, coffee, flowers, and handicrafts. Ecuadorian tourism is dominated by neighboring Colombia and Perú, with the United States accounting for approximately 19 percent of its visitors. The peaks in January, July, and December are related to the influx of visitors from the United States during those months.

Tourist Destinations and Attractions

The country's high mountains and volcanic ranges are important attractions, offering spectacular beauty with Indian culture. Quito, the capital and third largest city in Ecuador, is set in a hollow at the foot of a volcano. It is very picturesque. The old colonial area has been preserved with its buildings painted white and blue. Quito has many churches such as San Francisco, Monastery of Santo Domingo, and La Compañía. Quito also has a number of excellent art museums such as the Casa del La Cúltura Ecuatoriana, the Museum of Colonial Art, the Muséo de Santo Domingo, the Muséo de San Agustín, the Archaeological Museum, and the Muséo Colonial y de Arte Religioso. From Panecillo Hill there is a glorious panoramic view of Quito. The enormous statue of the Virgin of Quito is located on the hill's summit.

One of the most interesting market towns in South America is at Otavalo. In addition to its colorful *Indian markets*, Otavalo offers a number of other interesting features such as cockfights, bullfights, and a unique ball game. There are actually three markets taking place: a woolen fabrics and shawls market, an animal auction, and a produce market. It is a very busy place on Saturdays.

Santo Domingo, a scenic 80 miles from Quito, is the center for trips into the Colorado Indian villages. Guayaquil is the most important port city in Ecuador and is also the departure point for visits to the Galápagos Islands. The city has many monuments and churches including Santo Domingo and the Church of San Francisco. Built in 1548, the Church of San Francisco is the oldest church in Ecuador. Across the street from the Church of San Francisco is Parque Bolívar, the home of many land iguanas, with trees filled with the prehistoric-looking reptiles.

A fascinating attraction in Ecuador is the Galápagos Islands with their unique plant and animal life. Located six hundred miles off the west coast, they consist of six main islands and twelve smaller islands. The islands are the peaks of volcanoes. Darwin described the Galápagos Islands as "a separate center of creation," and they served as an inspiration for his origin of species theory. A number of plants and animals found here are unique to these islands. The most fabled species are the giant tortoise, marine iguana, land iguana, hammerhead sharks, Galápagos albatross, and a number of exotic birds. The land iguanas are so abundant that visitors almost step on them. Santa Cruz is home to the Charles Darwin Research Center, where visitors can visit the breeding pens of the giant tortoises and land iguanas.

Perú

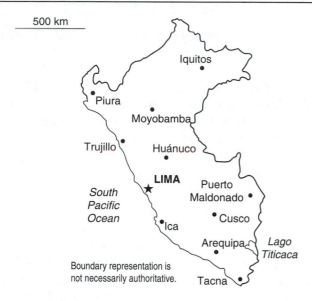

500 km

Iquitos

Piura

Moyobamba

Trujillo   Huánuco

LIMA

South
Pacific   Puerto
Ocean   Maldonado

Ica   Cusco

Arequipa   *Lago
Titicaca*

Boundary representation is
not necessarily authoritative.   Tacna

Capital Lima
Government: Republic
Size: 496,223 square miles (slightly more than three times the size of California)
Language: Spanish and Quechua, Aymara
Ethnic Divisions: 45% Indian, 37% Mestizo, 15% European, 3% Black, Japanese, Chinese, and other
Religion: Predominantly Roman Catholic
Tourist Season: Year-round
Peak Tourist Seasons: January, July, and August
Currency: Sol (SOL)

 ## TRAVEL TIPS

Entry: Passport and proof of round-trip or onward transportation required.
Transportation: Good international access to North America, Europe, and other Latin American countries. Within-country travel is by bus, air, and rail. Private cars with a driver make semi-regular trips between larger cities for a reasonable price as well. The scenic Central Railway connects Lima with the central highlands of the Peruvian Andes.
Health: Concern for malaria and yellow fever. Check with your local health officials before traveling.
Caution: Care should be taken because of drug traffickers and the Shining Path guerrilla group. Some areas are unsafe for tourists. It is best to travel with groups.
Shopping: Common purchases include alpaca goods, gold, silver, and handwoven fabrics.

CULTURAL CAPSULE

The people of Perú are ethnically diverse, consisting of Indians (45%), mestizos (37%), and Hispanic Europeans (15%). Other minorities include Blacks, Japanese, and Chinese. Spanish and Quechua (Indian) languages are both officially recognized. Another Indian language, Aymara, is spoken

widely. English is understood in businesses and tourist attractions. Most people are Roman Catholic, and the Indians mix their traditional Indian beliefs with their Christian beliefs. There are also Protestant and evangelical churches in the country.

Cultural Hints:
*   Shake hands upon greeting and departing.
*   Eye contact is important.
*   To beckon, all of the fingers are waved with palm facing down.
*   Ask permission to photograph Indians.
*   Eating and food:
    Keep hands above the table.
    No elbows on the table.
    When finished eating, place your knife and fork parallel
        across your plate.
    Summon the waiter by waving.
    If service is included in bill, a small tip is given.
    Typical food includes rice, beans, corn, fish, potatoes,
        and tropical fruits.

Physical Characteristics

The high Andes in the center are bounded by the coastal plains on the west and the lowland jungle of the Amazon Basin to the east. The climate is tropical in the lowland jungle region, cool in the mountains, and hot and dry in the western desert.

Tourism Characteristics

Since Perú's economy is underdeveloped, the government encourages tourism and hopes for its rapid growth. Tourism almost doubled between 1970 and 1975, but by 1996 they were only receiving about 500,000 tourists a year. The largest hotel chain, ENTURPERU, a state-owned chain, was privatized in 1994 and 1995. If the current growth rate of tourism continues there will be insufficient hotel capacity. Through government incentives over 100 projects had begun by the end of 1995. To further increase the hotel capacity, Perú is negotiating with the World Bank to further stimulate hotel growth.

Per's national air carrier, Aeroperu, was also privatized in 1993, and growth in airline capacity has increased. Along with this privatization, fares were deregulated, increasing accessibility both domestically and internationally.

Perú is actively promoting itself as an international tourist destination. However, the country lacks funding for essential infrastructure and private sector investment in hotels. Domestic air services have reached the saturation point at certain times of

Figure 5–4   Machu Picchu, Perú

is watching the sun rise over the Andes. In addition to Cuzco and Machu Picchu, the Urubamba Valley has a number of ruins, two well-known folk markets, the town of Puno, and Lake Titicaca, which combines scenery with the floating islands and archaeological ruins at Tiahuanaco to attract tourists to the southeast of Perú.

Lima, the capital of Perú, was the major city of Spanish South America. Perú has tried to maintain the colonial days in the heart of the city. The Plaza de Armas was the site of Spanish conquistador Pizzaro's palace, and the Museum of the Inquisition at Plaza Bolívar is where inquisition trials took place. The city has important museums, such as the Gold Museum, the National Museum of Art, the Museum of Anthropology and Archaeology, the Museum of Peruvian Culture, and the Bullfight Museum. These and others display the rich Incan and Spanish history of the region. At Nazca, some 280 miles south of Lima, flights can be taken over the Nazca lines, which are tracings of symbols, animals, and other features (a dog, monkey, birds, a spider, and a tree) extending for miles across the desert. The valley is full of ruins, temples, and cemeteries. Between Lima and Nazca, there are a number of coastal towns and a national park with sea lions and condors. The Colca Canyon is the world's deepest canyon and has a string of Spanish colonial churches in villages, with a culture and costume distinct from other areas. The government is trying to develop the area for tourism.

The Amazon, centering on Iquitos, has become a popular trip for a jungle adventure. River trips are taken from Iquitos into the jungle to observe jungle activity. Belén, a floating village, has a floating market of canoes canopied with palm thatch. Visitors may observe the buying and selling of tropical fruits, fish, and vegetables. The jungle camps provide access to jungle flora and fauna in unique settings.

the year and need to be expanded. Some 24 percent of Perú's visitors are from Anglo America, with the United States sending 20 percent of all tourists, primarily in July and August.

Tourist Destinations and Attractions

The most famous attraction in Perú is Machu Picchu, the legendary "Lost City of the Incas," Figure 5–4. It sits in the high Andes on a saddle of a mountain with terraced slopes. At least a day is required to see the ruins, consisting of staircases, terraces, temples, palaces, towers, fountains, sundials, and the Muséo de Sítio below the ruins. A hike up an adjacent mountainside provides a tremendous view of the site. The most popular tour consists of a visit to Machu Picchu by a train that departs from Cuzco at 6:15 A.M. and returns at 10:15 P.M. the same day. As a result, most tourists miss the most spectacular experience, which

Bolivia

Physical Characteristics

The Andes are located in the eastern portion of Bolivia, with plains and lowlands on the west. The climate varies from hot and tropical to cold and semiarid in the higher elevations (from the tierra caliente to the tierra fría).

Tourism Characteristics

Tourism to Bolivia has not been important, and its government has done little to encourage it. Only 300,000 to 400,000 tourists a year visited Bolivia in the 1990s. There are, however, a number of excellent resources to attract tourists.

400 km

Cobija

Trinidad

Lago Titicaca
★
LA PAZ   Cochabamba

Oruro   Sucre   Santa Cruz

Potosí

Tarija

Capital: La Paz
Government: Republic
Size: 424,162 square miles (about the size of California and Texas combined)
Language: Spanish, Quechua, and Aymara
Ethnic Division: 30% Quechua, 25% Aymara, 25–30% mixed, 5–15% European
Religion: 95% Roman Catholic, Protestant minority
Tourist Season: Year-round
Peak Tourist Season: May through November
Currency: Bolivian peso

CULTURAL CAPSULE

The population is approximately 60 percent indigenous Aymara and Quechua Indian, 30 percent mestizo, and 15 percent European (mostly Spanish). Spanish, Quechua, and Aymara are all official languages. Ninety-five percent of the people are Roman Catholic with a number of Protestant minority groups and some indigenous tribal religions that mix Indian beliefs with Catholic.

Cultural Hints:
- A warm handshake is a common greeting.
- Close personal space.
- Making a fist with the thumb between the index and middle fingers is rude.
- To beckon, hold palm facing down and move the fingers in a scratching motion.
- Eating and food:
  Summon waiter by raising hand.
  Never eat with fingers.
  Do not eat on the street.
  When tip is included in bill, leave a little extra.
  Eat everything on plate.
  Keep hands above the table.
  Pour wine with your right hand and with the palm face down.
  Common foods are potatoes, rice, soups, and fruits. A typical dish is saltenas (meat or chicken pie with potatoes, olives, and raisins).

TRAVEL TIPS

Entry: Visa is not required. Passport required.
Transportation: La Paz has airline service connections with North America, Europe, and other Latin American countries. Internal transportation is mostly by air as surface transportation is poor due to rugged terrain. Public transportation includes buses (crowded), minivans (less crowded and faster), and taxis.
Health: Concern for malaria, yellow fever, and cases of plague. Tap water is not safe. Altitude sickness is common.
Shopping: Local items include vicuna ponchos, alpaca sweaters, fabrics, gold and silver jewelry, wood carvings, and pottery.

Tourist Destinations and Attractions

La Paz, the highest capital in the world at twelve thousand feet, is in a natural basin or canyon, with Mount Illimani towering over the city. There are some colonial buildings left, particularly in the Calle Jaen. Around the Plaza Murillo in the center of town, tourists can visit the huge cathedral, the Presidential Palace, the National Congress, the Muséo Nacional del Arte, and a central market (Mercado Camacho) where Indian vendors sell their goods. The market is characterized by Indians sitting on the ground or in

stalls, selling everything from cheese empanadas, to steel wool, canned goods, powdered soup, brazil nuts, sausages, and so forth. The monastery of San Francisco, which was built in the colonial period; Santo Domingo; La Merced; and San Sebastian, the first church to be built in La Paz, are attractive churches in La Paz.

Near La Paz, the ruins of Tiahuanaco near the southern end of Lake Titicaca are impressive and are being reconstructed. Lake Titicaca provides a number

Figure 5–5 Reed Boat, Bolivia

of good attractions for visitors. Copacabán, an attractive little town on the lake, is noted for its restored church and miracle-working Dark Virgin of the Lake.

The most popular excursion is to ride on the lake to visit the Island of the Sun, a worship site of the Incas, Figure 5–5.

Where Else But Bolivia? Moonscapes, Witch Doctors and Reed-Boat Builders

By Wayne and Saima Wirtanen

Cochabamba Market

The central market in the city of Cochabamba was the cleanest and most photogenic of any market we've ever seen in South or Central America. The merchants took great pride in the display of their goods. Stacks of cow hoofs, silvery fish, farm produce, and a bewildering array of colorful spices had been magically turned into art displays for our cameras.

Then there were potatoes—more kinds, sizes, and colors than we ever imagined existed! We saw pure-white ones, jet-black ones that looked like stones, almost fluorescent red-orange ones and many variations in between. A sun-drying process is used to preserve the bountiful Andean potato crop for long-term storage. The prune-like tubers add another whole spectrum to the overwhelming potato scene.

Valley of the Moon

A few miles from La Paz there is a large area of soft sandstone that rainfall erosion has sculpted into an eerie landscape. As far as the eye can see are oddly shaped pinnacles of harder sandstone that has eroded more slowly than surrounding areas. This appeared to be a favorite spot for a wide variety of bird life; the extremely rough landscape makes intrusion by man very unlikely. This area is included in all day trips of La Paz and also can be reached by city bus.

The Street of Witch Doctors

A couple of blocks uphill from La Paz's central square is the street of witch doctors, the source of Andean magical goods that have served this culture for a very long time. In the street of "good" witch doctors, one can purchase a mummified llama fetus

that, buried under the foundation of a new house, will assure a peaceful home.

Photography is encouraged on the good-witch-doctor block and forbidden by the vendors in the bad-witch-doctor area. There's an interesting concept at work here: "good spirits" and "bad spirits" exist that must be dealt with in everyday life. Purchase of appropriate amulets, potions and other unidentifiable bits from each street of "specialists" is required to achieve success in love, business, health, and a happy home. . . .

Andean Cultural Display

Darius Morgan, Jr., has collected a unique all-in-one-place, Andean cultural exhibit. For starters, there is an authentic floating reed island with homes of the local Indian fishermen. In addition, stone and adobe buildings from very remote villages (three to five days away by four-wheel-drive vehicles) have been brought to the hotel grounds for reassembly in typical village surroundings.

Why is it that the adobe homes look exactly like ice igloos? Educated speculation is that these people originally made their homes of ice blocks during a remote time with a very cold climate.

As the climate warmed, the traditional construction was so established that, as the ice disappeared, adobe blocks gradually were substituted. The villagers only say, "They've always been built this way."

Kallawaya Fortune Teller

The Kallawayas are a small group of Andean healers and fortune tellers. On the hotel grounds is a museum that displays their herbal medicines and healing techniques. At midnight—the most auspi-

continues

continued

cious hour—our group went to the resident Kallawaya fortune teller for insight to the future.

On the floor of a dimly lit corner of the museum, an elderly Indian sat crosslegged. He was dressed in dark woolen pants, a heavy striped woven poncho, and a traditional colorful Andean knit cap that came down over his ears. He was surrounded by the obscure tools of his trade, which included a crate of used beer- and wine-bottles containing dark fluids. He spoke only a Kallawaya language, so all dialogue was interpreted from Kallawaya to Spanish to English and back.

The Indian was reputed to be able to read one's future by studying the pattern produced when his "client" tossed a small handful of coca leaves onto the braided blanket between them.

Following instructions carefully, Wayne tossed his coca leaves and asked, "What does the pattern predict for my wife's and my health in the next few years?" After careful scrutiny and a few moments of eyes-closed meditation, the response came back through the two interpreters: "You worry too much about that. You will have no serious health problems in your family for many years."

All the forecasts were not as rosy. Others in the small group were touched by the responses they received to sometimes very personal questions and afterward were reluctant to discuss how they felt about their midnight experience.

Source: International Travel News.
May 1993, pp. 51–57.

Chile

1000 km

Arica
Antofagasta
La Serena
★ SANTIAGO

South Pacific Ocean

Concepción
Puerto Montt

Easter and Sala y Gomez islands are not shown.

Boundary representation is not necessarily authoritative.

Punta Arena

Capital: Santiago
Government: Republic
Size: 473,094 square miles (three times the size of California)
Language: Spanish
Ethnic Division: 95% European and European-Indian, 3% Indian, 2% other.
Religion: 89% Roman Catholic, 11% Protestant
Tourist Season: December through March
Peak Tourist Season: December through February
Currency: Chilean peso (CHE)

 ## TRAVEL TIPS

Entry: No visa is required. A passport is required.
Transportation: Good international connections to North America, Europe, and other Latin American countries. Good service to cities within Chile. Public transportation is very good. Santiago has a subway, and all cities have inexpensive bus systems.
Health: Some areas have yellow fever.
Shopping: Local items include copperware fabrics, Chilean wine, woolen rugs, wooden carvings from Easter Island, leather goods, black pottery, and lapis lazuli jewelry.

CULTURAL CAPSULE

Chile is an urbanized nation with 85 percent of its population living in urban centers. The largest group of people are Spanish or mestizo (over 95 percent). Only 3 percent are Indians, and the rest are Irish, English, German, Italian, Yugoslav, French, and Arab. More than 80 percent of the population is Roman Catholic with minority groups of Protestant, Christian, Jewish, and some Indians. Spanish is the official language, but unlike the rest of South America's Spanish dialect, Chile uses *Castellano*. English is taught in schools and understood by many in the large cities. Chile has a booming economy, and its people enjoy one of the highest standards of living found in South American countries.

Cultural Hints:
* A handshake is a common greeting.
* Eye contact is important.
* Men rise when women enter the room.

- Good posture while seated is important.
- Making a fist and slapping it up into the palm of the other hand is very rude.
- Eating and food:
  Summon waiter with a raised finger.
  Pour wine with your left hand.
  Do not eat with your fingers.
  Eating anything but ice cream on the street is considered rude.
  Common foods are fish, seafood, chicken, beef, beans, eggs, and corn. Typical dishes are empanadas de horno (meat turnovers with beef, hard-boiled eggs, onions, olives, and raisins), humitas (grated corn, fried onions, sweet basil, salt, and pepper), pastel de choclo (beef, chicken, onions, corn, eggs, and spices), and cazuela de ave (chicken soup).

Physical Characteristics

Chile has low coastal mountains in the west, with a fertile central valley and the high Andes in the east. The climate is temperate, desert in the north and cool and damp in the south.

Tourism Characteristics

The country has a tourist industry in transition. It received 1.4 million tourists in 1996. Over 56 percent of them came from neighboring Argentina. The government put considerable effort into developing the tourist industry, and it still encourages new hotel development and personnel training in tourism. However, it does little to attract Americans. It has no tourist office in the United States. Less than 5 percent of the total visitors are from the United States.

Chile's tourist industry is very seasonal. The summer months of January and February are the strongest, drawing 50 percent of total visitors.

Tourist Destinations and Attractions

The country has a variety of attractions to offer. Located in the lush central valley, Santiago, the capital and main tourist city, has a Mediterranean-type climate. Nearly 70 percent of the population is concentrated in this central heartland. Santiago was founded in 1541 and is a well-planned city. The beautiful snow-covered Andes provide a picturesque panorama. The center of the city contains the Cathedral and the Archbishop's palace, the Palacio de La Real Audiencia with the Muséo Histórico Nacional inside, the Congressional Palace, and Casa Colada, which was the home of the Governor in colonial times and is now a museum of the history of Santiago. There is an excellent view of the city from the first Spanish fort built in Chile at the top of Santa Lucia.

Valparaíso, the second largest city and major port, is also a favorite tourist spot. It is built on a bay with a crescent of hills around it. The snow-capped peaks can be seen in the distance. Few buildings remain from the colonial times because of a number of earthquakes. The city does have a variety of landscapes, from the narrow, clean, winding streets around the center to the hills with tattered houses and shacks and littered back streets. There are a number of excellent seaside resorts around Valparaíso, including the Viña del Mar, which is the most famous and is the summer palace of the president. Visitors can go by ship from Valparaíso to legendary Easter Island, which has huge stone monoliths and has only recently been developed as a tourist attraction. However, since it is nearly 2,400 miles west, most visits are by air. Juan Fernandez, the setting for the classic story of Robinson Crusoe, is another island to visit.

Located between the Lastarria Range and Reloncavi Sound, the lake region is one of the most picturesque areas in Chile. Chile has also developed a number of mountain resorts in an effort to utilize the many ski slopes in the country.

MIDDLE-LATITUDE SOUTH AMERICA

Argentina, Paraguay, and Uruguay are located in the middle latitudes. They have a climate that does not share tropical conditions with the bulk of Latin America. Historically, this region did not have the advanced Indian civilizations of Mexico and the highlands of the Andes, so its development is based on European immigration. The presidents of the countries of Brazil, Argentina, Uruguay, and Paraguay signed a treaty in 1991 to create a common market and pledged to drop tariffs gradually, removing them by 1995.

Argentina

1000 km

San Miguel
de Tucumán

Córdoba

Mendoza

BUENOS AIRES

Bahía Blanca

Mar del Plata

San Carlos
de Bariloche

Viedma

*South Atlantic
Ocean*

Comodoro Rivadavia

Boundary representation is
not necessarily authoritative.

Ushuaia

Capital: Buenos Aires
Government: Republic
Size: 1,056,636 square miles (four times the size of Texas)
Language: Spanish, English, Italian, German, and French
Ethnic Division: 85% European, 15% Mestizo, Indian, other
Religion: 90% Roman Catholic, 2% Protestant, 2% Jewish, 6% other
Tourist Season: Year-round
Peak Tourist Season: December through March
Currency: Austral

TRAVEL TIPS

Entry: No visa required. Passport required.
Transportation: International connections with direct flights to North America, Europe, and other South American countries exist. Travel within the country is by train, air, bus, or auto. Buenos Aires has an extensive subway and bus system. Taxis are readily available.
Shopping: Local items include leather goods, furs, silver work, and gaucho souvenirs.

CULTURAL CAPSULE

Argentina's population has been influenced by the waves of European immigrants who came in the nineteenth and twentieth centuries. Italian and Spanish are the dominant groups (85 percent). Mestizos and Indians make up the remaining 15 percent. There is a sizable number of Syrian, Lebanese, and other Middle Eastern immigrants; most are city dwellers. More than 90 percent of Argentines are Roman Catholic. Although Spanish is the official language, many people speak some English, German, French, or Italian. Argentina is famous for its horse ranches and *gauchos* (cowboys) in the *Pampas* region. Beef is the single most important food. It is so much a part of the culture that steak is even eaten for breakfast. Also, Argentina was the place of origin

and is still home to the tango. It was started in Buenos Aires by a Frenchman, Carlos Gardel.

Cultural Hints:
- A warm handshake is a common greeting.
- Argentine culture includes close personal space, so people stand close when talking.
- Eye contact is important.
- Hands on hips indicates anger or a challenge.
- Yawning in public is rude.
- Closing the hand into a fist and extending the little and index finger is a rude gesture.
- Eating and food:
  Hands should always be above the table.
  Using a toothpick in public is bad manners.
  Summon a waiter by raising your hand with the index finger extended.
  Eating in the street is not proper.
  When finished eating, cross the knife and fork in the middle of your plate.
  Beef is the most important staple. Common foods include beef, corn, potatoes, and hot tea. Popular meals feature barbecue, meat pies, and locro (a stew of meat, corn, and potatoes).

Physical Characteristics

The northern half of Argentina consists of the rich plains of the Pampas. Southern Argentina is dominated by the flat-to-rolling plateau of *Patagonia*. The high Andes mountains run along the western border. The climate is mostly temperate, with subtropical and steppe climates dominating.

Tourism Characteristics

The National Tourist Office is actively engaged in promoting tourism. It has sought assistance from the Organization of American States for technical advice on the preservation of its colonial cities and towns. Gross receipts from international tourism are now the largest single item in export earnings. As a result, tourism now represents over 20 percent of total foreign exchange receipts from commodity exports, double what it was 10 years ago. Improved economic conditions have brought about an increase in domestic tourism and more travel by Argentines to other countries, mostly Chile and Uruguay.

Argentina has a well-developed tourism infrastructure, with excellent accommodations to support the largest and most rapidly growing tourist industry in South America. The 4.2 million visitors in 1996 represent a 40 percent increase over 1990. Most arrivals are from neighboring countries. The two leading European countries of origin, Italy and Spain, have long-established immigration and language ties with Argentina. The United States has also become an important visitor source, accounting for over 10 percent of Argentina's non-Latin market in the 1990s.

Tourist Destinations and Attractions

The country has a wide variety of landscapes, from tropical rain forests to the glaciers of Antarctica. Argentina's most famous tourist attraction is the capital city of Buenos Aires, the location of the world's widest thoroughfare and the world's largest opera house (Teátro Colón). Although the city has very few of its old buildings left, it has maintained its original design with narrow one-way streets. The historic Cabildo (the town hall), the pink Casa Rosada (Presidential Palace), and the cathedral are located in the Plaza de May, the heart of the city. The city also has numerous museums, libraries, and art exhibitions. The historical landmarks, cathedrals, palaces, and museums are all tourist inducements that complement the country's excellent cuisine. The famous Iguazú Falls of the Parana River can be reached from Argentina, but most visitors come to the Brazil side of the falls.

Outside of Buenos Aires, there are many other tourist attractions. Tigre is a popular weekend and holiday spot, situated in a delta of the Parana River 18 miles from Buenos Aires. The long coastal areas offer a number of excellent seaside resorts with casinos and wide, sandy beaches. The Mar del Plata, about 250 miles south of Buenos Aires, is a famous resort and playground with private clubs and summer estates of the wealthy.

In the northwest region, Córdoba, the capital city of Córdoba Province, is the second largest city of Argentina. It has a mixture of old churches and modern buildings. Some points of interest are the old

Figure 5–6 Barbecue in Argentina

colonial building (the Viceroy's House), the Church of La Merced, and the Church of La Companía.

The foothills of the Andes are in southern Argentina in Patagonia. Patagonia stretches from Central Argentina to the Strait of Magellan. This region contains two completely different geographical areas. First is the towering Andes and a vast terrain covered with sheets of ice and glaciers that spill into huge lakes. The second area, the Peninsula of Valdés in the east of Patagonia, offers a perfect vantage point for the observation of whales, penguins, huge sea elephants, and all kinds of marine life. The area includes the Bariloche and the southern lake district, which attract tourists for a multitude of sporting activities such as hunting, fishing, skiing, and golfing. Even further south, Tierra del Fuego has a large number of species of birds, snow-capped peaks, waterfalls, deep red forests, lakes, and glaciers for the hardy traveler.

Paraguay

Physical Characteristics

The country's topography consists of grassy plains, wooded hills, and low, marshy plains. The climate varies from temperate humid subtropical in the east to semiarid steppe in the Gran Chaco region of the west, which accounts for about 60 percent of the territory but is home for less than 4 percent of the population.

Tourism Characteristics

The country is now stressing the development of tourism by organizing tourist weeks, national festivals, and other special promotions. In 1996 Paraguay attracted 400,000 tourists. Argentina and Brazil account for over 52 percent of the tourists to Paraguay, again indicating the considerable intraregional travel

200 km

Mayor Pablo Lagerenza

Fuerte Olimpo

La Esmeralda

Pedro Juan Caballero

Concepción

San Pedro

★ **ASUNCIÓN**

Boundary representation is not necessarily authoritative.

Villarrica

Pilar

Encarnación

Capital: Asunción
Government: Republic, under authoritarian rule
Size: 254,219 square miles (about the same as Texas)
Language: Spanish and Guarani
Ethnic Division: 95% Mestizo, 5% European and Indian
Religion: 97% Roman Catholic, Mennonite and other Protestant
Tourist Season: Year-round
Peak Tourist Season: December through March
Currency: Guaranu (GUA)

within South America (World Tourism Organization, 1995).

Tourist Destinations and Attractions

There are a variety of attractions, from the vast Chaco, which for years was inhabited only by scattered Indian tribes and Mennonite settlements, to Asunción, the capital, to the Paraguay (Parana), Alto Parna, and Pilcomayo rivers that form Paraguay's boundaries. Asunción is usually the traveler's first choice of a city to visit. It is the largest city, containing many palaces, churches, and museums. The large modern church of La Encarnación is the focal building in the city. Asunción has a number of excellent parks such as Parque Caballero with waterfalls and plantations and the Botanical Gardens.

The small, ancient town of nearby Itaugua with its reddish tile roofs is another frequently visited attraction. Famous for spider-web lace, it has all types

TRAVEL TIPS

Entry: No visa is required for stays up to three months. A passport is required.
Transportation: There are connections to Asunción with the United States, Europe, and other Latin American countries. Travel between cities is by bus, but roads are not good. Paved roads connect the capital with Brazilian and Bolivian borders. Asunción's public transportation relies on streetcars and taxis.
Health: Yellow fever and malaria are a concern. Check with local public health officials before traveling. Tap water is not safe outside of Asunción.
Shopping: Local items include alpaca goods, gold, silver, and handwoven wool fabrics.

CULTURAL CAPSULE

Paraguay's population is the most homogeneous in South America. It is about 95 percent Spanish, Guarani Indian, and mestizo. There are small minority groups of Italians, Germans, Koreans, and Japanese. The two official languages are Spanish and Guarani. Nearly 90 percent of the population belongs to the Catholic Church.

Cultural Hints:
- A handshake is commonly used in greeting and departing.
- Women should dress conservatively and modestly.
- Paraguayans have a close personal space during conversations.
- The "OK" sign is considered rude.
- Keep feet on floor when seated.
- Winking is only used romantically or sexually.
- Eating and food:
  Keep both wrists on the edge of the table.
  Do not eat while walking.
  Common foods are chicken, pork, beef and corn, rice, and vegetables.

of other handicrafts, from hammocks to dresses. Ypacarai and Ypoa are Paraguay's major lakes. Both are resort centers with beautiful tropical trees and flowers. Other important attractions are the Indian culture, the open-air markets, and the excursions into the primitive Chaco jungles. Iguazú Falls is on the border of Brazil, Argentina, and Paraguay. However, Paraguay benefits far less from it as a tourist destination than the other two countries.

Uruguay

125 km

Boundary representation is not necessarily authoritative.

Rivera
Salto
Embalse del Río Negro
Paysandú
Melo
Laguna Merín
Mercedes
San José
Minas
South Atlantic Ocean
Rio de la Plata
MONTEVIDEO

Capital: Montevideo
Government: Republic
Size: 110,138 square miles (about the same as the state of Washington)
Language: Spanish
Ethnic Division: 88% European, 8% Mestizo, 4% Black
Religion: 90% Roman Catholic, plus Mennonite and other Protestant
Tourist Season: Year-round
Peak Tourist Season: December through March
Currency: Peso (URP)

TRAVEL TIPS

Entry: Visa not required for stays up to three months. A passport is required.
Transportation: There are international connections to Montevideo from United States, Europe, and Latin American countries. Buses, with some air service, provide the major form of intercity travel. Within Montevideo, bus service is inexpensive and taxis are reasonable and available.
Shopping: Local items include furs, leather goods, woolen goods, ostrich bags, jewelry and precious stones, and gaucho souvenirs of dolls and bombillas.

CULTURAL CAPSULE

The population is mostly Spanish and Italian (over 80 percent). Mestizos only account for 8 percent and Blacks 4 percent of the population. Most are Roman Catholics (65 percent), with the rest belonging to various Christian and Protestant faiths. There is a small minority of Jewish faithful.

Cultural Hints:
- A warm, friendly handshake is the common greeting.
- Uruguayans have close personal space.

- Keep feet on the floor.
- The "OK" sign is rude.
- Eating and food:
  To call a waiter, raise hand.
  Keep hands above the table.
  When finished eating, place utensils side by side on the plate.
  Using a toothpick in public is rude.
  Common foods are meats, fish, vegetables, and fruits. Typical dishes are roasts, stews, and meat pies.

Physical Characteristics

The country consists mostly of rolling plains and low hills. There are some coastal lowlands. The climate is warm and temperate subtropical with very infrequent frosts.

Tourism Characteristics

With the assistance of the Organization of American States, Uruguay has been developing programs to improve its tourist industry. Argentina and Brazil account for over 77 percent of all visitors to Uruguay. The country has not been successful in attracting visitors from the United States or Europe because there are few direct flights and Uruguay is not included in the Latin American circuit by tour operators.

Tourist Destinations and Attractions

The principal attraction is Montevideo, the capital, which is situated on a bay with beautiful beaches. The major attraction in Montevideo is the Palacio Salvo. The Municipal Palace contains two fine museums: the Museum of Art History and the Museum of Pre–Columbian and Colonial Art. The Palacio Legislativo has pink granite pillars, mosaic floors, and historic wall murals. The Teátro Solís (Theater of the Sun) and the Museum of Natural History are significant attractions. On top of the Cerro (Hill), there is an old fort, which is now a military museum, and the oldest lighthouse in the country. Extending north toward Brazil, there are a number of beaches and resorts, all popular with Argentine and Brazilian tourists. The most popular is Punta del Este, which has excellent beaches backed by sand dunes covered with pines.

BRAZIL AND THE GUYANAS

Brazil

1000 km

North Atlantic Ocean

Belém
São Luís
Manaus
Recife
Rio Branco
Salvador
Cuiabá
BRASÍLIA ★
Belo Horizonte
Corumbá
Rio de Janeiro
São Paulo

South Atlantic Ocean

Pôrto Alegre

Boundary representation is
not necessarily authoritative.

Capital: Brasília
Government: Federal republic
Size: 3,286,487 square miles (slightly larger than the United States, excluding Alaska)
Language: Portuguese, English
Ethnic Division: 55% European, 38% mixed, 6% Black, 1% other
Religion: 70% Roman Catholic, 30% other
Tourist Season: January through March
Peak Tourist Season: February
Currency: Cruzeiro

CULTURAL CAPSULE

Brazil is the largest and most populous country in Latin America. Most of the people live in the south-central area, which includes the industrial cities of São Paulo, Río de Janeiro, and Belo Horizonte. Four major groups comprise the Brazilian population: indigenous Indians of Tup and Guarani language stock; the Portuguese, who colonized in the sixteenth century; Africans brought to Brazil as slaves; and various European (German and Italian) and Asian immigrant groups. Soccer is the national sport and is played and watched passionately.

Cultural Hints:
- A warm, friendly handshake is the common greeting and departing gesture.
- Good friends embrace (Abrazo).
- Brazilians have close personal space.
- The "OK" with three fingers protruding outward is vulgar.
- To get someone's attention people say "pssst."
- Eating and food:
  Do not touch food while eating.
  Summon a waiter by holding up the index finger.
  Do not cut food with the side of the fork.
  Do not smoke during meals.
  Do not drink directly from a can or bottle.
  Common foods are bread, cheese, beans, rice, meat, and fruit. Typical dishes are imbu (potatoes and bread), feijoada (black beans with beef, pork, sausage, tongue), and meat with egg and French fries.

TRAVEL TIPS

Entry: A visa is required. Also, proof of sufficient funds and onward or round-trip transportation are required.
Transportation: Brazil has excellent international direct flights to the United States, Europe, and other Latin American countries. Travel to major tourist regions is by air and is expensive. São Paulo and Río de Janeiro have rapid transit systems. Buses provide more general coverage, and taxis with red license plates (fixed meters) are best.
Health: Malaria, yellow fever, and cholera are of concern.
Caution: Street crime is common. Tourists should not wear jewelry, flash money, or call attention to personal belongings.
Shopping: Local items include jewelry, gemstones, hardwood items, clay figurines, pottery, soapstone carvings, bone carvings, leather work, snake skin, tiles, basketwork, cotton fabrics, antique silver, and Indian miniature souvenirs.

Physical Characteristics

Brazil has mostly flat to rolling lowlands in the north, with some plains, hills, and mountains in the south with a narrow coastal belt. The climate is mostly tropical with a temperate subtropical area in the south.

Tourism Characteristics

Brazil continues to improve its tourist industry but it still has negative balance-of-trade payments. In 1971, Brazil had only 291,000 visitors; by 1975, the number had increased to 517,967, an increase of 78 percent (International Tourism Reports, 1985). In 1996 there were 2.2 million visitors. Like the other South American countries, Brazil has a strong intraregional tourist bias, with over 63 percent of the visitors coming from other South American coun-

Figure 5–7 Copacabana Beach, Rio de Janiero

older parts of the city are now a national monument, and considerable restoration work has been completed. As in many Brazilian towns, Carnival in Salvador is exciting and entertaining. There are a number of outstanding beaches in the region. With its 34 islands, the Bahía de Todos os Santos provides all types of water experiences.

Río, with its famed Copacabana Beach, Figure 5–7, architecture, monuments, and festivals, forms one corner of the tourist triangle, and the capital city of Brasília forms another. The triangle is completed by São Paulo, a modern city with gourmet food, waterfalls, and beautiful beaches, all important to the development of the strong tourist industry in this area.

Brasília, the capital, is a completely new city designed to attract some of the population inland from the coast. The public buildings were designed by architect Oscar Niemeyer. The center is the Plaza of the Three Powers, with marble buildings, reflecting pools, and metal sculpture. Brasília is famous for its large number of modern sculptures.

São Paulo, the largest city in Brazil and South America, has a modern dynamic skyline. The Butanta Institute, a snake farm, and the old Municipal Market are on the outskirts of town. São Paulo has fine beaches and resorts and small colonial villages.

Iguazú Falls, Figure 5–8, in the south, is visited heavily from Brazil since the Brazilian side offers the best panoramic view.

tries, 22 percent from Europe, and 7.8 percent from the United States.

Tourist Destinations and Attractions

The three principal tourist areas are Amazonia, the northeast, and the triangle formed by Río de Janeiro, Brasília, and São Paulo. In Amazonia, the Amazon River's exotic wildlife and vast rain forests offer an experience unequaled anywhere. Amazon tourist activity centers in the area of Manaus. The river trip from Belén to Manaus is becoming increasingly popular. Dominating Manaus is its famous theater (opera house).

Attractive local culture, beautiful church architecture, and pretty towns and cities such as Recife, the "Venice of America," can be found in the northeast. Salvador, the capital of Bahía State, has many churches, fortifications, and other old buildings. The

Figure 5–8 Iguazu Falls, Brazil

Guyana

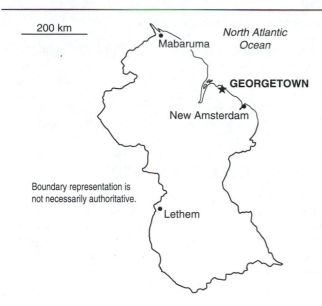

200 km

Mabaruma

North Atlantic Ocean

GEORGETOWN

New Amsterdam

Boundary representation is not necessarily authoritative.

Lethem

Capital: Georgetown
Government: Republic within Commonwealth
Size: 83,000 square miles (about the size of Idaho)
Language: English, Amerindian dialects
Ethnic Division: 51% East Indian, 43% Black and mixed, 4% Amerindian, 2% European and Chinese
Religion: 57% Christian, 33% Hindu, 9% Muslim, 1% other
Tourist Season: August to October
Peak Tourist Season: August to October
Currency: Guyana dollar

 ## TRAVEL TIPS

Entry: A visa is required. Proof of round-trip or onward transportation is also required.
Transportation: Some direct international flights from United States. Most must connect through Caracas and/or the Port of Spain.
Health: Malaria, yellow fever, and cholera are of concern. Drinking water should be boiled. Buses within Georgetown are irregular. Taxi service is available.
Shopping: Local items include Indian handicrafts, such as beaded aprons, basketwork, blowpipes, pottery, and clothing.

CULTURAL CAPSULE

The population comprises five main ethnic groups: East Indian, African, Amerindian, Chinese, and Portugese. The population is concentrated along the coast. Religion is an expression of the population, consisting of a number of Christian faiths, large numbers of Hindus, and a sizable minority of Muslims.

Physical Characteristics

The terrain is mostly rolling highlands with a low coastal plain. The climate is tropical hot and humid, moderated by northeast trade winds. The two rainy seasons are May to mid-August, and mid-November to mid-January.

Tourism Characteristics, Destinations and Attractions

Guyana has only a limited tourism industry. The major attraction is the capital, Georgetown, which contains attractive Georgian-style houses of wood supported on stilts. Some of the better sights are the City Hall, St. George's Cathedral, the Law Courts, the president's residence, and the Parliament Building. The botanical gardens have a large number of birds as well as a collection of palms, orchids, and ponds. The Kaieteur Falls on the Potaro River is in a class with Niagara and Victoria falls. The falls are nearly five times the height of Niagara Falls. Located in a jungle, they can be reached only by small aircraft.

Suriname

Physical Characteristics

Suriname is mostly rolling hills with a narrow coastal plain with swamps. The climate is tropical hot and warm.

Tourism Characteristics, Destinations, and Attractions

Suriname has the best-developed tourist industry of the Guyanas. It receives most of its tourists from the Netherlands. The United States accounts for only about two percent of the total visitors. Paramaribo, the capital, is a modern city with a diversity of cultures ex-

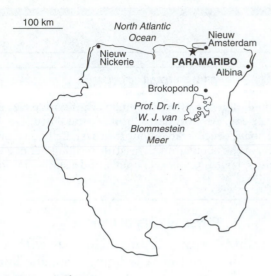

Capital: Paramaribo
Government: Military-civilian rule
Size: 63,077 square miles (about the size of Georgia)
Language: Dutch, English, Sranan Tongo
Ethnic Division: 37% Hindustani, 31% Creole, 15.3% Javanese, 10.3% Bush Black, 2.6% Amerindian, 1.7% Chinese, 1.0% European, 1.1% Other
Religion: 27.4% Hindu, 19.6% Muslim, 22.8% Roman Catholic, 25.2% Protestant, 5% indigenous beliefs
Peak Tourist Seasons: July, September, December 15 through January 15, and March 15 through May 15
Currency: Suriname guilder (SFL)

 TRAVEL TIPS

Entry: A visa is required. There are currency restrictions and exchange regulations.
Transportation: International connections are mostly through other Latin American and Caribbean countries. There is direct service with Amsterdam. Paramaribo has adequate bus and taxi service. There is little land travel between cities due to lack of adequate roads and bridges.
Health: Malaria and yellow fever are of concern. Check with health authorities before visiting.

CULTURAL CAPSULE

The population of Suriname is one of the most varied in the world. The major ethnic groups are Hindustani, Creole, Javanese, Maroon (Bush Black), Amerindians, and Chinese. Social relations tend to stay within ethnic groups. The population clusters along the narrow, northern coastal plain.

pressed in the variety of Catholic cathedrals, Moslem mosques, and Hindu temples. The People's Palace (the old Governor's Mansion), a number of eighteenth- and nineteenth-century Dutch-style buildings, and the restored Fort Zeelandia add flavor to the city. The country has a number of nature reserves providing a rain forest experience with a number of species such as sea turtles and a host of birds.

French Guyana

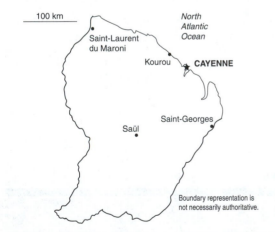

Capital: Cayenne
Government: Overseas Department of France
Size: 35,135 square miles (about the size of Maine)
Language: French
Ethnic Division: 66% Black or Mulatto, 12% European, 12% East Indian, Chinese, Amerindian, 10% other
Religion: Roman Catholic
Tourist Season: August to October
Currency: French franc

 TRAVEL TIPS

Entry: A visa is not required. A passport is required. There are currency restrictions on money taken from the country. Proof of onward or round-trip transportation is necessary.
Transportation: There are direct flights from France. International connections with the United States is through other Latin American and Caribbean countries.
Health: Malaria, yellow fever, and cholera are of concern.

Physical Characteristics

Low-lying coastal plains rise to hills and small mountains in the interior. The climate is tropical hot and humid with little seasonal variation.

Tourism Characteristics, Destinations, and Attractions

French Guyana has the most underdeveloped tourist industry in South America. Most of its visitors are from France. Cayenne, the capital, is on the island of

Cayenne and is the jumping-off place for visits to the jungle and the notorious penal colony, Devil's Island. The second city, Kourou, is the home of the French National Space Agency's Guiana Space Center, from which the European Space Agency's Ardiane rockets are launched.

In Javouhey and Cacao at opposite ends of French Guiana, two Hmong villages contain some 1,200 tribespeople, resettled in areas resembling their former villages in Laos. Tourists can view a wide array of colorful tapestries woven by the Hmong women and purchase traditional Southeast Asian vegetables.

THE ANDES

DAY 1   LA PAZ

Today we will tour the capital city of La Paz, Bolivia. Like many other South American cities, La Paz is divided into an old section and a more modern section, which is divided by the Choqueyapu River. We will begin our tour on the "right bank" at the Plaza San Francisco and Church and Monastery of San Francisco. This contains some of the best examples of Colonial art and architecture in La Paz. The architecture includes Baroque, Gothic, and Colonial. Next, we proceed down Calle Mercado where we find Mercado Negro (Black Market). This is La Paz's main business street. There are many fine shops selling a rich abundance of food, colorful clothing, Indian handicrafts, and produce. Also in this area, we will find Avenida Camocho and the city's most elegant street, the Prado. Moving on to the "left bank" from the Prado, we will visit the military museum, which contains valuable arms collections and exhibits of the nation's military glories. Further up the street, we will tour the National Museum of Tiahuanaco. This is a large stone building that contains arts and crafts in the style of an ancient Indian civilization. The museum also contains a large library. To finish off our tour of La Paz today, we will visit the Church of Santo Domingo and the Plaza Murillo, which honors heroes from Bolivia.

DAY 2   LA PAZ–PUNO

We will begin the day with a ride to the town of Huata Jata, a Bolivian naval base located on the shores of Lake Titicaca. This is the starting point of a Crillón Tour that provides hydrofoil services to the town of Copacabana. Copacabana is located on a peninsula in Lake Titicaca and is the site of Bolivia's most famous pilgrimage. The Virgin of Copacabana statue, to which many miracles have been attributed, is found here. The Islands of the Sun and the Moon, which are sacred to Inca mythology, are also found nearby. The most impressive Incan structure, the Palace of the Virgins of the Sun, is found on the Island of the Moon. A rowboat or a motorboat can be hired on the beachfront from the Copacobana area to the Islands of the Moon and Sun. Lake Titicaca is set in the beautiful mountains of Bolivia and lies on the Bolivia/Perú border. The lake itself is legendary and is enjoyed by many tourists. Sail, fish, or sightsee around the lake and see the Uros Indians and their islands made of reeds and rushes. From here, we will take one of the famous cruises on a steamship to the other side of Lake Titicaca. This is a twelve-hour ride, with overnight accommodations, that will end up in Puno, Perú.

DAY 3   PUNO–AREQUIPA–CUZCO

After arriving in Puno, there are a few sites to be seen before moving on. Puno is a famous site for archaeological ruins at Sillustain, Juli, Pomata, Chucuito, Sonderhuasi, and Pucara, all of which are the locations of ceramic ceremonial bulls. From Puno, we will catch a train down to the city of Arequipa, the second city of Perú. Arequipa is in a fertile valley at the foot of the snow-topped volcano El Misti. The city of Arequipa is one of the country's most popular stopovers for tourists traveling into the land of the Incas because of its tree-fringed boulevards, flower-filled gardens and patios, and its quaint colonial atmosphere. While we are in Arequipa, we will see the twin-towered cathedral of the Church of La Companía; the Plaza de Armas, around which the city was planned; and the beautiful suburbs of Tingo. From Arequipa, we will take the train to Cuzco, Perú. The railroad passes through many beautiful valleys and climbs to incredible altitudes. Along the way, you will see many signs of ancient terraces along the hillsides, records of the Perú of the Inca.

DAY 4   CUZCO

Today we will be in and around the city of Cuzco, Perú. With its adobe houses and red-tiled rooftops in a peaceful green valley, Cuzco is often referred to as the "sacred city." Many of the buildings and houses in the streets of Cuzco have been built on top of the old ruins of the Incas. The Church and Convent of Santo Domingo were even built upon the site of the most sacred Incan structure in the city, the Temple of the Sun. This is a beautiful Catholic convent. Other sites to be seen are the Church of Jesus and Mary and the Church of the Triumph. The University of Cuzco is a great cultural center and a liberal and progressive institution. One of the most original churches is that of La Merced, which contains many fine paintings and has a library of over seventeen thousand volumes and many unique altars, including one made of solid gold and decorated with diamonds, pearls, emeralds, and rubies. The markets of Cuzco are also a must for they are famous for their rugs and skins of llama and alpaca.

continues

continued

DAY 5 INCAN RUINS

This day will be spent on the outskirts of Cuzco in the lands of the Incas at different ruins. About fifteen minutes from town is the mighty fortress of Sacsahuamán. This is where giant boulders of incredible size were brought from long distances across the valley and strategically placed so that only a few men were needed to defend the fortress on the top of the hill from the attack of many men. At Tampo Machaí, another fort outside of Cuzco, a fountain of water emerges mysteriously out of the stones. There are many ancient Incan beliefs about this fountain. The remnants of a big amphitheater, altar, and sacrificial stone that were built by the Incas can be seen at Kkenco. We will also visit Puca Pucara, where the Incas built a subterranean passage that led all the way back to Cuzco in the Temple of the Sun.

DAY 6 MACHU PICCHU

One more excursion that is a must while in and around the city of Cuzco is a side trip out to Machu Picchu, the lost city of the Incas. Machu Picchu is a large city built on a narrow saddle in the mountains. It is surrounded by forested mountainsides that were terraced right to the edge to provide land for the inhabitants. The town of Machu Picchu is still intact except for the straw roofs, which have, of course, rotted. Now, the city is a maze of empty plazas, chambers, and palaces that are connected by stairways that are carved out of solid rock. You will also see massive stones that were carved to fit together perfectly without the aid of mortar and have stood up through time. How the Incas got these huge rocks up this mountain is still a great mystery, especially since they didn't have the use of wheels.

DAY 7 LIMA

Today, we will see the sites and scenery in and around the capital city of Lima, Perú. We will begin in the heart of the downtown at the historic Plaza de Armas. From there, we will go to the government palace found in the central square. This building houses many historic mementos of the old conquistadors. Plaza de Acho, which is nearly two hundred years old, is the oldest and most famous bullfight arena on the continent.

REVIEW QUESTIONS

1. What are the advantages and disadvantages of tourism to South America?
2. Describe the altitudinal zonation in South America.
3. Why does South America receive so few tourists?
4. What countries in South America have the best tourist industry?
5. What South American countries are likely to have the most tourists? Why?
6. Which South American countries are tourists from the United States most likely to visit? Why?
7. What are the major attractions of South America?
8. Describe the landforms of South America.
9. Describe the climate of South America.
10. Compare and contrast tourism to South America with tourism to Central America.

GEOGRAPHY AND TOURISM IN
Western Europe

CHAPTER 6

MAJOR GEOGRAPHIC CHARACTERISTICS

- Western Europe has a highly urbanized, skilled, and well-educated population.
- The climate is moderate for its northern location.
- Western Europe is the home of the Industrial Revolution.
- Western Europe is one of the wealthiest regions of the world.
- Western Europe has an outstanding network of transportation and communications.
- Western Europe is the most densely populated region of the world.
- Most of the countries of Western Europe were colonial powers and still have considerable influence in countries that were former colonies.
- Western Europe is one of the major trading centers of the world.
- Western Europe's economy is based on service industries, technology, and heavy manufacturing.
- The region is characterized by cultural fragmentation.

MAJOR TOURIST CHARACTERISTICS

- Western Europe generates more tourists than any region of the world.
- Western Europe receives more tourists than any region of the world.
- Western Europe has a long and well-established history of travel.
- Europe leads the world in reducing frontier barriers between countries.
- Western Europe has a highly efficient tourism industry.

MAJOR TOURISM DESTINATIONS

European capitals
London, Stonehenge, Stratford-upon-Avon, and York in England
Dublin and surrounding area
Cork and Kerry, Ireland
Amsterdam and Polder cities northwest of Amsterdam in the Netherlands
Brussels, Bruges, and Ghent in Belgium
Paris and the Chateau Region of the Loire Valley
Cathedral of Notre Dame (Paris, France)
French Riviera
French Alps
Rhine River between Köln and Wiesbaden
Bavaria
Berlin
Swiss Alps and Lakes
Tyrol area around Innsbruck
Salzburg region
Vienna (Danube Basin)

KEY TERMS AND WORDS

Anglican	Glacial drift
Basques	Glockenspiel
Cathedral Cities	Hanging Valley
Celtic	Lochs
Chateau	Massif Central
Cirque	Medieval
Continental Europe	North Atlantic Drift
Druids	Polder
English Channel	Queues
European Union	Riviera
European Plain	Tyrol
Fens	"White Gold"
Gaelic	

Table 6-1 International Tourism to Western Europe

Country	Number of Visitors (thousands)		1996 Receipts (millions of US $)	1996 Average Expenses per Visit (US $)
	1986	1996		
Austria	15,092	17,090	14,039	821
Belgium	2,454	5,753	5,893	1,024
France	36,080	61,500	28,241	459
Germany	12,217	15,205	15,815	1,040
Netherlands	3,142	6,546	6,256	956
Switzerland	11,400	11,097	8,661	780
United Kingdom	13,772	26,025	19,738	758
Ireland	2,378	5,280	3,003	569
Luxembourg	457.5	771	295	382

INTRODUCTION

The countries of Western Europe combine with the nations of Southern and Northern Europe to form the most important tourist region in the world. Five of the world's top destination countries are from this region (France, Austria, United Kingdom, Germany, and Switzerland). In addition, three other countries of this region (Netherlands, Ireland, and Belgium) are in the top thirty. Together, these countries account for nearly 30 percent of total world tourist arrivals. They are also major contributors to world expenditures in tourism. These countries, without Ireland, account for over 36 percent of the total world expenditures in tourism. Western Europe is extremely accessible, with major transportation routes both within the region and outside the region.

The region has excellent connections to Anglo-America. The nature of tourism to Western Europe from North America varies considerably from country to country. Germany, Belgium, the Netherlands, and Switzerland are "short stay" countries that tourists visit in connection with a multi-country visit or tour. Austria, France, Ireland, and the United Kingdom are more likely to have a stronger one-country emphasis or be the main destination, Table 6-1. All have a high per capita visitor expenditure, but average visitor expense differs markedly from country to country, primarily reflecting differences in length of stay.

Increasing cooperation associated with the European Union combines with deregulation of the airlines to make European travel easier and less expensive. The deregulation of the airlines in Europe has been much slower than in the United States. The latest step in open skies allows airlines to fly between any two cities in the European Union, even on domestic flights inside another country. As in the United States this is creating a new challenge for the national flag carriers as low-cost airlines develop in Europe. Airfares are being driven down on formerly monopolized routes, and discounts are given on heavily traveled routes. The European Union is also in the process of removing border requirements between member nations.

POPULATION CHARACTERISTICS, 1997

Country	Population (millions)	Annual Growth Rate (percent)	Time To Double Pop. (years)	Per Capita GNP	Life Expectancy (years)	Daily Calorie Supply	Percent Urban
Austria	8.1	0.1	990	26,890	77	3,495	65
Belgium	10.2	0.1	693	24,710	77	N/A	97
France	58.6	0.3	204	24,990	78	3,465	74
Germany	82.0	-0.1	—	27,510	77	3,443	85
Ireland	3.6	0.5	147	14,710	76	3,778	57
Luxembourg	0.4	0.4	178	41,210	77	N/A	86
Netherlands	15.6	0.3	223	24,000	77	3,151	86
Switzerland	7.1	0.3	231	40,630	79	3,562	68
United Kingdom	59.0	0.2	433	18,700	77	3,149	90

Figure 6–1 Western Europe

However, border requirements vary as some countries are reluctant to remove restrictions for fear undesirables will enter a European Union country with lax border procedures and then have access to them. The European Union has increased investment in tourism development in the countries of Southern Europe and Ireland, increasing travel to these areas.

PHYSICAL CHARACTERISTICS

Landforms

The landforms of Europe can be divided into four general types. All are found in Western Europe and the British Isles, Figure 6–2. They include the Northwest Highlands, the European Plain of Western Europe, the central uplands of France and Germany, and

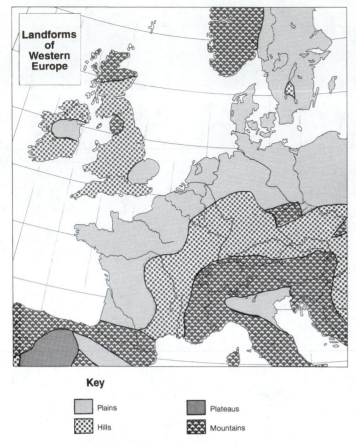

Key

☐ Plains   ■ Plateaus

▨ Hills   ▨ Mountains

Figure 6–2 Landforms of Western Europe

the rugged mountains of Switzerland, Austria, and Southern Europe. Part of the Northwest Highland that is characteristic of Northern Europe extends into Scotland, Northern England, Wales, and Ireland. These mountains are less rugged than the Alpine mountain system of Switzerland and are low, rounded, glaciated mountains. Glaciation has created such unique features as the lochs of Scotland, the Lake District of northwest England, the scenic Pennine Mountains of central England, and the spectacular mountain highlands of Scotland. The Scottish mountains are not high, but they have rugged portions that offer scenic vistas for visitors. They are visited by both international tourists and hikers and climbers escaping the cities of their respective countries.

The *European Plain* is an area of low, gently rolling topography and dense populations. This is the major agricultural and industrial region of continental Europe. It has been important historically for migrations of peoples and movements of armies, including the German armies in World War II. The European Plain includes Southern England and Western Europe. It extends across the northern half of France, Belgium, and the Netherlands through Germany and Poland and into Russia, where it is called

the Russian Plain. Important rivers cross this plain, including the Thames, Rhine, and Seine—three of the most important rivers in Europe. Numerous tourist attractions dot the Plain including the Shakespeare Country of Stratford-on-Avon in England, London, Paris, and other great European cities, and Versailles and other architectural remnants of Europe's colorful past.

To the south and east of the European Plain are the Alpine mountain systems of the Swiss and Austrian Alps, where elevations reach more than 15,000 feet. Between the European Plain and the Alps lie the central uplands and plateaus of Western Europe. These uplands and plateaus have eroded over the centuries and have low relief. They are found in discontinuous locations throughout the region. The most notable of these are the rugged landscapes of the Black Forest area of Germany and the *massif central* highland of France. The Alps are characterized by dramatic landforms that were created by mountain glaciation and water erosion. Picturesque amphitheater-like *cirques*, ridges, and deep valleys with waterfalls pouring forth from *hanging valleys* hundreds of feet above the main valley floor make this one of the most scenic areas of the world. The combination of landforms in Western Europe makes the region an important tourist destination for such activities as hiking, camping, and skiing.

Climate Characteristics

All of the British Isles, the Netherlands, Belgium, Luxembourg, and much of France and Germany have a marine west coast climate. The *peninsular* nature of Europe allows the water surrounding Western Europe to moderate the temperature. Winter temperatures in southern England (at a latitude north of the United States northern border) are similar to those found in Virginia in the winter. Summer temperatures are cooler than those in Virginia, creating a moderate climate throughout the year, with rain during most seasons. The region receives between twenty and forty inches of precipitation in most areas, with higher precipitation totals in Ireland, Scotland, and the other highland regions. On the continent, the marine influence is modified by the land. Winter temperatures in eastern France and in Germany are lower than those in the British Isles, and summer temperatures are higher. The moderating effect of the Atlantic Ocean is the result of the *North Atlantic Drift* (Gulf Stream), which brings warm water from the Gulf of Mexico to the European Continent.

Austria and Switzerland have greater climatic variations due to differences in local elevations and the direction a specific valley faces. There are great differences in climate, with January temperatures dropping below –30 degrees Fahrenheit in the high Alps. During July, temperatures range from 50 to 60 degrees Fahrenheit in the high mountains to 70 to 80 degrees Fahrenheit in the lower valleys.

TOURISM IN WESTERN EUROPE

Ireland

Capital: Dublin
Government: Republic
Size: 27,136 square miles (slightly larger than West Virginia)
Language: Irish (*Gaelic*) and English
Ethnic Division: Celtic with some English
Religion: 93% Roman Catholic, 4% Anglican, 3% other
Tourist Season: April to September
Peak Tourist Season: July and August (33%)
Currency: Irish pound

 ## TRAVEL TIPS

Entry: Visas are not required. Passports are required. You may be asked to show proof of onward or round-trip transportation.
Transportation: There are good connections between North America and Shannon. Other connections are available to Dublin and Shannon from European countries. Excellent and frequent ferry service to Great Britain and France is available. Ireland is part of the Eurail system. There is good train and bus service within the country. In major cities, public transportation is provided by bus and is efficient and reasonably priced. Taxis are expensive.
Shopping: Common items are Irish tweeds, jackets, suits, skirts, ties, knee rugs, tartans, Irish linen, laces, poplins, knitted goods, fishermen's sweaters, pottery, silver work, Connemara marble souvenirs, and world-famous Waterford glass.

CULTURAL CAPSULE

The Irish people are of Celtic origin. There is a significant minority descended from the Anglo-Normans. English is the common language, but Irish (Gaelic) is also an official language and is taught in the schools. The Irish are very friendly and cheerful. The people are about 94 percent Catholic.

Cultural Hints:
- A warm and friendly handshake is a common greeting.
- Lines (*queues*) are common and respected.
- The "V" for victory sign with back of hand facing out is offensive.
- Avoid gestures that use the fingers.
- Eating and food:
  Charges are generally included in the bill. If not, a tip is customary.
  Typical food includes fresh vegetables, dairy products, breads, seafood (especially smoked salmon), potatoes, chicken, pork, beef, and mutton.

Physical Characteristics

Ireland's terrain consists of a level-to-rolling interior plain surrounded by rugged hills and low mountains. The soils of this fertile central plain consist of *glacial drift* (rocks and soil carried by glaciers) deposited during the Ice Age. The climate is temperate marine, modified by the North Atlantic Drift, creating mild winters and cool summers. The mild, moist climate accounts for Ireland's famous green landscape and the woolen clothing that is worn much of the year.

Tourism Characteristics

The Republic of Ireland has not had the volume of tourists received by other Western European countries, but it now has some 5.2 million. This represents a 65 percent increase in visitors over 1990. Tourism now accounts for 6.8 percent of the country's GNP and 7.5 percent of its total employment. Since joining the *European Union* (EU) Ireland has had one of the fastest-growing economies in Europe.

The greatest number and percentage of visitors to Ireland are from the United Kingdom. Excluding

Northern Ireland, Great Britain accounts for nearly 48 percent of total tourists to Ireland. Including Northern Ireland, it would be 62 percent. Visitors from the United States rank a distant second. There has been significant growth in tourists from *Continental Europe,* more than doubling the number of visitors since 1985. Germany (265,000) and France (242,000) are the two leaders. North American visitors account for 12 percent of Ireland's visitors, but this has declined from 17 percent in 1985. The domination of Ireland's tourism by visitors from the United Kingdom and the United States is a reflection of historical and cultural ties. During the period between 1840 and 1860, Ireland's population declined from five million to just over two million, as a blight struck the staple crop of potatoes. Millions migrated to the United Kingdom and the United States, creating strong cultural and family ties that still exist.

Travel linkages with the United Kingdom have been improved with some deregulation of the airline industry and greater competition on the London-Dublin route. The results have been a dramatic drop in airfares and an increase in traffic. These linkages are also expressed in the length of visitor stay of 10.8 days, which is the longest of Western Europe. This destination character of tourism to Ireland reflects the family and cultural linkages as well as Ireland's physical separation from Western Europe. Further, Ireland's membership in the European Union increased European visitors. Today 23 percent of visitors come from Continental Europe. Most indicate holiday as the primary purpose of their visits. Growth in European routes has also increased air service from the *Continent.* TAP Air Portugal, Alitalia, KLM, Cityhopper, and Air Littoral all have begun service to Ireland in the last few years.

The past political troubles in Northern Ireland have hampered the growth of tourism to the Republic of Ireland from North America, as many potential visitors wrongly perceive the problem to be occurring on all of the island. Recognizing the importance of tourism to Ireland, the government established a National Tourist Board (the *Bord Failte Eireann*) in 1955, which is responsible for promotion, development, and marketing of tourism to Ireland. In 1964, eight regional tourist organizations were established to promote local areas and provide information services and accommodation reservation facilities.

Tourist Destinations and Attractions

The most important attraction of Ireland is the combination of a scenic cultural landscape in a lush, green setting. The beautiful pastoral scenery that results is a unique characteristic of the countryside. The Irish people are some of the most friendly and helpful in all of Europe. Descriptions of the major travel regions follow.

Dublin and Surrounding Area. Dublin is the capital and cultural center of Ireland. It contains a number of important historic buildings such as the Abbey Theater; St. Patrick's Cathedral, built in 1191; Tailor's Guild Hall, built in 1706; Christ Church on the edge of the liberties section of Dublin, which has a history of eight hundred years, Figure 6–3; the National Museum; the Custom House, dating from 1791; and the O'Connell Bridge, built in 1880. The single most important attraction in Ireland is Trinity College, which was founded by Queen Elizabeth in 1591. It has in its library the remarkable eighth-century *Book of Kells.* To the north of Dublin in the Boyne River valley there are a number of ancient burial places and ruins of both pagan and Christian Ireland. At Newgrange, there is a prehistoric burial mound as impressive as Stonehenge. Archaeologists and tourists alike have marvelled at the "Light Box," where at daybreak on a midwinter day (Winter Solstice) the sun's rays penetrate into the recessed area of the chamber. The light box is the slit above the entrance through which the sun's rays shine. The ancient kings of Ireland are buried in the burial mounds along the Boyne at Newgrange and Knowth. The great palace at the Hill of Tara was the seat of government from the Bronze Age to the Middle Ages.

The Upper West Coast. This region was the home of poet Yeats and is central to his writing. It is a rugged region, where the sea pounds the shores and picturesque castles are located. It is an area much acclaimed for its coastal scenery of cliffs and sandy beaches. Bloody Foreland is named for the intense blood-red beauty of its sunsets. The road to Bloody Foreland twists and climbs around the spectacular coastline, which includes the tallest marine cliffs in Europe. These cliffs tower up to a mile above the sea. Behind the coastal plain rise mountains interspersed with deep glens and innumerable crystal lakes. This is the heart of Yeats country, which inspired his poetry. An important site, Lough Derg, is one of Ireland's most noted places of pilgrimage. In Glencolumbkille, there is a specially created folk village showing how three centuries of Irish have lived in thatched cottages.

Courtesy Irish Tourist Board

Figure 6–3 Christ Church, Dublin

Galway and Galway Bay. This is a region of the Irish landscape that inspired legends in song and deed. It has attractive fishing villages and shepherds' whitewashed, thatched-roof cottages. *Castles, cathedrals,* and Spanish architectural remnants are readily viewed in the landscape. Columbus is reputed to have stopped in Galway as his last port of call in Europe.

Galway City is the gateway to three distinctive regions: the horse-raising and fox-hunting country to the east; the two large lakes, Lough Corrib and Lough Mask to the north, which provide salmon and trout fishing; and Connemara to the west, the harsh land stripped to its rock bone by glaciation, suffused with liquid light and smoky colors, which have been the subject of many Irish painters. The area includes the fjord-like Killary Harbor and Leenane and the beautiful Clew Bay near Westport. Rising from its shores and dominating the surrounding countryside is Ireland's holy mountain, Croagh Patrick.

Limerick. Limerick was protected by King John's castle, whose drum tower and ramparts still stand. St. Mary's cathedral tower and fragments of the old city walls add to the historic character of the region.

Just to the north of Limerick, the Bunratty castle has been fully restored and furnished in its original style. Its Folk Park, a historical village, depicts the housing styles and history of Ireland, Figure 6–4. To the west on the Atlantic Coast in County Clare, there are a variety of mighty cliffs, caverns, and sandy bays culminating in the fortress-like Cliffs of Moher. They rise seven hundred feet straight above the sea. Burren County provides a lunar landscape and the Poulnabrone Dolmen, another of the Stone Age structures found throughout the country.

Cork and Its Environment. Cork, the second largest city in Ireland, is a port city on the Lee River. It is a major gateway for visitors from the continent arriving by ferry from France. Its history dates back to the sixth century and reflects the influences of the Vikings, Normans, and Oliver Cromwell. The legendary Blarney Castle and its famous stone are near Cork. Thousands of visitors climb to the top of the Castle to lie down and slide out over a well-like structure to kiss the stone, which is reported to bring them eloquent speech. The drive northwest from Cork to Waterford passes through small market towns, sea-

Courtesy Irish Tourist Board

Figure 6–4 Bunratty Folk Park

side resorts, cliffbound coasts, and mountains. Waterford City is world famous for its handblown lead crystal.

The Dingle Peninsula and Killarney. With its three "magic" lakes, Killarney is reported to be one of the most beautiful spots in the world and is the major resort area in Ireland, with its nearby Macgillycuddy's Reeks Mountains. West, across Macgillycuddy's Reeks, the Dingle Peninsula and the Ring of Kerry have some of the most magnificent coastal scenery and mountain background in Ireland. The region is characterized by lakes, lost valleys, soaring passes, little harbors, and sandy coves. Slea Head is the most westerly point in Europe. The scenic landscape is dotted with peat bogs that are being mined.

The United Kingdom

300 km

Capital: London
Government: Constitutional Monarchy
Size: 94,092 square miles (about the same size as Oregon)
Language: English, Welsh (26% of the residents of Wales speak Welsh), Scottish (60,000 in Scotland)
Ethnic Division: 81.5% English, 9.6% Scottish, 2.4% Irish, 1.9% Welsh, 1.8% Ulster (North Ireland), 2.8% West Indian, Indian, Pakistani, and other
Religion: 27 million Anglican, 5.3 million Roman Catholic, 2.0 million Presbyterian, 760,000 Methodist
Tourist Season: April to October
Peak Tourist Seasons: July and August
Currency: British pound

TRAVEL TIPS

Entry: Visas are not required. Passports are required.
Transportation: Excellent international connections to several cities in the United Kingdom from many North American and European airports. The London area airports are among the world's busiest. Frequent ferry service to Continental Europe. The Channel tunnel between Britain and France began operation in 1995. Excellent train and bus transportation within the country. Public transportation is efficient and comprehensive.
Shopping: Common items are woolens; men's clothing, tweeds, raincoats, overcoats; high-quality porcelain, china and glass; pewter, silverware, cutlery; art works and antiques; fabrics such as cashmere, tartans, yard goods, mohair, and sheepskins; and Scottish handicrafts such as baskets, pottery, jewelry, printed textiles, and stone carvings.

CULTURAL CAPSULE

The United Kingdom is a mixture of ethnic groups—Celtic, Roman, Anglo-Saxon, and Norse. The many invasions from Scandinavia, Rome, and Normandy are blended in the Britons of today. More recent migrations have created sizable minorities of Indian, Pakistani, African, and Asian ancestry. There is a strong degree of regionalism in Wales, Scotland, and Northern Ireland. The Welsh are descendants of the Britons, who settled the island before the Romans. They have maintained a strong cultural identity through their literature and language.

Cultural Hints:
- A light handshake is the common greeting.
- Excessive hand gestures are not used.
- The "queue" (line) is very important. Crowding in is not done.

- Avoid staring in public.
- Loud behavior is offensive.
- The "V" for victory sign with palm facing you is offensive.
- Eating and food:
  Call the waiter by raising your hand.
  Ask for the bill by making a motion indicating signing your name.
  Common English foods include tea, eggs, stewed tomatoes, bacon, sausage, fish and chips, beef, mutton, potatoes, and vegetables. There are many ethnic restaurants throughout Britain as well, especially Asian.

Physical Characteristics

The United Kingdom is separated from the European Continent by the *English Channel*, the Strait of Dover, and the North Sea. At the closest point, England is twenty-two miles from France. The country is mostly rugged hills and low mountains with level plains and rolling hills in the east and southeast.

The climate is characterized by cool winters and mild summers. Because of prevailing southwesterly winds, the climate is temperate. The year-round rainfall is heaviest in the coastal areas and the highlands. Fall and winter clothing is needed from about September through April.

Tourism Characteristics

The United Kingdom consists of England, Scotland, Wales, Northern Ireland, the Channel Isles, and the Isle of Man. Most international statistics on tourism refer to this definition of the United Kingdom. Great Britain consists of England, Scotland, and Wales. Britain is a term that is used interchangeably with Great Britain. Great Britain is the area referred to by British statistics on domestic tourism. England is the most populous and largest area of the three political units in Great Britain. It also dominates both international and domestic tourism markets to the United Kingdom. Eighty-three percent of all domestic holidays and nearly 90 percent of all overseas trips to the United Kingdom include England. However, when adjusting for population base on a per capita basis, tourism to Wales is more important economically than to England or Scotland. The ratio of tourist to resident in Wales is 4 to 5 compared to 2 to 4 for Scotland and 2 to 3 for England (International Tourism Reports, No. 3, 1991).

Residents of the United Kingdom have a high propensity for holidays and travel. One of the strongest characteristics of British international travel has been the growth of package tours. Companies such as Thompson have specialized in packaging tours for the mass market. These package tours are generally for week-long trips to such places as Greece, Spain, the Caribbean, and other "major destination" areas and are priced and sold inclusive of accommodations, meals, and airfare for less than the typical airfare on regularly scheduled airlines. British companies lease and operate their own airline charter services and hotels in the destination area. Thus, little of the tour package sold to countries and regions outside of Britain actually ends up in the local economy. Hotels in the destination areas even hire British citizens who are willing to work cheaply for the opportunity to live in an "exotic" location for a few months to a year.

The combination of low-priced packaging and poor weather at coastal resorts in Britain has led to a decline in long domestic holidays. Long domestic holidays were historically for the purpose of visiting British seaside resorts. Large English and Welsh resorts such as Torquay, Brighton, Bournemouth, Blackpool, Rhyl, Colwyn Bay, Llandudno, and Aberystwyth have lost up to a third of their visitors (International Travel Reports, No. 1, 1991). The "short break" market is the fastest-growing market in the United Kingdom and companies are developing strategies to capitalize on this trend.

Domestic tourism has always been highly seasonal. The peak season, which occurs in July and August, accounts for 30 percent of total domestic trips. Adding June and September to July and August, 53 percent of all trips were taken during the summer. The shortness of the British summer season, the school year ending in July, Bank Holiday in August, and the traditional closing of factories the first week of August are the major factors in the sharp seasonality of domestic tourism in Great Britain.

International tourism to the United Kingdom is dominated by visitors from the United States and Europe. Seventeen percent of all visitors are from North America, with the United States representing 14.4 percent. Europe accounts for 66 percent of total visitors, but no individual European country equals the volume of visitors from the United States. France (12.9 percent) and Germany (12.1 percent) are the two major markets in Europe. The average length of stay in the United Kingdom of 11.6 days is the longest of all the nations of Western Europe, indicating the destination character of the nation. Visitors from the United States are comfortable with the language and have a strong cultural link with the country. The location that receives the most international visitors is London (almost 70 percent of all international visitors), with southeast England a distant second at almost 14 percent. Although most visitors enter through airports around London, visitors still concentrate in the city, in many cases taking short day trips to surrounding towns and tourist sites or departing for travel to the Continent.

The opening of the Channel Tunnel in 1995 increased travel between Britain and France, making day trips between the two nations more practical and increasing the already-established trend. The two nations have already begun to take advantage of the linkage by creating a joint rail pass.

The combination of domestic and international tourism employs six percent of the labor force. This is more employment than is generated by banking, finance, and insurance combined. The importance of tourism in the United Kingdom was recognized by the government in 1969 when four statutory, independent national tourist boards were created. They are the British Tourist Authority (BTA), which is primarily responsible for overseas marketing; the English Tourist Board (ETB), which is responsible for marketing and development of tourism in England; and the Wales Tourist Board and the Scottish Tourist Board, which are responsible for marketing and development of tourism in Wales and Scotland, respectively. The growing importance of tourism to employment caused Prime Minister John Major to create a new government department (National Heritage) with Cabinet rank bringing together tourism, arts, museums, sports, and broadcasting.

The United Kingdom is a crossroads for international travel and is highly accessible from the Continent by air, bus, and rail. A large ferry system carries people back and forth into several European ports and countries. Transportation within the United Kingdom is excellent by rail, bus, or automobile.

Tourist Destinations and Attractions

It is impossible to identify all the tourist attractions in the United Kingdom in a few pages. In almost every shire, village, or countryside, there are some interesting attractions. Many of the castles, mansions, and some villages have been preserved by *National Trusts* (British or Scottish) to preserve and maintain history. The National Trust protects or owns about 200 historical buildings, over 400 miles of unspoiled coastline, and more than a half million acres of land. It has thirty complete villages and hamlets, castles, and abbeys, as well as lakes and hills. It owns lengths of inland waterways, bird sanctuaries, natural reserves, wind and water mills, working farms, coastal waterways, conservation camps, gardens, gift shops, and restaurants.

The United Kingdom is famous for its many thousands of stately homes. Many are open to the public either by private individuals or the National Trust. Descriptions of a few of the major centers follow.

London and Surrounding Region. London is one of the world's greatest cities. It has been the center of government since Roman times. Although there were a number of settlements in the region before the Romans, it was under the Romans that London became an important city. It provided good access for shipping of Roman solders and supplies. England's role later as a colonial and industrial power caused London to expand to include surrounding communities, creating Greater London. Because London has avoided skyscrapers, the resulting combination of parks and low buildings gives a feeling of being in an urban village. Greater London is the focal point of all tourism, domestic and international. Tradition is the word that best characterizes much of the attractiveness of London. This tradition is expressed in pageantry: the daily changing of the guards (footguards at Buckingham Palace; horseguards at St. James's Place), the Ceremony of the Keys at the Tower (locking the Tower, a tradition that has existed for seven hundred years), the yearly special occasions, such as the Queen's birthday, the opening of Parliament, and new terms at the Law Courts. The institutions of Britain are expressed in Parliament, Big Ben, The Tower of London (which houses the crown jewels), and churches, such as St. Paul's Cathedral and Westminster Abbey. The large parks retained when Kensington, Chelsea, and Hyde were created combine with a lack of tall buildings to provide a much more human-scale city than is experienced in other world cities.

London has numerous markets, such as Petticoat Lane and Portobello Road; great museums, such as the British, Victoria and Albert, Transport, and Underground War Rooms; art galleries; famous homes, such as those of writers Dickens, Keats, and Ben Johnson; impressive monuments; and theaters that fill with visitors every night.

West of London, Greenwich keeps the world's time and is home to the clipper ship the Cutty Sark and the National Maritime Museum. Near London, there are important castles, such as Hampton Court, home of Cardinal Wolsey, and Windsor, home of Henry the Eighth. Windsor Castle is still used by the British Monarchs. Overlooking the River Thames and Eton College, it is the largest functioning castle in use today and can be visited when the Queen is not in residence. Windsor Castle also has its pageantry with the changing of the guard and the procession of Knights of the Garter to St. George's Chapel. Near Windsor is Runnymede, where King John signed the Magna Carta in 1215 (but the historical marker was placed there by the American Lawyers Professional Association only recently). Today there is also a memorial to John F. Kennedy. Just southeast of London in Canterbury are the Cathedral and the shrine of Thomas Beckett.

Shakespeare Country and the Cotswolds. The center of one of the most interesting and scenic regions of small towns and villages in all of England is Shakespeare's birthplace, Stratford-upon-Avon. Known as the Cotswolds, the limestone-and-thatched-roof cottages provide a picturesque setting. Moreton-in-Marsh, Broadway, Bourton-on-the-Water, Cirencester, Chipping Campden, Tetbury, and the Slaughters are a few of these Cotswold towns built with the local honey-colored limestone that are still maintained today. Some outstanding castles, especially Warwick and Kenilworth, are fascinating to explore.

Coventry was firebombed by the Germans in World War II, and the rebuilt modern cathedral is a monument to peace. A statue of Lady Godiva, who, according to local folklore, some nine hundred years ago saved the town from additional taxes by riding through the streets upon her horse with only her long hair covering her body, is Coventry's other unique attraction. To the west in Shropshire, the Stokesay Castle is an excellent example of a moated and fortified manor house, and the world's first iron bridge is at Ironbridge. The bridge symbolizes the Industrial Revolution, when mass production of cast iron (and steel) made bridges longer, higher, and easier to construct.

The city of Oxford, with its famous Oxford colleges and their traditions, medieval spires, domes, towers, and ancient walled gardens, is also near this area.

The South and Salisbury Plain. From Brighton, one of the oldest historical resort centers in England, to Dorset County, there are a variety of scenic villages and medieval country towns. Brighton is a reflection of eighteenth-century England when the Brighton Pavilion was built as a palace. Nearby is Hastings, near where William the Conqueror defeated the last Anglo-Saxon King, Harold, in 1066 A.D. The two great cathedral towns of Salisbury and Winchester provide a rich historical view of Saxon and early history. Stonehenge, one of the modern wonders of the world, is the focal point of this region, Figure 6–5. The

Figure 6–5 Stonehenge

standing rocks in formation remain only dimly understood by modern observers. It is impressive to consider that these very large stones, up to twenty tons each, were moved to the area and set in a pattern before the invention of the wheel. Early folklore associated the development with the *Druids*. This has been discounted, although the Druids perform special ceremonies at Stonehenge on the twenty-first of June, when the rays of the rising sun fall in harmony with the pattern of the stones. Near Stonehenge at Avebury, there is another large prehistoric site with over one hundred huge stones in a large circle.

The Southwest Country. The climate of this area is mild, and parts of the area serve as the "English *Riviera*" with scenic harbors and dramatic landscapes. Tiny coastal villages, such as Polpero, were noted for their smuggling activities. The region has numerous hidden sandy bays, cobbled harbors, and the ruins of King Arthur's legendary castle of Tintagel on a Cornish cliff. Inland in the area, there are the moors, an area of two national parks, Dartmoor in Devonshire and Exmoor in Somerset. Dartmoor is an area of streams and wooded valleys with small villages and market towns on the edge. Plymouth is noted as the place from which the Pilgrims set sail and from which Sir Francis Drake went to battle with the Spanish Armada. On the edge of the area, Bath, with its Roman ruins and unique eighteenth-century Georgian architecture, and Bristol, a large port city, attract an important tourist trade.

North England. On the west side of North England, the Lake District has some of England's most beautiful scenery, with green hills, lakes, and moors. It is the region of the author Wordsworth, with the wooded shores of Grasmere, and the rushing streams and jagged peaks of England's highest mountains. The largest lake is Windermere, a long and beautiful sheet of water with a wooded backdrop. The Lake District is a popular destination region for domestic tourism for hiking, fishing, waterskiing, or pony trekking. Two of the most popular towns are Grasmere and Keswick, which are part of the Lake District National Park. On the central and east sides are the *cathedral cities* of Lincoln, York, and Durham. York, the most famous of the three, has Roman walls, timbered houses, and narrow twisting lanes.

South of York are the dales and moors that served as the inspiration for the novel *Wuthering Heights*. North of York and the Lake District along the Scottish border, Hadrian's Wall was the northernmost bastion of the Roman Empire. The wall, over seventy-three miles in length, was built by the Emperor Hadrian starting in 122 A.D. The Romans built a fort every five Roman miles. At every Roman mile, a mile castle, a small fort with barracks for a garrison of eight to thirty-two men, was constructed. The purpose of the wall was to protect the English part of the Roman Empire from the Picts and Scots of Scotland.

Wales. Wales has a rugged, scenic landscape of mountains and coastal areas. It is a region of castles, coastlines, and wild landscapes. It too is a popular region for hiking and other outdoor activities, with national parks, mountains, and scenic villages with names such as Betws-y-Coed, Llanberis Pass, Capel Curig, Nant Gwynant, and Snowdon. Snowdon National Park is a mountainous area dissected by cascading rivers and waterfalls, interspersed with lakes, forests, and small country towns. Cardiff, the capital and largest city of Wales, has important attractions, such as the impressive Llandaff Cathedral, the historical village, and a mining village illustrating the history of the mining industry of Wales. Cardiff also has its restored castle with a considerable amount of the original foundations.

Scotland. The major focal destination in Scotland is Edinburgh with its Royal Mile, a succession of picturesque streets that wind through the Old Town. The Royal Mile connects Edinburgh Castle, high atop Castle Rock, to Holyrood Palace, at one time the home of Mary Queen of Scots. Museums such as the National Gallery of Scotland, the Royal Scottish Museum, the Scottish National Gallery of Modern Art, and the Scottish National Portrait Gallery are major repositories of the history, culture, and art of Scotland. The Edinburgh festival is one of the most famous in the world. It begins in mid-August with the spectacular and colorful Military Tattoo on the floodlit Castle Esplanada and continues for three weeks with music, opera, drama, and art.

Glasgow, Scotland's second-largest city, is a large industrial city and considered one of the finest art cities in Europe. Not far from Glasgow and Edinburgh are the fabled scenic landscapes of the *lochs*. The term loch refers to landform features created when glaciers deepened stream valleys, which have since been flooded. Loch Lomond is one of the most beautiful lakes in Europe. Small villages, such as Inverary, and beautiful fjords adorn the west coast near Glasgow. The Highlands are scenic with tiny villages bordered by lovely bays on the coast and by loch-dotted moorland and steep mountains inland. It is in the Central Highlands that the famous Loch Ness is located. The islands off the coast of Scotland, Orkney to the north and Western Islands to the west, provide both scenic and cultural attractions enjoyed mostly by British visitors. The Orkney Islands were settled more than a thousand years ago by the Vikings, while the Western Islands were a center of Gaelic culture and Scottish Christianity. There are many golf courses throughout Scotland. The most famous is in the *medieval* university town of St. Andrews.

Few international visitors arrive directly in Scotland. Only 7.6 percent of visitors to the United Kingdom enter through a Scottish international airport. Even those visiting Scotland via England arrive in the United Kingdom from the southern part of the country. Scotland's tourism industry is much more dominated by travelers from North America than the United Kingdom as a whole. The United States and Canada are the source of 40 percent of Scotland's total visitors. Although not as important, Australia and New Zealand also have a higher percentage of visitors to Scotland than the total to Great Britain. All four countries have strong ethnic linkages with Scotland, as many Scots emigrated to those nations.

Northern Ireland. North of the Republic of Ireland, Northern Ireland's major attractions are in the outdoors. Northern Ireland has many lakes, which combine with its coastline to offer many beaches, coves, caves, and cliffs. The cultural attractions are associated with its Celtic and prehistoric background, which are found in museums, such as the Ulster Museum in Belfast, and in the countryside where castles and other structures dot the landscape. One of the better marine drives is the Antrim Coast Road. It has delightful bays and pleasant villages and towns along the coastline.

France

300 km

English Channel   Lille

PARIS ★

Brest   Nancy
             Strasburg

             Orléans
Nantes   Dijon
Limoges
             Lyon
Bay of
Biscay
    Bordeaux
             Grenoble
    Toulouse
Perpignan   Nice
             Marseille
             Corsica
Mediterranean
Sea

Capital: Paris
Government: Republic, with the President and Prime Minister sharing power
Size: 60,661 square miles (four-fifths the size of Texas)
Language: French, with some regional dialects such as Breton, Corsican, Catalan, Basque, Flemish, and Germanic
Ethnic Division: Celtic and Latin with Teutonic, Slavic, North African, Indo-Chinese, and Basque minorities
Religion: 90% Roman Catholic, 2% Protestant, 2% Muslim, 6% other
Tourist Season: Year-round on the Riviera; April to October in most of the country
Peak Tourist Seasons: July and August
Currency: French franc

⊕ TRAVEL TIPS

Entry: Visas are not required. Passports are required.
Transportation: There is excellent international access to France from several North American cities and numerous other countries. There are outstanding rail and ferry connections to other European countries. France has one of the world's fastest passenger trains (LTV) with speeds up to two hundred miles per hour. In addition, it is part of the Eurail system, providing reasonably priced rail travel both to and from other countries as well as travel within France. All cities have excellent public transportation. Paris has an efficient and user-friendly subway system.
Shopping: Common items vary from high fashion to the Flea Market in Paris. Perfumes, antiques, paintings, and other art objects are found both in galleries and on the street.

CULTURAL CAPSULE

France has been at the crossroads of trade, travel, and invasion for many centuries. As such, the three basic European groups—Celtic, Latin, and Teutonic (Frankish)—have mixed over the centuries to create the present population. Historically, France has had a high level of immigration. Most immigrants are southern Europeans (Portugese) and North Africans (Algerian, Tunisian, Moroccans). There are a number of other ethnic groups such as a sizable group of South East Asians, especially Vietnamese. About 90 percent of the population is Roman Catholic. Migrants and their children comprise the nearly two million Muslims living and working in France. French is one of the official languages of the United Nations and other international organizations.

Cultural Hints:
- A light handshake is a common greeting and used on departing.
- Business cards are exchanged often.
- Do not rest feet on tables or chairs.
- Do not use toothpicks, nail clippers, or combs in public.
- Do not converse with hands in pockets.
- Slapping an open palm over the closed fist is obscene.
- The "OK" sign in France is made by turning your thumb upward.
- Eating and foods:
  Fruit is peeled with a knife and eaten with a fork.
  Keep both hands above the table.
  Do not speak with food in your mouth.
  Typical foods include sauces, soups, bread, croissants, crepes, cheese, desserts, wine, beef, chicken. Crepes with filling such as ham, cheese, jams, and honey are good street foods.

Physical Characteristics

Two-thirds of France consists of flat plains or gently rolling hills. The balance is mountainous. The European Plain covers most of northern and western France from the Belgian border in the northeast to Bayonne in the southwest and rises to uplands in Normandy, Britanny, and the east. This large plain is bounded on the south by the steeply rising ridges of the Pyrenees Mountains, on the southeast by the mountainous plateau of the Massif Central, and on the east by the rugged Alps. Northern and western France generally have cool winters and mild summers because of their proximity to ocean waters. Southern France has a Mediterranean climate, with hot summers and mild winters.

Tourism Characteristics

France has a long history of tourism and a well-established reputation of being the playground of Europe.

It was involved in the Grand Tour for the noble and wealthy of Western Europe in the eighteenth century and has been a political and art center of Europe for at least five hundred years. France receives more tourists than any other European country, approximately 60 million. In addition, they have a large number of short-term border crossings; but in the summer months of June, July, and August, traffic and hotel occupancies are high.

Some of the elements that make France such an important tourism destination are its location, centrality, the importance and size of Paris with transportation systems that focus on the city from throughout Europe, large land area, the variety of landscapes, and the multitude of attractions. French landscapes are among the most diverse found in Europe, from the Vosges on the east, which reminds tourists of the Black Forest of Germany; to the varied Atlantic coasts of Le Touquet, La Baukle, and Biarritz; the vitality and variety of Paris; the castles of the Loire; the highest mountain in Europe, Mont Blanc; to the sun and sea of the Cote D'Azur (Riviera), with world-renowned coastal resorts centered on Nice and Cannes. This diversity is even greater with large international theme parks, such as Disneyland Paris, the Hagondange (The New World of the Smurfs), and the Zygopolis Waterpark at Nice.

France has a strong centralized tourist industry, with the Commisariate General au Tourisme directly responsible to the prime minister of the country. It promotes tourism, creates and improves the infrastructure through loans, subsidies, and fiscal incentives, and coordinates the various segments of the tourism industry.

Like the residents of the United Kingdom, a high percentage of French people (58 percent) take a holiday of four days or more annually. However, unlike other European countries, 82 percent of the French stay in their own country. The French use the automobile for vacation travel more than any other Europeans (81 percent of vacations), and the French are second only to the Dutch in going camping or owning travel trailers. Domestic travel is highly seasonal, with July and August as the peak. Travel on major highways leaving Paris can resemble a parking lot during some weeks in July and August when many government offices and businesses effectively close for the month.

International arrivals increased rapidly in the early 1980s, as did the length of stay. Tourism declined briefly in 1986 because of perceived political and terrorist threats in Europe, which affected American tourism to Europe. This was only a short-term decline as tourism increased again in 1987.

European countries account for over 86 percent of foreign visitors to France, with Germany and the United Kingdom accounting for 19 and 17 percent respectively. The United States market contributes some 38 percent of total visitors. While the number of visitors from the United States has grown, its market share has decreased. The increasing markets have come from Southern and former Eastern Europe. A significant percentage of visitors from Germany, Switzerland, Belgium, and Italy visit France to see friends, family, and relatives. France receives few tourists from Africa, the Middle East, or Asia.

All indications are that the future for tourism to France is extremely bright. The completion of the Channel Tunnel (1995), connecting France to the United Kingdom funnels a large number of tourists into France, rather than the Low Countries where they used to enter the Continent by ferry.

Tourist Destinations and Attractions

France, one of Europe's largest countries, has multiple attractions and a varied tourist industry. The size and number of these attractions are impossible to detail, but they may be briefly described by dividing France into tourist regions.

Paris and Surrounding Environs. Paris is one of the most striking capitals of the world, rich in history and monuments. Paris was first developed on an island in the center of the Seine River called Ile de la Cité. By the Middle Ages it had grown and extended to both banks of the river. Walls were built around the city in approximately 1200 by King Philip Augustus. Later, additional walls were built to encompass an expanding village. Paris temporarily became the capital in the tenth century, then permanently by the twelfth century. In the mid-1800s, a system of boulevards and traffic circles were planned and built, which combined with the many parks and monuments creates the attractiveness of Paris.

The most famous monument is the Tour d'Eiffel (Eiffel Tower). Built a little over a hundred years ago as part of the World's Fair held in Paris, it now dominates the visual landscape both day and night. The Arc de Triomphe was erected by Napoleon at one end of the elegant and beautiful shopping street, the Champs Elysees. A new attraction, the Grand Arc, part of Europe's largest shopping center, provides an excellent view of the city and is a gathering place in a long, open-air, central court area. At the other end of this street, in the middle of Paris, is the Place de la Concorde where Louis XIV and Marie Antoinette were guillotined. Some of the world's largest and finest museums are in Paris. The Louvre, with its modern pyramid entrance, and the d'Orsay are two of the most famous. They contain important and noted works of art, such as the *Mona Lisa, Winged Victory, Whistler's Mother,* and the *Venus de Milo,* as well as famous works of Cezanne, Monet, Renoir, Van Gogh, and Lautrec.

Paris has important cathedrals; parks and gardens, such as Notre Dame (one of the finest Gothic cathedrals in the world), Sacre-Coeur Basilica, Sainte Chapelle (with a beautiful stained-glass window), Jardin du Luxembourg, Bois de Vincennes, and Jardin des Tuileries, as well as world-famous night life and cuisine. Boat trips occur on the Seine day and night. Several famous palaces are located near Paris. The most famous is the palace of Versailles, built by Louis XIV and considered one of the most magnificent and elaborate royal residences and grounds in the world. Others are Fontainbleau, Chateaux of Vaux-le-Vicomte, Thierry, and St. Germain-en-Laye. Now Euro-Disney, some twenty miles east, is attempting to rival the historic attractions.

South of Paris, the cathedral in the medieval town of Chartres rivals Paris's Notre Dame, with marvelous Gothic architecture and exquisite stained-glass windows. The Loire Valley contains a number of well-kept *chateaus* of all sizes and degrees of charm. Within this area alone, there are over a hundred castles that can be visited. Light and sound shows, which were started in the Loire Valley in 1952, bring to life the rich past of kings, queens, and nobility of France as the castles, fortresses, and abbeys of the Loire Valley are brought to life in the brightness of a thousand lights. A few are Blois, with the death chamber of Catherine De Medici; Amboise, where 1,500 Huguenots were massacred in 1560 and Charles VII died; or Chambord, a royal palace of King Francois I, set in a large park as large as Paris. The Loire Valley is also an area of important wine production for France, adding to the picturesque character of the area.

Brittany. West of Paris, along the coast of the English Channel, is a picturesque and distinctive coastal area of cliffs, beaches, and charming fishing and farming villages. The countryside is dotted with giant granite boulders and wild meadows on the moors and thickets and forests in a gently rolling landscape. Sea resorts, ancient cathedrals, religious festivals and pilgrimages, and castles add to the pic-turesque coastline of Brittany. The high point of a visit to Brittany is St. Malo, with its massive medieval ramparts overlooking the seafront, and the great chateau and fortress.

Normandy. North of Brittany is the traditional home of the Normans, who invaded England in 1066. They left their mark upon the landscape with their unique architectural style in the cities of Rouen, Caen, and Bayeux. The link between Britain and Normandy's history is expressed in the cathedrals of Rouen, Bayeux, Coutances, Sees, and Hambye. Rouen was where Joan of Arc was burned at the stake. The site is now a church, and a monument has been dedicated to this female patron saint. Bayeux is famous for the Bayeux Tapestry, depicting the Norman Conquest of England.

Normandy has three hundred fifty miles of contrasting coastline, with cliffs, pebbly coves, and long stretches of fine golden sand. Resorts along the Cherbourg Peninsula are warmed by the North Atlantic Drift. Inland are forests, tranquil streams, lush pastures, and fruit orchards. Two of the most impressive features of the region are the beaches where the Allied forces landed on D-Day in World War II and spectacular Mont-St.-Michel. Mont-St.-Michel is one of the world's great wonders. The first view of the granite offshore mount, surmounted by a gothic abbey with a tall spire, is breathtaking. It is a popular pilgrimage center where visitors walk through twisted passageways faced by old houses, shops, and restaurants up to the top of the rock to the abbey church, with its spire rising more than five hundred feet.

The major attraction for many North Americans and Britons are the D-Day beaches along the coast. The American Cemetery with its rows of white marble crosses and stars of David overlooking Omaha Beach is a sobering, yet impressive, sight. On the seafront at Arromanches is an excellent museum commemorating the war.

Northern France. This vast, flat land is famous as the path of armies. Towns along the coast, such as Dunkirk, Dieppe, Le Havre, and Calais, are important points of departure to, and entry from, England. They also bring thousands of day trippers from Britain to enjoy the coastal beaches.

The French Alps and Massif Central. The center for this region is the cities of two past Winter Olympics, Grenoble and Albertville. Grenoble serves as a base for visitors to the many ski resorts in the surrounding mountains. High mountains and beautiful lakes characterize this region. It is a region with a reputation for mineral waters for the treatment of specific illnesses and for mountain resorts for the alleviation of respiratory complaints. Famous centers such as Vichy, La Bourdoule, Chatel-Guyon, Mont Dore, Royat, and St. Nectaire were built to cater to visitors seeking health treatment. Second homes, holiday villages, and individual chalets are popular in this region.

Cote d'Azur and Principality of Monaco. The international playground of Cote d'Azur, or Riviera, with its picturesque little harbors, marinas, and beach resorts along the Mediterranean and casino in Monaco, equals Paris as a tourist destination in terms of visitors. The region is high on the list of dream places to visit. The climate and warm deep blue sea have fostered fashionable resorts such as St. Tropez, St. Raphael, Cannes, Antibes, Nice, and Menton, along with Monte Carlo. The two most popular cities for American tourists are Nice and Cannes. Both have wide avenues, palm trees, and palatial hotels. The Cannes Film Festival in the spring brings visitors and movie stars from all over the world to the world's largest and most famous film festival.

Languedoc-Roussillon. A new tourist area near the Spanish border, Languedoc-Roussillon, is designed to take advantage of the sandy Mediterranean beaches and take some of the pressure off the Riviera. Montpellier (one of the most attractive towns in southern France) and Narbonne are the major centers for this developing region. It is a culturally unique area with small towns, small buildings with red-tiled roofs, and ancient fortresses on the hills. One of the most impressive medieval fortress towns is inland at Carcassonne. It is impressive both by day and by night with its circle of towers and battlements built by Visigoths and Romans.

Pyrenees. Along the border with Spain is a scenic mountain area inhabited by a distinctive cultural group, the *Basques*. Also close to the area is the famous religious shrine of Lourdes. Lourdes is a small town in a beautiful mountain setting on the edge of the Pau Gorge, which attracts thousands of pilgrims to the site where the Virgin Mary reputedly appeared to a young girl near the Massabiel Rock in February 1858. Just north of the Pyrenees, there is an excellent wine-producing area with wineries to visit.

Corsica. This Mediterranean island, with its rocky coastline, is the birthplace of Napoleon. Corsica lies 100 miles south of the French Riviera, 50 miles from the Italian peninsula, and 8 miles from Sardinia. Half of Corsica's 220,000 inhabitants are concentrated in the two main towns of Ajaccio and Bastia. It is sometimes called the Isle of Beauty. The island is covered with jagged, forested mountains, with small villages perched on the sides of the valleys. The sprawling coastal beaches fringed with palm trees, ancient buildings, and open-air cafés are popular for visitors.

Monaco

The Principality of Monaco is the second smallest independent state in the world, after Vatican City. It is located on the Mediterranean coast some eleven miles from Nice, France, and is surrounded on three sides by France. Founded in 1215 as a colony of Genoa, Italy, Monaco has been ruled by the House of Grimaldi since 1419, except when it fell under French rule during the French Revolution. Designated a protectorate of Sardinia (1815–1860) by the Treaty of Vienna, its sovereignty was recognized in 1961. It is a constitutional monarchy headed by Prince Rainier III. The people are French (47 percent), Monegasque (16 percent), Italian (16 percent), and other (21 percent).

Monaco is divided into three sections—Monaco-Ville, the old city; La Condamine, the section along the port; and Monte Carlo, the new city, the principal residential and resort area. International air service is available to North America and other countries of the world through the international airport at Nice.

Monte Carlo has become famous as an exclusive resort for the rich and famous and royalty. Monte Carlo's famous casino is a major source of income for the Principality of Monaco. The mild winter climate with its sunny days makes the Riviera a year-round attraction.

Belgium

50 km

North Sea

- Oostende
- Antwerp
- **BRUSSELS** ★
- Kortrijk
- Liège
- Mons
- Charleroi
- Bastogne

Capital: Brussels
Government: Constitutional Monarchy
Size: 11,783 square miles (slightly larger than Maryland)
Language: 56% Flemish (Dutch), 32% French (Walloon), 1% German, 11% legally bilingual
Ethnic Division: 55% Fleming, 33% Walloon, 12% mixed or other
Religion: 75% Roman Catholic
Tourist Season: April to October
Peak Tourist Season: June to August
Currency: Belgian francs

TRAVEL TIPS

Entry: Visas are not required. Passports are required.
Transportation: There are international flights to North America and other European countries. Belgium has excellent road and rail connections with other European nations and ferry service to Britain. Its internal transportation is excellent by major highways and limited access roads between major cities. Public transportation includes subways, streetcars, buses, and taxis.
Shopping: Belgium lace and chocolates are the most famous items. Also tapestries, diamonds, leatherwork, linen, glass, and antiques are common purchases.

CULTURAL CAPSULE

The people of Belgium comprise elements of Celtic, Roman, German, French, Dutch, Spanish, and Austrian origins. Today, the Walloons (French speakers) occupy the southern half of the country, and the Flemish (Dutch speakers) the northern half, referred to as Flanders. French and Dutch are the official languages, but are spoken in their respective regions. English is understood in both areas. There are minorities of Italians, Spaniards, North Africans and Germans. The majority of the population is Roman Catholic.

Cultural Hints:
- A light, brief handshake is a common greeting.
- Pointing with the index finger is impolite.
- Being loud is rude.
- Do not talk with items in both hands, including food.
- Do not put feet on chairs or tables.
- Eating and food:
  Keep your wrists on the table.
  Generally, bills are paid at the table.
  The tip is generally included in the bill; extra is appropriate.
  Typical foods include pork, game birds, fish, cheeses, fruits, vegetables, breads, soups, wine, beer, and mineral water. Belgium is famous for its chocolates and waffles. French fries are served with a variety of dressings based on mayonnaise rather than ketchup.

Physical Characteristics

The north and west of Belgium constitute a great fertile maritime plain, which is scarcely above sea level. South of Brussels, central Belgium is a rolling country of pleasant hills and valleys, rising gradually eastward. Still further south and to the east, the hills give way to the mountainous Ardennes Forest, the river valleys of which have been invasion routes in wars dating back to the Middle Ages but which are now popular tourist and vacation spots.

The climate is cool, temperate, and rainy with mild winters and cool summers, typical of a marine west coast climate.

Tourism Characteristics

Belgium's tourism is characterized by short stays. Visitors stay only a fraction over two days. The majority of tourists to Belgium come from other Western European countries, with the Netherlands, West Germany, and the United Kingdom accounting for approximately two-thirds of its nearly 5.8 million visitors. The United States is the largest market outside of Europe, accounting for slightly less than seven percent of total visitors. Many residents from the United Kingdom come for day or weekend visits. Nearly half of the tourists are from the Netherlands, the largest single source of visitors. Belgium's location on major international and European transport routes is conducive to a large number of tourists visiting Belgium as part of a longer visit to Europe in general. As is the case in many European countries, tourism is highly seasonal with the summer months as the high season.

Tourist Destinations and Attractions

The historical cities of Belgium-Bruges, Brussels, Ghent, Liege, and Antwerp are picturesque, combining medieval with modern atmosphere. The town center of the capital, Brussels, is one of the most picturesque of all Europe. The Grand Place (the town center) consists of the Town Hall, Figure 6–6, Maison du Roi, and the Guild Houses. Excellent parks such as Parc de Bruxelles and the Parc du Cinquantenaire also attract visitors to Brussels. Antwerp, the major port and a diamond center, is the home of the Cathedral of Notre Dame, Rubens House, and the Gallery of Fine Arts. Bruges, a medieval city, and Ghent, Figure 6–7, the "Venice of the North," are famous cities with their own personalities. Museums, churches, and palaces

Courtesy Belgium National Tourist Office

Figure 6–7   Ghent, Belgium

maintain the character of the Flemish (Dutch) culture, especially their famous artists.

In the southern part of Belgium, the Ardennes Mountains are where the famous World War II Battle of the Bulge took place. This area is popular with both Belgians and international tourists who are attracted to its spas, parks, quaint villages, beautiful streams, woods, and nature reserves.

The European Community (EC) and the North Atlantic Treaty Organization, housed in Brussels, foster business travel to Belgium. Belgium's coast has some of the better beaches in Western Europe, with promenades, casinos, and aquariums. Beach cities such as Knokke-Heist, Oostende, and Le Zoute receive large numbers of tourists on day excursions from Britain.

Courtesy Belgium National Tourist Office

Figure 6–6   Town Hall on the Grand Palace in Brussels

The Netherlands

75 km

North Sea

Leeuwarden • Groningen •
Den Helder •   Assen •

AMSTERDAM ★

Zwolle •

The Hague •   • Utrecht
Europoort •   • Rotterdam
                      Nijmegen •
                   • Tilburg
                      • Eindhoven

Maastricht •

Capital: Amsterdam (but government is located in The Hague)
Government: Constitutional Monarchy
Size: 16,042 square miles (the size of Massachusetts, Connecticut, and Rhode Island combined)
Language: Dutch
Ethnic Division: 97% Dutch, 3% Indonesian and other
Religion: 34% Roman Catholic, 25% Protestant, 41% unaffiliated
Tourist Season: April to September; Tulips-April
Peak Tourist Season: April to September
Currency: Dutch guilder (FL.)

CULTURAL CAPSULE

The Dutch are primarily from the Germanic culture, with some minorities from Indonesia and Suriname, former colonies of the Netherlands. The two major religious groups are Roman Catholics (40 percent) and Dutch Reformed (27 percent). The Royal Family belongs to the Dutch Reformed Church. The official language is Dutch; however, English, German, and French are generally understood.

Cultural Hints:
* A handshake is common as a greeting and at departure.
* Eye contact is important.
* Rubbing the nose with the forefinger from the bridge downward indicates someone is cheap.
* Do not chew gum while speaking.
* Pointing the index finger to the forehead indicates a person is crazy, or foolish.
* Touching and contact are not common.
* Eating and food:
  Hands rest above the table.
  Do not eat before the hostess does.
  Leaving the table during a meal is considered rude.
  Sample all items of a meal.
  Typical food includes bread, cheese, meats, sausage, potatoes, vegetables, fish (herring, smoked eel), and pastries. There are a number of Chinese and Indonesian restaurants. French fries are served with a variety of dressings based on mayonnaise, rather than ketchup.

TRAVEL TIPS

Entry: Visas are not required. Passports are required.
Transportation: There is excellent international air service to numerous North American and European cities. Also, there is excellent surface transportation service to other principal European cities and between Dutch cities. Public transportation is available in cities by bus and streetcars, serving the city and its suburbs. Bicycles are a popular mode of travel in cities and the countryside. Bicycles are available for rent for a nominal fee at train stations.
Shopping: Important local items include diamonds, Delftware, porcelain, traditional dolls, cheese, paintings, and antiques.

Physical Characteristics

The country is low and flat except in the southeast, where some hills rise to one thousand feet above sea level. Nearly one-third of the land is below sea level and has been reclaimed from the sea (*polder* lands). The climate is a marine west coast with cool summers. The warmest weather occurs between June and September, while the other eight months are cool to cold. Winters are long, and the damp cold from the North Sea is uncomfortable even when temperatures are well above freezing.

Tourism Characteristics

Tourism to the Netherlands is characterized by short stays. Europe accounts for 66 percent of all visitors, with Germany and the United Kingdom contributing over half of all European visitors. The United States is the largest market outside of Europe and ranks third overall. In 1996, the Netherlands had nearly 6.5 million visitors. Tourism is significant for the economy of the Netherlands, as it has one of the highest daily per capita expenditures in Western Europe. It accounts for 230,000 jobs for the country.

Tourist Destinations and Attractions

The major attractions of the Netherlands include its famous flower auctions, particularly at Aalsmeer; flower bulb fields such as at Keukenhof Gardens at Lisse, which draws many tourists in the spring; its culture and small villages such as Volendam, Haarlem, Gouda, and Zandvoort with their old houses, gardens, and residents attired in folk costumes in stores and other places where tourists frequent; its countryside of reclaimed polder lands; and rich farmland with windmills and canals. The major city of Amsterdam, with its famous canals, includes other famous sites and museums, such as Rijksmuseum, the Van Gogh Museum, and Anne Frank's house where her family took refuge from the Nazis during World War II. The Rijksmuseum is the national museum of the Netherlands, built around 1885. The most famous work of art in the Rijksmuseum is Rembrandt's *The Night Watch*. The Van Gogh Museum contains about eighty of his works arranged in chronological order to show Van Gogh's stylistic development. The most popular tour of Amsterdam is the glass-topped boats through the canals, Figure 6–8.

The Hague (Den Haag), where the government is actually located, has the International Court of Justice (the Peace Palace) and historic Ridderzall (Knights' Hall). Near Amsterdam, the miniature village Madurodam offers a view of almost all of the notable landscapes of the country. Rotterdam is one of the most dynamic and efficient seaports in the world, with a large free-port center. Other major cities include Utrecht, which has one of the oldest and best-preserved Gothic cathedrals in Europe;

Courtesy Netherlands National Tourist Office

Figure 6–8 Museum Boat Tours in Amsterdam

Leiden, a university town where the Pilgrims lived before setting out for America; and Delft, with step-gabled houses and a famous porcelain factory.

Luxembourg

Capital: Luxembourg
Government: Constitutional Monarchy
Size: 998 square miles (smaller than Rhode Island)
Language: Luxembourgish, German, French; many also speak English
Ethnic Division: Celtic with French and German blend; guest workers from Portugal, Italy, and other countries
Religion: 97% Roman Catholic
Tourist Season: May to September
Peak Tourist Season: May to September
Currency: Luxembourg franc; Belgian franc also circulates freely

TRAVEL TIPS

Entry: Visas not required. Passports are required.
Transportation: International airlines connect Luxembourg with Chicago and New York in the United States. Luxembourg is a rail and road hub for Europe. Major international routes pass through Luxembourg. Luxembourg also has excellent public transportation.

CULTURAL CAPSULE

Luxembourgers are an ethnic mix of French and German (75 percent) and a number of guest workers from Italy, France, Portugal, and other European countries. The language is a reflection of French and German blend. It is Luxembourgish, a Franco-Moselle dialect mixed with many German and French words. English is widely understood. Over 90 percent of the population is Roman Catholic. The remaining population belongs to various Protestant denominations or is Jewish. In 1815, after four hundred years of domination by various European nations, Luxembourg was made a grand duchy by the Congress of Vienna. It was granted political autonomy in 1838 under King William I of the Netherlands, who was also the Grand Duke of Luxembourg.

Tourism Characteristics

Luxembourg's central location has been a major factor for its tourist industry. For years, it has been a primary access to Europe by low-cost, scheduled airlines, such as Icelandair. It is on several major transportation routes. Of its 700,000 plus visitors in the 1990s, 80 percent were from other European countries, mostly its neighbors, Germany, Belgium, and the Netherlands. Tourism is seasonal, primarily in the summer.

Physical Characteristics

The northern half of the country is largely a continuation of the Belgian Ardennes. It is slightly mountainous and heavily forested. A plateau extends from France into the southern part of Luxembourg, creating an open, rolling countryside. Luxembourg has a marine west coast climate much like that of the United States Pacific Northwest, with mild winters and cool summers.

Tourist Destinations and Attractions

Luxembourg City, the capital, is Luxembourg's major attraction. It has medieval bridges, spires, and ramparts, which are illuminated at night; a gothic cathedral; and museums. The Ademes and Moselle Valleys are green, scenic valleys with old fortresses dotting the landscape.

Germany

Capital: Berlin, with some government functions remaining in Bonn
Government: Federal Republic
Size: 96,019 square miles (the same size as Wyoming)
Language: German (English is understood by many)
Ethnic Division: Mostly German
Religion: 45% Protestant, 37% Roman Catholic, 18% other or unaffiliated
Tourist Season: May to September
Peak Tourist Season: June, July, August
Currency: German (Deutsch) mark (DM)

 TRAVEL TIPS

Entry: Visas are not required. Passports are required.
Transportation: There is excellent air access to Germany. A number of cities have direct international flights to North America, Europe, and the rest of the world. Frankfurt's international airport is a hub for much of Europe. The airport also has a train terminal. Both rail and road transportation are excellent. Germany has a number of express trains and an extensive network of highways. The Autobahn is world famous as a limited-access, high-speed (no speed limits) highway. Cities have excellent mass transportation in the form of trains, steetcars, and subways.
Shopping: Items include musical instruments, fine porcelain, crystal, silverware, cuckoo clocks, wood carvings, stainless stell cutlery, Bavarian leather shorts, Tyrolean hats, Mercedes Benz automobiles, and wine.

CULTURAL CAPSULE

The population of Germany is primarily German; however, there are large numbers of foreign guest workers from Turkey, Italy, and the Baltic States. Changes in East Germany since 1990 have prompted former Yugoslavians and others to migrate to Germany. An ethnic Danish minority lives in the north, and a small Slavic minority known as the Serbs lives in eastern Germany. In the western region there are refugees from the Middle East, India, Africa, and Asia. The reunification of Germany occurred on October 3, 1990. It has been difficult (and expensive) to try to bring the standard of living of Germans in former East Germany up to the levels of West Germany. German is the language of the country, and English is widely understood and taught in the schools. The two major religions are Roman Catholic (in the south and west) and Lutheran (in the north and east).

Cultural Hints:
- A handshake is a common greeting.
- Business cards are exchanged.
- Men rise when a woman enters the room.
- Coughing or restlessness at a concert is rude.
- Chewing gum in public is not appropriate.
- Do not talk with your hands in your pockets.
- Do not put your feet on the furniture.
- To indicate the number one, raise the thumb.
- To point the index finger to the temple and twist is considered very rude.
- Eating and food:

    To call a waiter, raise the hand with index finger extended.

    It is common to be seated with other parties if seats are not available at a private table.

    Do not cut potatoes, pancakes, or dumplings with a knife.

    Typical foods include potatoes, noodles, dumplings, sauces, vegetables, cakes, pastries, sausages, pork, chicken, and ethnic foods. German sausage, in dozens of different types, is world famous. Regional dishes, such as smoked eels in Hamburg, smoked ham and bacon in the Black Forest, and liver dumpling soup and roast pork in Bavaria, are but a few of the many regional specialties.

Physical Characteristics

The terrain of Germany varies from the plains of the northern lowlands through the central uplands and Alpine foothills to the Bavarian Alps. The highest peak is the Zugspitze, reaching 9,720 feet. In the southwestern corner of the country is the Black Forest, so named because of the deep green of its firs, which give a dark or black appearance.

The climate is a marine west coast, with cool, cloudy, wet winters and summers moderated by occasional warm winds.

Tourism Characteristics

While Germans represent one of the great international and domestic travel markets of the world, the German visitor industry consists primarily of short, one-day excursionists or travelers in transit. Germany's location on the borders of the Netherlands, France, Switzerland, Austria, Belgium, Luxembourg, Czech Republic, Poland, and Denmark brings many one-day visitors from these countries as well as travelers passing through to visit neighboring countries. Like other countries of Europe, many of Germany's visitors are from Europe itself, as 65 per-

cent of their visitors are European. The Netherlands is the largest single market for nights spent in hotels in Germany, accounting for 14.6 percent. The United States and United Kingdom rank second and third with 10.7 and 9.9 percent, respectively. Americans only stay a few days, indicating that Germany is part of a larger tour of Europe.

The major purpose for visiting Germany is listed by visitors as a "holiday." Two other reasons given are visiting friends and relatives and business. In addition, a significant number of visitors from Northern Europe (Denmark, Sweden, Norway, and Finland) indicated "in transit" as a major reason for visiting. Business as a tourist attraction is reflected in the increasing convention exhibitors and international fairs in Germany.

The summer months of June, July, and August are the most dominant season for both domestic and international tourism. Most visitors (84 percent) arrive by road from neighboring countries.

Tourist Destinations and Attractions

Descriptions of the major tourist regions of Germany follow.

The Rhineland-Palatinate. One of the most romantic areas of Europe is the Rhine River region. Castles dot the islands of the river and adjacent hills. Vineyards and picturesque towns are found along the river's length. Although it is one of the world's busiest rivers, the Rhine is also rich in history and legend with its castles and islands. One of the most popular tourist attractions is the Rhine Valley between Bingen and Koblenz. The Rhine cuts deeply into the Rhenish Slate Mountains and is lined with vineyards, castles, and beautiful villages, such as Bingen with its Mouse Tower, Kaub with its Pfalz (toll station) in the middle of the Rhine, St. Goar, St. Goarshausen, Boppard, and Koblenz. The mighty Prussian fortress of Ehrenbreitstein towers over Koblenz. The Rhine and Moselle rivers join near Koblenz.

East of the Rhine, Westerwald and Taunus have nature reserves, the historic old state spa of Bad Ems, and the famous potteries in the Kanenbackerland. West of the Rhine, Eifel and Hunsruck offer crater lakes and wildlife parks; the Benedictine Abbey of Maria Laach, the best-preserved Romanesque edifice in Germany and a historic jewel; and the Ahr Valley, the largest red wine producer in Germany. Between the Eifel and Hunsruck, the Moselle winds its way from Trier to the Rhine, past many renowned wine-producing villages, art treasures, and religious symbols. Trier, Germany's oldest city, prides itself in having the most splendid Roman architecture north of the Alps. The cities in the Rhine region from Cologne (Köln) on the north, through Bonn, Frankfurt/Main, and Heidelberg on the Neckar, contain important cathedrals, museums, and picturesque town halls. Cologne, an old Roman city, boasts a cathedral that dominates the landscape amid a city replete with Romanesque churches, a medieval city wall, and famous museums. To the south of Cologne are Frankfurt and Wiesbaden.

Wurzburg to Fussen. The "romantic road" from Wurzburg to Fussen connects a series of medieval walled cities. Rothenburg is one of the most famous well-preserved medieval towns overlooking the Tauber River. It offers an extensive network of footpaths, wall walks, thirty gates and towers, and magnificent houses and museums. Other communities, such as Dinkesbürhl and Nördlingen, are equally well preserved. Augsburg, an important trade and banking center even in Roman times, is an excellent example of Renaissance architecture. At the end of the romantic road is Fussen in Bavaria.

The Black Forest (Baden-Württenberg). The Black Forest is an area of scenic beauty, with vineyards, hills, meadows, woods, and splendid vistas of the Rhine plateau. Heidelberg is home to Germany's oldest university town with its world-famous student castle. The Black Forest is famous for its many health resorts, mineral springs, and wooden clocks. The most well-known health resort is Baden-Baden. Other centuries-old spas are at Wildbad, Bad Liebenzell, Baiersbronn, Bad Mergentheim, Bad Durrheim, and Triberg. The gateway to the southern Black Forest is the medieval town of Freiburg, which is referred to as the "Gothic city of woods and wines." With its orchards and vineyards, the area around Lake Constance adds to the tropical flora of Mainau Island in the lake to provide a diversity of beauty.

Bavaria. The center of German culture in Bavaria (southern Germany) is Munich, with its large cellar-like beer halls, Oktoberfest Fair, and Fasching, the carnival time preceding Lent. The museums, city halls, and palaces of Bavarian kings abound in the area. Munich was the site of the 1972 Olympic games, and the grounds are today a major attraction with their unique design. South of Munich in the German Alps are high mountains with cogwheel railroads and cable cars, lakes, and some of the best-preserved castles in all of

Europe. Lederhosen and yodeling with the Alps as a backdrop are the most familiar tourist images of Germany. Northeast Bavaria is a storybook land.

King Ludwig II built several castles (Linderhof, Herrenchiemsee, and Neuschwanstein) that represent the apex of castle building in the region. They are in excellent condition and set in very picturesque areas. Other important attractions are the passion play at Oberammergau, which occurs every ten years in memory of the town being saved from the Black Plague that swept Europe in the fourteenth century; Garmish-Partenkirchen, from which a train ride can be taken to Zugspitze high in the Alps; and Berchtesgarden near the border of Austria.

Two cities, Nuremberg and Regensburg, serve as examples of the area. Nuremberg has a well-preserved ancient Imperial castle. Regensburg is dominated by many churches and patrician homes. The cathedral of the Old Free City is one of the Gothic masterpieces in Bavaria. The Danube cuts through the region and is navigable from Regensburg to the Black Sea.

Berlin and Former East Germany. Berlin's importance as a travel region has been growing rapidly since the reunification of Germany. Berlin is the official capital of Germany, although it shares many administrative functions with Bonn, increasing its importance for business and government travel. It does offer some interesting comparisons between the former East Berlin and West Berlin. The principal attraction in Berlin is the old capital of Germany and its growing importance as a cultural center. The performance of opera, ballet, drama, orchestra, and chamber music is taken seriously. Berlin's attractions include many historic buildings that have been reconstructed or which are being rebuilt after suffering damage or destruction in World War II. These include the Schloss Charlottenburg, summer palace of the Hohenzollerns rulers; the Egyptian Museum and a number of galleries and fine museums; the Brandenburg Gate; Humboldt University; Neue Wache; the National Gallery; and Marienkirche, Berlin's oldest church.

Major cities for tourists in eastern Germany are Dresden, Potsdam, Leipzig, and, in general, the southern part of former East Germany. Although Dresden was destroyed completely by fire bombing in World War II, it has been rebuilt. The open plazas with fountains and gardens contrast with the old structures that are being rebuilt. The major attraction is the Zwinger Art Museum, which has an exceptional collection of paintings by Rembrandt and Michelangelo. Just downstream of the Elbe is Meissen, the "Porcelain City." Since 1720, Europe's most famous porcelain *"white gold"* has been continuously produced in this classic small city that lies on the steep banks of the Elbe. Potsdam, about an hour from Berlin, has been a significant town since the 1600s. The palace Sans-Souci has important works of art. Cecilienhof, a twentieth-century palace near Potsdam, is where the Potsdam Agreement was signed.

Leipzig was the site of a famous battle of Napoleon. During the twelfth century, Leipzig was a famous trade center. Some of the buildings from that period are still standing, reflecting Leipzig's early glory. Along the border region near the Czech Republic is a beautiful wooded mountain landscape with a number of attractive towns such as Freiberg, with its ancient fortifications and tiny miners' houses in narrow streets.

Northern Germany. In northern Germany, a distinctive landscape of woodland, fields and meadows, moors, sky and water, and ports attracts travelers. The fresh, salty, North Sea breezes travel across the blue waters of the countless lakes, bays, fords, inlets, fertile *fens* (low farmlands), and fishing villages. The coasts of the North Sea, the Baltic, the Frisian Islands, and Heiigoland offer fine sandy beaches and modern spas. Two cities important in the region are Hamburg and Bremen. Hamburg, a Free Hanseatic City in medieval times, has a large harbor and the Old City, which provides a good place to explore. Bremen is one of Germany's oldest cities. The city's historic buildings date from the eighth century. The oldest are grouped around the Market Square, where the Town Hall with its superb facade and one of Europe's finest banqueting halls, the Grosse Halle, may be found.

Austria

Capital: Vienna
Government: Federal Republic
Size: 32,377 square miles (slightly smaller than Maine)
Language: German
Ethnic Division: 99.4% German, 0.3% Croatian, 0.2% Slovene
Religion: 85% Roman Catholic, 6% Protestant, 9% none or other
Tourist Season: May to September
Peak Tourist Seasons: July and August
Currency: Austrian Schillings

TRAVEL TIPS

Entry: Visas are not required. Passports are required.
Transportation: Good international air service with a few direct flights to Vienna from North America. There is frequent and excellent service from other European countries. It has excellent European connections by both road and rail. Austria is part of the Eurail system providing inexpensive rail access. Public transportation is excellent by bus, streetcar, and subway.
Shopping: Common items include dirndls (dress), wood carvings, music boxes, felt hiking hats with pins from each place visited, Tyrolean leather goods, porcelain figurines, crystal, ski equipment and mountaineering clothing, and antiques.

CULTURAL CAPSULE

Austria is inhabited by a very homogeneous population (99 percent German speaking). In the last few years, there have been a number of immigrants from Central Europe and Turkey, many of whom work in the service jobs of the tourist industry. There are two significant minority groups, Slovenes in south-central Austria and Croatians on the Hungarian border. Nearly 85 percent of the population is Roman Catholic. The official language is High German. English is understood by many and is required in high schools.

The Austro-Hungarian Empire played a decisive role in Central European history, partly because of its strategic position astride the southwestern approaches to Western Europe and the north-south routes between Germany and Italy. Although present-day Austria is only a tiny remnant of the old empire, it still occupies this strategic position for tourism.

Cultural Hints:
• A handshake with eye contact is common as a greeting and at departure.
• Chewing gum in public is inappropriate.
• Hands in pockets when conversing should be avoided.

- To signal "one" when counting, use the thumb.
- Do not be loud.
- Eating and food:
  Wait for all to be served to eat.
  To call a waiter, raise your hand with the index finger extended.
  Keep hands above the table.
  Place knife and fork next to your plate when finished.
  Typical food includes potato dumplings, goulash, Wienerschnitzel, bread, beer, wine, cheese, boiled beef, and chicken.

Physical Characteristics

The terrain of Austria is mostly mountainous, with the Alps in the west and south. In the north and south, the relief is low with gentle slopes. The climate is humid continental, with cloudy cold winters and cool summers with occasional showers.

Tourism Characteristics

Tourism is very important to the economy of Austria. Austria ranks the highest in Europe for tourism contribution to GDP. Like Switzerland, Austria experienced a plateau in the middle 1980s for visitors. However, it has had growth recently, drawing between 17 and 18 million visitors a year in the 1990s.

Austria's tourism is extremely dependent upon the European market. Over 88 percent of its visitors are from other European countries. The United States, the major non-European market, accounts for only six percent of the visitors to Austria. Even the European market is dominated by one major source, Germany, which contributes 63 percent of all bed nights. The common language, history, culture, and common border are major factors in this domination by Germany. While the length of stay is much longer than for most of the other Western European nations, it does receive a number of visitors who are in transit from the Northern European countries to the Mediterranean countries of Italy, the Baltic States, and Greece. There has been an increased flow from the former Communist Central European countries because of Vienna's location. It has become a hub for travelers from both the west and the east to visit the other regions of Europe.

There are two seasonal peaks, the largest being the summer, which coincides with the school holidays and is a popular period for outdoor activities, such as swimming, fishing, and waterskiing. The second peak is in the Alpine areas in the winter for skiing. The summer season accounts for over 50 percent of the bed nights and the winter, 30 percent. Austria's cities experience a less seasonal pattern of tourist arrivals. Austria receives an overwhelming number of its tourists by road, with 93 percent coming by car. Most of these are from neighboring countries and are excursionists on short trips or on their way to another destination. Packaged tour groups from the United States and the United Kingdom represent the bulk of air arrivals.

Tourist Destinations and Attractions

Austria is famous for its nature tourism (skiing, hiking), culture, music, and pastry. Three cities in Austria—Vienna, Innsbruck, and Salzburg—are the centers for the three major regions. Vienna, the capital, has famous churches, such as St. Stephen's Cathedral; some of the finest palaces of Europe, including the Hofburg, the Schonbrunn (which rivals Versailles), and the Belvedere; museums associated with the history of the Hapsburg Empire; some of the finest musical productions in the world; the performing Spanish Riding School (the Lippizaner White Stallions); the Vienna Boys Choir; and the picturesque Vienna Woods. Vienna is the center of Austrian culture. The Kunsthistorisches Museum (Museum of Fine Arts) is one of the major art museums in the world. The Danube and the Vienna woods are other attractions near Vienna. Farther from Vienna, the countryside offers towers perched on the Alpine foothills, medieval cloisters, and monasteries. Dürnstein is a red-roofed, riverside village where King Richard the Lionhearted was imprisoned during the Crusades.

With its medieval city and fortress, Salzburg is the birthplace of Mozart and provided the location for the hit film *The Sound of Music*. Like Vienna, Salzburg is a center for music and theater and is surrounded by beautiful mountains and lakes. The mountain and lake scenery attracts winter sports enthusiasts and summer sightseers alike. Mozart's birthplace is now a museum displaying early editions of his works, models of sets for some of his famous operas, and other memorabilia. In addition, the medieval Salzburg Castle and St. Peter's monastery, set on a hill in the center of the town, are major attractions. One of the most unusual palaces in all of Europe, the Hellbrunn, is a short trip from Salzburg. It was built by a prankster, the archbishop Markus Sittikus. Hidden water nozzles in the benches, walls, sculpture, floors, and ceilings spray visitors today as they did in his time. In an area just east of Salzburg, Austria's lake country, the Salzkammergut has scenic lakeshore towns and picturesque countryside.

Innsbruck, which hosted the Winter Olympics in 1964, is the center for summer sightseeing travel to alpine peaks and glaciers, and in the winter is a skier's mecca. Gothic architecture adds to the atmosphere of the city. The city is full of beautiful buildings. The two most-noted sights are the Golden Roof on an ornate stone balcony of an ancient mansion and the Roman-style Triumphal Arch. Innsbruck is the main city of *Tyrol*. Throughout Tyrol, there are mountain lakes, green meadows, high mountain peaks, rambling streams, and picturesque villages.

Switzerland

Capital: Bern
Government: Federal Republic
Size: 15,943 square miles (about the same size as Vermont and New Hampshire together)
Language: 74% German, 20% French, 4% Italian, 1% Romansch, 1% other
Ethnic Division: 65% German, 18% French, 12% Italian, 1% Romansch, 4% other
Tourist Season: May to September
Peak Tourist   Seasons: July and August
Currency: Swiss franc

 ## TRAVEL TIPS

Entry: Visas are not required. Passports are required.
Transportation: There is good international air access from North America, Europe, and other countries to the international airports at Geneva and Zurich. Railroad stations are located in the terminals at both airports, providing excellent access to other cities in Switzerland and Europe. Switzerland is part of the Eurail system connecting Europe, but it also has a rail system that links some of the most dramatic Alpine views, tiny villages, and lush green meadows by special public trains. One of the most popular is the Glacier Express linking such famous places as Zermatt, Andermatt, Chur, and Davos. It also has a good system of limited-access highways throughout the country. Public transportation is efficient and provides good coverage.
Shopping: Common items include watches, wood carvings, chocolate, embroidered items, cheese, handicrafts such as music boxes, cuckoo clocks, wood carvings, and antiques.

CULTURAL CAPSULE

Switzerland has a number of ethnic groups, German (72 percent, living mostly in the east and central regions), French (18 percent, living mostly in the west), and Italians (10 percent, living mostly in the south). There are a number of foreign residents and guest workers from the Baltic states, Spain, Greece, Italy, and the Middle East. Switzerland has four national languages—German, French, Italian, and Romansch (based on Latin and spoken by a tiny minority)—but only three are official. English is widely known and understood. The canton (province) chooses which language will be official in that province, and all signs are generally in that language. Nearly half of the people are Roman Catholic, and the other half belong to various other Christian churches. There is a small Jewish minority.

Cultural Hints:
- Various customs identify the language groups; however, a handshake is appropriate for greetings and when parting.
- Chewing gum or cleaning fingernails in public is not appropriate.
- Talking with hands in the pockets is disrespectful.
- Exchanging business cards is important.
- Maintain good posture.
- Do not litter.
- Pointing the index finger to your head to indicate a person is foolish is an insult.
- Eating and food:
  Cut potatoes and other soft food with a fork rather than a knife.
  Keep hands above the table.
  Do not smoke while eating.
  If a restaurant is full, you may be seated with strangers.
  Typical foods include breads, cheese, meat, sausages, leek soup, fish, wines, and pork. The most famous dish is fondue, which is hot, melted cheese or meat in a chafing dish utilizing long forks to dip bread or meat. A regional dish at the eastern end of Lake Geneva is a potato fondue in which small potatoes are covered with hot, melted cheese.

Physical Characteristics

The Alps mountain chain in the southern part of the country (running east to west) constitutes about 60 percent of Switzerland's area. The Jura Mountains, an outspur of the Alps, stretch from the southwest to the northwest and occupy about ten percent of the territory. A lowland plateau between the two ranges comprises the remaining 30 percent of the country. Switzerland's climate is humid continental. It varies with altitude. The winters are cold, cloudy, and rainy or snowy (depending upon the altitude), while the summers are cool to warm, cloudy, and humid with occasional showers. Switzerland's winters have many snow-free days for visitors to enjoy the mountain skiing.

Tourism Characteristics

The Swiss have a high regard for nature and beauty, and it is reflected in their tourism. With its winter sports and summer sightseeing activities, Switzerland has a strong year-round tourist season; but the busiest months are July and August. Switzerland has a long tradition in the tourism industry. The federal character of Switzerland is reflected in its tourism offices. The Swiss National Tourist Office is primarily concerned with the promotion of Switzerland abroad. Switzerland's location in the center of Europe is an important factor in its tourism industry. Its reputation as an expensive country is not deserved as it provides accommodations and service in a range of prices.

Courtesy Swiss National Tourist Office

Figure 6–9 Klein Scheidess, Switzerland

Switzerland's major market is other European countries. Seventy percent of its visitors are European, with Germans (30 percent), British, and Dutch dominating in Europe. Visitors from the United States average about 10 percent of all visitors to Switzerland, normally exceeding British and Dutch visitors. The average length of stay, 3.8 days, indicates that many tourists come to Switzerland either in transit or as part of a larger trip or a short excursion. This is the case with a majority of the United States visitors, who make a multiple-country tour.

Tourist Destinations and Attractions

The main destinations in Switzerland are in the high, rugged Alps, Figure 6–9, with such ski resorts as St. Moritz, Davos, Arosa, Flims, Zermatt (near the Matterhorn), Gstaad (in the Saane Valley), Murren (which sits on cliffs above the Lauterbrunnen Valley), and Klosters. Mountain climbing is popular. The Matterhorn is one of the most recognizable mountains in the world. The Alpine lakes interspersed between the high mountain peaks offer abundant scenery. Lake Geneva, Lake Leman (the largest lake in Europe), Lake Thun, Lake Brienz, Lake Lucerne, Lake Maggiore (partially in Italy), Lake Lugano (partially in Italy), and Lake Constance (partially in Germany) are only a few of the summer attractions for tourists. Some of the major tourist towns are Lucerne, Bern, Interlaken, Geneva, Montreux, St. Gallen, Zurich, and Zermatt, Figure 6–10.

Lucerne is the center of American tourism to Switzerland. It is situated on the shores of Lake Lucerne with mountains nearby for excursions. The city is enhanced by a wooden bridge with seventeenth-century paintings, the turreted city walls, and the baroque interior of the Jesuit Church. Lausanne, which is an educational center, hosts many festivals of music, ballet, and opera. Other major tourist destinations are Interlaken with its view and gateway to the Bernese Oberland and the highest railroad line in the world (to the top of the Jungfrau, a ride of 11,333 feet); and Bern, the capital, which offers museums, Swiss handicrafts, and culture to the interested traveler.

Montreux, on the sunny side of Lake Geneva, is famous for its international music festivals. The vistas from the mountains near Montreux are impressive and easy to reach. Major financial and international cities include Zurich, the largest city, and Geneva, which claims the title of the world's premier international city. (Over two hundred international organizations, including the United Na-

Courtesy Swiss National Tourist Office

Figure 6–10 Zermatt at the foot of the Matterhorn

tions, have offices in Geneva.) Geneva was the site of the League of Nations, the forerunner of the United Nations. Basel, representing the Swiss emphasis on practicality, is an industrial town, an old university town, and the beginning of navigation downstream on the Rhine. Basel is also a city of arts and culture; its art gallery holds important collections. There are over twenty museums in Basel. In eastern Switzerland, St. Gallen has a magnificent baroque cathedral surrounded by an old town. A short distance from St. Gallen are Lake Constance and the famous Pestalozzi Children's Village of Trogen, which was established for the care of orphans.

Courtesy Swiss National Tourist Office

Figure 6–11 Lugano, the garden city in Ticino, Switzerland

Switzerland's Bernina Connection

by Jay Brunhouse

The problem train travelers had with riding Switzerland's most exciting train, the Bernina Express, was this: once you got to Tirano, Italy, what did you do?

Tirano, although a pleasant little town of mountain houses and terraced vineyards, is not on everybody's "must see" list. And connections to Milan are tenuous.

This summer, the Swiss Transportation System added a whole new dimension to scenic train travel by introducing postal-bus service between Tirano and Lugano.

Swiss postal buses are comfortable, fully appointed coaches with a musical horn. Lugano is one of Europe's most beautiful cities with excellent climate and lots to see.

Now Bernina Express riders have a great, convenient goal and a sensational way to get there. Just as exciting, you can make your trip aboard the Bernina Express in the opposite direction, by starting at Lugano.

Every visitor interested in the outdoors, however, will prefer to break his or her trip to stay in one of the charming mountain villages in the spectacular Engadine region of Graubúnden and in Lugano besides the lake.

Free with Railpass

All segments—including mainline connections, the narrow-gauge Rhaetain Railroads and the new postal bus—are covered by Swiss railpasses, Swiss cards, and Eurailpasses.

Coming from Zurich by Swiss National Railroads' train, you connect with the red Bernina Express cars of the private, narrow-gauge Rhaetain Railroads (RhB) waiting in front of Chur's mainline station.

There actually are several departures of the Bernina Express. Some require advance reservations and payment of a supplement, because there is an English-speaking guide aboard, and some don't.

Hikers push the panoramic windows down from the top to admit fresh mountain air. Photographers lean out, snapping photos nearly the whole length of the trip. They are able to focus on the magnificent scenery through pulled-down panoramic windows while traveling along at only a snail's pace.

Bends are so sharp that you can see both the locomotive and the end of the train.

Landwasser Viaduct

The high point of the 6 1/2-mile section from Tiefencatel to Filisure takes you across two famous viaducts. First, you pass the Schmittentobel viaduct, 6.1 miles out of Tiefencastel. Then, out of a 164-foot tunnel, you quickly glimpse ahead the five classic arches of the 1903 Landwasser viaduct curving to the right over the river far below. The viaduct's celebrated southern arch plunges you without warning into the Landwasser Tunnel.

The section past Bergun to Preda is one you will always remember. The direct distance is four miles, but engineers have bent the line into such extraordinary contortions of loops and spirals that you actually travel 7.6 miles, including 1.7 miles through seven tunnels.

If you climbed directly you would climb one foot for every sixteen, but the extensive spirals and reversals of direction safely reduce your grade to one in thirty.

Albula Tunnel

From Preda, your Bernina Express picks up speed through the 3.6-mile Albula Tunnel. It is the highest (6,242 feet) principal tunnel through the Alps and the most expensive and difficult engineering work of the RhB.

The stretch south to Tirano carries along the Bernina Line. You can board trains for only this segment in either Pontresina or St. Moritz. Trains south of Pontresina average only 20.5 miles per hour, including stops, making the train even slower than the Glacier Express.

Your Bernina Express reaches the summit at Bernina Hospiz (7,403 feet) where winter lasts seven months. You have climbed 5,973 feet by simple adhesion, even more than any Swiss rack railroad with cogs.

continues

continued

Descending follows a route that required surveyors to perform near miracles. Your train has to drop 4,034 feet through larch and spruce forests in a horizontal distance of only 4.7 miles.

Engineers solved this problem by designing a series of cautious, cascading cuts, circular tunnels, sharp zigzags, and astonishing loops.

First, you descend to the right in a semicircle, passing below Alp Grüm Station to the 833-foot Palu Tunnel, in which you make a three-quarter turn and emerge down the mountain.

For a second time, you pass below the restaurant terrace into the 948-foot Stabline Tunnel, emerging on the back slope of Alp Grüm before doubling back through the 745-foot Pila Tunnel and returning below the terrace for a third time.

Alp Grüm

In less than ten minutes, you look up from Cavaglia (5,553 feet) to see the restaurant at Alp Grüm, now 1,305 feet above you. The forests have turned to deciduous trees: hazel, aspen, alder, and birch.

Your coming descent to Poschiavo is the most miraculous of all. Your train takes four more zigzags and tunnel turnarounds. You see Poschiavo first on the left and then four more times on the right while your train loops above the towers of the city. Photographers race back and forth across the carriage in order to capture all of the kaleidoscopic scenery.

Past Miralago (the name of which, "Look at the Lake," refers to your view), you again descend steeply to Brusio.

Here you make one of the world's most amazing loops across a raised, corkscrew stone viaduct having only a 164-foot radius. Nearby highway traffic is brought to a standstill as drivers and passengers watch your train descend.

Your Bernina Express then continues down the valley past the Renaissance pilgrim's church of the Madonna di Tirano to the Italian frontier.

Source: International Travel News.
September 1992, pp. 59–61.

Liechtenstein

Located in the mountains between Austria and Switzerland, the small nation of Liechtenstein (27,825 people) draws tourists who want to buy stamps and mail letters from this tiny country. The population is homogeneous, stemming almost entirely from a Germanic tribe, the Alemanni. The official language is German, but most speak *Alemannic*, a German dialect similar to that used in eastern Switzerland. The rugged snow-capped mountain peaks, beautiful valleys, old cottages, medieval castles, and friendly people set an atmosphere helpful to hikers, skiers, and other tourists. While many tourists visit, the length of stay is the shortest in the world, as few stay overnight. The attractions offered to tourists are at least as varied as the topographical features of the country. The Rhine Valley, where Liechtenstein is situated, is characterized by a wide valley base and the steep western slope of the Dreischwestern mountain range. The mountainous eastern part of the country is made up of three high-altitude valleys, the best-known of them being the Malbun Valley. The Castle of Gutenberg dominates the village of Baizers. It is situated upon a 150-foot-high rock formation that rises above the plain.

GERMANY

DAY 1   FRANKFURT–HEIDELBERG–STUTTGART

We will leave Frankfurt for Heidelberg, a romantic university town at the head of the Neckar Valley. This has been a university town since 1386 and is the setting of the operetta "The Student Prince." Sightseeing here will include the Old Neckar Bridge, a visit to the ruins of the Castle of the Palatine Electors with its Great Vat, a 49,000-gallon, eighteenth-century wine cask that attracts particular attention. Then we will go on to Stuttgart, which is located among hills near the Black Forest. Stuttgart is the gateway to an attractive countryside dotted with spas and recreational areas.

DAY 2   STUTTGART

Although this is an industrial center (Mercedes® cars, and printing and publishing houses), wine grapes are harvested within three hundred yards of Stuttgart's main station. The Altes Schloss (old castle), which houses an interesting local museum, and the gothic Collegiate Church are located in the old town square, the Schillerplatz. Also flanked by a former princely residence and Royal Chancellery, the Schillerplatz is used as a vegetable and flower market. In the Schlossgarten Park are the baroque Neues Schloss (new castle), the modern State Parliament House, a theater, and an opera house. Stuttgart has a tradition of avant-garde architectural design, and the Liederhalle, a concert-hall complex, is one of its best. Daimler-Benz, in the Untertuerkneim suburb, is the oldest automobile factory in the world and has an interesting museum.

DAY 3   STUTTGART–MUNICH

We continue southeast to Lake Constance. This is Europe's largest fresh-water reservoir. Making our way through the Bavarian Alps, we encounter the realm of fairytale castles and palaces built by King Lugwig II, namely Linderhof, Herrenchiemsee, and Neuschwanstein. We will hike up a hill to the last-named castle and take a tour inside. Onward we go to Oberammergau, with its painted houses and wood-carving workshops. This is most famous for its Passion Play, which was first performed in 1634 as thanks for having been spared the plague. It has been performed at ten-year intervals ever since. We then head to Munich, where we will stay for the night.

DAY 4   MUNICH

The best buildings in the city are the Rathaus in the Marienplatz (the heart of town), where the *Glockenspiel* figures perform daily, and the gothic Frauenkirche, a block away, with its two onion-shaped domes. The

continues

Figure 6–12 Frankfurt Town Square

Figure 6–13 Herrenchiemsee Castle

continued

Hofbrauhaus, which is about one hundred years old, is the latest in a succession of brewery taverns that date back to 1589. Nymphenburg, the baroque summer palace of Bavarian kings, is a streetcar ride from the city center. Its splendid apartments are open to the public. Sightseeing also includes the Oktoberfest area, the Olympic Stadium, and the 1,000-foot-high Television Tower. Like most of the other German cities, Munich is a beautiful city full of greenery and parks.

DAY 5   MUNICH–NUREMBERG–ROTHENBURG

We leave Munich for a drive on the autobahn to the city of Nuremberg. It is located 125 miles north of Munich. Nuremberg is a lovely medieval city that has retained its double fortifications (with 125 towers) and ancient castle. Hans Sachs and Meistersinger lived here. In 1526, the first science university in Germany was founded here. St. Sebald's Church is rich in fourteenth- and fifteenth-century art, and St. Lawrence's has a lovely Annunciation by Veit Stoss. The National Museum has superb collections of fine arts and crafts, including works by Duerer. One local culinary specialty is Lebkuchen (gingerbread). We continue onward by following the Romantic Route to the medieval, walled city of Rothenburg. Sightseeing here includes the town's ramparts and towers, cobbled lanes, and sixteenth-century houses.

DAY 6   ROTHENBURG–FRANKFURT–BERLIN

A short drive this morning takes us to Frankfurt. From there, we take a quick flight to bustling Berlin. Sightseeing begins on arrival with the Brandenburg Gate. Then Charlottenburg Castle, an old surviving building, Olympic Stadium, the restored Reichstag Building, Kaiser Wilhelm Memorial Church, the Radio Tower, Schoenenberg City Hall with its Liberty Bell replica and Freedom Scroll, and elegant Kurfúrstendamm, which are all fascinating. In the afternoon, we will be sightseeing in the former East Berlin. While there, we will visit Frederick the Great's Palace of Sans Souci, with its great art treasures, and the ancient Cecilienhof palace, once the residence of the crown prince. We will also visit the Unter den Linden and Karl Marx Alee. Return to Frankfurt.

DAY 7   DEPARTURE

Return by air to the United States from Frankfurt, arriving home the same day.

REVIEW QUESTIONS

1. Describe the three major terrain types in Western Europe. What is the type of tourism in each?
2. Why is the climate of Western Europe more moderate than in the same locations in the United States?
3. Which countries of Europe have a tourism visitor profile that is more transitory in nature? Why?
4. What are the major tourist regions of the United Kingdom?
5. Where do the visitors to Ireland come from? Why?
6. Which countries of Western Europe have large numbers of winter tourists? Why?
7. How do you explain the fact that Germany, one of the largest countries in Europe, has such a short length of stay by visitors?
8. What factors explain the short length of stay by visitors to the Netherlands and Belgium?
9. France has the highest percentage of its residents who remain in their home country. What might explain this pattern?
10. What role do natural features (like the Alps or the Rhine River) play in tourism to Western Europe?

GEOGRAPHY AND TOURISM IN
Northern Europe

CHAPTER 7

MAJOR GEOGRAPHIC CHARACTERISTICS

- Northern Europe has a high-latitude location and rugged physical geography.
- Population centers are concentrated along the region's southern margins.
- Northern Europe is relatively isolated.
- The Lutheran religion predominates in Northern Europe.
- Northern Europe has a homogeneous population with few minorities.
- Individual countries have high standards of living.
- The lingua franca for the region is English.
- The population is highly urbanized, highly skilled, and highly educated.

MAJOR TOURISM CHARACTERISTICS

- The major attractions are scenic and outdoor sports related.
- The character of the travel industry varies greatly from country to country.
- Tourism is less important to the economies of these countries than to the rest of Europe.
- Fewer tourists visit Northern Europe than other regions of Europe.
- Most visitors stay only for short periods of time.

MAJOR TOURIST DESTINATIONS

Capitals of Northern Europe
Fjords of Norway (Bergen to Trondheim)
Bergen to Oslo, Norway
Jutland, Denmark
Turku to Helsinki, Finland
Lake Country (Finland)
Lapland
Odense, Denmark
Malmo, Sweden
Göteborg to Stockholm, Sweden

KEY TERMS AND WORDS

Archipelago	Maritime Influence
Capital	Midnight Sun
Fjord	Peninsula
Glaciation	Sagas
Glacier-burst	Sami
Hanseatic League	Scandinavia
Insularity	Skåne
Lingua Franca	Vulcanism
Lutheran	Welfare State

INTRODUCTION

Northern Europe, Figure 7–1, occupies a position in Europe comparable to that of Alaska in North America. Its southern point, the border of Germany and Denmark, is situated in the same latitude as the southern tip of the Alaskan Panhandle (55 degrees North). The northernmost point of continental Europe at the North Cape in Norway is at the same latitude as Point Barrow, Alaska (71 degrees North).

The distance from the eastern extremity of Finland to the western extremity of Iceland is as great as from the Alaskan Panhandle to the outermost islands of the Aleutian Chain. Northern Europe is nearly 90 percent as large as Alaska.

Northern Europe is one of the wealthiest regions of the world, which is remarkable given the marginal environment that has limited the agricultural base of the individual countries. The region is also referred to as *Scandinavia*. Anciently it was the name of the country of the Norsemen. Today the region encompasses Denmark, Norway, and Sweden and is sometimes expanded to include Finland and Iceland. All five countries jointly market tourism under the Scandinavian Tourist Board.

Humanitarianism, social concern, cooperation, and planning are the key elements in the political systems created in the region. The people and governments have been guided by the belief that every citizen has the right to low-cost health services, higher education, decent housing, productive jobs, and a clean environment. The people of Northern Europe have built a society that enables them to live as well or better than any region of the world, and the degree and nature of government involvement in residents' lives have led some to classify the countries as *"welfare states."*

Culturally, there is a strong similarity among the residents of Northern Europe. Historically, it was the last area of Europe to be free of *glaciation* and the last to receive human settlement. More than 80 percent of the people are nominally members of the Lutheran Church, and with the exception of Finland, the languages are Germanic in origin. Finnish is a Uralic language, closely related to Estonian and distantly related to Hungarian, but the Finns are also predominantly Lutheran. English is the *lingua franca* of the region. (Lingua franca refers to the use of a second language that can be spoken and understood by many peoples in regions although they speak other languages at home.) The populations of the countries of Northern Europe are small, with Sweden's 8.7 million being the largest and the 230,000 of Iceland being the smallest. The growth rates in all of the nations are very low, with all under 0.2 percent per year. Literacy rates are nearly 100 percent, and per capita incomes rival those of all industrial nations and are exceeded only by a few oil-rich countries of the Middle East.

The Northern European nations are on the periphery of Europe both geographically and in terms of tourism. The region receives the fewest tourists of the four major regions of Europe, Table 7–1.

There are a number of common cultural and physical geographical elements in these northern countries. Most have more of their own residents travel as tourists than they have nonresident tourist visitors. The three largest countries—Norway, Sweden, and Finland—have their major population centers in the south. With the exception of Iceland, proximity to the European core has led to air pollution from the industries of Europe causing problems for lakes, streams, and forests.

PHYSICAL CHARACTERISTICS

Landforms

Northern Europe is a region of *peninsulas* and islands, each separated from the others by bays or inlets of varying widths or open sea, Figure 7–2. The dominant physical feature of Northern Europe is its peninsular nature. Norway and Sweden comprise the Scandinavian peninsula, and Denmark occupies most of the Jutland peninsula. The second characteristic of the physical geography is its *insularity* (of or relating to an island or by extension to isolated conditions similar to an island). Major islands include Iceland and the Faeroes in the North Atlantic, Spitsbergen and Jan Mayen in the Arctic, the Danish *archipelago* (a group of islands), the Swedish islands of Gotland and Öland in the Baltic, and the Aland archipelago at the entrance to the Gulf of Bothnia. As a result of its peninsular and insular character, Northern Europe is relatively isolated from the rest of Europe. This isolation has played an important part in the historical and cultural development of the region and in large part explains the distinct regional consciousness of the residents of Northern Europe.

The important landform feature is the northern mountainous area composed of a core of relatively low mountains with elevations ranging from 1,000 feet to a maximum of 8,100 feet in the south of Norway at Mount Galdhøppigen.

POPULATION CHARACTERISTICS, 1997							
Country	Population (millions)	Annual Growth Rate (percent)	Time To Double Pop. (years)	Per Capita GNP	Life Expectancy (years)	Daily Calorie Supply	Percent Urban
Denmark	5.3	0.1	990	29,890	75	3,628	85
Finland	5.1	0.3	257	20,580	77	3,253	65
Iceland	0.3	0.9	79	24,950	79	3,058	92
Norway	4.4	0.3	204	31,250	78	3,326	74
Sweden	8.9	0.0	4,077	23,750	79	2,960	83

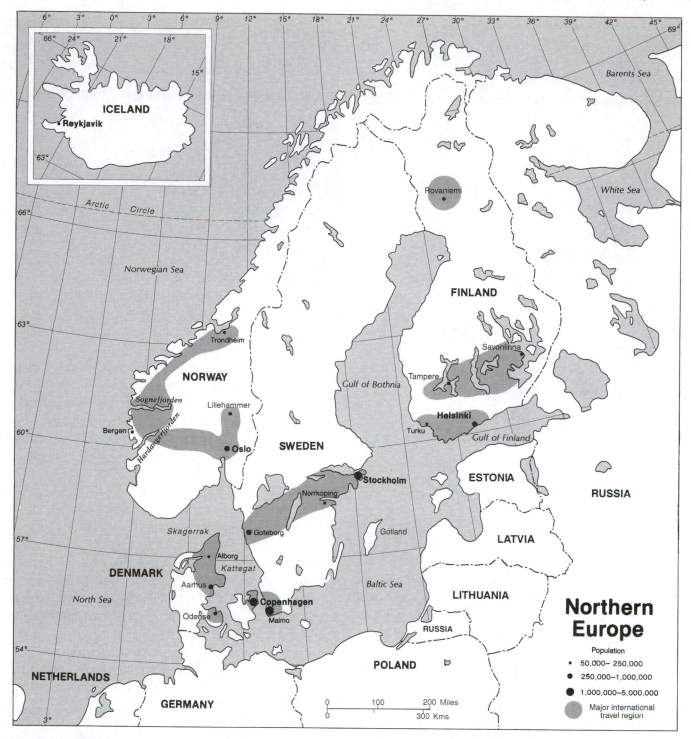

Figure 7–1   Northern Europe

These old mountains were covered by huge continental glaciers, and they are less rugged than the Alpine mountain systems of central Europe. The high-latitude location combines with the altitude of the northern mountains to make them some of the most sparsely settled areas of Europe, essentially uninhabited except for logging activities, mining, hunting, and other activities associated with isolated settlements.

Glaciation of the northwest highlands added many of the distinctive features to the present Scandinavian landscape that are important to tourism. Erosive glaciation formed a variety of distinctive landforms, including cirques, arrêtes, U-shaped valleys, hanging valleys, fjords, and rounded, polished, and striated rock. Glacial features such as moraines, sand and gravel outwash plains, kettles, drumlins, and eskers are seen on the landscape. The most im-

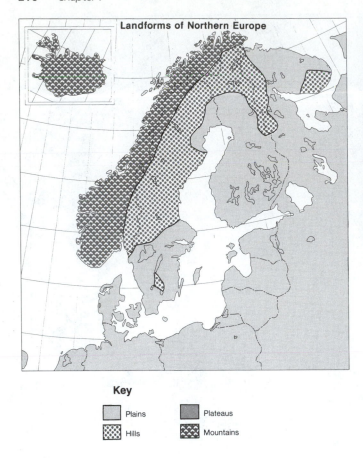

Figure 7–2 Landforms of Northern Europe

Key

Plains   Plateaus

Hills   Mountains

Courtesy Norwegian Tourist Board

Figure 7–3 Aurlandsfjord, Flam, Norway

portant of these to tourism are the *fjords*, Figure 7–3. Fjords are simply old river channels that were deepened and widened by glaciers flowing out of the mountains and into the oceans. After the ice melted, these were flooded by the sea, creating narrow deep bays. Many of the fjords have been scoured by the ice to depths of more than 3,600 feet (1,107 meters). Bordered by steep slopes and extensive forests, agriculture and settlements are concentrated where glaciers left narrow drift plains. Population is concentrated at the head of the fjords at such places as Aurland and Flam where the deposits of drift have been enlarged by rivers building deltas into the fjord.

South and east of the mountainous core of the Scandinavian Peninsula are the valleys of the Norwegian East Country and of the Inner Northland of Sweden with relatively broad and open plains. In the southern lowlands of Sweden, a small zone of highlands of undulating hills occurs, with elevations reaching about 1,000 feet.

Finland is basically a glaciated plain, with eskers, deltas, ground and terminal moraines, and lakes. One of the most distinctive areas of Finland is the lake plateau (or Salpanselka), where more than 60,000 lakes cover almost a quarter of the area. The mountainous region in the north of Finland is an extension of the northwest highlands of Norway and Sweden. Denmark is part of the North European Plain and its related glaciated landscapes.

Iceland, Europe's most westerly country, is a basaltic rock island that emerges above the surface of the waters of the North Atlantic. Three-quarters of Iceland is barren and treeless. It is rugged, mountainous terrain, largely covered by glaciers. *Vulcanism* is still common, with volcanic eruptions,

	Number of Visitors (thousands)		1996 Receipts (millions of US $)	1996 Average Expenses per Visit (US $)
Country	**1986**	**1996**		
Denmark	1,216	1,794	3,425	1,909
Finland	404	894	1,601	1,791
Iceland	114	201	154	766
Norway	1,637	2,746	2,497	909
Sweden	824	2,374	3,685	1,552

Table 7–1 INTERNATIONAL TOURISM TO NORTHERN EUROPE

earthquakes, and numerous hot springs, making Iceland one of the most active volcanic regions of the world. Volcanic activity occasionally occurs beneath one of the glaciers, resulting in the spectacular and destructive phenomenon, *glacier-burst*. Hot springs are found in virtually every part of the island. Many boil over periodically, sending great columns of super-heated water and steam into the air. Iceland is an island of mountains, fjords, rivers, waterfalls, green valleys, high plateaus, volcanoes, glaciers, geysers, and hot springs. Agriculture is severely restricted, and fishing is the basis for the largest export item. The rugged landscape is described by some as a "moonscape" and provided training for the United States space program.

Courtesy Finnish Tourist Office

Figure 7–4 Lapland, Finland

Climate

Because of *maritime influence* on the islands and peninsula of Northern Europe, the marine west coast climate prevails in Denmark and along the coastal margins of Sweden, Iceland, Norway, and islands as far north as the Arctic Circle. The weather is not as cold as the location would suggest, with even the islands north of the Arctic Circle affected by the relatively milder water temperature, reflecting the influence of the North Atlantic Drift. The northern location does dictate cool summers. Temperatures average near or above freezing during most winters and into the mid-60s during the summer. Precipitation, the bulk of which falls as rain, totals between 20 and 30 inches per year.

In northern Scandinavia there is tundra climate across the north of Norway. The mountainous core of the Scandinavian Peninsula and northern Finland have subarctic climates, Figure 7–4, while the inland plain areas of Finland, Sweden, and Norway have a humid continental, cool summer climate. The humid continental climate has winter temperatures below zero and summer temperatures similar to the marine west coast. The greater part of eastern Norway, Sweden, and Finland receive between 20 and 30 inches of precipitation a year, with maximum rainfall in the summer. Southern Sweden and southern Finland have a humid continental, warm summer climate. They have a hot, humid summer with maximum temperatures reaching the eighties during the daytime, and winters with sub-zero temperatures and permanent snow cover.

Because of insularity, both the Faeroes and Iceland have maritime climates. In the Faeroes, winter temperatures rarely dip to the freezing point, and summer temperatures seldom rise above 50 degrees Fahren-

heit. About 60 inches of precipitation are received each year, the maximum in winter and almost all in the form of rain. Because of the North Atlantic Drift, the south and west coasts of Iceland have a milder and wetter climate than the northern and eastern coasts. Winter temperatures in the southwest seldom average below freezing, but in the north and east they normally drop into the low twenties. Snow is more common and longer lasting in the north and east regions. Precipitation averages between 30 and 60 inches a year in the south and west. Over most of the northern half of Iceland, it usually amounts to less than 20 inches.

The high-latitude location of the region causes an additional physical geographic phenomenon that affects both the region's inhabitants and tourism, the twenty-four hours of daylight in the summer. North of the Arctic Circle, the sun does not set for twenty-four hours at a time because of the tilt of the earth. This phenomenon is called the "*Midnight Sun*" and is an important tourist attraction. In the winter, of course, there are an equal number of days without the sun rising. Even south of the Arctic Circle in northern Europe, the summer night is only a few hours long.

TOURISM CHARACTERISTICS

The similarities of economic, geographic, cultural, and historic development among countries in this region are also found in their tourism. The four major countries (Denmark, Norway, Sweden, and Finland) have a similar tourism profile: outdoor activity; high season in summer due to cold, dark winters and cool summers; a relatively small number of tourists compared to other European countries; the heavy use of the automobile by international tourists; a relatively short stay; the lack of overall importance of tourism to their economies; and more individual tourists and tourist itineraries. Cruises have become popular in this region and one of the major factors in the growth in the number of visitors. While the countries share some common tourism elements, there is also considerable variety in attractions from country to country.

Denmark

100 km

Faroe Islands and Greenland are separate entries

Capital: Copenhagen
Government: Constitutional Monarchy
Size: 16,633 square miles (about twice the size of Massachusetts)
Language: Danish, Faroese, Greenlandic, and a small Germanic minority
Ethnic Division: Scandinavian, Eskimo, Faroese, German
Religion: 91% Evangelical *Lutheran*, 2% Protestant and Roman Catholic, 7% other.
Tourist Season: April thru October
Peak Visitor   Season: July and August
Currency: Kroner (Dkr)

Shopping: Common items include Danish jewelry, furniture, wooden carving boards, salad bowls, and utensils. Also gold, silver, stainless steel flatware, ceramics, glassware, toys, and Danish cheese are popular items.

CULTURAL CAPSULE

The Danes are a Gothic-Germanic people who have inhabited Denmark since prehistoric times. Danish is the official language with a small German-speaking minority along the border with Germany. English is widely spoken and understood. Ninety-two percent of the people are Evangelical Lutheran; however, most are cultural Lutherans, limiting church participation to baptism, confirmation of family or friends, and major holidays, such as Easter and Christmas. The Danes are a friendly and informal people.

Cultural Hints:
- A handshake is the most common greeting.
- Eye contact is important.
- Politeness is important.
- Cover your mouth when yawning.
- Danes do not use hand gestures in conversation.
- Eating and food:
- In restaurants, the service charge is usually included in the bill.
- Call a waiter by raising the hand and index finger.
- Don't get up from dining until the host or hostess does. Typical food includes cheese, pork roast, fish, beans, Brussels sprouts, potatoes, fresh vegetables, and soup. A common breakfast in hotels is a smorgasbord of cheese, fruits, and pastries.

Physical Characteristics

Denmark occupies a peninsula and 406 islands north of the Federal Republic of Germany. Denmark consists of flat-to-rolling terrain. The climate is temperate, with mild winters and cool summers and strong prevailing westerly winds.

 TRAVEL TIPS

Entry: Visas are not required for stays of less than ninety days in Scandinavia. Passports are required.
Transportation: Direct flights are available between Copenhagen and a number of North American and European cities. There are excellent rail and ferry linkages to other major European centers. Copenhagen serves as a hub for train service into the other Scandinavian countries and western Europe. Public transportation in Copenhagen is excellent by bus, suburban train, and taxi service. The Danish government hopes to have its Kastrup Airport at Copenhagen become one of the major international airports in Europe and an intercontinental gateway, particularly for Northern Europe, similar to Heathrow at London or Schiphol at Amsterdam.

Tourism Characteristics

Tourism to Denmark increased only slightly in the last decade, but Denmark has the second largest tourism receipts of the northern European countries.

Tourism to Denmark is highly regional in origin, with Germany, Sweden, and Norway responsible for 65 percent of the bed nights. Germany is the dominant market, accounting for 28 percent of the bed nights in Denmark. The United States accounts for slightly less than six percent of Denmark's visitors. Tourists from Anglo-America are quite comfortable in Denmark as most of the population can speak the English language. There are a significant number of Americans who have Danish ancestors, in part accounting for the American tourists to the country. A large celebration, the Ribild Fourth of July celebration, takes place each year in recognition of America's independence. A site on Ribild Hills on the northern tip of the Jutland moor was dedicated in 1912 as a national park. In the park stands the Lincoln Memorial Cabin, built of logs from the original thirteen states, and the Immigrant Museum, devoted to mementos of Danish immigration to the United States. The tourist season is quite seasonal. The summer months are the most popular, with over half of all visitors.

Tourist Destinations and Attractions

Tourist attractions in Denmark are overwhelmingly cultural and historical, reflecting the lack of any individual outstanding physical feature. Most of Denmark's islands are small with very few inhabitants. The country can be divided into three regions in terms of tourism.

Copenhagen. Copenhagen, the capital, is one of Europe's most attractive cities. Located on the island of Zealand, the largest Danish island and a short ferry ride to the coast of Sweden, Copenhagen was founded in the twelfth century and today is home for a quarter of Denmark's five million inhabitants. Tivoli Gardens, the inspiration for most theme parks, is in the center of town. One block from the train station of Copenhagen, Tivoli, Figure 7–5, is one of the most beautiful theme parks in the world. Surrounding a lake are fountains, amusement rides and games, food establishments of all types and sizes, and theaters where concerts, plays, pantomime, skits, and acrobatic shows occur throughout the day. Copenhagen is a lovely city for dining, shopping, nightclubbing, and sightseeing. The major shopping street is alive with strollers, impromptu entertainment, and Danish ambiance.

The middle of Old Copenhagen is composed of a maze of pedestrian shopping streets offering shops of every conceivable type for every taste. One of the

Courtesy Danish Tourist Board

Figure 7–5 Tivoli Gardens, Copenhagen, Denmark

most charming and picturesque areas is the Nyhavn (New Haven) district. It was built along a canal with tall row houses that now express the Danish style of architectural design, handsomely painted in rich tones of blues and yellows. Nyhavn was originally sailors' quarters, but today consists of a jungle of bars, cafés, restaurants, and the home where Hans Christian Andersen wrote his first fairy tales. Boat tours leave the area to visit the harbor and attractions along the canals of Copenhagen.

There are a number of museums, such as the Glyptotek Art Museum, the Permanent Contemporary Crafts Exhibit, the National Museum (history), Christiansborg Palace with its collection of rare documents in the Royal Library (including pre-Columbian Viking logs of transatlantic voyages), the Royal Theater (1500), the Royal Museum of Fine Art, and the Citadel. "Langelinie Promenade" along the harbor is where the most photographed mermaid in the world, the Little Mermaid, sits, Figure 7–6. It is such an important figure that her head was once severed and held for ransom. The ransom was not paid, and the head was recast and reattached to the statue.

Copenhagen's architectural beauty is expressed in the four identical mansions in Amalienborg Palace Square. The Royal House of Glucksborg has always resided here, and the Royal Guard with their striking tall bearskin caps are impressive. The changing of the guard brings tourists and residents to the square. Rosenborg Castle is a beautiful Renaissance palace that is now a museum housing

Figure 7–6 The Little Mermaid

fine tapestries and royal possessions, including the Danish crown jewels. Surrounding the castle, the Kongens Have (the King's gardens) features beautiful flowers, majestic trees, and walks lined with sculptures.

Many of the morning activities center on the square opposite the Stock Exchange where many vendors have their colorful booths. The Fish Market is the place to watch the daily catch being sold by fishermen's wives. Across the canal, from which many canal and harbor tours depart, is Thorvaldsen's Museum, which contains a large collection of his work.

Outside of Copenhagen and Zealand. North of Copenhagen is a Deer Park near which is the royal hunting lodge of Eremithagen with a fine view over the Sound to Sweden. A large number of old Danish farms, windmills, and historical houses from all over the country have been assembled at Sorgenfri.

Some twenty-five miles north of Copenhagen in the heart of the Grib Forest lies Hillerød. The Frederiksborg Castle, Figure 7–7, a fairy-tale castle dating back to 1560, is the main attraction of Hillerød. Near Hillerød is the Ebleholt Abbey from the Middle Ages. Northeast of Hillerød is the Fredensborg Palace, the summer residence of the Danish Royal Family, which was built in Italian style in the early eighteenth century. Further north is Helsingør, a busy port and a major crossing point to Sweden. Kronborg Castle in Helsingør was built in the late sixteenth century and is famous as the setting of Shakespeare's *Hamlet*. Helsingør is one of the best preserved towns in Denmark, and its old section illustrates the old buildings and narrow streets of bygone years. Near the North Zealand fishing ports of Hornbaek, Gilleleje, and Tisvildeleje, there are extensive beaches and pinewoods, which have excellent bathing facilities for the visitor.

West of Copenhagen is Roskilde, one of Denmark's ancient leading cities. The twelfth-century cathedral is compared to Westminster Abbey and is the burial place for more than thirty-eight Danish kings and queens. The Viking Ship Museum has on display five Viking ships, found in Roskilde Fjord.

South of Copenhagen on the island of Amager is the old fishing port of Dragør, which has an old-world charm. From Dragør, tourists visit the bird sanctuaries on the island of Saltholm. Odense, the birthplace of Hans Christian Andersen, is on the nearby island of Funen. A museum with Andersen's books, letters, drawings, and personal belongings is located at Odense. The island of Funen has the greatest concentration of manor houses and castles in Denmark. Egeskov Castle is one of Europe's best-preserved Renaissance castles, built on oak piles that have been driven down into the lake.

Jutland. The Peninsula of Jutland has miles of broad white sandy beaches that attract many campers from Germany, Sweden, and Norway. Extending out from Aarhus, Denmark's second largest city and seaport, is a series of beaches, lakes, and picturesque small villages and towns. Old Town in Aarhus has narrow cobblestone streets and an open-air museum illustrating life in the sixteenth century. Along the eastern coast of the Jutland Peninsula are jagged fjords, tree-studded slopes, and rolling meadows, with heather moors and fertile fields. The medieval town of Ribe, where storks nest on the roofs of attractive old houses, is located in the moors. Founded in

Courtesy Danish Tourist Board

Figure 7–7 Frederiksborg Castle, Denmark

948 A.D., Ribe is Denmark's oldest town. The peninsula has numerous small museums in most of the small towns. These museums house Viking relics and depict Viking life. The south islands of Fano, Aero, Samso, and Bornholm offer glimpses of Danish village and rural life.

Finland

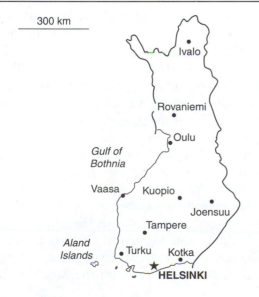

Capital: Helsinki
Government: Republic
Size: 130,558 square miles (slightly smaller than Montana)
Language: 93.5% Finnish, 6.3% Swedish, some Lapp and Russian minorities
Ethnic Division: Finn, Swede, Lapp, Gypsies, Tatar
Religion: 89% Evangelical Lutheran, 1% Greek Orthodox, 1% other, 9% none
Tourist Season: May through September
Peak Tourist Seasons: June (14%), July (17%), and August (16%)
Currency: Finnmarks (FIM)

TRAVEL TIPS

Entry: Visas are not required for stays up to ninety days in Finland. Passports are required.

Transportation: There is international air service to Helsinki from North America and other European countries. Trains and ferries connect Finland, via Sweden and Denmark, with the rest of western Europe or east to Russia and the Baltics. Finland has excellent domestic air, rail, and highway networks. Public transportation is excellent by bus, train, and subway (Helsinki).

Shopping: Items include furniture, jewelry, leather goods, furs, toys, glassware, ceramics, textiles, foods such as crispbread, herring, cheese, and liquor.

CULTURAL CAPSULE

The majority of the population is Finnish. It is thought their original home was in what is now west-central Siberia. As the Finns moved into the area they pushed the Lapps into the more remote northern regions. Finland has a small minority of Lapps and some Gypsies. The Finnish language, which over 93 percent speak, is a Finno-Ugric member of the Uralic language family and not Indo-European. Lappish is spoken by a minority of Lapps. Swedish and English are widely understood. Over 90 percent of the population belongs to the Evangelical Lutheran Church, but weekly church attendance is very low. The small minority of Eastern Orthodox results from Finland's past ties to the Russian Empire.

Cultural Hints:
- A handshake is a common greeting even with children.
- Punctuality is important.
- Do not eat food while walking on the streets.
- Eye contact is important.
- Do not cross your legs at the ankles.
- Do not talk with your hands in your pockets.
- Do not fold your arms while talking. It is considered arrogant.
- Eating and food:
  Avoid eating anything with your fingers.
  The check is given and paid at the table.
  Eat small portions and everything on the plate.
  Typical foods include fish, seafood, salmon, wild game, reindeer, vegetables, potatoes, cheese, wild berries, milk, and rye bread. Smorgasbords are common in hotels and restaurants, especially for breakfast.

Physical Characteristics

Finland's landscape is not as rugged as the neighboring countries of Sweden and Norway. Relatively flat, the country's rolling hills nearly exceed 1,500-foot elevation. The mountains in the northwest corner on the Norwegian border, however, are about 5,000 feet above sea level.

Even though Finland extends far north, the climate is moderated by the influence of the North Atlantic Drift, the Baltic Sea, and more than 60,000 lakes. However, it is cold in the winter, and its high latitude does create short summers.

Tourism Characteristics

Finland's tourist arrivals have been increasing over the past few years. In the past, Finland received few tourists because of its relative remoteness from the prime European markets, higher airfare from America, and its short summer. Finland is second only to Iceland in lowest length of stay in Northern Europe. However, with the breakup of the former Soviet Union, Finland now benefits from its location as an origin point for tours (particularly cruises) to Russia, Estonia, Latvia, and Lithuania. Tourism numbers to Finland have doubled in the 1990s.

Finland does benefit from a special relationship with Russia. A former possession of the Russian Empire, Helsinki has long been a business center for East-West trade and is home to a number of international organizations. This location and relationship is seen in the origin of Finland's visitors. The three major markets for Finland are Sweden, Germany, and Russia. Together, they account for over 50 percent of tourists to Finland. Outside of Europe, only the United States has a significant number of visitors to Finland (8 percent of bed nights).

Summer seasonality of visits is the norm, in part reflecting the large number of Germans and Swedes who come to camp.

Tourism Destinations and Attractions

Finland's major attractions can be divided into four regions.

Helsinki. Helsinki, the capital, was founded in 1550 by King Gustaf Vasa when Finland was still united with Sweden. The city was completely rebuilt after the Great Fire in 1808. It has a very Scandinavian architectural style with many parks. Over 30 percent of its area has been retained as open space. Helsinki is one of the smaller capitals of the world but has been the site of the Olympic games. The places of interest begin with the old center around the Senate Square, much of which is in a neoclassic style, forming a homogeneous and attractive whole, Figure 7–8. It serves as an example of planned, single-style harmony on a large scale.

Other places to visit within Helsinki include the Art Museum of the Ateneum, with its comprehensive collection of Finnish paintings; Kansallisteatteri, the Finnish National Theater; the Morning Market

Figure 7–8   Lutheran Cathedral on Senate Square in Helsinki

Turku.   Turku is Finland's oldest city, dating from the fourteenth century. It is the southwestern gateway to the country. Formerly the administrative and cultural capital of the country, old Turku has a well-preserved medieval cathedral and castle. There are a number of museums of interest, including the Handicraft Museum, which is a block of houses that survived the 1827 fire, and Sibelius Museum, which has a collection of musical instruments. Turku contains over twenty old shops from the medieval period.

Lake Country.   Tampere, second in size only to Helsinki, is on the headland between Näsijärvi and Phhajarvi lakes. It is a good location for excursions into the countryside by motorboat for hiking and camping. From Tampere and Aulanko north and east, the country is dominated by lakes and magnificent scenery. The area is popular for chalet and camping holidays combined with watersports on Finland's many lakes and rivers. In the eastern part of the lake district, Savonlinna is one of Finland's most popular tourist destinations for all tourists (domestic and international). The Olavinlinna Opera, established in 1475 on a small island near the center of Savonlinna, is the stage for the Savonlinna Opera Festival each July. It is the biggest cultural event in Finland, attracting over 100,000 visitors. About 15 miles from Savonlinna is what the Finns claim is the world's largest wooden church.

Lapland.   Visits to the North Pole center around the towns of Rovaniemi on the Arctic Circle and Kemijarvi, north of the Arctic Circle. Both have winter sports centers and facilities. The emphasis at Rovaniemi are the Lapps, winter sports, and the lumber industry. Near Rovaniemi is the reported home of Father Claus, the original inspiration for the American Santa Claus.

Square at Kauppatori, with its colorful array of flower and fruit stalls and handicrafts booths; the Mannerheim Museum; the Observatory Hill Park, which provides an excellent view of the harbor and waterfront; the Parliament Building; and the Finnish National Museum, which has a section devoted to the Finno-Ugric culture. Helsinki also has a unique church that is built into a rock and has an impressive interior. Carved from a rock outcrop, the pantheon-like interior is enhanced by the rugged granite walls and the copper-plated cupola. Seurasaari Island is an open-air museum illustrating the original farm and manor buildings from early history, with folk dancing and folk music performances in the summer. Nearby is Tapiola, the forerunner of planned communities.

Sweden

Physical Characteristics

The terrain is flat or rolling in south and central Sweden and along the Gulf of Bothnia to the north. Mountains stretch along much of the frontier with Norway Forest covering 50 percent and lakes covering 9 percent of Sweden. Like other Scandinavian countries, Sweden has a more moderate climate than its northern location would indicate. The warming influence of the North Atlantic Drift makes the climate similar to Northern New England rather than Alaska, which is at the same latitude. Small steamers and pleasure craft can traverse between Stockholm and Göteborg via lakes, rivers, and the Gota Canal. This has become a popular tourist route for those spending larger periods in Sweden. The rivers cross-

400 km

Kiruna

Tärnaby

Luleå

Umeå

Gulf of Bothnia

Sundsvall

Gävle

Uppsala

Karlstad

★ STOCKHOLM

Jönköping

Göteborg

Gotland

Kattegat

Öland

Baltic Sea

Malmö

Karlskrona

Capital: Stockholm
Government: Constitutional Monarchy
Size: 173,780 square miles (about the size of California)
Language: Swedish, with Lapp and Finnish-speaking minorities
Ethnic Division: Homogeneous Caucasian with small Lappish minority. 12% foreign-born or first-generation immigrants (Finns, Yugoslavs, Danes, Norwegians, and Greeks)
Religion: 93.5% Evangelical Lutheran, 1% Roman Catholic, 5.5% other
Tourist Season: May to September
Peak Tourist Seasons: July (39%) and August (22.5%)
Currency: Swedish Krona (SEK)

TRAVEL TIPS

Entry: Visas are not required for stays up to three months. Passports are required.
Transportation: International airlines connect North America, Europe, and other countries with Stockholm and Goteborg. There is excellent connection by rail and road to other countries. Sweden is part of the Eurail system. The longest road and rail bridge in Europe is under construction between Copenhagen, Denmark, and Malmo, Sweden, which will increase visitors to Sweden. At present, however, ferries are required to cross from Denmark to Sweden. Public transportation is excellent by train, bus, subway, and streetcars.
Shopping: Common items include Swedish glass and ceramics, handwoven textiles, wood carvings, antiques, reindeer-skin products, and tableware.

ing Sweden have lost their significance for transport but remain important for defense and hydroelectric power generation.

Tourism Characteristics

Sweden has a large deficit in tourism trade balances, with its citizens spending much more money out of the country on tourism than is brought in by visitors. Sweden had a good growth rate in tourism during the 1980s, and 1990s.

Tourism to Sweden is highly regional. Germany and Norway account for 32 percent (20 and 12 percent, respectively) of the total bed nights in Sweden. The United States accounts for under 10 percent of the total bed nights. Less than 16 percent of Sweden's visitors are from outside of Europe and North America, and no one country dominates.

CULTURAL CAPSULE

Sweden has one of the world's highest life expectancies and one of the lowest birthrates. Over 85 percent of the people are ethnic Swedes. The country's ethnic and linguistic minorities include 17,000 Lapps (*Sami*) and 50,000 indigenous Finnish speakers in the north as well as over 700,000 immigrants, mostly from the Nordic countries, Yugoslavia, Turkey, and Iran. Non-Swedes account for about 12 percent of the population. The Sami live in the north and traditionally herd reindeer for a living.

Swedish is a Germanic language related to Danish, Norwegian, and Icelandic. The Sami speak their own language, and the large Finnish minority speaks Finnish. English is understood by many throughout the country. Most Swedes belong to the Evangelical Lutheran Church, but most rarely attend church services. There has been a growth in Muslims and Jews due to recent immigration.

Cultural Hints:
- A firm handshake is common at greeting and departure.
- Eye contact is important.
- Do not break into lines.
- Do not put your hands into your pockets when talking.
- Swedes recognize most of the popular gestures.
- Eating and food:
  Hands should be kept above the table.
  Toasting is common in Sweden.
  When finished eating, place utensils side by side on your plate.
  Typical foods include meat, fish, cheese, vegetables, fruits, seafood, yogurt, and potatoes. The smorgasbord is a common breakfast in hotels, providing many of these items.

Tourist Destinations and Attractions

There are three general tourist regions: Stockholm and the Central Region; the South, centered on Malmö; and the North.

Stockholm and the Central Region. Stockholm, the capital of the old kingdom of Sweden, is built on a group of islands in Lake Mälaren and Saltsjön, part of the Baltic Sea. Founded in the early thirteenth century, it has grown into a modern metropolis incorporating the islands and spreading out over the mainland. The most-visited tourist area is the Gamla Sta'n (Old Town), which has quaint, narrow cobblestone streets and old houses. The Royal Palace is on the same island. Across from Gamla Sta'n are Skansen, an open-air museum of Swedish life and culture; a number of other museums and art galleries; park lands; and the seventeenth-century warship *Vasa*, a symbol of Sweden's former sea might. Boat excursions take visitors to the magnificent eighteenth-century palace of Drottningholm or through the Swedish Archipelago. To the north is the medieval city of Uppsala, with its old university, cathedral, and burial mounds of Viking kings. Uppsala is the seat of the archbishop and the leading university town of Sweden. Near Stockholm on the northern shore of Lake Mälaren is Sigtuna, the oldest town in Sweden. It was founded by Sweden's first Christian king, Olof Skotkonung, and for one hundred fifty years it was the country's capital. There are ancient towns, quiet villages, farms, large lakes, forests, and many castles and manors throughout the area.

The South, including Skåne and the Lake Country. *Skåne* is the chateau country of Sweden. There are many castles and manor houses, some of which are open to the public. Glimmingehus and Torup are among the oldest castles. They are thick-walled medieval fortresses. This area is the most fertile area in Sweden. Beautiful farms with half-timbered homes and ancient towns can be seen throughout the countryside. North of Skåne in Smaland, the land is not as fertile or productive. It has rocky soil and dense forests. On the coast of Smaland, the medieval castle at Kalmar is one of Scandinavia's most impressive. The area is filled with meadows, windmills, ancient forts, and Viking burial sites.

To the west, the lake country centers on Lake Vanern and the Göta Canal, which connects the Baltic in the east to Lake Vanern in the west, making it possible to travel by boat from Göteborg to Stockholm. It is an attractive area with castles and scenic countryside of narrow valleys, forests, lakes, and waterfalls. On the coast is Göteborg, Sweden's second-largest city and hub of the west coast. Three of the most popular attractions at Göteborg are Liseberg (Sweden's largest and most famous amusement park, particularly noted for its floral displays), an excellent maritime museum, and an aquarium.

The North. The area northwest of Stockholm to the Norwegian border is characterized by the wooded hills and valleys of Varmland and Dalarna. Jämtland and Lapland contain one of Europe's few remaining wilderness areas, a sportsman's paradise providing varied outdoor activities.

Norway

Capital: Oslo
Government: Constitutional Monarchy
Size: 149,158 square miles (near the size of New Mexico)
Language: Norwegian; small Lapp and Finnish-speaking minorities
Ethnic Division: Germanic (Nordic, Alpine, and Baltic) and minority of 20,000 Lapps
Religion: 88% Evangelical Lutheran, 4% other Protestant and Roman Catholic, 3% none
Tourist Season: May to September
Peak Tourist Seasons: June (15%), July (21%), August (18%)
Currency: Norwegian Kroners (NKR)

 TRAVEL TIPS

Entry: Visas are not required for visits up to three months. Passports are required.
Transportation: International air service provides access to Oslo from North American and European cities. Rail connections through Sweden and Denmark connect Norway with Western Europe. It is part of the Eurail system. Ferry

service from Bergen and Stavanger connect to Newcastle, England. Other ferries connect along the west coast to Western Europe. Major cities have excellent public transportation.

Shopping: Common items include arts and handicrafts such as silverware, handblown glass, carved wood, pewter, ceramics, knitwear, and furniture.

CULTURAL CAPSULE

Norwegians are predominantly Germanic. There is a minority of Lapps (Sami), who live mostly in the north. Norwegian is the official language. There are two forms, Bokmal, or "book language," which is used in most writing and spoken by the majority of people, and Nynorsk, influenced by the Dutch, a rural dialect. The Lapps speak Sami and learn Norwegian as a second language. English is widely understood and spoken. Norway is in the top rank of nations in number of books printed per capita, even though Norwegian is one of the world's smallest language groups. The Evangelical Lutheran Church is a state church, and over 85 percent of the population are members.

Cultural Hints:
- A firm, brief handshake is a common greeting.
- There is little personal touching except among relatives.
- Do not speak in a loud voice.
- Most popular gestures are understood.
- Cover your mouth when yawning.
- Courtesy and good behavior are important.
- Eating and food:
  Don't start eating until the host does.
  A service fee is usually included in the bill, but a small tip is customary.
  Typical food includes seafood, particularly salmon, meat, potatoes, cheese, yogurt, vegetables, soup, and cod. Some specialties are fish balls, smoked salmon, cod, cabbage and mutton, and sheep's head. The smorgasbord is common in most hotels, serving a variety of the foods listed.

Physical Characteristics

Norway's terrain is glaciated with mostly high plateaus and rugged mountains broken by fertile valleys. There are scattered plains. The coastline has numerous islands and is deeply indented by fjords. Arctic tundra is found in the north. The climate is temperate along the coast as it is modified by the Gulf Stream, while winter temperatures in the interior are extremely cold. Spring and summer are moderately warm, with maximum temperatures reaching about 70 degrees Fahrenheit.

Tourism Characteristics

Norway has the largest tourist industry and the second-greatest rate of growth in the 1990s of the Northern European countries. The discovery of oil in the North Sea allowed the government to develop its tourism infrastructure in a steady manner. The largest markets are Denmark, Germany, and Sweden. They account for 23, 16, and 13 percent, respectively, of the bed nights in Norway. The United States accounts for some 10 percent of the visitors. A large number of Norwegians migrated to the United States in the late 1800s and early 1900s. This cultural tie between the United States and Norway combines with the environmental attractions in Norway to attract travel from the United States to Norway. Ecotourism is important to Norwegians, and over one-third of the families own or share a cabin in the mountains or by the sea.

Tourist Destinations and Attractions

Norway is known as fjord country. No country in the world evokes the mental image of deep valleys and spectacular coastal and lake views as does Norway. The three major tourist regions are Oslo, Bergen and the Fjords, and Trondheim and the Land of the Midnight Sun.

Oslo and Southern Norway. Oslo, the capital, is over nine hundred years old. Oslo's climate is tempered by the waters of the fjord and surrounding lakes. Winter sports are evident even in Oslo itself, with the Holmenkollen ski jump overlooking the city and a ski museum as a part of the city's winter complex. Across the harbor on the Bygdøy Peninsula are a number of attractions. The Folk Museum has over one hundred fifty buildings and houses from various parts of Norway and from various eras. The Folk Museum hosts folk-dancing and craft demonstrations in the summer. It also contains a collection of author Henrik Ibsen's works. Also on the peninsula are museums housing Viking ships and *Kon-Tiki*, the raft on which Thor Heyerdahl floated from Latin America to the Polynesian Islands in the 1950s to prove that the people in the two areas were related. The Arctic polar exploration ship, the *Fram*, sailed by Nansen and Amundsen seeking the North Pole, is also found here.

Much activity centers on the harbor area for short excursions to the local fjord and downtown sites of the fourteenth-century Akershus Fortress, the Town Hall with its famous murals, Frogner Park with an outstanding collection of granite statues by Gustdav Vigeland, and other art museums. There has been extensive development around the harbor, where a large shopping complex is a major focal point.

Courtesy Norwegian Tourist Office

Figure 7–9 Bergen, Norway

The surrounding area has old towns, scenic countryside with red barns, old fortresses and churches, lakes, and relics of Norway's past. North of Oslo at Lillehammer is the site of the 1994 Winter Olympic games.

Bergen and the Fjord Country.   Bergen, the former Hanseatic League city of the Middle Ages, is the second-largest city in Norway in the heart of the fjord country, Figure 7–9. (The *Hanseatic League*, of German origin, was a mercantile association of towns that was founded during the medieval time period by wealthy merchants to control maritime commerce and trade originating in the Baltic and North Seas.) Many excursions can be undertaken from Bergen to the fjords, both north and south. Along the waterfront are the old buildings, museums, old homes, and shops of the Hanseatic port. Near Bergen is the home of the composer Edvard Grieg.

Throughout the fjord country, spectacular natural scenery and panoramas combine with fishing villages to create stunning vistas. Hardangerfjord south of Bergen is the most striking. Sognefjord, north of Bergen, is the world's longest and deepest fjord. The Hardangervidda plateau, Europe's largest mountain plateau, is the home of the largest herd of wild reindeer in Europe. A most interesting combination of train, bus, and ferry rides, the Voss-Stalheim-Flam Myrdal route that branches off from the Bergen-to-Oslo route ranks high in scenic panoramas. The train, in fact, stops so passengers can see and photograph the best possible views of magnificent scenery and roaring waterfalls. Legendary Notre Dame football coach Knute Rockne was born at Voss.

South of Bergen, Stavanger is an attractive fishing city that emphasizes its historical role as a fishing village. Today, Stavanger is a major oil center. Steam-

Views from the Tourist Office

Vigeland Park

Vigeland Park forms a part of the largest and most beautiful park in Oslo—the Frogner Park. The sculpture park is laid out along an 850-meter-long axis (a little over a half a mile), stretching from the

Courtesy Norwegian Tourist Office

Figure 7–10 Vigeland Park in Frogner Park, Oslo, Norway

main entrance at Kirkeveien to the Wheel of Life westward.

Without the assistance of pupils or other artists, Gustav Vigeland modeled every one of the 192 sculptures, containing 650 figures in all, Figure 7–10. He also conceived the architectural setting and the design of the grounds with their far-stretching lawns and the long, straight avenues to the west of the Frogner lakes. Even the children's ferry sailing on the lake during the summer was Vigeland's idea and was designed by him. There has been a great deal of controversy about the Vigeland Park, and the debate is still going on, though with less fervor. Some will find that there are too many sculptures too close to each other and that the whole layout is too severe and rigid. There have also been strong reactions to the content and the form of the sculptures. Few however, remain unaffected, whether they like the park or not.

Vigeland Park is an immense documentation of one artist's life's work and of the city of Oslo's will to realize this gifted artist's greatest ambitions. Moreover, Vigeland Park is a documentation of a deep interest in Man in all ages, in life's most typical situations, common to all human beings, which is the main motif of all the sculptures. The sculptures were created at a time when the leading trends in art turned from the figurative tradition to the abstract and non-figurative. Vigeland never took part in this development; to him Man was the all-essential. Vigeland expresses his program in the following sentence, "Human life is the highest in art and literature."

Source: Tone Wilborg, *Guide to the Vigeland Park.* Vigeland Museum.

ers connect the two cities and provide excellent views of the coastal fjords.

Trondheim and the Land of the Midnight Sun. Trondheim is the gateway to the north country and summer trips to the Arctic Circle and North Cape,

where the sun never sets between May 14 and the end of July. Trondheim sights include the famous Nidaros Cathedral (English Gothic style), the royal residence Stiftsgarden, and the Bishop's Palace, a relic of Trondheim's medieval glory. The countryside is beautiful, offering an excellent location for those interested in winter sports.

Iceland

125 km

Greenland Sea

Ísafjördhur

Húsavík

Akureyri

Seydhisfjördhur

Borgarnes

Höfn

REYKJAVÍK

Hafnarfjördhur

Vík

North Atlantic Ocean

Capital: Reykjavik
Government: Republic
Size: 39,769 square miles (about the size of Virginia)
Language: Icelandic
Ethnic Division: Mixture of descendants of Norwegians and Celts
Religions: 95% Evangelical Lutheran, 3% Other Protestant and Roman Catholic, 2% no affiliation
Tourist Season: May to September
Peak Tourist Seasons: July and August
Currency: Kronur

TRAVEL TIPS

Entry: Visas are not required for stays up to three months. Passports are required.
Transportation: There is international air service from Chicago and New York and Luxembourg to Reykjavik, the capital. Iceland Air uses it as a stopover en route to Europe and the United States. There are no railroads or streetcars in Iceland. Public transportation is by bus and taxi.

CULTURAL CAPSULE

Icelanders are descendants of Norwegian settlers and Celts from the British Isles. The official language, Icelandic, is close to the old Norse language and has remained relatively unchanged since the twelfth century, making it more similar to ancient Norwegian than modern Norwegian. The state church is the Evangelical Lutheran Church or other Lutheran churches. There are a few other Protestant and Roman Catholic congregations.

Cultural Hints:
- A handshake is a common greeting.
- Names in a phone book are alphabetized by the first given name. It is necessary also to know the last name.

- After dinner, shake hands with the host.
- Icelanders use very few hand gestures when talking.
- Smoking is prohibited in public buildings.
- Do not eat on the street.
- Eating and food:
  A service charge is included in bill.
  Icelanders do not tip.
  Typical foods include fish (cod, haddock, halibut, plaice, herring, salmon, and trout), lamb, and dairy products. Specialties are smoked mutton, yogurt, and potatoes.

Physical Characteristics

Nearly 80 percent of Iceland's land area is composed of glaciers, lakes, and mountainous lava. The terrain is essentially a plateau interspersed with mountain peaks and icefields. The inhabited areas are on the coast, particularly in the southwest. Much of the island's land area is of recent volcanic origin. The climate, influenced by the North Atlantic Drift, has damp, cool summers and mild, but extremely windy winters. In Reykjavik, the average temperature is 52 degrees in July and 30 degrees in January.

Tourism Characteristics

Iceland has the least number of visitors in Northern Europe. Its insular location is a major factor in its small number of visitors. Iceland had the largest percentage growth in tourism of northern European countries, however, during the 1980s. Between 1986 and 1996 the number of visitors doubled, but this was only an additional 85,000 visitors. Iceland's income resulting from tourism is low, as the per capita expenditure on tourism is the lowest in the Northern European countries.

The tourist industry is highly dependent upon North America and Europe. The two regions account for over 96 percent of the visitors to Iceland. Germany and the United States represent the largest individual markets for Iceland, accounting for about one-third of its visitors. Northern European countries account for 43 percent, with Denmark, Sweden, and Norway each contributing 11 percent of Iceland's tourists.

Tourism Destinations and Attractions

Reykjavik, the capital, was founded over 1,100 years ago. It has an international airport and receives the most visitors. It also is home of almost half of all the population. Attractions in Reykjavik include the Old Town near the harbor, the University, the National

Figure 7–11 Iceland landscape

Museum and Art Gallery, Nordic House, a center for Nordic Studies, the Einar Jonsson Museum, the Asgrim Jonsson Museum, the home of Asmundur Sveinsson, and the Folk Museum at Arbaer.

Iceland's proudest cultural achievement is its literary contributions. In the twelfth and thirteenth centuries, Icelandic writers recorded Eddic and Akaldic poetry portraying many of the legends, religious beliefs, and ideas of the pre-Christian Nordic-Germanic people, thereby preserving much of the heritage. These *Sagas*, almost all of which were written between 1180 and 1300, remain Iceland's best-known literary accomplishments. The Sagas present views of Nordic life and times up to 1100, and they have no counterpart anywhere in the Nordic world. The twentieth-century artist and modern sculptor Asmundur Sveinsson (1893–1982) drew his inspiration from Icelandic folklore and the Sagas.

A short distance from Reykjavik is the national park Thingvellir, where the world's first parliament convened. Also, the region has a unique open plain between tall lava walls and Iceland's largest lake. There are also many fishing villages and towns along the coast. The landscape, Figure 7–11, consists of glaciers, swift rivers, mountain peaks, flower-strewn grasslands, and birchwoods.

All through the islands, hot springs and volcanoes provide spectacular sights. Two of the most famous are Gullfoss, known as the "Golden Waterfall," and Geysir, a spouting hot spring. Gullfoss is a waterfall that plummets two hundred feet into a deep gorge, creating rainbows. Geysir and other geysers erupt frequently.

NORWAY

DAY 1   BERGEN–STALHEIM

In Bergen, we begin our Norwegian itinerary with a visit to the fish market. Then we proceed to the base of the cable rail cars to the top of Mount Fløjen and enjoy a spectacular view of the city. Late this morning, we begin our walking tour of old Bergen. A highlight of our tour will be a visit to the Hanseatic Museum.

This afternoon, we travel north by train into the heart of fjord country, passing magnificent scenery on the way to Voss. We transfer to motorcoach on our way to the Stalheim Hotel, which offers some breathtaking views overlooking the Neryadal Valley. Enjoy a leisurely stroll prior to this evening's dinner. The Stalheim Hotel is renowned for its superb cuisine. A special treat is in store as you retire to your rooms: one of Norway's most spectacular views is visible from your room.

DAY 2   FJORD CRUISE

This morning, we descend by motorcoach along the hairpin road to Gudvangen, for our mini-cruise on the majestic Sognefjord, queen of the fjords. We arrive in the village of Flam and walk to our lodge, which is only four minutes from the dock. Spend a peaceful afternoon paddle-boating in the fjord. You may want to watch the family of goats on the cliffs. Enjoy a tasty Norwegian dinner of salmon.

DAY 3   FLAM TRAIN

We depart this morning for what is considered the most scenic rail route in Europe. The Flam train departs for Myrdal. The 300-mile-long track must pass through 200 tunnels and 18 miles of snow in addition to crossing more than 300 bridges. This road has 21 hairpin bends. The train proceeds slowly for the best possible views of magnificent scenery. Passengers can get off and walk closer to an enormous raging waterfall that cascades close to the train. From Myrdal, we continue on to Oslo, enjoying the glacier countryside.

We arrive in Oslo in time to enjoy an evening meal at Ludwick's Restaurant, where everything is upside down! After dinner, stroll through the Vigeland Sculpture Park, where unusual statues depict family life. Retire for a good night's sleep.

DAY 4   OSLO

This morning, we will take the ferry across the Oslofjord to Bygdoy Peninsula to see the fascinating Viking Ship and Kon-Tiki museums. Tour the Norse Folke Museum while on the island. The rest of the day is free for shopping.

DAY 5   RETURN FLIGHT

Spend the morning shopping for that special Norwegian sweater or visiting Frogner Park and the museum. A motorcoach will bring us to the airport in time to catch our return flight home.

REVIEW QUESTIONS

1. Describe the climates of Northern Europe. How do they affect tourism?
2. What geographic features do the countries of Northern Europe have in common?
3. Why do you think Sweden has such a large deficit in its tourism trade payments?
4. Compare Scandinavia with Alaska and explain why the climate is different.
5. Where are the major population centers of Northern Europe? Why are they there?
6. Describe the general characteristics of tourism to Northern Europe.
7. Why does Finland receive so many fewer visitors than the other Scandinavian countries?
8. What are the major tourist regions of Norway?
9. What are the major tourist regions of Denmark?
10. Where are the major tourism markets for the Northern European countries? Why?

GEOGRAPHY AND TOURISM IN
Southern Europe

CHAPTER
8

MAJOR GEOGRAPHIC CHARACTERISTICS

- Nearly all of Southern Europe has a mediterranean climate.
- Mountains have formed a barrier between Western Europe and Southern Europe.
- Southern Europe occupies three major peninsulas.
- Southern European nations have increased in wealth as a result of joining the European Union.
- The nations share a common cultural heritage created from the Greek and Roman empires.
- The region lacks major deposits of important minerals.
- Populations are located on coastal or riverine plains.
- Agriculture is concentrated in coastal and river plain locations.
- Agricultural productivity is lower than in Western and Northern Europe.

MAJOR TOURISM CHARACTERISTICS

- The region's major tourism emphasis for Europeans is sun-sea-sand.
- Tourism costs are lower than in Western and Northern Europe.
- Religious pilgrimages are important to the region.
- Cruises and excursions are popular in the region.
- Tourism to the region is mostly destination oriented.
- Tourism is highly localized to specific regions within each country.
- The archaeological and cultural heritage of Western civilization is an important attraction.

MAJOR TOURIST DESTINATIONS

Capitals
Venice, Italy
Florence, Italy
Rome and the Vatican City
Area around Naples
Balearic Islands and the Coasts of Spain (Brava, Blanca, and Sol)
Central Region around Madrid
Andalusia
Barcelona
Lisbon and Its Environs
Agarve
Athens and Its Environs
Island of Peloponnisos
The Greek Islands

KEY TERMS AND WORDS

Acropolis	Mediterranean
Alhambra	Mezzogiono
Alluvial	Moors
Ancient Cities	Mosque
Andalusia	Old Quarter
Casbah	Ottoman
Christianity	Pilgrimage
Eastern Orthodox	Po Valley
Greco-Roman	Punic
Greek Islands	Revelations
Holy Week	Romance Languages
Island	Visigoth
Medieval	Western Culture

INTRODUCTION

Southern Europe has become the playground of Europe. While there are various places throughout Europe (such as the Riviera) that also claim to be Europe's playground, as an entire region, Southern Europe best epitomizes the concept of a continental playground. While there are major cultural and historical attractions in the region, the massive number of European tourists to the region return regularly because of the favorable climate, warm sea, and excellent beaches. By contrast, Americans visit mostly for the antiquities and cultural experiences.

The four major countries of Southern Europe—Portugal, Spain, Italy, and Greece—form a group that is distinct from Western, Northern, or Central Europe and the Balkans. Climatically, there is less variability from country to country. Economically, these nations have been slower to industrialize. However, since joining the European Union (EU) Spain and Portugal have experienced rapid economic growth. The average per capita income is still lower than those found in Western or Northern Europe but above those in Central Europe and the Balkan states. Italy has the highest per capita income in the south, but it is only 52 percent of that of its neighbor, Switzerland.

Membership in the EU will continue to provide a boost to their economies. The EU removed most trade barriers among its European members in 1992. It is hoped that this will allow the nations of southern Europe to capitalize on lower wage rates to expand their production and sale of industrial goods. At present, the EU is working toward a standard basis for the currencies of all the EU. Whatever form this takes, it will further benefit the Southern European countries.

PHYSICAL CHARACTERISTICS

Landforms

Southern Europe includes three peninsulas: the Iberian (Spain and Portugal), the Italian, and the southern tip of the Balkan (Greece). This inter-fingering of land and water creates long coastlines with outstanding beaches. The landforms are generally quite rugged, Figure 8–2, and mountains form a barrier between the Southern European nations and other nations of Europe. The Pyrenees, which are young mountains, form a barrier between France and Spain. They rise to an elevation of more than eleven thousand feet. The Alps, ranging west to east through Switzerland, Austria, and northern Italy, have tended to isolate Italy from Western Europe. To the south and east, the Pindus Mountains occupy much of northern Greece and separate it from Eastern Europe. Further, mountains are an important element creating the distinctive landscapes found within each

Figure 8–1a Southern Europe

country. The Pindus occupy much of Greece; the Apennines and Dolomites form a rugged backbone of the Italian peninsula; and the Cantabrian Mountains and Sierra Nevada form the boundary of Spain's central plateau. All of the mountains of Southern Europe are young and still geologically active. Consequently, the region is subject to earthquakes.

Population, economic activity, and tourism are concentrated in coastal lowlands around the mountains of the region. Important lowlands are found along the coasts, in the central plateau of the Iberian Peninsula, in the north of Italy, and along the rivers of the region. The coastal lowlands of the Iberian Peninsula vary from rocky and picturesque strips to broader expanses of coastal plain, such as around

		POPULATION CHARACTERISTICS, 1997					
Country	Population (millions)	Annual Growth Rate (percent)	Time To Double Pop. (years)	Per Capita GNP	Life Expectancy (years)	Daily Calorie Supply	Percent Urban
Cyprus	0.7	0.8	90	N/A	78	3,779	53
Greece	10.5	0.0	1,773	8,210	77	3,825	72
Italy	57.4	0.0	—	19,020	78	3,504	67
Malta	0.4	0.5	136	N/A	77	3,486	89
Portugal	9.9	0.0	1,733	9,740	75	3,634	48
Spain	39.3	0.1	1,386	13,580	77	3,572	64
San Marino	0.03	0.2	289	N/A	76	N/A	91

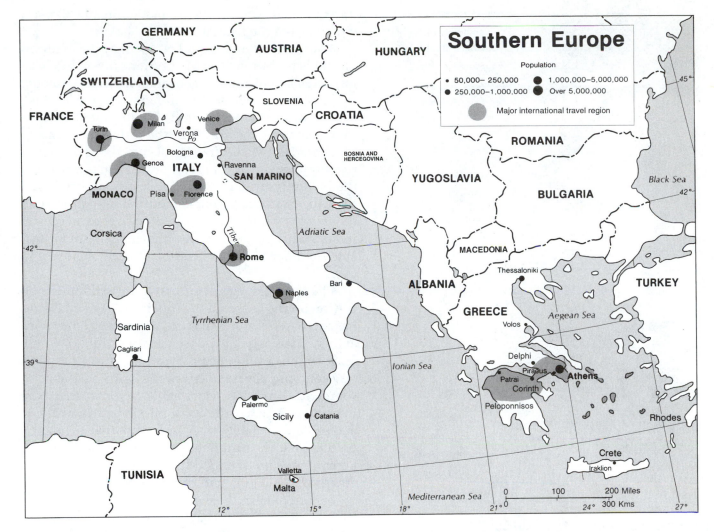

Figure 8–1b Southern Europe

Valencia, where the area is wide enough to support considerable agriculture. The coastal plain at Valencia relies on irrigation, and here the emphasis is on intensive irrigation agriculture. Such coastal lowlands produce vegetables (especially tomatoes), citrus fruits, and rice. They are sometimes referred to as the "gardens" of Europe. The majority of the interior of Spain consists of the Iberian Plateau or Mesa. Wheat, barley, and animal grazing are important here.

The coastal plains in Italy are narrow, but form important agricultural regions on both the west and east coasts. The area around Rome is an example, as the coastal lowland produces vegetables, small grains, and other products for the urban market. The coastal lowlands are subject to earthquakes and volcanic hazards from the Apennines. The eruption of Mt. Vesuvius near Naples in 79 A.D. destroyed the Roman cities of Pompeii and Herculaneum, whose excavated ruins have become popular tourist attractions today. On Sicily, Mount Etna has been very

active all during modern history. In spite of this, the coastal lowlands are densely populated.

Italy has more people than the other three countries of Southern Europe combined. The *Po Valley* of northern Italy is the focus of economic development in the country. The broad floodplain of the Po River represents one of the most fertile areas in all of Europe. It is rimmed by the Alps and Apennine Mountains and has a chain of natural lakes, such as Como, Maggiore, Iseo, and Garda. The valley is an area of fertile *alluvial* (water-deposited) soils. It is both the major agricultural region of Southern Europe and the industrial heart of Italy, with such industrial cities as Turin, Milan, Parma, Modena, and Bologna.

The rivers of Southern Europe have a strong seasonal flow, reflecting the summer drought of the *Mediterranean* climate. The Duoro, Tagus, and Guadiana of Portugal and Spain; the Guadalquivir and Ebro of Spain; and the Po and Tiber of Italy are important both for their lowlands, where population

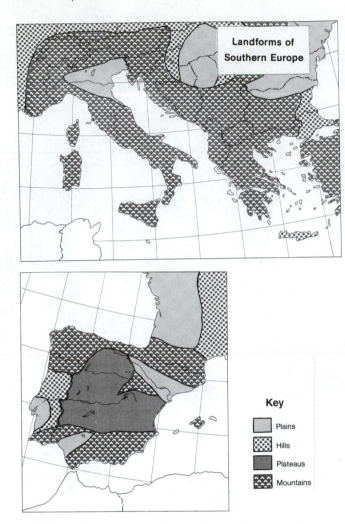

Key

- Plains
- Hills
- Plateaus
- Mountains

Figure 8–2 Landforms of Southern Europe

and agriculture are concentrated, and for their cities, historic sites, and tourist attractions. In their respective countries, they are heavily utilized to provide water for cities and agriculture.

A host of small *islands* dot the Mediterranean around the countries of Southern Europe. Like the mainland, they tend to be rocky and mountainous and have similar climates, beaches, and historical attractions. Because sailing was the most efficient form of transportation until the development of the railroad, many of these islands were important trading centers in ancient times. Major islands or island groups include (from east to west): Cyprus, which is now divided between Greek and Turkish people; Rhodes (Greek); a plethora of Greek islands in the Aegean Sea; Crete (Greek); the Ionian (Greek) and other islands of the Adriatic Sea that are part of the territory of individual countries in the region (Greece, Albania, Slovenia, Croatia, Bosnia and Hercegovina, Montenegro, and Italy); Sicily, Sardinia, and smaller

Italian islands west of the Italian Peninsula; Corsica (French); and the Balearic Islands (Spain).

A serious environmental problem in the Mediterranean is pollution. The Mediterranean Sea has been impacted by pollution for several reasons. With only narrow straits, such as the Gibraltar and the Turkish Straits, where the water in the Mediterranean can be exchanged with water from the Atlantic Ocean or Black Sea, the Mediterranean accumulates the pollution dumped into it. This combines with the fact that the Mediterranean is nearly tideless, with little tidal scouring or strong permanent currents to move sediments and pollutants deposited by rivers and coastal industries. Thus, the Mediterranean is more vulnerable than open seas and oceans to permanent pollution.

The rapid development of tourism and industrialization on the coasts of the Mediterranean countries has increased the pressure on the Mediterranean Sea at a rate faster than the governments could or would react to the developing problem. Emphasis has been on economic development rather than on the environment, as creation of jobs has been considered more important. Much of the economic growth has been in activities associated with high amounts of marine pollution, such as tourism, steel, petroleum refining, petrochemicals, metal refining, metallurgy, heavy chemicals, and pulp and paper mills.

For the tourist, the pollution problem of the Mediterranean Sea is noticeable only in the garbage left on the most heavily used beaches or in the busy harbors where oil slicks create iridescent sheens. Environmentally, however, continued economic development in the Mediterranean Basin poses a serious threat to the ecology of the Mediterranean Sea.

Climate Patterns

For the most part, Portugal, Spain, Italy, Malta, and Greece have Mediterranean climates characterized by summer drought and winter rainfall. Nearly 80 percent of precipitation falls between December and March. The temperatures of the region are warmer than the rest of Europe because of a more southerly location and a lower incidence of cloudiness. The summers are hot, except along the Atlantic shore in Portugal and Spain, with July temperatures averaging between 70 and 85 degrees Fahrenheit. The relative humidity in the summers is very low and fairly rapid nighttime cooling is common, making coastal areas very comfortable and very attractive to tourists. The winters are mild. Extended periods of frost are unknown, except in the mountains. Groves of citrus fruit trees dot the landscape of the lowlands of the Mediterranean.

It was in the Mediterranean climate that the *Western culture* was born. This was the home of the Minoan, Mycenaean, classical Greek, Etruscan, Roman, and Byzantine cultures, upon which much of Western civilization is based. Many of the ruins of early cultures are based on abandonment of cities due to extended drought, earthquakes, volcanoes, or conflict.

The Po Valley in Italy is a small zone with humid subtropical climate. Temperatures are similar to those of the Mediterranean region, but it does not have the intense summer drought. In the Iberian Peninsula, there are areas of steppe climate found where the mountain ranges block rain-bearing winds from the ocean. Two of these are the southeast coastal area of Spain and the Ebro Valley northeast of Madrid.

The growth of major cities such as Rome, Milan, Madrid, Barcelona, and Athens has so clogged the road arteries of the cities that air pollution is extremely high. Air pollution is so high that the Acropolis in Athens and other important ruins are in jeopardy. Some cities have completely banned auto traffic from downtown historic districts and have closed antiquities such as the Parthenon on Athens's Acropolis and the Altamire caves at Santander, Spain.

Cultural Characteristics

Southern Europe shares important cultural characteristics. The Catholic Church has been the dominant religious force in the area. The languages, with the notable exception of Greek and a few minor tongues, are based on Latin. Since Latin diffused from Rome, these and other languages based on Latin are known as *Romance languages*. Greece retained its linguistic integrity when it was part of the Roman Empire; unlike the rest of the region, it is dominated by the *Eastern* (Greek) *Orthodox* Church.

Tourism Characteristics

Tourism in Southern Europe in the twentieth century has rivaled manufacturing as a source of national income. Florence and other cities of the Mediterranean, however, were the focal point of visitors as far back as the Renaissance. As Europe experienced the Industrial Revolution, residents of the more industrialized and wealthy nations of Western Europe turned south to the warm climates of Southern Europe bordering the beautiful Mediterranean. Italy was the earliest destination because of its history and transport connections to Northern and Western Europe. After World War II, tourism increased to Spain and Greece. The Swedes, Germans, and British have historically escaped temporarily from the cloudy, damp, cool lands of the north to the sunny lands of the Mediterranean. Generally, they have grouped in various coastal cities and resorts. Along the Costa Del Sol in Spain, specific communities and resorts are dominated by French, German, British, or Swedish visitors. These communities provide familiar language and food for each nationality group.

Pilgrimages are an important element of tourism, especially to Southern Europe. The Catholic Church has a long tradition of pilgrimages in the region. Pilgrimage sites vary in importance, ranging from small shrines that attract only those faithful who live in the immediate surroundings to world-renowned sites that are visited by Catholic people from all over the world. Fatima, north of Lisbon in Portugal, Santiago de Campostela in Spain, and the Vatican in Rome draw millions of visitors each year. The landscape is dotted with monasteries and impressive churches both large and small. Many early monastic orders were established as agricultural settlements engaged in land reclamation and colonization. Most were secularized over time, but the monasteries remained on the landscape.

Southern Europe can be characterized as a tourism destination region, with a greater number of travelers visiting the area than leaving it. The percentage of Southern Europeans taking a vacation in which they travel to another country, while lower than among Western or Northern Europeans, is rising. Italy is the leader, but the Spanish are rapidly becoming world travelers based on their new affluence resulting from membership in the EU. The low percentages of citizens leaving the region are the result of two factors: the lower standard of living of the nations of Southern Europe and the greater distances of the population centers from other European countries. All four capitals—Lisbon, Madrid, Rome, and Athens—are spatially less accessible from other European countries.

The three major attractions common to the four countries can be classified as sun-sea-sand, religion, and historic sites. The tourism industry in Southern Europe is both highly seasonal and geographically concentrated in coastal areas and capitals.

Table 8–1 illustrates the size of the travel market. Spain and Italy have the greatest number of visitors and have a travel industry as large as any in Europe. Together they account for nearly 14 percent of the world's arrivals. Both Portugal and Greece have a

Table 8–1 International Tourism to Southern Europe

Country	Number of Visitors (thousands)		1996 Receipts (millions of US $)	1996 Average Expenses per Visit (US $)
	1986	1996		
Cyprus	828	2,005	1,860	928
Gibraltar	101	71	92	1,296
Greece	7,025	8,987	3,660	407
Italy	24,672	32,853	27,349	832
Malta	574	1,054	618	586
Portugal	5,409	9,900	4,260	430
Spain	29,910	41,295	28,428	688
San Marino	454	530	N/A	N/A

significantly smaller number of visitors. This is due to their relatively isolated locations and the similar attractions of sun-sea-sand of Spain and Italy, which are closer to the major markets of Western Europe. Greece has only slightly more visitors than Portugal, reflecting its cultural importance, its location between Europe and the Middle East, a more favorable climate, and its numerous attractive islands (World Tourism Organization, 1995). Tourism to Southern Europe grew more than 50 percent in the decade of the 1980s, slightly more than the rest of western and northern Europe (44 percent).

Greece

150 km

Capital: Athens
Government: Presidential parliamentary
Size: 50,944 square miles (about the size of New York)
Language: Greek
Ethnic Division: 97.7% Greek; 1.3% Turkish; 1.0% Vlach, Slav, Albanian, and Pomach
Religion: 98% Greek Orthodox, 1.3% Muslim, 0.7% other
Tourist Season: Year-round
Peak Tourist Season: May to September
Currency: Drachma (DRA)

 ## TRAVEL TIPS

Entry: Visas are not required for stays up to three months. Passports are required.
Transportation: International air service from several North America cities, most via other European countries to Athens. Train and ferry from Patras connects Greece with Italy. The Eurail passes are good on the ferries between Patras and Brindisi, Italy. Train service is available to most cities, but not to Delphi. Streets and highways are hard-surfaced, but smaller roads are sometimes rough and ungraded. Tourists must have an international driver's license to rent a car. Public transportation in Athens via subway, buses, and taxis is good and relatively inexpensive. Taxis are difficult to obtain during rush hours and at some locations. Many of the taxis at hotels only take guests of that hotel unless business is slow.
Shopping: Common items include local handicrafts, woven fabrics, linen, wool carpets, sheepskin jackets, embroidered blouses, fabric bags, silver jewelry, and ceramics.

CULTURAL CAPSULE

Some 98 percent of the population is ethnic Greek, with small groups of Turks, Albanians, Pomachs, and Slavs. The same percentage (98) belongs to the Eastern (Greek) Orthodox Church, which is supported by the state through taxes. During the centuries of *Ottoman* Turkish domination, the church preserved the Greek language, values, and national identity and was the central point in the struggle for independence. The Greek language dates back at least 3,500 years. English and French are widely understood. There is a Muslim minority.

Cultural Hints:
- A warm, friendly handshake with good eye contact is a common greeting.
- A slight upward nod of the head means yes.
- To tilt the head to either side means no.
- Greeks smile both when happy and upset.
- Waving the hand palm outward and fingers spread apart is rude.
- The "OK" sign is the fist closed and thumb up, but is impolite.
- The fist closed and thumb between index and middle finger is obscene.
- To beckon extend the arm, palm down, and make a scratching motion with fingers.
- Eating and food:
  The appetizers before and after lunch are finger food.
  Tip the waiter and busboy.
  When finished eating, place utensils in an X shape and the napkin next to your plate.
  Keep your wrists on the table.
  Typical food includes lamb, seafood, olives, cheese, potatoes, rice, beans, breads, chicken, fruit, and vegetables. For cooking, oil, garlic, onions, and spices are commonly used.

Physical Characteristics

The country consists of a large mainland, with mountains and hills accounting for 80 percent of the area, the Peloponnisos connected to the mainland by the Isthmus of Corinth, and more than 1,400 islands, such as Crete, Rhodes, Corfu, and Dodecanese. The climate is Mediterranean, with mild winters and hot, dry summers.

Tourism Characteristics

The importance of tourism to Greece was demonstrated in 1986 when the number of visitors decreased dramatically after a series of terrorist events in Europe, including the hijacking of a TWA airliner departing from Athens and a bomb blast aboard a TWA airliner approaching Athens for a landing. The Greek government began an intensive promotional campaign during the latter half of 1986 and during 1987 and tourism rebounded. However, after a decade of growth in the 1980s, growth has slowed in the 1990s. Greece is still a relatively inexpensive location for the visitor compared to the rest of Europe. It has a shorter length of stay than other southern European countries, due in part to the fact that it is a gateway to the Middle East for both cruises and air travel.

Europe is the overwhelming market area for Greece. Over 93 percent of the visitors to Greece are from Europe, with the United Kingdom and Germany accounting for 44 percent of European travelers. The dominance of these two countries results from the development of Greece as a major charter destination area by large travel companies in the United Kingdom and Germany. The United Kingdom and Germany lead the world in destination development for mass tourism. The majority of the European market desires a relaxing holiday in which sun, sea, and sand are the most important elements, things that Greece can provide. The United States accounts for 25 percent of visitors to Greece. The United States market reflects three facts: the gateway character of Athens to the Middle East, the cultural connectivity between Greece and the United States created by the historic migration of Greeks to the United States and the cultural antiquities of Greece itself. In the islands, as well as at Delphi, Olympia, Knossos, and Athens, there are large hotel developments.

Greece is a mecca for youthful travelers, who favor cheap accommodations in campsites, hostels, or unlicensed rental rooms. The government does not encourage or market to this group, yet hundreds of thousands of youthful tourists visit Greece each year.

Although the climate of Greece is pleasant year-round, the peak tourist season is from May to September. Seasonality is largely a result of institutional holidays, such as school vacations, in the major market countries of Europe and the United States.

Tourist Destinations and Attractions

The major attractions of Greece are its classical historical and architectural remains, its scenic islands, picturesque ports, and sheltered coves. The Greek culture is expressed in the villages, flea markets, food, festivals, and friendly people. All are important factors in the future of Greece's tourism. Tourism destination regions can be divided into four broad groups.

Athens and Surrounding Environs. The major destination is Athens. Athens is the largest city in the Balkan peninsula with a population in the greater Athens area of over three million residents. The city itself is surrounded by an amphitheater of mountains. The focal attraction of Athens is the *Acropolis*, which dominates the city. The major site on the Acropolis is the Parthenon, a temple of Athena built between 448 and 438 B.C., and Erechtheion, with its Porch of Maidens. Other Acropolis attractions include the Temple of Olympia, Zeus, and the Theseum. Around the base of the Acropolis are other classical ruins, such as the Temple of the Wingless Victory. Other sites in Athens are the Arch of Hadrian, the Monument of Lysirkates, the Olympic Stadium, the Theater of Dionysos, the Odeion of Herodes Atticus, and the Theseion, a focal point of ancient Athenian community life. The history of Christians and Muslims in Greece is on display at the Byzantine Museum and the Benaki Museum.

The Plaka is the oldest and most picturesque quarter in Athens, spreading around the Acropolis with winding, narrow alleys, single-story houses, and elegant mansions. There are small taverns, nightclubs, and shops. The market offers all types of handcrafted goods such as woven fabrics, linen, wool carpets, sheepskin jackets, embroidered blouses and fabric bags, handmade silver jewelry, ceramics, and gold icons and ornaments. The Parliament is guarded by colorfully dressed soldiers called Evzones. The periodic changing of the Parliament guard is an attraction in its own right. It is a carry-over from the old changing of the guard at the Palace before Greece became a republic. The Greek House of Parliament is a neoclassical building overlooking the Tomb of the Unknown Soldier. Formerly used as a residential palace of Greece's first king, Otto (1832–1862), it has been the Greek Parliament since 1933.

Near Athens, there are a number of easy and interesting one-day excursions. To the south is the Temple of Poseidon overlooking the sea. To the west is Delphi, with its extensive outstanding ruins, including the Temple of Apollo, the Treasuries along the Sacred Way, the Theater, the Stadium, the Temples of Athena, and the sacred Castalian spring from which pilgrims drank on their way to the Delphic Oracle. It is considered by many as the most spectacularly beautiful ancient site in Greece evoking the classical past. Set on the slopes of Mount Parnassos, it offers a view of the plain below and the surrounding countryside.

Between Delphi and Athens is Osios Loukás monastery (the Monastery of St. Luke Stíris). It sits on the brow of a hill with commanding views of Helikon and the surrounding country. The monastery is dedicated to a local beatified hermit, the Blessed Luke (Osios Loukás) of Stíri. His family fled from Aegina during its invasion by the Saracens, and Luke was born in the region. It has beautiful mosaics, which combine with the physical setting to provide a pleasant attraction.

Also near Athens is Marathon, where the ancient Athenians stopped the invading Persians. The 26.2-mile marathon race was derived from the military runner who carried the news of the victory to Athens. South of Athens is Piraeus, which is the major port for Athens and the home of many cruise ships visiting the Greek islands and the eastern Mediterranean.

The Island of Peloponnisos. At the Isthmus of Corinth, the Corinth Canal is a major geographical feature. The canal is 4 miles long, 27 yards wide, and 26 feet deep. It was built to save vessels from going all the way around Peloponnisos. The *ancient city* of Corinth is spread out at the foot of the huge rock of Acrocorinth. Its ruins are largely Roman. Corinth includes a Temple of Apollo, one of the oldest in Greece; a marketplace; a theater; and the Odeon. Mycenae on Peloponnisos is a city of pre-Hellenic Greece. It has impressive stone ramparts and tombs. Mycenae was the most powerful, brilliant, and sovereign influence in Greece until 1100 B.C., when it was destroyed by fire. While most of the treasures have been moved to the National Archaeological Museum in Athens it still offers a glimpse of Greek civilization. The Lion Gate entrance is the oldest example of monumental sculpture in Europe. Excavations have uncovered the palace complex of houses, sanctuaries, royal tombs, and other important buildings.

Nauplion, which was the first capital of modern Greece, has *medieval* fortresses. Epidaurus was the center of the worship of Asklepios, the god of healing. The area is near vineyards and age-old olive groves with mountains in the distance. On a hillside, within the sanctuary, lies the theater of Epidaurus (third century B.C.). It is the most famous and best preserved of all the ancient theaters in Greece. It is built of limestone and can seat twelve thousand spectators. Each summer it offers ancient drama. The acoustics are so good that the merest whisper can be heard in the last row.

Olympia was the site of the first Games, which started in 776 B.C. and continued every four years for a thousand years. The Olympic Games were revived in 1896 by the French historian and educator Pier de Coubertin. Since then, every four years a torch bearer, like the ancient heralds, starts out from Olympia bearing the sacred flame to the place where the Games are held. Near the ancient site the modern village of Olympia has a Museum of the Olympic Games.

Thessaloniki (Salonika) and the North. Thessaloniki is the second largest city in Greece and historically the crossroads of international trade. The old Byzantine city walls still dominate part of the town. Thessaloniki has a number of outstanding Byzantine churches, some with important mosaics. The area also reflects other conquerors, such as the Ro-

Greece—Cruising the Cycladic Jewels of the Gods

by Lauren Tague

The air is cool and the sun brings a breath of warmth over the port on the island of Naxos. A fisherman rearranges the octopus to dry in the warm afternoon sun as it hangs from a wooden pole braced between two old black cane chairs. He was an older man, a knotted tan hat covering his head. The clothes were in browns and greys. I don't know why the colors remain so vivid in my memory. Perhaps it was the contrast of the blue sea against his form. He posed with grace for a photo while holding up the largest of the octopuses. I began to wonder in which taverna he sells his catch . . . and if I would be eating this sea creature tonight.

We are cruising among the Cycladic Islands on the Zeus III. The name Cyclades derives from the Greek word for circle, and the group is described as a circle of islands centered on Delos, the sacred island of the Antiquity.

We leave the port of Piraeus for our cruise of the Cycladic Jewels. For seven days we visit and explore the islands of Kea, Tinos, Delos, Mykonos, Paros, and Naxos.

Zeus III made its way the next day to the egg-shaped island of Paros. The Church of the Hundred Doors, Greece's second valley of the butterflies, excellent beaches, and exciting nightlife place Paros somewhere in between the traditional and the present day. On Paros nothing is in excess. The island is also noted for its marble, considered among the world's best and once used in the Temple of Solomon in Jerusalem and in the sacred temples of Delos. The ancient quarry at Marathi is worth a visit.

Parikia, the major port, is unusual in that its back streets, the Agora section, are more appealing than the harbor area. It is noted for excellent restaurants, good hotels, a good archaeological museum, and the thirteenth-century Kastro, with architecture dating back three thousand years. The Church of Ekatontapyliana (Lady of the Hundred Gates) is Greece's oldest church in continual use. While its exact age is unknown, traces remain from the six-teenth century. Next to Chios' Nea Moni Church, it is architecturally the Aegean's most important church. It is reputed to have one hundred doors and windows, and according to legend, when the hundredth is counted, Constantinople will return to Greece.

There is excellent shopping in Paros, and the Aegean School of Fine Arts attracts artists from all over the world every summer. A popular excursion is to visit neighboring Antiparos Island to ride mules and enjoy splendid views over the southern islands. Luckily, the island escapes overcrowding even during the heavy months of July and August.

On to Naxos, one of the most beloved of the Cyclades, fortressed and Venetian-towered. The lifestyle scale is different here, with a grander, more monumental sense of things. The vistas stretch for miles. It is a romantic, aristocratic island.

According to mythology, when Theseus journeyed forth to slay the half-man, half-beast Minotaur in the Labyrinth at Knossos, he was helped by Ariadne, the eldest daughter of King Minos of Crete. Ariadne, infatuated with Theseus, provided him with a ball of string to retrace his steps out of the maze. Filled with gratitude, Theseus took her away with him. On the voyage home, however, he left Ariadne on the shores of Naxos, whether by design or by accident, it is unclear. Here she was rescued by Dionysus.

From the moment of arrival, Naxos gives the impression of power and broad-shouldered strength. You enter the harbor with its view of the Portara, the great marble gateway shaped like the Greek letter "pi," with the ruins of the never-completed Temple of Apollo on your left. Today the Temple and its massive doorway serve as a dramatic welcome to his island.

The vineyards and olive groves of the interior sweep down and fill the deep valleys of this island. Naxos presides over what is often called the most dramatic view in the Cyclades. If you choose to head

continues

continued

inland, you will find a wealth of charming villages. While the best beaches, in the sense of the more sheltered ones, are strung out along the west and south coasts, the road network is such that the most accessible ones are in the north. Naxos is an island rich in resources enough to embrace many worlds.

It is late afternoon when we reach the infamous island of Mykonos. This is cosmopolitan Greece at its best and worst. Undeniably beautiful, I am told by everyone that I will not want to return from this island.

We sit and have afternoon café in a bar overlooking the port and the sea. The day is cool and the wind picks up off the sea as we walk through the village along the twisting tunnel-like streets. Smooth cube-like houses with brightly painted doors line the streets. Every surface is being freshly painted again in anticipation of the upcoming season, now about a month away.

It is now late evening in a taverna somewhere in the village past "little Venice." You can only find your way by being lost. The moussaka sizzles as it reaches your table. The red wine is light and refreshing. A table of men, old acquaintances, sit and relax in the corner. One of the men, with the years etched deeply in his face, begins to sing along with the music … no one really listens or ignores.

The island is said to have acquired its name from a mythological hero named Mykonos, a direct descendant of Apollo. Also in mythology, Hercules slew and buried some giants there, whose tombs became the island's granite hills. Curiously, for an island of almost four hundred churches, *Christianity* came later to Mykonos than to most of the surrounding islands, and the worship of Dionysus survived longer.

Mykonos's long promenade stretches from a tiny beach where only the most undiscriminating will venture into the water, to the Church of Paraportiani and Folk Museum at the other end of the waterfront. The town's two squares both open up onto the waterfront and are lined with shops, restaurants, and bars. The maze of narrow streets run back from the sea.

It is impossible to single out the best beaches on an island of excellent beaches. The most appealing are, of course, the least accessible; buses and boats carry the main flow of visitors to the major ones, and dirt bikes or cars can be rented to reach Ilia, Psarrou, Agrari, and San Stefano. Bathing suits are optional at all of the beaches on Mykonos. If you prefer surf, you should head north for Panormos, but only on a windless day.

Tinos was our last island on this trip. It remains one of the most traditionally Greek islands. With 90 percent of its visitors Greek, it is an agricultural, mountainous island of some fifty villages.

A wide, paved street leads up from the harbor to the Church of Evangelistria, a neoclassical structure faced in white marble. The icon of the Virgin is festooned with diamonds and pearls, and the church itself is hung with offerings in gold and silver.

The Tinos "dovecotes," visible as soon as you leave town, are fantastically decorated two-story stone fortress-like towers, with openings arranged geometrically for the birds.

Most Greeks get no further than "Tino" town, with the island's reputation for wind greater than its beaches. But if you must bronze, try Kolimbithia, on the protected north coast near Koumi, or Porto on the southeast coast. These will be your best choices.

Source: Jax Fax Travel Marketing Magazine. May 1993, pp. 14–16, 156–158.

mans and the Ottomans. The region of northern Greece (Macedonia) has numerous beaches, beautiful villages (some with beaches), and a rugged terrain. Athos, southeast of Thessaloniki, is one of the most beautiful places in Greece. It is the home of many monasteries interspersed among the rocky paths, scrubs, and trees of Mt. Athos. Northeast of Thessaloniki is the beautiful beach town of Kavalla.

The Greek Islands. The *Greek Islands* have become the playground of the rich and famous, Figure 8–3. Names such as Corfu, Rhodes, Crete, Mykonos,

Naxos, Santorini, and Ithaka have become highly recognized and associated with outstanding Mediterranean islands. These are part of four major island groups: the Sporades, Cyclades, Dodecanese, and Ionian islands. Crete is the largest and most visited of all the islands. It is distinguished by its ruins of the Minoan civilization. It is the fourth-largest island in size in the Mediterranean, following Sicily, Sardinia, and Cyprus. Because of its size, it offers a variety of settings, from mountains capped with snow to palm-lined beaches, caves, and coves. The Minoan ruins are most impressive at the Palace of Knossos.

Courtesy Greek National Tourist Organization

Figure 8–3 Gregolimano on Euboea Island

Located off the west coast of Greece, the Ionian Islands include Corfu, which is probably the most popular of this group. Corfu has lush vegetation, hotels, and beautiful beaches. Other islands in this group are Paxos, Ithaka (an impressive mountainous island with ports, coves, and caves), Sami, and Zakynthos ("the Venice" of the Ionian Sea). Southeast in the Cyclades are Mykonos, with its dazzling white buildings; Santorini, with its volcanic remnant landscape; Rhodes, with its walled medieval city built by the Knights of Saint John; Syros, a center of Catholicism in Greece; and Paros, with its white-washed houses and bougainvillaea draped from balconies and staircases.

In the Sporades Islands, Samos features the three wonders of the ancient world—the harbor mole, the kilometer-long tunnel of Eupalinos cut through Astypalala for a water supply when under siege, and the Temple of Hera. Other islands in this group are Chios, which is reported to contain the home town of Homer, and Lesvos.

The Dodecanese, like part of the Sporades, closely follow the Turkish coastline. One of the most famous islands for tourism in this group is Patmos, which is a holy island for Christians as it is reputed to be the island where St. John wrote *Revelations* and received his vision of the Apocalypse. Other attractive islands are Le'ros, Kalymnos, Kos, and Rhodes. Rhodes was the home for a time of the Knights of St. John, who created a walled, medieval town around the harbor.

Cyprus

Religion: 78% Greek Orthodox, 18% Muslim, 4% Maronite, Armenian, Apostolic, and other
Tourist Season: Year-round
Peak Tourist Season: May through September
Currency: Cyprus Pound and Turkish Lira

 TRAVEL TIPS

Entry: A visa is issued upon arrival for stays up to three months. Passports are required.
Transportation: International air service is available through Turkey or Greece. Boat service from Turkey, Greece, and Middle East countries.
Shopping: Common items include silver work, leather goods, and handmade lace.

Capital: Nicosia
Government: Republic. Divided between two ethnic groups, Turkish and Greek. Turkish Cypriot President has declared Northern Cyprus a Turkish Republic.
Size: 3,572 square miles (slightly smaller than Connecticut)
Language: Greek, Turkish, English
Ethnic Division: 78% Greek; 18% Turkish; 4% Armenian, Maronite, Christian, and other

CULTURAL CAPSULE

The majority of the people (called Cypriots) are divided between Greek (78 percent) and Turkish (18 percent). The language and religion of Cyprus follows this division: Greek and Turkish for language; and Greek Orthodox and Muslim the dominant religions in the same percentages as ethnic divisions. In 1974 hostilities divided the island into two de facto autonomous areas—a Greek area controlled by the Cypriot government (60 percent of the island's land area) and a Turkish-Cypriot area (35 percent of the island's land area). The two are separated by a narrow buffer zone controlled by the United Nations.

Figure 8–4 Cyprus

Physical Characteristics

Cyprus, Figure 8–4, is the third largest island in the Mediterranean after Sicily and Sardinia. The central plain from Morphou Bay in the west to Famagusta Bay in the east has mountains on both the south (forest-covered Troodos Mountains) and the north (barren Kyrenia Range). The climate is Mediterranean, with hot, dry summers and damp, cool winters.

Tourist Characteristics

The conflict between the two major ethnic groups, Greeks and Turks, combined with the problems in the Middle East to seriously affect tourism to Cyprus. This is true particularly for tourists from the United States and Canada, which account for a little over 2 percent of the visitors. Most visitors are from Europe (91 percent) and the Middle East (5 percent). Although the political division still exists, tourism has recently increased, reaching 2 million visitors in 1996. However, travel is complicated by the fact that visitors who arrive in areas controlled by the Turkish Cypriots are not permitted to visit the Republic of Cyprus (Greek Cypriot control).

Tourist Destinations and Attractions

The major tourist destinations and attractions are historical and archaeological, with sites from the Neolithic, Hellenic, Macedonian, Roman, Crusader, and Ottoman periods. This illustrates the crossroads nature of the island in the eastern Mediterranean. It is a major cruise stop at the ports of Limassol and Larnaca. The major sites are Nicosia, with its Venetian walls ringing the old town; Kyrenia, with its Crusader Castle; Famagusta, with its walled Turkish quarter; and the Monastery of Stavrovouni at Larnaca. The island is popular for both water and snow skiing.

Italy

Capital: Rome
Government: Republic
Size: 116,319 square miles (about the size of Arizona)
Language: Italian (Some northern regions have German- and French-speaking minorities.)
Ethnic Division: Italian, with small clusters of German, French, and Slovene
Religion: Almost 100% Roman Catholic
Tourist Season: Year-round
Peak Tourist Seasons: June, July, August, and September. Compounded by nearly 40% of Italians taking their vacations in July and August
Currency: Lire (LIT)

 TRAVEL TIPS

Entry: Visas are not required for visits up to three months. Passports are required.
Transportation: Excellent international air service connects Italy with North America, Western Europe, and the

Middle East. Italy has excellent rail service both for international service and domestic. They are part of the Eurail system and have their own rail passes. Cities and towns have good public transportation.

Shopping: Common items include cameos, glass objects, pinochio, embroidered tablecloths, mosaic jewelry, alabaster statues, fruit, leather, shoes, knitwear, and antiques.

CULTURAL CAPSULE

While Italy is generally ethnic Italian there is great cultural, economic, and political diversity in the country. Some minority groups are French, German, Slovenes, and Albanians, all of which are expressed in the languages in the various regions of these minorities. Nearly all Italians are nominally Roman Catholic.

Cultural Hints:

- A handshake is common for greeting and parting.
- Italians often touch one another when conversing: physical contact is common.
- Dress modestly when visiting churches. Women cover their heads and do not wear shorts or sleeveless blouses.
- It is not considered rude to push and shove in crowds.
- The closed fist raised with the index and little finger extended is obscene.
- To wave goodbye, hold the palm up and waggle fingers back and forth.
- Cover the mouth when yawning.
- Eating and foods:
  Do not start to eat before hostess.
  Meals are a time to visit.
  Keep hands above the table.
  Do not leave the table until all have finished.
  A knife and fork are used for dessert.
  Service charge is often in the bill, but a small tip is still appropriate.
  Restaurants in which clients stand are less expensive than those in which they are seated.
  Typical foods include pasta, cheese, fish, meat (particularly veal), and vegetables. Salad dressing is oil and vinegar, without spices. Pasta is served by itself and meat follows later.

Physical Characteristics

With the exception of the Po Valley, the south in the "heel of the boot," and coastal lowlands, Italy is a rugged and mountainous nation. The climate is generally mild and Mediterranean with considerable variation. In the south, Sicily is comparable to Southern California, although somewhat warmer. In the mountainous north, the climate is more humid and alpine.

Tourism Characteristics

Tourism is extremely important to Italy's economy. Tourism is a ministry-level responsibility in Italy under the Ministry of Tourism, with each of the twenty-one tourist regions having a tourist board. Each province within a region has a provincial tourist office. The Entre Nazionale Turismo Italiano (ENTI) under the Ministry of Tourism is responsible for promoting tourism abroad. The Ministry of Tourism has the overall political responsibility for tourism through promotion and development strategy. The ministry is responsible for licensing, training, and investment subsidies. The ministry is concerned with negative factors, such as terrorist incidents, public order, and disruptions in the transportation sectors. Italy is concerned with competition from Spain and Portugal for the mass budget-minded, sun-sea-sand markets of Northern Europe, especially since Italy is becoming more expensive. Italy has a long history of tourism, from the Renaissance to the eighteenth century when it was the major destination of the "Grand Tour" taken by the wealthy and nobility of Europe, to the mass tourism of the present.

With its diversity of attractions, Italy is one of the world's leading tourist destinations, ranking fourth in total visitors. It is difficult to determine the exact nature of Italy's market because the data is incomplete and a number of visitors are in transit across Italy to the former Yugoslavia and Greece. The World Travel Organization reports 26.6 million tourists and 33.6 million excursionists. However, general patterns indicate that an overwhelming majority of the visitors to Italy are from Europe, which accounts for more than 91 percent of the visitors. Switzerland, Germany, and France are the three largest individual markets, with 16.7 percent, 16 percent, and 15.5 percent of the total market, respectively. The United States sent 1.3 million visitors to Italy in 1996, accounting for 2.5 percent of Italy's visitors. Americans stay longer, accounting for 7.8 percent of the hotel bed nights. Only Germany has a significantly larger number. The large German market is illustrative of the transit nature in that many used to be on their way to the former Yugoslavia, which received a larger number of visitors from Germany than did Italy.

Forty-five percent of all international visitors to Italy were attracted by artistic/historical attractions, the climate (43 percent), natural environment (26 percent), or visiting friends and relatives (9 percent). Thirty-two percent indicated a combination of events. The Vatican is a major attraction. Many visitors, whether Catholic or not, combine visiting the historical attractions and the Vatican. Visits to friends and relatives by tourists from the United States are declining as the population of the United

States ages and there is less direct connectivity to Italy by United States citizens.

Tourism is highly seasonal, with a summer peak. August alone accounts for 30 percent of all foreign and domestic bed nights, while July accounts for an additional 21 percent. International tourism is more dispersed through the four summer months of May through August. There is a seasonal peak in the winters in the mountains. Mountain resorts account for 19 percent of all tourist arrivals. Tourism in Italy is highly regional, with approximately 60 percent of all international visitors visiting northern locations where most of the cultural attractions and best beaches are located. A major concern of the Italian government is the development of southern Italy (called the *Mezzogiono*). Because of its poor economy and the potential of tourism to help solve the economic problems of the South, the Mezzogiono is the focus of tourism development attempts. In 1996, the travel regions south of Naples received only 9 percent of the total visitors, and one region—Puglia, in which the tourists catch ferries to Greece—accounted for 25 percent of these. Because of its distance from the main European markets, the South must depend upon air-inclusive tour traffic, which puts it in competition with Spain, Greece, and North Africa.

The impact of tourism has reached such a level that there is concern over the quality of life for the residents as well as the ecosystem. UNESCO has funded a study of a number of art cities of Europe, trying to assess the impact of visitors and establish measures to negate the negative consequences. Venice plans to be the first city to limit the number of visitors to the number of bed spaces plus a set number of day visitors. Some days Venice has in excess of fifty thousand day visitors in the city.

Tourist Destinations and Attractions

The Southern Alps and Lake Country. As in Switzerland and Austria, the glaciated lakes, such as Maggiore, Como, Garda, and the high mountain Alps, provide scenic winter and summer resorts. The site of the 1956 Winter Olympics held at Cortina d'Ampezzo is the centerpiece of winter sports in the Dolomites, providing gentle beginning slopes to spectacular runs and late-season skiing, some years into late June or early July. The lake district is full of beautiful lakes with blue waters at the foot of high scenic mountains. The district centers on Maggiore, the most famous lake, with its luxuriant vegetation, much of which is tropical, and sometimes rugged shores. Italy shares Lake Maggiore with Switzerland.

The Lake District has a mild climate resulting from its location on the southern side of the Alps, which block the cold winds from the north.

In the northwest corner of Italy the Aosta Valley is a land of great natural beauty with medieval villages and views of some of Europe's highest mountains, Mont Blanc and Monte Rosa. Like the rest of northern Italy, the region has some excellent winter sports resorts with fine skiing. Remains of the Roman Age can be seen along the road from Ivrea to the Piccolo San Bernardo and in Aosta itself. Gothic influence is visible in buildings in Aosta and in the romantic castles of Fènis, Issogne, and Verrès.

Some important tourist cities are Turin, a major industrial center, noted for its cars and typewriters, featuring several museums and the cathedral in the Piazza San Giovanni, which houses a relic of the Holy Shroud; Milan, another major industrial city and a fine art city centered on the Piazza del Duomo with its great Gothic cathedral, which is the second largest church building in Italy, the home of one of the most famous opera houses in the world, La Scala, and many important artworks such as da Vinci's "Last Supper" and Michelangelo's "Pieta"; and Bolzano, the capital of Alto Adige, which was once the South Tyrol of Austria and is German in character still today.

Italy's Coastal Environment (including the Riviera). Having five thousand miles of coastline, Italy offers not only excellent beaches, but hilltop villages, white rock stairways, fishermen's villages, reefs, island-rocks, high cliffs over transparent water, and a host of cultural and archaeological sites both along and within easy distance of the coastal areas.

Stretching from the French border to Tuscany is the Italian Riviera. The mild climate has given it a lengthy beach season, which, in turn, extends the tourist season. The area has numerous pocket beaches of sand and rock, woods, prehistoric grottoes, romantic villages and hamlets, plus larger towns and cities with olive-, palm-, and magnolia-lined boulevards. The most famous resort is San Remo, with its casino and funicular railway to the top of Mount Bignone. The capital of the Italian Riviera is Genoa, a busy seaport and birthplace of Christopher Columbus, with an interesting section of medieval churches and houses. Along the coast from the Riviera to Sicily are expanses of coast beaches and scenic beauty. A variety of resorts on the Adriatic coast take advantage of the long, sandy beaches and clear water of the sea.

The Cities in Central Italy from Venice to Ancona and Tuscany. Venice is built on over 115 islands

Figure 8–5 St. Mark's Square, Venice, Italy

separated by 177 canals but connected by 400 bridges, gondolas, and a style of living unlike any city in the world. The Rialto Bridge, Piazza San Marco, the Basilica of San Marco (Figure 8–5), the Bridge of Sighs, and doges' palaces are household names that remind visitors of Venice. A number of islands are easily reached from Venice. They include the Lido, with its fashionable seaside resorts; Murano, famed for glassblowing and shaping; and Burano, where lace is made.

Florence, the capital of Tuscany, is the center of the art world and was the focal city of the Renaissance. Florence was at one time called the City of the Medici and is the city of Michelangelo, whose famous statue of David is in the Academia of Florence. Much of the art can be seen in the Uffizi Palace, the Piazza della Signoria, the Bargello Museum, the Palazzo Pitti, and the Academia. The center of Florence is the Piazza del Duomo, with its thirteenth-century Baptistery of San Giovanni and Ghiberti's famous bronze doors. The Cathedral of Santa Maria del Fiore in Florence is one of the largest churches in the world. The thirteenth-century Church of Santa Croce is the burial place of both Michelangelo and Machiavelli. High on a hill above the Pitti Palace is the Piazza de Michelangelo, with a most-photographed view of Florence. Florence is noted for its leather goods and market, some of which is on Ponte Vecchio over the Arno River.

In addition to these two gems, there are a host of villages and towns that fascinate visitors. Verona, with its rose-red brick architecture; Ravenna, famous for its fine mosaics; Vicenza, with its palladian architecture; Siena, a walled town; and Pisa, with its leaning tower, Figure 8–6, are only a few.

Rome and the Vatican. The Vatican is the center of the Roman Catholic Church. St. Peter's and St. Peter's Square are the heart of pilgrimages to the Holy City. The Vatican City occupies an area of 109 acres situated entirely within the city of Rome. In addition to St. Peter's Basilica and the Vatican Apostolic Palace, its museums, archives, and library, the Vatican City consists of a number of administrative and ecclesiastical buildings, a village of apartments, and the Vatican Gardens. Its population is about one thousand. The cathedral dome and the youthful "pieta" were designed and sculptured by Michelangelo. The canopy of the main altar and St. Peter's Square were designed by Bernini. In addition to housing one of the great museums of the world, the Vatican is the location of the Sistine Chapel. Its fresco ceiling was done by Michelangelo.

Apart from the Vatican, a visitor can keep busy in Rome. Ancient Rome is evident in the Colosseum, the Forum, the Palatine Hill, the Pantheon, the Via Appia Antica, the Roman baths, and the Castel Sant' Angelo, which dominates the Tiber River. Relics of early Christianity can be seen in the Catacombs, an underground burial place for early Christians. Other popular attractions include the Spanish Steps, the Villa Borghese, the Trevi Fountain, and the Palazzo Venezia, which was the official home of Mussolini. Other important and interesting churches are the Santa Maria Maggiore, St. John Lateran, St. Paul Without the Walls, and St. Peter in Chains.

Near Rome, Tivoli is a small town on the Aniene River that is well-known for its wine, villas with their

Figure 8–6 Leaning Tower of Pisa

cascades and beautiful gardens, and Lido di Roma, a fashionable resort.

Naples and Surrounding Area. Naples and many of the ancient cities in the region, such as Pompeii and Herculaneum, were resort towns for ancient Rome, built in the shadow of Mount Vesuvius. The eruption of Vesuvius destroyed both Pompeii and Herculaneum, and the excavated cities are excellent historical sites detailing life in the Roman era. Naples is a city built around a lovely bay that is bounded by Vesuvius, the Sorrento Peninsula, and islands just beyond the harbor. The crowded streets of Naples are alive with vendors, festivals, refreshment kiosks, and friendly people.

North of Naples in Caserta, the remarkable palace of Charles III rivals Versailles in size and splendor. The Mediterranean is best enjoyed from Capri and Ischia, little islands off the coast of Naples. Capri's most famous natural wonder is the Blue Grotto. The Sorrento Peninsula, with its colorful villas, scenic villages, shops, and views of the sea, is best observed along the Amalfi Drive, Figure 8–7. Further south of Pompeii are the remains of an extremely well-preserved Greek Temple of Poseidon and a beautiful example of Doric architecture at Paestum.

Sicily. Sicily has a tremendous potential for tourism. Palermo, the largest city, has a fine Greek temple, and there are a number of Greek ruins, such as an amphitheater at the Greek City of Syracuse. Taormina has a rugged picturesque setting, including a fine view of Mount Etna and access by bus to some good beaches. In addition to the Greek temples throughout Sicily, there is architectural evidence of Roman, Norman, and Moorish influence.

Figure 8–7 Sorrento, Italy

Sardinia. Sardinia, the second largest island in the Mediterranean, is the popular luxury resort of the Aga Khan, who built Costa Smerelda. Sardinia is rugged, with mountain ranges extending to six thousand feet in elevation. It has beautiful scenery, excellent beaches, and many historic attractions from the Phoenicians and Romans.

San Marino. San Marino, the world's smallest republic, is in the Apennine Mountains. It is about one-third the size of Washington, D.C. Located in the north central area of Italy near the east coast, it has few visitors as its tourism facilities are limited. About two million tourists visit San Marino each year, attracted by its medieval fortresses and panoramic views. It is only accessible by highway. Most visitors are day visitors. Its language is Italian, and its currency is the Italian lira.

Spain

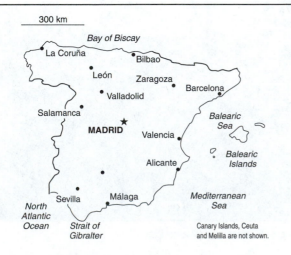

Capital: Madrid
Government: Parliamentary Monarchy
Size: 194,882 square miles (about the size of Arizona and Utah combined)
Language: Castilian Spanish; second languages include 17% Catalan, 7% Galician, and 2% Basque
Ethnic Division: Spanish with a Basque minority, growing numbers of North and West European retirees.
Religion: 99% Roman Catholic, 1% other
Tourist Season: March through October
Peak Tourist Seasons: July, August, and September
Currency: Pesetas (PTS)

CULTURAL CAPSULE

Spanish people are a mixture of Mediterranean and Nordic ancestry and are considered a homogeneous ethnic group, although the Basques disagree. There are four official languages in Spain. Castilian is the main language of business and government. The other three are Catalan (17 percent), Galician (7 percent), and Basque (2 percent). English is common in the tourist centers. While there is no official religion, more than 90 percent of the people belong to the Roman Catholic Church.

Cultural Hints:

- A firm handshake is common in greeting or when parting.
- Business cards are commonly exchanged.
- Eye contact is important, but women should be careful in doing so.
- The "OK" sign is an obscene gesture.
- The hand in a raised fist with the index and small finger extended is an insult.
- Do not put your hands in your pockets when talking.
- Chewing gum in public is rude.
- Eating and food:
  Keep your wrists on the table.
  When finished eating, place the knife and fork parallel across the plate.
  Do not eat while walking in the streets.
  The service charge is generally in the bill. Tip a small amount also.
  Typical food includes meat, eggs, chicken, fish, fresh vegetables, potatoes, onions, pork sausages, lamb stew, roasted meats, cold vegetable soup (gazpachos), and rice. Churros, a batter made of flour and butter, deep-fried and sprinkled with sugar, are sold throughout the cities.

Physical Characteristics

Spain has a large flat-to-dissected plateau surrounded by rugged mountains and hills. The coastal plains offer considerable opportunity for sun-sea-sand recreation. The climate depends on location. The interior has clear, hot summers and cold winters, while along the coast is mild and moderate, with most of the rainfall in the winters.

Tourism Characteristics

Spain has become one of the largest destination countries for international tourists in Southern Europe. Along with France and the United States in visitors it is one of the world's leaders, ranking fourth in total tourism receipts. Most of its importance as a destination for tourists has developed since the end of World War II. Tourism is the most important single element in the Spanish economy, accounting for the highest percentage of export trade in any European country. The character of tourism emphasizes low-priced package tourism oriented towards the coastal areas and the Balearic Islands. In addition, Spain has a large number of visitors (some 16 million) that stay less than 24 hours. These short-stay visitors come mostly from France and Portugal and are not included in the 41 million total foreign tourists Spain receives annually.

Europe is the most important market region, accounting for almost 84 percent of Spain's total visitors. Germany and the United Kingdom (33.5 and 28.3 percent, respectively) lead in total bed nights in hotels. French and Portuguese are the greatest total number of visitors, but they are short term and campers or are passing through Spain. Spain and Portugal account for some forty percent of the total visitors, but only ten percent of the bed nights. This indicates the imbalance in the number of visitors and the number of bed nights spent in Spain. Tourism from the United States and Canada accounts for less than three percent of all visitors, again indicating the dominance of Europe as the major market (World Tourism Organization, 1995).

Tourism to Spain is both highly seasonal and geographically concentrated. The peak season is the summer from June to September, with August being the largest tourism month. Summer tourism is compounded by Spanish holidays in August, when the Spanish move from the hot interior of Madrid and other major cities to the coasts. This high level of seasonality creates serious problems in labor and hotel usage. On the Balearic Islands, the industry has tried to adjust to this problem by closing some hotels and emphasizing a few large hotels in each complex during the off-season. They have developed a program of unemployment compensation that provides for payments to workers during the off-season.

There is a heavy regional concentration, with the Balearic Islands and the Costa Brava (north of Barcelona) having the largest number of visitors.

Figure 8–8 Bullfighter, Spain

The Costa Brava and Barcelona. North of Barcelona along a coastline of cliffs and pines are secluded coves, wide sandy beaches, and picturesque seaside villages. South of Barcelona are a number of seaside resorts, such as Stiges and the ancient town of Tarragona, with its Roman, Visigoth, Moorish, and medieval ruins.

Near Barcelona, Montserrat and the Benedictine Monastery sit high in the mountains in a spectacular setting. Barcelona itself is the largest and busiest port in Spain. It was the home of the 1992 Summer Olympics and from where Columbus set sail for America. About six thousand new hotel beds were added in preparation for the Olympics. Located near the Ramblas (the principal pedestrian street), the Gothic Quarter features a series of beautiful restored medieval structures and a cathedral dating from the twelfth century. Throughout the city, there are interesting churches. The unfinished but original Church of the Sagrada Familia by Antonio Gaudi and the oldest church (the Church of San Pablo del Campo) are quite interesting. Pueblo Espanol, a Spanish village built for the Exposition of 1929, depicts architectural styles and workmanship from the various regions of Spain at that time.

The Costa Blanca, centered on Alicante, and Costa del Sol, between Algeciras and Malaga, are the second ranking destination. Saturation of the coastal areas creates a distinctive cycle of bustling summer seasons versus the high vacancy rates in the winter months.

Although it is handicapped by its interior location, the area around Madrid is the major interior location for international tourists.

In 1992, Spain was the center of world attention, hosting the Summer Olympics in Barcelona and the World's Fair in Seville. Madrid was selected as the European City of Culture for 1992. There were also a number of celebrations marking the five–hundredth anniversary of both Columbus's discovery of America and the unification of the country under King Ferdinand and Queen Isabella, which ended eight centuries of Moorish domination.

Tourist Destinations and Attractions

Destination regions in Spain can be divided as follows.

Balearic Islands. The Balearic Islands—Majorca, Minorca, Ibiza, and Formentera—are best known for their sun-sea-sand and mass tourism. There are some outstanding cathedrals and fortresses, which provide a diversion from the beaches. Throughout the islands, there are traces of prehistoric, Greek, Roman, *Punic*, and Arab civilizations.

Costa Blanca and Valencia. The Costa Blanca, which extends north and south of Alicante, was at one time a series of coastal fishing villages. They were "discovered" by tourists from Northern and Western Europe and have become large tourist developments focusing on wide, sandy beaches and the warm waters of the Mediterranean. Valencia is a port city that provides ferry access to the Balearic Islands. Valencia is set in a rich agricultural area with gardens of lemon, almond, olive, pomegranate, palm, and orange trees. The city has many fine ancient mansions and gardens and a number of museums.

Andalusia. *Andalusia* (the south of Spain where Moorish influence is still visible) and the Costa del Sol are often pictured on travel posters and brochures of Spain. The combination of white-washed houses with red-tiled roofs and the Moorish architecture reflecting the Islamic culture makes this area unique. In the coastal area from Malaga to Algeciras, near the Rock of Gibraltar, the small coastal villages have been overwhelmed with tourist developments. The region offers splendid beaches, mild climates, and a host of cities and towns in Andalusia to visit. In Malaga, there is a Renaissance cathedral and a Moorish Alcazaba. Throughout Andalusia, there are fine examples of Moorish culture.

The city of Granada is replete with Moorish architecture, the most famous of which is the *Alhambra Palace* with its stunning towers, halls, fountains, courtyards, gardens, mazes, and gold mosaics. Below the hill on which the Alhambra is located are gypsy caves and a cathedral where King Ferdinand and Queen Isabella are buried.

Northwest of Granada, Cordoba has more ruins from the Moorish period. The *Mosque* at Cordoba is considered by many to be the greatest surviving example of Moorish architecture. The third major city in Andalusia affected by the *Moors* is Seville, the unofficial capital of Andalusia. The Moors were a combination of tribes (Arabs, Berbers, Syrians, etc.) from North Africa united by Islam and the Arabic language. Seville was under Roman, Visigoth, and Moorish rule, all of which left their mark. The Cathedral of Seville is one of the most beautiful Gothic cathedrals in Spain. The Moorish Christian Alcazar also adds to the beauty of the city. The Giralda Tower is one of three original Moorish towers that is still erect. The Santa Cruz quarter with its twisting byways, dignified old houses, and flag-stoned patios and the Tower of Gold are but two of the many attractions this fine city offers. One of the most-celebrated *Holy Week* festivals takes place in Seville. The mountains in Andalusia provide some outstanding attractions. Two of the most famous are Jerez de la Frontera (sherry country) and Ronda, one of the oldest towns and bullrings in Spain. It has an outstanding Roman bridge spanning a deep, rocky cleft. The movie "Lawrence of Arabia" was filmed in Almeria, in southeast Spain.

Madrid and Central Spain. Madrid, the capital and cultural center of Spain, has one of the world's great museums, the Prado. The works of El Greco, Velasquez, Goya, and other Spanish masters are found here. The Royal Palace is one of the beautiful palaces of Europe with Flemish tapestries, porcelain furniture, fifteenth- to eighteenth-century armor, Goya portraits, and an outstanding and attractive garden. Madrid's cathedral was built in the seventeenth century and is a blend of Gothic and Renaissance styles. Madrid is the home of the World Tourism Organization.

A number of interesting and important towns, cities, and countrysides lie within a day's travel from Madrid. Probably the most famous is Toledo, the religious center of Spain. Toledo has outstanding churches, such as its thirteenth-century Spanish Gothic cathedral, the Church of Cristo de la Luz, which was a tiny mosque in the tenth century, and two former synagogues of the city, Santa Maria and El Tránsito. Toledo was the home of El Greco. His most famous paintings and his restored house can be seen here. The most visual feature of the landscape is the fortress that was rebuilt following the civil war of the 1930s. The scenic landscape with windmills on hilltops that was made famous in the book about Don Quixote is near Toledo.

North of Madrid, the Romanesque city of Segovia has impressive ruins and one of the most beautiful castles in Spain, and Avila, a medieval walled city. Close to Madrid are El Escorial, a huge monastery-palace and burial place for the kings of Spain; the Palace of Aranjuez, inspired by Versailles and the Trianons; and the Valley of the Fallen, a burial place and monument to the former Spanish dictator Franco and the civil war heroes of Spain.

Northern Spain. Santiago de Compostela, one of the major pilgrimage cities of Europe, and the famous government hotel, Hostal de las Reyes Catolicos, one of the most magnificent hotels in Spain and a showcase in itself, are in the Northwest. On the Asturian coast, visitors can tour the city of Santander and see the world-famous 13,000-year-old Altamire cave paintings. (A replica of the caves is located at the national museum in Madrid.) Northern Spain has one of Spain's busiest coasts because of its close proximity to France, San Sebastian, and the port city of Bilbao. An hour south of San Sebastian is Pamplona, which is famous for its once-a-year festival of the running of the bulls July 6 and 15. Ernest Hemingway was enamored with Spain and its culture. He spent considerable time in Spain and wrote part of his *For Whom the Bell Tolls* at the Casa Botin, an old restaurant in Madrid, first opened in 1725. Both Hemingway and Orson Welles watched a few bullfights in Ronda. Welles's ashes were scattered in Ronda after his death.

Canary Islands. Off the coast of Morocco and about 650 miles south of Spain are the volcanic Canary Islands. Las Palmas on Grand Canary Island and Santa Cruz de Tenerife are the two most frequented locales. The Canaries have been "discovered" by the large tour operators of Germany and Great Britain and have become a highly commercialized sun-sea-sand vacation destination.

Gibraltar

Capital: Gibraltar
Government: Colony of the United Kingdom
Size: 2.25 square miles
Language: English, Spanish
Ethnic Division: Italian, English, Maltese, Portuguese, and Spanish descent
Tourist Season: March through October
Peak Tourist Seasons: July and August
Currency: Pound sterling

Physical Characteristics

The Rock of Gibraltar dominates the landscape. The climate is mild in the winter and warm in the summer, with most precipitation in the winter.

Tourism Characteristics

Gibraltar, famous as "the Rock," has been under control of the British for many years and is a political issue for the Spanish. For many years, the border between Gibraltar and Spain was closed. In order to visit from Spain, tourists had to travel to Morocco and then return to Gibraltar or vice versa. The border with Spain is now open, but Gibraltar's visitors are mostly British. In the 1990s, Gibraltar received approximately 100,000 visitors a year. The major attraction is "the rock," which can be ascended by cable car to see the Barbary apes. It has good beaches, water sports, duty-free shopping, a Moorish castle, and St. Michael's Cave, prominent for military defense, overlooking the Strait of Gibraltar.

Andorra

Capital: Andorra la Vella
Government: Co-principality
Size: 175 square miles (about two and one-half times the size of Washington, D.C.)
Language: Catalan (official); French and Castilian

Ethnic Division: Catalan stock; 61% Spanish, 30% Andorran, 6% French, 3% other
Religion: Roman Catholic
Tourist Season: May through September
Peak Tourist Seasons: July and August
Currency: Pesetas (PTS) and Franc (FFR)

Cultural Characteristics

The population is concentrated in the seven urbanized valleys that form Andorra's political district. Andorran citizens are a minority, outnumbered three to one by Spanish residents. The national language is Catalan and is spoken by more than six million people in the region comprising French and Spanish Catalonia.

Physical Characteristics

The terrain consists of rugged mountains that are dissected by narrow valleys. The climate is temperate, with snowy, cold winters and cool, dry summers.

Tourism Characteristics

Andorra is high in the Pyrenees on the Spanish and French border. Andorra's major attraction is its location and the lowest–cost duty-free shopping in Europe, which attracts visitors from adjacent Spain and France. Andorra's setting in the mountains is outstanding, and attractions such as lakes, hiking, camping, and skiing are available. It has resorts such as Pas de la Cosa and Envalira, which are good winter sports areas.

Portugal

125 km

North Atlantic Ocean

Braga
Porto
Covilhã
Coimbra
Portalegre
LISBON ★
Beja
Faro

Azores and Madeira Islands are not shown.

Capital: Lisbon
Government: Republic
Size: 35,516 square miles (about the size of Maine)
Language: Portuguese
Ethnic Division: Mediterranean, with some 100,000 African
Religion: 97% Roman Catholic, 1% Protestant, 2% other
Tourist Season: April through October
Peak Tourist Seasons: July (14.65%) and August (20.65%)
Currency: Escudos

 ## TRAVEL TIPS

Entry: Visas are not required for visits up to sixty days. Passports are required. There are currency limits on importing and exporting escudos.
Transportation There are direct flights from North America, European countries, and Brazil and elsewhere to Lisbon. There is good road, rail, and air service within the country. Lisbon has a good, inexpensive taxi, bus, streetcar, and subway system.
Shopping: Common items include wine, glaxed tiles, porcelain, textiles, embroideries, tapestries, leather gloves, filigree jewelry, and decorative pieces in gold and silver.

CULTURAL CAPSULE

The Portuguese are a mixture of an Ibero-Celtic tribe and Germanic, Roman, Arabic, and African peoples. There is a small minority of Africans who migrated to Portugal after decolonization of Portugal's African territories. Portugal is one of the oldest states in Europe. It traces its modern history to 1140 A.D. when, following a nine-year rebellion against the king of Leon-Castile, Afonso Henriques, the Count of Portugal, became the country's first king. After a series of expansions, the present-day boundaries were secured in 1249. The official language is Portuguese. English, French, and German are taught in the schools and understood by many. Over 95 percent of the people are Roman Catholic.

Cultural Hints:
- A firm handshake is a common greeting.
- To get someone's attention, the Portuguese will extend the arm upward, palm out, and wag the fingers up and down.
- Do not point directly at a person with the index finger.
- The thumbs up with both hands means everything is well.
- Do not make the V for victory sign behind someone's head. It is an insult meaning lack of morals.
- Eating and food:
  Dinner is a social event taking time.
  When finished eating, place the knife and fork vertically on the plate.
  Eat fruit with a knife and fork.
  A special knife and fork are used for eating fish.
  Do not use bread to wipe up gravy or juices.
  Typical food includes fish (cod is popular), chicken, rice, pork, partridge, quail, rabbit, potatoes, vegetables, fruits, and pastry. Olive oil is the favorite cooking oil, and garlic is a popular seasoning substance.

Physical Characteristics

Portugal is divided into two distinct topographical and climatic regions. North of the Tagus River, the country is mountainous and the climate is moderately cool. The area south of the Tagus has rolling plains, less rainfall, and a warm climate, particularly in the interior. The Azores are a series of nine rugged, mountainous islands of volcanic origin lying about 800 miles west of Lisbon. Their climate is moist and moderate. The Madeira Islands, located about 350 miles west of Morocco, are more rugged than the

Azores. Their mild year-round temperatures are attractive to tourists.

Tourism Characteristics

Portugal has had the largest percentage growth of arrivals in southern Europe in the last decade. Tourist arrivals increased over 165 percent in the 1980s. It now has an industry comparable to Greece, with 10 million visitors in 1996. Its relative location and attractions have been factors in the past that hindered its tourist trade, but it has overcome them. Portugal's better beaches are similar to those in other Southern European nations; but they are located in the south of Portugal, far from markets, and they are not on the Mediterranean.

Portugal's single largest market is Spain, accounting for some 50 percent of its arrivals. However, they represent less than 10 percent of its bed nights. The United Kingdom, the source for 14 percent of Portugal's arrivals, accounts for 19.4 percent of all bed nights. Germans comprise 22.7 percent of its bed nights. In the 1960s and 1970s, Portugal cultivated the sophisticated traveler and the luxury market from North America. In the 1980s, however, they began to market to countries and companies with a strong reputation for mass tourism. This change is expressed in the high volume of visitors from the United Kingdom and Germany. Further development will, of necessity, need to emphasize air travel. The crowded Spanish beaches are making Portugal an attractive alternative.

Since Portugal joined the European Union, the wealthier countries of the EU have assisted Portugal in funding major improvements in roads, railways, and airports. The tourist boom in the Algarve has attracted a host of real estate speculators from all over Europe.

Tourism Destinations and Attractions

The main attractions are found in three areas: Lisbon and its environs, the Algarve, and the Madeira Islands. Coimbra is a smaller destination.

Lisbon and Its Environs. Lisbon, the capital, and the Tagus estuary coast are the major centers for tourism to Portugal. Lisbon is one of the oldest capitals in Europe. The city of Lisbon is spread over seven hills. It was founded by Phoenicians in 1200 B.C. It is a city of contrasts between the old and the new, with wide, shady avenues contrasting with the narrow streets and alleys of picturesque old districts. Lisbon is the chief center of administration, business, and diplomatic activity. The influence of the Moors can be seen in the buildings and castles. A number of museums, such as the Museum of Popular Art, the Maritime Museum, the National Coach Museum, and the National Museum of Ancient Art, are excellent. The Tower of Belem, built in 1515, is a part of a fortress marking the spot of Vasco da Gama's first sailing for India. Jeronimos Monastery is a Manueline Renaissance structure where da Gama is buried. Both of these sites are found in the city. On the hilltop dominating Lisbon is the Castle of Sao Jorge, an old Moorish fort with a medieval village around its base.

The *old quarter* of Lisbon is called the Alfama, a Moorish and Visigoth district of winding, narrow *casbah* (bazaar) streets and houses. Near Lisbon, the towns of Estoril and Cascais are resort centers with beaches and casinos. Queluz (National Palace) is described as a miniature Versailles, with outstanding gardens. Three important buildings at Sintra are the Royal Palace, Pewna Palace, and Moorish Castle. All along the coast north from Lisbon are scenic fishing villages and towns, such as Nazaré, a fishing village that is rich in folklore and has a fine beach. A little over one hundred miles north of Lisbon, Fátima is the location where the Virgin Mary is reputed to have appeared to three shepherd children. Fátima is now an important pilgrimage site in Portugal.

Algarve. The Algarve is Portugal's answer to the Costa del Sol and other coastal beach resorts in Spain. The Algarve is in the southern part of the country and offers the best beaches and water in the country. It stretches from Sagres in the west to the Spanish frontier in the east. It is a sheltered, south-facing coastal strip with a string of small towns and fishing villages that has become Portugal's vacation zone. Its fishing villages are very picturesque, with white houses topped by gracefully carved chimneys. Orchards of oranges, figs, carob, and almond trees dot the landscape.

Madeira and the Azores. Madeira is the main tourist island of the volcanic Madeira Islands, about four hundred miles off the coast of Africa, west of Morocco. Its mild climate, moderate rainfall, and mountainous countryside with deep ravines, vineyards, banana groves, pines, and eucalyptus trees provide a number of resorts and favorable attractions. Madeira is referred to as a garden of thousands of flowers. Funchal, the capital of the island, and the center of tourism, is surrounded by parks and gardens overlooking the ocean. The city itself is worth exploring with its narrow streets and passages in the old part of the city. Santa Catarina's chapel dominates the city from its position on one of the plains along the coast. The builders used violet lava, grey volcanic stone, and black or white stones in its construction. Its appearance is brightened by white and yellow climbing plants. Relics of the fifteenth and sixteenth centuries are seen in Fort Sao Lourenco, the Santa Clara Convent, the old Customs House, and the Sao Tiago Fort. All can be discovered by walking through streets and squares paved with black and white stones, patterned in such a way that they are often a reminder of the waves on the sea.

The Azores are a group of nine islands some eight hundred miles west of Portugal. The Azores have some seaside resorts and excellent spas. Ecotourism is becoming important in the Azores. The sea is rich in tuna, blue and white marlin, swordfish, and albacore.

Coimbra. The city of Coimbra was founded by the Romans and was the capital of Portugal in the early days of the kingdom. The university here was one of the first in Europe. Coimbra is rich in art, monuments, and historical buildings. Near Coimbra are Conimbriga (ruins of a Roman town), Lorvao (monastery), Pombol (Castle), and Cantanhede (the churches of Sao Pedro and Varziela). West of Coimbra at the mouth of the River Mondego, Figueira da Fox is a resort area and fishing port that offers gambling and an excellent climate to the visitor.

Malta

Capital: Valletta
Government: Republic
Size: 122 square miles (about twice the size of Washington, D.C.)
Language: Maltese, English
Ethnic Division: Mixture of Arab, Sicilian, Norman, Spanish, Italian, English
Religion: 98% Roman Catholic
Tourist Season: Year-round
Peak Tourist Season: June through September
Currency: Maltese pound

Cultural Characteristics

Malta was first colonized by the Phoenicians, following by the Arabs, the Italians, and the British. Most of the foreign population consists of retired British people. Roman Catholicism is established by law.

The two official languages are Maltese (a Semitic language) and English. Malta is one of the most densely populated countries in the world. Flights to Malta are available from Europe and Northern Africa. There is car ferry service from Naples and Sicily.Physical Characteristics

Malta consists of three islands, approximately 58 miles south of Sicily in the Mediterranean. They are mostly low, rocky, and flat, with dissected plains and coastal cliffs. The climate is Mediterranean, with mild, rainy winters and hot, dry summers.

Tourism Characteristics

Malta gained its independence from Britain in 1964. The island was historically an island fortress because of its strategic location in the Mediterranean. Although the islands' topography consists of low, barren hills, the climate is warm and clear, particularly in the winter. Over fifty percent of Malta's visitors are from the United Kingdom. Malta's previous ties combine with its warm winters to make it very attractive to the British. Germany and Italy are the other two markets of significance, accounting for approximately ten and eight percent of the visitors, respectively. Malta has a very long average length of stay, illustrating the destination character of visitors.

Cultural attractions of Malta are associated with the Phoenicians, Romans, Arabs, Normans, Knights of St. John, French, and British. Monuments and remains from temples and idols of prehistoric civilizations are also found.

A SPANISH ADVENTURE

DAY 1   MADRID

The day in Madrid will be spent visiting the El Prado Museum, one of the finest in Europe; the Royal Palace, which was built between 1737 and 1764 and was the home to Spanish monarchs for over 200 years until the 1930s; and the Plaza Major, the heart of the old quarter of Madrid, which is a maze of narrow streets, small churches, and charming squares.

DAY 2   AVILA–SEGOVIA–LA GRANJA

A drive north of Madrid will take us to Avila, Segovia, and La Granja. Avila, "city of stones and saints," is a well-preserved medieval city surrounded by walls that extend over one and a half miles with eight gates and 88 semicircular towers and battlements. Part of the day will be spent walking through the narrow streets and along the battlements of its incredible walls, providing an unforgettable experience of this medieval city. Segovia is an ancient Roman town with a well-preserved Roman aqueduct and one of Spain's finest cathedrals. The Alcazar fortress palace is in an impressive setting on a hill overlooking a valley. Returning to Madrid, we will stop at La Granja, the royal palace with beautiful fountains and gardens.

DAY 3   TOLEDO

Toledo is an easy drive south of Madrid. Toledo was first settled by the Romans and was the capital city for the Visigoths. It later became the religious center for the Catholic kings. It was at one time under the control of the Moors and was the medieval center of learning and capital of Spain until Madrid was named the capitol in 1561. Sightseeing will include El Greco's home; Alcazar, an ancient fortress; the Sinagoga de Santa Maria la Blanca, the main synagogue of Toledo in the twelfth century; the Cathedral, one of the largest and most magnificent in Spain; and the Puente de Alcantara, a dramatic bridge spanning the Rivere Tajo between high cliffs.

DAY 4   CORDOBA–SEVILLE

Today we will drive through the La Mancha plains to Cordoba. The tour of Cordoba will include the Mosque, the most famous Moorish structure in Western Europe and now a Gothic-Baroque-Rococo cathedral; the Alcazar, which was built in the thirteenth and fourteenth centuries and has Moorish courtyards and Roman mosaics; and the Juderia, the Jewish quarter of the city. We will arrive in Seville in the late afternoon.

DAY 5   SEVILLE

The morning sightseeing will include the Alcazar, which was built in the fourteenth century utilizing portions of an ancient Almohad palace; the Cathedral, which is the third largest in the world, exceeded only by St. Peter's in Rome and St. Paul's in London; the Giralda, which adjoins the Cathedral and is the only structure remaining from an ancient Arab mosque; and the Barrio de Santa Cruz, the Jewish quarter of the city, with its whitewashed homes, red-tiled roofs, inner courtyards, decorative iron lanterns, and balconies covered with flowers lining the cobblestone streets. Seville's Plaza de Toros is one of the most famous arenas for bullfighting in the world. This afternoon you will be at leisure to enjoy the city.

DAY 6   GRANADA–MADRID

A stop in Granada will provide you an opportunity to visit the Alhambra, a famous fortress and supreme monument of Arabic architecture; the gorgeous gardens of the Generalife, where you will enjoy the panoramic view of the city; and the gypsy quarters below the fortress. We will return to Madrid for the evening.

DAY 7

Return home from Madrid.

REVIEW QUESTIONS

1. What are the advantages and disadvantages for the tourism industry of the physical environment of Southern Europe?
2. Which Southern European country has the most diverse tourism industry? Justify your response.
3. Which country has the shortest length of stay? Why?
4. What are the problems of tourism to Cyprus?
5. Compare and contrast tourism to Spain and Portugal.
6. What are five reasons for visiting Greece?
7. Why is tourism so important to the economies of most of the Southern European countries?
8. What are some of the major problems that Spain has with tourism? How can Spain overcome the problems?
9. Identify and describe tourism to the small nations of Southern Europe.
10. What are some general concerns visitors have about going to Southern Europe?

GEOGRAPHY AND TOURISM IN
Central Europe and the Balkan States

CHAPTER 9

MAJOR GEOGRAPHIC CHARACTERISTICS

- Central Europe and the Balkan States are fragmented culturally and politically.
- The region is located between more powerful countries, which hindered its political development, resulting in repeated conflicts.
- The region historically had a central monarchy and a nobility whose palaces and other relics are important tourist attractions.
- There is a wide range of economic and tourism development, standard of living, and political stability.
- Central Europe is characterized by physical and cultural diversity.

MAJOR TOURISM CHARACTERISTICS

- There is a diversity in entry requirements, but all countries are encouraging international tourism.
- The countries of Central Europe have increased their interest in tourism development.
- There is a wide variety of tourist attractions and landscapes.
- Tourism from the West has expanded dramatically since the revolutions of 1989 overthrew the Communist governments in the region.
- Many attractions, highways, and accommodations have been destroyed because of ongoing conflicts in former Yugoslavia, which was a major destination before 1990.

MAJOR TOURIST DESTINATIONS

The capitals of Central Europe and the Balkan States
Black Sea Resorts
Karlovy Vary, Czech Republic
Adriatic Sea Coast
Transylvania
Carpathian Mountains
Tatra Mountains
Krakow
Lake Balaton
Julian Alps
Dubrovnik
Valley of Roses
Dinaric Alps
Romanian Riviera
Dalmation Coast

KEY TERMS AND WORDS

Adriatic
Austro-Hungarian Empire
Danube
Eastern Orthodox
European Cities
European Plain
Gothic
Hidden Economy
Industry

Iron Gate
Karst
Masurian Lake District
Medieval
Mountains (Carpathian, Tatra, Dinaric Alps)
Turkic Ottoman Empire
World War II

In 1991 Croatia and Slovenia declared independence from Yugoslavia; Bosnia-Herzegovina followed in 1992. Macedonia also declared independence from Yugoslavia in 1992, but it is recognized only by a few countries. In 1997 Bosnia-Herzegovina was divided into Croat, Serb, and Muslim territories, with United Nations peacekeeping forces stationed in each.

CENTRAL EUROPE: CONTRASTS IN THE FORMER COMMUNIST REALM

Introduction

The countries of Central Europe and the Balkan States (Figure 9–1) are distinct geographically and as a tourism destination region in three readily identifiable ways. First, the region has only recently (1989) emerged from communist domination. Communist governments made visiting difficult to varying degrees depending upon each individual country's policies. Second, the region spans a wide range of climatic, scenic, and cultural settings, providing a great variety of tourism experiences. Third, portions of this region are a living relic of *medieval* Europe, something which is unusual because of the extensive conflicts that have affected the continent in the last two centuries.

Some of these countries, such as Albania, avoided any tourism contact with the West in the past and are now opening to tourism with limited contact. At the other extreme was Yugoslavia, which endeavored to develop its tourism industry as an integral element of its economic base. Visits by tourists to these countries prior to 1990 were indicative of their policy towards tourism. Yugoslavia and Hungary had millions of visitors, primarily from Western Europe, while Albania numbered tourists in the thousands. Analysis of the geography of these various countries illustrates the differences that exist between countries, the impact of government policies on tourism flows, and the tremendous changes now occurring.

The Political Geography of Central Europe

The political geography of Central Europe is a function of its location and physical geography. The location is peripheral to the core of Europe centered in France, Germany, and the British Isles. The location is also important because certain countries lie along the trade routes between Asia and Europe, Russia and Europe, and the Middle East and Europe. In consequence they have been invaded and re-invaded, creating an ever-changing mosaic of boundaries and countries. The physical geography of Central Europe that contributed to the fragmentation of the region still affects the area. The contrast in physical geography between the *European Plain* of Poland and the mountainous peninsula occupied by Yugoslavia and Albania helps explain the present cultural fragmentation, which is partially reflected in the political boundaries of the region. Taken together, the location and physical geography of Eastern Europe continue to be expressed in the extraordinary changes presently occurring within the region.

The nations of Central Europe today share a long history of political and cultural evolution. At varying times, they have been invaded from Russia and the former Soviet Union, Germany, Austria, Turkey, and Rome. The resulting pattern of peoples, languages, and cultural characteristics makes this one of the most complex areas in the world. The most recent factors affecting the political geography of Central Europe and the Balkan States were the impact of *World War II* and the emergence of the Communist Party as the sole political party in each of these countries and the revolution of 1989 that overthrew the Communists, leading to both democracy and conflict. These changes in turn reflected events that transpired at the end of World War I, illustrating the importance of the past in explaining the present geography of the region. At the present (1996), the final political boundaries in this area, particularly in what was Yugoslavia, still remain to be defined.

POPULATION CHARACTERISTICS, 1997							
Country	Population (millions)	Annual Growth Rate (percent)	Time to Double Pop. (years)	Per Capita GNP	Life Expectancy (years)	Daily Calorie Supply	Percent Urban
Albania	3.4	1.7	41	670	72	2,605	37
Bulgaria	8.3	-0.5	—	1,330	71	2,831	68
Czech Republic	10.3	-0.2	—	3,870	73	3,632	77
Hungary	10.2	-0.4	—	4,120	70	3,644	64
Poland	38.6	0.1	573	2,790	72	3,301	62
Romania	22.5	-0.2	—	1,480	70	3,155	55
Yugoslavia	10.6	0.2	279	N/A	72	3,634	51
Bosnia-Herzegovina*	3.6	0.6	122	N/A	72	N/A	34
Croatia	4.8	-0.0	—	3,250	70	N/A	54
Slovenia	2.0	0.0	—	8,200	74	N/A	50
Macedonia	2.1	0.8	86	860	72	N/A	58
Slovakia	5.4	0.2	408	2,950	73	N/A	57

Figure 9–1 Central Europe and Balkan States

THE MODERN STATES OF CENTRAL EUROPE AND THE BALKAN STATES

The countries of the region range in size from Poland (largest in population and area) to Macedonia (smallest in population and area).

The development of *industry* came late to this region. Industrial development primarily reflects developments since World War II. Even in the Czech Republic the bulk of industrial development historically occurred in the region adjoining Germany. The initial industrial development in western Czech Republic spread to southern Poland. Since World War II the industrialization of Central Europe has proceeded more rapidly. The general pattern of industrial development is from north to south, with the Czech Republic and Poland still having the highest level of industrialization. This reflects both their earlier beginnings in industrial development and the amount of assistance that they received from the former Soviet Union. Albania is the only country in which employment in industry does not exceed employment in agriculture.

The relative standard of living across the region reflects the level of economic development. As measured by per capita gross national product (GNP), Slovenia is the highest. It is misleading to assume, however, that the per capita GNP effectively measures the standard of living. The growing importance of private ownership of farms, small shops, and industries and service activities create a *hidden economy* that is not measured by the official GNP. Changes since 1989 have created inflation, private enterprises, and challenging economic situations for all of these countries, even affecting the ethnic divisions in the region that led to the breakup of Yugoslavia and the division of Czechoslovakia.

The conflict in Bosnia continues to create problems to the economic infrastructure of the region. How soon or whether recovery can occur in this region is questionable. In consequence, the economies of countries created from Yugoslavia have fallen from among the region's highest standards of living to among its lowest. Continued killing and destruction, of course, make even measurement of living standards meaningless.

THE PHYSICAL GEOGRAPHY OF CENTRAL EUROPE

Landforms

The physical geography of Central Europe and the Balkan States has contributed both to the political fragmentation and the attractiveness of the region for tourists, Figure 9–2. The landforms of Central Europe can be divided roughly into four broad areas:

1. The North European Plain
2. The Central Mountains
3. The Plains of the Danube River
4. The Mountains and Coasts of the South

The North European Plain is an extension of the major landform feature of Western Europe that ex-

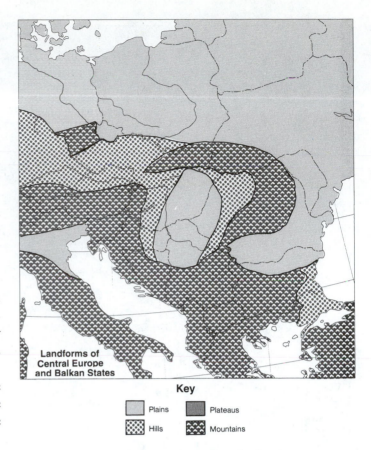

Key

☐ Plains   ▨ Plateaus
▨ Hills   ▨ Mountains

Figure 9–2 Landforms of Central Europe and Balkan States

tends on to Russia as the Russian Plain. Most of the plain varies from 200 to 300 miles in width. Few features in the plain are higher than 900 feet above sea level. The landforms of the plain are not level and reflect the historic development of the North European Plain and its subsequent glaciation.

The first zone of the plain lies adjacent to the Baltic Coast. It is made up of glacial moraines of sand and gravel. These moraines create a series of hills or ridges that extend in an arc across the North European Plain from Denmark through Lithuania to Russia. These hills are a series of terminal moraines from glaciation, and in the northeast of Poland they have blocked the natural water drainage, creating the *Masurian Lake District*. Soils in this region are infertile, and much of the area is planted in pine forests.

South of these hills is a zone of sand and gravel that was stratified by melted water draining from the glaciers to the north. The soils are relatively infertile and are used for growing oats, rye, and potatoes. This zone creates the characteristic north Polish landscape of pine trees separated by large fields of rye, potatoes, or oats. Cutting across the sand and gravel deposits are the large shallow valleys created by the rivers of melt water that flowed from glaciers as they advanced and retreated over a period of a million years. The rivers of Poland (the Oder, Warta, and Vistula) are all found in these great valleys. Because they are broad, flat, and often marshy, they are also used for the canal routes that link the rivers of the European Plain. The soils are poorly drained and are often used as pasture for livestock.

Located north of the *mountains* that form the southern margin of the European Plain is a fertile plain where fine wind-blown material called loess was deposited near the end of the glacial period. These are the most fertile soils in Central Europe and are used for wheat, sugar beets, and other important crops.

The Poles, the largest cultural group in Central Europe, developed their distinctive cultural characteristics in the various zones of the North European Plain. The Poles created a number of capital cities over time on this plain, the most important of which were Poznan, Krakow, and Warsaw. Poznan was located on the Warta River and had access to the Vistula River by a glacial valley. Population growth led to a shift of the capital to Krakow because of its location on the upper Vistula River proper. Continued population growth and political changes ultimately prompted removal of the capital to Warsaw on the middle Vistula River. Warsaw has a more central location on the main route from Central Europe to Moscow, a fact that is important even today in trade and tourism.

The Central Mountain Zone

The Northern Plain ends as it meets the mountain ranges of the Carpathians, the Ore (Erzgebirge) and Sudeten Mountains. The most important of these are the *Carpathian Mountains*, which constitute a long arc of mountains ranging from 3,500 to over 8,000 feet elevation and extend a distance of over 1,000 miles. These are part of the Alpine geologic system of Europe. Portions of these mountains are rugged and scenic and are important for tourism. In the southern part of the Carpathians, the rugged nature is reflected in their designation as the Transylvanian Alps. The western ranges of the Carpathians include the high *Tatra Mountains* on the border between Slovakia and Poland. An important tourist area, the Tatra Mountains exceed 8,000 feet in elevation. Other ranges of the Carpathians are also very scenic and are the location of popular resorts in several of the countries of Central Europe.

The Ore and Sudeten Mountains are lower than the Carpathians. Their primary importance lies in the

fact that they completely enclose the Bohemian Basin of the western Czech Republic. The Ore and Sudeten Mountains rise to 2,500 to 4,500 feet and represent old mountains that have been worn down by erosion over long periods and later uplifted. The Bohemian Basin contained within the Ore, Sudeten, and Carpathian Mountains is the location of the 1,000-year-old capital of the Czechs, Prague. The Sudeten and Ore Mountains are important for their mineral resources of iron ore and coal, and the Czech and German peoples have had a great amount of interaction over time in developing these mineral resources.

The Basin of the Danube

The *Danube* River is the largest and longest river of Europe. It cuts through a series of basins that are, in turn, the focus of individual cultural groups of the region. These basins begin with the Great Hungarian Plain of Hungary, Austria, and Slovakia. Farther down the Danube, the Wallachian Plain is found in Romania. The Hungarian Plain and the Wallachian Plain are separated by a resistant rock mass, which creates the gorges of the Danube River known as the *Iron Gate*. Historically a barrier to navigation, this is more important today as a unique scenic area of the Danube River. Agriculture in the Hungarian and Wallachian Plains forms the most important agricultural region of each of the countries that include portions of these plains. Their generally level nature has allowed transportation and urban areas to develop across them in response to population growth.

The Southern Mountain Systems

South of the Danube River Plains, a series of mountain ranges of alpine origin dominate the landscape of Central Europe. The *Dinaric Alps* run along the *Adriatic* Sea of the Mediterranean, forming the backbone of Bosnia and Herzegovina, Croatia, and parts of Yugoslavia. North and east of the Dinaric Alps are the Hungarian Plains of northern Serbia, Croatia, and eastern Slovenia, while to the south and west the land drops rapidly to the Adriatic, creating scenic landscapes characterized by marginal agricultural activities interspersed with resort communities and a few cities occupying the small plains adjacent to the coast.

Approached from the sea, the coastline is imposing as it rises abruptly from the water. Agriculture utilizes terraces built over hundreds of years to produce olives, grapes, and corn, and to graze goats and sheep. The Dinaric Alps are made of limestone, which has been eroded by water to create a unique landscape form known as *karst*. The mountains extend as an unbroken barrier for 350 miles, with elevations varying from 4,000 to 6,500 feet. The highest point in the Dinaric Alps is 8,272 feet in the south of Bosnia-Herzegovina.

East of the Dinaric Alps, a series of hills and mountains dominate the Balkan Peninsula. The most important of these are the Balkan Mountains of Bulgaria. The Balkan Mountains generally run east-west and reach elevations over 8,500 feet, but a series of interlinked valleys provides a variety of routes between the Danubian Plains and the Mediterranean coastal region. The highest point in the Balkans is at Mount Musala, which rises to 9,610 feet. South of Mt. Musala are the narrow plains of northern Greece.

The combination of the Dinaric and Balkan mountains and the intervening hills was especially important because historically it led to isolation. A wide variety of cultural groups including Serbs, Slovenians, Macedonians, Turks, Croats, Bulgars, and Albanians lived over long periods of time in the isolated valleys of this mountainous region. Even today the cultural contrasts are highly recognizable as one travels across the countries created from Yugoslavia, adding to the potential attractiveness of the region for tourists.

Climate of Central Europe and the Balkan States

The climate of Central Europe and the Balkan States is transitional between the maritime climates of Western Europe, the Mediterranean climate of Southern Europe, and the continental climate of Russia. In the north in Poland, the Czech Republic, and Slovakia, the climate is primarily humid continental, with cool summers similar to Wisconsin and Minnesota summers. The summer temperatures tend to be in the 70s or low 80s for the daytime maximums. These three countries are generally humid, but the relatively moderate daytime highs make summers comfortable. The areas south of the Sudetes in the Czech Republic, such as Prague in the west, are less humid because the mountains create a rainshadow effect. Slovakia and Poland are wetter in the summertime.

Poland, the Czech Republic, and Slovakia have winter temperatures that rarely drop below 20 degrees Fahrenheit. This region has a winter climate analogous to that found in areas of the United States such as St. Louis. The humid continental warm summer climates of Central Europe have a summer maximum of precipitation, with most countries receiving between 20 and 30 inches. Across the entire region, the only areas that have more than 30 inches of precipitation are associated with the mountains and highlands. The result is a climatic pattern of moderate to warm summers with seasonal extremes of winter cold in the north, but delightful and extensive autumn periods. North of the Dinaric Alps of Croatia and Bosnia-Herzegovina, snow covers much of the East European region for a prolonged period. The average duration of snow cover ranges from 40 days in northern Poland to 10 to 30 days over most of the highlands of Bosnia-Herzegovina, Hungary, Romania, and Bulgaria. The snow cover lasts longer in the mountains of the Carpathians and Dinaric Alps, making them an important winter resort region.

The highest temperatures found in the region are recorded in the coastal areas of Croatia, Albania, and southern Bulgaria, while the coldest temperatures are found in northeastern Poland, where the continental and latitudinal influences are greatest. The Black Sea Coast regions of Bulgaria and Romania have summer temperatures similar to those found in the Carolinas and Virginia of North America, which makes them attractive to tourists.

A Mediterranean climatic type is found along the Adriatic sea coast of Croatia, Bosnia and Herzegovina, and Albania. The Mediterranean climates of the Adriatic are characterized by long, hot, dry summers and moderate humid winters. Across the Mediterranean region, the precipitation is between 20 and 30 inches, most of which falls in the winter season. The hot dry summers combine with the beaches of Croatia, Bosnia and Herzegovina, and Macedonia to make it a most attractive destination for foreign tourists in Central Europe when it is not handicapped by armed conflict. The winter season in the coastal Mediterranean climate has temperatures that range between 30 and 55 degrees Fahrenheit range. The climatic variety found in Central Europe provides a mirror image to that found in Western Europe. The range from the cool continental climates of northern Poland to the Mediterranean climate of Croatia is very similar to the range found from northern Germany to Spain or Italy with their Mediterranean climates.

TOURISM IN CENTRAL EUROPE AND THE BALKAN STATES

Tourism in Central Europe and the Balkan States reflects the physical and cultural geography of the region. *European cities* and towns are central to tourism to Central Europe. The pattern of urban development reflects both the recent changes in industrialization and economic development and the historic population distribution based on the physical geography of the region. Major industrial cities remain the primary economic centers of the individual countries. From Warsaw in Poland to Prague in the Czech Republic to Budapest in Hungary to Belgrade in Yugoslavia, the old cities remain dominant. In part, this reflects their political role, but it also reflects their development over long periods of time as economic and trade centers.

The emergence of *medieval* states in the Middle Ages was associated with the development of a capital city in each. These capital cities became the focus of the castle and the cathedral in that state. The close association of government and church is manifested in the role the church played in selecting the kings, crowning them, and providing them with skilled administrative staff. These old cities developed on a hill or defensible site such as the Wawel at Krakow, the Hills of Buda in Budapest, or the Hradcany Castle of Prague. Within the fortification was located the castle of the king and the cathedral of the bishop or archbishop. The Wawel at Krakow best retains its appearance of a medieval capital and is a major tourist attraction. The Hradcany of Prague preserves its *Gothic* Cathedral of St. Vitus, but most of the present buildings on the hill date from the eighteenth century. The other capitals such as Budapest, Zagreb, and Warsaw have been destroyed by wars and later rebuilt.

Other cities developed in the region primarily for trade purposes. The majority of these cities have a castle or monastery as the nucleus around which they developed. The cities were generally planned with at least a number of straight streets intersecting at right angles to create rectangular blocks. One of these central blocks became the marketplace, which is typical of the older merchant cities of Central Europe. The towns contain parish churches, but the churches are rarely as ostentatious or pretentious as the town or guildhall. Because of the role of the merchants in most of the cities of Central Europe, the guildhall emerges as the dominant architectural attraction where it has not been destroyed.

The coastal town, whether along the Baltic or the Mediterranean coast, is related to merchant trade of the late Middle Ages. The few towns along the Baltic Coast reflect the trading of the Hanseatic League. Houses are tall and richly decorated, with warehouses built along the waterfront as at Gdansk, Poland. They reflect the tradition of Hamburg and the German traders who came to the Baltic Coast. Mediterranean coastal settlements generally derive from Italy. Rijeka, Croatia (formerly the Italian community of Fiume), was originally a Roman settlement. Split, Croatia, grew around the palace built by the Roman Emperor Diocletian for his retirement.

Some of the older towns have surviving relics from the Roman Period, or churches dating from the second and third centuries. Dubrovnik, Croatia, was originally a small island settlement of Italian merchants. By filling in the narrow channel that separated it from the coast, it was able to expand onto the mainland. Unfortunately, Dubrovnik, which was once one of the premier attractions in Yugoslavia, was heavily damaged by Serbian shelling when Croatia declared its independence in 1991. Most of the medieval towns in Central Europe date from medieval times and medieval trade rather than from the Romans or the early Italian state. Initially established for trade, the old core is generally recognizable even today. The medieval settlement was surrounded by a wall or fortification for defense, and the line of these walls is visible in the parks or boulevards that still are found in some cities, such as Budapest or Prague. In a few instances, the medieval walls survive, as at Zagreb in Croatia or in Warsaw, Poland. The newer areas of these towns (1800s forward) are recognizable because of larger or stylistically distinct buildings with wider streets.

An important characteristic of a medieval town was its division into sectors, in each of which there was some specialization by occupation or trade. Prior to World War II, this segregation into districts was most evident in the persistence of Jewish ghettos. The calculated destruction of these overcrowded ghettos during World War II destroyed much of the uniqueness of the ghettos of Central Europe, but the old Jewish cemeteries and tabernacles still exist in some communities, adding to the character of the communities.

The *Turkic Ottoman Empire* had an influence on Bulgaria, parts of Romania, the south of Yugoslavia, Bosnia-Herzegovina, and Albania for many centuries. In these areas occupied by the Turks, the cities' sections were divided on the basis of religious belief or ethnic group rather than occupation. Cities in these regions have characteristic architecture, including mosques dating from the Islamic religion of Turkic invaders and cathedrals of the Eastern Orthodox Church, which share many of the architectural characteristics of the mosque. The onion-shaped domes, arches, and uses of tile are typical of the Islamic influence in the Byzantine architecture of this area of Eastern Europe, greatly enhancing its attraction to tourists. Many have been damaged or destroyed by ethnic conflict between 1991 and 1995.

Grafted onto the old towns of Central Europe are the structures of the post–World War II communist period. These are more homogeneous and better planned than the early towns in terms of ease of movement, but they are less interesting. The characteristics of these areas include large apartment blocks, state-run shops, children's playgrounds, and a generally monotonous and egalitarian community. The Communist presence of monumental architecture (Palace of Culture, the Party Headquarters), fountains, and boulevards with gardens are designed to make the quality of life less crowded and more efficient. They succeed in this, but because they were repeated over and over throughout the region, they are less interesting to tourists than the towns from the previous era. Until 1989, tourism reflected the impact of the Communist governments. With the exception of Yugoslavia, tourism was normally operated by a national government travel agency, which owned and operated the major hotels and national tourist offices and controlled most tourism.

Most international tourism in the past was characterized by planned movements of groups between the eastern European countries themselves. The overthrow of communism has transformed the character of tourism to the region. Western tourism to the Czech Republic, Poland, and Hungary has soared in the past five years. It is estimated that over 37 million tourists visited the Czech Republic and Hungary in 1996. Poland has also had marked increases as Western visitors come in response to easing of entry requirements, the emergence of private travel agencies and tour companies, and the low costs of travel there compared to the rest of Europe. Poland, the Czech Republic, and Hungary had the largest numbers of visitors in 1996, Table 9–1, while in Romania, Bulgaria, and the countries created from Yugoslavia the numbers have declined. Much of the decline in the 1990s was caused by the decline of organized tours from the former Soviet Union to Bulgaria and Romania and the ongoing conflict in the former Yugoslavia. Bulgaria

Table 9–1 Tourism in Central Europe and the Balkan States

Country	Total Tourists, 1990 (thousands)	Total Tourists, 1996 (thousands)	Tourist Season
Albania	30	38	May–Oct.
Bulgaria	4,500	2,795	May–Oct.
Czech Republic	8,100*	17,000	May–Sept.
Slovakia		650	May–Sept.
Hungary	20,510	20,670	May–Sept.
Poland	3,400	19,420	May–Sept.
Romania	6,533	2,834	May–Oct.
Bosnia-Herzegovina	N/A	N/A	May–Oct.
Croatia	N/A	2,649	May–Oct.
Yugoslavia	N/A	162	May–Oct.
Slovenia	N/A	832	May–Oct.

*Total for United Czechoslovakia

has the potential to increase due to the inexpensive nature of trips and the relatively stable and peaceful transition in governments. Other factors affecting the number of visitors to individual countries reflect the tourism infrastructure.

As would be expected, the level of tourism facilities in Central Europe is a reflection of the Communist system. With few exceptions, hotels and other accommodations are clean and adequate, but not luxurious. A few luxury hotels have been constructed in major cities, such as the Hilton in Budapest, but most have been designed to meet the needs of the East European tourists at lower costs. There still exist a few major hotels that predate the Communist Revolution in Central Europe, with all of the elegance expected by the wealthy travelers of the pre–World War II era. As with most of the public facilities in the countries of Central Europe and the former Soviet Union, however, these luxury hotels are but a shadow of their former elegance. The service level is also lower than is normally experienced in Western Europe and other countries where the staff has an incentive to insure that the service provided is outstanding. New hotels are being rushed to completion in the three leading tourism destination countries as Western hotel chains invest in the region.

Poland

150 km

Baltic Sea
Gdynia
Gdańsk
Szczecin
Bydgoszcz
Białystok
Poznań
WARSAW ★
Łódź
Wrocław
Lublin
Katowice
Rzeszów
Kraków

Boundary representation is
not necessarily authoritative.

Capital: Warsaw
Government: Democratic Republic
Size: 120,728 square miles (nearly identical to New Mexico)
Language: Polish
Ethnic Division: 98.7% Polish, 0.6% Ukrainian, 0.5% Belarussian, less than 0.05% Jewish
Religion: 95% Roman Catholic, 5% Russian and Greek Orthodox, Protestant, Other
Peak Tourist Season: May through September
Currency: Zloty

 ## TRAVEL TIPS

Entry: Visas are not required for stays up to 90 days. Visitors must register with hotel or police within 48 hours of arrival in country.
Transportation: Good air and rail connectivity to major cities and tourist destinations. Within the cities public transportation is efficient and inexpensive. Purchase tickets from kiosks on board and punch the tickets in machines mounted near the door.
Currency: Do not convert large sums of currency. In many cases it is better to use hard currency (dollars, German marks, French francs, British pounds) to purchase goods and service.
Shopping: Common items include regional costumes, handwoven rugs, lace, embroidery, ceramics, woodcarving, amber jewelry, coral jewelry, leather work, metalwork, peasant dolls, wooden toys, crystal, and art.

CULTURAL CAPSULE

Poland has the largest population in Central Europe and has the seventh largest population in Europe. It is ethnically homogeneous with 98 percent Polish. Poland is predominantly active Catholic. The Catholic church was strong during the Communist regime and has been strongly nationalistic.

Cultural Hints:
- Shake hands to greet, with men waiting for women to extend hand first.
- Generally do not embrace or touch while talking.
- Don't chew gum when talking with Poles.
- Toasting during meals is common.
- Eating and foods:
  Tips are expected.
  Wait to eat until all are served.
  Common foods include pierogi (dumplings with cream cheese and potatoes), cabbage dishes of all kinds, and potatoes.

Physical Characteristics

Poland is part of the European Plain that continues to the Ural Mountains. It is bordered on the north by the Baltic Sea and the Carpathian Mountains to the south along the Czech border. The climate is moderately severe in the winters, with mild, cool summers with frequent showers and thundershowers.

Tourism Characteristics

Poland has some of the greatest cultural attractions of Central Europe, but it is handicapped by the fact that it lacks the major attractions for tourists—sun, sea, and sand. The Polish government is desperately trying to increase the number of tourists to Poland. Tourism was up marginally in 1989, and by 1996 it was estimated at over 19 million. When East Germany became part of Germany and citizens gained the freedom to travel, many chose to visit Poland. The majority of these visitors are Germans on day trips who benefit from the low prices in Poland. Visitors from the United States increased from 93,000 in 1989 to a projected 140,000 in 1993. The Polish populations in the United States and Canada account for much of the travel from Anglo-America. With the change in government it is anticipated that future visitors to Poland will be more diverse. The currency (Zloty) is stable and readily convertible, but in the past there was a shortage of hotel rooms in Central European countries. That has changed as a number of American companies opened new hotels in the 1990s. Warsaw has a 444-room Marriott, 355-room Sheraton, and 328-room Holiday Inn. A number of other international standard hotels have opened. Occupancy rates are now around 60 percent. Poland is experiencing a boom in private enterprise bringing a growth in street markets, new retail shops, restaurants, private hotels, car hire firms, and travel agencies.

Poland to Prague

Sharon and Nelson Helm

Gdansk

We made arrangements with the Orbis office in the hotel for a morning tour of Gdansk ($16 each) including an organ recital on an 8,000-pipe organ in a former Cistercian abbey in the suburb of Oliwa. The tour itself was with a guide using his nearly new small Fiat for just the two of us.

Among the other highlights of the tour were Gdansk's huge Church of Our Lady, the largest Gothic brick church in Poland (capable of holding 25,000 people); the Old Crane, which is a 1443 vintage dock house; the seventeenth-century Golden Gate entrance to the old city, and the Three Crosses Monument dedicated to the shipyard workers who were killed in the civil disturbances of 1970, leading to Poland's drive to democracy.

Warsaw

On the road to Warsaw, we took a route by the city of Malbork to get a picture of the Castle of the Teutonic Knights. The magnificent castle dates back to 1308 and supposedly is one of the most impressive fortresses in Europe.

The next morning we signed up for a tour of Warsaw ($18 each); it took about five hours and was very good.

Included were the old-town (where we saw a twenty-minute film showing the almost-total destruction of Warsaw by the Nazis), the many important statues on the Royal Road, Chopin Park, the Polish "White House," the Opera House, the Tomb of the Unknown Soldier with its hourly changing of the guard and the impressive Wilanow Palace, still used for important state functions.

On Friday evening we went to a terrific folklore dinner show at the Europejske Hotel; it cost about $27 for two.

Krakow

The 200-mile drive to Krakow passed quickly and we pulled into the parking lot of the Hotel Cracovia around noon.

During the drive, we went through the city of Czestochowa. This city is the pilgrimage destination of thousands on Assumption Day (August 15) paying homage to the famous Black Madonna, an icon located in a monastery there.

An inquiry at the Orbis office in the hotel resulted in our attending a concert that evening of organ and choir music in a Benedictine abbey. The abbey was founded in 1044 and is located in the small village of Tyniec about 18 kilometers southwest of the city. Cost of the tickets for this excellent program was about 72 cents each!

After the concert we returned to our hotel, then walked along the Vistula River and took a few pictures of Wawel Castle, which was begun in the fourteenth century and was the residence of many Polish kings. Along the banks of the river were several tables where the men of the city were spending their leisurely evening hours playing chess.

The next morning, after enjoying a large buffet breakfast, we walked about five minutes to the old center of town.

Where the original walls once stood there now is a lovely green belt surrounding the old town. There were large trees and landscaping with benches and paved walks; it was obviously a popular location for strollers and a place to meet friends.

Krakow sustained only minimal damage during the war, so it is a treasure of seven centuries of Polish architecture. Sadly, what the war did not do is now being done by the high level of industrial air pollutants from nearby factories in the area. It still is a joy to wander around in the city, however.

Time for Shopping

Krakow's Market Square is the largest medieval town square in Europe. In the center is the Sukiennice, or Cloth Hall. This 328-foot-long structure is crammed full of small, beautiful folkart and craft shops.

We also found many shops in Krakow's old town full of crystal, lace blouses, leather goods and other items. We had not found much to purchase thus far in Poland, so this city seemed like a jackpot.

continues

continued

Zakopane

We reluctantly left Krakow for the resort city of Zakopane in the High Tatra Mountains of southwest Poland. In driving just 60 miles, the scenery changed very rapidly from a flat plain to a scenic mountain setting.

It was very obvious that this part of Poland has more wealth. The single-family homes have a multi-story design with steep roofs and a foundation and lower level that use large native stones with a very distinctive appearance.

The town was full of families on holiday; however, we heard no English spoken on the streets. Once again there were good bargains in crystal and we could not resist a few more items.

Paczkow

From Zakopane we headed northwest, paralleling the Czech border, toward the small town of Paczkow, which Fodor's described as "a magnificent little town, a kind of Polish Carcassonne, completely ringed by medieval walls with towers and bastions."

After a long day's drive on many secondary but good roads with much more traffic than anticipated we arrived at Paczkow.

What a disappointment! Yes, there were some walls and a few towers, but to compare this to the magnificent fortress of southern France was a farce!

The only restaurant in town, surprisingly, was named Carcassonne, but it served only beer and soft drinks.

A City for Walking

Prague is a lovely city that must be enjoyed by walking. The flavor of several centuries of culture surrounds you. The buildings are covered by wall paintings, sculpture, ornate windows and unusual rooflines.

There are beautiful domes, spires, steeples and statues everywhere you look, and all of this is enhanced by parks, green belts and an untold number of flowers—an exquisite feast for the eyes.

The city also is known for its music and there usually are several events from which to choose each evening. If you want to attend a concert or opera in the Smetana Theater, plan ahead of time as tickets are sold out very quickly.

We did attend two concerts: one an organ soloist and the other an organ with soprano soloist as well as a trumpet soloist. Both were very good and the tickets were only $3 and $4 per person.

Both of these concerts were in churches, one a ten-minute walk from the apartment across the Charles Bridge and the other just around the corner from the apartment. Tickets were available at the American Hospitality Center.

We did spend a morning at the Prague Castle in the Hradcany district wandering through the squares and around the towering Gothic spires of the St. Vitus Cathedral. We also spent some time on the Charles Bridge with hundreds of others admiring its statues and browsing among the assorted vendors all across its span of the Vltava River.

The main attraction, of course, was the splendid buildings of Stare Mesto and the old town square where it was easy to spend an afternoon just taking in the atmosphere of the surroundings and a superb Czech beer as well.

Another location we visited was the old Jewish quarter with its fifteenth- to eighteenth-century cemetery. The stones there are packed in like many slices of a spilled loaf of bread.

We used the excellent and inexpensive Prague underground to go from the National Museum at the upper end of Wenceslas Square to the Hradcany district. We had no sooner begun looking at the map and fare chart when a man offered to help us. He was very friendly and seemed justifiably proud of his city.

Worth a Return

All in all, we heartily recommend independent travel to these two friendly and interesting countries.

Would you believe it? We are planning to include Krakow and Prague on our next itinerary!

Source: International Travel News.
September 1992; pp. 5–8, 46–49.

Figure 9–3 Old Town Poznam, Poland

Tourist Destinations and Attractions

The major destinations in Poland are the cities of Warsaw, Krakow, and the Baltic Coast, especially the port city of Gdansk. Warsaw was the third capital of Poland and was built in the seventeenth century. Destroyed during World War II by the Germans as they resisted Russian attempts to take the city in 1944, it has since been reconstructed. The old structures were rebuilt using street scene paintings, which can be seen in the national museum. The museums and reconstructed architecture are major tourist attractions, particularly the monument to the heroes of the Jewish ghetto. The monument remembers the nearly half-million Jewish people of Warsaw who were killed by the Nazis during World War II. Near Warsaw is the birthplace of Chopin (at Zelazowa Wola). The Pulski's museum at Warka, the Wilanow and Lazienki palaces of the kings of Poland, and the restored "old town," Figure 9–3, are also fascinating.

Krakow was not destroyed or even damaged during the war. The Wawel Mount is still dominated by the royal castle, which dates from the 1500s. Originally the second capital of Poland, the royal castle houses crown jewels, royal tapestries, and historical exhibits. The cathedral on Wawel Mount houses the crypts of the Polish kings and reflects the relationship of the church to the state during much of Poland's history. The old town in Krakow is a treasury of old architecture. The important structures are the Gothic Collegium Maius, now the Museum of the Jagiellonian University, the Main Market Square with the Cloth Hall, and the Church of Our Lady. Some of Krakow's architecture and art collections date from the early Middle Ages.

Poznan, an ancient Polish city, has become an important business travel center. The old Market Square with the town hall has a number of classical and baroque-style buildings. Near Poznan is Kornik, the medieval castle of Zamoyskis, with a library of priceless manuscripts.

The Baltic Coast has a length of 365 miles with sandy beaches. Water temperatures tend to be cool, but it still attracts numerous visitors during the short summer season. The coastal resort of Sopot and the reconstructed portions of Gdansk and Szczecin, two Hanseatic cities in the north, are major attractions.

The southern mountains have the winter resort area of Zakopane, near the Czech border. It is visited year-round, offering hiking and alpine climbing in the summer and skiing and other winter sports in the winter. Throughout the Tatra mountains, there is a beautiful scenery with steep, austere ridges and peaks, mysterious caves, beautiful forests, swift-flowing streams and waterfalls, and dozens of lakes of all sizes.

THE CZECH REPUBLIC AND SLOVAKIA

Physical Characteristics

The terrain is a mixture of hills and mountains separated by plains and basins. Bohemia, the westernmost region in the Czech Republic, consists of rolling plains, hills, and plateaus surrounded by low mountains to the north, west, and south. Moravia, the eastern part of the Czech Republic, is more hilly than Bohemia and is bordered on the north by the Carpathian Mountains. Slovakia has mountains in the central and northern part and lowlands in the south that are important for agriculture. The climate of the Czech Republic is temperate, with cool summers and cold, cloudy, humid winters. Slovakia has wider extremes—warmer summers in the south and colder, more severe winters in the mountains in the north.

Tourism Characteristics

The Czech Republic and Slovakia have a long tradition of tourism concentrated in the Czech Republic. It was part of early European tourism during the development of resort spas in the 1800s. It has a growing tourist industry. Visitors to the Czech Republic and Slovakia increased from 4.5 million in

The Czech Republic

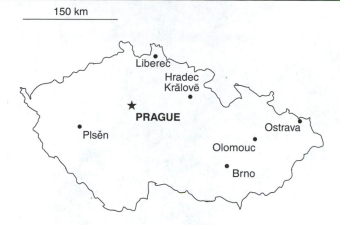

Capital: Prague
Government: Democratic Republic
Size: Approximately 30,000 square miles (slightly smaller than Maine)
Language: Czech and some Slovak
Ethnic Division: 94% Czech, 3% Slovak,
Religion: 39% Roman Catholic, 4.6% Protestant, 3% Orthodox, 13% other, 40% atheist
Tourist Season: April through October
Peak Tourist Season: June through September
Currency: Crown

 ## TRAVEL TIPS

Entry: Visas are not required for stays under 30 days.
Visiting: The former Czechoslovakia travel organizations, Cedok and CSA (Czechoslovak Airlines) are still the prime organizations for selling travel to both countries.
Transportation: There is an excellent network of bus, rail, and air service. Public transportation in the cities is good. Direct air service is available from the United States as well as the European gateways of Paris and Brussels.
Shopping: Common items include Bohemian crystal, Carlsbad China, handicrafts, and ceramics in the Czech Republic and Slovak ceramics and embroidered articles in the Slovak Republic.

1983 to over 8 million in 1990. By 1996 the Czech Republic was the dominant destination, receiving 17 million visitors more than Slovakia. They also receive a large number of day visitors, who would bring the total visitors to over 25 million during 1990. Famous historical spas offering high-quality service are Carlsbad (Karlovy Vary), Marienbad (Marianske Lazne), and Piest'any. Its central location, wide network of transport, and cultural linkage with the rest of Europe have allowed the Czech Republic to have a strong tourist tradition. Slovakia is more rural and has always had only a fraction of the tourists visiting the Czech area.

Slovakia

Capital: Bratislava
Government: Democratic Republic
Size: Approximately 19,000 square miles (equal to New Hampshire and Vermont)
Language: Slovak and Czech
Ethnic Divisions: 86% Slovak, 10% Hungarian, some Czech, German, Polish, Ukrainian, Russian
Religion: 60% Roman Catholic, 20% Protestant, Orthodox and other, 10% atheist
Peak Tourist Season: April through October
Currency: Koruna

CULTURAL CAPSULE

The division of Czechoslovakia into the Czech Republic and Slovakia represented ethnic differences. Other ethnic groups include 60,000 Hungarians in Slovakia. Both have some Ukrainians, Germans, and Poles. There are about 250,000 Gypsies, mainly in Slovakia, who represent the fastest-growing minority. Czechs and Slovaks were united after World War I and remained so under Communist control. In 1993 Czechoslovakia split into the two independent states. The division was largely an urban (Czech) and rural (Slovak) division.

Cultural Hints:
- Shake hands on greeting, with men waiting for women to extend hand first.
- Eye contact is important.
- A stiff forefinger turned on the temple of the head indicates someone is crazy, and is very rude.
- A good topic of conversations is sports.
- Eating and foods:
  When finished eating, place your knife and fork to one side of your plate.
  Don't put your elbows on the table.
  Toasting is common.
  Food differs somewhat by ethnic group, but pork roast, dumplings, sauerkraut, ham, and sausage are the most popular.

The Czech Republic and Slovakia appear to have the best future for tourism in Eastern Europe. They have natural beauty and an outstanding wealth of places of historic, cultural, and architectural interest. They are within easy accessibility to Europe's main origin markets and do not have the problems of Bulgaria or Romania or the economic difficulties of the Baltic states.

Tourist Destinations and Attractions

The premier tourist destination in the Czech Republic is Prague (Praha). The medieval city of Prague is built on seven hills on both sides of the river Vltava. The old Charles Bridge (now closed to vehicular traffic) carries visitors to the ancient city and fortress. The beautiful medieval castle city of Prague with its well-preserved buildings of all social classes from the Middle Ages is one of the most important attractions in Central Europe, Figure 9-4.

The architecture and atmosphere of Prague make it one of the most delightful cities in Europe. Because Prague's old city was not destroyed by war, it allows visitors to see something of what life was like several hundred years ago. Tourist accommodations are limited, and hotel reservations must be made up to a year in advance for visits that coincide with festivals. Reservations should be made at least several months in advance for hotel accommodations in Prague during the entire summer season.

Today much tourism to the Czech Republic is related to the health spas, which have attracted visitors for centuries. The most notable of these are Karlovy Vary and Marienbad. The principle attractions here and at the more than fifty other spas are the waters, which are impregnated with sulfur. The odor is breathtaking, but they are reputed to be remarkably effective in terms of health. Giant Mountains National Park has excellent ski facilities.

The primary destination in Slovakia is Bratislava, which was once the capital of Hungary. As the capital, it developed an international and cosmopolitan atmosphere. The Bratislava castle is 200

Figure 9–4 Clock Tower in Prague

feet up on a hill overlooking the city. The architecture, museums, and other attractions make Bratislava an interesting visit. It also has the longest beer hall in Europe.

The Tatra Mountains and Tatras National Park are the second major destination for tourists in Slovakia. The mountains have a number of ski resorts and have a relatively long ski season. Tatranska Lomonica is the most famous summer and winter resort in the region.

Hungary

Physical Characteristics

The terrain is mostly flat with rolling plains. The climate is temperate, cold, cloudy, and humid in the winters, with warm, humid summers.

Tourism Characteristics

Hungary has had a long history of tourism and has an excellent transportation network. Europe accounts for over 97 percent of the visitors to Hungary with

125 km

Miskolc

• Györ   ★   • Debrecen
          BUDAPEST

Dunaújváros •

          • Szeged
• Pécs

TRAVEL TIPS

Entry: No visa is required for stays less than 90 days.
Transportation: International airlines offer direct services to Budapest from North America and Europe. Train service is available via Vienna, and Hungary is part of the Eurail system. Public transportation is good in cities. Budapest has an inexpensive subway, trolley, and bus system.
Telecommunications: Telephone and fax services are readily available at standard international rates.
Shopping: Common items include hand-embroidered material, peasant pottery, Herend and Zsolnay china figures, and leather work.

Capital: Budapest
Government: Democratic Republic
Size: 35,921 square miles (slightly smaller than Indiana)
Language: 98.2% Hungarian, 1.8% other
Ethnic Division: 89.9% Hungarian, 4.0% Gypsy, 2.6% German, 2.0% Serb, 0.8% Slovak
Religion: 67.5% Roman Catholic, 20.0% Calvinist, 5.0% Lutheran, 7.5% atheist and other
Tourist Season: April through October
Peak Tourist Seasons: July (20%) and August (28%)
Currency: Forints (FOR)

CULTURAL CAPSULE

Magyars (the Hungarian name for both the people and the language) comprise 98 percent of the population. There are small groups of Germans, Slovaks, Gypsies, and Romanians.

Cultural Hints:
- Greet with a handshake, with men waiting for women to extend hand first.
- Avoid uninvited touching of others.
- Avoid discussions of politics or religion.
- Eating and foods:
  Tips are customary.
  Popular food includes goulash, a stew of meat, potatoes, onions, pork, chicken, noodles, potatoes, and dumplings. Paprika is a popular spice. Strudel and pancakes are popular desserts.

Austria, Germany, and Romania the major market areas. Most of the Romanian visitors are on one-day trips, having less impact than the long-term visitors from Western Europe. The United States accounts for only one percent of tourists, many of whom are on side trips from Vienna. Tourism from Anglo-America has grown rapidly in the 1990s as Budapest has become one of the most popular destinations of Central Europe.

Hungary has both medieval communities and the grandeur of the relics of the *Austro-Hungarian Empire*. (Budapest is often referred to as the Vienna of Central Europe.) Prices on some consumer goods in Europe are fair as well. Hungarian-made clothing, musical instruments, handicrafts, and artwork are relatively cheap when purchased with foreign currency.

Tourist Destinations and Attractions

The major tourist attraction in Hungary is Budapest, but hotel space is at a premium in spite of more than 16,000 hotel rooms in the city. Budapest is the primary destination because of its beautiful location along the Danube, Figure 9–5, and the sense of being in one of the most beautiful cities of the world.

The city consists of two parts: Buda, which is the hill side of the river and includes Castle Hill with its

numerous Gothic structures, Figure 9–6, including the former Royal Palace; and Pest, on the other side of the Danube, the newer, low-lying part of the city. The designation as new is somewhat misleading, as even the newer part dates from the Middle Ages. Post–World War II structures are built in the areas surrounding the city. The major attractions include

Figure 9–5 Danube River at Budapest

Figure 9–6 Mathias Church, Budapest, Hungary

the Parliament Building, Varosliget (the city park, which contains both a zoo and a fun center), and the Corso. The Corso is a broad boulevard running along the Danube River's edge. It is popular with residents and tourists alike. Budapest has nightclubs, gambling casinos, and modern hotels that rival western European countries. The final attraction is the excellent shopping opportunities at relatively low costs. Budapest is the starting place for cruises to the Black Sea.

The second tourist area of Hungary is Lake Balaton. This is the largest freshwater lake in Central Europe, and it is surrounded by campgrounds, which attract Hungarians, Italians, and Germans. Water temperatures are in the high seventies in the summer because of the shallow nature of the lake. Spas have always been popular in Hungary, dating back to the occupation of the region by both the Romans and the Turks.

Romania

200 km

Capital: Bucharest
Government: Democratic Republic
Size: 91,699 square miles (slightly smaller than Oregon)
Language: Romanian, Hungarian, and German
Ethnic Division: 89.1% Romanian, 8.9% Hungarian, 0.4% German, 1.6% Ukrainian, Serb, Croat, Russian, Turk, and Gypsy
Religions: 70% Romanian Orthodox, 6% Roman Catholic, 6% other, 18% unaffiliated
Tourist Season: March through December
Peak Tourist Season: June (10%), July (18%), and August (20%)
Currency: Lei (LEI)

- Eating and foods:
  Hands should be kept above the table.
  Toasting is common.
  Foods include mititei (grilled meat balls), patricieni (grilled sausage), and mamaliga (cornmeal mush), soups, and pastries.

Figure 9–7 Romanian Historical Village

Physical Characteristics

Romania is mostly flat to undulating plains with hills and mountains in the northwest (Carpathians and the Transylvanian Alps). The climate in the mountains is extreme, with cold, cloudy, snowy winters. The climate is moderate in Transylvania and along the Black Sea.

Tourism Characteristics

Since the early 1970s, Romania has developed its tourist structure rapidly. Romania has an abundance of good hotels and restaurants because the number of visitors has declined since the 1989 revolution. Most of its tourists in the past were from surrounding Eastern European countries and the Soviet Union, but many of these choose to go to Poland or western Europe now. Romania's tourism is centered around its rich cultural tradition, some of which predates the Roman occupation. The traditional folk arts, including dance, wood carving, ceramics, weaving, and embroidery of costumes combine with folk music to provide interest for visitors. The country's many Orthodox monasteries along with the Transylvanian Catholic and Evangelical churches have rich history and many artistic treasures.

Tourist Destinations and Attractions

Three major areas attract the bulk of tourists to Romania. These are the Black Sea Coast; the capital, Bucharest; and Transylvania. Coastal resorts begin in the north near Constanta and extend over 150 miles south to Mangalia. The main attractions include the sun and sea, thermal springs, health spas (including medicinal mud), and ruins that are 2,700 years old. Bucharest is a large and sprawling city with a variety of architectural relics dating from the influence of Rome to the Turkic Byzantine Empire to the neoclassic styles of the late Renaissance. Modern construction includes the conventional bland apartment buildings, skyscrapers, and a unique circular department store. The presence of the village museum adjacent to Bucharest is also a major tourist attraction. The village museum has nearly 500 peasant houses, churches, barns, and other relics that show how peasants in the Danubian Plains lived during past centuries. These peasant dwellings include underground homes, brush homes, log homes, and adobe dwellings, Figure 9–7.

The Transylvania area is important because of its association with Dracula in the minds of Western visitors. In actuality the castle of the fifteenth-century prince Vlad Tepes (from whom Dracula is derived) is located in Wallachia rather than Transylvania. Vlad's castle is accessible from the Black Sea Coast. Transylvania has the second largest city in Romania, Brasov. The primary attractions are the scenic open mountain countryside and peasant villages. The "Romanian Riviera" of the Black Sea stretches south from Constanta for 150 miles. Throughout this region are the typical beach resorts of high rise hotels and an abundance of nightclubs, restaurants, discos, and bars. Constanta was founded by the Greeks in the sixth century B.C. and was an important seaport under the Romans and the Turks.

Yugoslavia and Montenegro

Physical Characteristics

The terrain is varied. There are rich fertile plains. To the east are ranges and basins; to the southeast, ancient mountains and hills; to the southwest, a high shoreline with no islands off the coast. The climate in the north is continental with cold winters and hot, humid summers. In the south along the coast it is hot and dry in the summer and relatively cold in the winter.

Capital: Belgrade (Podgorica for Montenegro)
Government: Democratic Republic
Size: Yugoslavia: 34,135 square miles (slightly larger than South Carolina)
     Montenegro: 5,298 square miles (about the size of Connecticut)
Language: Serbo-Croatian
Ethnic Division: Serb (majority), Albanians, Montenegrins, Hungarians
Religion: 65% Eastern Orthodox, 19% Muslim, 4% Roman Catholic, 1% Protestant and 11% other minority religions
Tourist Season: April through October
Peak Tourist Season: July and August
Currency: Yugoslav New Dinar

 ## TRAVEL TIPS

Entry: No visa needed. Entry stamp allows a 90-day stay.
Transportation: International connections by rail and air connect Belgrade with other European countries.
Caution: The collapse of the Yugoslav federation and the ethnic warfare have destabilized the area.
Shopping: Common items include peasant handicrafts, embroidered blouses, gold and silver filigree jewelry, carpets, leather goods, carved wooden goods, laces, and pottery.

CULTURAL CAPSULE

The people are Serbs and ethnic Montenegrins. All are adherents of the Serbian Orthodox Church. There are a few Roman Muslims and Roman Catholics, but the future for minorities is uncertain.

Cultural Hints:
• Handshake upon greeting.
• Dress conservatively
• To beckon a waiter raise your hand.

Tourism Characteristics

Yugoslavia stood in marked contrast to the rest of Central Europe prior to 1990. The primary source of tourists to Yugoslavia was not Central Europe, but West Germany, which accounted for nearly one-third of the visitors to Yugoslavia. In total, nearly 80 percent of all visitors were from Western Europe, and only 14 percent were from Central Europe. Two and one-half percent of the visitors to Yugoslavia came from the United States (*The Economist Publications Limited*, 1988).

The accommodations within Yugoslavia were somewhat uniform in that they tended to reflect the prevailing philosophy of the centrally planned economies of Central Europe in providing basic accommodations. Although Yugoslavia had four classes of hotels plus accommodations in private homes and campgrounds or youth hostels, there was not a marked difference between the highest- and lowest-class hotels in terms of basic accommodations. The hotels of Yugoslavia tended to be geared directly to mass tourism of the middle class from Europe. Primary differences were in the nature and quality of the entertainment and the amenities offered rather than in the accommodations themselves.

Some of the factors that attracted Western tourists to Yugoslavia (relatively low cost, good accommodations and attractions, and excellent beaches) also attracted Eastern Europeans to Bulgaria, Hungary, and Romania. Since the breakup of the country in 1991, tourism has declined drastically. Europeans remain the dominant visitors, accounting for nearly 96 percent of visits. Conflict and destruction of facilities make it inadvisable to visit the new countries created from Yugoslavia or the remnant country of Yugoslavia itself.

Tourist Destinations and Attractions

The Adriatic coastline in Montenegro attracted a large number of visitors before the division of Yugoslavia. Today, it is isolated and remote from major industrial countries of Europe. There is a ferry to Italy from Bar on the south coast. While there are no major islands off the coast, there are excellent long, sandy beaches. Budva is the largest tourist center on the Montenegrin coast, drawing mostly inexpensive package visitors. Budva is a restored old-walled town in the center of a beautiful beach. Further north the Bay of Kotor is the longest and deepest fjord in southern Europe, providing picturesque ferry and bus rides.

The major destination in Yugoslavia is the capital, Belgrade. The dominant attraction in Belgrade is the

Kalemegdan Citadel, a hilltop fortress at the junction of the Sava and Danube rivers. Orthodox churches, medieval gates, Turkish baths, and Muslim tombs are all part of the citadel. The Monument of Gratitude to France and a large Military Museum are here also. Nearby, Stari Grad, the oldest part of Belgrade, contains the National Museum and the Ethnographical Museum with a collection of Serbian costumes and art. Belgrade's most important museum is the Palace of Princess Ljubice, an authentic Balkan-style palace built in 1831 and still furnished in that time period.

Marshal Tito's grave and former residence is a few miles south of Belgrade.

Southern Yugoslavia has a number of Orthodox monasteries with thirteenth- and fourteenth-century frescoes. Near the village of Despotovac is Manasija Monastery built in 1418 and completely enclosed in defensive walls and towers. The oldest and one of the greatest monasteries of medieval Serbia is south of Kraljevo. There are a number of monasteries in the region and Novi Pazar, which is a Muslim town. There are old Turkish mosques, inns, and bathhouses.

Slovenia

Capital: Ljubljana
Government: Democracy
Size: 7,836 square miles (slightly larger than New Jersey)
Language: 91% Slovene, 7% Serbo-Croatian, 2% other
Ethnic Division: 91% Slovene, 3% Croat, 2% Serb, 1% Muslim, 3% other
Religion: 70.8% Roman Catholic, 2% Muslim, 27.2% other
Tourist Season: April through October
Peak Tourist Season: July and August

 TRAVEL TIPS

Entry: Visas are not required. Tourist cards are obtained at the border.
Transportation: There are good rail and road connections to Slovenia. The cities have good public transportation.
Shopping: Common items include peasant handicrafts, embroidered blouses, gold and silver filigree jewelry, carpets, leather goods, carved wooden goods, laces, and pottery.

CULTURAL CAPSULE

The people are predominantly Slovenes, 89 percent, with some Croats and Serbs. The first Slovenes settled in the region in the sixth century A.D., but by the ninth century it was part of the Holy Roman Empire and became Germanized.

Cultural Hints:
- Greetings are made with a handshake.
- Eating and foods:
  Don't put your elbows on the table.
  Foods are Germanic in taste and type. Sausages and sauerkraut, game dishes, Austrian strudel, dumplings, and pastries are all tasty.

Physical Characteristics

Much of the region consists of mountains and valleys with a short coastal strip on the Adriatic. The climate of the coastal regions has hot, dry summers and cool wet winters. The plateaus and valleys are mild to hot in the summers and cold in the winter.

Tourism Characteristics

Slovenia has been affected less by the division of Yugoslavia and is consequently better able to handle tourists than the other republics. Slovenia is a transition between Central Europe and the Balkans. Much of the area reminds a visitor of the Austrian Alps or Bavaria with its wooded slopes, fertile valleys, scenic rivers, and neat little villages. The limited tourism data available indicates tourism is slowly increasing. Slovenia draws a significant number of visitors from the nearby countries of Italy, Austria, Croatia, and Germany.

Tourist Destinations and Attractions

The two major destination regions of Slovenia are the area around the capital, Ljubljana, and the Julian Alps. Ljubljana is a small city on the banks of the Sava River. Castle Hill dominates the landscape. Castles, cathedrals, museums, and markets are spread throughout the town. The most famous destination near Ljubljana and the road to Rijeka are the famous

Postojna Caves. Visitors are taken by train and on foot through 3 miles of the nearly 17-mile cave. The Skocjan Caves were placed on UNESCO's World Heritage list in 1986 but are more difficult to visit due to their remoteness.

The Julian Alps, shared with Italy, provide both summer and winter activities. The region is one of the finest hiking areas in Central Europe. The area contains the Triglav National Park, which was founded in 1924. It provides mountain huts scattered throughout the region. Hikers pass outstanding waterfalls, narrow gorges, glacial lakes, and scenic valleys. The most fashionable resort in the Julian Alps is Bled, set on a beautiful crystal-clear emerald lake.

Croatia

100 km

Capital: Zagreb
Government: Parliamentary democracy
Size: 21,800 square miles (slightly smaller than West Virginia)
Language: Croatian
Ethnic Divisions: 78% Croat, 12% Serb, 10% Muslim, Hungarian, Slovene, and others.
Religion: 76.5% Catholic, 11.1% Orthodox, 1.2% Slavic Muslim, 0.4% Protestant, 10.8% other
Tourist Season: April through September
Peak Tourist Season: July and August
Currency: Croatian dinar

TRAVEL TIPS

Entry: Visas are required and can be obtained at the border.
Transportation: Serious transportation problems in some regions resulting from war. Ferry service from Italy gives some access to southern region of country. Some areas remain unsafe because of the political situation at present.
Shopping: Common items include peasant handicrafts, embroidered blouses, gold and silver filigree jewelry, carpets, leather goods, carved wooden goods, laces, and pottery.

CULTURAL CAPSULE

The population is largely Croat with the Serbs the largest minority. There are some Slovenes, Italians, and Slovaks. The Croats are mostly Roman Catholics. German and English are widely used through the country—German because of the number of migrant workers to Germany in the past, and English because of the popularity of English in general.

Cultural Hints:
- Shake hands when meeting.
- Single women may be harassed and should avoid sunbathing and hiking alone.
- A closed hand with the index and little fingers raised is an insult.
- Eating and foods:
  Check prices before ordering.
  If there is no service charge, tip when paying. Leave tip on the table.
  Food consists of Italian pizza and pasta, seafood on coast, brodet (mixed fish stewed with rice), mushrooms, manistra od bobica (beans and fresh maize soup), and strukle (cottage cheese rolls). Italian-style espresso coffee is popular.

Physical Characteristics

The terrain is diverse with flat plains along the Hungarian border and low mountains and highlands near the Adriatic coast. The coast is hot, with dry summers and wet and mild winters. The interior has hot summers and cold winters.

Tourism Characteristics

The war has created serious problems for the tourist industry. In general the area of Zagreb, Istria, and the islands of northern Croatia are safe and can be visited without problems. The Adriatic resorts have been affected by the war. In some cases considerable destruction has occurred, and in others there is limited access because of war damage. This is particularly true farther south at Osijek and Dubrovnik. The mountain regions are inaccessible at this time. Although the effects of the war will be noticeable for some time, tourists are beginning to return to some coastal attractions. The majority of visitors are from the region and Italy.

Tourist Destinations and Attractions

The capital, Zagreb, is a medieval city, on the banks of the Sava River. There are many lovely parks, galleries, museums, and cafés. St. Stephen's Cathedral, built in 1899, has Renaissance pews, marble altars, and a Baroque pulpit. The Baroque Archiepiscopal Palace and sixteenth-century fortifications surround the palace. A number of other churches, such as the St. Catherine's Church (Baroque), Stone Gate, and St. Mark's Church (Gothic, painted-tile roof), have important art works. A number of museums, including the Historical Museum of Croatia, the National History Museum, the City Museum, the Archaeological Museum, and the Ethnographic Museum, recall the history and people of the past and present.

The most important coastal destination is the Dalmatian coast, which occupies the central 150 miles between the Gulf of Kvarner to the Bay of Kotor and includes the offshore islands. The offshore islands are comparable in beauty to those of Greece.

The most important resort is at Dubrovnik. Dubrovnik has beautiful beaches, Renaissance palaces, Venetian-style architecture, old stone streets, and massive city walls of the ancient city. It has been hit hard by the war, and much destruction has occurred, especially to hotels. Three other major cities occupy the Dalmatian Coast and attract tourists. Split is built around a well-preserved fourth-century Roman palace. With its fine Roman ruins and much of the old city wall, Zadar is one of the most beautiful towns on the Adriatic.

Numerous smaller communities and resorts have been built along the Dalmatian Coast, all capitalizing on the beautiful pebble beaches, islands, climate, and clear water. Along the coast and inland there are seven national parks that remain in Croatia from what was formerly Yugoslavia. One park that is important to domestic tourism and should gain in international popularity is Plitvice Lakes. It is midway between Zagrab and Zadar. Accessible either by auto or tour bus, it has sixteen lakes that are connected to each other by waterfalls and are set in a beautiful forest. If the armed conflict can be peacefully resolved, tourism is expected to be the primary source for restoring Croatia's damaged economy.

Bosnia and Herzegovina

Capital: Sarajevo
Government: Democracy
Size: 19,791 square miles (slightly larger than Tennessee)
Language: Serbo-Croatian
Ethnic Divisions: 38% Muslim, 40% Serb, 22% Croat
Religion: 40% Slavic Muslim, 31% Orthodox, 15% Catholic, 4% Protestant
Tourist Season: April through September
Peak Tourist Season: July and August
Currency: Croatian dinar in ethnic Croat, Yugoslav dinar in other areas

 ## TRAVEL TIPS

Entry: No visa is required unless issued at border.
Caution: At this time it is not a safe area due to the aftermath of the civil war.
Transportation: There are direct flights from Rome to Sarajevo.
Money: Traveler's checks and credit cards are not presently accepted.
Shopping: Common items include peasant handicrafts, embroidered blouses, gold and silver filigree jewelry, carpets, leather goods, carved wooden goods, laces, and pottery.
At present (1997) little can be anticipated concerning travel to this region because of the ongoing ethnic conflict.

CULTURE CAPSULE

While the civil war supposedly ended in 1996, the location of Serbs, Croats, and Muslims in the region and the final borders are yet to be determined. All three groups speak the same language. It presently appears that most of the territory will be controlled by Serbs who want to join Yugoslavia to create Greater Serbia.

Physical Characteristics

The terrain is mountainous. It has hot summers and cold winters. The high elevations have short, cool summers and long, severe winters.

Tourism Characteristics

Presently little can be said concerning tourism to the region.

Tourism Destinations and Attractions

The three cities, Sarajevo, Mostar, and Jajce, were the principle destinations for tourists. Sarajevo, the capital, by the Miljacka River, had 73 mosques. It was ruled by the Turks from the mid-fifteenth century until 1878. Thus, it offered the strongest Turkish flavor of any city in the Balkans. It had picturesque Turkish mosques, markets, and color. However, what will remain after the war is uncertain. Sarajevo was the site of the 1984 Winter Olympic Games. It was shelled by Serbs for nearly two years, with tremendous loss of life and property damage.

The second destination city, Mostar, was founded by the Turks in the fifteenth century on a river crossing. It also offered the visitor a view of Islamic culture with its old quarter, mosques, and Turkish Bridge (destroyed by Serbian shelling in late 1993). Like Sarajevo, it has been badly damaged and is now off-limits to tourists. Jajce is a medieval walled city with cobbled streets and old houses set in a hilly country. It was briefly the capital of liberated Yugoslavia in 1943. Medjugorje has been a heavily visited pilgrimage site in the 1980s.

Bulgaria

125 km

Capital: Sofia
Government: Democratic Republic
Size: 42,823 square miles (a little larger than Virginia)
Language: Bulgarian with some German and French
Ethnic Division: 85.3% Bulgarian, 2.5% Gypsy, 8.5% Turk, and 6% other Eastern European minorities
Religion: 85% Bulgarian Orthodox, 13% Muslim, 2% other
Tourist Season: April through October
Peak Tourist Season: July and August
Currency: Lev (LEV)

🧭 TRAVEL TIPS

Entry: Visas not required for visits of less than 30 days.
Transportation: There are direct flights from other European capitals and North America to Sofia. Rail accommodations are available to the rest of Europe and the Black Sea resorts near Varna and Burgas. Sofia has a good public transportation system with streetcars, trolley-buses, and buses.
Shopping: Items include embroidery, woodcarving, pottery, leather and fur clothing, blankets, and carpets.

CULTURAL CAPSULE

The people are primarily Bulgarian (85 percent). The most important minority is Turkish. The principal religion is the Bulgarian Orthodox Church. Other religions include Islam, Roman Catholicism, Protestantism, and Judaism. Bulgaria's name is derived from a Turkic people, the Bulgars, who originated in the steppe north of the Caspian Sea. The Slavic people absorbed the invading Turkic people and were, in general, the precursors of the present-day Bulgarians. The official language, Bulgarian, is a Slavic language using Bulgarian Cyrillic. It is very similar to the Russian alphabet.

Cultural Hints:
- The handshake is the form of greeting.
- Nodding your head up and down means yes.
- Nodding your head back and forth means no.
- Eating and foods:
  Rest both wrists on the table.
  Tip 10 to 15 percent.
  Food specialties are lamb, pork, beef, fish, cheese, and Turkish-type desserts with espresso coffee.

Physical Characteristics

The country is mostly mountains with lowlands in the north and south. The climate is temperate, with cold, damp winters and hot, dry summers.

Tourism Characteristics

The Bulgarian government views tourism as an important source of foreign exchange to modernize and expand their economy. While the industry in Bulgaria is small compared to the developed tourist-receiving countries in Europe, its visitor numbers in the 1990s have changed little. Most of its visitors are from the region, particularly Yugoslavia. Most of the accommodation facilities are in beach-resort holiday centers along the Black Sea. Turkey is the major market for Bulgaria, followed by Germany, Italy, and Russia. However, many of the Turks are passing through on their way to Western Europe, mainly Germany. The numbers from the United States are small but are increasing gradually as Bulgaria is a good bargain and has had a peaceful transition from communism to democracy. Direct nonstop service was established in 1993 between New York and Sofia. The new private hotels, restaurants, and shops are eager to please tourists from North America. The major purpose of visits are to transit the country. However, for those visiting, holidays and recreation are the main purposes for visiting the country.

There is an abundant supply of hotel rooms since tourism has declined as the historic flow of Russian and East European organized tourism has essentially ended.

Tourist Destinations and Attractions

The tourist destinations in Bulgaria can be classified into three groups: the Black Sea Coast, the capital city Sofia, and the Valley of the Roses. The Black Sea Coast is the dominant international tourist attrac-

tion. Balkantourist, the national tourist organization, developed three modern beach resorts on the Black Sea in combination with the traditional center of Varna and Burgas. Varna, the largest city on the Black Sea, was founded in the sixth century B.C. by the Greeks. It later became a major trading post in the Roman Empire. In addition to swimming and sunbathing, the Black Sea Coast has numerous spas that are reputed to be beneficial for rheumatism, arthritis, and other joint afflictions. One of the more famous is Pomorye, where mudpacks and salt baths are used for the treatment of arthritis and sciatica. The new resorts of Drouzhba, Albena, Zlatni Piassatsi, and Slunchev Bryag (Sunny Beach) provide foreign tourists all of the amenities for a sea-and-sand vacation experience.

Sofia is an ancient city in a basin near the Balkan Mountains. Culturally the influence of both Roman and Ottoman Turk rule is evident in the architecture. The Alexander Nevsky Memorial Church, built in the nineteenth century as a tribute to Russians who liberated the country from the Turks, is one of the most impressive architectural structures. In addition, the Balkan Hotel contains the remains of the fourth-century church of St. George within its courtyard. Several mosques and the archaeological museum contain important relics from the Turkish past with its Islamic influence.

The third area that attracts tourists is the Valley of the Roses. This is the premier producing region for the roses from which essentially all the world's attar of roses comes for use in perfumes and soap. During May and June, the scent of the harvesting of millions of roses makes this a unique tourist attraction.

Albania

Capital: Tirane
Government: Nascent democracy
Size: 28,750 square miles (slightly larger than West Virginia)
Language: Albanian (Tosk is official dialect), Greek
Ethnic Division: 95% Albanian, 2% Greeks, 2% other
Religion: 70% Muslim, 20% Albanian Orthodox, 10% Roman Catholic
Tourist Season: May through August
Currency: Lek

TRAVEL TIPS

Customs: Visas are required.
Accommodations: Very limited.
Money: Credit cards and traveler's checks are rarely accepted.
Transportation: Somewhat limited.
Shopping: Common items include black embroidery, linen, native wood carvings, and rugs.

CULTURAL CAPSULE

Ninety-six percent of the people are ethnically Albanian, descendants of the ancient Illyrians who once occupied much of the Balkan Peninsula. Today's Albanians are divided into two groups—the Gegs to the north of the Shkumbin River and the Tosks to the south. Their differences in physical traits, dialects, religions, and social customs are distinguishable but not dramatic. A number of minorities in Albania include Greeks, Vlachs, Bulgars, Serbs, and Gypsies.

Physical Characteristics

Albania is mostly hills and mountains covered with scrub forests. It is subject to destructive earthquakes and tsunamis. The only navigable river is the Buene (Bojana). The climate is mild with cool, wet winters and dry, hot summers. The interior is cool and rainy.

Tourism Characteristics

Tourism under Communism was virtually non-existent, and Albania was withdrawn from the world. It has now opened to the world, and tourism has grown slowly during the 1990s. Although a few hardy tourists come from Western Europe, most are from Italy and central Europe. The main tourist centers include Tirane, Durres (an ancient city), Sarande, and Shkoder. The Roman amphitheater at Durres is one of the largest in Europe. The ancient towns of Apollonia (dating from Roman times) and Berat (known as the "city of a thousand windows"), which is a museum-town with a medieval fortress and mosque, are two of the major historic towns.

CONCLUSION

Tourism continues to grow in Central Europe both as a result of the increasing standard of living among the residents of the individual countries of the region and because of increasing attempts by most governments in the region to attract tourists from Western Europe, the United States, and elsewhere. The variety of cultures, physical geography, and resorts provide opportunities for tourists at costs below that found in Western Europe. The combination of variety, low cost, and personal safety created by the traditional strong police force in most countries makes these countries increasingly attractive. In the absence of renewed political problems as in Croatia, Bosnia-Herzegovina, and Yugoslavia, it can be expected that tourism to Central Europe will increase at an even greater rate as the investment in tourism facilities and amenities continue to provide for the tourist.

The Best of Hungary

DAY 1   VIENNA–FERTOD–SOPRON

Relax today as we drive over the Austrian border into some of the richest agricultural land in Hungary. Fertod is our first stop, where the mansion of the Princes of Esterhazy stands. Patterned after the great palace of the French kings, it is called "Magyar Versailles." Then travel a few miles southwest to the town of Sopron. The composer Goldmark lived here, and Franz Liszt gave his first concert here as a child. Enjoy the afternoon sightseeing and exploring the many noteworthy homes and monuments in Sporan, such as the Storno house and the Benedictine Church. Then prepare for a delightful evening of Hungarian goulash and music.

DAY 2   SOPRAN–SZOMBATHELY–PECS

Travel south today to the town of Szomibathely, founded by Emperor Claudius in A.D. 41. Remnants of the Roman era are preserved in the Garden of Ruins. Enjoy the beauty of the Cathedral and the Bishop's palace. After lunch, travel farther south near the border of Yugoslavia to the town of Pecs, home of the first Hungarian university. Enjoy the evening dining in a quaint Hungarian inn.

DAY 3   PECS–KALOSCA–BUDAPEST

In the morning visit Pecs' 1,000-year-old cathedral, an early Christian cemetery, and a triple-arched underground chapel. Enjoy lunch in a quaint café, then travel northward along lush green countryside toward the Danube River to the town of Kalocsa, remarkable for its folkloric tradition and fine embroidery. Time is yours to shop or bask in the traditions of this country town. Then more beautiful landscape lines the way to Budapest as we travel up the Danube River. Tonight the delights of Budapest await you.

DAY 4   BUDAPEST

The twin cities of Buda and Pest are yours to review from Gellért Hill, capturing the eight bridges that span the Danube River. Buda is on the right bank, surrounded by wooded hills, and Pest is on the left bank, lying on flat land that spreads both east and south. Today visit Margaret Island, stroll through her well-kept park, and visit several pools fed by warm springs. To the north visit Castle Hill and step back in time at the Royal Palace or at Fishermen's Bastion. Capture a beautiful evening listening to the Budapest Philharmonic.

DAY 5   BUDAPEST

Today discover rich culture in Budapest as you enjoy St. Stephen's Basilica, the National Museum, the Museum of Fine Arts, and the National Gallery. The afternoon is yours to delve deeper into Hungary's artistic talent or to shop. If shopping, Hungary is best for pottery, woodcarving, Herend china, embroidery, and lace. In the evening, enjoy celebrating Hungarian-style with the State Folk Ensemble.

DAY 6   BUDAPEST–EGER

Traveling outside cosmopolitan Budapest, you may spot horses and their herdsmen in traditional costumes on the way to Eger. The historic town of Eger lies in a broad valley between two mountains. It is one of the most interesting towns in Hungary. Tour the Church of Minorities, a Turkish minaret, the palace of the Archbishop, and the Serb Orthodox Church. Lower hills around the town are thickly covered with vineyards. The evening is open to enjoy Hungary's rich folkloric heritage.

DAY 7

Return to Budapest for return flight home.

REVIEW QUESTIONS

1. Which Central European countries have the most developed tourism industry? Why?
2. What impact do climate and the physical geography have on tourism to Central Europe?
3. Describe tourism to Bulgaria. What are the major attractions?
4. Describe the attractions and major markets for Slovenia and Croatia.
5. How are the countries of Central Europe distinct geographically and as tourism destinations from Western Europe?
6. What role does the Danube play in Central and Eastern Europe?
7. Describe tourism to Hungary.
8. If you had to select one country to visit that would give you the greatest diversity, which Central European or Baltic country would you select? Justify your answer.

GEOGRAPHY AND TOURISM IN
Russia and the Countries of the Former Soviet Union

CHAPTER 10

MAJOR GEOGRAPHIC CHARACTERISTICS

- The environment in many of the countries created from the Soviet Union is harsh, resulting from high-latitude location or desert climates.
- Russia has the largest territorial expanse in the world, creating long-distance travel.
- The new countries of the former Soviet Union are in the process of changing from socialist to free enterprise economies at varying speeds.
- The population is ethnically diverse with Russians found in every new country.
- There are limited coastal areas to attract tourists.
- The countries created from the Soviet Union are differentiated by their distinctive physical and cultural geography.

MAJOR TOURISM CHARACTERISTICS

- International visitors generally visit the large cities of Russia, Ukraine, and the Baltic States.
- There is regional concentration of international tourist facilities in a few large cities.
- International tourism is an important revenue source, and most of the countries of this region are building new hotels and entering into agreements with Western businesses to enhance their attractiveness to international tourists.
- There is a limited variety of activities and facilities for all tourists.
- Visitors generally have limited knowledge of Russia and other countries created from the former Soviet Union.

MAJOR TOURIST DESTINATIONS

Moscow and St. Petersburg (formerly Leningrad)
Tallinn and the other capitals and coastal areas of the Baltic States
Kyyiv, the Black Sea Coast, and the Crimean Peninsula in the Ukraine
Tashkent and the ancient cities of the Silk Road in Uzbekistan
Eastern coast of the Black Sea in Russia and Georgia
Lake Baikal and Siberian Russia
Novogorod and the ancient Russian cities of the Northwest

KEY TERMS AND WORDS

Asiatic Russia	Kremlin
Caucasians	Madrassa
Central Planning	Perestroika
Commonwealth of Independent States	Privatization
Republics	
Communist Party	Siberia
Czar	Slavic
Demokratization	Soviet
European Russia	Taiga
Glasnost	Trade Unions
Golden Ring	Tundra
Intourist	Turkic

INTRODUCTION

The former Union of Soviet Socialist Republics (USSR or simply the Soviet Union) was and, even in its present form of fifteen independent countries, is one of the greatest potential tourist destinations in the world. The Soviet Union disintegrated as a unified country in the fall of 1991. Three of the countries—Estonia, Latvia, and Lithuania (collectively known as the Baltic States)—chose to remain com-pletely independent. The twelve remaining countries, Table 10–1, have formed a loose political organization called the *Commonwealth of Independent States* (CIS). Within these fifteen countries is one of the largest ranges of ethnic cultures, climates, and vegetation of any comparable group of countries in the world.

The actual powers of the CIS organization are related to coordinating the transition from the unified Soviet state to a system by which the new states are

Figure 10-1a Map of Region

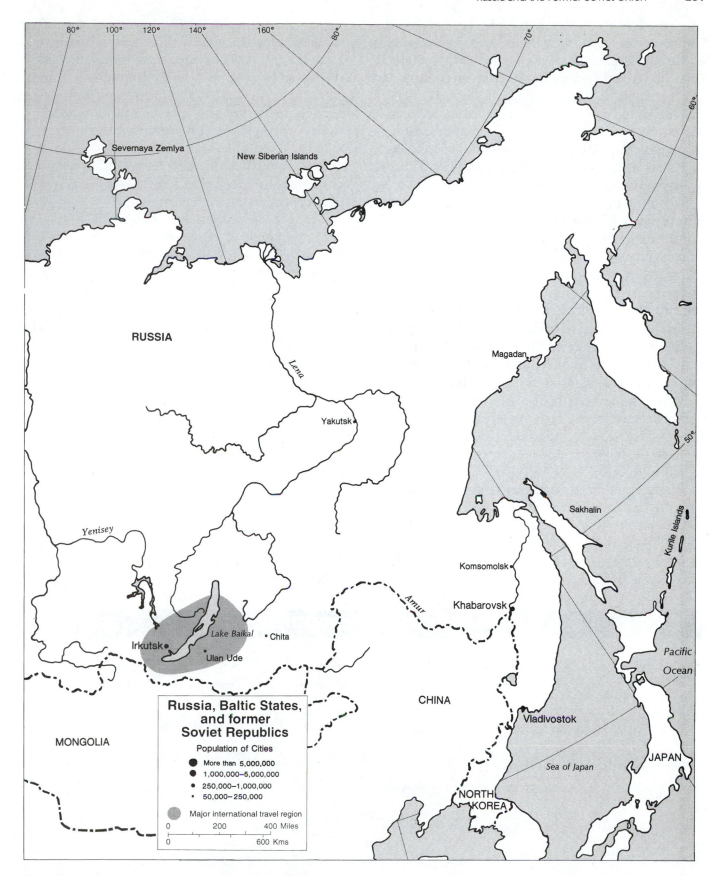

Figure 10–1b   Map of Region

connected by trade, defense, and other agreements. Unfortunately, the individual countries remain unstable, and the future of the region is unpredictable. The economies of nearly all of the fifteen countries are lower today than before 1990, as the breakup of old trade relationships has negatively affected individuals and countries. The political and economic arrangements that the CIS federation and the three independent states ultimately arrive at will greatly affect tourism to this remarkably varied area.

For most people, the countries created from the former Soviet Union, Figure 10–1, remain an enigma. Three important time periods have combined to create the present geography and tourism patterns of these fifteen countries. The first was the emergence of the Russian Empire. Beginning in the fourteenth century, Russian princes expanded their control over the land that stretched from the Baltic Sea in the west to the Pacific Ocean in the east. The centuries of Russian expansion added numerous peoples and cultures to the Russian Empire and resulted in the construction of many beautiful cities, palaces, museums, and churches. These structures remained as major tourist attractions during the other two major time periods that have affected the tourism industry of the region.

The second major time period affecting the countries created from the former Soviet Union began in 1917. The USSR was created from the Russian Empire after the revolution of 1917 that ended with the *Communist Party* dominating the country. Under Communist leaders' direction, fifteen republics were recognized within the USSR. Russia was the largest of these, comprising nearly three-fourths of the territory of the USSR. The transformation of the historical Russian Empire into the Communist-dominated Soviet Union was one of the most significant events affecting the nature and character of tourism in the country at the present. Important results of the 1917 revolution were the establishment of a single-party political system (Communist Party) and an economic system based on the work of Karl Marx as interpreted and expanded by Lenin, Figure 10–2.

During the seventy years of communist domination, large industrial cities with featureless blocks of housing were constructed as suburbs of old cities or as new cities across the Soviet Union. Many of the old palaces and churches were maintained as tourist attractions, and large new exhibits, museums, and monuments glorifying the Communist state were constructed. Many of the most imposing of these were statues of Lenin or museums to his honor. Chief among these is Lenin's tomb in Red Square in Moscow. Until 1987, the USSR relied on a rigidly planned economy controlled by the government. Tourism was a part of this economy, and numerous hotels, camps, and health spas were constructed for citizens of the Soviet Union and the relatively few international tourists who arrived.

The third time period affecting tourism in this region began in the late 1980s. After nearly sixty years of government control, the Soviet Union began to experiment with some modifications to their system to encourage elements of free enterprise. Using the

		Annual	Time To		Life	
	Population	Growth Rate	Double Pop.	Per Capita	Expectancy	Percent
Country	(millions)	(percent)	(years)	GNP	(years)	Urban
Estonia	1.5	-0.5	—	2,860	68	70
Latvia	2.5	-0.7	—	2,270	66	69
Lithuania	3.	-0.1	—	1,900	70	68
Armenia	3.7	0.6	108	730	72	67
Azerbaijan	7.6	1.2	56	480	70	53
Belarus	10.3	-0.4	—	2,070	69	69
Georgia	5.4	0.3	204	440	73	56
Kazakhstan	16.4	0.5	133	1,330	69	56
Kyrgyzstan	4.6	10.6	43	700	66	35
Moldova	4.3	0.1	866	920	68	46
Russia	147.3	-0.5	—	2,240	65	73
Tajikistan	6.0	2.3	30	340	68	28
Turkmenistan	4.6	2.1	33	920	66	45
Ukraine	50.7	-0.6	—	1,630	68	68
Uzbekistan	23.7	2.1	33	970	70	38

POPULATION CHARACTERISTICS, 1997

Figure 10–2 Lenin

concepts of *glasnost* (free exchange of information and ideas), *perestroika* (restructuring of industry to emphasize quality and profitability rather than simple volume of production whether profitable or not), and *demokratization* (democratic ideals), the leaders tried to change the economy of the Soviet Union. The result was far from what they planned, as the ideas of glasnost and demokratization were adopted into the political arena, resulting in the breakup of the country and the emergence of the fifteen republics as independent countries after 1990.

The democratic movement that has created fifteen new countries is the third period that affected tourism. Each of the newly independent countries has adopted elements of the free enterprise economic system and a democratic government. The official role of the Communist party has been all but obliterated as even the statues of Lenin and other Communist leaders have been removed from most public places, Figure 10–3. The economic changes created uncertainty as the various governments debated attempts to transfer government-owned farms, factories, banks, stores, and other aspects of the economy into private ownership. Inflation and shortages of many items are causing many residents of the new countries to question whether the dramatic changes were worth the cost. Territorial and other disputes between the various groups in some of the countries create ongoing conflict.

The revolutionary nature of the events in the Soviet Union in 1991 have created a host of issues that are still unresolved, and at the time of this writing it is impossible to predict the end result of the momentous changes of 1991. The geographic and historical relationships that will ultimately shape these emerging countries and their tourism patterns, however, will be related to the past and present patterns of tourism in the former Soviet Union.

THE GEOGRAPHIC BASE OF THE COUNTRIES CREATED FROM THE FORMER SOVIET UNION

The geographic characteristics of the countries created from the Soviet Union are distinctive because of their tremendous size and location. With nearly 6.6

Table 10–1 Countries Created From the Soviet Union

Name	Capital	Area (thousands of miles^2)	Population (thousands)
Russia	Moscow	6,520	147,300
Kazakhstan	Almaty	1,031	16,400
Ukraine	Kyyiv	223	50,700
Turkmenistan	Ashqabat	181	4,600
Uzbekistan	Tashkent	160	23,700
Belarus	Minsk	80	10,300
Kyrgyzstan	Bishkek	74	4,600
Tajikistan	Dushanbe	54	6,000
Azerbaijan	Baky	33	7,600
Georgia	T'Bilisi	27	5,400
Lithuania	Vilnius	25	3,700
Latvia	Riga	24	2,500
Estonia	Tallinn	16	1,500
Moldova	Chisinău	13	4,300
Armenia	Yerevan	11	3,800

Sources: World Population Data Sheet. Population Reference Bureau, 1997.

Figure 10–3 Fallen statue of former Director of Soviet Secret Police, further defaced with paint

million square miles of area, Russia remains the largest country in the world, about twice the size of Canada, China, or the United States. Russia sprawls nearly halfway around the world, extending through 170 degrees of longitude and eleven time zones. Citizens in western cities of Russia, such as St. Petersburg, are just going to bed as those in the far east in Vladivostok are arising for work. If Russia were placed so that its westernmost border coincided with the west coast of Alaska, it would extend across Alaska, Greenland, and the North Atlantic to the west coast of Norway. The other former republics range in size from the tiny Baltic States to Kazakhstan, which is one-third the size of the United States.

The location of the former republics of the Soviet Union is highly varied. The southernmost is Turkmenistan, which extends from 35 degrees to about 42 degrees north latitude. Russia extends from about the latitude of Boston to its islands in the Arctic Ocean at about 78 degrees north. In spite of the northerly location and associated harsh climate, Russia and the Baltic countries are among the most densely populated high-latitude lands in the world. Remember that Moscow is north of the southern border of Alaska and St. Petersburg is located at the same latitude as Stockholm, Sweden, and you can understand the challenges created for any political and economic system attempting to develop Russia's vast land.

The Land

The northerly location of most of the lands of these countries handicaps development of agriculture and exploitation of mineral resources. Much of the cultivated land is of lesser quality than that found in the United States, with the result that the fifteen countries created from the former Soviet Union cultivate only about one and one-half times as much land as the United States even though they occupy nearly three times as much area.

The countries are also isolated because of their northerly location and the difficulty of utilizing their ports and harbors. Access to the Atlantic Ocean from Russia and the new Baltic countries is through the easily blocked narrows controlled by Sweden and Denmark. Access from Moldova, Ukraine, southern Russia, or Georgia is through the Dardanelles of Turkey. Northern Russia is accessible only between the Arctic icepack and the northern coast of Norway. To the south, the borders of the new countries are generally mountainous, rugged, and arid, which makes transportation and communication difficult. In such a vast area, there are major regional differences recognized by geographers and citizens alike. A common division of the region is into the Russian Plain, the Ural Mountains, the west Siberian Lowland, the central Siberian Uplands, and the eastern and southern mountain systems, Figure 10–4.

Figure 10–4 Landforms

The Russian Plain

The most densely inhabited portion of the former Soviet Union is referred to as the Russian Plain. The Russian Plain is nearly one-half the size of the United States. It stretches 1,100 miles from the Black Sea north to the Arctic, and 1,500 miles from east to west from the Polish border to the Ural Mountains. The topography of this plains area is one of rolling hills interspersed with rivers and streams. Highlands are low, rarely rising more than 1,000 feet above sea level. North and west of Moscow an elevated area known as the Moscow Plateau reaches 1,000 feet above sea level, and the Volga Heights rise to approximately the same elevation on the west bank of the Volga River. The Baltic countries, Belarus, Ukraine, Moldova, and western Russia, are located on this plain.

The Ural Mountains

The Ural Mountains are a series of parallel ranges some 1,500 miles in length that extend from the Arctic Sea southward toward the Caspian Sea. They are similar to the Appalachians of the United States in geological origin and structure, except there are not as many parallel ridges. The maximum elevation is 6,185 feet at Mount Narodnaya. Most of the peaks in the Ural Mountains are between 750 and 2,000 feet above sea level. The range is some 50 miles wide in the north, but it widens to 140 miles in the south. The highest elevations are found in the north, and because of their generally low nature and the presence of numerous passes they are not a major barrier to transportation. They are primarily of importance because they are the traditional division between *European Russia* and *Asiatic Russia* and the rest of Asia. In addition, as the root of an old mountain system that has eroded away, major deposits of minerals are located around their flanks.

The West Siberian Lowland

Stretching eastward from the Ural Mountains to the Yenisey River lies one of the most level expanses of land in the world. The West Siberian Lowland extends over 1,200 miles from east to west and from 1,100 to 1,600 miles from north to south and covers an area roughly equal to that of the Great Russian Plain. At no place does the elevation exceed 400 feet above sea level. Two main rivers, the Ob and Yenisey, drain the west Siberian Lowland. Drainage is poor all year round because of the low gradient of the rivers. During spring when melt water flows downstream, large areas are flooded. The Ob Basin is especially important because large resource deposits of oil and natural gas have been discovered here. The extreme southern margin of this lowland was the producer of over one-half the wheat grown in the Soviet Union in a typical year and now comprises the main agricultural area of Kazakhstan, producing wheat for export to Russia.

The Central Siberian Uplands

East of the West Siberian Lowland is a rugged area of uplands and plateaus. The Yenisey River marks the eastern boundary of the West Siberian Lowland, and beyond it is a plateau region with elevations between 2,000 and 6,000 feet. The landscape is highly eroded, with streams incised into it to create a very rugged region that is a barrier to transportation. Numerous resources are found in the region, but it is very sparsely inhabited because of the rugged topography and harsh climate.

The Southern Mountain Ranges

The southern border of Russia, Uzbekistan, Turkmenistan, Tajikistan, and Kyrgyzstan is bounded by a series of high mountain ranges. Peaks rise to 16,000 to 20,000 feet in the Tien Shan and the Pamir Ranges. Their primary importance is that they serve as a barrier to communication and transportation to the south to Asia and prevent moisture from entering the deserts of Central Asia from the Indian Ocean to the south. This region lies in the most southerly latitudes of the New Central Asian countries and is important for irrigated agriculture like cotton and fruit. Moisture from the mountains provides the basis for the agriculture that is carried on in this arid region in the valleys and plains along the margins of the southern mountains. The mountains themselves are used for grazing and lumber production as well as mineral exploitation.

The Eastern Mountain Ranges

In the far east of Russia (roughly east of Lake Baikal and the Lena River) is a complex series of mountains, plateaus, and valleys. The highest peaks in this extensive region are between 10,000 and 15,000 feet. Some of the mountain ranges are characterized by volcanic activity, especially on the Kamchatka Peninsula in Russia's Far East. This region is still only sparsely populated, but is an important source for valuable resources such as gold. It has good potential for ecotourism because of the abundance of wildlife and natural landscapes found in the region.

Other Landscapes

In addition to the landform regions, the rivers, ports, and seas of the new countries are important in understanding their geography and tourism patterns. The rivers of Russia were primary arteries of transportation in historic times. Even today they are widely used for transportation of industrial raw materials and some manufactured goods, but their unique physical characteristics handicap their use. The majority of the rivers of Russia flow north into the Arctic Ocean, limiting their use to the short frost-free period of summer. This handicap is compounded because the movement of goods and people is primarily east to west, limiting the utility of the rivers. The rivers reflect the topography of the country with shallow gradients, broad shallow channels, and sand bars that require periodic dredging to maintain navigation. The most important river transportation system is that of the Volga and its tributaries. Unlike the majority of the rivers of Russia, the Volga begins in the northwest and flows east and then south. Between 1930 and 1980, the leaders of the old Soviet Union funded gigantic construction projects that created a series of dams and reservoirs on the Volga and connected it with the Don and Kama Rivers to allow for even greater transportation. This system is important to both Ukraine and Russia. The hydroelectricity and water for irrigation and culinary uses from the Volga are of much greater importance than the transportation of goods on the river during the short summer season. Cruises on these rivers in the summer are popular parts of domestic tourism and a growing interest for foreign tourists.

The Ob and Yenisey Rivers in the West Siberian Lowland are the largest rivers in Russia. Because of their isolation and location primarily in a subarctic climatic region, they are used little for tourism. The same is true for the Lena River at the eastern edge of the Central Siberian Uplands and for the Amur and its tributaries on the border of Russia's far east and China.

The Amu Dar'ya and the Syr Dar'ya are rivers of Central Asia that provide irrigation in the desert area of Turkmenistan, Uzbekistan, Tajikistan, and Kyrgyzstan. The cities and people that rely on them are distinctive and are particularly attractive to western tourists. Isolated by long distances from western markets, however, these rivers are visited by only a limited number of international tourists.

The former Soviet Union has a number of lakes and seas of tremendous size. The Caspian Sea, which has no external outlet, is more than 152,000 square miles in size, which is roughly five times the size of Lake Superior, the largest of the Great Lakes in the United States. Lake Baikal is the deepest lake in the world and extends 400 miles from north to south. It is only 50 miles wide, but it is a natural wonder because of fish and fauna that are found nowhere else in the world.

The former Soviet Union had important access to the world's oceans because of its long coastlines. However, in spite of having the longest coastline in the world, it was handicapped by inadequate ports. Nearly all the ports of Russia are icebound at least part of the winter. In the north along the Arctic Ocean, only the period from late July to early September can be used for shipping. In the east, Vladivostok is normally kept open year-round by icebreakers, but may suffer for two or three weeks from severe ice that prevents access. In the northwest of Russia, Murmansk is ice-free year-round because a tongue of warm water from the North Atlantic Drift swings around the Scandinavian Peninsula and keeps the water in the mid 30s Fahrenheit during the winter. St. Petersburg relies on icebreakers to remain open, but it is still frozen and inaccessible for two to three weeks out of the year. The Black Sea port of Odessa in Ukraine is normally open year-round.

The combination of mountains, plains, rivers, lakes, seas, and oceans provides a wealth of recreational opportunities that were developed for internal and external tourism by the Soviet Union. Such tourism activity is affected, however, by the harsh climates found within most of the new countries.

CLIMATE: TOURISM IN HARSH LANDS

The climatic reality of the countries created from the former Soviet Union is one of extremes. Climates tend to be either extremely cold or extremely dry. Few exceptions exist to this generality, but both the reality of the extremes and the existence of the exceptions are important in understanding the geography that affects tourism in the area. The climate of the countries of the former Soviet Union is controlled by five factors:

1. Size of the land mass of the continent.
2. The high-latitude location of Russia and the Baltic Countries.
3. The lack of physical barriers across the country to prevent movement of air masses.
4. The mountains to the south, which block the warmer moister air from lower latitudes entering the area, creating a rain shadow that

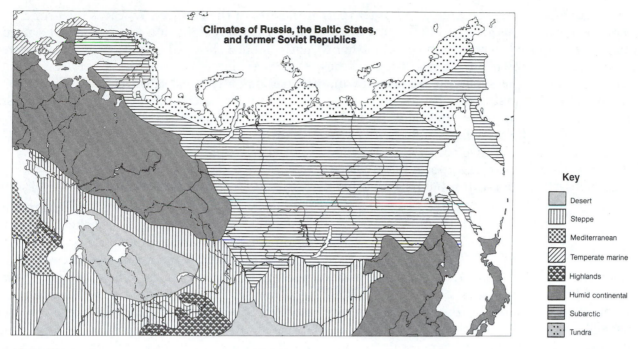

Figure 10–5 Climates

causes the arid zone in Uzbekistan, Tajikistan, Turkmenistan, Kyrgyzstan, and Kazakhstan.

5. The isolation of much of the land mass from moisture sources.

The countries created from the former Soviet Union have areas that represent seven climatic types, Figure 10–5, but only four cover large areas.

The Tundra Climate

In the far northern margin of Russia, there is a narrow belt of *tundra* climate. Temperatures in this region drop to below –50 degrees Fahrenheit in the winter, and summer temperatures occasionally exceed 60 degrees Fahrenheit. Vegetation in this region is primarily low growing: shrubs, willows, lichen, mosses, and grass. The summer is short and cool, and there are few inhabitants and little use of the land. Primary economic activities are resource exploitation and reindeer herding.

The Subarctic Climate

The largest climatic region in Russia is the subarctic. The subarctic climate has extreme seasonal contrasts in temperature. Winter temperatures have reached –98 degrees Fahrenheit, and summer temperatures as high as 90 degrees Fahrenheit have been recorded. With nearly 200 degrees Fahrenheit

potential difference between summer and winter temperatures, this climate epitomizes the seasonal extremes associated with continental climates. Summer temperatures regularly exceed 60 degrees, and winter temperatures regularly dip below –60 degrees Fahrenheit. The extreme seasonal difference is compounded by the presence of permafrost in much of the subarctic and much of the tundra. Permafrost is an area of permanently frozen subsoil. While the top few inches melt in the summer, the soil below remains frozen as there is no place for the moisture to go. The cool climate retards evaporation and results in much of the subarctic and all of the tundra being marshy and boggy.

Vegetation in the subarctic is coniferous forest, and geographers have adopted the Russian word for coniferous forest, *taiga*, to refer to the great coniferous forests of the high latitudes. The taiga region of Russia represents the greatest forested area of the world. Approximately one-fifth of the forested land of the earth is found in Russia, but much of it is slow-growing, scrubby, and deformed because of the extreme cold and short growing season. Much of the taiga, especially in the north, is unsuited for timber production.

Use of the subarctic for agriculture is limited because of the short growing season and permafrost. The 70 to 110 days when there is not frost is suitable only for plants that grow quickly. Because of the long period of sunlight in the short summer season, plants such as cabbages, radishes, potatoes, and other root crops are produced. Yields are low, but because of the great distances required to provision these northern locations, they are grown out of necessity. In the southern margins of the subarctic, longer growing seasons, absence of permafrost, and better soils allow production of wheat and other small grains. Yields per acre still remain below what would justify production in a market enterprise society but they are produced in Russia to provide for local needs. Tourism in the subarctic region is limited to its southern margin.

The Humid Continental Climate

Immediately south of this subarctic climate is a narrow zone of humid continental climate. This is an important climatic zone in the Baltics, Russia, Belarus, and Ukraine, one which receives ample precipitation in most years and has good soils for agriculture. The winters tend to be long, gray, and overcast, with snow cover for from six months in the northern portion to three months in the south of the zone. Summers are humid and generally are not extremely hot. Winter temperatures in the humid continental climatic zone go as low as –40 degrees Fahrenheit while summer temperatures generally do not exceed the mid 80s. In the major tourist cities of Moscow and St. Petersburg, summer temperatures normally do not exceed 80 degrees Fahrenheit in the summer, but occasionally early June or August temperatures in St. Petersburg are as low as 50 degrees Fahrenheit. The most pleasant season of the year in the humid continental zone is generally the autumn, when skies are clear, temperatures mild, and the foliage colorful.

Vegetation is a mixture of coniferous and deciduous trees. In the fall when the colors change, they create a beautiful scenic aspect. Agriculturally the humid continental climate is one of the most significant regions in the countries of the former Soviet Union.

Steppe

The steppe climate is a zone of transition between humid continental and desert climates. The transition zone between the humid continental and the steppe climate is a zone of very fertile black chernozem mollisol soils in Russia, Ukraine, and Kazakhstan. Although they are fertile, these soils suffer from an unreliable precipitation regime. In spite of this, the steppe remains the premier agricultural area of the country. Wheat is the primary crop, but because precipitation is variable and erratic, the potential of a shortfall in grain production is present each year. Precipitation totals between 8 and 16 inches annually, most of which comes in the form of heavy thunderstorms in the summer. Winter snowfall is light; consequently the soil is subject to extreme frost action.

The Desert Climates

The desert climates of Kazakhstan, Turkmenistan, Tajikistan, Kyrgyzstan, and Uzbekistan have hot summer temperatures. Temperatures rise to over 120 degrees Fahrenheit. In the winter, they drop below freezing for short periods. Where adequate water is available, agriculture is important. The desert area is devoted to grazing, primarily of sheep; but where irrigated, it produces fruits, cotton, grain, and dairy products. Because the desert climate is not frost-free all year, special measures have to be taken for producing specialty crops such as oranges. Protection from the periodic frost is obtained by heating small orchard areas or covering the trees.

Minor Climatic Types

In addition to the large climatic regions found in the countries created from the former Soviet Union, small areas of other climates that are important are found in individual countries. Most important from the standpoint of tourism are a small area of humid subtropical climate on the eastern margin of the Black Sea in Georgia, Russia, and Ukraine and a tiny area of Mediterranean climate in Ukraine on the Crimean Peninsula in the Black Sea. The humid subtropical climate exists because it is protected by the Caucasus Mountains to the north and receives warm moist air masses from the Black Sea. The area has a warm and moist climate that allows production of citrus fruits and tea and has made it a major summer resort area. Beaches of the Black Sea attracted millions of Russians, Georgians, Ukrainians, and some foreigners before 1991. Sanitoriums in the surrounding area are used for health spas.

Directly west of the humid subtropical region is a small region of Mediterranean climate on the Crimean Peninsula of Ukraine. The Crimean Mountains limit the influx of cold air from the north and maintain mild winter temperatures, while the area's location with respect to the prevailing winds combines with the mountains to prevent it from being extremely damp. The result is a climate that is warm and dry in the summer and mild with periodic rainfall in the winter. Precipitation totals between 20 and 30 inches, resulting in a very attractive region for tourism.

The small areas of Mediterranean and subtropical climates appear insignificant on a map, but they are of primary significance to tourism and agriculture in countries created from the former Soviet Union because of the dominance of the harsh climates discussed earlier.

The mountains of the southern margins of the countries created from the former Soviet Union have undifferentiated climates. Temperature and precipitation varies widely depending on elevation and exposure to the sun. The mountains are important because they provide hiking, climbing, and skiing opportunities for tourists.

THE PEOPLE OF THE COUNTRIES CREATED FROM THE FORMER SOVIET UNION

In spite of great ethnic differences, it is possible to divide the population of the fifteen new countries into three broad ethnic groups. The largest group is the Slavic people, consisting of Russians, Ukrainians, and Belarussians. The actual number of each ethnic group does not equal the population of individual countries such as Russia because members of each group are found in many of the new countries. Russians number some 150 million and comprise 51 percent of the fifteen countries' total population. The next largest group is the Ukrainians, with about 50 million people or 17 percent of the population. Between them, these two groups constitute nearly 70 percent of the total population of the countries created from the former Soviet Union. They represent a substantial minority population even in areas where other nationalities are more numerous. There are 10 million Belarussians, making up about 3.5 percent of the population. Thus, the Slavic population group represents more than 70 percent of the total population of the former Soviet Union.

The second most important population group is comprised of *Turkic* people: Kirghiz, Tatars, Uzbeks, Kazakhs, and Azerbaijanis. In total, these people constitute approximately 11 percent of the total population of the countries created from the Soviet Union. The *Caucasians* constitute a third group. They are a diverse people made up of Armenians, Georgians, and a host of smaller ethnic groups. The multiplicity of groups in the Caucasian family results from the isolation of small groups over long periods of time in the Caucasian Mountains. A final group, labeled "other," includes people ranging from Estonians who speak a language similar to Finnish to the Aleutian and Yakut tribal groups of Russian Siberia.

FOREIGN TOURISM

Foreign tourism is not yet an important sector of the economy of most of the fifteen countries created from the former Soviet Union. The new governments hope tourism will become a primary economic activity, attracting foreign and domestic tourists, however. Tourism was of minor importance in the Russian Empire before the communist revolution of 1917, as it was before the era of mass tourism. Under the communists, domestic tourism was internal since the official policy maintained that the Soviet Union had sufficient variety of natural and cultural features for its residents. Even so, it was not until the 1980s that residents of the Soviet Union could travel relatively freely within the country, and internal passports were required until 1992. Foreign travel for nearly all Soviet citizens was simply not allowed before 1990. Suspicion that outsiders would undermine the socialist society effectively limited the number of foreign tourists entering the Soviet Union until the 1980s.

All tourism in the Soviet era was a state monopoly run by the government agency, *Intourist.* Intourist controlled hotels, airlines, restaurants, bus systems, spas, and other activities related to tourism. In 1971, foreign visitors totaled 2.1 million, a figure that increased to some 3.5 million by 1981. Approximately half of these visitors were from other socialist states, primarily those in Central and Eastern Europe. During the 1980s the number of visitors from these socialist states increased, reaching 63 percent in 1984. In the late 1980s and 1990s, the number of foreign tourists continued to increase, reaching a peak of nearly 7.8 million in 1989. Since then, tourist numbers have fluctuated wildly. In 1992, there were only some 3 million visitors to the former USSR. By 1996, Russia had rebounded to 14.6 million foreign visitors, Table 10–2. This figure, however, is misleading, since 78 percent of all visitors to Russia in 1996 were from the 14 other new countries created from the former Soviet Union, Table 10–3. Subtracting these visitors leaves a figure comparable to total visitors to the USSR in 1992 (3.2 million), indicating that tourist numbers from outside the region are quite stable. The value of tourism to Russia totaled only five billion dollars in 1996, only 60 percent that of Poland and one-fifth that of France. The other

Table 10–2 Tourist Arrivals in Russia, 1992–1996			
Year	Number (thousands)	% Change from Previous Year	% of Total Arrivals in Europe
1992	3,009	N/A	N/A
1993	5,898	96.0	1.9
1994	5,823	-1.3	1.8
1995	9,262	59.1	2.8
1996	14,587	57.5	4.1

Source: Travel and Tourism Intelligence, 1997, p. 35

Figure 10–6 Russians are the largest group in the former Soviet Union. The photo shows veterans of World War II.

countries created from the former Soviet Union have only a fraction of the tourist visitors or income of Russia.

Foreign tourists visit the newly independent countries primarily between the first of May and the end of September. The average length of stay is approximately five days, about a day and a half less than the average in Western European countries.

The majority of tourists came for business purposes in 1996. Business travel is four times greater than leisure travel to Russia from Ukraine and ten times greater than from Georgia. The majority of visitors from countries that were not part of the former Soviet Union also cite business as their reason

for visiting Russia, reflecting the rapid economic changes in Russia since 1991.

Since the independence of the individual republics, the tourism industry in this entire region has been in a state of flux. Prior to 1989 three separate state agencies handled all tourism to the Soviet Union: *Intourist* (which handled foreign tourists), *Sputnik* (which handled youth tourism from within the USSR and "friendly" nations), and the CCTE (tourism of Soviet people through the *trade unions* where they worked). These groups were completely split up in 1991 and 1992, as *privatization* (the process by which ownership changed from state to private individual or corporation) ended many state enterprises. Numerous joint-stock corporations were founded in Russia and elsewhere, but the extent and nature of privatization is different in each of the fifteen new countries.

There were an estimated 8,000–9,000 independent tourist-related companies in Russia in 1996, but most are insignificant. Fewer than 25 agencies handle the great majority of inbound tourists to Russia. VAO Intourist, the relic of the vast Intourist enterprise of the Soviet Union, still handles 27 percent of tourist arrivals from countries that were not part of the former Soviet Union, and even more of that from the countries that were. VAO Intourist remains so dominant primarily because of its direct or indirect control of a significant part of the infrastructure of hotels, transportation, restaurants, and entertainment in Russia.

To provide for the needs of foreign visitors, the umbrella organization that linked the Intourist companies—Intourist-Holding—had more than 57,000 rooms in the hotels that they owned and operated in 1991. This comprised approximately 75,000 of the

Table 10–3 Origins of Visitors to Russia, 1996.			
Nationality	1995	1996	% Change 1996–1995
Ukraine	2,031	5,029	147.6
Finland	1,276	1,363	6.8
Georgia	521	1,275	144.7
Armenia	330	1,160	251.5
Moldova	199	1,102	453.8
Poland	666	874	31.4
Uzbekistan	73	547	649.3
Lithuania	441	535	21.3
Kazakhstan	218	358	64.2
China	390	349	- 10.5
Belarus	1,178	329	- 72.1
Turkmenistan	44	297	568.2
Tajikistan	59	294	398.3
Germany	323	280	-13.3
Azerbaijan	285	269	-5.6
Estonia	188	249	32.4
Latvia	186	179	-3.8
United States	216	179	-17.1
Turkey	134	160	19.4
Mongolia	170	144	- 15.3
TOTAL (incl. others)	N/A	16,208	N/A

Source: Travel and Tourism Intelligence, 1997, p. 37

total of 100,000 beds in the fifteen countries of the former Soviet Union. The largest hotel is the Rossiya near Red Square in Moscow with 3,060 rooms. Built in the early 1970s, it typified the Soviet approach to tourism. Facilities were concentrated in one location, with the hotel having three large restaurants and a store where foreign visitors could purchase goods with foreign currency. In the past, the availability of goods was much higher in the foreign currency stores than in the stores available to the masses. Like the rest of the centrally planned economy under communism, the Rossiya was bland, drab, and inefficient in both service and operation. The Rossiya typified the Soviet Union's approach to foreign tourism, which emphasized *central planning* and control of tourism through use of very large facilities.

There were several advantages to the Soviet Union of having a few very large tourist facilities for foreign visitors. First, this provided a simple means to process and handle foreign visitors as they arrived and departed. Second, it allowed for economies of scale in providing both food and lodging. Third, it facilitated a high degree of organization of tours so that the transportation system could be used effectively and efficiently. Fourth, it minimized the possibility of contact between Soviet citizens and foreigners.

The new countries created from the Soviet Union have seen some change in their approach to tourism, but it remains far below international standards. New hotels have been constructed or planned in major destinations (primarily Moscow and St. Petersburg), and Western companies have acquired partial or complete ownership or management of many of the new structures. Names like Radisson, Marriott, or Intercontinental will be familiar to American visitors, and Holiday Inn, Hilton, and Hyatt were all negotiating for a presence in Russia at the end of 1997.

In spite of the changes taking place in the old tourist industry of the former Soviet Union, the industry is far different from that in western countries. Many workers in the hotel sector still feel that service is demeaning, the bureaucracy remains entrenched, food is at best indifferent in hotels, and private restaurants, while increasing in number, are still insufficient. Also, there is little nightlife outside the hotels and few opportunities for individual tourists to travel without the benefit of organized tours unless they are fluent in Russian.

Future prospects for international tourism to the countries of the former Soviet Union are mixed. Economic and personal ties between Russia and the former republics indicate that most international tourism will continue to be between the new countries themselves. Foreign tourism from beyond the region is handicapped by a variety of factors. First is the strong competition from other East European destinations such as Prague, Budapest, or Warsaw. A second factor, the difficulty of getting a visa to many of the former Soviet Union countries, makes other East European countries even more attractive since visas are not required or easily acquired for most East European countries. The third problem is the continued poor quality of rooms and service at most hotels and other tourist-related establishments. A fourth problem is created by the economic changes that have occurred since 1991. Many of the fifteen new countries still use a two-tier pricing structure, charging foreigners substantially more for hotel rooms and opera, museum, ballet, train, or concert tickets than residents of the former Soviet Union. This is exacerbated by the tendency to charge "Western" prices for hotels and restaurants that clearly do not meet Western standards of quality or service. A fifth problem is the substantially increased crime rate and greater fear for personal safety in the new countries than in other European countries that compete for international tourists. Together these factors suggest that international tourism from beyond the boundaries of the fifteen new countries created from the former Soviet Union will experience only slow growth until these issues are resolved.

INTERNAL TOURISM IN THE FORMER SOVIET UNION

Internal tourism dominated the tourism industry of the former Soviet Union. More than 155,000,000 vacation trips were taken inside the Soviet Union by its citizens yearly. Soviet citizens were granted 15- to 48-day vacations annually by law. Variation in vacation length depended on profession, age, and length of service. Over 50 percent of the working population and more than 75 percent of school children were legally entitled to vacations of 23 days or longer. The provision of vacation tourism for Soviet citizens was under the direction of the trade unions. Most workers had their vacations highly subsidized by the place where they worked, resulting in extremely cheap vacation excursions. The various national and local trade union organizations provided a total of about two million beds for vacationing citizens of the Soviet Union. These facilities rarely meet minimal standards for international tourism, and the tumultuous changes associated with the disintegration of the Soviet Union has left this sector of the industry in disarray. The subsidies from the trade unions have largely evaporated, and the emergence of fifteen independent countries has disrupted the old organization for internal tourism within the Soviet Union. Ongoing strife in some of the more popular destinations for citizens of the former Soviet Union (the Black Sea coast, central Asia, and Georgia) have further affected domestic tourism.

In the process of privatization of the old tourism industry, many employees have been made redundant. The numbers of internal tourists decreased, and the length and cost of vacations provided by the newly emerging private sector have changed dramatically. It is impossible to provide accurate statistics at the present time because of continued turmoil in the economies of the individual countries. The one area in which tourism by citizens of the countries of the former Soviet Union has increased is foreign travel beyond the boundaries of the old Soviet Union. The loss of the former subsidies from trade unions, a relaxation or removal of limits on foreign travel, and the continual problem of the low quality of the tourism experience in the fifteen new countries have prompted many of their residents simply to save until they can visit other countries. European countries have received many of these tourists, but Turkey, China, and even Japan are destinations for residents of the former Soviet Union. Many of these tourists travel abroad for leisure and business, purchasing goods for resale in their home countries.

LOCATION OF TOURIST-RELATED ACTIVITIES IN THE FORMER SOVIET UNION

Domestic Tourists

For the internal tourist of the former Soviet Union, the primary vacation destinations are associated with the sea coasts of the Black Sea in Russia and Ukraine, the Baltic Sea Coast in Estonia, Latvia and Lithuania, the Southern Mountains of Central Asia, and to a lesser extent, the Volga River. Vacation facilities along the Black Sea coast are the basis for a wide variety of communities from Sochi to Batumi and Yalta. Accommodations range from sparse dormitory-style facilities in converted monasteries or large mansions predating the revolution to medical and health spas and to large hotels.

The Baltic Sea coast is another destination for the CIS and Baltic state tourist. The Volga River is the destination for a popular Russian pastime, a Volga River cruise. The various travel organizations of Russia operate a wide variety of tour boats that provide

extended tours on the Volga, including stops at the cities, beaches, and parks along the river.

The mountains in the south of the CIS are a destination for tourists who enjoy hiking in the summer or skiing in the winter. The Caucasus Mountains in Russia and Georgia have the greatest development of these activities. The development of regional recreation centers, such as one on Lake Baikal, capitalizes on unique local features to benefit regional residents. The importance of the trans-Siberian Railroad as a vacation experience should also be mentioned. Tens of thousands of CIS residents take one-to-two-week vacations simply traveling on the trans-Siberian. Transportation prices remain relatively inexpensive for residents of the CIS, and entire families vacation by traveling on the railroads.

Foreign Tourists

It is possible to recognize eight broad tourist regions in the new countries of the former Soviet Union that foreign tourists visit. The Central Region consists of Moscow, St. Petersburg, and Kyyiv. This region receives more tourist visitors than any other in the new countries. It is characteristic of the attractions of the former Soviet Union: Czarist structures, a unique culture, and a distinctive lifestyle. Moscow is the most important tourist city in the former Soviet Union. The major attractions in Moscow include the *Kremlin* and Red Square. The Kremlin, takes its name from the Russian prefix *kreml*, which refers to a fortification. The Kremlin of Moscow is equally as important because it was the location of the head of government for the Soviet Union historically and now for Russia. The Kremlin consists of a complex of old and new buildings on 64 acres surrounded by fifteenth-century walls. The Kremlin contains the cathedrals of the *Czars* and Czarinas and the Armory Museum, Figure 10–7. Adjacent to the walls of the Kremlin is Red Square. It contains the mausoleum in which Lenin is embalmed, the exquisite St. Basil's Cathedral, and the Military Museum. Other important sights in Moscow include several remaining homes of important writers like Pushkin, Tolstoy, and Dostoevski. Famous museums in Moscow contain some of the most important icons, Russian paintings, and European Renaissance artwork in the world.

St. Petersburg, Figure 10–8, remains the second largest city in size and attraction for foreign visitors to the former Soviet Union. The buildings and morphology of St. Petersburg reflect the influence of French and Italian architects and artists employed by

Peter the Great. The city has been repainted to reflect the original color scheme, and the canals used to drain the swamplands of the Neva River make it the "Venice of the North." The museums are outstanding, especially the Hermitage. The Hermitage has one of the greatest collections of Western paintings in the world. The summer palace of Katherine the Great is another important attraction.

Kiev (now Kyyiv) was largely destroyed during World War II and has been rebuilt as a modern city. The wide boulevards and modern buildings are typical of most centrally planned cities in the former Soviet Union. The presence of Russian Orthodox cathedrals and the few remaining architectural gems create an interesting counterpoint to this scene. One of the important attractions is the series of fountains and statuary in honor of those who gave their lives in the Great Patriotic War (World War II), Figure 10–9.

Smaller towns around these three major cities in the Central Region are interesting for tourists, but the vast majority of foreign tourists visit only these three. Those who do go to smaller towns in the St. Petersburg region opt to visit the wooden villages around Lake Ladoga or Lake Onega. These communities date from the time of the Scandinavian invasion of what is today Estonia and Russia, from the eighth century A.D. onward. They have some of the finest old churches found in Russia. Other trips go out from St. Petersburg to such places as Petrodvorets with its

Figure 10–7 Churches in the Kremlin, Moscow

Figure 10–8 Street scene in St. Petersburg with Soviet-style rectangular buildings and memorial plaza.

Figure 10–9 World War II Memorial at Kyyiv

ous tourists from the East European satellite countries of the Soviet Union, but tourism is now mostly domestic.

The Southern Coast of the Crimean Peninsula of Ukraine

Major cities of this region include Yalta, Alupka, Miskoorr, and Simeiz. The region has been developed for tourism, including prohibition of direct air flights into cities such as Yalta. Incoming tourists land to the north at Simferopol and are taken to Yalta and the surrounding resorts by bus. Automobile traffic is limited within the region, resulting in a very attractive resort setting. The beaches, climate, historical attractions, and spas are among the best in the former Soviet Union. With their alternating appearance of stark rock and pleasant vegetation, the Crimean Mountains combine with the Black Sea and its beaches to make this one of the most attractive locations in the CIS. The primary users of the Crimean Coast are domestic tourists.

Cities of the Caucasian Region (T'Bilisi, Yerevan, and Baku)

The cities of the Caucasus include the birthplace of Stalin, a variety of health resorts that utilize mineral waters of the region, and winter sport facilities. The distinctive culture found in each of these cities makes each of them a unique destination in terms of foods and cultural activities; but as with the Crimea, this region primarily attracts domestic tourism.

landscaped gardens, fountains, and parks; to Pushkin's home outside of Moscow; or to Zagorsk near Moscow where the historical role of the Russian Orthodox Church can be recognized.

In combination, the remaining seven regions visited by foreign tourists do not attract the number of visitors that come to the Central Region.

The Baltic Region

The Baltic region focuses on the cities of Tallinn, Riga, and Vilnius, capitals of the three Baltic countries. This region is characterized by its European-influenced (particularly Scandinavian) medieval architecture and by sandy beaches on the Baltic. Tallinn has a particularly beautiful old town within its walled fortifications, dating from the Middle Ages.

The Black Sea Region

The Black Sea region includes Odesa in Ukraine, Sochi in Russia, and Batumi in Georgia. The region attracts tourists because of its coastal location, its excellent resorts, and the Black Sea beaches. The Black Sea region used to be a destination for numer-

The Central Asian Region

The Central Asian region is perhaps the most distinctive region in the the former Soviet Union. The major cities (Tashkent, Almaty, Samarkand, and Bukhara) are filled with architectural monuments that reflect the many people who have inhabited this area. The cities are ancient trading centers that now serve as focal points for the cultural groups that are the basis for each of these Central Asian countries. The climate, landscape, language, and old sectors of the communities are distinctively different from anything else found in the CIS. Newer sections of the cities reflect the Soviet penchant for central planning and mass production of buildings and are less interesting than the older section. Because of the distance and limited numbers of hotels, this region receives far fewer visitors than does the Central Region.

Siberia

Siberia is a part of Russia. Major cities in Siberia include Novosibirsk, Irkutsk, and Khabarovsk. This region reflects the vastness of the taiga and the harsh Russian climate. Novosibirsk has a winter carnival that attracts some foreign tourists, and Lake Baikal is visited by those coming to Irkutsk, but the total foreign tourist flow to Siberia is extremely low. The trans-Siberian railroad attracts a few foreigners who traverse this region and may visit many of the cities along the route, but the lack of an architectural heritage in the new towns of Russian Siberia combines with the distance to minimize foreign tourist visitors to the area. Beyond the regions that dominate tourism in the former USSR, only minor tourist activity occurs in the balance of the large region that was once the Soviet Union.

TOURISM: PROBLEMS AND POTENTIALS

The tourism industry of the region suffers from the same problems that the general economy must face. For the domestic tourist, the industry provided an opportunity to escape from the cities with their seemingly endless blocks of apartment complexes, but the services that were provided were at a basic level. The underlying theoretic guidelines of the Communist party dictated that the quality of hotels and recreation it provided would be generally uniform throughout the country. Consequently standards tend to be much lower than those found in typical Western countries. In spite of this, since the domestic tourist has no other choice, tourism is a major economic activity. The present independent governments' emphasis on free enterprise may eliminate some of these problems. If it is effective in the tourism industry, we could expect that individual hotels or resorts would provide their workers an incentive as they generate more profit. If this occurs, it can reasonably be expected that there will be variation in quality of tourism, accommodation, services, and experiences that will change the bland and uniform nature of the domestic tourism experience

in the individual countries created from the Soviet Union.

The foreign component of the tourism industry in the former Soviet Union is small, but each of the new countries proposes its expansion. The general low level of service experienced in the industry usually discourages foreign tourists from returning more than once. The exception to this is in the new joint-venture hotels operated by private interests, where the level of service is more typical of what might be found in Western Europe.

In spite of these problems, the countries of the former Soviet Union have attractions that could lead to a major increase in foreign tourism flow if they were exploited. The appeal associated with the unique and the unknown is perhaps the greatest attraction that the new countries have for foreign tourists. The majority of the people of the world know little about Russia or the other countries. Their enigmatic natures continue to attract limited numbers of foreign tourists. Continued improvement in services and goods and development of tourist attractions by each individual country may result in a major change in the number of foreign tourists to the region.

For the individual or organization involved in the tourism industry that interfaces with the countries created from the former Soviet Union, it is important to recognize the strengths and weaknesses of the existing tourist industry. Tourists to the new countries should be made aware that they will not receive the same level of service that they might expect in Western Europe and that facilities will not be at the same standard. If tourists go with a desire to learn more about the cultures of the fifteen new countries and their distinctive geography, they will not be disappointed. A visit to these countries can be one of extreme enjoyment if unrealistic expectations are not held. The continuing changes in the region, including efforts to implement incentives in the economy, will lead doubtlessly to an even better experience for foreign tourists in the future. For the present, however, the region remains in a state of flux.

Armenia

Physical Characteristics

Armenia occupies the Armenian Plateau south of the Lesser Caucasus Mountains. Less than 10 percent of the country lies below 9,000 feet, and the highest

point reaches above 15,000 feet. The majority of the population is located on the plateau proper, whose elevations are between 7,000 and 8,000 feet above sea level. Armenia is subject to earthquakes, that in

75 km

- Kumayri
- Kirovakan
- Sevan
- **YEREVAN** ★
- Ozero Sevan
- Zod
- Angekhakot
- Kafan

Capital: Yerevan
Government: Republic
Official Name: Republic of Armenia
Size: 11,505 square miles (slightly smaller than Maryland)
Language: 93% Armenian and 2% Russian
Ethnic Division: 93% Armenian, 1.5% Russian, 1.7% Kurd, 3.5% Other
Religion: 94% Armenian Orthodox Catholic
Tourist Season: April through October
Currency: 1993 Russian ruble

CULTURAL CAPSULE

Armenia has a long history as a Christian country. An important part of the Roman Empire, Armenia adopted Christianity as the state religion in about 300 A.D. As part of the expanding Byzantine Empire, it was ultimately conquered by Muslim Arabs in 661 A.D. During the late 1000s and 1100s, Armenia was allied with European Crusaders, but was again conquered by the Muslims and became part of the Turkish Ottoman Empire. Nationalistic movements in Armenia in the late nineteenth and early twentieth centuries led to the massacre of as many as 1½ million Armenians and the flight of many to Western countries at the end of World War I. Incorporated into the newly created Union of Soviet Socialist Republics in 1923, Armenia remained a part of the Soviet Union until it declared itself independent on the 23d of September 1991. The Armenian Orthodox Church has remained dominant throughout the Communist period and today. The Armenians are highly nationalistic and are presently engaged in conflicts with Azerbaijan over Azerbaijani enclaves within its territory and an Armenian enclave in Azerbaijan.

Cultural Hints: Armenia is said to be the place the Middle East meets Europe, so there is great variety in foods and architecture.
- Shake hands upon meeting, with men waiting for women to extend hand first.
- Friends embrace and touch cheeks.
- Chewing gum in public is generally unacceptable.

- Toasting during meals is common.
- Eating and foods:
  Tipping is appreciated, and a gift of money will help you find a seat in a crowded restaurant. Lamb is Armenia's staple meat, and boiled lamb is a specialty. Trout from Lake Sevan are a luxury meal. Brandy is the primary beverage specialty. A variety of Middle Eastern food types are also found here, such as rice pilaf and a wide variety of fruits and vegetables.

 TRAVEL TIPS

Entry: A passport and visa are required and should be obtained before entering the country. Visas can be obtained at the border or airport, but it is easier to do so before going to Armenia. Visitors with a valid visa from any of the CIS countries automatically receive a three-day transit visa. Fees are required for all visas.

Transportation: Air transport is available to the countries of the former Soviet Union, the Middle East, and Europe. At present, air, road, and rail transportation are available to Armenia via Tbilisi, the capital of Georgia. Transportation within Armenia is best accomplished by taxi, although there is an efficient bus service in Yerevan and other major cities.

Currency: The Armenian Dram is the official currency. Armenia is essentially a cash-only society at present. Traveler's checks and credit cards are rarely accepted. Dollars, French francs, or German marks are preferred forms of currency for most exchange. In most cases it is better to use hard currency from Western countries to purchase goods and services.

Shopping: Common items purchased include handicrafts such as folk costumes or other clothing or fabrics, dolls, jewelry, and wooden carvings.

December 1988 killing 25,000 people and leaving a half a million homeless. The town of Spitak was nearly destroyed in that earthquake. The plateau is incised by deep ravines that were cut by rivers and streams from the mountains. The climate is humid continental with hot summers subject to drought. Winters have freezing temperatures and snow while the mountains of the Lesser Caucasus provide opportunities for hiking in the summer and skiing in the winter as a result of their highland climates.

Tourism Characteristics

Armenia is a beautiful land with sophisticated people. Armenia's history provides both important tourism opportunities and a great sense of tragedy. Lacking any of the traditional attractions of sun-sea-sand, Armenia has traditionally attracted visitors with ethnic ties to the country or those interested in its long and varied history. Under Communist rule the only city open to foreign visitors was Yerevan, the capital. Since independence, the government has lifted many of the restrictions on travel, and tourists are rarely stopped by the authorities. Tourism to Armenia is limited because of ongoing conflicts. Reports of these conflicts frighten potential visitors to the area.

Tourism has always been a minor part of the economy of Armenia although currently it is virtually halted as a result of conflicts. Nevertheless, Armenia has great tourism potential because of its varied and beautiful mountain scenery and the unique Armenian culture and architecture. Someday it may have the stability to capitalize upon its potential.

Tourist Destinations and Attractions

The major destination in Armenia is Yerevan and the surrounding area. Yerevan is a Soviet-built city that is basically drab and featureless, but the vitality of its markets and the emerging cooperative restaurants provide a unique experience. The central plaza in Yerevan has a lovely series of fountains that are enhanced by colored lights at night. The government house on the east side is the seat of the government, and two important hotels are nearby. The Hotel Armenia is being reconstructed and is the best hotel in the city presently. Other places to visit include the Armenian History Museum and the Ancient Manuscripts Library. The library houses over 12,000 Armenian manuscripts dating back to the ninth century. The display of illuminated manuscripts is particularly impressive. The other major site in Yerevan is its memorial to the victims of the 1915 genocide.

Near Yerevan are two important sites. Echmiadzin, the capital of Armenia from 184 to 340 A.D., is a very holy place to Armenians as the site of their most important orthodox cathedral and the residence of the church's leader, the Supreme Catholicos. Sixteen miles east of Yerevan is Garni, where the temple to the Roman god Mithrus was built by the Armenian king in the first century A.D. After Armenia converted to Christianity, Armenian rulers used the temple as a summer residence. Damaged by earthquakes, it was restored in the 1960s and 1970s. There are also ruins of a seventh-century church and a third-century bath house with a mosaic floor in the Roman style.

Geghard is an operating monastery 22 miles east of Yerevan. It has marvelous carved churches dating from the early 1200s. There are lovely old Christian sites located in or near all of the major cities of Armenia. The most important medieval Armenian cultural center is at Agartsin. Located 70 miles from Yerevan, it has a classic Armenian church built between the tenth and thirteenth centuries.

Azerbaijan

150 km

Khachmas

Sheki

Mingechaur

Gyandzha

Sumgait

BAKU ★

Kyurdamir

Stepanakert

Caspian Sea

Nakhichevan'

NAKHICHEVAN

Astara

Capital: Baku (Baky)
Government: Democratic Republic
Official Name: Azerbaijani Republic
Size: 33,436 square miles (slightly larger than Maine)
Language: 89% Azeri, 3% Russian, 2% Armenian, 6% other

Ethnic Division: 90% Azeri, 2.5% Russian, 2.3% Armenian, 3.2% Daghestani, 2% other
Religion: 93.4% Muslim, 2.5% Russian Orthodox, 2.3% Armenian Orthodox, 1.8% other
Currency: Manat

TRAVEL TIPS

Entry: A passport and visa are required. Travelers arriving without a visa cannot register at hotels and will be asked to leave immediately.

Transportation: Transportation to Azerbaijan is somewhat difficult. Air transportation is available through Moscow on a more or less regular basis, and to other capitals of the former Soviet republics. Train transportation also comes from the former Soviet republics and weekly from Iran and Turkey. At the present time Azerbaijan is attempting to imrove other air links to Iran, Turkey, Pakistan, and other Middle Eastern countries as well as Europe. There is a modest subway system in Baku, and taxis provide transportation within the country and to cities adjacent to the capital.

Currency: Azerbaijan is a cash-only economy. Travelers checks and credit cards are rarely accepted. Do not convert large sums of currency into manats.

Shopping: Common items include handicrafts such as copper bowls and other ornate metal objects, distinctive folk costumes, and objects related to the Muslim heritage of the country.

blow. The term Baku literally means "place where the wind blows." Winters are moderate, and summers are long and hot.

Tourism Characteristics

Azerbaijan is a picturesque and culturally and geographically diverse country. It has received little tourism in the past and receives even less today. During the Soviet period, most visitors were Russians or Georgians and Armenians going to the beaches and spas along the Caspian. Western visitors were extremely few and typically visited only Baku for one or two nights and then the ancient town of Sheki as part of an Intourist tour to the Caucasus and Central Asian republics. Foreign tourism to the southern half of the republic has been basically nonexistent. Ongoing conflict with Armenia and the resurgence of Islam in the country have reduced tourism to a trickle. Azerbaijan is strengthening its ties with Turkey and Iran and may benefit from tourism from these areas in the future if it is able to develop its Caspian Sea coast.

Tourist Destinations and Attractions

The major destinations in Azerbaijan are Baku, Sheki, and the Caspian coast. Baku is by far the most important tourist attraction. With a quarter of Azerbaijan's population in its limits Baku is the biggest metropolis in all of the Caucasian area and was the fifth largest city in the Soviet Union. It is built on the Apsheron Peninsula, and owes its growth to the discovery of oil in the Caspian Sea and along the coast of Azerbaijan. The city is the site of a school (*Madrassa*) for Shia Muslims, opened in 1989 as the first in the former Soviet Union. The most interesting tourist attractions in Baku are associated with the old town, a medieval fortress that withstood the Mongol Tartar siege in the thirteenth century. Much of the city heart is pedestrian only. The Dzhuma holds the museum of carpets and applied art. This is the best and most impressive museum in Azerbaijan and includes displays of woven and knotted Azerbaijani carpets, carved wood, metalwork, jewelry, and European and Russian paintings.

Sheki is perhaps the oldest city in Azerbaijan. Located on the southern slopes of the Caucasus Mountains 235 miles from Baku, evidence indicates it was founded over 2,500 years ago. It was the home of a ruler in Azerbaijan in the eighteenth century, and the Summer Palace and Riverside Fortress are still standing. Sheki is especially important for locally

---

CULTURAL CAPSULE

Azerbaijan was one of the Muslim republics in the former Soviet Union. Culturally it is an extension of the Soviet Central Asia region in terms of its culture and traditions, but its language and ethnic background are tied to Turkish. It shares with the central Asian republics a tradition of Islam, which has been highly secularized as a result of the seventy years of Soviet rule. Since independence, there has been a resurgence of interest in the Muslim tradition and visitors should be aware of Muslim values in dealing with the people. Most people understand Russian, but a Turkish phrase book will allow you to use basic words that will be understood by the Azeri majority. The written form of Azeri uses the Russian Cyrillic alphabet.

Cultural Hints:
- A common greeting is to shake hands, but friends will embrace and may kiss one another upon the cheek.
- Shake hands with everyone at an office or other gathering.
- Public displays of affection are usually not acceptable.
- Before taking photographs, ask permission, especially in mosques or of individuals (who may ask for a small fee).
- Alcohol should only be consumed in hotels or restaurants catering to foreign visitors or secularized Muslims.
- Eating and foods:
  Tips will result in better service. Food is served with the traditional black tea, which is drunk in large quantities. Common foods include richly spiced lamb; a pilaf of rice fried with meat, fish, vegetables, or fruit; shish kebabs; minced lamb and vegetables steamed in grape leaves; and soups made from lamb stock. Azerbaijan is famous for its desserts, which are similar to those found in Turkey.

Physical Characteristics

Azerbaijan occupies the large, flat Kura lowland south of the Great Caucasus Mountains. To the west, the uplands leading into Armenia separate it from that country, while to the south the mountains of northern Iran further isolate the Kura lowland. The population is concentrated on the Aspheson Peninsula jutting into the Caspian Sea and along the Kura River and the Caspian Sea coast. The climate is a dry, semiarid steppe subject to drought. Summers are sunny and warm, but gale-force coastal winds often

made silk, and its caravanserais (historic inns dating from centuries ago) and bazaars are still famous. The Caspian Sea coast was an important tourist destination during the Soviet period, with Russians and Armenians joining Azerbaijanis in experiencing the sun-sea-sand. Since the independence of Azerbaijan, this tourism has declined precipitously. The beaches have good potential if they are ever developed properly and the economy and political situation are stabilized.

Belarus

150 km

Boundary representation is not necessarily authoritative

with some ten daily trains passing through. Minsk can also be reached by car as Poland's border is only 20 miles away along a very good road. Transportation in Minsk relies on a subway and an efficient bus system. Inexpensive and simple to use, this is the best bet for tourists. Travel between cities utilizes trains primarily.

Currency: Belarus is essentially a cash-only economy. Traveler's checks and credit cards are accepted only sporadically. Do not convert large sums of currency into rubles. In many cases it is better to use hard currency (dollars, German marks, French francs, British pounds) to purchase goods and services.

Shopping: Common items include intricately carved wooden boxes (whose geometric designs are made of lacquered straw), wooden trinkets, ceramics, and woven textiles.

Capital: Minsk

Government: Democratic Republic

Official Name: Republic of Belarus

Size: 80,155 square miles (slightly smaller than Kansas)

Language: Belarussian is the official language, closely related to Russian. Russian is understood everywhere and shares many words with Belarussian.

Ethnic Division: 80% Belarussian, 13% Russian, 4% Poles, 3% Ukrainian, 1% Jews

Religion: Secularized Russian Orthodox, estimates of 20–35% practicing in 1993. Protestant and Roman Catholic congregations presently being organized.

Tourist Season: May through September

Currency: Belarussian ruble (BR)

 ## TRAVEL TIPS

Entry: A visa and passport are required. The visa must be obtained before entering the country at Russian consulates or embassies. Visitors without visas will not be allowed to register at hotels and will be asked to leave the country immediately.

Transportation: The capital of Belarus is served by air transport from Moscow and St. Petersburg on a daily basis. Air transport to European cities is less frequent, but cities such as Warsaw are typically served two to four times a week. Minsk is on the main Moscow-Warsaw-Berlin rail line,

CULTURAL CAPSULE

Belarus is a flat region along the shortest route between Moscow and Poland. Its name means "White Russia," which seems to derive from its ancient inhabitants' clothes. It is a border region that has been fought over for centuries by Russians, Poles, Germans, and others. It suffered grievously during World War II, and was one of three Soviet Republics with a seat in the United Nations before the great independence movements of the 1990s. The people are Slavs who settled the region in the sixth to eighth centuries. The region was dominated by a powerful Lithuanian state in the Middle Ages, and subsequently by Poland. Roman Catholicism became the official religion in 1386. Expansion of Russia caused the peasants who had remained Russian Orthodox to revert to their orthodox religion. During the Soviet period, religion was publicly practiced primarily by the elderly, but since independence there has been a return to the church by many of the young. The language is so similar to Russian that the Russian language is still widely used in spite of independence.

Cultural Hints:

- Shake hands in greeting, but close friends may engage in a hug and a brief kiss to alternate cheeks.
- As you enter a row of a theater to occupy your seat, if you pass in front of other seated people turn and face them.
- People stand in line, and it is rude to cut in.
- Public display of affection is avoided.

- Eating and foods:
  Tips are appreciated. During meals toasting with vodka, wine, or beer is common. A typical Belarussian meal includes potatoes, mushrooms, and sausage or other pork. Soups (especially borscht, with its distinctive red color from beets) are common. Potato dumplings are often served with soup. Cucumber-and-tomato salad is common in the summer with lunch and dinner. Sour cream is added to borscht and other soups. Pastries filled with meat are a common main dish. Pies, strudels, and other desserts are a mainstay of major meals.

Physical Characteristics

Belarus is a part of the Russian plain, which is an extension of the European plain. Nearly flat with low elevations, the Russian plain in Belarus is characterized by poor drainage, marshlands, and easy access. The climate is mild and is transitional between the humid continental climate of Russia and the wetter maritime climates of Europe to the west. Summers tend to be moderate with temperatures rarely exceeding the mid 80s, while winters are cold and snowy. Summers have frequent thunderstorms, but are otherwise an ideal time to visit. Fall is the most scenic because of the fall foliage.

Tourism Characteristics

Belarus has relatively little to offer in the way of tourism. The major role of Belarus has been as a transit route between Europe and Russia. Consequently, its tourism has been associated with either travel or any disasters that have occurred in the region. As the location of conflict between competing groups, there is a variety of historic sites to visit. In 1996 Belarus entered into a joint economic and political union with Russia. What this will mean concerning Belarus' independence remains to be seen.

Tourist Destinations and Attractions

Major destinations in Belarus are Minsk, the hamlet of Khatyn, and Brest on the border. Minsk has an old town, which included the marketplace in the twelfth century. There is a small area of housing on the east bank of the river that has been restored to the seventeenth- and eighteenth-century style to make a quaint attraction. There are craft shops and functioning churches found in the old center of town. Essentially all of Minsk was destroyed during World War II, and its new buildings reflect the Soviet architectural style. The restored main street of Minsk is the site of major shops and a Belarussian art museum is located only 1½ blocks south. There is a museum of the Great Patriotic War (World War II), which gives a vivid introduction to the destruction and suffering of Minsk during World War II. The art palace exhibits Belarussian arts and crafts, and some reproductions are available for tourists.

Near Minsk are pleasant pine forests and a reservoir (the Minsk Sea) where camping and picnicking are enjoyed by the residents.

The small village of Khatyn is 60 kilometers north of Minsk. Burned to the ground with all of its inhabitants in 1943 as a reprisal by the Germans against local partisans, it is now a memorial to the Great Patriotic War. There is a sculpture and a graveyard commemorating 185 other Belarussian villages destroyed by the Germans. (Do not confuse Khatyn with Katyn, where the Soviets murdered thousands of citizens of the USSR.)

Brest is primarily important for the Brest fortress located here. A fort was built in the 1800s and destroyed in the German invasion of 1941. Rebuilt in a monumental style as a memorial after World War II, it features recorded explosions and gunfire to provide atmosphere for visitors. The Defense of Brest Museum is adjacent to the fortress. Also on the outskirts of Brest each Saturday and Sunday is one of the largest markets in the former Soviet Union. Poles and Belarussians sell Western products of all types from guns to computers.

Estonia

Physical Characteristics

Estonia is generally a level area of the North European Plain. The highest point in Estonia is only about 1,000 feet above sea level, and this is the highest point in all three Baltic countries. Estonia includes over 800 islands, the largest of which are accessible to visitors. The climate of Estonia is less extreme but damper

Final boundaries of Estonia, Latvia and Lithuania with the former Soviet Union are expected to be confirmed by agreement

150 km

Gulf of Finland

Narva

★ **TALLINN**   Kohtla-Järve

Baltic Sea   Haapsalu

Hiiumaa   Võhma   *Lake Peipus*

Saaremaa   Pärnu   Tartu

Gulf of Riga

Valga

Capital: Tallinn
Government: Democratic Republic
Official Name: Republic of Estonia
Size: 17,413 square miles (twice the size of New Jersey)
Language: Estonian is the official language: 66% speak Estonian, approximately 30% speak Russian, some Finnish, Belarussian, and Ukrainian also spoken.
Ethnic Division: 64% Estonian, 27% Russian, 3.2% Ukrainian, 1.8% Belarussian, 1.1% Finn, 2.13% other (1992 estimates)
Religion: Lutheran is the primary denomination, but there are significant numbers of Russian Orthodox and others. Secularization during Soviet rule has been replaced by strong nationalistic feelings associated with Estonian language and the Lutheran Church.
Tourist Season: May through September
Currency: Kroon (Estonian crown)

than the humid continental climate of Russia. The summers range between 70 and the low 80s for the highs, but from November to February temperatures rarely rise above the low 30s. December and January are the coldest months, and there is usually snow on the ground from mid December to mid March. The warmest months are July and August, but they are also the wettest with persistent showers.

Tourism Characteristics

Estonia is unique among the former republics of the Soviet Union in that it maintained a much stronger connection to the West during the entire Soviet period. On a regular basis a long-standing ferry service between Tallinn and Helsinki covered the 50 miles of the Baltic separating them. Estonians were able to receive Finnish television and understand most of it because of the language similarities. The Estonians were highly nationalistic and resented the Russian

CULTURAL CAPSULE

Estonia is unique among the former Soviet republics in that it has a language unrelated to any of the *Slavic* tongues. Estonian is related to Finnish. Estonia has a long tradition of orientation to the West, and several of its cities were dominated by Germans as part of the Hanseatic League. The combination of German, Danish, and Finnish influence has created a Scandinavian feeling in Tallinn and other Hanseatic cities. The major tourist attractions reflect its varied history and are among the most attractive in the former Soviet Union.

Cultural Hints:
- Shake hands to greet. Old friends may embrace.
- When dining, the fork is kept in the left hand and the knife in the right.
- Western gestures are generally recognized, but not used as frequently as in the West.
- Eating and foods:
  Toasting during meals is common.
  Tips are expected.
  Ice cream is a favorite summer delicacy, available in numerous shops and outdoor stalls.
  Typical foods include roast pork with onions and mushrooms, soups (including borscht) and a variety of pastries, cakes and open sandwiches. Fish, chicken, potatoes, cabbage, cheese, pork, and bread are common foods.

migration into their country during the Soviet period. Of all of the former republics, Estonia had the reputation for the highest-quality consumer goods and the greatest availability of goods and services. Its long connections to Germany and Scandinavia resulted in a culture that is Western oriented and more similar to Scandinavia than to Russia. The country is determined to increase its tourism, particularly short-break tourism from Scandinavia and Western Europe. As more facilities are built and older facilities are renovated, it can be expected that tourism to this beautiful country will increase.

Tourist Destinations and Attractions

The major destinations in Estonia are the cities of Tallinn, Tartu, and Parnu. Tallinn is a lovely Hanseatic League city. In few areas of Europe can you experience the feeling of the fourteenth and fifteenth centuries as you do in Tallinn with its old medieval walls and winding cobbled streets climbing its hills and the needle narrow spires of its churches. It has been judiciously restored to make it extremely attractive. It is divided into the upper town (Toompea) and the lower town. Both are medieval and include a variety of lovely architectural styles in the stores, houses, and churches. The upper town occupies the hill overlooking the harbor. The entrance is through a gate tower built in 1380, which separates the upper town on the hill from the lower town. Leading between high walls to the upper town, its cobbled streets are vivid reminders of life during the medieval period. Upper town includes the Toompea castle, the Russian Orthodox Alexander Nevsky Cathedral, and a variety of beautiful buildings. The castle built by the Danes in 1219 has been largely destroyed, and a baroque replacement dating from the time of Catherine the Great dominates the hill. The castle is now home to the Estonian parliament. Another major attraction in the upper town is the Lutheran dome church (Toomkirik). There are observation platforms in the upper town that provide a dramatic view of the medieval lower town and the Baltic.

The second major attraction is the lower town and its square (Raekoja Plats), which is dominated by the only surviving Gothic town hall in Northern Europe. The square was the center of the first markets held here, from the eleventh to the end of the nineteenth century. In the streets leading off the square are old Lutheran and Catholic churches as well as lovely

Figure 10–10 Baltic Coast Beach

homes dating from the fifteenth to the seventeenth century. Roads through the medieval gates of the town are lined with the houses of merchants and gentry built in the fifteenth century or later. Many of the Tallinn guilds (associations of artisans or traders) can also be seen in the medieval lower town.

The second largest attraction in Estonia is the city of Tartu (Dorpat). It is noted for its classical architecture, which results from the comprehensive rebuilding after the town burned down in 1775. Tartu is also home to the most famous university in Estonia. Founded in 1632 when the country was under Swedish control, Tartu University became one of the premier centers of learning in nineteenth century Europe, and its scientific emphasis still persists. Tartu is also home to the Estonian National Museum.

Parnu is a coastal resort 130 kilometers south of Tallinn. This is one of the oldest occupied sites in Europe, with archaeological relics found just inland from the site dating back 9500 years. It was a Hanseatic port in the fourteenth century, and in the mid nineteenth century emerged as a sanitorium utilizing its mud baths. Today several sanitoria provide mud baths as well as access to the resort area oriented towards the beach, Figure 10–10.

Latvia

Physical Characteristics

Latvia is part of the Russian Plain, which is an extension of the European Plain. It is squeezed between Estonia on the north and Lithuania on the south, but does have a coast on the Baltic Sea.

Latvia received relatively few visitors during the Soviet regime. In It is still a minor tourist destination in Europe.

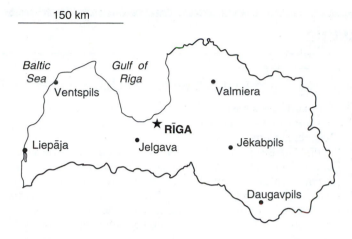

150 km

Baltic Sea

Gulf of Riga

Ventspils

Valmiera

★ RĪGA

Liepāja   Jelgava   Jēkabpils

Daugavpils

Final boundaries of Estonia, Latvia, and Lithuania with the former soviet Union are expected to be confirmed by agreement

Capital: Rīga
Government: Democratic Republic
Official Name: Republic of Latvia
Size: 24,595 square miles (approximately the same size as West Virginia)
Language: Latvian is the official language, but approximately one-third of the population speak Russian, while there are small groups speaking Belarussian, Ukrainian, and Polish
Ethnic Division: 51.8% Latvian, 33.8% Russian, 4.5% Belarussian, 3.4% Ukrainian, 2.3% Polish, 4.2% other
Religion: Lutheran, Roman Catholic, and Russian Orthodox, with small congregations of Protestants
Tourist Season: May through September
Currency: Lats

Tourist Destinations and Attractions

The principal destinations in Latvia are Rīga, the Baltic Coast, and the valley of the Gauja River. Rīga is the largest city in the former Baltic Republics of the Soviet Union and is a major commercial and industrial site. It has many old buildings dating from its centuries of occupation, especially by Germans. Old Rīga is the most picturesque of these, containing whole rows of Germanic buildings dating from the seventeenth century. Its crooked streets are mainly pedestrian only, providing the sense of a gigantic outdoor museum. Two towering churches and their squares dominate the old town. The oldest is the brick Dom Cathedral founded by the Germanic Knights in 1211 A.D. Rīga Castle dates in part from the thirteenth century. It contains three museums, the most interesting being the history museum on the fourth floor.

The Baltic coast of Latvia is home to a strip of resorts stretching about twenty miles. The water of the Baltic is cool, and at present so polluted that

TRAVEL TIPS

Entry: A passport is valid for six months and is required. No visa is required for stays up to 90 days by citizens of the United States and some European countries. A visa is required for others. Latvian visas are valid for Estonia and Lithuania, and Estonian and Lithuanian visas are valid for entry to Latvia. Travelers who plan to enter Russia or another member of the Commonwealth of Independent States (even in transit) will also need a Russian visa.
Transportation: Latvia is connected by air to most capital cities of Europe. There are no direct flights from the United States currently. Trains provide access to Moscow and the Baltic Republics as well as other countries of the CIS. City transport relies on buses and trams, which are inexpensive and frequent.
Currency: Traveler's checks and credit cards are accepted. It is convenient to bring some cash (crisp, clean, newer bills) to convert into Lats at exchange booths.
Shopping: Common items include amber and amber jewelry, woolen textiles, linen fabric, lace, wooden dolls and other trinkets, and embroidery.

CULTURAL CAPSULE

Latvia has suffered from outside intervention more than any other of the Baltic States. It was not until the late nineteenth century that the idea of a separate country became widespread among the Letts, who are the majority population. The principal city, Rīga was founded by Germans as a storehouse for traders to the North European Plain. The Germanic Knights occupied the area until the sixteenth century, after which Poles, Russians, Swedes, and Russians controlled it.

Cultural Hints:
- Shake hands to greet, with friends embracing and kissing one another's cheeks. Flowers are often presented by visiting guests.
- Public displays of affection are discouraged.
- Eating and foods:
  Toasting during meals is common.
  Small bribes are often required to get into popular restaurants.
  Tips are expected.
  Common foods include borscht, smoked sausage, pork rolls stuffed with carrots, fish, soup, cheese, potatoes, and bread.

swimming is prohibited. The main attractions are the sanatoria dating from the nineteenth century, the long sandy beaches, and the pine-covered dunes.

The Gauja River Valley is known for the castles perched above the river valley. Some remnants of the 1207 Germanic Knights' Castle are still standing, and its ruins remind visitors of the host of occupiers and their associated wars that have afflicted the small country of Latvia.

Lithuania

150 km

Final boundaries of Estonia, Latvia, and Lithuania with the former Soviet Union are expected to be confirmed by agreement.

Capital: Vilnius
Government: Democratic Republic
Official Name: Republic of Lithuania
Size: 25,174 square miles (slightly larger than West Virginia)
Language: Lithuanian is the official language. Russian and Polish are important minority languages.
Ethnic Division: 80% Lithuanian, 8% Russian, 8% Poles, 1.5% Belarussian, 2.5% other
Religion: Secularized Catholic and Lutheran dominated under communists. A resurgence of belief in old traditions since independence. No data on actual membership.
Tourist Season: May through September
Currency: Litas

CULTURAL CAPSULE

Lithuania has a position on the open European plain that has made it a focus of repeated invasion. At one time the Polish-Lithuanian empire occupied much of the North European plain. The European influence is obvious in the dominance of the Roman Catholic Church in the culture. Decades of occupation as part of the Soviet Empire did not dull the nationalistic tendencies of the Lithuanians, and Lithuania was one of the first Soviet Republics to demand and obtain independence. The economy is being privatized and is ahead of Estonia and Latvia. Lithuania receives many day tourists from Poland.

Cultural Hints:
- Shake hands upon greeting. Close friends may embrace and kiss cheeks. Flowers are often presented by visitors.
- Generally do not touch while talking unless it is a close friend.
- Public display of affection reserved for greeting friends.
- Eating and foods:
  Toasting during meals is common.
  Tips are expected.
  Pork is a common dish.
  Typical foods include caviar, pork, beef, chicken, wild game, eggs, soups, meat pies, potatoes, vegetables, and bread.

Physical Characteristics

Lithuania lies on the North European plain. The land is basically level, with many small lakes. The soil is very fertile and productive. The climate is a modified maritime with cool damp winters and warm summers. Winters experience freezing temperatures and snow, especially as you move inland from the Baltic Sea. Summers are warm, but temperatures rarely reach the 90s. July and August are the hottest months and have frequent showers.

Tourism Characteristics and Tourist Destinations and Attractions

Europe accounts for over 90 percent of visitors to Lithuania, with Russia the largest single market (30 percent). The United States represents approximately 5 percent of its visitors. The primary destination in Lithuania is the capital, Vilnius, but tourism to Lithuania has never had very large numbers. In 1994, it ranked fifth of the fifteen countries created from the former Soviet Union. Vilnius, however, is often described as the prettiest and greenest capital of the Baltic countries. Attractions in Vilnius include the

TRAVEL TIPS

Entry: A visa is not required for residents of the United States and many European countries. A valid passport is required. Unexpired Estonian and Latvian visas are also accepted. Travelers who plan to visit Russia or other members of the CIS, even in transit, will require a Russian visa.
Transportation: Good air connections from Europe and the CIS. There are daily trains to Poland, Germany, Russia, and the other Baltic republics. There are taxis in the cities, but most tourist destinations have sites accessible by walking.
Currency: Litas. Traveler's checks may be cashed at major hotels and banks, and credit cards are rarely accepted at most hotels, major restaurants, shops, and banks.
Shopping: Common items include woolen and linen textiles, amber and amber jewelry, embroidered folk costumes, scarves, dolls and other wooden objects, and art objects of tin or other thin metal.

red brick tower on the 150-foot-high hill. Part of the old defenses of Vilnius, it provides a good view of the city. The cathedral is now a national shrine, as it was reopened for worship in 1989 and became a symbol of Lithuanian independence. Rebuilt many times since the Gothic structure built in the 1400s, it is now essentially done in the classical style. The old town of Vilnius was built in the fifteenth and sixteenth centuries. Much of this area was a Jewish ghetto during World War II. Lithuanians were involved in the Holocaust, in which essentially all of Lithuania's Jewish population was murdered under German direction. Parts of the old town have been restored to better-than-new condition, while others are dilapidated. The narrow streets and old buildings are among the most interesting attractions in Vilnius. The university in Vilnius was founded in 1579, and today has about 16,000 students. There are numerous other attractions, including lovely Catholic churches, museums, and shops.

At Paneriai about four miles from Vilnius is one of the German death camps, where 100,000 Lithuanian Jews were exterminated. The pits where the thousands of bodies were disposed of are grassed over, but still evoke in visitors a deep sorrow over the inhumanity of the Holocaust.

Kaunas is Lithuania's second largest city. Destroyed repeatedly over the centuries, it contains some lovely restored fifteenth- and sixteenth-century German merchant houses around the old town square. The new town is dominated by a pedestrian street, where the most interesting museums and shops in the town are found. On the outskirts of town is the Ninth Fort, which was turned into a death camp by the Germans. About 80,000 Jews were killed here.

Moldova

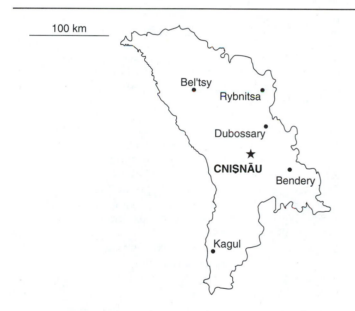

100 km

Bel'tsy
Rybnitsa
Dubossary
★ **CNIŞNĀU**
Bendery
Kagul

Capital: Chisināu (formerly Kishinev)
Government: Democratic Republic
Official Name: Republic of Moldova
Size: 13,012 square miles (slightly larger than Maryland)
Language: Officially Moldovan, which is actually Romanian; Russian and Ukrainian spoken by about 13% each
Ethnic Division: 64.5% Moldovan, 13.8% Ukrainian, 13% Russian, 3.5% Gagauz, 2% Bulgarians, 1.5% Jews, 1% other
Religion: 98.5% Eastern Orthodox, 1.5% Jewish
Tourist Season: No distinct season
Currency: Romanian Leu and Russian ruble

TRAVEL TIPS

Entry: A visa and passport are required. Visas can be obtained at the border with Romania or at the airport. Visas are required to travel to other CIS countries and are very difficult to acquire in Moldova. Visitors (except Romanian citizens) without visas will be unable to register in hotels and will be forced to leave the country.
Transportation: Air connections to Moscow, Romania, and Ukraine operate daily. Daily trains run to Moscow and on to Bucharest in Romania. Travel by car from Romania is also relatively easy. Within Moldova, trains and buses provide transport in and between cities.
Currency: Moldova is essentially a cash-only economy. Traveler's checks or credit cards are rarely accepted. Do not convert large sums into local currency, as Western currency is often more useful in obtaining goods and services.
Shopping: Common items include embroidered cloth, ceramics, pottery, glassware, and wooden hand-painted icons.

Physical Characteristics

Moldova occupies a gently rolling plain that slopes toward the Black Sea. The climate is a humid continental warm summer. Winters are mild, with occasional periods of freezing temperatures and snow. Summers are hot, with temperatures reaching into the 90s. Summers are characterized by thundershowers. Moldova was the center of grape production in the former Soviet Union, producing nearly a quarter of all wine. Brandy is also a major product in Moldova. It was also the center of tobacco production, producing one-third of all tobacco. Fruits, especially apples, are also an important crop.

Tourism Characteristics

Moldova was a minor destination for tourism in the former Soviet Union. Less than one percent of all tourists to the fifteen new countries created from the Soviet Union went to Moldova in 1994. Since independence from the Soviet Union, Moldova has stated its intention to rejoin Romania. The eastern industrial part of the country, which is predominantly Russian, has declared itself an autonomous republic. Its greatest number of tourists is from Romania at the present, as many come to visit former friends and family separated for fifty years.

Tourist Destinations and Attractions

The major attraction in Moldova is Chisinau (Kishinev). In 1990 it was the seventh most visited city in the former Soviet Union. It was largely destroyed during World War II, but has some interesting parks and museums. The old town consists of a few streets of wooden houses near the river. Wine tasting is offered as a form of entertainment.

Other than Chisinau, the road from Romania to Chisinau provides a scenic drive through rolling countryside of vineyards and fields of corn (maize), sunflowers, and sugar beets. There are a number of old monasteries found in the countryside of Moldova. Other cities are less interesting, but provide visitors a view of brandy manufacturing (in Beltsy) or the old forts from the Russian-Turkish conflict over the region (at Benderey and Tiraspol).

Ukraine

250 km

Boundary representation is not necessarily authoritative.

Capital: Kyyiv (formerly Kiev)
Government: Democratic Republic
Official Name: Ukraine
Size: 233,090 (slightly smaller than Texas)
Language: Ukrainian, Russian, Romanian, Polish
Ethnic Division: 73% Ukrainian, 22% Russian, 1% Jewish, 4% other
Religion: Secularized Ukrainian Orthodox, Ukrainian Catholic, Protestant, Jewish
Tourist Season: May through September
Currency: Karbovanets (Ukrainian coupon) being replaced by Hryvnya

 TRAVEL TIPS

Entry: A passport and visa are required and should be acquired before arrival. Travelers to Ukraine without a visa must obtain one upon arrival at the border point or within 24 hours of arrival.
Transportation: The capital of Ukraine has reasonably good air connections, with at least weekly flights from major European cities and more frequent flights from Moscow via Aeroflot. Ukraine has created its own airline from Aeroflot, which flies to Russian and European cities.
Currency: Hryvnya. Ukraine is essentially a cash-only economy. Do not convert large amounts into local currency. Western currency is generally more useful when purchasing goods and services.
Shopping: Common items include Pysanky (Ukraine's famous painted eggs), embroidered cloth and clothes, carved wooden boxes and spoons, and ceramics.

CULTURAL CAPSULE

Ukraine is second only to Russia in population in the newly created countries in the CIS. With nearly 52 million citizens, Ukraine approaches the population of France and the United Kingdom. Ukrainian is a Slavic language that is very closely related to Russian. The word Ukraine means "borderland," and this describes the geographic location of Ukraine that has so greatly affected its culture. Affected by repeated invasions and occupations, it developed some major differences from Russia.

One of the major cultural differences is in the Ukrainian Church. Poles occupying what is now Ukraine established the Uniate Church (also known as the Ukrainian Catholic

Church) in 1596. This church accepted the Roman Pope as leader, but practiced Russian Orthodox forms of worship involving the old Slavonic language. While many people remained loyal to the Orthodox Church, the combination of distinct church and language ultimately led to independence at various times, culminating with the demands of the Uniate Church for independence from the USSR that began in 1988. Since then the Ukrainian Orthodox Church has separated from the Russian Orthodox Church. The Ukrainian language differs from Russian because of the persistence of old Slavonic pronunciation and the modification caused by centuries of interaction with Poles, Lithuanians, and other countries, which controlled the country at various times.

Cultural Hints:
- Shake hands as a greeting. With friends, Ukrainians embrace and kiss cheeks.
- Toasts are common at dinner.
- Shaking the raised fist signifies anger.
- Do not cut into lines.
- Eating and foods:
  The fork is kept in the left hand while eating.
  Bribes may be required to get into popular restaurants.
  Typical foods include chicken (as in chicken Kiev); cucumber-and-tomato or egg salad with sour cream; borscht with sour cream; small pastries like ravioli filled with meat, potatoes, or almost any combination of meat and vegetables; pancakes with a meat or other filling; potatoes; breads; beef; chicken and pork; and a variety of pastries and cakes.

Physical Characteristics

Ukraine consists primarily of rolling plains known as the steppes. In the west it rises to the Carpathian Mountains, and in the south are found the Crimean Mountains on the Crimean Peninsula. The climate is transitional between the humid continental to the north and the desert to the east, creating both areas of steppe and humid continental climates in Ukraine. The very tip of the Crimean Peninsula has a subtropical climate. Summers are quite hot across the entire Ukraine, with temperatures in the 90s. Winters are mild along the Crimean coast, cool along the rest of Ukraine's Black Sea coast, and cold further inland with snow.

Tourism Characteristics

Ukraine has some of the best attractions for tourism in the former Soviet Union. Beaches along the Black Sea, while generally covered with small pebbles, provide a sun-sea-sand experience, making them a major destination for residents of the former Soviet Union. The breakup of the old subsidized system of vacations has caused a sharp drop in non-Ukrainian visitors to this area. Ukraine was second only to Russia in economic importance and power in the former USSR. It has a strong industrial base with numerous resources. As it makes the transition to its own currency and creates new markets for its manufactured goods, its economy could become one of the most robust in the CIS. At present, inflation rates are still very high, and the economic problems tend to inhibit potential tourists.

Tourist Destinations and Attractions

The major destinations in Ukraine are Kyyiv, the Crimean Peninsula, and the Black Sea coast centered on Odessa. A variety of other cities have important historic sites, but are minor when compared to these three.

Kyyiv is one of the most historically important cities of Europe. The first Russian state, Kyyiv Rus, existed here from the ninth to the eleventh centuries, and it was here that the Eastern Orthodox Church was adopted by the rulers. St. Sophia Cathedral dates from the eleventh century, and its interior is an outstanding example of the decorative scheme followed by the Russian Orthodox Church for 900 years. It was opened for Christian services in 1990 following nearly seventy years as a museum under Soviet rule. The second major site in Kyyiv is the Caves Monastery, a series of gold-domed churches, underground labyrinths where the mummified remains of generations of monks are placed, and museums with world-class collections of artifacts relating to the earliest occupants of this region. Other sites in Kyyiv include museums, a variety of churches with outstanding architecture, and the monument to the 100,000 Jews killed at Baby Yar, a ravine outside of Kyyiv.

The Crimean Peninsula has been an important tourist destination for Russians since the nineteenth century. It was the number one destination for internal tourists in the former USSR because of its combination of sun-sea-sand and health sanatoria. The major beaches and sanatoria are around Yalta, which was a protected city during the Communist era. Arriving tourists flew into Simferopol and were then bussed to Yalta to maintain its peaceful atmosphere. Yalta is the main attraction with its pedestrian-only area. The beaches have more pebbles than sand and the water is polluted, but there are lovely parks, the famous Russian author Chekhov's house, an aerial tram to the peak behind Yalta for the view, and some lovely old homes to enjoy. The coast near Yalta has some beautiful palaces, parks, and spas that attract tourists. One was the site of the famed Yalta conference between Roosevelt, Churchill, and Stalin where the division of Europe after World War II was finalized. The beautiful scenery and lovely climate make the coast of the Crimea one of the loveliest spots in the former Soviet Union.

Odessa is the biggest Black Sea port and the historic locale for interaction between the Mediterranean to the south and the Ukrainian steppes to the north. It has some good museums that are small enough to be easily enjoyed in a few hours, the famed Potyomkin steps descending from the hill overlooking the harbor, and nearby beaches. Of poor quality and badly polluted, they are extremely crowded in the summers.

Russia

2000 km

Boundary representation is
not necessarily authoritative.

Capital: Moscow
Government: Democratic Republic
Official Name: Russian Federation
Size: 6,592,849 square miles (twice the size of the United States)
Language: 80–90% Russian, 5% Ukrainian, plus some Tatar, Estonian, Latvian, Lithuanian, and Belarussian
Ethnic Division: 82% Russian, 3% Ukrainian, 4% Tatar, 11% other
Religion: 80% Secularized Russian Orthodox, 10% Roman Catholic, and 5% Muslim, 5% Protestant (1993 estimates)
Tourist Season: May to September, but Moscow and St. Petersburg attract tourists year-round.
Currency: Russian ruble

TRAVEL TIPS

Entry: A passport and visa are required. Visas must be obtained at a Russian consulate or embassy before entering the country.
Transportation: Russia has good air connections to Europe via the Russian airline Aeroflot and some American and European carriers. Travel between cities in Russia and to neighboring countries created from the USSR is via Aeroflot, which has frequent scheduled flights. Recent fuel and parts shortages mean that not all of the scheduled Aeroflot flights actually depart. Train transportation is frequent, efficient, and of fair quality. Transportation within the larger cities includes efficient, clean, and inexpensive subways, trams, and buses. (The subways were one thing that worked in the former USSR). Taxis are available, but very expensive compared to the public system.

Currency: Do not convert large amounts into rubles. Traveler's checks can be cashed at some banks, American Express offices, and at some hotels, especially non-Russian owned, in Moscow and St. Petersburg. Dollars (and to a lesser extent German marks, British pounds, French francs or currency from the Scandinavian countries) are useful in obtaining goods and services.
Shopping: Common items include Matryoshkas (painted, nested wooden dolls), enameled wooden boxes, bright woolen scarves, brightly painted wooden spoons and other trinkets, and artificial fur hats.

CULTURAL CAPSULE

Russia has the largest population of the former countries created from the USSR. While Russians are the dominant group, there are important subgroups, such as the Tatars, that create an exciting cultural mosaic. The Russian culture has been shaped by centuries of autocratic government, the Russian Orthodox Church, and a vast, harsh land. From the czars who ruled the Russian Empire to the communist governments of the twentieth century, democracy has been limited and survival the main goal. The Russian people have developed an amazing resilience to withstand hard times, and their culture is characterized by stoicism and tolerance for suffering unknown in the Western world. The church was of paramount importance in people's lives before the revolution, and in spite of 70 years of persecution, it is estimated that there are still some fifty million believers among the Russians. The changes associated with the breakup of the USSR has brought new challenges for the Russian people, but they will no doubt persevere once more.

Visitors note that Russians seem to rarely smile while walking the streets, but in the privacy of their homes and among family and friends the Russians seem more happy and friendly than other Europeans. Visitors will find that Russians are a helpful and accommodating group, particularly if they take the time to learn even a few Russian words.

Cultural Hints:
- Use a firm handshake and direct eye contact upon greeting someone.
- Friends typically embrace and kiss cheeks. Flowers are often presented as a gift by visitors.
- Whistling at public performances is a sign of disapproval.
- Clapping in unison by the audience is the equivalent of a standing ovation for performers.

- Always face people in a theater if you must pass in front of others already seated.
- Long lines, while less common than in the past, are still the norm. Do not cut into them.
- Toasting during meals is common.
- Eating and foods:

  Tips help to get a seat in crowded restaurants.

  The fork is kept in the left hand, the knife in the right while eating.

  Individual travellers should tip waiters. Members of groups will find they receive better service at the next meal if they leave a small tip.

  Typical Russian foods include borscht (or other hearty soups) served with sour cream, caviar served in hard-boiled eggs, cucumber and tomato salad, beef stroganoff, meat-stuffed grape or cabbage leaves, chicken, filled pancakes, fish, cabbage and potato dishes of all kinds, small pastries filled with meat and vegetables, breads, and of course the famous Russian ice cream.

Physical Characteristics

Russia is a vast land with all types of terrain, ranging from the broad expanses of the Russian plain in the west to high mountains in the south and east. The climate is equally varied, varying from tundra and subarctic to a small area of humid subtropical along Russia's Black Sea coast. In general, we can say that Russia has very limited opportunities for typical mass tourism associated with sun-sea-sand, but its great variety of other climates provides recreational opportunities of all types. The scenic beauty of Russia's diverse landforms provides unlimited potential for experiencing the beauties of this vast land.

Tourism Characteristics

Russia has always been the primary destination of tourists to the region encompassed by the former USSR. In the 1990s, some 70 percent of all foreign tourists to these fifteen countries were to Russia. The two leading destinations have been and remain Moscow and St. Petersburg. More than 50 percent of all beds owned by Intourist were in Russia.

Russia has always suffered from the perception that its facilities and services were below the standards found in other European countries. This is basically true, as under the old system there was little incentive for workers to provide good service, and facilities reflected the planning orientation of the ministry of tourism. Hotels were large, drab, and designed for group travel. Restaurants for tourists were generally found in the hotels. Unless you were a part of a group, getting served was a near impossibility. Nightlife was basically going to the restaurant or

cultural events, often designed specifically for foreign tourists. The distinctive culture, economy, and political system attracted visitors willing to endure the mediocre experience, but it was typically for one visit only.

With the breakup of the USSR and the emergence of free enterprise, these characteristics are changing. New privately owned restaurants are opening regularly, a variety of tour agencies are available to provide assistance, and new or newly remodeled hotels provide better accommodations and entertainment such as casino gambling. Nonetheless, as of 1997, tourism in Russia still involves many of the old characteristics of poor service, unhelpful bureaucracy, and redundant employees, such as the women on each floor of many hotels still giving out and collecting keys. Aeroflot still loads foreigners on planes for internal flights, lets them sit on the runway in a baking plane for seemingly endless time periods while Russian residents are loaded, and then provides minimal service in flight (no food on flights under four hours, for example). Offsetting this is the genuine hospitality of individual Russians, a culture and history that are available nowhere else in the world, and the marvels of the famed buildings and museums of the country.

Tourist Destinations and Attractions

There are almost innumerable tourist attractions in Russia, but the major destinations are Moscow and the surrounding area known as the Golden Ring; St. Petersburg and the surrounding region; the Russian Black Sea coast centered on Sochi; the Russian Northwest; and Siberia.

The number and variety of attractions in Moscow are so great that only a few can be mentioned. The greatest attraction is the Kremlin and related cathedrals. In the square in front of the Kremlin is Lenin's tomb and St. Basil's Cathedral, Figure 10–11, whose colorful onion domes surmounted by gold crosses symbolize Old Russia. Now open to the public, it is being restored as a house of worship. The Kremlin is the brick fortress built by Ivan the Great. Inside are some of the loveliest examples of Russian Orthodox churches as well as the Armory Museum exhibiting items from the Czars. The Moscow Subway is an attraction in its own right, with beautiful mosaic walls and statues. Clean and attractive, the Metro (subway) moves millions of Muscovites daily. There are a variety of other museums and churches of interest in Moscow, as well as shops and stores selling Russian souvenirs and western products, such as

Figure 10–11 St. Basil's Cathedral, Moscow

reflect the original color scheme, and the canals used to drain the swampland of the Neva River make it the "Venice of the North." There are a number of outstanding churches, St. Isaac's and the Kazan Cathedral on Nevsky Prospekt (street) being the two most famous. The museums are outstanding, especially the Hermitage. The Hermitage has the greatest collection of Western paintings in the world and is one of the great art museums of the world. The palace of the czars and czarinas ruling Russia for a century and a half, the Hermitage is one of the greatest treasures of Russia. Near St. Petersburg are five palaces, the most impressive being Peter the Great's palace at Petrodovorets on the Baltic. The Catherine Palace at Pushkin is a Baroque extravaganza that shouldn't be missed.

The Black Sea coast of Russia is centered on the city of Sochi. Nearby is probably the best resort in Russia, Dagomys, which is a completely self-sufficient resort for foreign tourists built by Intourist in the 1980s. The beaches of both Sochi and Dagomys are of pebbles, but Dagomys is less crowded as Russians are concentrated at the beaches of the much larger (340,000) city of Sochi. This small stretch of the Black Sea's coast comprises Russia's sun-sea-sand attraction.

The Russian northwest is a large area stretching from the Gulf of Finland west of St. Petersburg to the Barents Sea in the north. It provides innumerable op-

McDonald's hamburgers, Pizza Hut pizzas, and Baskin Robbins ice cream, Figure 10–12. Locally made handicrafts and paintings attract foreign shoppers, Tigure 10-13.

There are many cities of interest around Moscow, but some of the more important for tourists are known collectively as the *Golden Ring*. Located northeast of Moscow, they provide a wonderful introduction to Russian history and culture. Suzdal is the best known and was preserved by the Soviet Union as a "museum town." It remains a small town of some 12,000 people with no industry, and its beautiful old Russian Orthodox churches, monasteries, and convents are outstanding. Other cities in the Golden Ring with outstanding old structures are Vladimir, Yaroslavl, and Kostroma.

St. Petersburg remains the second largest city in size and attraction for foreign visitors to Russia. The buildings and morphology of St. Petersburg reflect the influence of French and Italian architects and artists under Peter the Great. The city has been repainted to

Figure 10–12 Western shops are now found in GUM Department Store, Moscow

Ports from St. Petersburg to Moscow

by Lei Chatfield

The places we visited on our river cruise were awash with history, yet everything along the way was in a state of change. The Volga-Baltic Canal waterways between the two tsarist capitals were opened only recently to Westerners—for the first time since 1917. Thus, we were plying waters that have long been enjoyed by Russian vacationers, but were new to us, visiting fascinating historic ports en route.

Our Russian guide would proudly point out a sight of "Leningrad... oh, er, St. Petersburg." Street signs didn't match new maps as the names changed. New holidays were being created to replace the old as we visited in May.

The government was trying to give value to the ruble as vendors asked (legally, in the new political climate) for dollars. And people were very open about politics.

It was an exciting time to visit.

New Route

On this eleven-day itinerary between St. Petersburg and Moscow I joined a group of travel writers.... We all were looking for something new to report to our readers and we were not disappointed.

Our water route took us to destinations that previously could be visited overland by Westerners only with difficulty and/or red tape. Now, with the tape cut, we cruised into such ports as the island of Kizhi with its wooden, twenty-two-domed Church of the Transfiguration built in 1714 without a single nail.

Or, later, on the Volga River, the city of Yaroslavl where we happened upon a festival. As we strolled along the esplanade we saw people selling artwork and playing traditional musical instruments and singing....

However, to me, the real highlight was the enthusiastic and warm—and even reserved or timid—reception we received in these newly-visited-by-Westerners ports.

Smooth Sailing

Sometimes, the more things change, the more they seem to stay the same. As we arrived at the ship docking area in St. Petersburg, we were met with bureaucratic confusion. Yes, we were a couple of hours early, but the ship we were to board had no record of us.

Upon a little prodding from our EuroCruise's representative, however, it turned out that there was a "simple solution": our riverboat had not been cleared for our particular itinerary. Instead, we were put on an identical sister ship, the MV Sergei Kirov, which had been cleared.

The captain was Russian, the management staff and chefs were Western and the other crew members were Russian—instructed by Western managers.

The passengers mainly were from Switzerland, Germany, the Netherlands, and America. The "official currency" on board was the U.S. dollar. The official languages were German and English.

Although there still was a language barrier for many of the Russian dining-room staff, they know enough basics to be able to serve passengers—and what they lacked in vocabulary they made up for with enthusiasm and an eagerness to please....

Ships Facilities

Our English-speaking guides who lectured on board and lead our land and bus excursions were representatives of a new, privately owned agency in St. Petersburg, Valentina Travel. Both had been with Intourist for years and, being founts of information, Valentina lured them away in the new free-market climate.

One afternoon I attended a class, expecting to learn how to make borscht. We got as far as the ingredients, but then the cost of ingredients came up. The cooking lesson turned into an "economics-in-changing-Russia" class.

Contrary to the previous controlled economy, the goods now are available. However, there's something new: inflation.

I can learn about borscht at home. The economics were fascinating. The Russians we were to meet, from St. Petersburg to Moscow, were eager to expound on the subject....

continues

continued

Haunting Ports

I find Russian history fascinating, perhaps because it is so incomprehensible.

This huge, disparate conglomerate came under one umbrella with Peter the Great. But, whatever the political changes over the years, one thing remains constant: the Russian toughness and resolve, evidenced in our first port, St. Petersburg.

Needing extensive road repair and refurbishment of its buildings, St. Petersburg, built from an unforgiving marshland, stands as a beautiful tribute to the vision of its founder.

Peter's admiration of Europe inspired him to build this window to the west, relocating the capital from Moscow to St. Petersburg.

Whatever the driving force, the result is pure magic; it's hard not to be mesmerized by this city.

Yes, of course, there's the obvious, the magnificent Hermitage, but on our tour we also were taken to see the Marble Palace ... with portraits of royalty so long kept under wraps, our guide was more excited than we to see them being displayed for the first time in decades.

A side trip took us to Pushkin to see the very overindulged European-style palace of Catherine. We saw only the grounds as it was closed that day, so we were taken instead to the Pavlovsk Great Palace, "risen from the ashes" after World War II.

Going through this palace we saw photographs of the burnt destruction from the war. Then we looked around us at what had been restored.

Although I want to go back to see the inside of the Catherine Palace, I'm glad I saw Pavlovsk....

Continuing On

Other highlights included:

- Kizhi—This island in Lake Onega is a folk museum. Most outstanding of the collection of wooden structures (peasant houses, windmill, sauna, etc.) is the twenty-two-dome Church of the Transfiguration.

- Goritzy—The claim to fame at this port is the huge Belozersk Monastery founded in the fourteenth century and now a museum. It was one of the biggest and richest monasteries, once served by 20,000 serfs.

- Uglich—This small town on the Volga claims an infamous place in Russian history. It was here that the last child of Ivan the Terrible, Dmitrii Ivanovich, died a mysterious death at the age of nine. Thus, a major attraction there is the Church of Dmitrii's Blood. For the shoppers, there's a very good craft store en route back to the ship. There are also many street vendors selling watches manufactured there.

- Moscow—In this original (and now once again) capital of Russia, the obvious highlight is the Kremlin. Don't leave without visiting the Armory Museum there. The collections include the famous Fabergé eggs, but equally fascinating to me was the display of royal costumes.

No matter how limited your time in Moscow might be, be sure to see the subways. Just as the churches used to convey messages to the people pictorially with paintings and mosaics, the subways do now. They are indeed works of art.

Much More

...To sum up about Russia, I'd like to bow to a statesman who had a knack for putting things in a nutshell:

I cannot forecast to you the action of Russia. It is a riddle wrapped in a mystery inside an enigma; but perhaps there is a key. That key is Russian national interest.

Thank you, Sir Winston Churchill.

To sum up the new travel experience to this land, I can say only this: Russia will continue to change and, being the enigma she is, we don't know how. I'd suggest visiting now.

Source: International Travel News,
October 1992; pp. 5–8, 52–57

Figure 10–13   Paintings for sale in Moscow illustrate the growing private sector in the former Soviet Union.

portunities for ecotourism, as well as a number of important towns and cities with architecture reflecting the history of the region. Novgorod is a city dating back to the 800s. It has some of the most diverse and lovely architecture in Russia. Karelia is the name given to the vast area stretching north through forest, lakes, and bogs to the far north of Russia. On Kizhi Island in Lake Onega is found an amazing collection of wooden churches and other buildings. The most impressive of these is the 22-dome Church of the Transfiguration.

Siberia is the vast land stretching east of the Ural Mountains. The most widely known attractions within it are the Trans-Siberian Railroad and Lake Baikal. The railroad skirts the southern margins of Siberia, introducing Russians and hardy foreign tourists to Siberia's vast forests. Lake Baikal is one of the most pristine water bodies in the world and is known as the "Blue Eye of Siberia." Architecturally, Siberia has interesting wooden houses with intricately carved wooden Siberian lace panels. The cities reflect Soviet planning, but have some interesting museums and churches. The far east of Siberia has good potential for Japanese and American tourists interested in experiencing Russia now that travel is possible to this eastern rim of Russia. Vladivostok on the east coast of Russia has seen explosive growth as tourists and business travelers from the United States and Japan flock to this region that was closed to non-Soviet citizens until after 1991. Alaska Airlines and Japan Air offer flights to Vladivostok and other cities of the far east of Siberia, reflecting the growing importance of tourism to this region.

Georgia

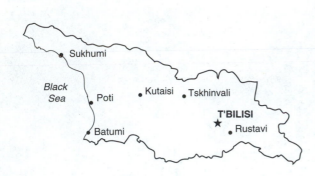

150 km

Capital: T'Bilisi (Tbilisi)
Government: Democratic Republic
Official Name: Republic of Georgia
Size: 26,911 square miles (slightly smaller than Montana)
Language: 71% Georgian, 9% Russian, 7% Armenian, 6% Azerbaijani, 7% other
Ethnic Division: 70% Georgian, 8% Armenian, 6% Azeri, 6% Russian, 3% Ossetian, 2% Abkhaz, 5% other
Religion: 65% Georgian Orthodox, 10% Russian Orthodox, 8% Armenian Orthodox, 11% Muslim, 6% unknown
Tourist Season: May through October
Currency: Russian ruble

TRAVEL TIPS

Entry: A passport and visa are required. Visas are necessary to register at hotels, and visitors without them will be asked to leave the country immediately.
Transportation: Georgia's capital and major tourist destinations are served by Russian and European airlines. Transportation within Georgia is good by road from the Black Sea resorts to T'Bilisi and city transportation relies on a limited subway in T'Bilisi and buses, trolley buses, and taxis in the larger cities.
Currency: Georgia is a cash-only economy. Traveler's checks and credit cards are rarely accepted. Do not convert large sums into rubles. In many cases it is easier and preferred to use Western currency.
Shopping: Common items include local handicrafts of wood or embroidered fabric, jewelry, and hand-painted icons.

CULTURAL CAPSULE

Georgia is one of the most distinctive of the new countries created from the former Soviet Union. Even during the Soviet era, Georgians prided themselves on their freewheeling economic system, which relied unofficially on a strong free enterprise ethic. The Soviet era brought modernization, but Georgia and Georgians experienced a degree of freedom and nonconformity not found elsewhere in the former USSR. Georgia is ethnically heterogeneous, with ancient

differences between the individual groups being the basis for conflict with Azerbaijan and with a breakaway northern Black Sea coastal portion of Georgia known as Abkhazia. Nonetheless, the Georgians are a friendly and hospitable people who welcome guests and treat them like family. Georgia is in many ways reminiscent of a Middle Eastern country with its spicy foods and vocal and friendly people.

Cultural Hints:
- Handshakes are a common form of greeting, but Georgians often embrace upon meeting with a kiss on the cheek.
- Toasts are common during meals.
- Public displays of affection are generally avoided.
- Eating and foods:
  Food is an important part of the culture of Georgia, with meals being a time of hospitality that may extend to people at other tables at restaurants. Toasting with wine or with Georgian brandy or vodka is the norm. Typical foods involve strong spices, herbs, and garlic and include a wide variety of meats, vegetables, and cheeses as well as delicious breads. Typical dishes include green or red beans served with walnuts, beet root, or spinach leaves pounded into a paste with herbs and spices, boiled pigs feet, spicy meat broth, chicken soup with eggs beaten into it, and tomato and onion used in cooking chicken, mutton, and all kinds of meat.

Physical Characteristics

Georgia has one of the most varied landscapes among the countries created from the former USSR. It is largely mountainous, with the Great Caucasus Mountains to the north rising above 15,000 feet and the lesser Caucasus to the south extending above 10,000 feet. Between these mountain ranges is the Colchis lowland which extends west from T'Bilisi to the Black Sea coast, and the Kura lowland, which extends eastward from T'Bilisi. The climate along the Black Sea coast has a warm and pleasant climate, grading from Mediterranean to humid subtropical. Moving inland up the Colchis lowland, the humid subtropical climate becomes dryer, but is still characterized by hot summers with precipitation and mild pleasant winters.

Tourism Characteristics

Georgia has some of the most scenic tourist attractions among the fifteen former republics of the Soviet Union. If the beaches of the Black Sea were not so pebbly, Georgia would rival much of the Mediterranean in attractiveness. During the Soviet era the coast of Georgia was the ultimate sun-sea-sand tourist destination for Russians. It also has a remarkable vitality among its people that is missing in other areas of the former Soviet Union and ancient cities, such as T'Bilisi, which attracted both domestic and foreign tourists. In the 1990s Georgia is the fourth largest destination for foreign tourists in the former Soviet Union.

Georgia's tourism has suffered dramatically since the breakup of the Soviet Union. The attraction of the Black Sea coast has been destroyed by ongoing conflict between the residents of Abkhazi and the central government in T'Bilisi. Foreign tourism has dropped to a low not experienced since the isolation of the Stalin era. The beaches and spas in the hills and mountains between the Black Sea coast and T'Bilisi, which formerly attracted the citizens of the Soviet Union, have also experienced a precipitous decline in visitors. The ending of the Soviet system of trade union–sponsored and–subsidized holidays has meant that the patronage of these sites has decreased and the industry is suffering serious problems of overcapacity.

Tourist Destinations and Attractions

The major destinations in Georgia are the Black Sea coast, the city of T'Bilisi, and the Caucasus Mountains. With a population of 1.3 million, T'Bilisi is a large sprawling city set in a bowl between the greater and lesser Caucasus. Its red-tiled roofs, narrow streets, and ancient buildings stand in contrast to the industrialization brought by the Soviet era. The air is highly polluted, but there are still important attractions for visitors. Most important are the museums that detail the unique history of this land, which has been overrun by invaders repeatedly through history. The Georgian state museum and the Georgian state art museum are two of the best. Equally attractive is the old city with its narrow, winding streets that create a maze for visitors and the thirteenth-century Metekhi Church. A second church of importance is the Sioni Cathedral and Caravanserai (inn). This is the center of the Georgian Orthodox church and contains its holiest relic, a cross supposedly from the fourth century.

The Black Sea coast of Georgia is a second major attraction, with primary destinations including the cities of Sukhumi and Batumi and the Georgian coast between. The road from T'Bilisi to the Black Sea coast also takes travelers through Gori, the birthplace of Stalin. Abkhazia, formerly known as Sukhumi, is a city of over 300,000 that combines a resort function with its port and industrial role. For the visitor, the attraction is a warm, sunny climate and the palm and eucalyptus trees that suggest a tropical setting. The beachfront is backed by a pedestrian promenade with vegetation typical of a tropical climate. North of Sukhumi to the border with Russia, there are some resort towns and beaches. From Sukhumi south there is also beachfront, with important resorts at Poti, Kobuleti, and Batumi. All of the towns along the coast have both access for swimming and sun bathing and sanitoria in the hills behind the beach. Batumi is a port resort that includes many of Georgia's Muslims. It has the highest rainfall of any city in the former Soviet Union, typical of a subtropical climate. Citrus and tea production in the surrounding country attracts tourists, but the beach is the main attraction.

The most famous attraction in the Caucasus Mountains is the famed Georgian military road that climbs north from T'bilisi to cross the Caucasus. The switchbacks on the road as it climbs the steep southerly slopes of the Caucasus provide some of the most breathtaking views available in any of the fifteen former republics of the former Soviet Union. Along the highway, a route formerly used by the ancient Greeks, are found lovely churches, small towns, and even a small ski resort at Gudauri near the summit of the highway at the Krestovy Pass. At nearly 8,000-feet elevation, it has snow from November to May and a luxury Austrian-built and -run hotel completed in 1990. Hiking to the peaks of the Caucasus are also attractions in this area.

The Central Asian Countries Created from the Former Soviet Union

Tajikistan

150 km

Boundary representation is
not necessarilt authoritative.

• Khudzhand

★ **DUSHANBE**

Kulyab •

Murgab •

Kurgan-
Tyube

• Khorog

Turkmenistan

300 km

Tashauz •

*Caspian
Sea*

• Krasnovodsk

• Nebt-Dag

Chardshou •

★ **ASHGABAT**   Kerki

• Mary

Kushka •

Uzbekistan

300 km

*Aral
Sea*

• Nukus

Andizhan

TASHKENT

• Urgench   ★

Fergana

• Bukhara

Karshi •   Samarkand

Termez

Kyrgyzstan

150 km

★ **BISHKEK**

Talas •   • Przheval'sk

Issyk-Kul'   *Ozero
Issyk-Kul'*

Dzhalal-
Abad •   Naryn •

• Osh

Kazakhstan

800 km

Petropavl •

• Kustanay

Pavlodar •

Oral •

Qaraghandy •   Semey
(Semipalatinsk)

• Atyraū

*Lake
Balkhash*

*Caspian
Sea* Aqtaū •

Qyzylorda •   **ALMATY**

Zhambyl •   ★

Shymkent •

Physical Characteristics

The tremendous cultural diversity is matched by the
physical characteristics of this area. Stretching from
the Caspian Sea to Mongolia, and from the Hindu
Kush Mountains and Tibetan plateau in the south to
the Siberian forests of Russia to the north, it is highly
varied. Much of it consists of inland steppes and
deserts rising to the snow-capped mountains to the
south. Important inland seas, such as the Aral Sea and
great rivers like the Amu Darya and the Syr Darya,
have been important from prehistoric times. The
great deserts—the Kyzyl Kum and the Kara Kum—
contrast with the fertile oases along the streams and
in the valleys of the region.

TRAVEL TIPS

Entry: All of these countries require a passport and visa. A visa must be obtained before entering the country. Visitors without a visa will be forced to leave the country immediately.

Transportation: Good rail and air connectivity to Moscow from all of the cities. The largest city, Tashkent, has air connection to Pakistan, India, and other Asian cities. Air transportation is handicapped by the penchant of the new countries' airlines to cancel flights or delay flights due to mechanical problems or lack of fuel. Train connections are reliable and on time to major cities along the rail route.

Currency: All of these countries are essentially cash-only societies. Credit cards and traveler's checks are accepted rarely if ever, and then only in Tashkent. Do not exchange large amounts of currency into local currency. Dollars are often the preferred currency.

Shopping: Items purchased by tourists are similar across these countries and include local handicrafts such as embroidered rectangular skullcaps worn by Muslim men, colorful scarves worn by Muslim women, wool products (including Persian lamb coats, sweaters, etc.), brightly colored cotton and silk fabrics and clothing, and copper or tin utensils or art objects.

The climate of this region is characterized by desert conditions. Temperatures in the summer are hot, rising above 110 degrees Fahrenheit regularly in the lowland towns and cities and exceeding 120 degrees Fahrenheit periodically in some of the cities on the margins of the desert such as Bukhara. The evening temperatures are much lower, dropping to the 70s in the cool of the night. Rainfall is limited, with some places averaging less than four inches per year. These are mid-latitude desert climates, and winters are characterized by cool to cold temperatures with periodic frosts and occasional snow.

Tourism Characteristics

The five countries of the former Soviet Central Asia have never had a large tourist flow. In 1990, Uzbekistan ranked third among the former republics with 2.2 percent of all tourist arrivals, but Kazakhstan, Kyrgyzstan, Tajikistan, and Turkmeni-

CULTURAL CAPSULE

The five countries created in former Soviet Central Asia are distinctive because of the dominance of Islam. The natives were all Muslim at the time of the Communist Revolution, and in the intervening years of official denigration of religion it has become somewhat secularized. Since independence, however, the Muslim people have begun to exercise their former beliefs and practices as they are given control of the mosques that were once museums. The region of countries is highly diverse ethnically, but each is based on a predominant ethnic group. Historically these countries have been the location of kingdoms controlled by either local rulers such as the Uzbeks, or foreign invaders such as the Tatars. The unifying role of Islam combined with these kingdoms to create famous holy and educational cities in the region in the past. The resurgence of Islam means that many of the architectural relics of the bygone era in these countries require that women visitors be clad modestly in either a longish skirt or dress or long pants.

The combination of ethnic diversity and Middle Eastern traditions makes this one of the most culturally vibrant regions in what used to be the Soviet Union. Women dress in colorful dresses covering equally bright trousers. Men in the various republics have distinctive headwear, such as the intricately embroidered square skullcap worn by the Uzbeki men. The veil found in some Islamic countries is rarely seen in this region, but many women cover their hair with scarves.

The people are very friendly and willing to assist tourists, whom they treat with respect. The foods are among the best in the former Soviet Union, relying heavily on the use of mutton, spiced vegetables, and rice. Fruit and vegetables are a regional specialty, as well as delicious flatbread, shish kabob, soups with meat, onion, chilies and noodles, and a variety of rice dishes such as rice pilaf using meat, vegetables, or fruit. Green tea is the common beverage because of the Islamic prohibitions on alcohol. Remember that this is an Islamic country, and while seventy years of Soviet rule have decreased the intensity of many people's commitment to their beliefs, the use of the right hand in touching or passing food is still essential as you have no way of knowing the degree to which the people with whom you associate are committed Muslims.

stan in combination only received 1.1 percent of tourists. The greatest attraction for tourists to this area, the Islamic and Middle Eastern flavor of the society, was not an important draw during the Soviet

Country	Capital	Language	Currency	Sq. Mi. and State Comparison Size
Kyrgyzstan	Bishkek (Frunze)	Kyrgyz (Kirghiz)	Som	76,641 (South Dakota)
Tajikistan	Dushanbe	Tajik	Ruble	55,251 (Wisconsin)
Turkmenistan	Ashgabat (Ash-khabad)	Turkmen (72%)	Ruble	188,456 (California)
Uzbekistan	Tashkent	Uzbek (85%)	Ruble	172,472 (California)
Kazakhstan	Almaty (Alma-Ata)	Qazaq (Kazakh)	Ruble	1,049,156 (four times Texas)

Country Profiles

era. The architecture dating from the earlier ruling period is magnificent, but the distance and difficulty of traveling to this area during the Soviet era kept visitors to a low number.

Since 1991, the number of visitors to these new countries has apparently fallen even further. Political instability and ethnic conflict have plagued some of these new countries, and the breakup of the old tourist monopoly on travel has further disrupted tourist flows. Economic uncertainties combine with increasingly unreliable air transport to further frighten potential visitors. Estimates vary, but tourism from Western Europe and Russia is generally less than one-fourth pre-1991 levels. While there are now more visitors from Asia and the Middle East, especially business related, tourism is far below previous levels.

There are tremendous opportunities for tourism in this region, but at the present time it is effectively disrupted. It is doubtful whether it will see a resurgence in the near future.

Tourist Destinations and Attractions

The two major general destinations for tourists to this region are the capital cities of each country and the famed cities of Samarkand and Bukhara, which were part of the ancient Silk Road and were the capitals of various historic kingdoms in this region. Each of the capitals has lovely architectural relics from the golden age of the empires in this region. Typically associated with mosques or madrassas, they are often characterized by their lovely blue or green glazed tiles, Figure 10–14. Many of the capital cities also have museums that illustrate the ethnic background of the people and their arts, particularly in weaving and carved wood, or provide access to native crafts. Every city has a marvelous bazaar or market, Figure 10–15.

The main tourist attraction in this region, however, are the cities of Uzbekistan associated with the famed Silk Road and the kingdom of Timur (Tamerlane). Samarkand and Bukhara have some of the most spectacular architecture anywhere in the world. The cities were key stops on the famed Silk Road, and Samarkand was the capital of Timur's empire and contains some of his greatest structures. Bukhara was the capital of a later empire and is a virtual outdoor museum.

Samarkand is the principal attraction in all of Central Asia. Even from the air its beautiful mosques and minarets are visible. The most famous attraction is the Registan, which is a group of large madrassas.

Figure 10–14 Mosque and Madrassa at the Registan in Samarkand

Covered with brilliant blue mosaics, it was once Samarkand's medieval commercial center and market. Other sites are too numerous to mention, but include the gigantic Bibi-Khanym mosque on the northeast of the Registan. Nearby is the Shakh-i-Zinda, a street of tombs, apparently the burial site for the wives, daughters, and other favored family members belonging to Timur and his son and grandson. This has recently been restored to local Islamic control, and a tiny fee is charged, but it provides a good opportunity to see how the wealthy provided for their dead a millenium ago in a Muslim state.

Bukhara is very different from Samarkand. It is a low city built on the edge of the desert, and its brown appearance is deceptive. Much of the center has been preserved to maintain its architecture, and the streets are lined with ancient madrassas and old bazaars. Historically the center of Bukhara was a large marketplace with specialists trading their wares in the traditional Islamic city fashion. The buildings have been largely protected and preserved, and visiting is

Figure 10–15 Market in Uzbekistan

one of the truly amazing tourist experiences left in the world. Bukhara was the capital of Central Asia's empire before Timur and by the tenth century was its religious and cultural heart, known as the Pillar of Islam. It was a second capital of a sixteenth-century empire and owes much of its appearance to that period. The central bazaar is one of the most fascinating in all the Islam world, and it has a wide variety of minarets, mosques, and madrassas to fascinate the visitor. Bukhara is one of 100 cities recognized by UNESCO as part of a world architectural heritage. Visitors are well repaid for the distance, heat, and poor accommodations found there.

New hotels built by Indian interests were opened in Samarkand and Bukhara in the mid-1990s, and they will make the experience of visiting these famed Silk Road cities even more enjoyable. Because of the summer heat, the best times to visit are April through May, and September to November.

Tashkent is Central Asia's biggest and most European city and was fourth in size after Moscow, St. Petersburg, and Kyyiv in the former Soviet Union. A transportation hub, it is primarily a city built during the Soviet era. A major earthquake destroyed most of the old town, but there are a few sites including the Kukeldash Madrassa that are of interest. Tashkent

Figure 10–16 Islamic Men

has a huge market north of this madrassa where visitors can experience the daily life of the local people.

There are a variety of other attractions in these new countries, but tourism continues to decline because of the problems associated with the changing political and economic picture, Figure 10–16.

RUSSIA: A FIRST VISIT

DAY 1 UNITED STATES–HELSINKI

Depart the United States for Helsinki.

DAY 2 HELSINKI

Arrive in Helsinki in the morning. Afternoon free to adjust to time change and jet lag.

DAY 3 HELSINKI–ST. PETERSBURG

Morning tour includes the Cathedral, the Market Square at the harbors, and the old romantic houses of Eira. Also visit the Senate Square, Sibeiius Park and Monument, and the Taivallahti Church, which is built into solid rock. Leave Helsinki at 12:00 N by train. Arrive Leningrad at 8:05 P.M.

DAY 4 ST. PETERSBURG

The morning city tour of St. Petersburg includes the Nevskv Prospect thoroughfare, which is lined with palaces, churches, and museums; the Neva River embankment; winding canals; Admiralty Building; Pushkin Drama Theater; Catherine I Monument; St. Isaac's Cathedral; the equestrian statue of Peter the Great; and the Fortress of Peter and Paul. The afternoon sightseeing of the city features the world-renowned Hermitage Museum with more than two million exhibits in its six buildings. Housed here is the priceless collection of art and other treasures amassed by the Russian rulers from history's beginning. Also see one of the Hermitage's buildings and the Czar's Winter Palace with its lavish apartments and Halls of State.

DAY 5 ST. PETERSBURG–MOSCOW

The morning is free. Afternoon sightseeing of beautiful points of interest. Depart in the evening at 11:00 P.M. by train for Moscow.

DAY 6 MOSCOW

End on Tverskaya (formerly Gorky). Start near the Kremlin where you can visits shops and stores. The afternoon will be free.

DAY 7 MOSCOW

The day will be spent touring the historical monuments of Moscow and the Kremlin. This will include the Bolshoi Theater, Red Square, Lenin Mausoleum, St. Basil, GUM, skyscrapers, Orushezhnaya Palace, and the government building known as the "White House."

DAY 8 MOSCOW–HELSINKI

After a leisurely morning in Moscow we will fly to Helsinki for an evening of relaxation and overnight stay before tomorrow's flight home.

REVIEW QUESTIONS

1. How many countries comprise the former USSR? What are their names?
2. What is the difference between European Russia and Asiatic Russia? How does tourism differ in the two areas?
3. Identify and describe the five major features of the physical geography of Russia.
4. What are the five factors that control the climate of the former Soviet Union?
5. Describe how climate effects tourism to the former Soviet Union.
6. What are some reasons the number of international tourists to Russia has fluctuated so widely in the past twenty to thirty years?
7. What changes have occurred in tourism in this region since it broke up into independent countries?
8. Describe the major tourist destinations in the countries created from the former Soviet Union. How do you explain the dominance of the most important destinations?

GEOGRAPHY AND TOURISM IN
The Middle East and North Africa

CHAPTER 11

MAJOR GEOGRAPHIC CHARACTERISTICS

- The Islamic religion dominates the entire region.
- The region is the hearth of early civilization and three major religions: Christianity, Islam, and Judaism.
- Population concentrations reflect water availability.
- The region is one of the driest areas of the world, but is strategically important, especially for oil.
- Political and social conflict in the region affects the region and the world.

MAJOR TOURISM CHARACTERISTICS

- Pilgrimages associated with Christianity, Judaism, and Islam are important to tourism.
- International tourism is concentrated in a few countries of the region.
- With their distinctive landscapes, the cities of the region attract regional and international tourists.
- Travel within the region is often difficult.
- Historical and archaeological sites of ancient cultures are major tourist attractions.

MAJOR TOURIST DESTINATIONS

Islamic capitals
Petra and Jerash (Jordan)
Jerusalem
Holy Land sites
Cairo, the Great Pyramids, and the Sphinx (Egypt)
Luxor, Egypt
Abu Simbel (Egypt)
Istanbul (Turkey)
Ismir
Central Anatolia
Damascus
Tunis and Coastal resorts (Tunisia)
Algiers
Casablanca, Tangier, and Marrakesh (Morocco)

KEY TERMS AND WORDS

Arabian Plateau	Islamic World
Ashkenazim	Jewish
Baksheesh	Koran
Bazaar	Lake Kinnereth
Bedouin	Lifestyle
Caliph	Medina
Casbah	Mediterranean
Christian	Middle East
Coptic	Mosque
Cultural Hearth	Muslim
Desert	Nile
Desert Pavement	Oasis
Druze	Pilgrimages
Friday Mosque	Riverine Basins
Greco-Roman	Sahara Desert
Islam	Sephardim
Islamic	Shiite
Islamic Cities	Souk (Suq)
Islamic Fundamentalist	Steppe
Islamic Law	Sunni

INTRODUCTION

Tourism to the Middle East and North Africa increased slowly in the last decade. In the 1990s, visitors to North Africa and the Middle East represented only about 3.3 percent of total global international arrivals, but North Africa alone accounts for nearly 45 percent of all tourism to the entire continent of Africa. Tourism is very important to specific areas and countries of the Middle East, but specific destinations have changed in the last few decades as a result of political problems in the Middle East and North Africa. Lebanon, Iran, and Iraq, for instance, have declined as tourist centers because of the conflict in their countries.

The region is dominated by the *Islamic* religion. (Islam refers to the religion; a *Muslim* is a believer in Islam.) Most countries (other than Israel, Iran, and Turkey) are part of the Arab realm. Most of the Arab countries in the region have joined an Arab Tourism Union (ATU) to promote and develop local tourism.

The chief emphasis has been on developing a Pan-Arab integrated tourism market, with hopes for increasing the flow of tourism traffic between the Arab nations. To date they have met with little success in developing a Pan-Arab integrated tourism market. In some of these countries, European and American tourists are not encouraged and are often faced with restrictions that curtail movement and curiosity. There has been a wave of anti-Western sentiment accompanied by a movement to revive Islamic traditions in countries such as Iraq, Libya, Algeria, and Iran. In addition, there have been *Islamic fundamentalist* movements in Tunisia and Egypt, creating concern among potential visitors. Some of the wealthier countries that export petroleum, such as Saudi Arabia, Bahrain, and Dhubai, are not interested in Western tourists, because they do not need the income from tourism. Dhubai has a large duty-free airport and acts as a hub for travel through the region and eastern Africa, but these Arab states are concerned that tourism will affect their population's

POPULATION CHARACTERISTICS, 1997						
Country	Population (millions)	Annual Growth Rate (percent)	Time To Double Pop. (years)	Per Capita GNP	Life Expectancy (years)	Percent Urban
MIDDLE EAST						
Afghanistan	22.1	2.8	25	N/A	43	18
Bahrain	0.6	2.0	35	7,840	72	88
Cyprus	0.7	0.8	90	N/A	78	53
Gaza	1.0	4.6	15	N/A	72	94
Iran	67.5	2.7	26	N/A	67	58
Iraq	21.2	2.8	25	N/A	59	70
Israel	5.8	1.5	47	15,920	77	90
Jordan	4.4	3.3	21	1,510	68	78
Kuwait	1.8	2.2	32	17,390	75	96
Lebanon	3.9	2.2	32	2,660	70	87
Oman	2.3	3.4	20	4,820	71	72
Qatar	0.6	1.7	41	11,600	73	91
Saudi Arabia	19.5	3.1	23	7,040	70	80
Syria	15.0	2.8	25	1,120	67	51
Turkey	63.7	1.6	43	2,780	68	63
United Arab Emirates	2.3	1.8	38	17,400	74	82
West Bank	1.7	3.4	21	N/A	72	N/A
Yemen	15.2	3.5	20	260	59	25
NORTH AFRICA						
Algeria	29.8	2.4	29	1,600	67	50
Egypt	64.8	2.1	34	790	64	44
Libya	5.6	3.6	19	N/A	63	85
Morocco	28.2	2.0	35	1,110	68	51
Tunisia	9.3	1.9	36	1,820	68	58

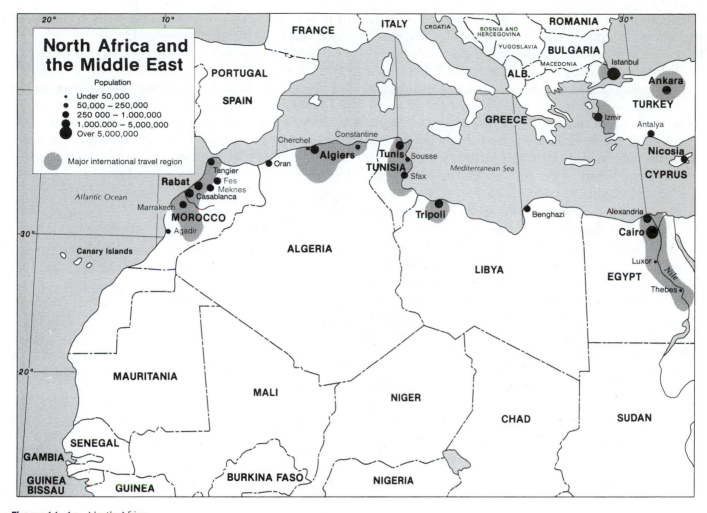

Figure 11–1a North Africa

attitudes toward alcohol and lead to adoption of Western dress, behavior, and values, which they feel are decadent.

The importance of Islam to this region makes it possible to identify specific tourist types in the *Islamic World*. The first characteristic is attraction to cities. Muslims enjoy visiting the cities of their region and the world for both *pilgrimages* and business purposes. The traditional *Islamic cities* offer attractions, such as the *mosques* where daily prayers are to be offered, the baths, and the *bazaars*. The business capitals of the Islamic world such as Damascus, Syria; Beirut, Lebanon; and Cairo, Egypt, are the centers of trade and commerce carried out under *Islamic law*. Muslims also visit cities for burial pilgrimages. It is the desire of many Muslims to be buried in a sacred place. Holy pilgrimages to Mecca in Saudi Arabia or the Dome of the Rock in Jerusalem involve several million Muslim visitors a year. Residents of the region are attracted to water because of its coolness and the rest it offers to desert-tired eyes. Muslims are not

attracted to the sandy beach as are Western tourists, but visit for the water itself. Tourists in this area also make summer visits to the mountains in search of relief from the heat of the cities. A final form of tourism within the region is family-related tourism. Family members visit relatives abroad or return home from foreign residences (Ritter, 1975).

GEOGRAPHIC CHARACTERISTICS

The Middle East and North Africa, Figure 11–1, is a widely misunderstood region. In much of the Western world the term the *Middle East* evokes images of oil-rich sheiks, conflicts between Arab and Arab or Arab and Israeli, terrorist groups, and nomadic *Bedouins* crossing the Sahara desert in camel caravans. Popular stereotypes of the region are misleading, and even efforts to define the region have problems of agreement. Most of the area is dry, with precipitation totals under twenty inches per year and in many places less than ten inches per year. Culturally, North

Africa and the Middle East are considered a single region by geographers and many others because of the influence of the Islamic religion. The Middle East is the hearth of the *Islamic* religion. At least 80 percent of the people of the region, including North Africa, are Muslim. Areas suitable for human occupancy are widely scattered, and most of the lands of North Africa and the Middle East have high population densities only in more favorable sites associated with water. Thus for most of the region, the population density of individual countries is low.

Population is concentrated in riverine or *oasis* locations, and the vast majority of the people have little to do with nomadism, camels, or the *Sahara Desert*. The view of the region as the home of wealthy Arab sheiks engaging in conspicuous consumption from their oil wealth is equally erroneous. Not only is the oil wealth concentrated in only a few countries, but within them a significant portion of that wealth is being channeled into development efforts to benefit a broader segment of the population. Even the aridity of the area is modified by elevation and increased precipitation in the highlands. The idea that the Sahara is entirely sand is another error, since most

of it is covered by a rocky gravel surface known as *desert pavement* rather than sand.

The importance of the region to the world centers on its vast reserves of oil and oil-related wealth; its role as *cultural hearth* for the world's major religions of Judaism, Christianity, and Islam; the importance of the area historically as a cradle of civilization; and its present strategic location and repeated conflicts that threaten to draw other regions of the world into global war.

Landform Characteristics

The landforms of the Middle East and North Africa, Figure 11–2, influence the local climatic conditions and affect the availability of the lifeblood of the region—water. There are three general landform regions:

1. The generally level terrain associated with deserts in North Africa, and the plateaus of Arabia, Iran, and Turkey.
2. The mountain ranges in northwest Africa (the Atlas), and those surrounding the plateaus of

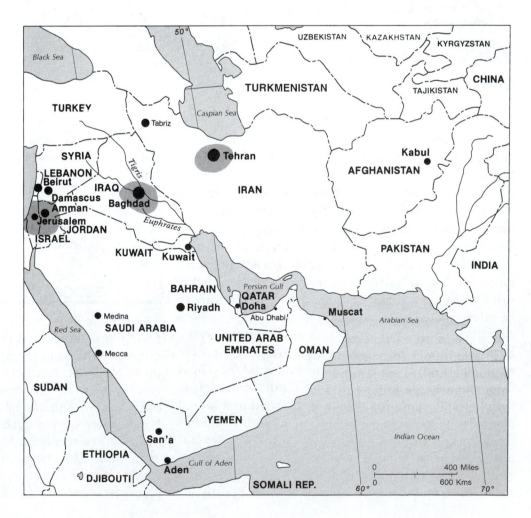

Figure 11–1b Middle East

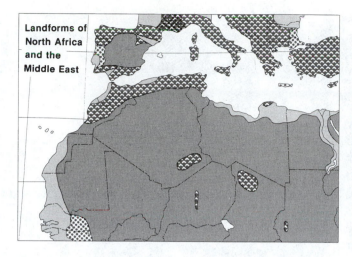
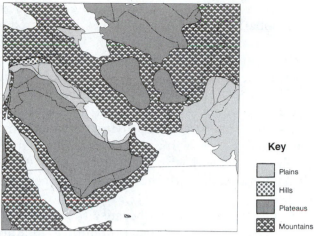

Key

☐ Plains
▦ Hills
▨ Plateaus
▩ Mountains

Figure 11–2 Landforms of North Africa and the Middle East

Iran and Turkey (Zagros and Taurus), and on the west of the *Arabian Plateau*.

3. The *riverine basins* of the Nile, Euphrates, Tigris, and smaller streams.

Critical differences exist between these regions based on the presence or absence of water. Population is concentrated along the rivers, in the highlands, or near highlands where moisture is available. The mountains of North Africa and the Middle East are the primary geographical factor affecting the distribution of water and, consequently, the population. In northwest Africa, the Atlas Mountains provide an orographic barrier, and the water from the mountains is the lifeblood of the agricultural areas of this region. The *Nile*, one of the most important rivers in the world, starts south of the North African region in mountains that provide it with water. The Nile River valley is home to over 60 million people, and over 90 percent of Egypt's population lives along the river. The Nile provides water for irrigation, for drinking, for transportation (including for tourism), for the fishing industry, and for the hydroelectricity upon which industry is based. In addition to providing water and electricity, the High Aswan Dam on the Nile, which was completed in the early 1970s, is a tourist attraction.

In Afghanistan, Iran, Pakistan, and Turkey, the Taurus, Zagros, and other mountain ranges reach elevations of over 18,000 feet. These mountains are the source of streams and rivers that provide water for a host of small rivers and for the Tigris and Euphrates Rivers as well. The Tigris and Euphrates were the early cradle of civilization, and Iran (Persia) and Iraq (Mesopotamia) have been battling over Shatt-al-Arab, the mouth of these important water-ways, since the seventeenth century. Like the Nile, the Tigris, the Euphrates, and smaller streams such as the Jordan River provide life to the arid regions through which they flow.

CLIMATE CHARACTERISTICS

The Middle East and North Africa are not as arid as commonly assumed, but in general, the region does have a dry climate. The predominant climatic type is desert or steppe, with precipitation totals of ten inches or less per year. The driest portions are the Sahara and the great deserts of the Arabian Peninsula.

Important areas of Morocco, Algeria, Tunisia, Turkey, Syria, Israel, and Jordan have *Mediterranean* climates. Precipitation totals of fifteen to thirty-five inches make farming more profitable in these areas, particularly fall-planted crops such as barley and wheat, which utilize the winter rainfall.

The temperatures of the Middle East and North Africa are almost uniformly high during the summer months. The highest average daily temperatures during the summer nearly always exceed 80 degrees Fahrenheit and in Libya and Egypt and the lowlands of the Persian Gulf often exceed 100 degrees Farenheit.

ORGANIZATION OF LIFE

Of interest to tourism is the organization of life in the region. There are three distinctive *lifestyles*: city, village, and nomadic. For tourists and residents, the cityscape is dominated by narrow streets, the mosque, and the bazaar. The mosque is the focal point of the city and its neighborhoods, for Muhammad revealed that the faithful Muslim must bow in prayer five times daily while facing Mecca. Fridays are the sabbath, and the great mosques are referred to as *Friday Mosques*. Each section of the bazaar specializes in one category of goods, making shopping easier than the maze of winding narrow passageways might suggest to the uninitiated visitor. Closest to the mosque are the merchants selling articles necessary for worship, then those skilled artisans working with silver or gold. Farthest from the mosque are textiles and goods associated with food preparation, which are least compatible with the worship service of the mosque.

Streets remained narrow because the *Koran* (the words of Allah to the prophet Muhammad) did not provide for public space greater than that needed for a laden camel to pass. The construction of buildings in the Islamic city provides the individual with security and privacy. Islamic architecture is interior-oriented rather than exterior-oriented, with a central court bounded by the rooms of the home and no windows in the exterior walls. Each quarter of the city was set apart for different groups, separated by walls and strong gates for protection.

Early Islamic cities became great learning centers where scholars were responsible for many scientific advancements. Today, these large cities, such as Baghdad, Amman, and Cairo, are the homes of both the very wealthy and the very poor. Contrasts between the rich and poor abound in city life. Problems of sanitation, water supply, unsafe housing, and access to adequate food contribute to a low standard of living among the urban poor. Cairo's sewage and water system, for example, was built to serve three million people, and today its population is in excess of eleven million people. In spite of the dichotomy between rich and poor, the Islamic city is a magnet to tourists and a haven to its residents. The myriad architectural attractions, fascinating street scenes, and tantalizing glimpses into the Islamic lifestyle make the great Islamic cities a unique tourist attraction.

The second lifestyle (which tourists generally only glimpse) is found in the villages. The villagers focus on agriculture—wheat, dates, barley, and other small grains and vegetables for local and national consumption. The location of villages depends upon water. The villages are composed of houses of various sizes and amenities depending upon social and economic level, the mosque, the market or bazaar (Figure 11–3), and the fields surrounding the village. The village lifestyle is more traditional than the lifestyle in the cities. The pace of life reflects centuries of evolution of a social and political milieu that pro-

Figure 11–3   Arab Market

vided for the needs of each village member. The contrast with the city is apparent to even a casual visitor. For the tourist who has braved the traffic-congested streets of a city, such as Cairo, the villages in the region offer an opportunity to pause and reflect on the relative progress brought by the industrial revolution. Nearly one-half of the people of this region live in villages, and even city residents return frequently to family homes in the village.

The third major lifestyle is found among the nomads. The nomads account for only 5 to 10 percent of the population of the region, and national boundaries and politics are pressuring them to become sedentary. The nomads use a part of the environment not used by villagers, herding their animals throughout the region. They provide meat, cheese, leather products, and animals for the village and city dwellers. It has become increasingly popular with tourists to visit a Bedouin tent, Figure 11–4. They observe and learn of the lifestyle of the nomad and feel the trip to the region is more complete having had such fleeting contact with the local peoples.

TOURISM IN THE MIDDLE EAST

World attention is focused upon this region of the world both because of the political situation and its

Table 11–1 International Tourism to the Middle East

Country	Number of Visitors (thousands)		1996 Receipts (millions of US $)	1996 Average Expenses per Visit
	1986	1996		
Afghanistan	N/A	10	2	200
Bahrain	96	2,669	300	112
Egypt	1,311	3,675	3,200	871
Iraq	1,004	345	13	38
Israel	1,101	2,097	2,800	1,335
Jordan	1,912	1,103	700	635
Kuwait	84	75	109	1,453
Oman	88	435	99	228
Qatar	98	263	N/A	N/A
Saudi Arabia	857	3,454	1,308	379
Syria	618	888	1,478	1,664
Turkey	2,079	7,966	6,000	753
Yemen	52	75	39	520

Source: Yearbook of Tourism Statistics, World Tourism Organization, 1997.

potential. The political situation has changed the tourist map of the region. Lebanon's ongoing civil war has destroyed its formerly important tourist industry. The continuing stress between Iran and Iraq, Iraq and Kuwait, the Gulf War, the Israeli-Arab dispute, the rise of Islamic fundamentalism, and difficulties between the moderate and radical Arab states combine to inhibit tourism in many areas of the region. Government decrees against Western lifestyles (as in Iran) and prohibition of Western tourists in Saudi Arabia and Yemen limit tourist activity. In spite of this, the historical importance of the region as a cradle of Western civilization continues to attract visitors, Table 11–1.

The major tourist countries of the Middle East today are Egypt, Israel, and Turkey. Syria's tourism has dropped significantly in the past five years. However, historically other countries of the region, such as Jordan, Lebanon, Syria, Iraq, and Iran, have been major international tourist centers. If the political situation were to stabilize they could conceivably become important again. Jordan's tourism was hurt by the Gulf War of 1990-1991. However, in 1995 Jordan and Israel signed an accord opening their borders. Access to Israel's markets and tourists will increase tourism to Jordan. Libya's current government would be a major handicap to tourism from the United States even if the region were more politically stable. The region continues to be plagued by war, terrorism, and religious fanaticism. In recent publications, the World Tourism Organization does not even include Lebanon because tourism as we know it today is virtually nonexistent there. The Arab states of the Persian Gulf issue visas only for visitors there on business, travelers in transit, or (in the case of Saudi Arabia) for Muslims on pilgrimage to the holy sites of Islam.

Figure 11–4 Bedouin Tent, Middle East and North Africa

Egypt

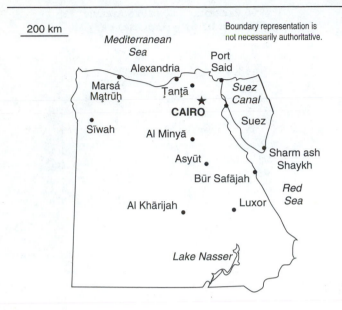

200 km

Boundary representation is not necessarily authoritative.

Mediterranean Sea

Port Said
Alexandria
Marsá Maţrūh   Ţanţā   *Suez Canal*
★ CAIRO   Suez
Sīwah   Al Minyā
Asyūt   Sharm ash Shaykh
Būr Safājah   *Red Sea*
Al Khārijah   Luxor
Lake Nasser

Capital: Cairo
Government: Republic
Size: 386,650 square miles (slightly smaller than Texas, Oklahoma, and Arkansas combined)
Language: Arabic, English, French
Ethnic Division: Egyptian, Bedouin, Arab, Nubian
Religion: 94% Sunni Muslim, 6% Coptic Christian
Tourist Season: Year-round
Peak Tourist Season: No significant tourist peak
Currency: Egyptian pound

CULTURAL CAPSULE

Egypt is the most populous country in the Arab world and the second most populous on the African continent. The Egyptians are homogeneous (90 percent), with Mediterranean (Egyptians) and Arab influences in the North. There are some Nubians of northern Sudan in the South and minorities of Bedouin, Greeks, Italians, and Syro-Lebanese. Arabic is the official language in Egypt with English and French used in business and education. Over 90 percent of all Egyptians belong to the *Sunni* sect of Islam. There is a fairly large number of *Coptic Christians* (over five million).

Cultural Hints:
- A warm, friendly handshake is a common greeting.
- Men only shake hands with a woman if she extends her hand.
- Personal space between men is very close.
- The right hand only is used for eating.
- Do not offer the left hand or offer food with the left hand.
- Do not show or point sole of foot to another person.
- Pointing at a person is impolite.
- Tipping (*Baksheesh*) is important for personal services. Carry a lot of small change.
- Eating and foods:
  Eat finger food only with the right hand.
  It is considered impolite to eat everything on your plate.
  Tips should be provided for all.
  Typical foods include rice, bread, fish, lamb, chicken, turkey, tomatoes, yogurt, cucumbers, and stuffed vegetables.

TRAVEL TIPS

Entry: Visas and passport are required. If arriving by air, tourists can obtain visas at the airport. It is best to obtain visas prior to travel. Arrival and departure taxes are collected. Currency exchange requirements exist.

Transportation: International flights from North America via western Europe connect Cairo with North America. Overland buses travel between Israel and Egypt. There is good domestic air service from Cairo to major cities. Rail service along the Nile connects Cairo to major tourist centers at Alexandria, Luxor, and Aswan. Public transportation in Cairo is best by taxi.

Health: Concern should be taken for yellow fever, malaria, and cholera. Typhoid, tetanus, polio, meningitis, and hepatitis immunizations are recommended by the State Department. Care should be taken not to drink tap water and eat fruits and vegetables that can be peeled.

Shopping: Common items include cotton and linen, gold and silver jewelry, local crafts such as copperware, wood carvings, leather goods, Nubian basketwork, and camel saddles. A cartouche with the visitor's name is also a popular souvenir.

Physical Characteristics

Egypt is a desert country bisected by the Nile Valley and its delta. The climate is hot and dry in the summers and winters are moderate.

Tourism Characteristics

Egypt has serious economic problems resulting from the sharp drop in oil prices in the last few years, resulting in fewer Egyptians working abroad in other oil-producing countries, and from the decline in tourism caused by a fear of terrorism and political conditions resulting from the rise of Islamic fundamentalism in the Middle East. In the 1990s, there have been a number of attacks on tourists by such groups in Egypt. Certain areas in Egypt should not be visited, but most of the major tourist attractions have had few problems. The country's tourism is further constrained because of the high cost of travel from the main tourist-generating countries of the United States and western Europe.

Egypt's moderate stance toward Israel has created a shift in its tourist market. Egypt has had a history of tolerance between its religious factions of Muslims and Coptic Christians. The bulk of Egypt's tourists in 1975 were from other Arab countries, accounting for 62 percent of the accommodation nights recorded. This dropped considerably following Egypt's treaty with Israel in 1978. However, the increased ease of travel between Egypt, Jordan, and Israel and the increased emphasis on tourism arrivals caused Egypt to experience rapid growth from 1978 to 1985. Arabs represent about 32 percent of the market today, with Sudan and Saudi Arabia the two dominant market countries in the region. Arrivals from western Europe (led by Germany and the United Kingdom) accounted for over 55 percent of the arrivals. There were about 136,000 visitors from the United States in 1996. This shift from a regional to a worldwide emphasis has reduced the length of stay. In the 1950s, the length of stay was for almost one month. Today it is approximately six days. A visit to the pyramids and either a cruise up the Nile River or a quick trip to Luxor or the Aswan Dam can be completed easily in a week or less. Arab visitors still stay longer than do those from industrialized countries, however. Most of the visitors from the industrialized countries include Egypt in a two-or-three country visit as part of a regional visit. Egypt is working with Jordan to create a two-center visit that is attractive to Arab visitors.

Tourism demand is year-round, with Arab visitors preferring the summer, the Europeans and North Americans preferring the winter, and the central Europeans and Russians preferring the spring and autumn (*International Tourism Reports*, 1991).

Tourist Destinations and Attractions

Four regions and the Nile cruises comprise Egypt's major attractions. Nile cruises between Luxor and the Aswan Dam, or Cairo to Luxor and then on the Aswan reservoir (Lake Nassar) are the most popular, especially for North American and West European visitors.

Three regions are more important than the fourth. They are Cairo and the surrounding area, Luxor, and Aswan. Cairo, Egypt's capital, is the political and cultural center of much of the Arab world, although it has lost some political leverage because of its treaty with Israel. In Cairo, the two major attractions are the Egyptian Museum (one of the world's great museums, featuring a collection of ancient artifacts, including mummies, art objects, the King Tut collection, and other historical relics) and the Khan Khalili

Bazaar (an enormous marketplace where visitors can purchase almost anything they desire, particularly a variety of gold and silver works, embroidered clothing, leather, and other handicrafts). In the old city there are a number of Christian churches and monuments illustrating the influence of the Coptic Christians. The city also offers the Arab culture and a host of mosques set in the landscape of a major Arab city.

Near Cairo, the famous Pyramids of Giza and the Sphinx, Figure 11–5, are a must for travelers. The most famous of the group is the Great Pyramid built by King Cheops (IV Dynasty) around 2650 B.C. It is composed of almost 2.5 million blocks of stone. Near the Pyramid of Cheops are three small pyramids dedicated to either his wives or family members. Pictures do not do justice to their impressive nature.

Also near Cairo are Memphis and Sakara. Memphis is the oldest capital of Egypt, built by King Menes. The statue of Ramses II is the most beautiful representation of him in Egypt. The Step Pyramid of King Zoser at Sakara near Cairo is the oldest stone building in the world, dating from before 2500 B.C. It lies on a desert plateau southwest of Cairo.

The second region is Luxor and the Valleys of the Kings and Queens upstream on the Nile. With the magnificent temples of Luxor and Karnak, Luxor (or Thebes as it was known in ancient time) was the summer palace of the Pharaohs. At Luxor is the famed Temple of Luxor. It was built by two pharaohs— Amenhotep III and Ramses II. The second temple at Luxor, Karnak, is one of the impressive archaeological sites in the Middle East and North Africa. A visit starts with a walk through the Avenue of the Rams, representing Amun, a symbol of fertility and growth. It has one of the best sound and light shows in the world. The temple was a major setting for the movie *Death on the Nile*. The Valley of the Dead, across the Nile from Luxor, is the ancient burial place for the historic leaders of Egypt, including King Tut. The

Figure 11–5 The Pyramids and Sphinx

tombs are multichamber works of art, and several, including those of Ramses VI, Serti, Armenophis, and King Tutankamen can be visited.

Further up the Nile near Aswan were the two funerary temples built by Ramses II for himself and his queen. They have been removed from an area now covered by Lake Nasser and have been restored at Abu Simbel on a height overlooking the lake.

The fourth important region is Alexandria and the surrounding area, which receives fewer visitors. Alexandria is a *Mediterranean* resort and port city that was founded by Alexander the Great and was an important post for the Romans. The Greco-Roman ruins today combine with the superb sand beaches along the coast to attract visitors to Alexandria.

Many Mediterranean cruise ships use Alexandria as a port of call.

Egypt has been developing holiday villages along the Mediterranean and Red Sea. The combination of dramatic mountain scenery and the clear blue waters of the Red Sea combine to provide a rich resource for tourism development in this area. With the traditional attractions of the Nile cruise and the archaeological ruins, Egypt feels its beach tourism has the potential to increase the number of visitors by providing a more diversified tourism destination. If political calm can be achieved in the region, Egypt's location and many attractions should assist the country in becoming an important tourist center.

Israel

Capital: Jerusalem
Government: Parliamentary democracy
Size: 7,850 square miles (about the same as New Jersey)
Language: Hebrew, Arabic, English
Ethnic Division: 82% Jewish, 18% minorities, mostly Arabic
Religion: Judaism, Islam, Christianity, Druze
Tourist Season: March through October
Peak Tourist Season: March through July and December
Currency: Israeli shekel (ILS)

 ## TRAVEL TIPS

Entry: Visas are issued on arrival for stays of less than 3 months. Passports are required. Travelers wishing to visit Arab countries should have their visas inserted on removable paper rather than placed into a passport. Some Arab countries will not admit visitors with the Israeli visa in their passport. Airport departure tax is collected. Visitors need proof of sufficient funds and return or onward transportation.

Transportation: International airlines connect Israel with regularly scheduled services to North America, Europe, and parts of Africa and Asia. Israel has a good nationwide bus service. Public transportation in cities is reasonable and provides good service.

Health: Tap water is potable and immunization is only required when coming from infected areas of the world.

Shopping: Common items include locally made sportswear, jewelry, beachwear, copper and glass, ceramics, leather, suede, carved olive wood, religious ornaments, and handicrafts.

CULTURAL CAPSULE

There are three broad *Jewish* groupings: the *Ashkenazim*, or Jews who came to Israel from Europe, North and South America, South Africa, and Australia; the *Sephardim*, who trace their origin to Spain and Portugal; and the *Eastern* or *Oriental* Jews, who descend from ancient communities in Islamic countries. The Ashkenazim have generally dominated religion and politics in Israel. The 4.47 million population includes about 200,000 Israeli settlers in the West Bank of Jordan occupied by Israel, the Gaza Strip, the Golan Heights, and East Jerusalem. Seventeen percent of Israel's citizens are Israeli Arabs and members of the Druze and Circassian ethnic groups. The remainder (83 percent) is Jewish. In the occupied West Bank and Gaza Strip are nearly 2 million Palestinian Arabs.

Hebrew is the official language of Israel. Arabic is taught in the public schools and is also an official language. English is understood widely and is used in commerce. In the West Bank and Gaza Strip the Palestinian Arabs speak Arabic. A large percentage also speak English or French. Of the Palestinian Arabs, about 92 percent are Muslims (mostly Sunni) while the rest are Christian (Greek Orthodox or Roman Catholic). Stores and shops in Israel, the West Bank, and Gaza Strip are closed on Friday, Saturday, or Sunday, depending upon the owner's religion.

Cultural Hints:
- A warm, friendly handshake is a common greeting.
- "Shalom" (peace) is a usual greeting in Israel.
- "Salaam alaikum" (Peace be upon you) is a usual greeting by Palestinians.
- Both Israelis and Palestinians have close personal space.
- Pointing at a person with the index finger is rude.
- Israelis understand most common hand signs.
- Men need to wear a skullcap (kipah) when visiting Jewish religious sites.
- In Palestinian areas it is impolite to point the bottom of the shoe at another person.
- In Palestinian areas it is impolite to pass objects or shake hands with the left hand.
- Eating and foods:
  There is a variety of food in the region because of the great cultural diversity. Some typical foods are falafel (pocket bread filled with beans, lamb, or chicken); stuffed grape leaves; spiced rice; kebab (meat and vegetables on a skewer); gefilte fish; vegetable salad, mixed with olive oil, lemon juice, and spices; and fruit and eggs. Israelis do not mix dairy products and meat during meals because of their religion; therefore, breakfasts will be meatless with lots of fruit, vegetables, and dairy products.

Table 11–2 World Jewish Population

Region	Jewish Population
Africa	300,000
Asia	3,900,000
Europe	1,500,000
Latin America	1,000,000
North America	7,900,000
Oceania	100,000
Eurasia	3,100,000
World	17,800,000

Source: The Universal Almanac, 1996.

Physical Characteristics

Israel is a combination of coastal plains, desert, and mountains. The climate is temperate, but hot and dry in the deserts.

Tourism Characteristics

Israel, the Holy Land of three religions—Islam, Christianity, and Judaism—is an important world tourist center. Tourism increased annually until terrorist events in 1985 and early 1986 and civil unrest in 1987–1988 resulted in a major decline. Tourism has leveled out at just over one million visitors a year. In 1996, foreign tourism was the largest export income source for Israel, totaling 2.8 billion dollars. The United States is the largest source area for international tourists to Israel, accounting for 400,000 visitors a year in the 1990s.

The government recognizes the importance of tourism and has assisted in the development of hotels and other segments of the tourist infrastructure. It has developed a central electronic reservation system for hotels and encouraged the development of more hotel rooms. It works actively to promote tourism and since 1986 has organized a vigorous campaign to regain previous visitor levels from the United States and Europe. In September 1992 Israel joined with Egypt, Greece, and Cyprus to promote travel from the United States to these four countries. Although Israel receives fewer total tourists than Egypt, Israel receives more from countries outside of the region. Its average length of stay of some 21 days is one of the highest in the world. This is due to the nature of the tourists. The United States is the leading source of tourists to Israel, accounting for 22.5 percent of the total, 75 percent of whom are American Jews. Table 11–2 illustrates potential markets for travel to Israel. Many have family ties and have a tendency to stay longer in the region. The Western European countries account for over 27 percent of total tourists to Israel, with Germany and France the leading contributors (World Tourism Organization, 1992). The importance of religion other than Judaism cannot be overlooked. Both Christian and Islamic faiths have important religious sites in Israel. In 1996, even a few pilgrims from Iraq and Libya visited holy sites in Jerusalem.

Tourism Destinations and Attractions

The principal attraction of Israel is religion, centering around the old city of Jerusalem and Bethlehem, with holy sites located throughout the country. Jerusalem, Figure 11–6, offers much of religious significance for all three major religions. The Dome of the Rock is second only to Mecca as a sacred site for Muslims. It is the spot where the Prophet Muhammad is reported to have ascended into Heaven. It is also the site of Solomon's temple. Near the Western Wall is the Wailing Wall, which is important to Jews. Jews call

Courtesy of the Israel Ministry of Tourism

Figure 11–6 Jerusalem: View of the Old City

the wall the *Kotel Ha'naaravu* (the Western Wall). The name "Wailing Wall" was applied to it as Jews came here to pray and bewail the destruction of the Temple, the Exile, and the hard fate of the Jewish people. Men and women pray at different sections of the Wall in accordance with Orthodox Jewish cus-

toms. Sites associated with Christ, such as Golgotha where Christ was crucified, the Garden of Gethsemane, the Via Dolorosa (the last path Christ walked), the room of the Last Supper, the Church of the Holy Sepulchre, and so on, attract Christians. Some areas of Jerusalem are closed to traffic on the Jewish Sabbath. Also, modern Jerusalem has a beautiful Israel Museum containing the Dead Sea Scrolls, the famous Chagall windows, and the Museum of the Holocaust. Old Jerusalem, surrounded by a wall, has Arab, Christian, and Jewish quarters and markets. It is only a short trip to Bethlehem to visit the site of Christ's birth and Rachel's tomb.

North of Jerusalem is the Sea of Galilee, which is called *Lake Kinnereth* by Israelis. Surrounding the sea are a number of holy sites, such as the Mount of Beatitudes and Capernaum, Figure 11–7. It is difficult to travel anywhere in Israel without coming in contact with sites of significant meaning for some segment of the three great religions. For example, the Dead Sea and Negev area, two other major centers of attraction, are associated with locations from Biblical times: Masada, the Dead Sea Scrolls, Beersheba, and Sodom. Masada is famous because of a long siege by

Figure 11–7 Temple at Capernaum

the Romans that ended in the deaths of all the Jewish defenders. Now Air Force pilots fly over from time to time to emphasize Masada's symbolic importance to Israel today.

The Dead Sea provides a unique experience of swimming and floating. Negev is also a resort and garden center for the region. Israel shares the Gulf of Aquaba with Jordan. Elat on the Gulf is a well-developed beach resort that provides some excellent water recreation in the clear water of the Gulf of Aquaba. Many Europeans are attracted to the modern cities of Haifa and Tel Aviv and the nearby coastal resorts. Near

Tel Aviv is the ancient city of Jaffa. The Israeli government and other private organizations are conducting excavation projects throughout the country. These areas are becoming important attractions for visitors.

The occupied territories of the West Bank and Gaza Strip are predominantly Arab and contain many of the region's religious sites. Continued unrest in the West Bank has created some problems for the traveler desiring to visit those sites. In 1993 an agreement was signed leading to self-rule in Gaza and Jericho. The impact of terrorism on tourism in the future remains to be seen.

Jordan

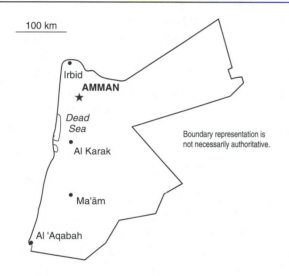

100 km

Boundary representation is not necessarily authoritative.

Capital: Amman
Official Name: Hashemite Kingdom of Jordan
Government: Constitutional monarchy
Size: 35,135 square miles (slightly smaller than Indiana)
Language: Arabic, English
Ethnic Division: Arab, with minorities of Circassians, Armenians, and Kurds
Religion: 92% Sunni Muslim, 8% Christian
Tourist Season: June through December
Peak Tourist Season: June through August
Currency: Jordan dinar (JOD)

TRAVEL TIPS

Entry: Visa is required and can be obtained on entry. Passports are required.
Transportation: Amman is serviced by a number of Middle Eastern and European airlines from North America, Europe, and Cairo. Road transportation between major cities is good. Within cities taxis are most used by tourists, although there is bus service.
Health: Avoid tap water, uncooked vegetables and unpasteurized milk products. Drink only boiled or bottled water.

Shopping: Common items include gold and silver jewelry and local crafts such as wood carvings, leather goods, Nubian basketwork, and camel saddles.

CULTURAL CAPSULE

Jordanians are Arabic. There are a few communities of Circassians, Armenians, and Kurds. The largest minority today is some 1.5 million Palestinian Arabs, which includes some 850,000 registered refugees. Most Palestinians living in Jordan are citizens. About one-fourth of the Arabs are of Bedouin descent; however, less than 5 percent are currently nomadic. Many of the Bedouins still live in tents. Arab is the official language of Jordan, but English is widely spoken among the educated. Approximately 90 percent of the population is Sunni Muslim. The Jordanians are good-natured, friendly, and hospitable. While appointments are important, Jordanians may be late as time is not as important in Jordan. Some Palestinians, although having Jordanian citizenship, consider themselves Palestinians first and support the establishment of a Palestinian homeland.

Cultural Hints:
- A warm, friendly handshake is a common greeting.
- "Salaam alaikum" (peace be with you) is also common.
- Avoid touching members of the opposite sex in mosques and on the street.
- Avoid excessive admiration of any object owned by hosts.
- It is an honor to be invited into a home.
- Excessive praise for children is considered bad luck.
- Do not offer the left hand or pass and accept objects with the left hand.
- Do not point sole of foot or shoe at another person.
- Good posture is important.
- Eating and foods:
  It is polite to leave small portions of food on your plate.
  Eat with the right hand, never the left.
  Refuse offers of additional food for at least two times, then accept on the third offer if you wish more.
  Coffee is important. If not wanted tip the cup back and forth.

Physical Characteristics

Jordan is a country of rocky deserts, mountains, and rolling plains. The dominant topographic feature is the great north-south Jordan Rift Valley, which is an extension of the African Rift Valley. The climate is Mediterranean with a rainy season from November to March.

Tourism Characteristics

Jordan has benefitted from the relative calm along its border with Israel over the past few years, but like Israel and Egypt it has been hurt by the political conflicts and border changes in the area. During 1991 the Gulf War reduced its tourism to almost zero. However, in 1992 and 1993 tourists began to return to Jordan. Jordan's tourism was crippled by the loss of the West Bank and Eastern Jerusalem to Israel following the 1967 war with Israel. Jordan benefits from tourists crossing the border into Israel. Jordan serves as a transit country for visitors to Israel due to some favorable airfares. Along with Israel and Egypt, Jordan is also part of a regional destination area. Jordan is bordered by Syria on the north, Iraq and Saudi Arabia on the east, Saudi Arabia on the south, and the occupied West Bank on the west. The transit nature of Jordan serves two markets: tourists going to Israel and Islamic pilgrims from countries such as Turkey who visit the holy places in Saudi Arabia by land. The major rail line between Turkey and Saudi Arabia traverses Jordan, making such linkages possible.

Eighty-five percent of visitors to Jordan are Arabic, and have far less economic impact on the country than the Western visitors to Israel do there. Low expenditures reflect the fact that relatively few of Jordan's visitors are true leisure travelers. The largest number of Arab visitors are Egyptians who are either working in Jordan or passing through Jordan on their way to or from Syria, Iraq, or the Gulf. The other two large Arab groups are from Syria and Saudi Arabia and contain few leisure tourists.

Tourist Destinations and Attractions

The major attractions of Jordan are archaeological relics, such as the city of Petra ("The Rose City"); desert castles; Kavak, a citadel built by the crusaders; Jerash, a preserved Roman Colonial city; Amman, the capital; Roman ruins; and the country's many museums. Petra, a Nabataean capital, is carved into solid rock. It is considered one of the wonders of the world. It can only be reached by walking or by riding donkeys or horses down a canyon, which is the more popular method. It even has a hotel at the bottom of the canyon. Jerash includes well-preserved examples of *Greco-Roman* architecture, including a Triumphal Arch, the Temple of Aratemis, the Street of Columns, and an amphitheater. Madaba, which dates back to the Middle Bronze Age (2000–1500 B.C.), is mentioned in the Bible as a Moabite town.

Amman has an archaeological museum that emphasizes the life of Nabataean Muslims and other artifacts of the region. Also, there is a fine Roman amphitheater cut out of a hillside in Amman. Jordan has a beach resort with excellent beaches at 'Aqaba at the head of the Gulf of 'Aqaba.

Lebanon

Capital: Beirut
Government: Republic
Size: 4,015 square miles (smaller than Connecticut)
Language: Arabic, French, Armenian, English
Ethnic Division: 95% Arab, 4% Armenian, 1% other
Religion: 70% Muslim and Druze, 30% Christian
Tourist Season: Year-round
Currency: Lebanese pound

CULTURAL CAPSULE

Nearly 93 percent of the population is Arabic, and about 7 percent are Armenians, who live mostly in Beirut. The major religious groups are Muslim and Christians. *Shiite* Muslims make up the single largest religious group. Many Christian sects are represented in Lebanon, including Maronite, Greek Orthodox, Greek Catholic, Armenian Apostolic, Roman Catholic and Protestant. The *Druze*, a group derived from Shiite Islam, constitute another significant minority. Arabic is the official language. French and English are widely understood. The Armenian minority also speak Armenian, and some speak Turkish.

Physical Characteristics

Lebanon consists of a coastal plain, a mountain range, the Bekaa Valley, and a mountainous region to the east. The climate is Mediterranean, mild to cool with wet winters and hot, dry summers.

Tourism Characteristics

Lebanon has been decimated by conflict in the last 10–20 years. At one time, it was a major destination and a financial center with outstanding connectivity, sometimes called the "Switzerland of the Middle East." It had very good accommodations and other tourist facilities. It is trying to rebuild its economy, and it is not recommended for travelers from the West.

Tourist Destinations and Attractions

Beirut, the capital, has good beaches and caves to explore from the sea. A day's trip from Beirut are the Biblical Cedars of Lebanon, from which the cedar for King Solomon's Temple came. South along the coast are the Biblical cities of Sidon and Tyre, which remain centers of conflict and unrest. Tripoli is an ancient Phoenician city. It has a crusader castle overlooking the city. As in other Middle Eastern cities, mosques are common throughout Lebanon.

Syria

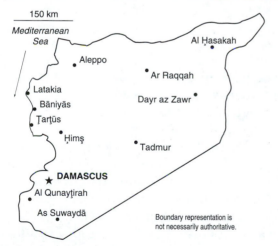

Boundary representation is not necessarily authoritative.

Capital: Damascus
Government: Republic
Size: 115,738 square miles (about the same as North Dakota)
Language: Arabic, Kurdish, Armenian, Aramaic, Circassian, French, and English
Ethnic Division: 90.3% Arab, 9.7% Kurds, Armenians, and other
Religion: 74% Sunni Muslim, 16% Alawite, Druze, and other Muslim sects
Tourist Season: July through December
Peak Tourist Season: July
Currency: Syrian pound (SYL)

CULTURAL CAPSULE

Syrians are of Semitic stock and about 90 percent of the population is Arab. Muslim (Sunnis) constitute the majority (74 percent). The Alawites represent about 16 percent, and Christians represent approximately 10 percent of the population. Arabic is the official language, and English and French are spoken by some of the educated.

Cultural Hints:
- A friendly handshake is a common greeting.
- Do not point at other people.
- Do not point the sole of the foot at another person.

- Items are passed with the right hand, never the left.
- Do not offer the left hand to another person.
- Eating and foods:
  Eat with the right hand.
  Syrians generally refuse an invitation for more food twice and accept the third offer.
  Alcohol and pork are taboo.
  Typical foods include chickpeas, eggplant, meats, breads, and beans.

Physical Characteristics

Syria is mostly desert with a narrow coastal plain and mountains in the west. The climate is characterized by hot and dry summers and a mild, rainy winter.

Tourism Characteristics

Although Syria officially encourages tourism and has a national tourist office to promote the development of an infrastructure, the current political problems have decreased the volume of tourism from Western nations. Its close ties to Iran provide Syria with oil, but result in few tourists from the West. Visitors from Europe and the United States have increased by one-third in the 1990s. The Islamic neighbors of Jordan, Lebanon, Turkey, and Iran provide the majority of visitors to Syria. Of the Arab states that promote tourism, Syria has the shortest length of stay, indicating a somewhat transit character to their tourist trade. Syria has little trade from the United States. However, if the political situation were to change, it would offer a number of attractions of interest to North Americans.

Tourist Destinations and Attractions

Syria has a number of interesting places to visit, such as the Arab citadel of Aleppo with its mosque and museum; the ruins of ancient Tadmor at Palmyra; desert palaces, such as the Krak des Chevaliers, one of the best-preserved Crusader castles in the Middle East; and the Convent of Saint Takla, the oldest convent in the world, where Aramaic is still spoken. The capital, Damascus, is an Arab city with a rich history. The House of Ananias, the Tomb of Saladin, St. Paul's Church, and the Street Straight in Damascus are all referred to in the Bible. *Souks* (marketplaces) full of copper inlays, brass, wood, and spices provide important handicraft items for the visitor. Roman ruins and a typical Arab bazaar are additional attractions.

Through Visitors' Eyes

Syria: A Showcase of Antiquities

by Eloise Larson

Archaeological Wonderland

In our opinion, Syria is second only to Egypt in abundant, diverse, and well-preserved archaeological sites of interest to the tourist.

Damascus, the world's oldest continuously inhabited city, has many historic places of interest: the covered sulks, massive Omayyed Mosque, the Mausoleum of Saladin, Al-Azem Palace, the Chapel of Ananias, and the remains of the Roman temple of Jupiter—as well as the new palace of President Assad.

Shops in the old Christian quarter delight the eye with local handicrafts and shimmering brocades of famous Damascene textiles. They sell for $75 per meter.

Palmyra lies northeast of Damascus across the stony Syrian Desert. For centuries this oasis of palm and olive groves sheltered camel caravans en route from the Persian Gulf and the Orient Silk Road to Aleppo and the Mediterranean world.

The ruins of this second-century-A.D. city have been extensively excavated and restored to reflect its former wealth and grandeur. Its ancient monuments, built in the Roman style, include the Great Colonnade, the huge temple of Baal, the Monumental Arch and the agora, theater and tetrapylon.

In the Valley of the Tombs to the west, five-story, stone-tower tombs dot the barren landscape. Like an ageless sentinel, a seventeenth-century medieval Arab fortress crests a lonely hilltop in the distance. As a unit, it was a setting of rare beauty under intense blue skies—a photographer's delight.

Syria's hundreds of tells cloak the remains of ancient cities that reached their zenith during Biblical times. Excavations at the tells of Mari, near the Iraqi border, and Ebla, south of Aleppo, brought to light the remains of third-millennium-B.C. city states.

continues

continued

Their palace libraries have yielded thousands of cuneiform tablets, greatly enriching scholarly knowledge of those early eras. Some of Ebla's tablets contained the world's earliest bilingual dictionary of Eblaite and Sumerian words. Examples of these clay tablets can be seen in Syria's excellent museums.

For my husband, Del, our visit to Ebla was the highlight of the entire tour. Beehive-shaped houses are disappearing in Syria, but we were fortunate to see some near Ebla. Plastered outside with brown mud, they resemble eggs sitting on end in a carton.

Ghost Cities

Greek lieutenants of Alexander the Great's army founded the walled cities of Doura Europus, Apamea, and Raqqa, introducing Hellenistic architecture to the Middle East. Now the partially uncovered ruins reflect additions by succeeding cultures, as well.

The martyriums at Rassafeh and Qalaat Simeon (Basilica of St. Simeon) were important pilgrimage sites for Christians around the fifth century A.D. during Byzantine times. The majestic ruins of St. Simeon's basilica surround a huge boulder, all that remains of the famous 50-foot pillar atop which St. Simeon lived and preached for 40 years.

The numerous dead Byzantine stone cities near Aleppo are relatively well preserved, but their decline started about 1,200 years ago with the coming of Islamic rule. Today the ruins are deserted save for Gypsies and their flocks of goats.

Aleppo

In Aleppo, our room in the Amir Palace Hotel overlooked the massive Citadel, which rests on top of a natural tell in the middle of the city. Built in the thirteenth century, this medieval fortress is the best remaining example of true Arab citadel architecture.

The city of Aleppo vies with Damascus in its ancient beginnings. The city's monotone earth color makes the brown, stone buildings look like square crystals rising from the surrounding soil. For centuries it was a major commercial center on the great camel caravan routes; at one time it had 18 miles of vaulted souks.

Today this labyrinth of narrow alleys, open stalls, former caravansaries, old mosques, etc., still covers about five acres. Shops are grouped according to the goods they sell and bargaining is expected.

Phoenician Legacy

Continuing west from Aleppo, we drove through the Orontes River valley. This is the most fertile valley in Syria, and little wonder, for erosion has denuded the hillsides and deposited the soil on the valley floor below. The city of Latakia, on the balmy Mediterranean coast, is surrounded by orchards of bananas, oranges, and lemons and fields of Latakia tobacco.

Nearby are the extensive excavations of the ancient Phoenician city of Ugarit. During its golden age, in about the sixteenth to thirteenth centuries B.C., it became an important center of trade and learning. Its royal palace, built of stone, was one of the most imposing and famous buildings in the Middle East, covering over 2½ acres.

In the palace library a clay tablet was found containing what is considered to be the world's first consonantal alphabet from which all of today's alphabets are derived.

Crusader Castles

Next we visited one of the most imposing medieval fortresses in Syria, Marqab Castle. Used by the Arabs and Crusaders, it rests atop a steep mountain, overlooking Syria's coastal region. Made of black basalt, it is dark and foreboding with a 360-degree view of the surrounding area.

Even more impressive was the Crak des Chevallers, mightiest of the Crusader castles and headquarters of the Hospitallers—the Knights of St. John. Crowning its hilltop summit like a huge stone dreadnought, it commanded a vital pass that linked inland Syria with the sea.

It is the world's best-preserved example of crusader architecture and contains a fascinating maze of vaulted rooms, corridors, intricate defense mechanisms, turrets with spiral staircases, courtyards, gates, moats, and parapets to explore.

Untapped Treasures

At Hama the view from our room was spellbinding; huge, centuries-old wooden waterwheels (novias) cast their perfect reflections in the still water of the Orontes River in ever-changing light—a sight we shall never forget. No longer used, they sit idle as electrical pumps irrigate the local gardens.

We found the old Byzantine church at Maaloula, with its pagan altar and beautiful icons, and the Seidnaya Monastery, built by Emperor Justinian, very interesting.

continues

continued

itnessing a Greek Orthodox baptism at Seidnaya provided an unexpected insight into the culture of Syria's Christians as well. The proud family had the ceremony videotaped for future reference.

Our travel adventure ended with a day trip to Bosra, near the Jordanian border, to see the best-preserved Roman amphitheater in existence. An Arab citadel built around the theater protected it for centuries.

W It is surprising to enter a fortress and find a freestanding open-air, 15,000-seat theater inside. The raised stage is backed by Corinthian columns and still is used for performances today.

Syria's treasures of antiquity seems without end. If it were situated elsewhere in the world, it would surely be a prime tourist attraction.

Source: International Travel News.
October 1992; pp. 43–46.

Turkey

400 km

Capital: Ankara
Government: Republican parliamentary democracy
Size: 487,863 square miles (about three times as large as California)
Language: Turkish, Kurdish, Arabic
Ethnic Division: 80% Turkish, 20% Kurd, 3% other
Religion: 98% Muslim (mostly Sunni), 2% other (Christian and Jewish)
Tourist Season: May through October
Peak Tourist Season: July through September
Currency: Turkish lira (TUL)

TRAVEL TIPS

Entry: Visa is not required for stays up to 3 months. Passports are required. Currency declaration is necessary for large amounts.
Transportation: International air carriers connect Istanbul, Ankara, Izmir, Antalya, and Dalaman to North America and Europe. Turkey has rail and intercity bus service to many points in Europe. Domestic air, rail, and road transportation are available. However, driving at night should be avoided because of many poorly lit vehicles on the roads.
Health: Bottled or boiled water should be used at all times. Fruits and vegetables should be cleaned and peeled before eating.
Shopping: Common items include jewelry, ornaments, copper, brass, silver, meerschaum pipes, daggers, ceramics and pottery, animal skins, rugs, and carpets.

CULTURAL CAPSULE

Nearly 80 percent of the population are Turks, with a sizeable minority of Kurds. Although 98 percent of the population is Muslim (Sunni), Turkey is officially secular. Turkish is the official language of the country. It is related to the Uralic-Altaic languages spoken in Asia. The Kurdish minority speaks Kurdish. English is somewhat popular, and in major cities many understand it.

The legendary Mustafa Kemal, a Turkish World War I hero later known as "Ataturk" or "father of the Turks," founded the republic of Turkey in 1923 after the collapse of the 600-year-old Ottoman Empire.

Cultural Hints:
- A handshake is a common greeting.
- Many Turks remove their shoes when entering a home.
- Showing the sole of your shoe or pointing is an insult.
- Do not eat or smoke on the street.
- It is an insult to pass an item with the left hand.
- The hand clenched in a fist with the thumb between the index and middle finger is a rude gesture.
- Do not cross your arms over your chest when talking with someone.
- Remove shoes when entering a Turkish mosque.
- Before taking pictures ask for permission.
- Eating and foods:
  Some restaurants include a service charge. If so, tip 5 percent. If not, tip 15 percent.
  Typical food includes seafood, Turkish coffee, tea, cheese, bread, soup, shish kebabs (chunks of lamb on a skewer), vegetables prepared in olive oil, rice, baklava (syrup-dipped pastry), and milk pudding.

Physical Characteristics

Turkey is mostly mountainous with a central plateau and a narrow coastal plain. The climate is hot and dry in the summers, with mild, wet winters. It is somewhat harsher in the interior.

Tourism Characteristics

Tourism has been an important element of Turkey's development plans. As such, the government has emphasized the development of the tourism industry, stressing the importance of income generated by tourists.

Turkey's location makes it a Mediterranean, Middle Eastern, and Balkan country. Its long (for the region) history of relative political stability encourages the growth of tourism. Tourism in Turkey tripled between 1986 and 1996. Germany, the United Kingdom, and the former USSR (mostly from the Muslim southern republics) are the leading generators of tourists to to Turkey, but the United States accounts for only a small percentage of the visitors. Cruises are an important element in the tourist industry, with approximately 25 percent of all arrivals coming by ship. Still, the average of 9.5 days per visitor is impressive, indicating Turkey is a destination country. Americans constitute the largest single source of visitors from cruise ships on day trips from Greek islands close to the Turkish coast.

Tourist Destinations and Attractions

Turkey's tourist regions can be divided into four areas. They are Istanbul and the Northwest, Izmir and the West, Central Anatolia, and the Black Sea and the East.

Istanbul and the Northwest. Istanbul's location on the Bosphorus has long been a geographical and cultural crossroads, and the cultural landscape expresses that interaction. Constantine's St. Sophia, the "Blue" mosque of Sultan Ahmet, Figure 11–8, the Suleymaniye mosque, and the city walls from the Byzantine era are but a fraction of the many mosques and minarets. The Topkapi Palace (the home of the Ottoman sultans) is well worth a visit. In addition, museums, palaces, and narrow streets crowded with shops and people bring to life the old history of Istanbul.

Throughout northwest Turkey, there are resorts on the Black Sea and other evidence of the history of the region with mosques, famous battle sites such as

Figure 11–8   Sultan Ahmet Blue Mosque, Istanbul, Turkey

Gallipoli, the Ottoman capital Bursa, and Greco-Roman ruins.

Izmir and the West. This area has one of the most-unspoiled and least-developed coastlines in the Mediterranean, with sandy bays, islands, and fishing ports. St. Paul preached in the area, and many sites he visited have become attractions. Greek and Roman ruins (including the birthplace of Herodotus); one of the original seven wonders of the ancient world, the great tomb of King Mausolus; rock fortresses; caravan routes; spectacular waterfalls; and assorted ruins dot the landscape in this region. At Ephesus, some 50 miles from Izmir, is the site of an ancient city that dates back to 4000 B.C. and contains the Temple of Diana, another of the ancient seven wonders of the world, and the statue of the Mother

Figure 11–9   Valley of Goreme, Turkey

Goddess of Earth. Nearby is the Basilica of St. John, which is believed to contain the tomb of St. John. The region also contains an early Turkish citadel, the beautiful Mosque of Isa Bey, and the ruins of the Greek cities of Troy and Aphrodisia.

Central Anatolia. This is a region of spectacular snow-capped mountains forming a backdrop for the coastal plain with its great castles and scenic towns and cities. The region centers on Ankara, a modern city. Old Ankara features the Citadel. However, the most important structure is the Mausoleum of Ataturk, founder of the Turkish Republic, which is built on the highest hill and is visible from throughout the city. The Ethnographical Museum houses

exhibits of Turkish history, folklore, and art. Around Ankara, there are a number of other ruins with remains of the Hittites and the Phrygian capital of Gordion, where Alexander the Great cut the famous Gordion Knot that gave him the key to Asia. The Valley of Goreme, Figure 11–9, is a unique area where human activity has blended unobtrusively into the landscape.

The Black Sea and the East. To date, this is the least-developed region of Turkey. The region offers miles upon miles of deserted sandy beaches, charming fishing villages, cities with bazaars, and remains of former civilizations—Greek, Hittite, Roman, and Seljuk.

Iran

CULTURAL CAPSULE

Just over 50 percent of the population are ethnic Persians. Other groups include Azerbaijanis (25 percent), Kurds (9 percent), Gilakis and Mazandaranis (8 percent), Lurs (2 percent), and a number of other groups. The official language is Persian (Farsi), but there are many languages and dialects representing the various ethnic groups. Turkic, Kurdish, Luri, and Arabic are the major other languages. The state religion is Shiite Islam. It is an Islamic Republic, in which women are expected to be covered from wrist to ankle, veils and hair covering are mandatory, and makeup is frowned upon. Enforcement of these and other strict Islamic prohibitions on alcohol, Western movies, and pork is by young men or women who stop offenders on the streets. They may lecture, warn, or arrest those breaking these rules.

Capital: Tehran
Government: Islamic republic
Size: 636,296 square miles (slightly larger than Alaska)
Language: Farsi, Turkish, Kurdish, Arabic
Ethnic Division: Persians, Azeri Turks, Kurds, Arabs, Turkomans, and others
Religion: 89% Shi'a Muslim, 10% Sunni Muslim, with minorities of Christians and Jews
Tourist Season: April to mid-June and mid-September to mid-November
Currency: Rial

Physical Characteristics

Iran consists of a rugged mountainous rim surrounding a high interior basin. The basin is composed of desert plains and two smaller mountain ranges. There are three relatively small plains near the Caspian Sea, along the Persian Gulf and the Gulf of Oman, and in the southwest (the Plain of Khuzistan). Iran's climate is quite variable with seasonal changes. Most of Iran experiences long, hot, dry summers. In the winter, temperatures are low in the north.

TRAVEL TIPS

Travel to Iran is not recommended by the United States State Department. A visa and passport are required. (The Algerian Embassy represents Iran in the United States.) Travelers are expected to conform to Islamic law.

Tourism Characteristics

The combination of the Islamic revolution and the war with Iraq has left Iran with little tourism from outside of the region. The World Tourism Organization currently does not include data from Iran.

Tourist Destinations and Attractions

Pilgrimages to Iran's holy cities of Isfahan and Qom and the sites and museums of the once-great Persian empire, such as Shiraz, Persepolis, and Tehran, are Iran's most important and unique attractions. Tehran provides a contrast between the modern styles and the ancient Muslim buildings. The Shahyad Monument, which was built in 1971 to commemorate the 2,500th anniversary of the Persian Empire, is an impressive structure. The old and historical character can be observed at the Golestan Palace, the Decorative Arts Museum, the National Arts Museum, and the Sepahsalar Mosque. Near Tehran is Rey, considered to have been one of the great ancient cities.

Isfahan was once the capital city of Persia. It has many decorated mosques, regal palaces and gardens, old bridges, and a busy bazaar. Shiraz, which was also once the capital of Persia, includes the New Mosque, one of Iran's largest; the tombs of the lyric poets, located in typical Persian gardens; the Mashidi-I Jumeh Attiq; and the Eram and the Khalili Gardens.

Darius the Great founded Persepolis in 521 B.C. It contains the tombs of Xerxes, Darius, Cyrus, and Artaxerxes. The ruins of Pawargadae, the capital of Cyrus the Great, and the ruins of Naqshe Rustam are nearby.

Iraq

200 km

Mosul
Irbīl
Karkūk
Sāmarrāʾ
BAGHDĀD ★
Ar Ruṭbah
Al Ḥillah
Al Kūt
An Nāṣirīyah
Al Basrah
Persian Gulf

Capital: Baghdad
Government: Ruling Council
Size: 167,924 square miles (about the size of California)
Language: Arabic, Kurdish, Assyrian, Armenian
Ethnic Division: 75% Arab, 15–20% Kurd
Religion: 60% Shi'a Muslim, 35% Sunni Muslim, 5% Christian
Tourist Season: September to January and April to June
Currency: Iraqi dinar (IRD)

✵ TRAVEL TIPS

Since 1991 U.S. passports are not valid for travel to or through Iraq.

CULTURAL CAPSULE

Iraq's two largest ethnic groups are Arabs and Kurds. Other groups are Assyrians, Turkomans, Iranians, Lurs, and Armenians. Most Iraqi Muslims are members of the Shiite sect, but there is a large Sunni population as well. Small communities of Christians, Jews, Bahais', Mandaeans, and Yezidis exist. Most Kurds are Sunni Muslims, but differ in language, dress, and customs from Iraqis. Iraq, known as Mesopotamia, was the site of flourishing ancient civilizations, including the Sumerian, Babylonian, and Parthian. Muslims conquered Iraq in the seventh century A.D. In the eighth century, the Abassaid caliphate established its capital at Baghdad, which became a famous center of learning and the arts. By 1838, Baghdad had become a frontier outpost of the Ottoman Empire. Iraq became a British mandated territory at the end of World War I. In 1932 it was declared independent and ruled by the Hasemite family, who also ruled Jordan.

Physical Characteristics

Iraq consists primarily of the plains of the Tigris and Euphrates Rivers, with mountains in the north and northeast. The climate is desert, hot, with very dry summers and cold winters. Most of the rainfall occurs from December through April.

Tourism Characteristics

Iraq concentrates its program for the promotion and development of tourism in its own region. As a result, there are few European and American visitors. Tourists from Europe and the United States accounted for only ten percent of the total visitors to Iraq before the Gulf War of 1990–1991. The countries around Iraq are its major source region, with Arab countries contributing 80 percent of Iraq's total tourists. The total number of tourists was slightly more than 700,000 in 1990 but dropped to less than 400,000 in 1996 as a result of the Gulf War and the subsequent United Nations embargo on Iraq. Until the region stabilizes, the tourism industry in Iraq will not contribute to its economy.

Tourist Destinations and Attractions

Iraq has a number of monuments and remnants of such early civilizations as the Assyrians, Babylonians, Sumerians, and Akkadians. Many of the artifacts from these civilizations are in the National Museum in Baghdad. Baghdad also has Tell Harmal, a walled city dating back to Hammurabi; palaces; mosques; minarets; and bazaars. Baghdad is home to one of the world's oldest universities, the Mustansiriyah, founded in 1234 A.D. Some early important landmarks are the Abbasid Palace, the Minaret in Suq al-Ghazil, the Arms Museum, Bab al-Wastani, the Sheik'Abdul Qadir al-Gailani Mosque, and Zubaida's Tomb. One of the holy pilgrimage places for Shiite Moslems is the Mosque of Kadhimain near Baghdad. Also in the region is a large palace built by Sassanian Persians in the fourth century A.D. (Ctesiphon), with its still-standing arch that is the longest single-span nonreinforced brick arch in the world.

A number of ancient city ruins are added attractions in Iraq. Hatra with the Temple of the Sun; Babylon, Khorsabad, a capital built by Sargon II who ruled Assyria from 721 to 705 B.C., with a palace and the Temple of Sebiti; the site of Jarmo, one of the most ancient cities in the world; Nimrud, with extremely thick walls and massive gateways; Nineveh, ruled by three ancient kings; and Samarra with the great Friday Mosque and the ruins of Beit al-Kalifa, a maze of terraces, artificial lakes, gardens, and pavilions. One of the better cities to visit of the many ancient cities is Mosul. It has over 100 mosques and numerous Christian churches.

Iraq has a number of holy shrines such as Karbala, which is one of the holiest cities in the world for Shiite Muslims, and Najaf, where Ali (the early leader of Shiite Muslims) is entombed. Ur, the home of Abraham, is important for Christians and is one of the earliest cities of the world.

The ruins of Babylon (including the Hanging Gardens, one of the seven wonders of the ancient world) are near Baghdad. They have been rebuilt by the Iraqi government. In addition to the Hanging Gardens, Procession Street, Ishtar Gate, the South Palace, and the Tower of Babel (now being restored) were all in Babylon.

Afghanistan

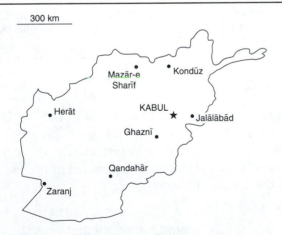

 TRAVEL TIPS

Travel to Afghanistan is not advised. Visas are required and must be approved in Afghanistan. Passports are required. Travel is risky because of the political situation.

Capital: Kabul
Government: Democratic republic
Size: 260,000 square miles (about the size of Texas)
Language: Dari (Afghan, Persian), Pushtu
Ethnic Division: Pukhtun/Pushtun (Pathan), Tajik, Uzbek, Hazara, Aimaq, Turkoman, Baluch, Nuristani
Religion: 84% Sunni Muslim, 15% Shiite Muslim
Tourist Season: Spring and Fall
Currency: Afghani (AFG)

CULTURAL CAPSULE

Afghanistan is ethnically and linguistically mixed. The Pukhtun (40 percent), Tajik, Uzbek, Turkoman, Hazar, and Aimaq ethnic groups make up the bulk of the Afghan population. Dari (Afghan Persian) is spoken by a third of the population, and Pushtu is spoken by about half. Turkoman and Uzbeki are spoken widely in the north. There are more than 70 other languages and dialects throughout the country. Afghanistan is a Muslim country. Eight percent of the population are Sunni, and the remainder are Shiite. Islamic practice pervades all aspects of life, and Islamic religious tradition and law provide the principal means for controlling conduct and settling legal disputes.

Physical Characteristics

Afghanistan is a mountainous country with small fertile valleys. The climate is dry with cold winters and hot summers.

Tourism Characteristics

Afghanistan has only a token tourism industry due to civil war, invasion by the Soviets, and a poor infrastructure with only a few hotels of poor quality. Government data indicates there are approximately 10,000 visitors per year, generating approximately $2 million a year in income.

Tourist Destinations and Attractions

Two cities, Kabul and Mazar-I-Sharif (an ancient city of the kingdom of Bactria), and the hidden valley of Bamian (with relics from prehistoric times and one of the largest Buddhas in the world) dominate the limited tourist attractions. Herat is the home of a mosque that is considered by some to be one of the greatest in the world. It was built in the twelfth century and has been restored several times. Afghanistan is the gateway to the Khyber Pass with its magnificent scenery.

ARABIAN PENINSULA

The countries of the Arabian Peninsula limit tourism to business travel and Islamic religious pilgrims. Two of the most important Islamic sites are Mecca and *Medina* in Saudi Arabia. Today, Saudi Arabia limits the number of pilgrims in order to maintain control over the territory. The countries of Saudi Arabia, Kuwait, Bahrain, Qatar, United Arab Emirates, Oman, and Yemen comprise the area.

TOURISM IN NORTH AFRICA

North African countries have gone through the process of being discovered by Europeans seeking the warm coastal beaches of the Mediterranean. The three most visited countries are Morocco, Algeria, and Tunisia, Table 11–3. The physical attraction of the beaches in a Mediterranean climate combined with the lure of a culture much different from Europe's intrigues many Europeans. In addition, French is used widely as a lingua franca. The tourist is much more comfortable, therefore, than would be the case with a completely foreign tongue. Tunisia, Morocco, and Algeria cater to Europeans and have developed resort centers, allowing the tourists to escape the puritanical milieu of Islam while still being able to enjoy the cultural landscape. Libya, however, does nothing to attract Western tourists. Strict enforcement of Islam's dietary and social restrictions makes most visitors from the Western industrial world uncomfortable in Libya.

The Sahara Desert and its oases, common to all countries of North Africa, are also becoming major tourist attractions. The Sahara provides contact with what Europeans and other Westerners might consider to be exotic cultural experiences. A number of ancient and modern ruins left by the Phoenicians, Romans, Arabs, Spanish, and French serve to augment the modern attractions.

Table 11–3 International Tourism to North Africa				
	Number of Visitors (thousands)		**1996 Receipts (millions of US $)**	**1996 Average Expenses per Visit (US $)**
Country	**1986**	**1996**		
Algeria	849	605	16	26
Morocco	2,128	2,695	1,387	514
Tunisia	1,502	3,885	1,436	370
Libya	120	88	6	68
Source: Yearbook of Tourism Statistics. Madrid: World Tourism Organization				

Morocco

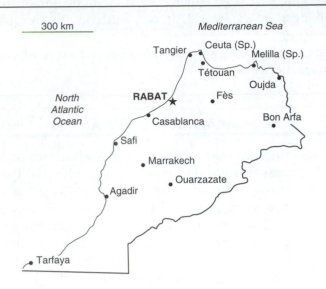

300 km

Mediterranean Sea

Tangier · Ceuta (Sp.)
Tétouan · Melilla (Sp.)
RABAT ★ · Oujda
North Atlantic Ocean
· Fès
· Bon Arfa
· Casablanca
· Safi
· Marrakech
· Agadir · Ouarzazate
· Tarfaya

Capital: Rabat
Government: Constitutional monarchy
Size: 279,094 square miles (about the same size as Texas)
Language: Arabic, French, and Berber
Ethnic Division: 99.1% Arab-Berber, 0.7% non-Moroccan, 0.2% Jewish
Religion: 98.7% Muslim, 1.1% Christian, 0.2% Jewish
Tourist Season: February through September
Peak Tourist Season: July and August
Currency: Dirham (MDH)

TRAVEL TIPS

Entry: Visas are not required for visits up to 3 months. Passports are required.
Transportation: International air carriers provide access to North America, Europe, North Africa and Africa. Ferry services via Tangier and Ceula, Morocco, to Algeciras and Malaga, Spain, provide access from Europe. There are good air and rail connections between major cities.
Health: Water in urban areas is clean, but do not drink water in rural areas. Eat only carefully prepared fruits and vegetables.
Shopping: Common items include copper ware, tooled leather, silver, gold, pottery, camel saddles, and other handicraft goods.

CULTURAL CAPSULE

Morocco is the oldest kingdom in the Muslim world, having been independent since the arrival of Moulay Idriss, a grandson of the prophet Mohammed in the eighth century. The two major groups (99 percent) are Arab and Berber or mixed Arab-Berber. The official language is Arabic. French is a second language particularly in government and commerce. In the northern zone Spanish is spoken. In rural areas any of

---

three Berber vernaculars are spoken. The earlier-known settlers of Morocco were the Berbers, believed to have come from southwestern Asia. After a succession of invasions the Arabs invaded in the seventh century and brought Islam to Morocco. Islam is the country's official religion. Most Moroccans are Sunni Muslims.

Cultural Hints:
- A handshake with foreigners is a common greeting.
- Close contact, such as kissing cheeks, is common among close friends.
- Do not show the sole of your shoe or point it at someone.
- Take shoes off to enter a mosque.
- Do not offer the left hand to another person.
- Eating and foods:
  Finger food is common, but only eat with the right hand. The host will bring water for guests to wash their hands. Restaurants often include service charge. If not, tip 15 percent.
  Typical food includes lamb, beef, chicken, meat stew, vegetables, milk, and dates. Muslims do not eat pork or drink alcoholic beverages. Couscous is the national dish. It is generally composed of wheat (semolina) steamed over a stew of lamb or chicken accompanied with vegetables and garbanzo beans. It is traditionally eaten with the fingers.

Physical Characteristics

Morocco is mountainous, but with extensive coastal plains. The climate is mild along the coasts, but hot and dry in the interior.

Tourism Characteristics

Morocco (and Tunisia) compare favorably with Israel and Egypt in terms of tourism industry. Morocco receives more visitors and income than the other North African countries. Tourism is the second largest foreign exchange earner after phosphates. The importance the government places on tourism is reflected in the creation of a Ministry of Tourism in 1985. Morocco has been one of the most politically stable countries in North Africa, which should allow the industry to continue to develop. Its relatively large number of visitors reflects five factors:

1. Cruise ships call at the ports of Casablanca and Tangier. Morocco thus benefits from the large Atlantic ports of Europe.
2. Morocco is close to Spain, and encourages tourists in coastal resort areas in southern Spain to participate in one- to three-day trips to Morocco. Its close proximity to Europe and

its excellent beaches make it a major attraction for sun-sea-sand participants in Europe. This proximity effect is very important to tourism in Morocco. Also, this is the principal path for visitors from the United States.

3. The opening of the Algerian and Moroccan border and reestablishment of air service to restore communications between the two countries. Algerians have flocked across the border to visit family and friends and to shop.

4. Morocco has an excellent network of roads and railroads linking the major cities and tourist destination regions with both ports and cities with international airports.

5. The relative inexpensiveness of travel to and through Morocco makes it attractive to tourists. Morocco has benefitted from the devaluation of its currency (the dirham), and the increase in hotel prices in Spain in the past few years contributes to the existing favorable price structure in the country.

The combination of location, attractions, and relatively low price have led to a rather extended length of stay of eleven days, by far the highest of all countries in North Africa. In part, this reflects visits by Moroccans living overseas. Of the more than 3 million annual visitors, some 600,000 are Moroccan residents working abroad. The major market area is Europe, with four countries (France, Spain, United Kingdom, and Germany) accounting for one-third of all international visitors other than Moroccan residents returning home. The United States and Canada account for slightly less than three percent of visitors to Morocco. While seasonality is not a problem, the low season is in the winter months. Part of the winter visitors are the wealthy wintering in Morocco. Europeans prefer visiting in April and in the fall, with the exception of the Spanish, who follow the traditional patterns of June and August (*International Tourism Reports*, The Economist Publications Ltd., 1987, and *Yearbook of Tourism Statistics*, 1995).

Tourist Destinations and Attractions

Cultural and political landscapes compete with the sun-sea-sand of coastal resorts in attracting visitors. Morocco's attractions can be divided into seven regions: Tangier and the surrounding area; Agodir with its beach resorts; Marrakesh; Casablanca; the Imperial cities; Ouarzazate (the "Hollywood" of Morocco); and Tarfaya and its beach resorts.

The capital, Tangier, and the surrounding beach resorts of Restinga-Smir, M'Diq, Al Hoceima,

Nadord, Saidia, and Asilah are an obvious attraction. Tangier once was considered a pearl, but has lost much of its attraction for tourists. It is still a destination for day trips from Spain.

Agadir, the "Miami Beach" of Morocco, has all the trappings of a major coastal resort attraction and a third of all Moroccan bed nights. Agadir is also a base for tours to the Atlas Mountains. At the foot of the High Atlas Mountains, the famous trade center Marrakesh is one of four Imperial cities. It has many musicians, magicians, snake charmers, storytellers, and markets that immerse visitors in the Moroccan culture. The souk (*suq*) amid covered alleyways displays traditional handicrafts. To escape the heat of the desert, the Agdal Garden was created in the twelfth century. The garden stretches over an area of some 1,000 acres. It has several pools surrounded by fruit trees.

Casablanca, the major cruise port in Morocco, has the best-developed market for tourists. The old native quarter with the Great Mosque is impressive. A number of beautiful public buildings such as the Courthouse, Town Hall, Post Office, and Bank of Morocco, which is designed in neo-Moorish style, surround the United Nations Square.

The Imperial cities, Rabat, Marrakesh, Fèz, and Meknes, constitute an important attraction in their own right. Fèz is the oldest and is both a cultural and religious center of the country. Important attractions are the Karaouine Mosque, Mesbahia Medersa (an old school that is remarkable for its traditional architecture), and Souk. Rabat, the political capital, is also an ancient city with a *Casbah*, the Tower of Hassan, the Dar es Salaam Summer Palace, and the Royal Palace. Also of interest are the minaret Tour Hassan, the Mohammed V Mausoleum (an outstanding example of Moroccan architecture), and the Oudaias with its traditional garden, the museum of handicrafts, and antique Moorish café.

Meknes was built in the seventeenth century to rival Paris. It has a most impressive 25-mile girdle of defensive ramparts. Other important sites are Moulay Ismail's magnificent tomb; the monumental gates of Bab Mansour, Bab Berdain, and Bab Djema En Nouar; and the Dar Jamai Palace, now the Museum of Moroccan Arts. Just outside of Meknes are the historically important town of Moulay Idriss and the splendid 2,000-year-old Roman ruins at Volubilis. A tour of all four Imperial cities is one of the most popular tourist activities in Morocco. The least-developed region for tourists is centered on the film capital of Ouarzazate, near the Algerian border. From Ouarzazate, tourists can visit Berber villages, desert oases, and the Dades valley (the "Grand Canyon" of North Africa). The coastal desert region near Tarfaya has many virgin white beaches. This area still re- quires considerable development, but it does have some luxury hotels developed by Club Med.

Tunisia

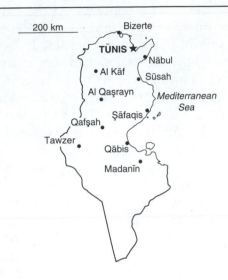

Capital: Tunis
Government: Republic
Size: 63,170 square miles (about the same as Missouri)
Language: Arabic, French
Ethnic Division: 98% Arab, 1% European
Religion: 98% Muslim, 1% Christian, 1% Jewish
Tourist Season: Year-round
Peak Tourist Season: July and August
Currency: Tunisian dinar (TUD)

TRAVEL TIPS

Entry: Visas are not required for stays up to 4 months. Passports are required.
Transportation: International Air service is good through Europe and other North African countries. Tunisia has a good network of roads and domestic air transport between cities. Railroads service the northern and coastal areas. Public transportation is good. There is an excellent light rail system.
Shopping: Common items include blankets, rugs, pottery, copper, silver, leather goods, carved wooden items, brass, ceramics, lace, and embroidery.
Caution: There have been a number of killings of village people by the Islamic fundamentalists.

CULTURAL CAPSULE

Some 98 percent of the population is Arab. There are small minorities of European descent. Arabic is the official lan- guage, and French is widely used. Many Tunisians also speak some English. Ninety-eight percent of the people are Muslim. The majority are Sunni Muslims. In recent years there has been a movement toward Islamic fundamental- ism. This has created social unrest and government controls. Tunisia has been undergoing a transition from a one-man dictatorship to a much more open society. Tunisia considers itself a Westernized country, and Western clothing is com- mon in both urban and rural areas.

Cultural Hints:
- A handshake is the most common form of greeting.
- Good friends brush each other's cheeks and kiss the air on greeting.
- Personal warmth is characteristic of all greetings.
- A toss or movement of the head backward means no.
- Take off your shoes when entering a mosque.
- Do not point or show sole of the foot to another person.
- To beckon hold the palm down and wave all fingers toward the body.
- Do not use the index finger to point at objects or people.
- Eating and foods:
  Family style or a common plate is customary.
  Tips are usually included in the bill.
  "Hamdullah" (thanks to God) means it was a good meal.
  Wash hands before and after meals.
  Typical foods include fish, lamb, fruits, chicken, toma- toes, potatoes, onions, olives, oil, and peppers. Al- cohol and pork are forbidden by Islam. Couscous is Tunisia's national dish. It is made of steamed and spiced semolina and topped with vegetables and meats.

Physical Characteristics

Tunisia is composed of a hot, dry central plain, the Sahara Desert, and mountains in the north.

Tourism Characteristics

Tunisia has a growing tourist industry. Tourism de- velopment is a major goal of the government's eco- nomic development plans. It is the largest earner of foreign exchange. The only cloud on the horizon that may affect tourism is the growing militancy among many of its Muslims. Tunisia is one of the most modern Arab countries and draws visitors mostly from its neighbors and Europe, principally France and Germany. The United States accounts for only about one percent of the tourist trade to Tunisia. The num- ber of visitors from the United States fell in 1991 due to popular support for Saddam Hussein of Iraq in

Figure 11–10   Ribat de Sousse, Tunisia

Tunisia during the Gulf War. The lack of tourists from the United States and the high number from Europe reflect the type of attractions offered.

For the Europeans, Tunisia is mainly a sun-sea-sand center. It has 750 miles of coastline on the Mediterranean, with a number of modern hotels from Tunis to Hammamet on down the coast to Sousse, Sfax, and Djerba. The hotels are some of the best in Africa, and the beaches are wide, sandy, and attractive. United States travelers can find similar amenities available much closer to home. The beaches attract the Europeans, who come by package tours from Germany, Netherlands, France, Britain, and Italy. Europeans account for over 60 percent of the total visitors to Tunisia. The average length of stay is 8.4 days with an average expenditure of $338 per visitor, which fits well within a week's package from Western Europe.

Tourist Destinations and Attractions

As indicated, the principal attraction is the beautiful Mediterranean setting with wide, sandy, attractive beaches. The historical cultural landscape reflects a variety of groups: Berbers, Phoenicians, Romans, Vandals, Byzantines, Arabs, Turks, and the French. The culture of the area offers opportunities for excursions into the Sahara that are different enough from the Mediterranean resorts in Spain, France, and Italy to attract those seeking experiences other than sea-sun-sand. The first Club Med vacation village was founded in Tunisia.

Tunis, the capital, is an attractive city with broad boulevards and the ruins of Carthage, which was founded by the Phoenicians and conquered by the Romans, nearby. With its bright homes with iron balconies and sky-blue doors, Sidi Bon Said is popular with artists. Sousse, some 70 miles from Tunis, has extensive Christian catacombs. Near Sousse, Monastir is a picturesque walled city; and Kairouan, one of the most Holy Cities of Islam, has the Grand Mosque of Sidi Okba, which dates back to the eleventh century.

Algeria

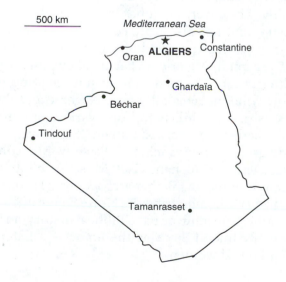

Capital: Algiers
Government: Republic
Size: 918,497 square miles (about one-third the size of the United States)
Language: Arabic, Berber, French
Ethnic Division: Arabs and Berbers
Religion: 99% Sunni Muslim
Tourist Season: Year-round
Peak Tourist Season: March through October
Currency: Algerian dinar (ALD)

TRAVEL TIPS

Entry: Visas are required for visits up to 90 days. Passports are required. Visitors will not be admitted if they have visas in their passport from Israel. Visitors need proof of onward or round-trip transportation. Currency declaration is required and exchanges recorded.

Transportation: International airlines provide access to Algeria from Europe and other North African countries. Algeria has good intercity transportation by air, rail, and road to its northern cities, and good connections between Algeria, Tunisia, and Morocco.

Health: Typhoid, tetanus, polio, and cholera vaccinations are recommended. Water should be boiled or bottled water purchased. Peel or cook all fruits and vegetables.

Shopping: The *souks* have a multitude of things to buy. Common items include Moorish-style jewelry, leather slippers and handbags, baskets, toys, brass trays, chiseled copperware, tapestries, antiques, silver-inlay daggers, and woven rugs.

Caution: Muslim fundamentalists have killed villagers.

CULTURAL CAPSULE

About 83 percent of the population is Arabic and 16 percent are native Berber. There is a very small European minority. Most of the population (91 percent) lives along the Mediterranean. Nearly all are Sunni Muslim. Arabic is the official language. French is commonly used along the coastal areas for business and among the older generation.

Cultural Hints:
- A light handshake and sometimes an embrace are common forms of greeting.
- Do not use the index finger to point at objects or people.
- Use the right hand to hand objects, shake, and eat.
- Sit properly without slouching.
- Do not show sole of shoe or point it at someone.
- Personal space is close.
- Long, direct eye contact is important (among men).
- Ask permission to take pictures.
- Do not hold hands or express affection in public with a person of the opposite gender.
- Tilting the head backward means no.
- Eating and foods:
  Do not touch food with your left hand.
  Leaving some food on the plate is a compliment to host.
  Typical food includes lamb, chicken, stews, pasta, vegetables, and fruits. Muslims do not eat pork or drink alcoholic beverages.

Physical Characteristics

The Mediterranean coast is a narrow plain. Behind the coastal plain is a mountainous and high plain region. The southern portion is desert. The climate is hot and dry with some rain along the coastal areas.

Tourism Characteristics

Algeria differs from Morocco and Tunisia in that its tourist sector is entirely state controlled, with the exception of a few small businesses that supply the industry with consumer goods. While Algeria has a host of rich natural attractions for tourism—expansive beaches on the Mediterranean, mountains, and archaeological sites of Roman, Berber, Arab, and French cultures—its tourism industry is small. In the last half of the nineteenth century, Algeria was the major destination for the wealthy from Britain. From then until 1984 the government did little to promote tourism. Although it began implementing plans and programs in 1984, the government has been slow to respond to tourism potential. The country has been negatively affected by the events of the Middle East, as the Palestinian Liberation Organization headquarters was moved to Algeria in the 1980s. The number of visitors to Algeria in the 1990s averaged less than 1 million a year, in part because of the actions of Islamic fundamentalists. Visitors stay only a short time, and individual tourist expenditures are the smallest for the North African region. Outside of North Africa itself, France is the major market region, reflecting former colonial ties. Most tourists are from other Arabic countries of North Africa.

Tourist Destinations and Attractions

Algeria offers the tourist a variety of scenery. It has broad beaches, rocky coves, scenic mountains, cascading waters, and desert sand dunes. In the mountains, there are picturesque fortified villages, such as Constantine (which sits on a precipitous rock overlooking a deep canyon). In addition, Algeria has Roman ruins, such as at Timgad, with an impressive number of villas, and temples and arches, such as at Djemila. The government has tried to stress the craft industry, and has also utilized the unique Moorish architecture in structures built for the tourist industry. The capital, Algiers, is a beautiful city on the blue Mediterranean. The medina is most interesting, with narrow winding lanes full of craftspeople and shops. The Casbah on a hill is full of a variety of cultures such as Berbers, Arabs, and Kabyles. Some important buildings are the Franchet-d' Esperey Museum, a fortress, and the Stephane Gsell Museum, containing Roman, Islamic, and Berber archaeology. The Greco-Roman city Cherchell and the Notre Dame d'Afrique are nearby. Constantine has a Biblical history, and the Palace of Almond Bey was the home of a harem of three hundred women.

Libya

400 km

TRIPOLI ★
Mişrātah
Gulf of Sidra
Surt
Ghadāmis

Mediterranean Sea
Tobruk
Banghāzī

Sabhā

Al Jawf

Capital: Tripoli
Government: Republic
Size: 1,099,713 square miles (larger than Alaska)
Language: Arabic, Italian, English
Ethnic Division: 97% Berber and Arab
Religion: 97% Sunni Muslim
Tourist Season: Year-round
Currency: Dinars

TRAVEL TIPS

Travel to Libya by Americans is restricted by the United States government. A U.S. passport is not valid for travel into or through Libya without validation by the Department of State.

CULTURAL CAPSULE

Libyans are primarily a mixture of Arabs and Berbers. Small tribal groups, Tebou and Touareg, are nomadic or seminomadic in southern Libya. There are a number of foreign workers, such as Egyptians, Turks, Pakistanis, Indians, Sudanese, Moroccans, South Koreans, and Europeans. Many foreign workers are employed in the oil fields, but many left in 1993 after atrocities by Islamic fundamentalists. Libya has a small population and a large land area. More than half of the population is concentrated in the two largest cities, Tripoli and Benghazi.

Physical Characteristics

Libya is mostly a barren flat plain and plateau country. The climate is warm and temperate along the coast and hot and dry in the interior desert.

Tourism Characteristics

Libya's tourist industry is at present small and is dominated by other Arab countries, which account for approximately 80 percent of the total visitors to Libya. The average length of stay and income generated as result of tourism is the smallest in North Africa. The current political situation in Libya is a major deterrent to travel. During the 1980s Libya's tourism industry remained stagnant at about 100,000 visitors a year. In the 1990s, it has declined in total number of visitors.

Tourist Destinations and Attractions

There are numerous beaches in the 1,242 miles of Mediterranean coast. The major cities, such as Tripoli and Benghazi, have modern hotels. Libya also has a number of archaeological sites from the Greek, Roman, Byzantine, and Islamic cultures. The traditional Islamic culture is very much in evidence, with women enveloped in veils and the social, legal, and political system based on the Koran. Tripoli, the capital, is an attractive city located on the Mediterranean. The Old City with its narrow, winding streets, the Hammam (bathhouse) of Sidi Dargut, the Mosque of Shaib el Ain, the House of Ali Pasha Karamanli, and the Roman Arch of Marcus Aurelius are major sightseeing areas of the city. Leptis Magna, some 75 miles from Tripoli, was at one time an important Roman city. Along the coast are many picturesque villages, beaches, and coves for swimming and sightseeing.

PATHWAYS IN THE HOLY LAND

DAY 1   NACHSHOLIM–HAIFA–MEGIDDO–MOUNT ARBEL–GALILEE

After an Israeli kosher breakfast (some may choose an early morning swim), we will visit the ancient site of Dor, where some of the cedars of Lebanon for Solomon's Temple were delivered by the Phoenician king Hyrum of Tyre. Today Kibbutz Nachsholim is the headquarters of the Underwater Archaeological Excavation Society of Israel and houses a unique museum, which we will visit. We will travel to the modern port city of Haifa. In Haifa, our bus will climb up Mount Carmel to Kaiser's Watch. From Kaiser's Watch—where the surrender of the Ottoman Empire was given to British general Allenby in 1917—we will be able to view the World Headquarters of the Baha'i faith, the port of Haifa, and the distant ancient port of Akko/Ptolemais. Traveling up the spine of Mount Carmel, we will pass the Haifa University campus, pass through the Druze communities, and arrive at the traditional site of Elijah's contest with the priests of Baal, Muhraka. Our travels will then take us to the Solomonic chariot city of Megiddo. The valley that stretches around this hill fortress takes its name from this strong citadel, Armageddon, where prophecy indicates one of the last great battles will be fought. Crossing this valley, also known by the names of Jezreel and Esdraelon, we will pass through the Nazareth hill country. We will arrive in Nazareth and visit the ancient well, the Church of the Annunciation, the old Jewish synagogue, and the precipice where Jesus was rejected by his own townspeople. Passing north over the Nazareth hills we will pass Sephoris, capital of the Galilee in Jesus's time; Kfar Cana, traditional site of the wedding feast where Mary asked Jesus to supply wine; and Gath-Hefer, birthplace of Jonah. The Horns of Hittin will loom before us as we approach Nebi Shueib, which is the tomb of Jethro according to Druze tradition.

DAY 2   CAPERNAUM–MOUNT OF BEATITUDES

Following an Israeli kosher breakfast, we will go to the En Gev dock to board a private boat made as a replica of the ancient fishing vessels of the early Apostles' days. As we cross to the western shore of the Sea of Galilee near Kibbutz Nof Ginnosar, our minds will reflect on the many miracles and events recounted in the scriptures that relate to this region. Next we travel north and east around the sea to Capernaum. We will visit the remains of this city Jesus called "mine own city." After sitting in the ancient synagogue, we will leave for a traditional Christian location called the "Primacy of the Rock," where the Apostle Peter was instructed by the resurrected Christ. Further up the hill is our next point of study, the traditional Mount of Beatitudes. Traveling along the western shores, we will pass Kinneret, which acted as a tolling city in Old Testament times along the Via Maris. Today at its base are the large pumping stations that supply water in the far southern deserts of the Negev. Traveling toward Tiberias, we will pass the town of Mary Magdalene, Magdala. To our right is the plain of Gennesaret. We will travel below Arbel to Tiberias. In Tiberias we will watch the multimedia presentation of the "Galilee Experience."

DAY 3   JORDAN RIVER–BEIT SHEAN–JERICHO–JERUSALEM

We will have our last kosher Israeli breakfast as we depart En Gev and the Galilee this day. We will head south along the shores of this famous sea and stop for a few minutes at the Jordan River, to put our hands in the water and recall some of the significant events that have occurred in and near this river. The bus will travel further south to Beit Shean, where we'll see the biblical and Byzantine ruins. Beit Shean was known as ancient Scythopolis. It was here that King Saul and his sons were hung on the city walls. The rebuilding of the Roman-Byzantine city surrounding the ancient acropolis is one of the most spectacular archaeological reconstructions in the country. We then turn south through the Jordan Valley on the border between Israel and Jordan. The Dome of Gilead and lands of the Joseph tribes will stretch before us as we recall the journeys of Israel and the Patriarchs. As we approach the end of the Jordan River near the Dead Sea, we will come to what archaeologists call the oldest continuously inhabited city in the world, ancient Jericho. Here are the sites of Elisha's Spring near what are believed to be the walls that tumbled down before Joshua's forces. Here, too, are the sycamore trees, recalling Jesus's stay with the publican Zachaeus, and Herod's winter palace at New Testament Jericho. Jericho today is one of the new autonomous cities of the Palestinian Authority. We will dine on fruits for lunch, after which we will follow the Old Roman Way through the Judean Wilderness that Jesus walked with his disciples. Like him, we will go on to Bethany (home of Mary, Martha, and Lazarus) to begin our walk over the Mount of Olives for our first view of Jerusalem.

continues

continued

DAY 4   JERUSALEM–WEST (NEW) CITY–BETHLEHEM

Breakfast will be followed by departure to the Panoramic Park on Jebel Mukkaber where an unusual view of Jerusalem may be seen looking from the south toward the three major valleys (the Kidron, the Tyropoeon, and the Hinnom or Gehinna) that shape the hills of ancient Jerusalem. From here we will proceed to West Jerusalem and the famous Model City at the Holy Land West Hotel. We will also visit the nearby museum of the Holocaust, Yad Vashem. Following this sobering experience, we will transfer to the major downtown business area on Ben Yehudah Street for lunch and shopping. In the afternoon we will bus to Bethlehem to visit the Church of the Nativity and Shepherd's Fields. We will end our day by returning to the Holy Land East Hotel for dinner and overnight. Some will want to shop in the area around the hotel (Bagdadi's, Jimmy's, Omar's, etc.).

DAY 5   DEAD SEA–MASADA–EIN GEDI–QUMRAN

Our day will begin with a 6:00 A.M. breakfast before our early departure to the Dead Sea (leaving early helps us to avoid the summer heat and possibly the "hamsheen," "sharav," or east wind that comes this time of the year). We will travel directly to Masada, visiting this Hasmonean-Herodian fortress. We will experience the tragedy and triumphs of biblical and post-biblical events through the physical remains and the discussions we have at this significant location. Next we will go to the shores of the Dead Sea near Ein Gedi, where stories of David and Samson will be reviewed, and those who so desire will float in this mineral-rich lake. We will hike the nature trails, see some of the biblical fauna and flora, and eat our sack lunches. Our next stop will be at the site of the Essene community of Qumran, where many of the Dead Sea Scrolls were found. In the early afternoon we will return to the hotel.

DAY 6   JERUSALEM

Following breakfast we will take a bus transfer to the Old City and enter it through Dung Gate. We will visit the Ophel Archaeological Gardens and continue to the Western (Wailing) Wall. Then we will ascend the path to the el-Aksa Mosque and Dome of the Rock, called by many the Holy Mount, where the temples of Solomon, Zerubabel, and Herod stood. Today it is the most sacred site to Jews, the third most sacred site to Moslems (next to Mecca and Medina), and the place of the final resurrection to many Christians. After the visit here, we will proceed up the Western Hill to the Jewish Quarter and visit the Cardo, the Holy Sepulchre, the Christian Quarter, and Jaffa Gate. Following a lunch of falafels or shwarmas, we will transfer to West Jerusalem and the Israeli National Museum and Shrine of the Book. Our visit will include what has been termed "the greatest archaeological find of the twentieth century"—the Dead Sea (Judean Desert) Scrolls. We will also visit the archaeological wing of the large museum to see artifacts that date to, and may have been used by, biblical personalities. As we leave the museum, we will stop for a view of the Israeli parliament building, the Knesset, and the national symbol donated by the British, the Menorah.

DAY 7   JERUSALEM (Events in the last week of Jesus's life)

After breakfast our bus will proceed to Mount Zion, site of the traditional Tomb of King David and of the Last Supper or Cennacle (Upper Room), and where the early Church of the Apostles was located. This visit begins our studies of the last week of the Christian messiah's ministry, which culminated in the Atonement. After a visit to the Church of the Dormition, we will proceed to Gethsemane and the Church of All Nations. We will then return to Mount Zion and the traditional house of Caiaphas (known as St. Peter en Gallicantu) to review the trials of Jesus by the high priests. We will transfer by bus for lunch in the Jaffa Gate area in order to see the Jaffa Gate Museum. En route we will drive through the very crowded section of orthodox Judaism called Mea Sha'arim to watch the community's preparations for the "Shabbat" or Sabbath. En route to the places of Jesus's judgment, we will visit another location of miracles, at St. Anne's Church, the site of the Pools of Bethesda. From here we will walk to Pilate's headquarters and the Hall of Judgment, which some say is located at the Antonia Fortress. We will stand on a portion of the pavement (Gabbatha) at the Sisters of Zion Convent. From the Antonia Fortress we will walk through the Old City streets to the Damascus Gate and then out of the city walls to the Garden Tomb.

DAY 8   BETHLEHEM–HEBRON–SHEPHELAH–BETH SHEMESH

Again our day will begin early with a 6:30 A.M. breakfast in order that we may return soon and avoid some of the heat of the afternoon sun. After breakfast we will board our motor coach and travel south past Rachel's Tomb and Bethlehem to Solomon's Pools. We will continue going south on the Patriarch's Way past the area of Tekoa, hometown of the prophet Amos, and stop on the outskirts of Hebron at a pottery and glass-blowing factory. We will proceed west from the Hill Country of Judah to the valleys of Shephelah, where many of the Old and New Testament events occurred. We will visit the Bell Caves and the Sidonian-Idumean city of Maresha (the Herodian family came from here). Below the hometown of Micah, we will do some spelunking (time permitting) and then

continues

continued

proceed to Midras and the first century A.D. "rolling stone tomb" for pictures. Next is the Valley of Elah, where David met the mighty Philistine, Goliath. We, too, will use a sling to try our luck at hitting a target. The next valley we enter is Sorek, where Samson (Zorah) and Delilah (Timnah) were born. We will stop for a recounting of the stories from the book of Judges at the ancient tel of Beth Shemesh, where the Ark of the Covenant was delivered from the Philistines. The final valley in our travels will be the Aijalon, where Joshua commanded the sun and moon to stand still for the children of Israel. Passing the Beth Horon, we will pass watchtowers that will remind us of ancient and modern parables and prophecies. If possible, we will stop at one and read some of these scriptures before proceeding to Nebi Samwil (traditional burial site of the prophet Samuel and place where Solomon prayed for wisdom) on the northern outskirts of Jerusalem. From here we can see nearly all of the Benjamin Plateau; here geographically 67 percent of Old Testament history occurred. Our return to Jerusalem will culminate the day's events with dinner and an overnight rest before the flight home.

REVIEW QUESTIONS

1. What are the six characteristics of Islamic tourism?
2. Why are North Africa and the Middle East considered a distinct region by geographers?
3. Describe the three most common characteristics of the topography of the area.
4. Why is the Middle East one of the most culturally complex regions of the world?
5. Describe the three major cultural groups of the Middle East and North Africa.
6. Discuss the three patterns for organization of life in the Middle East and North Africa.
7. What are the major tourist countries of the Middle East and North Africa? Why?
8. If tourists are thinking about visiting Egypt and Israel, explain why they should also visit Jordan.
9. Why is Jerusalem important to Arab travelers?
10. Which country of North Africa has the most-developed tourist industry? Why?

GEOGRAPHY AND TOURISM IN
Subsaharan Africa

CHAPTER 12

MAJOR GEOGRAPHIC CHARACTERISTICS

- Africa has the most rapid population growth rate in the world.
- Africa's physical environment can be labeled "harsh."
- The population distribution is highly rural.
- The physical geography makes access within Africa difficult and limited.
- Africa is rich in important resources needed in industrial nations.
- Conflict and boundary disputes are common, reflecting tribalism and nationalism.

MAJOR TOURISM CHARACTERISTICS

- Game parks dominate.
- There is a lack of tourism infrastructure.
- Africa has the smallest tourism industry of any major region.
- Tourism is mostly to coastal countries.
- Africa is relatively inaccessible to most of the world's potential tourists.

MAJOR TOURIST DESTINATIONS

The Great National Game Parks: Kenya, Tanzania, South Africa, Senegal, Zimbabwe, Zambia, and Namibia
Zimbabwe
Tanzania
South Africa
Senegal
Ivory Coast
Seychelles
Swaziland
Botswana
Coastal beaches and waters of Ivory Coast, Kenya, Mauritius, Seychelles, and South Africa

KEY TERMS AND WORDS

African Riviera	Nile
Afrikaaners	Plateau
Boers	Rift Valley
Cataracts	Safari Lodges
Game Reserves	Sahara Desert
Game Viewing	Sahel
Great Trek	Sanctuaries
HIV	Savanna
Horn of Africa	Serengeti
Ivory Coast	Swahili
Mt. Kenya	Tropical
Mt. Kilimanjaro	

INTRODUCTION

Africa is one of the largest continents, Figure 12–1, and is also one of the most sparsely populated and least visited. The entire continent of Africa totals 11,685,000 square miles, second only to Asia. The part of Africa south of the Sahara is itself a large area, totaling approximately 9 million square miles, roughly three times the size of the United States. The sheer size of this landmass has played a major role in its relationship with the rest of the world. Its size handicaps development of transportation and communication linkages, which remain concentrated along coastal areas or navigable waters. In addition to its large size and isolation, Africa generally has a climate that is either too wet or too dry for most agriculture.

Tourism in Africa is limited. Only three regions attract significant world tourism, East Africa (principally Kenya, Tanzania, and Mauritius), West Af-

POPULATION CHARACTERISTICS, 1997

Country	Population (millions)	Annual Growth Rate (percent)	Time to Double Pop. (years)	Per Capita GNP	Life Expectancy (years)	Daily Calorie Supply	Percent Urban
Angola	11.6	3.2	22	410	47	1,807	32
Benin	5.9	3.4	21	370	54	2,305	36
Botswana	1.5	2.6	27	3,020	54	2,375	27
Burkina Faso	10.9	3.0	23	230	47	2,288	15
Burundi	6.1	2.6	26	160	50	1,932	6
Cameroon	13.9	2.8	25	650	55	2,217	44
Cape Verde	0.4	1.9	36	960	65	2,805	44
Central African Republic	3.3	2.5	28	340	48	2,036	39
Chad	7.0	2.5	28	180	47	1,743	22
Comoros	0.6	3.6	19	470	58	1,897	29
Congo	2.6	2.3	30	680	46	2,590	58
Cote d'Ivoire (Ivory Coast)	15.0	2.6	27	660	52	2,577	46
Djibouti	0.6	2.3	30	N/A	48	2,338	81
Equatorial Guinea	0.4	2.6	27	380	48	N/A	37
Ethiopia	58.7	2.8	25	100	47	1,667	15
Gabon	1.2	2.0	35	3,490	54	2,383	73
Gambia	1.2	2.5	28	320	45	2,360	26
Ghana	18.1	2.9	24	390	56	2,248	36
Guinea	7.5	2.4	29	550	45	2,132	29
Guinea-Bissau	1.1	2.1	34	250	43	2,556	22
Kenya	28.8	2.6	27	280	54	2,163	27
Lesotho	2.0	2.6	27	770	58	2,299	16
Liberia	2.3	3.1	22	N/A	59	2,382	44
Madagascar	14.1	3.3	21	230	57	2,158	22
Malawi	9.6	2.8	25	170	42	2,139	18
Mali	9.9	3.0	23	250	46	2,314	26
Mauritania	2.4	2.5	27	460	52	2,685	39
Mauritius	1.1	1.2	60	3,380	70	2,887	43
Mozambique	18.4	2.7	26	80	46	1,680	28
Namibia	1.7	2.6	27	2,000	56	1,946	32
Niger	9.8	3.4	21	220	47	2,308	15
Nigeria	107.1	3.0	23	260	54	2,312	16
Reunion	0.7	1.6	43	N/A	74	3,245	73
Rwanda	7.7	1.9	36	180	40	1,971	5
Sao Tome and Principe	0.1	3.4	20	350	63	2,129	46
Senegal	8.8	2.7	26	600	49	2,369	43
Seychelles	0.1	1.4	50	6,620	70	2,287	50
Sierra Leone	4.4	1.9	36	180	34	1,799	35
Somalia	10.2	3.2	22	N/A	47	1,906	24
Sudan	27.9	2.1	33	N/A	51	1,974	27
South Africa	42.5	1.5	43	3,160	56	2,695	57
Swaziland	1.0	3.2	22	1,170	57	2,706	30
Tanzania	29.5	3.0	23	120	50	2,206	21
Togo	4.7	3.5	20	310	57	2,214	30
Uganda	20.6	2.9	24	240	41	2,153	11
Zaire	47.4	3.4	21	120	52	1,991	29
Zambia	9.4	2.1	33	400	44	2,077	42
Zimbabwe	11.4	2.7	26	540	51	2,299	31

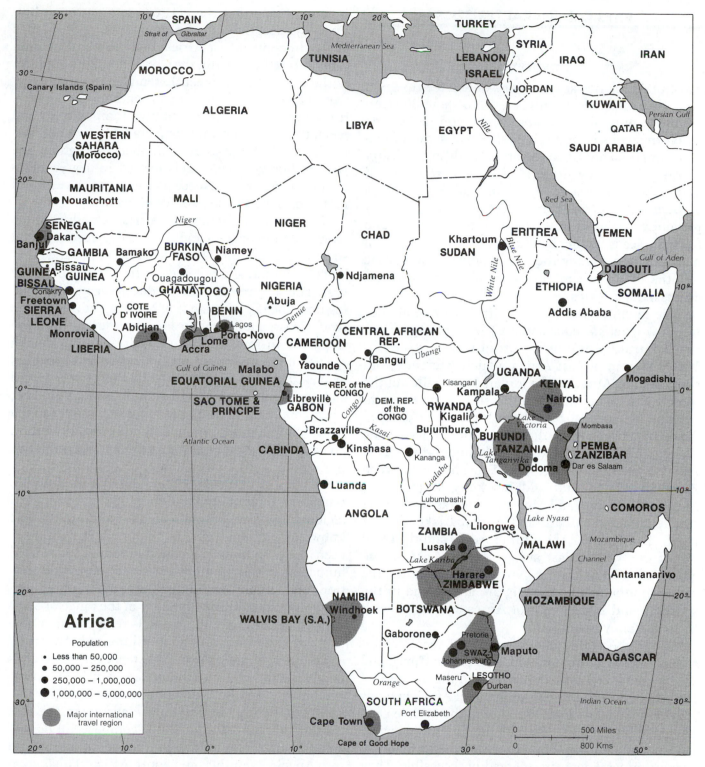

Figure 12–1 Africa

rica (Senegal and Ivory Coast), and Southern Africa (South Africa, Botswana, Zimbabwe, Zambia, and Swaziland).

Africa is a land of poverty, with the lowest per capita incomes in the world. In many countries, $100 a year or less is the norm. Low literacy rates, high birth and death rates, high infant mortality rates, and the predominance of rural village residence indicate the lack of industrial development of the continent. These factors also handicap the development of tourism to Africa.

PHYSICAL CHARACTERISTICS

Landforms

Most of Africa lies at elevations of 650 feet to 6,500 feet. True lowlands, from sea level to about 300 feet, comprise only a small area of the continent. The landforms consist of a relatively level series of plateaus imposed one upon the other, with sharp escarpments where they descend to the narrow coastal plain. This has created rapids and falls (cataracts) a short distance up the rivers from the coast, effectively preventing navigation to the interior. Access to and from the sea is further handicapped by the absence of natural harbors along the coast, sandbars across the mouths of the rivers, and reefs along the tropical coasts of East Africa.

The landforms of tropical Africa can be divided into low-level plateaus and high-level plateaus. The major feature of the high-plateau region is the Rift Valley system of East Africa, which stretches from southeastern Africa to the Jordan River valley of the Middle East. The rift features result from large continental blocks that have been lifted up or dropped down in an area of faulting, folding, and volcanic activity. This has created the high mountains of East Africa as well as the large Lake Tanganyika (between Zaire and Tanzania) and Lake Nyasa (between Malawi, Tanzania, and Mozambique), as well as the smaller Edward, Albert, and Turkana lakes farther north. The Red Sea, the Gulf of Aden, and the Dead Sea of the Middle East are geologically part of the great Rift Valley system. Volcanic mountains like Mt. Kilimanjaro in Tanzania are also found in the southern and eastern part of Africa associated with the Rift Valley system.

Lowland Africa rarely exceeds 2,000 feet in elevation. It includes the river systems of the Congo and the Niger as well as the major part of the drainage of the Nile. The dividing line of lowland Africa extends north from Angola to the Red Sea in the Middle East. Lowland Africa has undergone much less geological folding and faulting than other continents, and important mineral deposits are readily accessible. They contribute to the economy and importance of the region, as many are vital to the industrialized nations of the world.

Climate Patterns

The climates of Africa are characterized by too much, too little, or poorly timed precipitation. The location of almost all of the continent within 30 degrees of the equator means that the entire area is warm or hot. The only exceptions are the mountains and highlands of the rift zone of East Africa. Because of its location centered on the equator, the Congo Basin is the center of the tropical rain forest. Extending approximately five to eight degrees north and south of the equator, it is an area with year-round high temperatures and precipitation. Daytime temperatures average between 70 and 80 degrees Fahrenheit throughout the year, and daily ranges rarely exceed 15 degrees. Precipitation generally exceeds 45 inches per year, and in much of the region exceeds 60 inches.

The savanna climates of Africa extend from between 10 to 15 degrees and 20 to 25 degrees north and south of the equator. These climates are hot and rainy half of the year, and hot and dry the other half of the year. The savanna climate produces vegetation ranging from the tall grasslands of Nigeria, the Sudan, the Ivory Coast, and Kenya to a forest different from the tropical rain forest only in density and number of species of trees. Some savannas, such as those in areas of West Africa, probably resulted from the repeated and persistent burning by both the present and former occupants of the area. The savanna lands are also the home of the last great herds of wild animals and their predators. These have become a major tourist attraction.

North and south of the tropical savanna lands is a transition zone of steppe climate. The transitional region immediately south of the Sahara Desert is known as the Sahel, where the world's attention has been focused because of recurring drought and related human suffering for the past two decades. Precipitation totals from 7.5 to 20 inches yearly, and temperature maximums are constantly in the range of 80 to 100 degrees Fahrenheit. The daily temperature range is great, with nighttime lows falling to between 50 and 60 degrees Fahrenheit. This steppe region extends nearly the full width of the African continent, but it is relatively narrow in north-south extent.

South of the southern zone of savanna in Africa is another belt of steppe land. It is composed of Botswana, Zimbabwe, and Zambia, but portions extend into Angola, Namibia, and South Africa. This region is similar to the Sahel and has suffered from similar environmental problems such as drought. North and south of the steppe lands are the great deserts of Africa. To the north is the Sahara (approximately the same size as the United States), the world's greatest desert, and in the south is the Kalahari. These deserts are characterized by temperature extremes, limited precipitation, and isolated settlements. The desert regions of Africa have recorded the world's highest official temperatures of 136 degrees Fahrenheit. Precipitation ranges from two to six inches per year, making settlement difficult. Population is restricted to oases or the valleys of rivers, such as the Nile, which bring the much-needed water from the tropical savanna and tropical rain forest areas. Other rivers penetrate the margins of the Sahara and are the basis for settlements such as Tombouctou (Timbuktu) on the Niger and Kaedi on the Senegal River on the border between Mauritania and Senegal.

In southeastern and southwestern Africa, increased elevation or influence from prevailing winds creates areas of subtropical climate similar to the southeastern United States. The southwest tip of Africa around Cape Town has a Mediterranean or dry-summer, subtropical climate. The southeast coast has a humid subtropical climate caused by modification of the steppe lands by the higher elevations of the Drakensberg Mountains.

TOURISM IN AFRICA

Subsaharan Africa is the least developed and least visited region of tourism in the world and, with the exception of East and Southern Africa, travel and income to the region have been declining. A number of factors account for the overall general lack of a strong tourist industry in Africa. First is the region's long distance from the major tourist-generating countries of the world and the limited connectivity between North America, Europe, and Africa. There is direct connectivity into some countries, such as Kenya, Nigeria, and South Africa; but for the region as a whole, transportation is poor and infrequent. In some cases, little or no air travel connections exist to world tourist markets. Second, modern transportation systems within Africa are extremely poor or nonexistent. Travel both to and between countries can be circuitous at best. Third, in many countries, there is little or no infrastructure for tourists. Most of the countries are poor and have a difficult time financing their development, and funds have not been available from either international or local sources for tourism development. Fourth, the political unrest in many regions handicaps the tourist market. Fifth, the fear of *HIV* (human immunodeficiency virus) and reports of its high incidence in Africa is causing a decline in the limited number of tourists coming to Africa south of the Sahara. Sixth, some airlines in the past limited service to South Africa because of the racial policies existing in that country until 1992, limiting visitors to the African country that has the best transportation and cultural connectivity to major market areas. As yet, except for a few areas, such as those in East Africa, West Africa, and Southern Africa, there is little tourism of consequence in Africa. This region does have a higher percentage of travel for the purpose of business, which has led to the development of some world-class hotels in capital cities. Data are also sporadic, but some idea of the character of tourism to Africa can be illustrated for the various regions.

West Africa

Country	Capital	Language	Currency	Square Miles and State Comparison	
Benin	Porto-Novo	French, Fon, Yoruba	CFA franc	43,484	(Pennsylvania)
Burkina Faso	Ouagadougou	French, Sudanic	CFA franc	105,869	(Colorado)
Gambia	Banjul	English, Mandinka, Wolof	dalasi	4,361	(2 × Delaware)
Ghana	Accra	English, Akan, Moshi-pagoma	cedis	92,100	(Oregon)
Ivory Coast	Abidjan	French, Dioula	CFA franc	123,847	(New Mexico)
Liberia	Monrovia	English, Nigeran, Congo	Liberian dollar	43,000	(Pennsylvania)
Mali	Bamako	French, Bambara	CFA franc	478,766	(Texas and California)
Mauritania	Nouakchott	Arabic, Pular, Soniwk-wolof	ouguiya	397,955	(Texas and California)
Niger	Niamey	French, Hausa, Djerma	CFA franc	489,191	(3 × California)
Nigeria	Lagos	English, Hausa, Yoruha, Ibo, Fulani	Naira	356,669	(2 × California)
Senegal	Dakar	French, Wolof, Pulaan	CFA franc	75,955	(South Dakota)
Sierra Leone	Freetown	English, Mende, Temne	leones	27,925	(South Carolina)
Togo	Lome	French, Ewe, Mina	CFA franc	21,925	(West Virginia)

While the official languages and some African languages are listed, there are a wide variety of languages and dialects spoken in each of the countries, as in all of Africa. The official language is used in the large cities but not necessarily by a majority of the population.

 TRAVEL TIPS

Entry: Most of the countries with the exception of Senegal require a visa, and some require proof of sufficient funds.
Transportation: Direct flights from various European countries provide service once or twice a week to the West African countries. Transportation outside of major cities is difficult, and taxis are the best form of travel within major cities.
Health: Protection for yellow fever, rabies, malaria, cholera, tetanus, typhus, and typhoid should be taken. Also in most cases tap water is not potable. Meats should be well cooked and fruits and vegetables carefully cleaned and prepared. Visitors should avoid swimming in freshwater streams and lakes. In most countries there is a high incidence of HIV infection among prostitutes.
Shopping: Common items include hand-carved wooden objects, brass, leather goods, masks, jewelry, handwoven fabrics, and handicrafts of the individual country.

Tourism Characteristics

Tourism to West Africa is illustrated in Table 12–1. Senegal and the Ivory Coast are the major beneficiaries of tourism to the region. Senegal acts as a transit area connecting North and South America and Europe with many African countries. Of the areas in West Africa, the Ivory Coast not only vies with Ghana for the largest number of visitors, but has the best tourist infrastructure, with fine restaurants and good hotels. Both countries have strong links with France and stable governments, unlike many countries of the region.

Tourist Destinations and Attractions

The focal point of tourism on the Ivory Coast is its beautiful beaches set amid plantations and picturesque fishing villages. The Ivory Coast is trying to build an *African Riviera* on the beaches. In addition, inland towns and villages are "living museums" that demonstrate the culture and way of life of the people in the country. Abidjan, the capital, is a colonial town providing attractions, such as the IFAN Museum, the public market, and an interesting African sector. Near Abidjan at Buna, there is a wild animal preserve. President Houphouet Boigny has completed a multi-million-dollar Catholic basilica, which will hold

CULTURAL CAPSULE

West Africa is Subsaharan Africa's most populous region, and the southern half of the region is home to the majority of people. It was from this region that much of the slave trade came. With the exception of Liberia, all the states of West Africa were created by European colonial powers—France, Germany, Britain, and Portugal—during the late nineteenth century.

West Africa is composed of a number of tribal groups, such as the Malinke, Fulani, Hausa, Mandingoes, and Mossi. The Malinke journeyed from their early center in Mali to the coastal areas of Guinea, Senegal, and Gambia. Malinke also moved into Burkina Faso, Liberia, and Sierra Leone, where they came to be known as Mandingoes. The Fulani have been migrants throughout the region, spreading Islam. The Hausa mostly live in Northern Nigeria and Niger, but are widespread through West Africa; and their language is sometimes suggested as a possible lingua franca for Africa. There has been large regional migration in West Africa from the poor inland states of Burkina Faso, Mali, and Niger to the wealthier states of the *Ivory Coast* and Ghana. Many Ghanaians, Togolese, Beninois, and Cameroonians have taken up residence in Nigeria.

The two major destination countries, Senegal and Ivory Coast, have a number of ethnic groups, with both countries having a large European (dominated by French) population. The Ivory Coast has more than 5 million non-Ivorian Africans living in the country. Islam is the dominant religion of the two countries, at 90 percent in Senegal and 25 percent in the Ivory Coast. Tribal religions are strong throughout both countries.

The typical food dishes include fish, rice, oil, poultry, onions, ground peanuts, and spices. They have been influenced greatly by French cooking. In Senegal the sexes and different age groups eat separately. Clean hands and eating with the right hand are important.

Taxis are hailed by raising one arm. Men and women keep their distance in public and are expected to be dignified and reserved around the opposite sex. Shaking hands is a common greeting. Punctuality is important in the Ivory Coast.

18,000 people inside and 300,000 people outside in its adjacent square. It was built in the president's home village 160 miles north of the capital city of Abidjan. Pope John Paul II visited and consecrated this basilica in September 1990. It contains four times the stained glass of the cathedral in Chartres, France, and the dome is twice the size of the dome of St. Peter's Basilica in Rome.

Senegal is a hub for international flights and also offers beautiful beaches. The capital, Dakar, has a number of interesting museums, such as the House of Slaves on the island of Goree and a "French town" similar to that in New Orleans or St. Louis. Dakar is an attractive city with shining blue, white, and pink houses and walls covered with bougain-

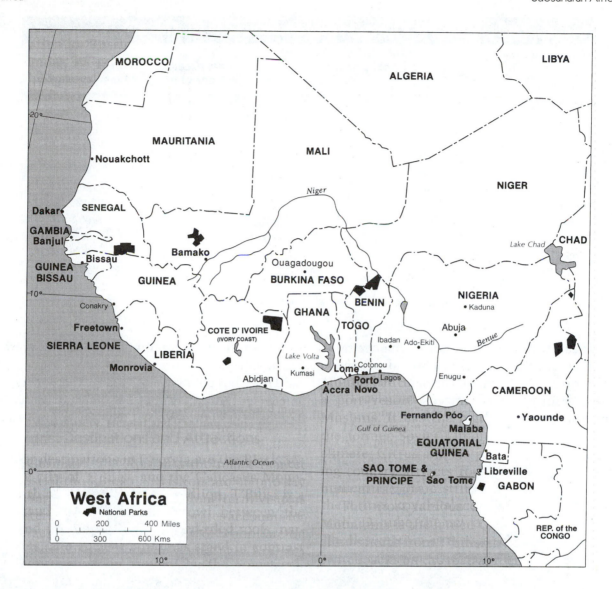

Figure 12-2 West Africa

villea. Senegal also has one of the finest game reserves in West Africa with a variety of wildlife and good accommodations. The game park, Niokola-Koba, also is the home of the Bassari people, who offer an interesting cultural experience, demonstrating their unique dress and festivals.

Although they do not have a well-developed tourist trade, the other West African countries have the potential for future tourism, relying upon a variety of African cultures, the wildlife, colorful scenery, and some excellent beaches. They will have to overcome serious political, economic, and environmental problems.

Nigeria suffers from overcrowding, poor sanitation, and high prices in its cities, but those who visit the capital, Lagos, will find a fine museum of African art, the Museum of Nigerian Antiquities, and one of the largest markets of Africa. Lagos is built on a series

of islands with connecting bridges and overpasses. There is a fine beach near Lagos. Ibadan, north of Lagos, is the site of the largest Black medical school in the world. The city is enclosed by thick sun-dried mud walls and has attractions such as markets and colorfully dressed members of the Yoruba tribe. Jos, Nigeria's mining center, has a museum that houses a terra-cotta display that is over 4,000 years old. The ancient mud-walled Islamic city of Kano in northern Nigeria exhibits the Islamic cultural environment to the visitor. Tribal cultures and ancient archaeological sites are important tourism attractions that could be developed in Nigeria.

Togo, near the Ivory Coast, has a tourist trade similar to Nigeria. It has made a serious attempt to improve its tourist business and draws heavily from its neighbors of Ghana and Nigeria. It too has good beaches, picturesque fishing villages, and some

Table 12–1 International Tourism to West Africa

Country	Number of Visitors (thousands)		1996 Receipts (millions of US $)	1996 Average Expenses per Visit
	1986	1996		
Benin	46	147	29	197
Burkina Faso	45	136	23	169
Gambia	74	77	22	286
Ghana	92	298	239	802
Cote d'Ivoire	184	157	43	274
Mali	33	50	20	400
Mauritania	N/A	N/A	11	N/A
Niger	29	17	17	1,000
Nigeria	311	303	55	182
Senegal	235	263	147	559
Sierra Leone	194	46	10	217
Togo	99	56	8	143

Source: *Yearbook of Tourism Statistics.* World Tourism Organization, 1997

unique African tribal cultures. Lome, the capital, is located on an excellent beach. It provides a scenic view of African life with picturesque fishermen's huts and colorfully dressed citizens. North of Togo, tours into the scenic highlands provide the visitor excellent views of mountain villages set above lush green valleys.

The other countries of West Africa receive only a small number of tourists. Most countries have good beaches and their people illustrate African tribal cul-

Figure 12–3 Mosque and prayer in Nigeria

Figure 12–4 Timbuktu

ture, but lack of facilities and promotion combine with political unrest to prevent significant growth in their tourist trade.

Benin has some national parks and game preserves, but their quality is questionable. There is a restored fortress at Ouidah that dates back to the Portuguese explorers, and it was the site of the last recorded slave ship from Africa, in 1870. For the more

daring, the Temple of the Serpents, which houses pythons, is also at Ouidah.

Ghana shares excellent beaches with the Ivory Coast. Accra, the capital, is a modern city in an African setting. Accra serves as a jumping-off place for trips to diamond and gold mines where visitors can observe the mining process. Near Accra along the coast, there are castles and forts that were built by the early Portuguese, Dutch, English, French, and Danish colonial powers. Liberia is worth mentioning as it received a large portion of its visitors from the United States in the past. Liberia was a nation created for freed slaves who returned to Africa from America prior to the American Civil War. Today a civil war has devastated the country, and it will be some time before the travel industry can recover.

The desert nations, such as Mauritania and Mali, have French settlements and offer camel caravan trips to such places as Timbuktu in Mali. Mauritania has some good beaches that can be developed, Chinguetti, the seventh holy city of Islam, and other Islamic buildings worth seeing.

East Africa

Country	Capital	Language	Currency	Square Miles and State Comparison	
Burundi	Bujumbura	Kirundi, French, Swahili	franc	10,747	(Maryland)
Comoros	Moroni	Arabic, French, Comoran	franc	838	(½ of Delaware)
Ethiopia	Addis Ababa	Amharic, Arabic	birr	472,434	(⅘ of Alaska)
Kenya	Nairobi	English, Swahili	shilling	224,961	(Texas)
Malawi	Lilongwe	English, Chichewa	kwacha	45,747	(Pennsylvania)
Mauritius	Port Louis	English, Hindi	rupees	790	(Rhode Island)
Rwanda	Kigali	Kinyarwanda, French, Kiswahili	franc	10,169	(Maryland)
Seychelles	Victoria	Creole, French, English	rupee	171	
Somalia	Mogadishu	Somali, Arabic	shilling	246,200	(Texas)
Tanzania	Dar es Salaam	Swahili, English	shilling	364,900	(2 × California)
Uganda	Kampala	English, Luganda, Swahili	shilling	91,134	(Oregon)

 ## TRAVEL TIPS

Entry: Visas are required by most countries, but in some (Kenya and Seychelles for example) they can be obtained at the airport. Most require proof of funds, onward or return transportation, and an airport tax.

Transportation: International service is provided through European capitals and other East African countries. Countries such as Kenya, Seychelles, and Mauritius have better international service and connectivity. Transportation within the major cities is best by taxi.

Health: In most areas tap water is not potable. Water should be boiled or filtered. Many large hotels in Kenya, Tanzania, and the Seychelles filter their water. Fruits and vegetables should be carefully cleaned and prepared. Cholera, yellow fever, and malaria are major concerns for travel to East Africa. Uganda has a serious AIDS and HIV problem, especially among prostitutes.

Shopping: Items include hand-carved wooden objects, brass, leather goods, masks, jewelry, handwoven fabrics, and handicrafts of the individual country.

CULTURAL CAPSULE

The East African region is an area of great diversity. The islands are the homes of distinctive civilizations with ties to Asia, yet their interactions with the African mainland require they be placed in this region. The region is one of animals, camels, cattle, goats, and sheep. People have migrated through the region since the existence of humankind; in fact, most of the human fossils of early people have been uncovered in this region.

The languages of the people are tied to either the Bantu or the Nilotic linguistic families. The official languages noted in the table are a result of European colonialism and are spoken by a minority in the major cities.

The area has had considerable Islamic influence through Muslim Arab traders or proximity to the Arabian Peninsula. Mogadishu, the capital of Somalia, began as an Islamic trading post in the tenth century. Islam dominates throughout the Horn of Africa, except in the Ethiopian interior and southern Sudan. In the first half of the nineteenth century the sultan of Oman moved his capital to Zanzibar. The region was a source of a large slave trade to Egypt and the Middle East, the Persian Gulf, and the Indian Ocean islands.

South Asian laborers were brought in by the British to build the East African railroad. Traders and business people settled in Kenya and Tanzania. South Asian laborers were brought in to work on the sugar plantations of Mauritius. East Asians now comprise two-thirds of this island's population. The region of the Horn can be characterized by drought and violence. The people of Kenya, Tanzania, Uganda, Burundi, and Rwanda have shared a similar background of tribal kingdoms and political division along ethnic lines. For example, the Tutsi—a ruling warrior class—and the Hutu—a peasant class—compete in Rwanda and Burundi.

The Comoros, Madagascar, Mauritius, and the Seychelles each has its own unique characteristics while sharing some common traits. All four islands have been influenced by contacts with Asia as well as with mainland Africa and Europe. Madagascar and the Comoros have populations that began in the Middle East, Africa, and Indonesia. The people of Mauritius and the Seychelles are a combination of European, African, and Asian origins.

All four have been influenced by France, with the British taking control of two islands during the 1830s and abolishing slavery. Local French Creole remained the major language on the islands.

The four major tourist destinations are Kenya, Mauritius, Tanzania, and Seychelles. While Kenya's population is largely African, it is divided into as many as forty ethnic groups along linguistic lines. English is the official language and widely used in large cities for business and official use. *Swahili* is the national language, and each ethnic group speaks its own language. The major religions are Protestant and Roman Catholic. The Muslims, who comprise about 6 percent of the population, live along the coast and in the Northeast. Tanzania's population is equally diverse. The majority of Tanzanians, including such large tribes as the Sukuma (the only group with more than a million members) and the Nyamwezi, are of Bantu stock. There are three Nilotic ethnic groups, two Khoisan, and two Afro-Asiatic. Zanzibar's population has a strong Arabic influence.

Mauritius was colonized in 1638 by the Dutch. Waves of traders, planters, and their slaves created a strong Asian influence. Mauritius' Creoles trace their origins to the plantation owners and slaves who were brought to work the sugar fields. Indo-Mauritians are descended from Indian immigrants who arrived in the nineteenth century to work as indentured laborers after slavery was abolished in 1835. Most Seychelles people are descendants of early French settlers and African slaves brought to the Seychelles in the nineteenth century by the British who freed them from slave ships on the East African coast. Indians and Chinese account for slightly over 1 percent of the rest of the population. Creole is the native language of 94 percent of the people, with English and French as common languages. English is the language of commerce and government. The handshake is the common greeting in the four major tourist destination countries. They understand most of the European gestures. In many cases using the left hand alone or to pass items is not polite. The verbal "tch-tch" sound is considered an insult in Kenya and Tanzania. Photographing people should not be done without permission. European cuisine (and Indian in major cities) is common in all four major tourist destination countries. The two island nations—Seychelles and Mauritius—have typical Creole, Indian, and Chinese food. Fresh seafood, fruits, and vegetables are common in these islands. Tanzania's foods include grains, fruits, rice, cooked bananas, and vegetables. Kenya's typical dishes are goat, beef, lamb, chicken, fish, red bean stew, and fruits.

Tourism Characteristics

Tourism is significant in East Africa, but a number of countries, especially the countries of the Horn of Africa, have low numbers of visitors due to the environmental and political problems of the region. Kenya, Table 12–2, receives the largest amount of visitors to the region, and it is second in Africa only to South Africa in total visitor numbers. Kenya leads Africa in non-African visitors. (South Africa has more visitors, but it has a strong regional flow from other African countries.) Tanzania has opened its borders with Kenya in order to take advantage of Kenya's large tourist industry. Kenya and Tanzania also benefit from tours combining the two countries. The largest number of visitors to Tanzania are by land, while Kenya's visitors come by air.

Along with the governments of other East African countries, Kenya recognized the importance of tourism early and has established governmental agencies to plan, develop, and promote tourism. All of the nations of East Africa have set out to improve their infrastructure for tourism by providing money to build hotels, lodges, airports, and so on. Kenya is beginning to have problems with its tourism. An economic recession resulted in badly maintained infrastructure, which makes tourist visits uncom-

Table 12–2 International Tourism to East Africa

Country	Number of Visitors (thousands) 1986	Number of Visitors (thousands) 1996	1996 Receipts (millions of US $)	1996 Average Expenses per Visit
Burundi	66	31	1	40
Comoros	6	25	9	36
Ethiopia	19	107	46	430
Kenya	604	907	493	544
Madagascar	27	77	61	792
Malawi	69	232	7	30
Mauritius	165	487	466	956
Reunion	165	339	N/A	N/A
Seychelles	67	131	102	778
Somalia	39	10	N/A	N/A
Tanzania	103	230	147	639
Uganda	32	240	100	417

fortable. Roads to game parks are in such disrepair that travel is alongside the road. Kenya has received adverse press pertaining to problems of security for the potential tourist. Other countries of Africa have been marketing their product more aggressively.

Figure 12–5 East Africa

Kenya has not tried to broaden its market outside of Europe and North America. European travelers make up the majority of Kenya's visitors, with Germans dominating. The United States is the most important country outside of Europe for tourists to Kenya. Some concern is expressed by officials that Kenya may be at the saturation point of its tourist-carrying capacity. Most visitors are associated with tours and groups. European visitors to Kenya (German and British) visit longer and combine visits to the game parks with a week on the coast for a sun-sea-sand vacation. North Americans typically visit for just a week and spend their time on safari, then return home.

The islands of Mauritius and Seychelles in the Indian Ocean enjoy a tourism trade that is as large as they can effectively handle and maintain. The Seychelles have targeted their tourism industry at the upscale market; consequently, they have the highest average expenditure per visitor. They feel this will provide them with the highest possible income and have less impact upon their islands. The Seychelles market is largely European, with minor markets from South Africa.

Mauritius had significant growth in the late 1980s. It now has the second largest volume of visitors to East Africa after Kenya. It is dependent upon three major markets: Europe (57 percent), South Africa (10 percent), and Réunion Island (19 percent). In an effort to diversify, Mauritius has tried to attract tourists from Japan and Singapore. A weekly flight to Singapore has been established, but direct flights to Japan are not presently operating.

Tourist Destinations and Attractions

The principal tourist attractions of Kenya are its forty national parks. The Nairobi National Park is important for observing African wildlife. Tsavo National Park, the largest national park in the world, offers spectacular scenery along with a wide variety of animals and birds. A major attraction in Tsavo is Mzima Springs. Elephants, hippos, and crocodiles are found in its waters while gazelle, zebra, and giraffe wander along the banks.

The Masai reserve, where the culture of the Masai people is partially protected, Figure 12–6, provides an opportunity to observe African wildlife and Masai culture. Masai Mara is one of the most visited game preserves in Africa, and its most prominent feature is the annual migration of the wildebeests from Serengeti in Tanzania. Lake Nakuru National Park has a variety of bird *sanctuaries*. At Lake Nakuru more than a million pink flamingoes can be seen feeding the shore. Close to Lake Nakuru, in the Nakuru National Park, is the first black rhino sanctuary constructed as part of the government plan to save the rhino from extinction.

Amberdares National Park exhibits the extraordinary mountain scenery of the Rift Valley and some picturesque villages, including an old town with narrow winding streets illustrating native culture. *Mt. Kenya*, Africa's second highest mountain, attracts climbers and hikers. Its slopes have two of the most famous hotels in Africa—Treetops and the Ark, which provide close-up viewing of game as they come out of the forest to salt licks. Nakuru and Thomson's Falls offer scenic views of the Great Rift Valley. Mombasa, on the Indian Ocean, is a Muslim center and has a host of mosques, a Portuguese fort, Fort Jesus, and a number of beaches.

Figure 12–7   Nairobi, Kenya

Nairobi, the capital, has a number of interesting attractions, including the National Assembly Building, the National Theatre, the University of Nairobi, and the National Museum with exhibits of African tribal lore and Kenyan history, Figure 12-7.

Of the other East African countries, Uganda has very little tourism due to the undeveloped nature of the industry as well as its unstable political situation. Uganda has three national parks, with the primary attraction being Murchison Falls (now called Kabalega), the source of the Nile, surrounded by mountain scenery and an excellent variety of wildlife. Uganda is considered by many to be one of the most beautiful countries in Africa. Lake Victoria is very picturesque. The two major cities are the capital city of Kampala and Entebbe. Both are on Lake Victoria, and travel between the two passes through small villages and farms. Kampala, like Rome, is built on a series of seven hills; it offers the visitor a mosque, the tombs of Kabakas, and the Uganda Museum.

The second most important country in East Africa is Kenya's neighbor, Tanzania. Tanzania receives less than one fourth as many tourists as Kenya and has the same general attractions as Kenya and Uganda. Game parks, mountain scenery, and one of the world's most famous mountains, Mt. Kilimanjaro, which attracts climbers and hikers, are part of its tourist destinations. Ngorongoro Crater is one of the largest craters in the world, nearly ten miles wide. A wide variety of wildlife, including antelopes and elephants, can be seen in the crater. Just outside of the crater is *Serengeti*, noted for its tree-climbing lions. *Serengeti* National Park has a large concentration of wildlife and is one of the better viewing parks in the world.

Figure 12–6   Tribal exhibition in Kenya

Dar es Salaam, the capital and port city of Tanzania, is an attractive city with attractions, such as the Ministries of the Government, the Arab Asian sectors, Tanzania National Museum, and the harbor area. Just off the coast is Zanzibar Island, which was a Persian and Arab trading center. With its ornate Arabian homes, Stone Town is most interesting in Zanzibar. Both Kenya and Tanzania have some excellent beaches that are attractive to Europeans who enjoy both the national parks and the sun-sea-sand environment.

Seychelles and Mauritius islands offer exotic Indian Ocean sun-sea-sand experiences for visitors. They offer beautiful scenery, placid lagoons, and coral reefs with spectacular snorkeling and skindiving. Madagascar, the fourth largest island in the world, receives few tourists. Ethiopia and Somalia have few tourists because of the conflicts in and between the countries. Both have suffered from extensive droughts, and the world news has emphasized the problems of the two countries and others in the semiarid Sahel.

Southern Africa

Country	Capital	Language	Currency	Square Miles and State Comparison	
Botswana	Gaborone	English, Setswana	pula	231,804	(slightly less than Texas)
Lesotho	Maseru	English, Sesotho, Zulu, Xhosa	loti	11,716	(Maryland)
Madagascar	Antananarivo	French, Malagasy	franc	228,880	(slightly less than Texas)
Mozambique	Maputo	Portuguese	metical	481,353	(2 × California)
Namibia	Windhoek	English, Afrikaans, German	rand	318,261	(½ of Alaska)
South Africa	Pretoria	Afrikaans, English	rand	433,680	(⅘ of Alaska)
Swaziland	Mbabane	English, Swati	lilangeni	6,704	(Hawaii)
Zambia	Lusaka	English	kwacha	290,585	(Texas)
Zimbabwe	Harare	English	dollar	151,000	(California)

 ## TRAVEL TIPS

Entry: Visas are required for some of the countries. In many cases they require proof of transportation and sufficient funds.

Transportation: The region is served from the United States with direct flights to South Africa and Zambia. Lusaka, Zambia, and Johannesburg, South Africa, are hubs for travel to and throughout the region. Connections to the other countries are via Europe, which provides service to the various countries of the region. Service from East Africa via Kenya to Botswana and Johannesburg is also available.

Health: Malaria, yellow fever, and in some cases cholera protection should be taken. Water in major cities of Southern Africa is potable, but care should be taken to use bottled and boiled water elsewhere. Visitors should avoid swimming in fresh water. Hepatitis has been a problem in some of the cities of the region.

Travel Advisory: The state department has advised that the political situation in South Africa is tense and travelers should be aware of problem areas. Travel to the most frequented tourist areas has been generally safe, but recently there have been some problems on the beaches.

Shopping: Common items include animal skins, precious stones, hand-carved wooden objects, brass, leather goods, masks, jewelry, handwoven fabrics, and handicrafts of the individual country.

CULTURAL CAPSULE

Southern Africa is a diverse region. The dominant theme in current history has been the evolving struggle of the region's indigenous black African majority for majority rule. The area was settled at least by the eighth century by a variety of black African ethnic groups who spoke languages belonging to the Bantu as well as the Khoisan linguistic classifications. The early groups practiced both agriculture and pastoralism. Some groups had organized into strong states by the fifteenth century as the Kongo of northern Angola and the Shona people of the Zimbabwean plateau. Others like the Nguni speakers lived in smaller communities.

In the sixteenth century small numbers of Portuguese began settling along the coasts of Angola and Mozambique. In 1652, the Dutch established a settlement at Africa's southernmost tip, the Cape of Good Hope. The Dutch expanded steadily into the interior throughout the eighteenth century, seizing land of the local Khoisan communities. The Dutch imported slaves from Asia as well as elsewhere in Africa. The region became racially divided between free white settlers and subordinated people of mixed African and Afro-Asian descent.

The British took over the Cape during the Napoleonic Wars and in 1820 began to send colonists to the region. During this period, the Zulu state emerged under the great warrior Prince Shaka. During the 1830s the British abolished slavery throughout their empire and extended limited civil

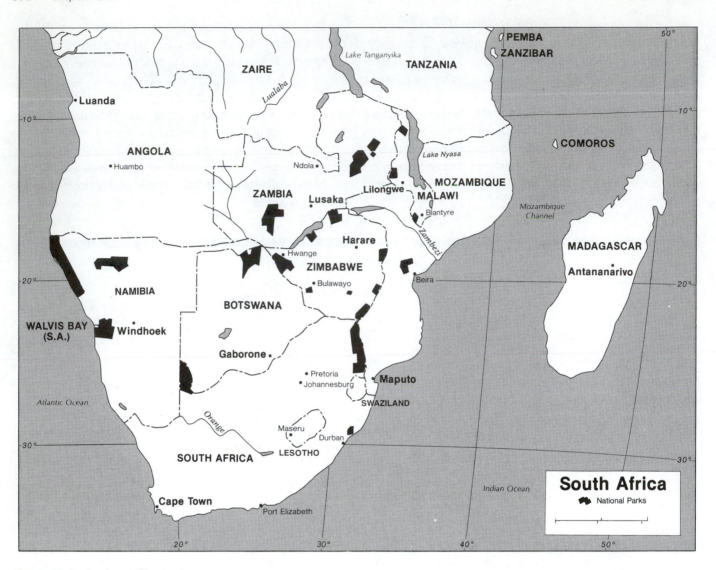

Figure 12–8 Southern Africa

rights to nonwhites at the Cape. A large number of white Dutch-descended farmers known as *Boers* migrated (the *Great Trek*) into the interior to be free of British control. Lesotho and western Botswana kingdoms preserved their independence from the Boers. During the second half of the nineteenth century, white migration spread throughout the rest of Southern Africa, dominated by British migrants. The discovery of diamonds and gold in northeastern South Africa brought further occupation and expansion by the British. Boer farmers moved to the growing towns and cities, and the term *Afrikaaners* was applied to all whites of Dutch ancestry.

In the 1890s the British South Africa Company occupied modern Zambia and Zimbabwe. British traders, missionaries, and settlers also invaded the area now known as Malawi. The Germans seized Namibia, while the Portuguese began to expand inland from their coastal enclaves. Thus by 1900 the entire region was under white colonial control.

After World War II movements advocating black self-determination developed throughout the region. By 1968 Botswana, Lesotho, Malawi, Swaziland, and Zambia had gained their independence. In 1974 Angola and Mozambique, 1980 Zimbabwe, and 1990 Namibia gained independence. South Africa is now a democratic country, after a 1992 vote by the whites to abolish official racial segregation. Until 1992 South Africa divided the population into four major racial categories: Africans, whites, coloreds, and Asians. The Africans are mainly descendants of the Sotho and Nguni peoples who migrated southward centuries ago. The largest African ethnic groups are the Zulu (6 million) and Xhosa (5.8 million). Whites are primarily descendants of Dutch, French, English, and German settlers, with small mixtures of other Europeans. Coloreds are mostly descendants of indigenous people and the earliest European and Malay settlers. They represent 9 percent of the population and live primarily in Cape Province. Asians are mainly descendants of the Indian workers brought to South Africa in the nineteenth century to work as indentured laborers on sugar estates in Natal. They constitute about 3 percent of the population.

As of 1996, South Africa has officially dropped its racist laws, and all individuals are equal before the law. In practice, the white minority still controls the wealth of the country, but the change to a democracy with Africans in the major political positions has occurred without the race war predicted by many.

Table 12–3 International Tourism to Southern Africa				
	Number of Visitors (thousands)		1996 Receipts (millions of US $)	1996 Average Expenses per Visit
Country	1986	1996		
Botswana	381	707	178	252
Lesotho	131	108	19	176
Namibia	N/A	405	265	654
South Africa	645	4,944	1,995	404
Swaziland	240	305	38	125
Zambia	123	264	60	227
Zimbabwe	357	1,743	219	126

Source: *Yearbook of Tourism Statistics.* World Tourism Organization, 1992.

Tourism Characteristics

Southern Africa suffers because of the great distances to the major industrial nations of the world and the political situation in the region. Of the nations of South Africa, three—Zimbabwe, Botswana, and South Africa—have a significant tourist industry, Table 12–3. Namibia, a newly independent nation, is only now building a tourist industry. Zimbabwe has an increasing tourist trade, as its political situation stabilized in the 1980s. Tourist numbers now exceed 1.7 million annually, a 376 percent growth since 1986.

The social and political problems in South Africa have hurt Zimbabwe as well as South Africa since traditionally Zimbabwe was included in tour programs with South Africa. Both tour operators and airlines had been canceling their South African trips due to South African racism. Tourism is now growing, and more cooperation is occurring in the region.

Much of Zimbabwe's tourist trade has been from the region. The greatest number of visitors to South Africa have been from the United Kingdom because of former colonial and commonwealth links. About 10 percent of South Africa's tourists are from the United States.

Namibia's independence in 1990 has led to the opening of the country to tourism. Currently a majority of its visitors are South Africans who comprise nearly 60 percent of the visitors. There is an increase in European visitors, with Germany being the main source, accounting for some 15 percent of visitors.

Botswana's visitors are mostly from other African countries (about 90 percent). Most travel independently, taking short camping safari vacations. The government has given priority to promote overseas tourism to the country. Its location and the location of its tourist resources provide opportunity to join its market with Zimbabwe, which will also help to in-crease the number of visitors. Non-African tourists are mostly European (English). The United States only accounts for 1 percent of the visitors to Botswana.

Tourism to South Africa itself has grown rapidly in the 1990s with the change in government. Nearly 75 percent of its visitors are from other countries in the region. Outside of Africa, the greatest number of visitors to South Africa are from the United Kingdom, because of former colonial and commonwealth links. About 2 percent of South Africa's tourists are from the United States.

Tourist Destinations and Attractions

The major attractions of Zimbabwe are the spectacular Victoria Falls and the upgraded *game viewing* areas. The falls are over a mile wide between Zimbabwe and Zambia and can be viewed from both countries. The Zimbabwe Ruins near Fort Victoria are impressive, with ruins of stone buildings dating from 700 B.C. The Wankie Game Reserve and the Inyanga National Park are excellent for observing African wildlife.

Figure 12–9   Hotel on Chobe River, Botswana

Figure 12–10   Goods in Market

Figure 12–11   Elephant Crossing

South Africa has game reserves, such as the Kruger National Park, the Kalahari Gemsbok National Park, and the Umfolozi Game reserve. The major cities of Cape Town, Pretoria, Durban, Port Elizabeth, Pietermaritzburg, and Johannesburg have museums and strong historical ties to the Afrikaaner culture. Reached by a cable car ride, Table Mountain provides a fantastic view of Cape Town and the coast. Cape Town has evidences of the Dutch and British colonial period. The most historic castle in South Africa is in Cape Town.

Pretoria, the administrative capital, has government buildings and the Voortrekker Monument in honor of the Boer trek to settle the Transvaal.

Figure 12–12   Durban, South Africa

Touching the Wild in Zimbabwe

Close to Nature

Makalolo is located 80 kilometers from Hwange Aerodome, in the southern, undeveloped part of Hwange National Park in Zimbabwe. Alan Elliott, local hunter and entrepreneur and fourth generation Zimbabwean, established the camp in 1980 as an alternative to the more traditional, luxurious safari lodges.

We were picked up in a Land Rover. (Transportation to and from the camp was provided.) The ride was one long game drive in itself.

Generally arrival at Makalolo is timed for just after dark, and the lights and the warmth of the fire are welcome after the almost two-hour drive.

Accommodations are large, green tents with awnings. We were impressed with their comfort and appeal. Bathrooms are mud huts that contain flush toilets and are centrally located in the complex of tents. Showers are bamboo structures with ten-foot ceilings, and the water is hot.

There is no landscaping here, nor is the camp set apart from the park in any way. Makalolo's location is moved every six months because no permanent camp installation is permitted in the park, due to possible ecological damage.

Our meals were served in a tented open-air clearing, and the food was excellent and plentiful. One morning on an early game drive, pancakes were prepared and served in the middle of a "vlei" (a large, open meadow).

The staff and drivers impressed us with their efficiency and friendliness, answering questions about wildlife and park ecology as if no one ever had posed that particular query before.

Game Drives, Walks

Hwange is famous for its game: elephants are so overpopulated that 4,000 will be culled from the herds within the next year. Cape Buffalo, giraffe, zebra, baboons, and wildebeest abound.

After a little time in the bush, Jim and I could distinguish between the sable antelope, kudu, duliter, steinbok, impala, and bushbuck. We also saw hippo, crocodile, jackals, and hyenas. The big cats presented more of a challenge, but we spotted both lion and leopard.

For bird watchers, this is a paradise. From the big birds—the Maribou Stork, the Secretary Bird, and the Kori Bustard—to the small—Bee-eaters, Lilac-breasted Rollers, and Crimson-breasted Shrikes—the wildlife of the air provides a fascinating study.

There generally are two game drives a day, one rather early in the morning and the second late in the afternoon. Actually we had little free time, perhaps an hour or so in the afternoon for a rest. In addition to the drives, Alan Elliott is licensed for game walks. Elliott carries a rifle for protection in case of an emergency but he has never had to use it. For those people to whom walking poses no problem, a walk in the wild should not be missed.

A few notes about seasons and the Zimbabwe climate: the wet season is December through March. The land becomes green and lush and due to plentiful water the animals disperse and are harder to spot. Most of the rain during those months falls at night and in the early morning.

The best game-viewing months are mid-July through October. As the moisture dissipates, the animals must gather at waterholes and thus are more easily seen. June probably is the coldest month, while October and November see temperatures of 115 degrees Farenheit....

Source: Judy Currie, *International Travel News.* Nov. 1986, pp. 16–17.

Durban, Figure 12–12, is the seaside resort center of South Africa. It also has Hindu temples and mosques and Indian markets that add to the area of best beaches in South Africa. It has a number of Bantu markets and is only a short drive from Zululand.

Kimberley is the diamond mining center, where visitors can watch the mining process.

The smaller countries of southern Africa receive few visitors from outside of Africa. A major development for Swaziland, Lesotho, and Botswana has been

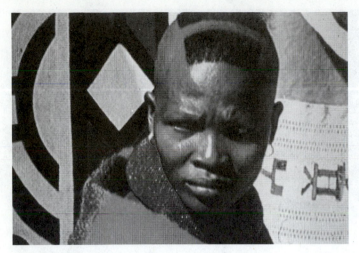

Figure 12–13 Xhosas woman, South Africa

the development of gambling casinos and large resort complexes. These places are very attractive to South Africans and other residents of the region, providing an important tourist industry to these countries.

Zambia, a landlocked country, shares Victoria Falls with Zimbabwe and also has a number of game reserves with abundant wildlife. In addition to Victoria Falls, Zambia has 19 game and wildlife parks. A specialty of the South Luangwa Park is walking safaris. Kafue National Park is one of the largest game sanctuaries in Africa, occupying an area as large as Wales. It offers both a rich variety of African wildlife as well as a spectacular array of bird life. Botswana

boasts of the most pristine and best-managed park and game reserves in Africa. Chobe National Park has a large concentration of elephants along with rhino, sable, and roan antelope. The Okavango Delta has a wide variety of birds.

Namibia is one of the few countries of the world where the black rhino still exists. In addition to the Etosha National Park it has 19 park and game reserves. Other attractions than game include the Fish River Canyon in the southwest, one of the biggest outside of the Grand Canyon, hot springs resorts, and the Cape Cross seal reserve on the northern coastline. Namibia's colonial history provides plenty of evidence of architectural gems in Luderitz and Swakopmund of the German colonial days.

There is little tourist data available for Angola and Mozambique. They have severe political problems, which hinder the development of tourism. Mozambique does have some natural attractions upon which to develop a tourism industry when the political problems are overcome. It has a rich variety of wildlife in its national parks, reserves, and the countryside.

Madagascar, the fourth largest island in the world, receives few tourists. It does offer secluded tropical beaches, coral reefs, ancient palaces, beautiful scenery, and considerable French influence. However, it is far from Europe and North America, and there are many sun-sea-sand exotic locations closer and more developed than Madagascar.

Central and Interior Africa

Country	Capital	Language	Currency	Square Miles and State Comparison	
Cameroon	Yaounde	English, French	franc	183,568	(California)
Central African Republic	Bangui	French, Swahili, Sanglo, Arabic	franc	242,000	(Texas)
Chad	N'Djamena	French, Arabic, Sara, Sango	franc	596,000	(Texas and California)
Congo, Democratic Republic of the	Kinshasa	French, Lingala, Swahili	zaire	905,063	(almost ¼ of U.S.)
Congo, Republic of the	Brazzaville	French, Lingala, Kilongo	franc	132,000	(Montana)
Gabon	Libreville	French, Fang, Myene	franc	102,317	(Colorado)
Sudan	Khartoum	Arabic, Nubian, Ya Bedawie	pounds	967,500	(¼ of U.S.)

 TRAVEL TIPS

Entry: Most of these countries require visas, sufficient funds, and proof of return or onward transportation.
Transportation: International flights are less frequent than other regions of Africa. Most flights are weekly through Europe or other African countries.

Health: Cholera, yellow fever, and malaria are major concerns. Also, typhoid, polio, and hepatitis inoculations are recommended. Raw fruits and vegetables should be carefully prepared. In most cases tap water is not potable. In most cities local transportation is crowded. Taxis are available.

CULTURAL CAPSULE

The countries of Central and Interior Africa incorporate a variety of people, cultures, resources, environments, and systems of government. Islam has influenced Chad, Sudan, and the northern part of Cameroon. In most areas Christianity coexists with indigenous tribal systems of belief. All of the states except Chad and Sudan encompass equatorial rain forests. French is the predominant language of the region as French was the principal colonial power in this region. Many of the ethnic groups, such as the Fang in Cameroon, Equatorial Guinea, and Gabon, the Bateke of the Congo, Gabon, and the Congo overlap national boundaries.

Table 12-4 International Tourism to Central and Interior Africa

Country	Number of Visitors (thousands) 1996
Cameroon	86
Central African Republic	29
Chad	7
Congo, Republic of the	27
Congo, Democratic Republic of the	37
Gabon	136
Sudan	10

Tourism Characteristics and Destinations

Tourism to Central and Interior Africa is very limited, Table 12-4. It is the most inaccessible region with the poorest tourist support facilities in the world. Cameroon has the best tourism development in the region, and along with Gabon receives the most visitors. Differing from the other countries in this region, it has a coastal location and offers a variety of attractions from coastal to scenic volcanic mountains. It has several fine game reserves with a great variety of wildlife.

Gabon is one of the most prosperous nations of Africa. Beaches, hunting, and photographic safaris are the major attractions of Gabon. Some important attractions are Kango, the M'Bei Waterfalls, and Ogooue' River. Franceville, Ndjole, and Booue are picturesque townships. Dr. Albert Schweitzer worked at Lambarene.

With its large game reserves, rivers, mountains, native villages, and pygmies, the Democratic Republic of the Congo has the potential for tourism, but it is a poorly developed industry. Albert National Park includes not only a variety of animals but a very scenic area that encompasses the Great Rift Valley with its volcanoes, grassy plateaus, alpine scenery, and tropical rain forest. Lake Kivu, the highest lake on the continent, is located in a picturesque setting. Kinshasa, the capital, is an attractive city providing good restaurants and accommodations. St. Anne's Cathedral, the King Albert Monument, the Museum of Native Life, and the markets provide good attractions for the visitor. Kinshasa serves as a good example of the weak tourism market. It is a city of crime, political collapse, poverty, and garbage. Founded by Henry Stanley, Kisangani reveals evidence of its Arab past and also has the pretty Bovoma Falls (formerly Stanley Falls).

The Central African Republic, too, is an undeveloped country with wildlife and national parks and pygmy cultures offering tourism potential. Bangui, the capital, has some interesting attractions in its colorful Central Market, Mamadou M'Baiiki (trading center), Kina, the Fatima Catholic Mission, and an arts and crafts center. Visits can be made from Bangui along the Ubangi River to observe life and visit coffee and rubber plantations and pygmy villages. However, like the Congo, the Central African Republic has not wanted to create a formal, highly visual tourist trade.

Sudan and Chad in the Sahel receive few visitors. Khartoum and Wadi Halfa are the most promising locations in Sudan. Khartoum, the capital, is the meeting place of the Blue and White Nile Rivers. Wadi Halfa has a number of antiquities in its museum and the Temple of Hatshepsut and Thutmose III at Buhen, which are close to Wadi Halfa. Excursions from Wadi Halfa visit ruins of temples, pyramids, tombs, and fortresses dating back to the Egyptian pharaohs. Chad has the potential to provide good excursions into either desert or tropical environments. N'Djamena, the capital, is a good central location to visit the region for safaris.

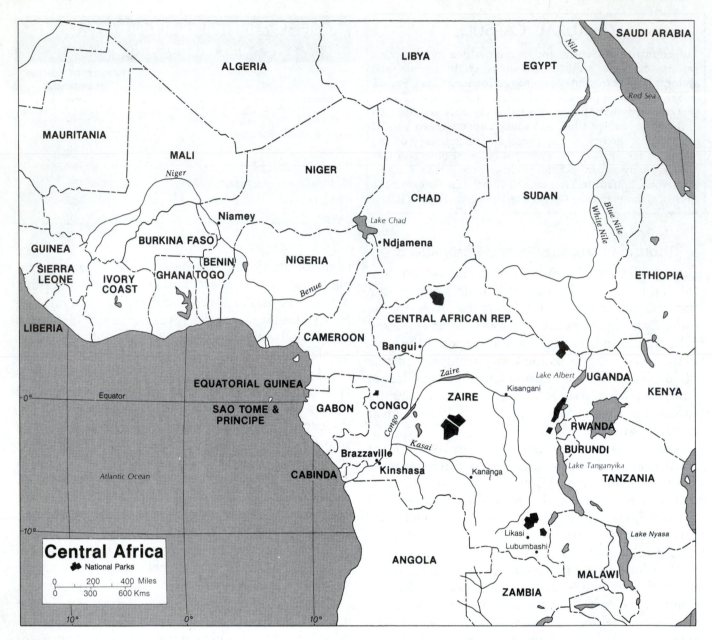

Figure 12-14   Central and Interior Africa

THE VARIETY OF TANZANIA

DAY 1   DAR ES SALAAM

Dar es Salaam is the capital of Tanzania and offers much to see. Today will be spent sightseeing the city. We will start with a walk down Independence Avenue, the main street in the new quarter of the town, which will give you a chance to enjoy the natural flora of this city. Government buildings, embassies, banks, shops, and curio stores line this street. We will then visit the Art Gallery Arcade located in the IPS building. It has many forms of the popular Makonde art. The Makonde are a proud, distinctive, and highly sensitive people. They tend to isolate themselves in small groups and are regarded by other people with both fear and respect. They are best known for their ebony sculptures, which are principally centered on the mother figure, but which sometimes embrace other themes that deal with life. After lunch, we will visit the National Museum, which is situated in the Botanical Gardens. Its outstanding attraction is the Hall of Man, where Dr. Leakey's first finds from Olduvai Gorge, including the skull of Nut-cracker Man and other human fossils, are displayed and where stages of man's development over the last two million years are clearly traced and illustrated. There is also a fantastic ethnographical collection displaying native handicrafts, witchcraft paraphernalia, dancing masks, and traditional musical instruments. The history of the coast is also displayed with Chinese porcelain, glazed Persian pottery, "trade-wind" beads from India, and a notable series of copper coins of the Sultans of Kilwa.

Tonight you will attend the National Dance Troupe at Lumumba Hall. This is a rare opportunity to see the ritual tribal dances and performances, including the famous Makonde masked stilt and snake dances.

DAY 2   MISASANI

Today you will travel to Village Museum, which consists of a collection of traditional, authentically constructed dwellings of various Tanzanian tribes. It displays several distinct architectural styles with building materials ranging from sand, grass, and poles to mud and rope. Villagers demonstrate their ancient skills of carving and weaving and offer their products for sale. You will enjoy lunching at the local restaurant built on the premises in an attractive style.

After lunch, you will travel to Misasani Village. Here you will be able to see the village life and habits of local fishermen who chisel their ngalawa boats out of logs. The tombs and pillars that exist here date from the seventeenth to the nineteenth centuries.

We will then continue traveling up the coast to Kaole, which contains the ruins of fourteenth-century mosques and tombs. Then we will continue our drive up to Kunduchi.

DAY 3   TANGA–ARUSHA

Tanga is the second largest town and port of Tanzania, following Dar es Salaam. It is the center of the important sisal industry. A number of sites to see here include: a sisal estate where you can see the spiny-leaved plants that are related to the amaryllis and how the fibrous tissue is harvested; the Amboni Limestone caves in Tanga, which are quite interesting to visit and explore; and Galanos, the hot sulphur springs for which Tanga is famous.

After exploring Tanga, you will depart for Arusha, which is the departing point for all safaris. You will visit Arusha National Park today. It is quite large and is made up of three separate parts: the five Momella Lakes with their prolific birdlife; the forested lower slopes of Mount Neru with its wealth of buffalo, elephant, rhino, giraffe, warthog, bushpig, waterbuck, bushbuck, and colobus monkey; the Ngurdoto Crater, the floor of which has been set aside as a reserve within a reserve "where there shall be no interference whatsoever from man." Visitors may view the wildlife only from lookout points on the crater rim.

DAY 4   NGORONGORO CRATER

You will travel to the Ngorongoro Crater. This is one of Africa's most beautiful areas of wildlife and certainly one of the most spectacular settings of scenic splendor anywhere. The drive to the crater is exceptional. Leaving Arusha, you start at the base of the Great Rift Valley Wall, pass the entrance to the Manyara National Park, pass by the Mbulu Plateau, the Karatu and Oldeani wheat and coffee farms, and finally through the temperate forest zone and up to the crater rim.

This crater is the largest intact crater in existence, exceeded in magnitude only by five damaged ones. There is absolutely no break in its 67-meter wall. Some eight million years ago, Ngorongoro was an active volcano until its cone collapsed, leaving a caldera some 20 kilometers in diameter. The crater rim (where all the hotels and lodges

continues

continued

are sited 2,286 meters above sea level) rises high over the Serengeti Plain. Inside, you will be able to see elephant, rhino, lions, leopards, and buffalo as well as 3,000 gazelle, 15,000 wildebeests, and cows. This is also the migratory point for flamingos.

DAY 5   OLDUVAI GORGE

You will travel to the Olduvai Gorge today. The Olduvai Gorge is where, under the direction of Dr. Louis Leakey, abundant material dating back at least two million years and possibly much longer,has been found. Remains of the prehistoric elephant, giant horned sheep, and enormous ostriches have been found in the Stone Age site, and more recently, the very early human remains of the Nut-cracker Man. Mary Leakey uncovered in 1969 the most intact Habilis skull ever found. It is thought to date from around 1.75 million years ago.

DAY 6   MOUNT KILIMANJARO

We will travel today to Mt. Kilimanjaro. This is Africa's most renowned and most beautiful mountain. It is located just three degrees south of the equator, and yet its summit is permanently snowclad. It is an extinct volcano with two peaks: Mawenzi (5,600 meters) and Kibo (6,447 meters). It takes a minimum of five days to climb, so instead we will visit the town of Moshi, which lies at the foot of Mt. Kilimanjaro. This town is the center of the coffee trade. There are also large plantations of sugar and sisal and wheat. Things to visit here are:

Mwarkio Art Gallery: Local artists display their talents and their creations in this museum. It will help you gain an insight into their ways of life.

Djamat ban Mosque: unique to this area.

Rest and explore the city and enjoy the breathtaking scenery of Mt. Kilimanjaro during your free time. You will begin your trip home from here.

REVIEW QUESTIONS

1. Why is Africa the least visited region of the world?
2. Describe the two major types of landforms in Africa.
3. Why has Senegal developed a relatively strong tourist trade?
4. Why are there few tourists to the interior nations of Africa?
5. Which region of Africa has the best-developed tourist industry? Explain why.
6. What are the three most visited attractions in nearly all of the countries of Africa south of the Sahara?
7. What are potentially attractive areas for tourism development in Africa?

GEOGRAPHY AND TOURISM IN
East Asia

CHAPTER 13

INTRODUCTION

East Asia consists of North and South Korea, the People's Republic of China, Japan, the Republic of China (Taiwan), Hong Kong, and Macau (Figure 13–1). The region had the greatest growth in international arrivals of tourists in the 1980s and 1990s. The opening of China to mass tourism in 1978 and its tourism development was the primary reason for this rapid growth. The interest in China has led to increased numbers of visitors for all the countries of the area. Japan and Hong Kong serve as gateways into China and visitors from industrialized nations normally combine a visit to China with visits to several other countries in the region. Hong King became a Special Administrative Region of China in 1997 by agreement with the United Kingdom. The agreement provides for a continuation of Hong Kong's unique social,

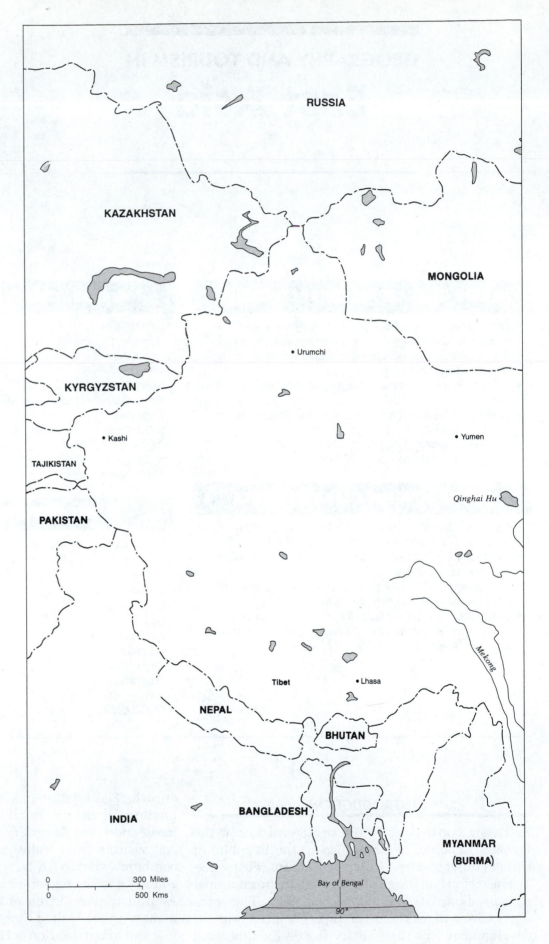

Figure 13–1a East Asia

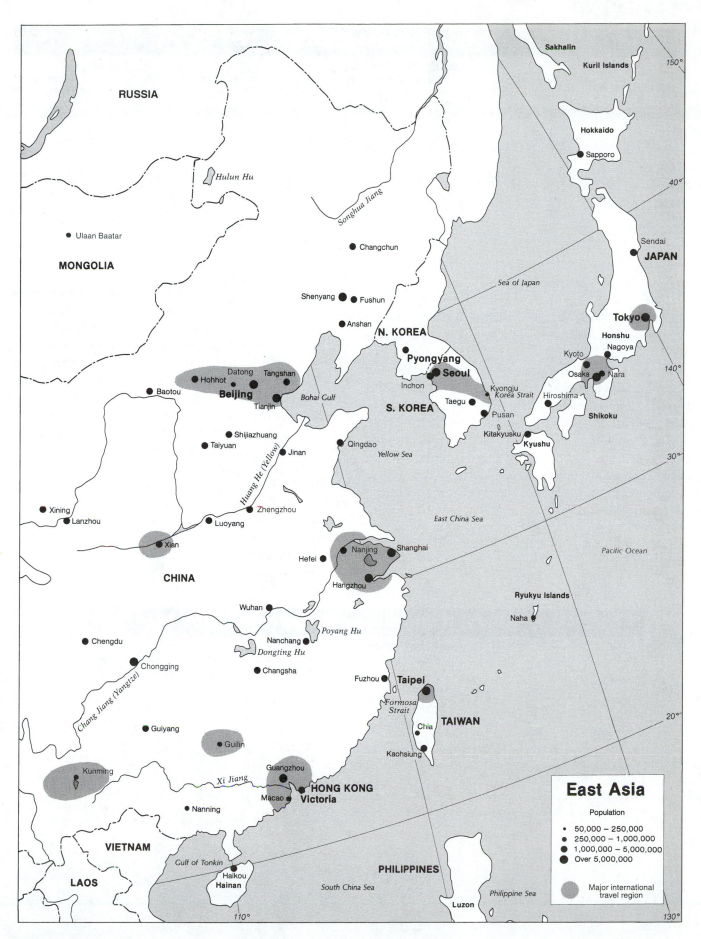

Figure 13–1b East Asia

POPULATION CHARACTERISTICS, 1997

Country	Population (millions)	Annual Growth Rate (percent)	Time to Double Pop. (years)	Per Capita GNP	Life Expectancy (years)	Daily Calorie Supply	Percent Urban
China	1,236.7	1.0	67	620	70	2,639	29
Japan	126.1	0.2	289	39,640	80	2,956	78
North Korea	24.3	1.8	39	N/A	70	2,833	61
South Korea	45.9	0.9	75	9,700	73	3,285	74
Macau	0.5	1.1	64	N/A	69	2,278	97
Taiwan	21.5	1.0	73	N/A	74	N/A	75

economic, legal, and other systems for 50 years. This will have considerable, but unpredictable, impact upon tourism to the region. Current data reflects the level of tourism before Hong Kong was returned to China.

East Asia is a very diverse region economically and geographically. It contains one of the most successful industrialized countries of the world in Japan, a number of growing newly industrialized countries (Hong Kong, Taiwan, and South Korea), and a developing country—China. Japan, and to a lesser extent South Korea, Taiwan, and Hong Kong, share in the greater wealth and higher standard of living of industrialized countries, and they are an exception to most of the countries of Asia. China's economy is increasing the most rapidly, however, resulting in dramatic economic changes in the country.

TOURISM IN EAST ASIA

The most significant feature of tourism to East Asia has been the opening and development of tourism to the People's Republic of China. East Asia accounts for more than 55 percent of all tourists to the larger Pacific Asia region. World Travel Organization data does not include Chinese living in Hong Kong, Macau, and Taiwan as tourists when they visit China since the Chinese government maintains they are all part of China. The number of tourists to the area and the significance of China would be even greater within the Pacific Asia region if these Chinese were included. Table 13–1 indicates the international tourism to East Asia. Each of the countries received over a million visitors a year. The region had an annual growth rate over 15 percent a year in the 1990s.

Table 13–1 International Tourism to East Asia

Country	Number of Visitors (thousands)		1996 Receipts (millions of US $)	1996 Average Expenses per Visit
	1986	1996		
China	9,000	22,765	10,200	448
Taiwan	1,761	2,358	3,075	1,304
Hong Kong	4,501	11,703	10,836	926
Japan	2,155	2,114	4,069	1,925
Korea, Rep. of	1,874	3,684	5,430	1,474
Macau	908	4,890	3,487	713
TOTAL	20,199	47,604	37,097	779

Source: Yearbook of Tourism Statistics. Madrid: World Tourism Organization, 1997.

Japan

500 km

Hokkaido
Sapporo

Occupied by
Soviet Union since
1945, claimed by Japan.

Sea of
Japan

Honshu

Sendai

Korea
Strait

★ **TOKYO**

Kitakyūshū

Osaka

North
Pacific
Ocean

Shikoku

East
China
Sea

Kyushu

Philippine
Sea

Okinawa

Capital: Tokyo
Government: Parliamentary democracy
Size: 145,856 square miles (slightly smaller than California)
Language: Japanese
Ethnic Division: Japanese, 0.6% Korean
Religion: Shintoism and Buddhism, 0.8% Christian
Tourist Season: April through October
Peak Tourist Season: October
Currency: Yen

CULTURAL CAPSULE

Japan is one of the most densely populated nations in the world with a population of 126 million (nearly half that of the United States), living on less than 5 percent of the total territory of the United States. The three major metropolitan areas of Tokyo, Osaka, and Nagoya contain nearly 45 percent of the population of Japan. The Japanese, about 99 percent of the population, are a Mongoloid people, closely related to the major groups of East Asia. There are small numbers of Koreans (675,000) and Chinese. Buddhism and *Shinto* are the major religions. Most Japanese still consider themselves members of one of the major Buddhist sects. Shintoism is an indigenous religion founded on myths, legends, and ritual practices of the early Japanese. Neither Buddhism nor Shintoism is an exclusive religion, and most Japanese observe both Buddhist and Shinto rituals, the former for funerals and the latter for births, marriages, and other occasions. Confucianism also influences Japanese thought. About 1.5 million people are Christians. Approximately 50 percent are Protestant and 40 percent Roman Catholic.

Devotion, conformity, loyalty, and hard work can best describe the Japanese people. The society is group oriented, and loyalty to one's superiors takes precedence over personal feelings. Conformity in dress is the general rule. Businessmen wear suits and ties in public. The traditional *kimono* or *wafuku*, which is a long robe with sleeves, wrapped with a special sash, is worn on special occasions and at leisure.

Cultural Hints:
- A bow is the traditional greeting. Japanese will shake hands with Westerners, but avoid an overly firm handshake.
- Avoid direct eye contact.
- Formal titles are important.
- Do not show signs of affectionate physical contact in public.
- It is impolite to yawn in public.
- Beckon with the palm down and waving all fingers.
- Point with the entire hand.
- Do not chew gum in public.
- Lines are respected.
- Avoid loudness and excessively demonstrative behavior.
- An open mouth is considered rude; cover your mouth when yawning.
- Correct posture is important.
- When counting, the thumb represents the number five.
- Blowing your nose in public is considered rude.
- Present gifts and business cards with both hands. Also, bow slightly.
- Eating and foods:
  Snack foods sold on the streets are generally eaten at the stand.
  Toasting is common in Japan.
  At public restaurants or private homes, remove your shoes before entering.

TRAVEL TIPS

Entry: Visas are not required for stays less than 90 days with proof of return or onward transportation.
Transportation: International air service connects Tokyo and Osaka with North America and the rest of the world. New developments include the new Kansai International Airport at Osaka, which opened in 1994, and a second terminal at Narita (Tokyo) which opened in 1993. These should increase Japan's accessibility. An express train began operating in 1991 from Narita Airport to Tokyo, carrying passengers to Tokyo in 53 minutes. This has greatly improved access into Tokyo from Narita. Japan has excellent domestic air service throughout the country. Japan has one of the most efficient and convenient rail services in the world, headed by its Shinkansen bullet train network.
Shopping: Common items include Japanese handicrafts and art objects, jewelry, silks, furs, pottery pieces, paper lanterns, dolls, and hand-painted dishes and bowls. The manufactured items known the world over can be purchased, but they are expensive and can be purchased for less in other cities such as Hong Kong.

Traditional meals are eaten with chopsticks from bowls that are held at chest level.

Western foods are eaten with Western utensils.

Typical foods are rice, fresh vegetables, seafood, fruit, and small portions of meat. Some typical dishes are miso (bean paste) soup, noodles, curried rice, sashimi (uncooked fish), tofu, pork, and sushi (combination of fish, cooked or uncooked, and rice with vinegar).

Physical Characteristics

Japan is a series of islands extending 1,400 miles from north to south, Figure 13–2. The islands are the peaks of a volcanic chain known as the Pacific "Ring of Fire," resulting in periodic destructive earthquakes. The hilly and mountainous terrain of three-quarters of Japan limits the area that is suitable for agriculture. Settlement is concentrated in the coastal plains, the level land in the small valleys between hills, and in the narrow river valleys. Rivers are short, and their steep gradients make them unsuitable for navigation, but they are important for the generation of electricity.

Japan extends through a wide latitude if all the islands in the archipelago are included, but the main four islands extend from just north of 30 degrees north (the latitude of New Orleans, Louisiana) to just north of 45 degrees (just north of Green Bay, Wisconsin). Climate ranges from humid subtropical to humid continental. There is sufficient rainfall for agriculture on the main islands, with no true dry areas. Precipitation totals range from 40 inches in the north to 100 in the south. Hokkaido and northern Honshu have cold winters, which limits agriculture to a single crop yearly. This northern area of Japan has a humid continental climate and commonly experiences snowfall in the winter season; in northern Hokkaido and in the higher elevations of the northern third of Honshu, there are many ski resorts. Sapporo on Hokkaido has hosted the Winter Olympics.

The southern two-thirds of Honshu and the islands of Shikoku and Kyushu have humid subtropical climates. They are warm and humid in the summers, and moderate and wet in the winter season. Snow in subtropical Honshu is limited to higher elevations. The level land of the coastal plains and interior valleys in this area is intensively cultivated, utilizing

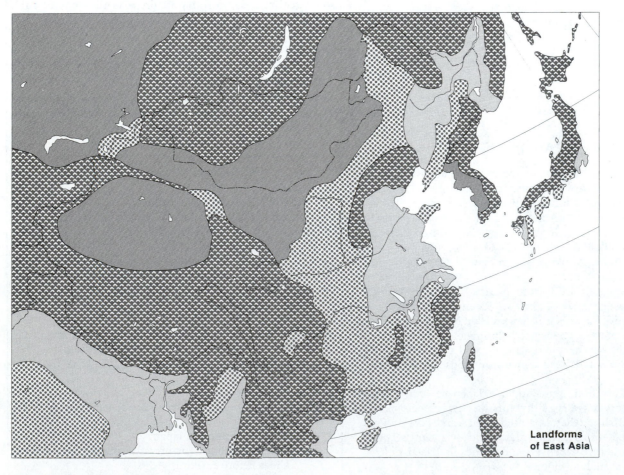

Key

Plains

Hills

Plateaus

Mountains

Landforms of East Asia

Figure 13–2 Landforms of East Asia

double-cropping with irrigated rice in the summer and dry grains or other crops in the winter.

Tourism Characteristics

Japan has not historically looked to tourism as a major foreign income earner as it had such a huge trade surplus in the 1980s. However, in the 1990s it has taken a more active role in promoting inbound tourism. Japan has a well-organized tourist industry. The government is involved with both domestic and international tourism, with offices in many cities of the world outside of Japan to promote and provide information about tourism to Japan. The government has also established a number of programs and offices to develop a broad variety of tourist attractions in Japan while maintaining the quality of its natural environmental settings.

The effort of the government of Japan can be illustrated by the following excerpts from *Tourism in Japan:*

Development of International Tourism in Japan: The rapid expansion of Japan's economy in recent years has exerted significant influences on other nations of the world. Frictional problems between Japan and other nations pose a problem of grave concern among the Japanese. The current lack of understanding about Japan by other nations indicates that Japan has been rather negligent in positively projecting itself to the world. International tourism is viewed by the Japanese as one of the most effective means to promote international cooperation and understanding.

Japan provides overseas promotional activities to motivate potential travelers to visit Japan and reception services to provide foreign visitors with opportunities to better understand the country upon arrival. Promotional activities to increase foreign tourist traffic to Japan are run by the Japan National Tourist Organization (JNTO), a nonprofit organization established by a special law and subsidized by the government. Since the language barrier is one of the biggest problems for foreign visitors while traveling in Japan, JNTO operates three Tourist Information Centers for foreign visitors (Tokyo, Kyoto, and the New Tokyo International Airport at Narita), where visitors are given free, multilingual information on travel in Japan.

To ease the language problems for foreign visitors, Japan has established a nationwide network of tourist information offices (called "i" system) where tourist information can be provided to foreign visitors in foreign languages. The system will be organized by JNTO under the direction of the Ministry of Transport with the cooperation of local governments.

To further ease the language problems that foreign visitors may face when traveling in Japan, the "Japan Travel-Phone" service was inaugurated on April 1, 1982. Calling "Japan Travel-Phone," foreign visitors can receive guide service through telephone talks from any place in the country. The service is free, using a collect-call system, except in the Tokyo and Kyoto areas. The service is operated by JNTO with financial assistance from about 80 Japanese export and tourism companies.

Tape-recorded telephone information on travel topics, entertainments and major calendar events in and around Tokyo and Kyoto is available around the clock. The "teletourist" service is provided in English and French in Tokyo, and is provided in English in Kyoto. The service is offered by the Tokyo Information Center (TIC) and the Kyoto TIC, respectively. With an increase in the number of foreign visitors to Japan, a movement to invite foreigners to Japanese homes has developed among the Japanese. This meet-the-Japanese-at-home movement, called the "Home Visit System," has been institutionalized by major local governments. In Japan, applicants for guide interpreters are subject to a national examination. No one, without passing the examination and holding a license issued by the Governor of the Prefecture where he lives, is qualified to work as a guide interpreter for foreign visitors. The "Good-Will Guide" program . . . is to help foreign visitors in case they have some problems on the street or in other public facilities. (The Japan National Tourism Organization)

Three factors appear to limit Japan's growth from the main generating markets of North America and Europe: (1) its prime attractions are culture, history, customs, and traditions that appeal to a relatively narrow segment of the long-haul tourist market; (2) there is a language and cultural barrier that deters some people from visiting, hence the program previously described; (3) high travel and land costs limit market demand. The image that Japan is expensive limits the number of visitors to the country.

Tourists arrive in Japan from throughout the world. The largest origin countries are South Korea, Taiwan, and the United States, combined for about 60 percent of the total visitors in 1996. The United

States is third, accounting for 15.6 percent of all foreign visitors. Increased travel to Japan has come from neighboring South Korea and Taiwan. Europe, led by Great Britain, accounts for 15.5 percent of visitors. Most of the European visitors are business travelers. Europeans have the highest incidence of business travel of any region's visitors to Japan.

The most popular time for visitors is October, followed by July and August. The winter months are the slowest, and the government desires to encourage and promote more winter events and conventions to level out the seasons. Travel to Japan increased in the 1990s due to the Asian Games in 1994 and surged again during the Winter Olympics in 1998.

Both domestic and international tourism have risen dramatically in Japan over the past ten years. The decreasing work days and increasing prosperity of the country are beginning to overcome the traditional cultural restraints against taking vacations. However, many Japanese still work on their days off and refuse to take vacations. This is changing slowly, which has an important effect on tourism. Tokyo's financial firms are no longer open on Saturdays. The government is encouraging the establishment of a five-day work week. Government offices are now closed two Saturdays a month. Students must take one Saturday a month off since 1993. The average annual holidays per firm is about sixteen days. Domestic tourism is characterized by short stays, and small groups are preferred over other groups.

Tourist Destinations and Attractions

The attractions most frequently visited by the Japanese themselves are temples and historical and cultural places, especially in the older cities of Osaka, Kyoto, and Nara. Each of these was at one time the capital of Japan, and they have great historical value and ancient treasures. In Nara, for example, the Horyuji Temple, which was built over 1,350 years ago and is the oldest of all wood buildings now existing in Japan, attracts Japanese. National parks are the second most important vacation attractions. There are 28 national parks, 55 nationalized parks, and 299 state parks. National parks are maintained by the Natural Environment Preserve Committee. Another major attraction is hot springs, which have been popular for generations. Japan has an outstanding internal transportation system, by rail and by air, for both domestic and international visitors.

One of the remarkable achievements in the Japanese travel industry has been the increase in international travel by the Japanese. Since restrictions on overseas travel were reduced in 1964, overseas travel by the Japanese people has grown dramatically. One factor encouraging the Japanese to travel is that goods can be purchased abroad more cheaply than at home. The most popular destinations for Japanese are the United States (particularly Hawaii), Korea, Taiwan, Hong Kong, China, Malaysia, Indonesia, and New Zealand. One of the characteristics of Japanese travel overseas is that it too is seasonal, with August as the peak and April the low point.

There are eight travel regions in Japan that serve as the major destinations for foreign visitors. First is Hokkaido, the northernmost island in the Japanese archipelago. Sapporo, the capital city, was the site of the 1972 Winter Olympics. Its annual winter carnival (Snow Festival) is a major attraction. It has a variety of gigantic snow images created by artists. Other attractions in the city are the Hokkaido University, Botanical Gardens, Historical Museum (illustrating Hokkaido treasures of Ainu and Giliak costumes, canoes, harpoons, and other objects), and Odori Promenade. The promenade is decorated year-round with flowers. Below it, there is an underground shopping arcade with some 150 restaurants, souvenir shops, and coffee houses. The characteristics of Hokkaido as a vacationland are its natural beauty and unique fauna and flora. The volcanoes, lakes, and spas form a rich variety of outdoor activities for the tourist. Hokkaido has five important national parks with a variety of volcanoes, caldera lakes, hot spring resorts, forests and wild flowers, and spas.

A second travel region is Tohoku, which is located in the northeastern section of the main island of Honshu. It has scenic areas that include three national parks and many hot springs. The parks offer mountaineering and skiing. The Tohoku region also boasts handicrafts, historical and traditional festivals, and folk dancing. The major tourist center in this region is Sendai, the capital of Miyagi Prefecture and the cultural, economic, and political center. Formerly a castle town, the city is very popular and serves as a center for trips to scenic spots in the district.

The third tourism region in Japan is Tokyo and the surrounding area. It has many shrines and temples along with the attractions of a great modern city. Historically Tokyo first became the seat of the Shogunate government in 1603. Under the Shogun's great influence, the city (then called *Edo*) enjoyed all the privileges of a virtual national capital for the next three centuries even though Kyoto remained the legal capital until 1868. Today Tokyo is the center of national politics, education, and finance. Although it is a highly westernized metropolis, it still retains much of its Oriental charm. Tokyo is particularly attractive to visitors because of its unique capacity to blend the East and the West, the old and the new. Side by side with the bustling activity of its business sections, there remain traditional ways and habits of old Japan interspersed with many colorful festivities.

An important attraction is the Imperial Palace surrounded by a high stone wall and moat. While visitors cannot enter the palace, the surrounding area is pleasant and interesting. The Meiji Shrine, which is located in a thickly wooded parkland and flower garden, is a popular attraction for Japanese and foreign tourists. One of the most popular attractions in Tokyo is the *Ginza*, the famous shopping district of Japan. It has many prestigious department stores, large and small specialty shops, restaurants and coffee shops, and bars and nightclubs. The Asakusa Kannou Temple, founded in 645 A.D., is surrounded by a multitude of souvenir shops, theaters, and amusement spots, indicating the importance of the temple as a tourist attraction. The surrounding area has lovely mountain scenery, hot springs, and many historic spots.

The most famous symbol of Japan is snow-capped *Mt. Fuji*, Figure 13–3. Five lakes on the fringes of Mt. Fuji and the mountain itself provide a variety of outdoor recreational activities. Hakone is a mountain resort and spa town with Mt. Fuji as a backdrop. Lake Ashi, boiling hot springs, and a splendid reflection of Mt. Fuji are among the attractions in Hakone. Kamakura, a small quiet town, was once a feudal government headquarters. It has a number of old temples and shrines. Some highlights are the Great Image of Buddha, the colorful Tsurugaoka Hachimangu Shrine, and the picturesque Enoshima Island. The gorgeous Toshogu Shrine, Lake Chuzenji, and the beautiful Kegon Falls, which fall 330 feet, are in and around Nikko.

Kamakura, 30 miles southwest of Tokyo, was also a seat of a feudal government. Today it is a lovely seaside resort. Kamakura is the site of *Daibutsu* or Great Buddha, a huge 700-year-old bronze image of Buddha, and the Tsurugaoka Hachimangu Shrine.

The fourth region, Chubu, is the center of the main island of Honshu, in which there are seven national parks and the "Japan Alps." The area has splendid mountain scenery, beautiful plateaus, swift rivers, hot springs, mirror-like lakes, and excellent ski resorts. The largest city of central Honshu is Nagoya, with a history that dates back to the seventeenth century when Ieyasu Tokugawa (1542–1616), the generalissimo who established his government in

Figure 13–3 Mt. Fuji

Edo (now Tokyo), built an imposing castle, which is now the city's symbol. Ise is considered the most sacred city in Japan. The Ise Grand Shrines, sacred to mythological creators of the country, are located there. The Grand Shrines have numerous pilgrims year-round.

One of the most scenic mountain areas in Japan is often compared to the European Alps, causing them to be called the *Japan Alps.* The center for travel into and through the Alps of Japan is Matsumoto. Matsumoto is a castle town, with a distinctive local culture and an unexploited countryside. Japan's oldest medieval castle is in Matsumoto and provides a panorama of the superb countryside. In the valley, from Shiojiri in the south to Otari in the north, there are charming old post towns and villages surrounded by lush agricultural land and flowing rivers. There are summer and winter resorts in the Japan Alps.

The fifth region is Kansai, with the metropolitan cities of Kyoto and Osaka on the southern half of the island of Honshu. This is a major destination for international visitors. The area has superb scenic beauty, like Ise-Shima National Park with its seascapes. In addition, the ancient capitals of Japan are in this area. Kyoto, the capital of Japan from 794 to 1868, has some 400 Shinto shrines and 1,650 Buddhist temples, as well as villas with elaborately designed gardens. One of the most impressive sites is the Kinkaku-Ji Temple (Temple of the Golden Pavilion). In the early 1300s the pavilion was constructed as a villa for the aristocrat Saionji Kintsune.

It was purchased in 1397 by the third shogun of the Ashikaga, Yoshimitsu. Yoshimitsu used the pavilion as a place to store his art and literature collection. After his death the palace became a Zen temple and remains the most recognized site in Kyoto. The gold-leafed temple consists of three different types of architecture: the first floor is traditional fujiwara court style; the second is Kamakura period samurai house style; and the third floor is Chinese Zen temple style. Kyoto is a city of festivals as well, with many centuries-old events to remind the visitor of life in the ancient world. It is Japan's top center for folk arts, silk fabrics, brocades, lacquerware, earthenware, porcelain fans, dolls, and bronze, all of superb workmanship.

The city of Nara, just south of Kyoto, is a popular day trip from Kyoto. Nara has an even older history than Kyoto and was the cradle of Japan's arts. It contains ancient tombs, ruins, and other historical relics. The most widely known symbol of Nara is the Kofukuji Temple, built in 710 A.D. Moved from Asuka to its present site, its five-story pagoda is a distinctive landmark.

Osaka serves as an excellent base for trips to Kyoto and Nara. Osaka has a long history as a commercial and transportation center of Japan. Contact between Japan and the countries of Korea and China took place in Osaka, and several emperors established their courts here. Kobe, near Osaka, is also an important port city. Its business and shopping centers vie with its architecture reflecting foreign influence, preserved from the Meiji Period, to attract visitors.

The sixth region is Chugoku, the western end of the island of Honshu. It has beautiful beaches, coastal plateaus, and the Inland Sea National Park. It includes Hiroshima, site of the first atomic bomb used in warfare, and one of the three most beautiful Japanese landscape gardens, Korakuen Garden. The central city in the district is Okayama, an old castle town. The attractions in Okayama include the Korakuen Garden and Washuzan Hill, which provides one of the best views of the Inland Sea. Hiroshima has been restored and has adopted the name "the City of Peace." The attractions in Hiroshima include Shukukeien Garden, Hiroshima Castle, Peace Memorial Park and Hall, Atomic Bomb Dome, Memorial Cenotaph for the A-bomb victims, and Memorial Cathedral for World Peace.

The seventh region is the island of Kyushu, which has a subtropical climate and six national parks and offers spectacular scenery, hot springs, and numerous historical sites. One major city in this region is Fukuoka, which is divided into the modern commercial district and the old trading port. Fukuoka has been undergoing development to stimulate more tourism. It is known for its Hakata-ori silk textiles and gala festivals of Hakata Dontaku. Nagasaki also contains a number of attractions, including some memorials to the suffering caused by the atomic bomb dropped on the city.

The eighth region is the Okinawa Islands, which have many historical ties to Japan. Okinawa has a wealth of natural beauty, including coral reefs and emerald water, sunny skies, and subtropical plants. Tourist attractions include Naminoue Shrine, dedicated to a god of land management, and Sogenji Temple, the mausoleum for successive Ryiukyuan kings and others.

South Korea

Capital: Seoul
Government: Republic with centralized power
Size: 38,000 square miles (about the same as Indiana)
Language: Korean
Ethnic Division: Korean, Chinese minority
Religion: Buddhism, Christianity, Shamanism, Confucianism
Tourist Season: Year-round
Peak Tourist Season: April through October
Currency: Won

CULTURAL CAPSULE

Korea is one of the most homogeneous countries in the world (ethnic Korean). Korea was first populated by a Tungusic branch of the Ural-Altaic family, which migrated to the peninsula from the northwestern regions of Asia. It has a small Chinese minority (50,000). Korean is a Uralic language remotely related to Japanese, Hungarian, Finnish, and Mongolian. The language uses numerous Chinese words. Many older people retain some knowledge of Japanese from the colonial period (1910–1945), and most educated Koreans can read English. Shamanism and Buddhism are the traditional religions of Korea. Shamanism, a folk religion, involves *geomancy*, the process of divination, avoiding bad luck or omens, warding off evil spirits, and honoring the dead. Nearly 30 percent of the population is Christian. The Confucian ethic of hard work and filial piety is important to the society. There are many rituals of courtesy, formality in behavior, and customs regulating social relations.

Cultural Hints:

- A slight bow and handshake is a common greeting between men.
- Women shake hands less often than men, usually just acknowledging with a nod.
- Good eye contact is important.
- Avoid touching, patting on arm, shoulder, or back unless good friends.
- Beckoning is done with palm down and a scratching motion.
- Do not place feet on desks or chairs.
- Use both hands to pass and receive objects.
- Cover mouth when yawning or using a toothpick.
- Lines are not common. People will push to enter bus.
- Shoes are removed before entering home.
- Avoid loud talking or laughing.
- Do not eat while walking along a street.
- Do not blow your nose in public.
- Remove your sunglasses during conversation with another person.
- Eating and foods:
  Periods of silence are common.
  Pass food and other objects with right hand.
  A service charge is usually included in the bill. Tipping is not expected.
  At a restaurant, one person usually pays for all.

When dining, the elderly are served first and the children last.
Typical food is spicy. Common foods are rice, spicy pickled cabbage, red beans, chicken, marinated and barbecued beef, barley tea, and fruit for dessert.

Physical Characteristics

South Korea occupies the southern portion of a mountainous peninsula. It consists of two major landforms: a coastal zone and a hilly backbone. The population of both South and North Korea is concentrated in the coastal zone. The most rugged areas are the mountainous east coast and the central interior. The climate is hot and rainy in the summer and cold and dry in the winter.

Tourism Characteristics

Tourism to South Korea is recognized as a national industry, and the government works to improve the industry and promote increased tourism to Korea. The South Korean tourism industry has increased dramatically for both outgoing and incoming tourists. The combination of Asian Games followed in 1988 by the Summer Olympics greatly benefited tourism to the country. Tourism in South Korea developed much later than in Japan. The Korean War, from 1950 to 1953, devastated the country and its economy. In 1962, there were only 15,000 foreign visitors to Korea. In 1996, there were 3.6 million. Today, Japan dominates the market, accounting for 46 percent of total visitors. Japan's proximity and the similarity of culture and language attract Japanese travelers, as do low prices for travel and consumer items. The United States accounts for 9.3 percent of the total foreign visitors to Korea. Presently few Europeans visit Korea, with only about 10 percent of the visitors being European. Visitors arriving for tourist purposes account for 70 percent of total visitors (Pacific Asia Travel Association, 1994).

The Olympics in Seoul (held in September 1988) helped the country develop accommodations and other tourist infrastructure, Figure 13–4, as well as showcased the country in Europe and North America as the pageantry of the summer games received broad coverage in those regions. The 600th anniversary of Seoul as the nation's capital takes place in 1994, and as such it has been designated as the "Visit Korea Year." The government is undertaking an extensive campaign especially in the United States to stimulate travel to Korea. Spring and autumn have been the peak seasons, but seasonality does not represent a

Figure 13–4   Olympic Stadium and Highway, Seoul, Korea

problem as it has not overloaded the accommodations to date.

Tourist Destinations and Attractions

There are three main attractions for tourists to South Korea. Seoul, the capital, has palaces and folklore museums with Korean architecture. Now an Olympic city, Seoul is the gateway to the Republic of Korea. Seoul's historic heritage is evidenced in the palaces, shrines, and monuments still standing through the city. A number of palaces are important attractions. Toksugung Palace blends both Western and Korean architecture. The Kyongbokkung Palace was built in 1395 by King Taejo of the Choson Dynasty and was rebuilt in 1868. Many of the nation's historic stone pagodas and monuments, including a ten-story pagoda, are on its grounds. The Secret Garden within the Changdokkung Palace contains 44 pavilions scattered amid small streams with bridges and other idyllic spots. Changgyonggung Palace has been restored and depicts the life and arts of the ancient royal family.

There are many other attractions in Seoul. The most current is a new museum to commemorate Seoul's 600th anniversary. The Great South Gate of Seoul (Nandaemum) has been designated as the foremost National Treasure. Chogyesa Temple (a large Buddhist temple) and the Temple of Heaven are two highly visible Buddhist temples in the city. In the vicinity there are the royal tombs, with the Tonggurung or East Nine Tombs as the best known and most accessible. The royal remains are entombed in huge mounds of earth, each surmounted by an altar stone on which sacrifices used to be offered on ritual days.

West of Seoul, at Inchon, is Chayu Park and the MacArthur Monument, commemorating the American Army's landing at Inchon in the Korean conflict, and the Memorial Hall for the Inchon Landing Operation. South of Seoul, the fortress city of Suwon boasts a restored fortress that was originally built in the late eighteenth century by King Chongjo to honor his father. The Korean Folk Village just outside of Suwon provides a view of Korea's past. Here in reconstructed farmhouses, residences of the nobility, and other buildings of several centuries ago, a functioning community of potters, millers, weavers, blacksmiths, pipemakers, and other craftsmen work as their ancestors did. At the Yongin Farmland, the Global Town exhibits various traditional cultural scenes from 21 different countries around the world. North of Seoul is the *Demilitarized Zone* (DMZ). P'anmunjom, in the middle of the DMZ, is the site of the armistice negotiations. East of Seoul, there are a number of lakes, providing a water vacationland for the visitor.

The second major area is the southwest area centering on Puyo and Kongju, former Paekche Kingdom capitals, known for their temples, museums, monasteries, sacred mountains, and royal tombs. Puyo, the last capital of the kingdom, has many ruins dating back to 600 A.D. A fortified castle sits on a steep hill in Puyo's city center. The Puyo National Museum is a fine example of Korea's modern architecture. Also, the government is building at Puyo an exhibition hall highlighting the Paekche culture, which flourished from 57 B.C. to 668 A.D. At Kongju, the Kongju National Museum houses the valuables of King Muryong's tomb. Near these ancient capitals at the town of Nonsan is the massive Unjin Miruk Buddha, Korea's largest stone Buddha, dating from the tenth century.

Figure 13–5   Traditional-style house and kimchi pots, Korea

Courtesy Korea National Tourism Corp.

Figure 13–6 Kyongbokkung Palace

A third major area is the southeast area centered around Kyongju. Kyongju was the capital of the Shilla Kingdom and at one time was one of the great cities of the world. In 1979, UNESCO selected Kyongju as one of the ten ancient historic cities in the world. The Chumsungdae Observatory, a bottle-shaped stone tower, may have been used for observing the stars. The layout of a series of stones around the base creates an attraction comparable to Stonehenge in England. Kyerim Forest, the remains of Panwolsong Castle, Anapchi Pond (a pleasure resort), and Tumuli Park (site of large royal tombs) are all impressive reminders of the Shilla period. Some of the tombs have been excavated and are open for viewing. At the Punhwangsa Temple, one of only five brick pagodas in Korea still stands. The Kyongju National Museum houses a treasure of objects from Shilla tombs, including the famous gold crowns, gold girdles, jewelry ceramics, sword hilts, and other artifacts. The countryside is dotted with temples, tombs, and fortresses, each of which is impressive in its own right.

At Pusan, the United Nations Memorial Cemetery serves as a reminder of the Korean conflict. Today Pusan is Korea's principle port, and its warmer southern location extends the season for ocean beach resorts and hot springs in the vicinity.

Throughout the country, there are many natural and cultural attractions that provide a rich potential for travelers. There are spectacular mountain scenery, clean sandy beaches, many natural harbors and waterfalls, distinctive cuisine, and many historical and archaeological sites. Health spas are in abundance and along with winter sports are important to a developing domestic market. One area the government feels has a tremendous potential is Cheju Island, which is an exotic semitropical island known for its female deep-sea divers, and Mt. Hallasan, the tallest mountain in Korea. Its striking scenery, lack of pollution, and warm climate make the island an important potential tourist attraction for Korea.

North Korea (Democratic People's Republic of Korea)

150 km

Capital: Pyongyang
Government: Communist state
Size: 47,000 square miles (about the same as Mississippi)
Language: Korean
Religion: Buddhism, Shamanism (religious activities nonexistent)
Currency: Won

TRAVEL TIPS

Entry: Travel from the United States is discouraged. The United States does not recognize the government and does not maintain diplomatic or consular relations with North Korea.

Transportation: International connections are through countries that have diplomatic relations with North Korea such as China. Internal travel is mostly by rail.

Shopping: Common items include lacquer boxes, costume dolls, brass and imitation antiques, and Koryo silk brocade.

CULTURAL CAPSULE

Korea was first populated by a Tungusic branch of the Ural-Altaic family, which migrated to the peninsula from the northwestern regions of Asia. The Koreans and Manchurians are physically similar. Koreans are racially and linguistically homogeneous. Korean is a Uralic language remotely related to Japanese, Mongolian, Hungarian, and Finnish. North Korea differs from South Korea in that it does not use a mixed script of Chinese and Korean. Russian, Chinese, and English are taught in the schools. Although religious groups (Buddhism, Shamanism, and Chondogyo) nominally exist in North Korea, the government severely restricts their activity. Chondogyo is an indigenous religion founded in 1860 as an eclectic combination of Buddhist, Confucian, and Christian beliefs. The government allows Christians to meet in small groups under the direction of state-appointed ministers.

Foods and customs are generally similar to South Korea.

Physical Characteristics

The Democratic People's Republic of Korea occupies the northern portion of a mountainous peninsula. It consists of numerous ranges of moderately high mountains and hills separated by deep, narrow valleys and small cultivated plains. The climate is temperate in the summer and cold in the winter.

Tourism Characteristics

Little data is available concerning North Korea's tourism. Entry is extremely limited and by invitation only. In the 1990s, they received about 100,000 visitors a year. Few visitors are South Koreans or Americans. The major market is Koreans living in Japan. A few Korean-Americans have been allowed to visit their families in North Korea. Few people visit beyond Pyongyang, the capital. The major attractions in the city are reconstructed Buddhist temples, which are no longer used as places of worship, and the Grand Theater. North Korea wants to increase its tourist industry and is offering group tours for rock climbing, bird-watching, sunbathing, and lessons in the martial arts.

Taiwan

Physical Characteristics

Taiwan (the Republic of China) is a mountainous island in an archipelago on the east side of the Asian continent. Its high mountainous backbone is oriented north-south and has elevations exceeding 10,000 feet. On the west side of Taiwan, there are low hills and an important coastal plain. The coastal plain is much narrower on the eastern side of Taiwan,

100 km

Chi-lung
Taipei
Taiwan Strait
Su-ao
Chang-hua
Pescadores
Hua-lien
Taiwan
Ma-kung
Philippine Sea
T'ai-nan
Kao-hsiung
T'ai-tung

Quemoy and Matsu islands are not shown

Capital: Taipei
Government: One-party presidential regime
Size: 13,900 square miles (about the size of Connecticut and New Hampshire together)
Language: Mandarin Chinese, Taiwanese, Hakka
Ethnic Division: 84% Taiwanese, 14% Mainland Chinese, 2% Aborigine
Religion: 93% mixture of Buddhism, Confucianism, and Taoism, 4.5% Christian, 2.5% other
Tourist Season: Year-round
Currency: Taiwan dollar

TRAVEL TIPS

Entry: A visa is required for stays up to two months. A transit visa is issued upon arrival for stays of less than two weeks.
Transportation: International connections are good from North America and other Asian countries to Taipei. Transportation within Taiwan is good, but most travel is by comfortable passenger express trains.
Health: Drinking water in major hotels is safe, but care should be taken elsewhere to drink bottled or boiled water.
Caution: Do not take photographs inside Buddhist temples without permission.
Shopping: Items include rosewood furniture, textiles, rattan, rare books, classical Chinese musical instruments, and traditional Chinese art and handicrafts.

concentrating the population on the west side of the island. The climate is subtropical, with a rainy season from June to September.

Tourism Characteristics

The government of Taiwan encourages and promotes tourism as an excellent source of income and a means of displaying Chinese culture. Originally called For-

CULTURAL CAPSULE

The native Taiwanese (21.5 million) are descendants of Chinese who migrated from the crowded, coastal mainland areas of Fujian and Guangdong provinces in the eighteenth and nineteenth centuries. There are also more than 2 million mainland Chinese who migrated after World War II. About 425,000 aborigines, inhabiting the mountainous central and eastern parts of the island, are believed to be of Malayo-Polynesian origin. The official language is Mandarin Chinese. Most native Taiwanese speak a variant of the Amoy (Hokkien) dialect of southern Fujian. Hakka, another Chinese dialect, is also spoken. Many Taiwanese over age 50 also speak Japanese. English is taught in urban areas as a second or third language.

The predominant religion is a combination of Buddhism and Taoism brought to Taiwan by the original Chinese settlers. The Confucian ethical code is considered by some to be the official religion of Taiwan. There are more than 600,000 Christians, mostly Protestant, in Taiwan.

Cultural Hints:
- A handshake is the most common form of greeting.
- A nod and a smile are considered appropriate for first meeting.
- Business cards are exchanged and should be read carefully.
- Use titles and full names.
- Remove your shoes before entering a home.
- Avoid touching a child on the top of his or her head.
- Use the open hand to point. Using the index finger is rude.
- Beckoning is done by waving all fingers with the palm down.
- Do not put your arm around the shoulder of another.
- Shaking one hand from side to side with palm forward means no.
- Winking is impolite.
- While sitting, place hands in your lap.
- Present and receive gifts with both hands.
- Avoid loud, boisterous, or rude behaviors.
- A balanced posture is important.
- Eating and foods:
  Toasting is common before and during dinner.
  Chopsticks are the normal eating instruments.
  Don't stick chopsticks upright in rice.
  When finished eating, place chopsticks parallel across your dish.
  Hold bowls of food directly under your lower lip and use the chopsticks to push the food into your mouth.
  Refusing food is impolite. Poke it around and move it to the side of your dish.
  Place long, slippery noodles in your mouth and slurp or suck.
  Don't use your chopsticks for communal dishes of food. Host will place food on your plate, or a separate pair of serving chopsticks will be near the serving dish.
  Bones are placed on the table or in a dish provided.
  When finished, leave a small amount on your plate or it will be refilled.
  Do not eat while walking in the street.
  Typical foods are rice, soup, seafood, pork, chicken, vegetables, and fruit. Sauces are important, and most foods are stir-fried.

mosa (meaning "beautiful") by Portuguese explorers, its first people were Polynesian. However, through time the population became dominated by Chinese influences, creating a distinctive Taiwanese population. Mainland Chinese fleeing the Communist Revolution in 1949 seized the island's government and ruled until 1987, when a Taiwanese native was elected president. Distinctive population groups today include the Taiwanese (80 percent of the population), Chinese (14 percent), aborigines, and sizeable communities from Korea, Vietnam, and Japan.

Taiwan's tourism industry has grown from a meager 15,000 visitors in 1956 to over 2 million visitors per year in the 1990s. Taiwan draws mainly from the East Asia region, which accounts for about 63 percent of its visitors. Japan is the major country of origin, accounting for 38 percent of Taiwan's visitors. North America, led by the United States with nearly 12.5 percent of the visitors, accounts for 14.7 percent of all visitors. Europe only accounts for 6.3 percent.

A unique feature of Taiwan's tourism trade is the large number of *"overseas Chinese"* who account for about 17 percent of tourists. These overseas Chinese represent mainlanders who have migrated throughout Asia to major urban centers. The vast majority of the overseas Chinese arrive in Taiwan from Hong Kong. It is difficult to assess the linkages other than ethnic in that many of the overseas Chinese do not state the purpose of their trip. For those that do state the purpose, over 63 percent are for pleasure. Taiwan has one of the highest average visitor expenditures in the world. The peak number of visitors occurs in the spring and autumn. This is largely caused by the climate, which is subtropical. There is a rainy season in May and June, and the highest temperatures occur between May and September. The December-to-March period is the coolest time of the year, but the Chinese New Year in February attracts some visitors.

While Taiwan has an excellent airline network to facilitate travel, entry visas are required of all visitors and in many cases they are difficult to obtain. The overseas Chinese have to produce an economic guarantee before a visa is granted.

Taiwan has a sizable domestic market. The increasing standard of living has been helpful in the growth of the domestic market. The government has created a network of national parks and resort development areas to facilitate travel. The leading attraction for domestic visitors is the China Lake (just outside Kaohsiung), which is visited by nearly 2.5 million people per year, followed by Yangmingshan (outside Taipei), with 2 million visitors annually, and Shihmen Dam, with 1.7 million visitors.

Tourist Destinations and Attractions

Taiwan has three main tourist areas. North Taiwan, an urban/rural region, contains the capital, Taipei, and has mountain resorts, a wildlife park, and numerous beaches. The main attraction in Taipei is the National Palace Museum, which contains a magnificent collection of Chinese art. Other important attractions in Taipei are the Presidential Mansion and the Taiwan Jinja Shrine. Lungshan Szu (Dragon Mountain Temple) is the oldest and most famous Buddhist temple in Taipei. The Martyr's Shrine is modeled after Beijing's *Forbidden City*. The aristocrats' compound in Panchio; the Taoist Chihnan Temple, 1,000 steps up Monkey Hill; and the ten monasteries atop Lions Head Mountain are near Taipei.

Central Taiwan is the second region and is an area of great natural beauty. Taroko Gorge, a twelve-mile-long, marble-sided natural feature, is the centerpiece of the region. Skiing and forest recreation are popular in this region. The city Tai-chung, in the center of the Sun Moon lake district, is one of the most scenic areas in the world.

The third region is in South Taiwan. This area around Kaohsiung is the intellectual center, the industrial center, and the main port of the nation. South Taiwan has Kenting National Scenic Area and some good beaches. The aboriginal villages of Taoyuan and Orchid Island are also in the south.

Hong Kong

Physical Characteristics

Hong Kong is on the southeastern coast of China. It consists of Hong Kong, the Lan Tao Islands, the Kowloon Peninsula, and more than 200 smaller islands. The islands are hilly and steep sloped. The only significant flatland is located in the New Territories. The climate is tropical, with a cool and dry period from September to March and a rainy hot season between March and August.

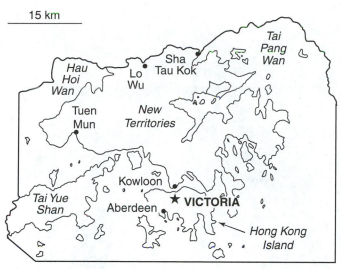

Lema Channel

Government: Hong Kong Special Administrative Region
Size: 411 square miles
Language: Cantonese and English
Ethnic Division: 95% Chinese, 5% other
Religion: 90% Eclectic mixture of local religions, 2% Christian
Tourist Season: Year-round
Peak Tourist Season: Year-round
Currency: Hong Kong dollar

TRAVEL TIPS

Entry: Visas are not required for stays up to 30 days. Proof of onward or return transportation is needed. Arrival and departure taxes are collected. Goods may be imported duty free except alcohol and tobacco products, motor fuels, cosmetics, and soft drinks.
Transportation: There are excellent international connections to North America, Europe, and other Asian countries. Buses and streetcars provide inexpensive local transportation. There is a modern subway system. The Star Ferry is used to travel between Kowloon and Victoria Island. Taxis are inexpensive and plentiful. Trains connect Kowloon and the New Territories.
Shopping: Hong Kong is a shopper's paradise. Items include rosewood furniture, textiles, rattan, rare books, classical Chinese musical instruments, and traditional Chinese art and handicrafts.

Tourism Characteristics

Hong Kong is a unique state, a special territory of China occupying the northeast side of the broad estuary of the Xi (Hsun) River, Figure 13-7. On July 1, 1997, the United Kingdom relinquished its claim to the territory, handing it back to China. China has pledged to keep Hong Kong's situation practically the same as under British rule, including tourism. Although skeptics claim that China will try to convert

CULTURAL CAPSULE

Hong Kong is ethnically homogeneous with nearly 98 percent being ethnic Chinese and 2 percent mostly European. Cantonese is the official Chinese dialect, and English is widely understood and also official. The religious characteristic is one of diversity. Strong elements of Taoism and Confucianism with folk religion practices are widespread. Ancestorial worship is important. Many homes contain brightly decorated boxes with pictures of deceased relatives, smoking incense sticks, or symbolic offerings of fruit to venerate ancestors. About 10 percent of the population is Christian.

Cultural Hints:
- Handshakes are a common form of greeting.
- The Chinese are reserved and modest when dealing with others.
- Aggressive behavior is offensive.
- Good posture is important.
- To beckon someone, hold the palm down and wave your fingers. Never use the index finger to beckon.
- Winking is impolite.
- Use an open hand for pointing.
- Place hands in your lap when seated.
- The people of Hong Kong are familiar with many Western popular gestures.
- Eating and food:
  Toasting is common.
  Chopsticks and knives and forks are used.
  For customs associated with chopsticks see section on Taiwan.
  To obtain check or bill, make a writing motion with your hand.
  Service is generally included in the bill, but it's still customary to leave a tip.
  Do not eat on the street.
  Typical foods are rice, fish, pork, chicken, and vegetables.

Hong Kong into a communistically dominated area, others maintain that China cannot afford to lose the strong economy of the area and therefore won't change anything.

Hong Kong is one of the most densely populated areas in the world. The majority of the population is concentrated on the island of Hong Kong itself, which is only 32 square miles in area. Geographically it is part of China, and even the population is 98 percent Chinese. Economically, it lacks natural resources and relies on China for food and water.

Hong Kong provided China access to the West during the life of Mao, when the government nominally refused relations with the industrial world. Contacts with Western firms were handled through the firms of Hong Kong Chinese, enabling China to gain needed technology without loss of face. Since the change in view of the Chinese government

Figure 13–7 Hong Kong

after Mao's death, China does not rely on Hong Kong as much, but the colony still provides an important arena for trading with the West. Hong Kong's own industrial productivity provides important technology for China and makes it one of the rapidly industrializing countries of the world. The continued importance of Hong Kong to mainland China as a supplier of manufactured goods and technology, as well as the potential for China to show Taiwan that former territories can rejoin China and still have local autonomy, suggests that China will fulfill its promises concerning the status of Hong Kong within China after reunification in 1997.

The government's Hong Kong Tourist Association is charged with the task of promoting, monitoring, and stimulating tourism. Hong Kong is second only to the People's Republic of China in the Pacific Asia region in number of tourists. It has had a long history as a tourist center because of its nature and relationship with mainland China. Tourism is the third largest earner of foreign exchange for Hong Kong after garments and electronics. Arrivals jumped from just under 2.3 million in 1980 to 11.7 million in 1996. Hong Kong has benefited from the increasing tourism to China as of its visitors also went to China. The

future of the tourism industry in Hong Kong depends upon its future as determined by China. However, as more direct connections are established between the industrialized countries of the world and China, Hong Kong's importance as a gateway to China may decline.

In terms of origin of visitors, Taiwan, with 17.8 percent, and Japan, with 14.3 percent, are the largest sources. Taiwan's dominance can be accounted for by increased travel to China by the Taiwanese and a liberalization of travel restrictions by the Taiwan government. The United States and Canada have dropped in importance into fourth position with a market share of 10.6 percent. Other major markets are Australia, the United Kingdom, Singapore, Philippines, Thailand, and South Korea.

The main purpose given for visiting Hong Kong is pleasure, but the role of the city as a financial center can be seen in the fact that during 1996 about 25 percent of visitors came for business reasons. The average length of stay is short, suggesting that it is a transit area combined with a large tour package or visit. The Hong Kong visitors Bureau has adopted a major slogan, "Stay an extra day," in an attempt to convince tour operators to increase the stay in Hong Kong.

Tourist Destinations and Attractions

Hong Kong's attractions are shopping and the scenery, including the skyline from the top of the peak reached by a tram ride. Hong Kong is synonymous with shopping. Merchants in Kowloon (across the bay from Hong Kong) and in Hong Kong present a variety of goods from stereo equipment and cameras to fine watches and jewelry. Ocean Park, an oceanarium and fun park, and Sung Dynasty Village, a model Chinese cultural village, add to its shopping attraction. Tiger

Balm Gardens are a complex of statuary and tableaux, depicting tales from Chinese mythology. The harbor offers fishing, restaurants, and an outstanding view of the skyline.

The New Territories provide an opportunity to observe Chinese rural culture without entering China. The oldest village in the New Territories, Kam Tin, is a miniature walled city, with the women still wearing large straw hats.

Macau

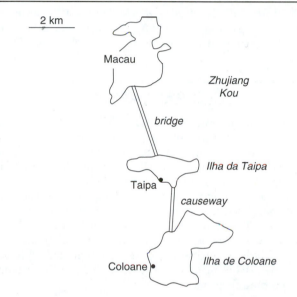

Capital: Macau
Government: Overseas Territory of Portugal, to be returned to China on December 20, 1999
Size: 6 square miles
Language: Cantonese, Portuguese
Currency: Pataca

U.S. passport holders must have visas to travel to Macau. They can be obtained from the Portuguese Consulate in Hong Kong or upon entry to Macau from Hong Kong. Visitors can go to Macau from Hong Kong either by ferry (3 hours) or by hydrofoil (1 hour). Taxis are plentiful and inexpensive.

Macau is located on the southern coast of China at the mouth of the Pearl River. Macau consists of the municipality of Macau, situated on a narrow peninsula, and Taipa and Coloane, two islands to the south. About 99 percent of Macau's population is Chinese, primarily Cantonese and some Hakka. The official language is Portuguese, although Chinese (Cantonese) is spoken extensively.

Macau, the oldest European settlement in the Far East, has a reputation for gambling and night life. Most visitors stay a very short while (1.5 days) and are usually on excursion from Hong Kong. Tourism and gambling account for 25 percent of its Gross Domestic National Product (GDNP). Since Macau was a Portuguese colony, many shows feature Portuguese folk dancing and Fado singing in addition to the Chinese shows.

China (The People's Republic of China)

Physical Characteristics

The central core of the region stretches from the deserts of West China through the Siberian Far East of Russia. This area is a series of desert basins, the largest of which is the Tarim Basin with elevations as low as 500 feet below sea level. South of this region is the *Qing Zang* (Tibetan) Plateau, consisting of plateaus over 12,000 feet above sea level. High above the plateaus are the Himalayan Mountains, reaching eleva-

tions of over 20,000 feet. East of the Qing Zang Plateau are two plateau regions averaging from 4,000 to 7,000 feet above sea level, separated by the Quinling Mountains from the important Sichuan Basin to the south.

North of the Quinling Range are a number of plains that are a major part of the populated East China area. In the far northeast, there is a large basin, the Dongbei Plain (formerly called Manchuria), surrounded by mountains on the north, west, and south-

1200 km

Boundary representation is
not necessarily authoritative.

Capital: Beijing
Government: Communist
Size: 3.7 million square miles
Language: Mandarin, Cantonese, other Chinese dialects
Ethnic Division: Chinese
Religion: Traditional Chinese religion consisted of a combination of Confucianism, Taoism, and Buddhism. Under communist rule the role of religion has been minor.
Tourist Season: Year-round
Peak Tourist Season: June to September
Currency: Yuan (foreign tourists use FEC)

east. The mountains to the south of the Dongbei extend into the central region of both North and South Korea. South of the Dongbei Plain in China is the Huabei (North China) Plain with its level lands along the Huang He (Yellow) River. This North China plain is the historic core of Chinese civilization.

Southeastern China is a hilly country with only limited areas of level plains. Much of this hilly region is cultivated. The Chang Jiang river (Yangtze) flows through this hilly region, and the second great population cluster of China is in the river valley. The Huang He and Chang Jiang River floodplains are home for approximately one-half of China's population. The Huang He of northern China originates in the high plateaus of west central China. From its source to its mouth in the Huang Hai (Yellow Sea), the Huang He is 3,388 miles long and drains an area of 290,519 square miles, an area of more than 49 million acres of agricultural land with a population of nearly 250 million people. The Huang He has always been important to the development of China. The ancestral home of today's China was in the Huang He basin.

The interior of East Asia is isolated from potential sources of moisture by either high mountains or the

TRAVEL TIPS

Entry: Visas are required for all purposes, even transits that do not leave the airport.
Transportation: China has direct flights from North America, Europe, and other countries to Shanghai, Beijing, and four other international airports. However, 88 percent of its visitors come by rail, mostly from Hong Kong. Domestic air service is provided through 195 domestic routes serving more than 90 cities. Efforts have been made to upgrade service and safety. China has added a number of new aircraft with orders from Boeing. The major form of travel between cities, except for the long distances for visitors, is by rail. Public transportation within cities is excellent.
Health: Concern should be taken for malaria and cholera. Outside of the large hotels water is not potable.
Shopping: Common items include Chinese handicrafts, art, historical artifacts, handwoven bags, hats, clothing, carved chess sets, leather coats and bags, and a host of souvenirs at major attractions.

CULTURAL CAPSULE

The largest ethnic group is the *Han* Chinese, who comprise about 94 percent of the total population. Fifty-five minorities make up 8 percent of the population, of which 15 have a population of more than a million people. They include Zhuangs, Hui, Uygurs, Yi, Mio, Manchus, Tibetans, Mongols, and Koreans. The national language is Putonghua (based on Mandarin). Other principle dialect groups include Cantonese, Shanghainese, Fujianese, and Hakka. Chinese does not have a phonetic alphabet. It uses characters to express words, thoughts, or ideas. A romanized alphabet (*pinyin*) is used to teach Chinese in school and for international communication.

Cultural Hints:
- A handshake is a common form of greeting.
- A nod or a slight bow is also used as a greeting.
- Use a person's title and last name when addressing him or her.
- Business cards are exchanged. They should be printed in both English and Chinese.
- Avoid touching or prolonged form of contact.
- Posture is important.
- Clapping is a sign of approval.
- Avoid direct eye contact in public.
- Ask permission to take photographs of people.
- When pointing, use the open hand, not one finger.
- To beckon someone, hold palm down and wave the fingers.
- Spitting and blowing the nose in public is common.
- Pushing and shoving in stores or boarding public transportation is common.
- Thumbs-up signal means everything is all right.
- Eating and foods:
  Chopsticks are used. (See outline under Taiwan for use of chopsticks.)
  Bones and seeds are placed on the table or in a dish.
  Refusing food may be impolite. Just poke it and move it to the side of your plate.

Toothpicks are common, but cover your mouth when using them.

Toasts are common.

Chinese will hold bowls directly under their lips and push food into their mouths with chopsticks.

While dining, guests sit at the left of the host.

Typical foods are rice, potatoes, corn meal, tofu, pork, beef, chicken, and fish. Specialties vary from region to region, including duck in Beijing or spicy dishes in Sichuan. Fruits and vegetables are eaten in season. Sauces are mixed with vegetables and meats and eaten with rice.

great Eurasian landmass. As a result of this continental influence, the large interior basins of China are deserts. In addition, because of the large landmass and northerly locations, winters are severe in northern China and Mongolia. The coastal areas of China have a more humid climate as a result of the effect of the summer *monsoon*. This eastern portion of China is commonly called *humid China*, while the north and west are called *arid China*. The monsoon in China does not result in the sudden onset of a persistently rainy sea-

son, but signals a wetter, more humid period. The precipitation of the summer monsoon is insufficient for consistently reliable production of crops in northern China, but is much heavier and more reliable in southern China, affecting crop types and yields.

Based on temperature and precipitation, it is possible to distinguish five climatic types in China, Figure 13–8. The largest is the desert of western China. In Mongolia and north central China, there is a transitional zone of steppe (almost desert), with typical grasslands. In the northern part of humid China, north of the Chang Jiang (Yangtze River), there is a humid continental climate. Dongbei (the northeast) has extremely cold winters with continuous winter snow cover influenced by Siberia. In Beijing (Peking) and along the Huang He in east China, there is a humid continental, warm summer climate.

South of the Chang Jiang River, China and Hong Kong have a humid subtropical climate with hot, humid summers and mild, humid winters. Xizang (Tibet) is typical of mountain regions, with a highly undifferentiated climate varying as a function of elevation and exposure.

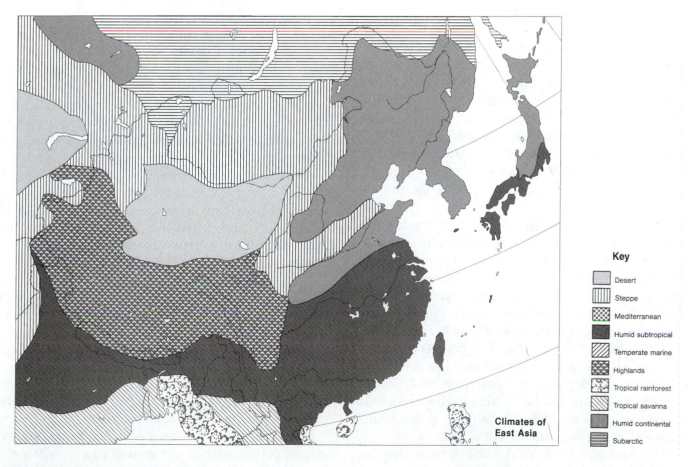

Key

- Desert
- Steppe
- Mediterranean
- Humid subtropical
- Temperate marine
- Highlands
- Tropical rainforest
- Tropical savanna
- Humid continental
- Subarctic

Climates of East Asia

Figure 13–8 Climates of Asia

Tourism Characteristics

One of the most significant features of world tourism has been the opening and development of tourism to China from the West. The first important year for Chinese tourism was 1978. In 1978, the Eleventh Party Central Committee of the Chinese Communist Party decided that tourism was a means to earn much-needed foreign currency. By 1984, China was receiving over $1 billion annually from tourism. This growth is remarkable not only in numbers but also because starting in 1978 there was little tourist infrastructure. The Civil Aviation Administration of China was operating with eighteen-year-old Soviet and British airplanes. In an effort to modernize, China needed currency from other countries and felt that tourism would help to provide this currency quickly.

The importance China has placed on tourism was demonstrated by its holding an International Tourism Conference in 1983, to stress to the world that tourism had arrived in China. A committee, the National Administration of Travel and Tourism, was organized directly under the State Council to formulate tourism policy, review plans, and coordinate the work of the governmental departments involved. Three organizations were established under the National Administration of Travel and Tourism to handle incoming visitors. They were the China International Travel Service, the China Travel Service, and the Youth Travel Service. Although the China International Travel Service (CITS) was founded in the 1950s, it played only a minor role in China until after 1978. Most foreign visitors prior to 1978 were Soviets or overseas Chinese. In 1978, CITS handled 120,000 foreign tourists, best by the mid-1990s, some 22 million foreign visitors (excluding overseas Chinese) visited yearly. About one-third are handled by CITS.

The growth in tourism results from the deregulation of tourism in China. State and locally sponsored tourism agencies can also negotiate and promote directly with foreign producers, issue visas, and receive payment in foreign currency. Branch offices of the CITS also have authority to deal directly with tour operators and issue visas. It has been estimated that by 1985, CITS branches handled 50 percent of the tour groups in China, utilizing 176 offices and more than 4,000 guides and interpreters. CITS also operated hotels and had contracts with foreign management groups for hotels in all the major tourist spots and major tourist cities of China.

The National Tourism Administration was reorganized in 1989. This led to significant changes in China's tourist industry structure. It allowed 44 new state-owned Grade "A" travel agencies (those allowed to deal with foreign operators, take foreign currency, and issue visas) to be established in each province and autonomous region and in the cities of Beijing, Shanghai, and Tianjin along with 14 other major tourism cities. The branch offices of CITS provincial branches were downgraded to a "B" status (permitted to handle foreigners, but not to allocate visas or do direct business). This was to decrease competition within its own ranks. Grade "C" handled domestic tourists only.

The China Travel Service (CTS) was established to handle overseas Chinese and Chinese *compatriots* from Hong Kong, Macau, and Taiwan, which accounts for the largest volume of travelers for their clients. CTS was created to permit overseas Chinese and compatriots special privileges, including a more generous import allowance, lower air and rail fares, and lower hotel prices, in part because they did not need to be of the same quality. Overseas Chinese were defined as ethnic Chinese living outside China apart from those living in Hong Kong, Macau, and Taiwan, who were designated compatriots, which the Chinese government officially maintains are part of China. By 1985, CTS had 270 offices with 20,000 personnel and 3,000 buses and cars. It also has offices in Hong Kong, Macau, the Philippines, Thailand, and the United States. Both CITS and CTS maintain different accommodations and levels of service for their clients. The Youth Travel Service (YTS) is responsible for helping young people to explore China at a lower price. It is also responsible for a number of exchanges between colleges and universities and China.

When China first began a major tourism program in 1978, it was designed for special interest groups such as doctors, nurses, and teachers. In October of 1982, China simplified admission procedures to allow individuals to visit and increased the number of cities that could be visited. In 1982, there were only 29 cities allowing visitors, although there were 120 cities open to foreign visitors. This was in part due to the lack of trained personnel and adequate facilities (both accommodations and air service), to provide proper service to visitors. Further liberalization occurred in 1986 when the State Council approved a law allowing foreigners to travel to all 274 open cities' areas without a travel permit. Today approximately 700 cities and places are open for visitors.

A tremendous growth has occurred in accommodations, particularly at the major centers of Beijing, Xi'an, Guilin, Shanghai, Hangzhou, and Guangzhou.

More areas have been opened and facilities built with the assistance of foreign investment and management skills established to support a more diversified travel industry. By mid-1990 there were over 250 joint-venture hotels in China. In addition, China has purchased new aircraft and opened several tourism programs in universities and colleges, bringing in specialists from all over the world to assist in providing service skills and teaching programs.

Domestic tourism is new for the Chinese, developing in the 1980s. By 1990 it was estimated that there were about 300 million domestic tourists visiting such places as the gardens of Suzhou, the Great Wall, Beijing, the West Lake in Hangzhou, Shanghai, and the seaside resorts of Qingdao, Yantai, and Qinhuangdao.

Of more than 19 million non-mainland visitors to China, over thirteen million (45 percent) were from Hong Kong, Macau, and Taiwan and are not counted as foreign visitors. In spite of the continual Chinese insistence that these are really Chinese citizens, they are in fact the largest group of international tourists to China. The most significant growth in the past 5 years has been the increased Taiwan market. Since Taiwanese visitors have been included in the compatriot count, data is somewhat limited. In 1993, it was estimated that 3 million visitors were from Taiwan. It was not until October 1987 that the Taiwan government first allowed its citizens to travel into China via a third country (usually Hong Kong). Travel regulations are continuing to relax, and Taiwanese businessmen were officially allowed into China in 1990 (The Economist Publications Limited: *International Tourism Reports*, 1990).

Of those classified as foreign visitors by China, Japan and the United States are the largest markets for China, accounting for 22 and 9 percent, respectively. Both have declined since 1988. Also, the American market is changing from upscale, high-income, to middle-income, budget-minded travelers. The average length of stay is 8.1 days, and for the foreign visitors seasonal, with April through June and September through November the peak periods. CTS indicates that there is a large demand to combine sightseeing with visiting friends and relatives for their clients, with major destinations being Beijing, Shanghai, Suzhou, Wuxi (for its lake and picturesque canals), Hangzhou (a scenic city known for its West Lake), Guangzhou, and Guilin. Hong Kong Chinese mostly go to the nearby special economic zones of Shenzhen and Zhuhai and to Zhongshan in Guangdong province.

Although there is a more liberal policy of travel, 70 percent of foreign visitors are still on inclusive tours. The most popular regions for foreign groups appear to include Beijing, Xi'an, Shanghai, Guilin, Guangzhou, Suzhou, Wuxi or Hangzhou, and sometimes Nanjing. Japanese tours tend to favor the ancient cities of Luoyang and Datong ("The Economist Publications Limited," *International Tourism Reports*, 1990). The crushing of student protests during the summer of 1989 (the *Tiananmen Square* incident) lowered tourism, but by 1991 tourist income of $2.8 billion represented an increase of 26.4 percent over 1988, the year before the incident.

Tourism Destinations and Attractions

The dominant attraction is the Chinese culture itself, as modified by subsequent experiments with socialism. The ten major cities in order for tourism are Beijing, Guangzhou, Shanghai, Shenzhen, Guilin, Xi'an, Hangzhou, Nanjing, Suzhou, and Wuxi. Visitors who return repeatedly to China note the changes that can take place even over a short period. Beijing, the capital with the Imperial Palace (the Forbidden City), serves as the anchor for tourism to China. The Imperial Palace covers 250 acres with golden roofs, marble balustrades, and the Palace Museum. Tiananmen Square is just south of the Forbidden City and is the center of Beijing. Its name comes from the huge gate (Gate of Heavenly Peace) on its north side that was built in 1412. It is a parade ground and has monuments, such as the tomb of Mao, and museums. On the west side of Tiananmen Square is the National People's Congress used for conventions and receptions of foreign dignitaries. In front of the Mausoleum of Mao Zedong are the Museum of Chinese History and the Museum of the Chinese Revolution. Northwest of the Forbidden City is Beihai Park, a beautifully landscaped park of artificial hills, pavilions, temples, halls, bridges, and covered walkways. The Beijing Zoo is one of the world's great zoos. The giant pandas are the star attraction at the zoo. The Temple of Heaven (Tian Tan) is a cluster of ceremonial buildings of the fifteenth century. The most impressive is the "Hall of Prayer for Good Harvest" (Zi Nian Dian). It is constructed entirely of wood without nails. Near Beijing is the Summer Palace of pagodas, pavilions, temples, courtyards, and nearby hills, lakes, and terraced gardens. The Summer Palace was the rest-and-recreation area of the royal families. It dates back to 1000 A.D. The grounds include Longevity Hall and Kunming Lake with the famous Marble Boat and the Seventeen Arched Bridge. The Long Corridor here with its Painted Gallery is most impressive.

Also near Beijing is one of the world's great cultural artifacts, the *Great Wall*, Figure 13–9, and the extremely interesting *Ming Tombs*. The Great Wall is 4,000 miles long and parts are 2,600 years old. The 13 Ming Tombs are equally as impressive, with the famous Sacred Way of Stone Animals guarding the entrance to the area. The tombs lie in a natural amphitheater, and the approach is lined with statues of men and animals. The tomb of the thirteenth emperor, Wan (1773–1620), has been completely excavated and can be visited. It is equal to the tombs of the pharaohs in Egypt.

Shanghai, the largest city and most European in design, also has an old Chinese town, with Yu Yuan Yu (the Mandarin's Garden), the Temple to the Town Gods, and the Garden of the Purple Clouds of Autumn. The Mandarin's Garden was built by the Pan family in the sixteenth century. It is noted for its many halls and pavilions, bridges, and towers. The Temple of the Town Gods next to the Mandarin's Garden is one of the few surviving such temples in China. The Garden of the Purple Clouds of Autumn behind the Temple of the Town Gods is known for its ornamental lake and pavilions. The Children's Palace, once the home of a wealthy merchant, is now one of the most famous attractions in China. It is a school for children learning dancing, singing, music, painting, and handicraft. The Temple of the Jade Buddha, the Carpet Factory, and the Jade Carving Factory are other important attractions in Shanghai.

A hundred miles south is West Lake near Hangzhou. The lake is extremely beautiful and is controlled by dikes, some of which were built around 820 A.D. Many pavilions and temples have been built around the lake. The Pagoda of Six Harmonies and the Lingyin Monastery are earlier reminders of the region. Buddhist rock carvings can be seen at the Lingyin Temple. The sunsets, sunrises, and misty days are exceptionally beautiful and are used often on pictures of China. A cable car between the temple and north peak provides a view of the lake.

At Suzhou (Heaven on Earth) is Huqiu Hill (Tiger Hill), the burial place of the father of King Wu. The pagoda on the top was built in 961 A.D. Suzhou has more than a dozen Chinese gardens dating from the eleventh century. Each was designed to represent an idealization of the natural world (rocks = mountains, ponds = oceans, shrubs = forests). Some are very small, while others are large multi-acre parks. The West Garden dates back to the Ming Dynasty and contains some 500 arhats that guard the temple.

Figure 13–9 *Chinese tourists at the Great Wall near Beijing, 1996.*

Nanjing, an ancient capital, has the tomb of China's first president, Dr. Sun Yat-sen, and the tomb of a Ming emperor, which also has a Sacred Way like Beijing. Around Nanjing, tourists also visit the Yangtze River Bridge and the People's Commune of National Minorities. Wuxi, some 80 miles west of Shanghai, is considered the Venice of China. Lake Taihu and the Grand Canal connect 72 islands with beautiful scenes, pavilions, and towers. Wuxi is noted for its silk factories and cement boats, which float on the Grand Canal.

Some 500 miles southwest of Shanghai, Lushan is a famous summer resort. The best-known attraction is the Fairy Cave or "Cave of the Immortals." The cave is located on a sheer cliff. Near Lushan, Hanpo Pass is the beginning of Poyang Lake, one of China's largest lakes. It is a scenic area, particularly at sunrise. Flower Path Park is one of the most fascinating

Figure 13–10 *Pagoda village cemetery in central China*

parks in China. There are miniature trees set in water in porous rock, rock formations, bridges, and so on.

Another region popular with tourists centers around Xi'an. The ancient city of Xi'an is the site of the excavation of Emperor Qin Shi Huang's gigantic buried army of terra-cotta soldiers and horses. Not long ago, bronze horses and soldiers were excavated in its vicinity. The Provincial Museum contains more than 2,000 ancient artifacts, including the oldest collection of stone tables (steles) in China and historical relics and the Gallery of the Stone Sculpture. Also in Xi'an are the Dayan Pagoda, known as the Big Wild Goose Pagoda; the Emperor Qin Shi Huang Mausoleum; the Ban Po Museum, a neolithic village of the Ban Po people who settled the area some 6,000 years ago; and the Bell Tower, which is 119 feet high and constructed of wood and brick.

Another important attraction in the broad region around Xi'an is Luoyang. Luoyang has the impressive Longmen Grottoes dating to 494 A.D. There are some 1,300 grottoes and 40 pagodas containing at least 100,000 Buddhas, the largest of which is 56 feet tall. In the Working People's Park, there are two Han tombs dating back to 206 B.C. Lushan is a famous summer resort for the Chinese.

Two of the most scenic cities are Guilin and Kunming. Guilin has been a popular attraction for international visitors since the opening of China in 1978. With its unique karst topography and river cruises on the Li River, Guilin is a delight to the visitor. There are sensational views of mist-covered hills and valleys, rock formations, rapids, and bamboo groves. Ludiyan (Reed Flute Cave) has a number of beautiful formations and colors and has a large grotto (Crystal Cave) that can hold 1,000 people. Kunming's most unique attraction is the Stone Forest, which was formed when limestone rose from the receding sea water. In Xishan Park, there are a number of ancient temples set on the shore of Kunming Lake. The atmosphere includes an interesting market, ruined pagodas, the Yuantong Temple, stores selling tribal handicrafts, and traditional Chinese teahouses. Nearby is the Stone Forest of Lunan, which consists of incredible, uniquely shaped rock formations created by erosion.

Far to the west on the Silk Road is Urumqi, the capital of the Xinjiang Uygur Autonomous Region, which provides visitors with an excellent view of western China, Figure 13–11. It has an outstanding museum of ancient artifacts dating to the Stone Age. The Lake of Heaven and the Carpet Factory are other important attractions in this remote city. Visits to Xizang (Tibet), under Chinese control, center in

Figure 13–11   Uygur man, Kashi, China

Lhasa. The Potala Palace on the slopes of the Red Hill in the Old City originally served as the Winter Palace of the individual Dalai Lama who was ruling the country at a specific time. Norbu Lingka, the Dalai Lama's Summer Palace, is located 62 miles west of the Potala Palace. The Jokhang Temple, with its golden tiles on the roof, was built in the seventh century A.D. Other attractions are the Drepung Monastery, constructed in 1416, and the Ganden Temple, which is one of the three major temples of the Ghelu Section of Tibetan Buddhism in Lhasa.

THE SILK ROAD TO ADVENTURE:
ARID CHINA'S ATTRACTIONS

When most people think of China, they automatically think of the eastern part of China. Eastern China is known to geographers as "China Proper." It is the China populated by the Han Chinese, the largest ethnic group in the world, consisting of over one billion Chinese. China Proper is the China of Beijing, with its marvelous Forbidden City where the Emperor ruled, carried from place to place and never allowed to walk upon the ground. China Proper is green and fertile, with each foot of ground intensively cultivated. It is home to more than 95 percent of China's citizens and to many of the world's largest cities—Shanghai, Beijing, Guangzhou, Wuhan, and Nanjing. China Proper is the China that most foreign tourists see as they travel to China.

China Proper is one of the most attractive and exciting places for foreign tourists to visit. The magnificent historic sites in and around Beijing (including the Great Wall of China, the Temple of Heaven where the emperor prayed yearly for good crops and good fortune for his people, the numerous Buddhist temples, and the Chinese people themselves) and Shanghai (the Jade Temple, the Bund, the bustling stores and markets) are almost overwhelming for a first-time visitor. Even the worst amateur photographer cannot help but take magnificent photos of the attractions and people found here.

But there is another China, one that shares only some of the characteristics that make China Proper so exciting. Most of China is not green and fertile, or densely populated, for it is desert and mountain country, and many of its occupants are not Han Chinese, but Tibetans, Kazakhs, Uygurs, Hues, and other groups defined by the Chinese government as "minority groups." The land and people of the great western interior of China are visited by only a relative handful of Westerners each year, but these visitors find a veritable wonderland that is amazing in its variety of attractions.

The western two-thirds of China is known to geographers as "Arid China." It is characterized by some of the driest deserts in the world, the Gobi and the Tarim Basin, with its dusty center occupied by the burning Takla Makan desert. The people of this broad region occupy oases on the margins of the deserts or river valleys in the mountains and deserts where streams flow from the high Tian Shan, Altun Shan, Qilian Shan, or Altai Mountains. Many of these mountain chains have peaks above 20,000 feet, which remain snow covered all year. Travel to this arid region has been occurring for thousands of years, most notably as a result of merchant traders who crossed the region to buy silk with goods brought from the west. The routes of these traders are known collectively as "the Silk Route," a series of trails that converged at central settlements but divided to form the northern, southern, and central silk routes. Marco Polo passed this way nearly a thousand years ago, and Buddhist holy men who introduced Buddhism to all of China and Eastern and Southeastern Asia created

memorials to Buddha nearly 2,000 years ago in the arid cliffs near villages along the Silk Road.

Modern visitors can only marvel at the tenacity that allows the creation and persistence of settlements and monuments in these arid places. Visiting the region in the summer of 1996, I was impressed by how little we in the West know about the Chinese and other occupants of this land that is larger than the United States. Some of the cities of the Silk Route are more than 2,000 years old. The arid climate has allowed preservation of the ruins of walls, temples, and art created by their early inhabitants. In a cliff on the margins of the farmland of Dunhuang, an oasis in the Gobi Desert, were carved 2,800 Buddhist temples, 482 of which are still in existence. Known as the Magao Grottoes, they are a United Nations World Heritage Site. The grottoes were dug out of the cliff over centuries by Buddhist monks and range in size from a few square feet to one large enough to hold a giant three-story Buddha. A visitor is overwhelmed by the devotions that prompted these artists of yesterday to devote their lives to creating memorials to their gods.

The Silk Route has more than archaeological attractions, however. The sights, sounds, tastes, and smells of these oasis towns are unique. Dress styles often combine styles from Chinese or local cultures with Western casual dress. In Linzia, the Hue Muslim women cover their hair with a scarf denoting marriage status (green, black, or white), while the devout Muslim men cover their heads with a white cap. At Xiahe, the Tibetan Buddhist women wear beautiful white, tan, or grey felt hats similar to the women of the Andes. The monks and their students at the Labrang Monastery, wear red robes, Figure 13–12. Labrang is one of six great Yellow Hat Sect monasteries, and its presiding monk (known as the incarnation of the living Buddha) is the third most important individual in Tibetan religion after the Dalai Lama and the Panchen Lama.

Food and dress vary from region to region along the Silk Route. The rice of Eastern China is replaced by wonderful handmade wheat noodles, some over two feet long. Round loaves of bread about eight inches in diameter and two inches thick are baked by wetting one side and sticking them on the inside of a domed adobe oven. Hot from the oven they are indescribably delicious. In summer melons, apricots, peaches, apples, and grapes are mouthwatering and present at every meal. Garlic is used in much of the cooking or is present at the table to be eaten whole. Some cities such as Hami (Hami melons), Turpan (white grapes and white raisins), or Lanzhou, Xining,

Figure 13–12   Tibetan student at monastery in western China

Hotel accommodations across western China are adequate, and many towns, including Kashi, Xining, Urumqi, and Linxia, have opened new Western-style hotels, often as a joint venture with Indian, Pakistani, or other foreign interests. Food is always abundant and delicious. The best times to visit this area are in April-May or September-October from the standpoint of climate, but then you will miss both the marvelous fruit of the summer and the scenic farms with their lush crops of wheat, corn, cotton, grapes, melons, rapeseed, and sesame seed.

Western China is a little-known travel destination, with fewer than 300,000 non-Chinese visitors a year, and most of these are Japanese. Whatever their nationality, however, tourists along the old Silk Road will find friendly people and a culture and history that cannot be appreciated until it is experienced. Tourism along the Silk Road is an adventure that may not be for the faint of heart, but anyone in reasonable health who desires to better understand the wonderful world in which we live will find it the trip of a lifetime.

and Kucha (watermelons) are famous across China, and Chinese tourists take boxes of delicious fruits back as they fly to eastern China.

Near the western border where China's borders join Pakistan and Kyrgyzstan, the Uygur Muslims are the largest population group. At Kashi (formerly Kashgar), the great Idkah mosque, the largest in China, is rivaled only by the giant concrete statue of China's former leader Mao Zedong a few blocks away. While the latter is increasingly irrelevant to the lives of the local people, the mosque is of renewed importance as a symbol of their distinct culture. Kashi is the western crossroads of the Silk Route, and its Uygur people are joined by Uzbekis, Kazakhs, Pakistanis, Afghans, and Han Chinese, creating an amazing and colorful ethnic mix, Figure 13–13. On Sundays the Kashi bazaar brings over 100,000 people to this teeming Kashi marketplace. Every imaginable product is on sale, including camels and other livestock, clothing and handicrafts, knives (the Uygur men all carry a knife—although the Chinese maintain that the Uygur are only allowed to wear them for decoration, they are very sharp decorations), spices, food, and even several pelts of the rare and endangered snow leopard.

Figure 13–13   Kazakhs in mountains near Urumqi, dressing tourists in Kazakh wedding finery

Many visitors entering China arrive from Hong Kong at Guangzhou (formerly Canton), considered the southern gateway to China. Attractions in Guangzhou include the Memorial Garden to the Martyrs (sometimes called the Red Flower Garden), which has a pure white stone tomb; the mausoleum of the 72 martyrs; the Zhenhai tower, which was built about 1480 and contains both a museum and an observation tower of the famous Pearl River; and the Dr. Sun Yat-Sen Memorial Hall. The Ancestral Temple of Foshan, an ancient Taoist temple, is near Guangzhou. The old European section has colonial architecture from the ninteenth century. The Qingping Free Market is an experience. Among the stalls visitors will find snakes being skinned alive, freshly slaughtered cuts of meat, and all kinds of live animals such as monkeys, cats, large wild birds, and so on.

Datong on the Mongolian border and Hohot in Mongolia are the major attractions in the Mongolian region. Datong contains the world-famous ancient Yungang grottoes. These cave temples, some of which reach heights of 60 feet, were carved in the period from 386 to 534 A.D. The Nine Dragon Screen, which is 147 feet long and 6 feet high, is colorful and impressive. Hohot provides a good view of the famous Mongolian grasslands and offers the experience of staying in a typical Mongolian *Yurt* (felt hut).

The Three Gorges on the Yangtze River can be viewed by visitors from cruise ships, but the Chinese have planned a dam on the river that will submerge these spectacular attractions. In the western Sichuan tourist district around Chengdu is the world's largest Buddhist statue. It is carved on Mount Leshan and surrounded by a region of unusual scenic beauty. In the tourist district of central Shandong Province is Confucius' hometown in Qufu, Mount Tai and Jinan City. The large palace-like Confucian temple, estate, and tomb are in Qufu. Near Qufu, Mount Tai is an imposing mountain with ancient architecture and cultural relics.

The attractions are as many and diverse as the size of the country itself. From the deserts and grasslands of the north and the high mountain region of Xizang (Tibet) to the hot, humid south, scenic beauty, ancient wonders, and modern ways are inviting to tourists. With the liberalization of the industry, further development of the infrastructure, and prices becoming competitive with other tourist destinations, China could well become one of the great tourist destinations in the world.

Mongolia

Capital: Ulaanbaatar
Government: Transition from Communist state to Republic
Size: 604,247 sq. miles (slightly larger than Alaska)
Language: Khalkha Mongol
Ethnic Division: 90% Mongol, 4% Kazakh, 2% Chinese, 2% Russian
Religion: 96% Tibetan Buddhist, 4% Muslim.
Tourist Season: June through August
Currency: Tughriks (Tug)

TRAVEL TIPS

Entry: A visa, a passport, and an invitation from a Mongolian host are required. Proof of sufficient funds and further transportation to leave the country are also required. There are currency restrictions in force.
Transportation: Most passenger travel is by the Trans-Mongolian Railway, which connects Ulaanbaatar with Naushki, Russia, and Erenhot, China.

CULTURAL CAPSULE

Over 90 percent of the people are comprised of subgroups of the Mongol nationality. The largest is the Khalkha (79 percent). Other Mongols are Buryads, Dorwods, Oolds, Bayads, Dzakhchin, Uriyankhais, Uzemchins, and Bargas. The largest non-Mongol ethnic group is the Kazakhs, about 6 percent of the population. The Mongols are pastoral nomads. Mongols have practiced a combination of Tibetan Buddhism and Shamanism. The Dalai Lama of Tibet is the religion's spiritual leader. The people practice ritualistic magic, nature worship, exorcism, meditation, and natural healing as part of their shamanistic heritage. While many monasteries were closed under communist rule, many have reopened; and Muslims are allowed to practice Islam.

Cultural Hints:
- A handshake is a common greeting.
- People are called by their given names.
- Use the right hand for making gestures.
- Passing items with the left hand is impolite.
- Use the open hand to point, not the index finger.
- Beckon someone with the palm facing down and wave the fingers.
- Avoid eye contact.
- Avoid touching or contact.
- Do not kick another person's foot.
- Eating and foods:
  Tea and milk are common.
  Guests give the hosts a small gift.
  At restaurants, meals are served European style.
  Tipping is not practiced.
  Typical foods are dairy products, meat (mutton, or beef), barley, and wheat. Rice is common in urban areas.

Physical Characteristics

Mongolia is a land of vast semi-desert and desert plains with mountains in the west and southwest. The climate is desert and continental with large daily and seasonal temperature ranges. Its winters are long and cold. The Gobi desert in the south can go years without rain.

Tourist Characteristics and Tourism Destinations

The tourism industry is small, and there is little data available pertaining to Mongolia. The major destinations and attractions are the dinosaur graveyard in the Great Gobi Reserve, the ancient city of Karakorum, the medieval Erdene-Dzuu monastery, and the summer palaces of the last living Buddha.

CHINA

DAY 1   SAN FRANCISCO–BEIJING

Depart from San Francisco for Beijing. Cross the International Date Line.

DAY 2   BEIJING

Arrive in Beijing at night. Beijing is the capital of the People's Republic of China. To the northwest are the mountains, and to the southwest are the plains.

DAY 3   BEIJING

Visit Tiananmen Square. The name of the square was derived from Tiananmen Gate, which is on the north side. It is the largest public square in the world. It covers 100 acres.

On the southern edge of Tiananmen Square is Qian Men Gate, which is the front gate. To the north of Qian Men Gate is the Chairman Mao Memorial Hall. It occupies the most important place in the square. Mao's stature as the great leader of the People's Republic of China is symbolized by this memorial hall.

On the western side of the Square is the Great Hall of the People, which covers an area of 560,000 square feet. It has a main assembly room large enough to seat 10,000 people.

In the middle of the square is the Monument to the People's Heroes. Its obelisk is 118 feet high. It was built to honor heroes who died because of the revolution. Mao's handwriting states: "The People's Heroes Are Immortal."

Two large buildings on the eastern side of Tiananmen Square are the Museum of the Chinese Revolution and the Museum of Chinese History. The Museum of the Chinese Revolution is in the left wing, and the Museum of Chinese History is in the right wing. An excellent museum guidebook is available here.

The northern gate of the square is the Tiananmen Gate, which is the northern entrance to the Forbidden City. It is a massive stone gate, painted red, which was built in 1417 and was restored in 1651.

The Forbidden City, also known as the Imperial Palace, is located in the heart of Beijing. The Wild Moat (palace moat) surrounds and protects the palace. The main entrance of the Imperial Palace is the Meridian Gate, also known as the Gate of the Five Phoenixes. The Imperial Palace has over nine thousand rooms and is divided into two areas—the Outer Palace and the Inner Court.

Smaller than the Meridian Gate is the Gate of Supreme Harmony, which is protected by two striking, stylized bronzed lions. Beyond the gate is a huge courtyard. The Hall of Supreme Harmony is one of the main buildings in the Outer Palace. It is also one of the tallest and largest of the palace buildings. It was used by the emperor for state occasions.

Going through the Hall of Supreme Harmony one will come upon the Hall of Perfect Harmony. The emperor received loyalty from his ministers in this hall.

Beyond the Hall of Perfect Harmony is the Hall of Preserving Harmony, which became the Palace of Examinations, the highest level of the nationwide civil examination system.

Next is the Palace of Heavenly Purity. The emperors from the Ming Dynasty to the early Qing Dynasty used to live in this Hall. Many symbolic objects surround the terrace. The Hall of Union displays one of the most marvelous scientific inventions of ancient China—a clepsydra (water clock). The Qing emperors used the hall for birthday celebrations. The palace where the Ming empresses lived is the Palace of Earthly Tranquility. In the Qing Dynasty, it was used as a shrine for worshipping gods.

The Imperial Garden is arrayed with statues, rock gardens, pebble walkways, and an artificial hill with a cave, waterfall, and a pavilion. It covers 3,400 square yards.

Visit Coal Hill, which is on the northern end of the Imperial Palace. The name of this hill is derived from the fact that coal was once stored here. Five White Pavilions, the Beautiful View Tower, and the Pavilion of Everlasting Spring are the main attractions of the park. The view of the Imperial Palace and modern-day Beijing from the summit is beautiful.

Visit Bei Hei Park, which is in the west of the Coal Hill. It is the most popular place for recreation. The Bridge of Perfect Wisdom, which is opened to Qionghua Island on North Lake to the southeast shore, is one of the park's famous places. Tibetan White Pagoda, which was built in 1651, occupies the center of this island. When China was under the Mongol's control, Kublai Khan established his palace in this park.

continues

continued

Visit the Temple of Heaven by bus. It is located in the southeastern part of Beijing. This is the largest park in Beijing. It has three main structures: the Hall of Prayer for Good Harvests in the north, the Imperial Vault of Heaven in the center; and the Circular Mound Altar of Heaven in the south. The Hall of Prayer for Good Harvests has a blue-tiled roof. The Imperial Vault of Heaven has the circular echo wall around the hall's outer courtyard. The three large stones known as the Three Echo Stones are in this hall. The Circular Mound Altar of Heaven consists of three marble terraces symbolizing earth, the mortal world, and heaven.

DAY 4   BEIJING

Today we will visit the Great Wall. This long wall was built for self-protection from the nomads of the northern border. It is the only man-made object that is visible from satellites in orbit. Today it is surveyed 3,750 miles from the Shan Hai Guan Pass to the Ju Yong Guan Pass in the Gobi Desert. The Great Wall has suffered serious damage from wind and water because of its geographical location. The view from the top of the Great Wall is magnificent, and by looking from this historic spot one can imagine the awful wars that occurred. The wall is steep and can be slippery so be sure to wear comfortable shoes with good soles. Helicopter tours of the Great Wall and the Ming Tombs are available for those wishing to see these great views from the sky.

Visit the Ming Tombs. These tombs are those of the Ming emperors. Their location was selected by the wind and water levels. There are thirteen tombs of the Ming Dynasty emperors. The road to the tombs is called the Sacred Way, which is 6.4 kilometers long. The largest and best preserved of the tombs is Chang Ling. This is the tomb of the Emperor Ching Zu. The tomb of the fourteenth emperor of the Ming Dynasty, Shen Zong, is called Ding Ling. The emperor's two wives are also buried here. It is also known as the Underground Palace.

DAY 5   BEIJING

Visit the Summer Palace. The Summer Palace is located northwest of Tiananmen Square. It is a very pleasing place for a relaxing walk. This park covers 632 acres, three-quarters of which is Kun Ming Lake. The remaining fourth is called Longevity Hill. On top of the hill is the Hall of Benevolence and Longevity, the Hall of Jade Billow, the Garden of Virtuous Harmony, and the Hall of Happiness and Longevity, which have been open to the public since 1979. The lake is very popular for swimming and boating in the summer and for skating in the winter.

In the afternoon, one may go shopping on the ancient street Liu Li Chang Jie, which is called "Beijing's culture street" because of its famous antiques, books, paintings, brushes, inks, ink-stones, rubbings of ancient inscriptions, and calligraphy known throughout the world.

DAY 6   NANJING

Travel to Nanjing by plane. Visit Yuhuatai Park. It is also called Terrace of the Rain Flowers. There are many springs in this park. They are like rainbow hues because of the colorfully grained pebbles in the area.

Visit Gu Lou. The view of the town from this observation point is very beautiful. It is called Drum Tower and was built during the Qing Dynasty.

Visit Nanjing Museum. The Nanjing Museum is located in the eastern suburbs of the city. Displayed and preserved inside are important historical objects discovered in the Jiangsu Province, such as bronze from the Shang Dynasty, Han pottery coins, weapons, and jewelry. Some artifacts date back 5,000 years.

DAY 7   NANJING

Visit Linggu Temple Park. It is located at the foot of Zijin Mountains. The park has several beautiful gardens with pine-tree forests. The Wuliang Temple and Pagoda are in this park.

Visit Sun Yat Sen Mausoleum. It is located on the southern slopes of Zijin Mountain and covers an area of 321 acres. Memorial Hall is reached by climbing 392 granite steps. Pines, cypresses, and fruit trees cover the ground.

Visit Ming Xiao Tomb. This is the tomb of the first Ming emperor, Hong Wu. A narrow sacred path with twelve pairs of stone animals leads to the tomb.

Visit Zijin Shan Observatory. This is on the third peak of Zijin Mountain. The observatory's museum is the main attraction. Collections of ancient astronomical instruments are displayed here.

DAY 8   NANJING–SUZHOU–SHANGHAI

Travel from Nanjing to Suzhou by train (crossing the Yangtze River Bridge) (approximately a three-hour trip).

Visit Suzhou Grand Canal. The Canal is located to the west of the city. This is the longest man-made canal in China and is crossed by cargo ships with agricultural products and raw materials. Its average width is 100 feet. Travel from Suzhou to Shanghai by train. Approximately one hour.

DAY 9   SHANGHAI

Visit Shanghai Museum. The museum is located on Henan Road. It is a three-storey museum, and it has one of the finest art collections in China. The collections from the Shang and Zhou Dynasties are located on the first

continues

continued

floor. Exhibited on the second floor are the collections from the Qin and Han Dynasties. On the third floor are the collections from the Tang, Song, Yuan, Ming, and Qing Dynasties.

Visit Jade Buddha Temple. This temple is located to the northwest of the city. There are many statues of Buddha in this temple, two of which are very famous. One is seated, and one is reclining. Twenty-four monks live in the temple.

Visit Children's Palace. This is the school where children between the age of seven and seventeen who have special talents can have specialized training. The children are the guides for tours of the palace.

Visit Long Hua Temple. This is the oldest and largest temple located in the southern suburbs of Shanghai. This is the only temple in Shanghai that has a pagoda. It also has four main halls with drum and bell towers.

Visit the Garden of the Mandarin Yu. This marvelous garden is divided into two parts. It was built by the governor Pan Yunduan. A small museum, called the Beautiful Spring Hall, is located in the outer garden. The garden also has a famous artificial mountain made of rocks. Included are streams of clear water, ponds with goldfish, and pavilions.

DAY 10 SHANGHAI–HONG KONG

Travel from Shanghai to Hong Kong by plane (approximately two hours).

Visit Tiger Balm Gardens, a public park built by the man who developed the medicine Tiger Balm. Its Hau Par Mansion has a marvelous collection of jade.

Visit Victoria Peak. A late evening ride up to the top of the peak (1,674 feet) is indispensable. The view of Hong Kong is breathtaking. Having dinner with this great view will make one of the great memories of this tour. Stay on Hong Kong Island.

DAY 11 HONG KONG– MACAU–HONG KONG

The excursion to Macau is by jet-foil, the fastest service available from the New Macau Ferry Pier on Hong Kong Island. Macau is the oldest European colony in the Far East. It is located on the peninsula extending out from mainland China. Its baroque churches, old mansions, and cobblestone streets show that Macau was founded by the Portuguese. Typical examples of the sixteenth-century style buildings are the Church of St. Paul Cathedral, and St. Dominic, St. Augustine, St. Lawrence, and St. Joseph cathedrals.

The rest of the day is free for shopping. Hong Kong is a shopping paradise. All the merchandise is duty-free. Enjoy the last night in Hong Kong.

DAY 12 HONG KONG– SAN FRANCISCO

Travel to the Kai Tak Airport by bus via the new tunnel to Kowloon. Leave for San Francisco.

REVIEW QUESTIONS

1. What advantage has Hong Kong's status as a colony of the United Kingdom provided for China?
2. What factors explain the rapid growth in tourism to China?
3. Why has Hong Kong, a tiny nation, had so many tourists?
4. What are the three major classifications of tourists to China?
5. Compare and contrast two of the major tourist regions of Japan.
6. Discuss the economic characteristics of the various nations of East Asia.
7. What are the major attractions of Taiwan?
8. What are the major markets for Taiwan's tourism industry?

GEOGRAPHY AND TOURISM IN
South and Southeast Asia

CHAPTER 14

MAJOR GEOGRAPHIC CHARACTERISTICS

- The population of this region is concentrated in the river basins.
- The monsoon impacts the economy and life in south Asia.
- Village life dominates throughout south and southeast Asia.
- There is fragmentation of the political, cultural, and physical geography.
- Large and rapidly growing populations combine with political and cultural conflict to make this region important.

MAJOR TOURISM CHARACTERISTICS

- This region is located far from the markets of the Western industrialized countries of the world.
- The exotic and sensual are emphasized in attracting tourists.
- The political problems of Southeast Asia retard the growth of tourism development.
- Tourism is localized in a relatively few countries and places in the region, such as the Himalayan Mountains.
- Tourists from industrialized countries visit only one country, but tourists from the region visit multiple countries.

MAJOR TOURIST DESTINATIONS

Kathmandu, Nepal
Bombay, Delhi, Agra, and Jaipur, India
Bangkok and Pattaya, Thailand
Singapore
Bali and Jakarta, Indonesia
Karachi, Pakistan
Kuala Lumpur and Penang, Malaysia
Manila and Luzon Island, Philippines

KEY TERMS AND WORDS

Archipelago	Population
Buddha	River Valleys
Circular Tours	South Asia
Coral Reef	Southeast Asia
Deccan Plateau	Stupa
Golden Triangle	Subtropical
Himalayas	Taj Mahal
Hindu	Temple
Monsoon	Village
Mosque	Wat
Pagoda	

INTRODUCTION

With the exception of a few countries, tourism to South and Southeast Asia involves few people. The region's isolated location from the major industrial countries of the world, the political problems of the region, and the poor economic character of the area are important factors in the lack of development of the tourist industry in South and Southeast Asia, Figure 14–1. Nearly all of the region's climate is either tropical rain forest or tropical savanna, which also hinders tourism development because of high temperatures and humidity during at least part of the year.

PHYSICAL CHARACTERISTICS

Landforms

The Indian Subcontinent of South Asia

South Asia occupies the Indian subcontinent. The most dominant and well-known landform feature of the subcontinent is the Himalayan Mountains, Figure 14–2. The *Himalayas* exceed 20,000 feet elevation, and the range presents a dominant barrier to movement of air masses and people. Invading groups and ideas have periodically moved through passes in the mountains, especially the Khyber Pass in the west. Movement to the north has been much more

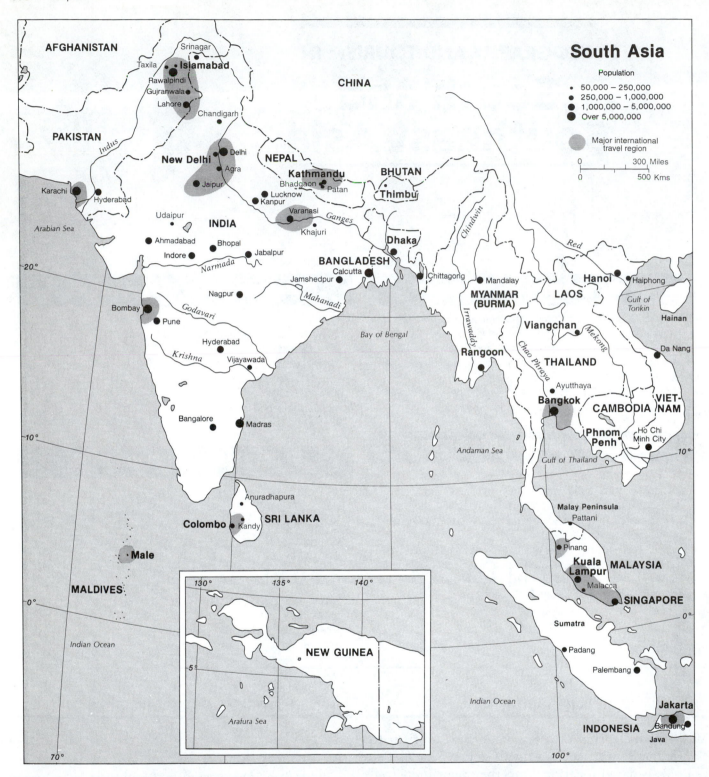

Figure 14–1A South and Southeast Asia

difficult, but the Karakoram Pass provides limited access from north central India through the Himalayan and Hindu Kush complex of mountains.

Four small regions occupy the Himalayas of South Asia: the countries of Nepal and Bhutan and the states of Kashmir and Sikkim. Kashmir is claimed by both India and Pakistan, and the resulting dispute has often had violent side effects. Sikkim became an Indian state in 1975. Except in the more favorable valleys, such as Nepal and the Vale of Kashmir, population in the Himalayas is limited. Bhutan has only 1.8 million people, and Sikkim has less than half a million. The populations of Nepal, Bhutan, and Sikkim are concentrated in the intermediate eleva-

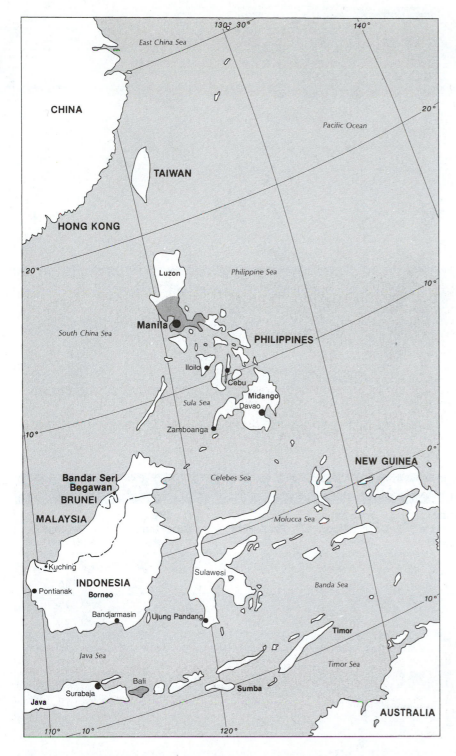

Figure 14–1B   South and Southeast Asia

tion zones where the climate is relatively moderate, ranging from *subtropical* to humid continental.

South of the Himalayas is the major area of the Indian subcontinent. The plains of the Indus, the Ganges, and the Brahmaputra rivers have the greatest population concentrations of the subcontinent, are the economic heart of the subcontinent, and were the center of the historic civilizations that dominated the subcontinent. These plains are from 200 to 300 miles in width and pass through the countries of Pakistan, India, and Bangladesh.

South of the plains of the large rivers of the Indian subcontinent is the peninsula of India with its principal landform, the *Deccan Plateau*. The plateau is an uplifted area, dissected by *river valleys* into a complex system of level plateaus, hills, and deep ravines.

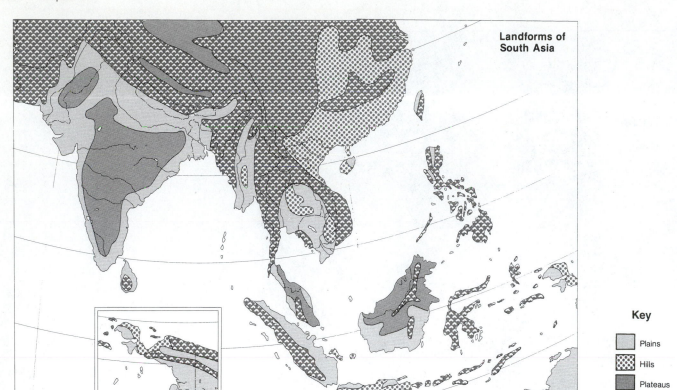

Figure 14–2   Landforms of South and Southeast Asia

POPULATION CHARACTERISTICS, 1997						
Country	Population (millions)	Annual Growth Rate (percent)	Time to Double Pop. (years)	Per Capita GNP	Life Expectancy (years)	Percent Urban
SOUTH ASIA						
Bangladesh	122.2	2.0	35	240	58	16
Bhutan	0.8	3.1	22	420	66	15
India	969.7	1.9	36	340	59	26
Maldives	0.3	3.6	19	990	72	26
Myanmar	46.8	1.9	36	N/A	61	25
Nepal	22.6	2.3	31	200	54	10
Pakistan	137.8	2.8	25	460	61	28
Sri Lanka	18.7	1.5	47	700	72	22
SOUTHEAST ASIA						
Cambodia	11.2	2.9	24	270	49	13
Indonesia	204.3	1.7	40	980	62	31
Laos	5.1	2.8	25	350	52	19
Malaysia	21.0	2.2	31	3,890	72	51
Philippines	73.4	2.3	30	1,050	66	47
Singapore	3.5	1.1	64	26,730	76	100
Thailand	60.1	1.1	63	2,740	69	19
Vietnam	75.1	1.6	43	240	67	20

The Deccan Plateau has elevations of approximately 1,000 to 1,500 feet above sea level. It is separated from the coastal plains by the Ghats mountain ranges parallel to the east and west coasts. The western Ghats reach elevations of 5,000 feet in a few areas, but the eastern Ghats are lower, with few elevations over 2,000 feet. At the very southern margin of the Deccan Plateau is a cluster of hills called the Blue Mountains, which reach heights in excess of 8,800 feet. The eastern and western Ghats are bordered respectively by the coastal lowlands of the Coromandel and Malabar coasts.

Southeast Asia

The landform diversity of *Southeast Asia* is different than the relative homogeneity of the climate of the region. The continental areas of Southeast Asia are dominated by a rugged and complex topography. Mountains rarely exceed 10,000 feet, but they are steep and covered with dense forest and are sparsely populated. The river valleys—the Red River of northern Vietnam, the Mekong River and its valleys, the Irrawaddy River basin, and the central lowland of Thailand—are the population centers of the various countries.

The islands and the archipelagos of Southeast Asia form part of the Pacific Ring of Fire and, unlike the continental areas of Southeast Asia, suffer periodic volcanic activity. Vulcanism and subsequent erosion and deposition have created a landscape of great complexity.

Climate Characteristics

South Asia

A common characteristic of the Indian subcontinent is the lack of freezing temperatures other than in the Himalayas where temperatures drop low enough to prevent double cropping. The dominant climatic element in the subcontinent is the *monsoon*. Except in areas of Pakistan, the monsoon brings heavy summer precipitation to the subcontinent. The monsoons result from the jet stream shifting north and south of the Himalayas with the changing seasons of the year. In winter, the jet stream in the northern hemisphere is divided, with one part south of the Himalayas.

This arm of the jet stream effectively prevents air movement and moisture from the oceans from moving into the core area of India along the Ganges, and dry conditions predominate. During this dry season, temperatures may exceed 95 degrees Fahrenheit.

During the summer, the jet stream moves entirely north of the Himalayas, in most years allowing moist air to penetrate the continent. During the summer season, when the monsoon winds blow from the ocean, the air mass rises as it moves over the continent, causing orographic precipitation. Some years, the jet stream remains south of the Himalayas late into the summer season, limiting precipitation. For tourists, the monsoon season of the year is most uncomfortable for travel.

Located in western India and Pakistan, the Indian desert stretches westward to the Indus River of Pakistan. The Coromandel and Malabar coastal regions of the subcontinent have a tropical rain forest climate as a result of orographic precipitation and latitudinal location. The eastern portion of the Ganges, known as the Delta region, also has a tropical climate, but it is a tropical savanna modified by the monsoon.

The Deccan Plateau has a humid subtropical climate that is plagued by inadequate summer moisture. The western Ghats cause a rain shadow on the Deccan Plateau, where agriculture often suffers from insufficient moisture at critical times. The Ganges Basin proper has a tropical savanna to subtropical climate that relies on the monsoon. Temperatures are uniformly high throughout the year, with winters typically having less precipitation.

To the west in the Indus valley of Pakistan, the climate is drier because of the rain shadow effect of the landmass of the Middle East. Only the coastal regions of Pakistan receive the full impact of the monsoons and have a hot, wet, tropical climate.

Southeast Asia

Southeast Asia is characterized by a homogeneous climate. No other area of the world of comparable size has such a uniform climate. The climate throughout the entire region is tropical, with temperatures exceeding 60 degrees Fahrenheit throughout the year. Although portions of the region have a dry period from a monsoon or a more savanna-type climate, there is no truly arid region in Southeast Asia. Prevailing winds in the islands and along the coasts of the continent cause rain shadows in some locales, but the region generally receives high precipitation. Abundant rain falls every month, but it comes in the form of convectional precipitation with brief, heavy showers each day.

North of the tenth parallel are the tropical savanna regions with alternating wet and dry seasons. Unlike India, where there is a prolonged drought during the dry season, the savanna lands of Southeast Asia generally receive scattered precipitation even in the dry season, with only certain areas of the mainland in a rain shadow receiving less than 60 inches per year. The wet season in the savanna regions may consist of a single wetter period in the high-sun months from May to September, or there may be two wet seasons with a dry period between. In either case, the wet season is characterized by heavy convectional precipitation modified by orographic barriers. The rainfall tends to be torrential. With the constant high temperatures, it causes high humidity and extreme erosion and leaching of the soils to a degree unknown outside the tropics.

POPULATION PROBLEMS

One of the impressions gained by tourists to this region is related to its people. South and Southeast Asia have large population numbers and a high growth rate. As of 1996, the absolute increase in numbers each year in India is greater than in any other country of the world, totaling nearly 18 million people per year—more than live in all but a few of the most populous states of the United States. India's population problem is typical of that of less industrialized countries. The perpetually increasing numbers of Indians help to keep India one of the poorest countries of the world. It is estimated that more than 300 million people in India's urban slums and rural areas live below the level necessary to maintain adequate health.

The impact of India's population on attempts to transform the economy is pervasive and insidious. The literacy rate of India is estimated at 36 percent, and the logistics of overcoming the mass illiteracy, even without population growth, would tax the resources of the entire subcontinent. Simply providing

one elementary school for each of the 580,000 *villages* is beyond India's present ability.

Pakistan's mushrooming population exceeds the country's food production. Pakistan is a nation of farmers, with a limited resource base that helps keep it in the less developed realm of the world. Bangladesh has similar problems. It has one of the highest rural population densities in the world. Food production is inadequate for the population, a population that at the present rate of growth will reach 160 million by the year 2000.

Population is also a major problem in Southeast Asia. The island of Java is one of the most densely populated locations in the world. As with the rest of Southeast Asia, however, the bulk of the country of Indonesia has low population densities. Indonesia has reduced its population growth rate, but as with other Southeast Asian countries, it still faces the difficult challenge of channeling its growing populations into less densely settled locales, improving literacy and health standards, and providing jobs for its burgeoning populations.

TOURISM TO SOUTH AND SOUTHEAST ASIA

South and Southeast Asia are exotic and sensual destination regions of the world. For most of the industrialized Western nations, both the environment and the culture are much different than those in which they live or with which they have considerable contact. Tourism is also localized in South and Southeast Asia, with a few countries receiving most of the tourists. Within the countries receiving the tourists, tourism is localized to a few specific regions. Tourism development and growth have been limited because of the political problems associated with wars, terrorism, and nationalistic movements. Most countries of the region lack accommodations for mid-

Table 14–1 International Tourism to South Asia				
	Number of Visitors (thousands)		**1996 Receipts (millions of US $)**	**1996 Average Expenses per Visit**
Country	**1986**	**1996**		
India	1,451	2,288	3,027	1,323
Bangladesh	129	166	38	228
Bhutan	3	5	5	1,000
Myanmar	47	165	60	364
Maldives	93	339	257	758
Nepal	223	404	130	322
Pakistan	432	348	112	322
Sri Lanka	230	302	168	556
Source: Yearbook of Tourism Statistics. Madrid: World Tourism Organization, 1997				

dle-income tourists. This situation is somewhat off-set by the lower food and labor costs that keep tour packages reasonable. A major tourist organization is the Pacific Asia Travel Association (PATA). It consists of 34 countries who work together to promote tourism through research, development, education, and marketing.

South Asia

South Asia averaged over 3.2 million visitors in the late 1980s and early 1990s, Table 14–1. This was less than one (0.6) percent of total world international tourists. The annual growth rate over the ten-year period from 1980 to 1990 of 3.4 percent has flattened over the past five years. This suggests that if the region can overcome the problem of distance from the major world markets and lack of adequate accommodations and political tension, there is still a considerable potential for tourism to the region.

A significant percentage of international tourism in the region is regional in character, Table 14–2. With its huge population, India provides the largest segment of international visitors to the other countries of South Asia. India also receives the most income from tourists, but in contrast to the other South Asian countries, visitors from within the region are far less important. India's international visitors come from many countries, but a significant

Table 14–2 Origin of Visitors to South Asia (1995 Market Share)

Country	United States	Asia/ Pacific	Europe	Others
Bangladesh	6.7	57.2	30.7	5.4
India	11.5	25.4	43.3	19.8
Nepal	6.2	48.6	39.5	5.7
Pakistan	9.9	22.2	49.9	18
Sri Lanka	2.2	31.9	63.2	2.7
Total for Region	9.2	29.9	45.8	15.1

Source: *Annual Statistical Report.* Pacific Asia Travel Association, 1995

percentage of those traveling from Europe are from the United Kingdom, reflecting ties from the colonial period. Many residents from South Asia, particularly India and Pakistan, migrated to Britain. Until recently, residents of former colonies of the United Kingdom that were members of the Commonwealth of Nations could migrate freely to the United Kingdom. With family ties in South Asia, visitors from England have trips of long duration, averaging nearly 20 days for India and 27 for Pakistan.

Tourism to India reflects the great regional variation in visits to the region. Climatic factors (the hot, humid monsoon), sociopolitical problems, and tourist attractions and development combine to determine the level of tourism activity in each individual country.

Bangladesh

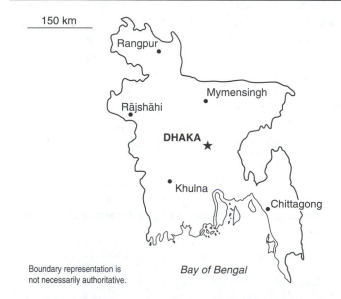

150 km

Rangpur

Mymensingh

Rājshāhi

DHAKA ★

Khulna

Chittagong

Boundary representation is
not necessarily authoritative.

Bay of Bengal

Capital: Dhaka
Government: Republic
Size: 55,598 square miles (about the same as Wisconsin)
Language: Bengali, English
Ethnic Division: 98% Bengali, remaining are Boharis and Tribal
Religion: 83% Muslim, 16% Hindu
Tourist Season: October through February
Peak Tourist Season: December through February
Currency: Taka

 TRAVEL TIPS

Entry: Visas are not required for stays up to 14 days. Proof of onward or return transportation is required. Arrival and departure taxes are collected.
Transportation: International connections to Dhaka are through Europe, India, and Thailand. Domestic airline service is adequate, and rail service is limited. Road transportation is limited, and most roads are not paved. Public transportation within cities is by bus (crowded), rickshaws, and babi-taxis (three-wheeled motor scooters).

Health: Malaria, cholera, typhoid, hepatitis, and yellow fever are concerns for protection. Do not drink water other than bottled or boiled. Do not eat food from street vendors. If you cannot peel it or it is not cooked, do not eat it.

Shopping: Items include pottery, products of papier-mache, textiles, carpets, leather goods, brass, wood carvings, and gold and silver filigree jewelry.

CULTURAL CAPSULE

Bangladesh is the most densely populated agricultural country in the world. The population of Bangladesh is about 98 percent ethnic Bengali and speak Bangla. They are of an Indo-European heritage, with some Arab, Persian, and Turkish influence. There are some Urdu-speaking non-Bengali Muslims of Indian origin (Assamese). They are often referred to as "Biharis" or stranded Pakistanis. There are also various tribal groups, mostly in the Chittagong Hill Tract. Most Bangladeshis (85 percent) are Muslims, and *Hindus* are the largest minority (14 percent). There are a small number of Buddhists, Christians, and Animists. English is understood and spoken in the urban areas and among the educated. Small groups along the southeast border speak their own language.

Cultural Hints:
- Women do not wear pants and men do not wear shorts.
- Men will shake hands and nod when introduced to a woman.
- The thumbs-up gesture is an obscene gesture.
- Remove shoes before entering a mosque.
- Do not take pictures without asking permission.
- Pushing and shoving is not impolite.
- Eye contact is important.
- Do not point the bottom of a shoe at a person.
- Do not whistle or wink in public.
- The OK sign with thumb and index finger touching is obscene.
- Beckon with palm down and all fingers waving.
- Eating and food:
  Never use the left hand to eat.
  Men and women often dine separately.
  Do not transfer food from one person to another.
  It is acceptable to eat with your fingers.
  Do not pass objects with your left hand.
  Bones and food wastes are placed on bone plates.
  Typical food is rice, fish, carrots, cucumbers, and tomatoes. Food is spicy (cumin, ginger, coriander, tumeric, and pepper) and often marinated.

Physical Characteristics

Bangladesh is a low delta plain with a marshy jungle coastline. Hills rise above the plain only in the extreme southeast and the northeast. The climate is semitropical monsoonal, with one of the world's highest amounts of annual rainfall. During the rainy season, May to October, travel can be difficult.

Tourism Characteristics

Bangladesh receives most of its visitors from Asia and the Pacific. Over 33 percent of the visitors are from India, with the rest of the Asian and Pacific countries accounting for an additional 30 percent of the visitors. Of countries outside of the Asian and Pacific realm, the United Kingdom contributes the most visitors, 12.1 percent. This is probably due to the colonial ties and linkages, which took a number of citizens of Bangladesh to the United Kingdom (Pacific Asia Travel Association, 1994).

Bangladesh is presently not an important world destination country. With only two major cities, it lacks both an infrastructure (roads, airports, sewage systems) and suprastructure (hotels, restaurants, entertainment). Most international visitors from the industrialized nations of the world are there for business or, as suggested, if from the United Kingdom, to visit friends and family.

Tourist Destinations and Attractions

Dhaka, the capital, and Chittagong, the major port city, have mosques, markets, and crowded, active street scenes. In Dhaka, a huge fort (the Lal Bagh Fort) and the tomb of Pari Bibi (a daughter of one of the moguls) are attractions. Near Chittagong, there is an excellent seaside resort (Cox's Bazaar), with beaches stretching 70 miles on the Bay of Bengal. On the Karnaphuli River around Rangamati, the local tribes build their bamboo houses in the jungle high on stilts. Bangladesh has a few archaeological sites and the Dhaka Museum of Antiquities, which displays relics of the early civilizations of the region.

Bhutan

Physical Characteristics

Bhutan is located in the secluded valleys on the south side of the Himalayas between the Tibetan plateau and the Assam Bengal Plains of northwest India. The country is extremely mountainous but has a plains area in the south, bordering India. The climate varies

75 km

Lingshi
Dzong

THIMPHU
★

Tongsa
Dzong

Tashi
Gang
Dzong

Paro

Samdrup
Jongkhar

Phuntsholing

Capital: Thimbu
Government: Monarchy
Size: 18,000 square miles (about the same as Vermont and New Hampshire together)
Language: Dzongkha (a Tibetan dialect) and English
Ethnic Division: 50% Bhote, 25% Nepalese, 25% Tribes
Religion: 75% Buddhism, 25% Hinduism
Tourist Season: November through March
Peak Tourist Season: December through March
Currency: Ngultrum

CULTURAL CAPSULE

The people of Bhutan are divided into three ethnic groups—Sharchops, Ngalops, and Nepali. Sharchops, the earliest major group, live in eastern Bhutan and appear to be closely related to the inhabitants of northeast India. The Ngalops are considered to be of Tibetan origin, arriving in Bhutan in the eighth century A.D. and bringing with them the culture and Buddhist religion that are dominant in the northern two-thirds of Bhutan. The Nepalis, most of whom are Hindus, arrived in the late nineteenth and early twentieth centuries. They farm Bhutan's southern foothill region. The official language of Bhutan, Dzongkha, is related to classical Tibetan and is written partly in a classical Tibetan script. Nepali predominates in southern Bhutan. English is the official working language and is taught in schools. It is widely used. More than 90 percent of the people are employed in subsistence farming and animal husbandry. Terrace agriculture is extensive, with rice paddies as high as 8,000 feet.

TRAVEL TIPS

Entry: Tourists are admitted only in groups prearranged with Bhutan's ministry of Tourism.
Transportation: Entry is by air or land from Pakistan or India only. Travel within country is mostly by foot or pack animal.
Health: Cholera, yellow fever, tetanus, typhoid, poliomyelitis, and hepatitis immunizations are recommended. Special food-handling methods and water purification are essential.

with altitude. The valleys of central Bhutan are temperate, while the southern plains and valleys are subtropical. Bhutan has heavy summer rain.

Tourism Characteristics and Tourist Destinations

Bhutan has little tourism. Before 1974, the few visitors allowed were official or business visitors. While it now accepts tourists, tourism continues to be very limited with only 30,000 total visitors between 1974 and 1994. In 1996, 5,000 tourists came to Bhutan. Bhutan has a very small private tourism sector, as tourism is organized directly by the government. It has little access and remains largely a mystery to the rest of the world.

Bhutan's main tourism attractions are the breathtaking Himalayan scenery and the country's culture. The Bhutan countryside has numerous monasteries, and the monks are a distinctive part of the culture. Punakha, the former capital, is the religious center of the country and beautiful *temples* and interesting fortresses are located in Paro, a city set in a scenic valley dominated by Mount Chomolhari. The Skimtokha Dzong in Thimbu is located on a high mountain perch. The Manas game sanctuary, with the rare golden langur monkeys, could become an important attraction if more visitors were allowed.

Myanmar (Burma)

Physical Characteristics

Myanmar is rimmed on the north, east, and west by mountains, with the population concentrated in the river valleys and coastal plains. The climate varies; lowlands are hot and humid with temperate higher elevations in the rugged highlands. It has the heavy summer rain associated with a tropical monsoon climate.

Tourism Characteristics and Tourist Destinations

In most geographies, Myanmar is considered a nation of South Asia. However, the World Travel Organization lists it as part of Southeast Asia. It has little tourism and for a number of years was closed to most of the world's tourist market countries. Tourism is still limited. It dropped from 47,000 visitors in 1986 to 21,000 in 1990. Since 1990, tourism to Myanmar

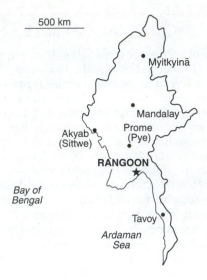

500 km

Myitkyinā

Mandalay
Prome
(Pye)
Akyab
(Sittwe)

RANGOON ★

Bay of
Bengal

Tavoy

Ardaman
Sea

Capital: Rangoon
Government: Military regime
Size: 262,000 square miles (slightly smaller than Texas)
Language: Burmese
Religion: 89% Buddhist, 4% Muslim, 1% Animist, 4% Christian, 2% others
Tourist Season: November through March
Peak Tourist Season: November through January
Currency: Ktat

 TRAVEL TIPS

Entry: Travel to Myanmar is tightly controlled by that country's government. There is limited entry at three border posts, including Tachilk for tourists who enter by land from Thailand. Visas are issued at the point of entry to individual tourists and certain groups.
Transportation: Access to Rangoon is from Bangkok, Singapore, Calcutta, Dhaka, and Kathmandu. Travel by car, train, or river steamer is arduous. Public transportation in Rangoon and Mandalay is inadequate, unsafe, and overcrowded.
Health: Inoculation for yellow fever, cholera, tuberculosis, typhoid, and malaria are needed. The plague and leprosy are endemic to the country. Boil all drinking water and eat only well-cooked meat and vegetables.
Shopping: Common items include local jade and other gemstones and native handicrafts.

CULTURAL CAPSULE

The dominant ethnic group of Myanmar is Burmans (25 million). More than 2 million Karens live throughout southern and eastern Myanmar. The Shans, ethnically related to the Thai, number some 2 million and live mainly in the eastern plateau region. Other major indigenous groups are the Rakhins in the west, Chins in the northwest, and Kachins in the north. There are large groups of ethnic Chinese, Indians, and Bangladeshi living in the country. Theravada Buddhism, an older form of Buddhism, is the major religion (85 percent). Other religions include Islam, Christianity, and traditional practices.

Myanmar's ethnic groups speak numerous languages and subsidiary dialects. Burmese is related to Tibetan and spoken by most of the people. English is a second language and spoken among the educated and official people.

has been increasing, but it will remain small compared with other countries in the region. The dry season from November to February is the best time to visit. Few cities outside of Rangoon have accommodations for travelers. Rangoon, the capital, has been influenced by the British and has old colonial public buildings and wide streets. It has parks, gardens, lakes, and colorful *pagodas*, of which the magnificent Shwedagon Pagoda is the focal point. The Shwedagon Pagoda historically served as the center of the religious and cultural life. A number of smaller shrines and temples, each with images of *Buddha*, surround the pagoda. Passageways and bazaars selling Burmese handicrafts, flowers, and incense are located around the pagoda.

Mandalay, in the northern part of the country, was the former capital and remains the cultural center of Myanmar. Like other Asian towns, its marketplace, bazaars, monasteries, and golden pa-

godas are the major attractions. Near Mandalay, Maymyo, which was the summer capital under the British, is now a popular resort for the Burmese people. Pagan, the ancient capital, has extensive ruins of more than 5,000 pagodas. The government is in the process of restoring some 30 of the most impressive temples. Moulmein, across the Gulf of Martaban, has been called the most beautiful town in Myanmar.

India

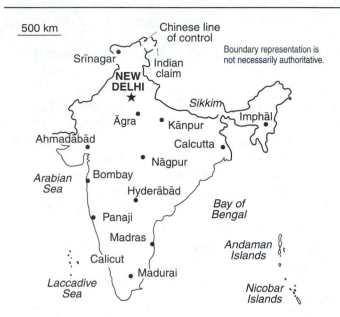

Capital: New Delhi
Government: Federal republic
Size: 1,268,884 square miles (more than twice the size of Alaska)
Language: Hindi, English
Ethnic Division: 72% Indo-Aryan, 25% Dravidian, 2% Mongoloid
Religion: 80% Hindu, 14% Muslim, 4% Christian, 2% Sikh
Tourist Season: November through March
Peak Tourist Season: November and December
Currency: Indian Rupee

 ## TRAVEL TIPS

Entry: Visas are required. Proof of sufficient funds and evidence of onward or return flight is required. Currency over $1,000 must be declared to customs. Import and export of Indian currency prohibited by law.

Transportation: There are good international connections by many carriers to New Delhi, Bombay, Calcutta, and Madras from Europe, Southeast Asia, the Middle East, and other South Asian countries. Indian Airlines provides service to many major cities within India. Rail service is good between cities, but distances between major cities are long. Local transportation includes buses, taxis, three-wheeled scooters, cycle rickshaws, and horsedrawn tongas. Buses are overcrowded and service is irregular. Taxis are plentiful in the larger cities and tourist regions.

Health: Typhoid, tetanus, hepatitis, diphtheria, cholera, and malaria shots are recommended. Water is unsafe. Drink bottled or carbonated water.

Shopping: Common items include handicraft goods, exquisite jewelry in gold and silver, Kashmir carpets, wood and ivory carvings, silks, fur, leather hides, saris, marble tabletops, and intricately inlaid items.

CULTURAL CAPSULE

India is a nation of villages. About 80 percent of the population live in the more than 550,000 villages throughout the country. Northern India has been invaded from the Iranian plateau, Central Asia, Arabia, and Afghanistan throughout its ancient and pre-modern history. The blood and culture of these invaders have mixed freely with those of the indigenous people to create the current character. Today Indo-Aryans make up 72 percent and the Dravidians account for 25 percent of the population. The remaining 3 percent is made up of a number of other groups including Mongoloids. Religion, caste, and language are major determinants of social and political organization. More than 1,600 languages are spoken in India, with 24 having more than a million users each. Sixteen are officially recognized languages, and English is an unofficial lingua franca. Hindi is the most widely used, with 30 percent of the people speaking it. English is particularly common in business and government. Although 83 percent of the people are Hindu, India also has approximately 100 million Muslims, giving it one of the world's largest Muslim populations. India also includes Christians, Jews, Sikhs, Jains, Buddhists, and Parsis. The Sikhs are recognizable because of their distinctive dress (including turbans for men). Extremely nationalistic, they are trying to create a Sikh state in Punjab. The caste system, comprising the traditional social categories of Indian society, has been historically based on occupation-related categories ranked in a theoretically defined hierarchy. Four castes were identified plus a category of outcasts (untouchables). However, there are thousands of subcastes. Despite laws against discrimination against lower castes and lower-end untouchables, the system remains an important factor in India.

Cultural Hints:
- A handshake is common with Westerners.
- Traditional greeting is palms pressed together, fingers up below the chin and a slight bow.
- The term "namaste" is a common greeting and goodbye.
- Do not touch women.
- Use titles when addressing others.
- Exchange of business cards is important.
- Do not stare in public.
- Whistling is impolite.
- Do not wink or whistle.
- Ask permission to take pictures.
- Do not touch another person with your shoes or feet.
- Do not pat youngsters on the head.
- Women should cover their heads when entering a sacred building.
- To grasp one's earlobes is to express remorse or honesty.
- To point, use the chin, full hand, or thumb but not a single finger.
- Remove shoes before entering a temple or mosque.
- Eating and food:
  Often utensils are not used.
  Eat with your right hand.

> Beckoning a waiter is done by a snap of fingers and hiss.
> Wash hands before and after meal.
> Transfer food from the communal dish to your plate with a spoon.
> Indian food is quite spicy. Typical food varies by region. In general it includes rice, wheat bread, and curry (eggs, fish, meat, or vegetables in a spicy sauce). Vegetarianism is common for religious reasons. Muslims eat no pork and drink no alcohol. Betel leaves and nuts are commonly chewed or eaten after meals.

Physical Characteristics

India has three main topographic areas: the sparsely populated Himalayan Mountains, extending along much of the northern border; the heavily populated Gangetic Plain, a well-watered and fertile area in the north; and the peninsula, including the Deccan Plateau, which is generally of moderate elevation. The climate varies from tropical in the south to temperate in the north. The cool season extends from November to March; a dry, hot season from March to June; and a hot, rainy season during the remainder of the year. Much of southeast India is subject to a second rainy period during the cool season.

Tourism Characteristics

India, the second most populous country of the world, receives nearly four times as many tourists as any other country in South Asia. Tourism grew slowly in the 1980s and early 1990s as a result of civil problems in the country, but many within India felt that the government stifled tourism growth because of a bureaucratic administration and lack of tax and investment incentive. Air fares, for example, are higher from Europe to India than they are to Hong Kong and other East Asian destinations, largely to protect the national airline, Air India. Hotel prices are high for a less developed country, mirroring prices in the industrialized world, which increases the cost of travel to India. Beginning in 1992 a National Action Plan for Tourism was introduced. The purpose was to encourage private investment, both domestic and foreign. The objective was to increase India's share of world tourist arrivals by upgrading the tourist infrastructure and the identification and development of selected areas. Seventeen tourist circuits and destinations were identified for development. Special targets were wildlife tourism, trekking, river rafting, mountaineering, rock climbing, water skiing, river running, paragliding and helicopter skiing.

India has the most dispersed world markets of all the South Asian countries, Table 14–2. Europe, led by the United Kingdom with its historical colonial ties, is the major source area. Migration of the Indian population throughout the world and their return home to visit is also illustrated in the fourteen percent of visitors from the Middle East, most of whom are migrant workers from India working in the oil fields. Also an indication of this migrant work force is that males represent almost 62 percent of total visitors to India. However, some caution needs to be applied in interpreting this ratio of males to females, because even among foreign nationalities arriving male tourists dominate, ranging from 70 percent of the Japanese visitors to almost 60 percent of the U.S. visitors. Seasonality is strong, with the monsoon months having the lowest number of visitors and the peak months being in December, January, February, and March during the dry season. India has one of the longest lengths of stay for foreign visitors in the world. The average stay of tourists is approximately 29 days. The combination of Indians returning home and the long distance and huge size of the country contribute to the long visit.

Tourist Destinations and Attractions

While tourist attractions are dispersed throughout India, the industry is concentrated in the north. The major tourism regions follow.

The Golden Triangle—Agra, Jaipur, and Udaipur. If there is a modern "Seven Wonders of the World," one would be the *Taj Mahal* in Agra, Figure 14–3. Along with the Great Wall and the Pyramids, the Taj Mahal is one of the best-known structures in the world. Pictures do not do justice to the beauty of the structure. The intricate artwork, using semiprecious stones, such as sardonyx, coral, amethyst, chalcedony, agate, lapis lazuli, and turquoise, and outstanding workmanship manifested in the marble screens and minarets make a visit to the Taj Mahal an overwhelming experience. The Taj Majal was built some 500 years ago by Shah Jahan as a tomb for his second wife and queen, Arjummand Bano Begam.

The Red Fort is also in Agra and nearby is the abandoned city of Fatehpur Sikri, a pilgrimage center for Indian women desiring larger families. Fatehpur Sikri, Figure 14–4, was developed as a new capital city several hundred years ago at great cost. It was abandoned due to lack of water, but all of the buildings remain. It is a fascinating attraction for international tourists, and the abandoned temple is a fertility sym-

Figure 14–3 Taj Mahal, Agra, India

is an excellent view of the Taj Mahal from the tower. Around Agra, there are a number of impressive structures, such as the Itmad-ud-Daula (a forerunner of the Taj) and Akbar's Tomb.

Located near the second city in the triangle, Jaipur (known as the Pink City), are the marble quarries from which the marble for the Taj Mahal was obtained. The old city contains both Hindu and Muslim architectural styles. The town was built in the eighteenth century on a grid plan with large plazas and extremely wide avenues, necessary for elephant parades. The focus of the old town was the Hawa Mahal, or the Palace of the Winds. The Hawa Mahal is a beautiful flamingo-colored five-storey structure. The Jantar Mantar, an observatory, is a remarkable attraction, Figure 14–5. Near Jaipur, the old fortified hill city of Amber was deserted after the construction and movement of the capital to Jaipur in the plains. Not only is the palace beautiful, but it offers a panoramic view of the surrounding countryside. One unique aspect of Amber is the use of elephants to carry many tourists.

The last of the *Golden Triangle* cities is Udaipur. A walled city in a desert state, Udaipur is in a fertile valley with lakes that add to the beauty of its white buildings, palaces, temples, and unique architecture. Elegant marble palaces appear to be floating on blue lakes, giving it a fairyland appeal. Gulab Bagh, a series of beautiful gardens, surrounds the lake.

bol because a Hindu priest's prayers successfully enabled the Maharajah's wife to bear him an heir when the city was occupied.

The Red Fort at Agra was built three-quarters of a century before Delhi's famed Red Fort. Within the area of the Red Fort, there are a number of buildings of interest. The Red Palace was believed to have been built by Akbar for his son, Jahangir. The Khas Mahal, or Private Palace, contains the Golden Pavilions, with beautiful curved golden roofs. The Sheesh Mahal, or Palace of Mirrors, and Musamman Burj, or Saman Burj (the Prisoner's Tower), are nearby. There

Delhi. Delhi, the capital, is two cities: Old Delhi and New Delhi, which was built by the British to be the capital of India. New Delhi contains the government buildings, which are dominated by the India Gate, built by the British in the style of the Arc de

Figure 14–4 Deserted city of Fatephpur Sikri near Agra, India

Figure 14–5 Jantar Mantar Observatory, Jaipur, India

Picturesque India

by Gordon Kilgore

Seeing for Oneself

...Most Americans have the wrong concept of India. It is depicted by our media as a hot, dirty, impoverished country with people sleeping in the streets. While these conditions can indeed be found in certain sections of a large city, such as Bombay, it certainly is not the norm.

This, in fact, would be like showing the most rundown block of an American large city or some guy sleeping in his cardboard "house" under a road bridge. While these conditions do exist and can be found in Atlanta, for example, it is not Atlanta.

India could be a nightmare experience: at the wrong time of the year, the temperatures can be unbearable; the best roads are no better than our worst secondary rural roads, and when traveling in open vehicles for long distances the rough roads and dust can be miserable. We flew to most places and were in air-conditioned coaches the other times.

There are plenty of cheap hotels that leave much to be desired in India. We stayed in the best, often palace hotels.

The food was hot and spicy and the bread was so good I wish we could have brought some home. Our food was a combination of Indian and Continental, so there usually was something for even the picky eaters.

A poor guide can add misery to misery. Most of our local guides were top-notch.

Our itinerary was very diverse. We saw the landmark sights such as the Taj Mahal in Agra, the pink city of Jaipur, bathing at the ghats in Varanasi, the city palace of Udaipur and the government buildings of New Delhi.

But we also attended the Pushkar Fair, the largest camel trading fair in the world, and visited small, isolated villages where we were allowed into the mud-and-dung homes.

We attended the Diwali (Hindu festival of lights) celebrations in Udaipur. A highlight was being invited to the Diwali ceremony at the home of a wealthy businessman and his family. They were of the Jain religion. It was a most unusual ceremony but still not too different from our own celebration of Christmas with family singing and feasting.

We visited two schools: a village grammar school and a prestigious prep school for the wealthy. We visited and witnessed religious functions in Hindu, Muslim, Buddhist, Sikh and Jain temples.

We sampled a variety of India's transportation that included Indian Airlines, trains, buses, private cars, taxis, scooter rickshaws, pedal rickshaws, camels and elephants. Margaret, Nino and I even ate dinner in an Indian home.

Photographers, Take Note

India is a large country composed of many princely states and districts. It is very diverse and one only has to go several hundred miles to find a different climate, different customs, and different people.

This was not a "kick back and relax vacation;" I would describe it as an educational trip. On the other hand, it was not a fast-paced, rush-rush type of trip. It was more of a steadily paced trip with extra personal time to photograph, shop or take a nap.

Our group was small, so we did more in a given period of time than a large group would do. I managed to expose 76 rolls of slide film and 16 rolls of black-and-white film.

At the end of our group tour, Margaret and I took a train to Sawai Madhopur and the nearby Ranthambore National Park. There we joined Sunjoy Monga, an Indian photographer and owner of Porpoise Photo Stock, a Bombay stock agency. The three of us traveled by car to Bharatpur Bird Sanctuary. These three additional days gave us an insight to another aspect of India that I did not know existed.

Of all the countries I have visited, India has the most to offer a photographer.

If you are a people photographer, the subjects are unlimited and, for the most part, willing.

If you like to shoot color, then the state of Rajasthan cannot be surpassed anywhere in the world.

continues

continued

A black-and-white shooter can have a field day with villages and small streets and the shapes and forms found in ancient temples and walled cities.

The architecture shooter will be blessed with more subjects than time, with continuous blue skies and only the direction of the light to contemplate.

Source: International Travel News. August 1996, pp. 22-27.

Triomphe in Paris. Several sites such as Connaught Place, Parliament Street, Rajpath, and Janpath are part of the well-planned New Delhi and provide an impressive visit. Connaught Place consists of three concentric circles radiating out from the center, with Janpath and Parliament Streets forming spokes of the wheel. The most impressive government buildings are the Parliament House and the President's House, a cream-and-red sandstone palace, that covers 330 acres. Old Delhi is a crowded, colorful bazaar of small shops and stalls. With its high walls and a complex of elegant palaces, the Red Fort is the focus of visitors to Old Delhi. Across the street from the Red Fort is the Jama Masjid, the largest mosque in India. Made of red sandstone inlaid with white marble, it is very impressive. Also not far from Red Fort, the Mahatma Gandhi Memorial marks the spot where he was cremated. The Imperial Palace of Shah Jahan, builder of the Taj Majal, is inside the Red Fort. The Muslim influence is evident in the 234-foot-high Qutub Minaret, a minaret built between the thirteenth and fourteenth centuries.

Bombay. Bombay, on the west coast, is a major international gateway into India. It is a cosmopolitan seaport and was the home of Mahatma Gandhi from 1917 to 1934. His home, Mani Bhavan, has become one of the featured attractions of Bombay. One of India's best museums, the Prince of Wales Museum, is in Bombay. Other places of interest are the Jehangir Art Gallery Colaba, a Jain Temple, and St. John's Church. The Elephant Caves, which contain splendid stone sculptures of religious figures, are nearby on an island. The Kamia Nehru Park includes the Towers of Silence, where the Parsis (a religious sect) place their dead. Vultures pick the flesh from the bones, after which the bones are cremated.

About 150 miles north and east of Bombay are the Aurangabad, Ellora, and Ajanta caves, which are among the modern wonders of the world. The rocky hills of the region became the home of rock-cut temples of various religious communities. The temples—12 Buddhist, 17 Hindu, and 5 Jain—were built between the fifth and seventh centuries. Construction of these temples ranks with the task of building the pyramids in Egypt.

Kashmir and the Floating Gardens of Srinagar. Kashmir is a fertile green valley at the foot of the Himalayas with lakes and gardens. Srinagar, the capital, is a city of canals, and the major transportation network is by water. The city has numerous mosques, Hindu temples, and brick and wooden houses that have grass growing on their mud roofs. Houseboats (long, elegant, flat-bottomed types) are common on the water. Specific sites of interest are the Juma Masjid Mosque, built of wood; the Mosque of Madani; the Mosque of Shah Hamada; the Mughal Gardens, which include the large Nishat Bagh or "Gardens of Delights"; Shalimar Gardens; the Shankaracharya Temple on a hill overlooking the city; the Sri Prata Singh Museum; and the Hazrat Bal Mosque, which is supposed to contain a hair of the prophet Mohammad that was preserved as a sacred relic. Near Srinagar, visits can be made into the high scenic areas of Gulmarg, Sonamarg, and Pahalgam.

Between Srinagar and Delhi in Punjab, Chandigarh, designed by the famed architect and city planner Le Corbusier, is the capital of Punjab. The city has broad avenues and gardens and a number of impressive buildings such as the Secretariat, the Assembly and the High Court.

The Holy City of Varanasi and the Erotic Temple of Khajuraho. Situated on the banks of the Ganges River, Varanasi is the holiest city in India. Hindu pilgrims flock to the city to bathe, perform their rituals, and cremate their dead. Scattered along its narrow, winding streets are over 3,000 temples that are visited by the Hindu faithful. Varanasi is considered to be one of the most ancient cities in the world and has other attractions, including the Durga Temple (Monkey Temple); the Golden Temple, or the Temple of Vishwanath; Benares Hindu University; the Motehr India Temple, a national monument; and an interesting bazaar area. Varanasi is also a principal departure point for trips into Nepal. A sacred city to Hindus, it is a pilgrimage site for visitors to its temples, the Ganges River, or those cremating their dead so that their ashes can be scattered on the Ganges.

Located approximately 200 miles west of Varanasi, Khajuraho is the home of the famous erotic temples built by the Chandella Dynasty between 950 and 1050 A.D. The temples may be the greatest examples of medieval Hindu architecture and sculpture in India. Of the 85 temples built, only 22 have survived, but they comprise an important and unique attraction.

Calcutta. Calcutta is India's largest city. It is also the city to which Western stereotypes of India (population, poverty, disease, etc.) are most commonly applied. Although there are problems in Calcutta, the stereotypes are exaggerated. The British left their mark on Calcutta with stately government buildings, which, combined with the Indian Museum and Zoological Gardens and Indian life, are the focal point of tourism. Some of the British influence and other attractions can be observed in St. John's Church; St. Paul's Cathedral, the Anglican center in Calcutta; the Raj Bhavan, the residence of the Governor of Bengal; famous Chowringee Street, noted for its fine shops and hotels; the Maiden, the city's principal park, with its cricket ground; the business district around Dalhousie Square; the Zoological Gardens; Calcutta University; Victoria Memorial Hall; Howrah Bridge, one of the largest in the world; and the Botanical Garden, which has a 200-year-old banyan tree. A number of temples are worth a visit, namely the Dakshineshwar Kali; Sheetalnathji, a Jain temple; the Kali Temple; the Belur Math Temple; and the Nakhoda Mosque, which is modeled after the tomb of Akbar at Sikandra near Agra. The Marble Palace has a fine collection of art, including works by Ruebens, Reynolds, Courbet, and Corot. Near Calcutta is the magnificent Sun Temple of Konarak near the city of Bhubaneshwar. It is designed in the form of a gigantic chariot, with carvings depicting the joys of earthly life.

Calcutta is the gateway for Darjeeling, known for beautiful sunrises on Mt. Everest, the nearby Annapurna, and the countries of Sikkim and Bhutan. Darjeeling provides excellent views of the Himalayan Mountains with excursions to Tiger Hill for the sunrise view of Everest. The Ghoom Monastery and St. Andrew's Church are also worth visiting.

Madras Region. Although it is much less important for international Western visitors, South India centered on Madras is the final major tourist region in India. On the southeast coast of India, Madras is the gateway for southern India. Madras offers excellent historical, artistic, and religious sites. The National Art Gallery, Government Museum, old Fort St. George, the Cathedral of San Thome, and the Kapaliwarer Temple associated with Shiva are important attractions in Madras that provide a diversity of experiences. The cave and rock temples and open-air reliefs of the Pallava Dynasty are near Madras. These caves have huge boulders carved into monolithic art forms. Madurai, an ancient town, has an unusual Meenakshi Temple that is adorned with gopurams, as well as other lovely carved temples.

Maldives

Capital: Male
Government: Republic
Size: 115 square miles (twice the size of Washington, DC)
Language: Divehi, English
Ethnic Division: Mix of Sinhalese, Dravidian, Arab, and Black
Religion: Sunni Muslim
Currency: Maldinian rupee

Physical Characteristics

The Maldives are an archipelago of atolls and islands about 400 miles southwest of Sri Lanka in the Indian Ocean. The Maldives have a tropical climate with two monsoon seasons, May to October and November to April. In spite of the monsoon seasons, it seldom rains for more than a day or two and there are usually periods of sunshine every day.

Tourism Characteristics

The travel industry is small, averaging 180,000 tourists a year, who stay for an average of 9.2 days. Direct charters to Europe have made Europe (Germany and Italy), the two largest markets, accounting for over one-third of the visitors. Japan is the third largest market with a 7 percent share, followed by France and Switzerland. Before 1983, visitors from India comprised a higher share of the visitors, but with the

CULTURAL CAPSULE

Of the 1,200 islands, 202 are inhabited, with the greatest concentration on the capital island, Male. The earliest settlers were probably from southern India, speaking languages of the Dravidian family. They were followed by Indo-European speakers from Sri Lanka in the fourth and fifth centuries B.C. In the twelfth century, Arab and East African sailors came to the islands. Maldivian ethnic character is a blend of these cultures. Unlike the rest of South Asia, the Maldivians have never been ruled by colonial powers for long periods of time. Originally Buddhists, Maldivians were converted to Sunni Islam in the mid-twelfth century. Islam is the official religion and is adhered to by the entire population. The official language is Dhivehi, an Indo-European language related to Sinhala, the language of Sri Lanka. The writing system, like Arabic, is from right to left, although the alphabets are different. Some social stratification exists on the islands, with the social elite concentrated in Male.

Indian government introducing import restrictions, duty-free shopping was curtailed.

Tourist Destinations and Attractions

The attractions in the Maldives are mostly sun-sand-sea, with diving and other water sports activities. The majority of the tourist resorts in the Maldives are located on Kaafu Atoll, with a limited amount of development on Alif Atoll.

Nepal

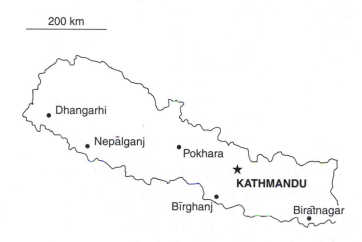

200 km

Dhangarhi

Nepālganj

Pokhara

★ KATHMANDU

Bīrghanj

Biratnagar

Capital: Kathmandu
Government: Constitutional monarchy
Size: 56,135 square miles (about the size of North Carolina)
Language: Nepali
Ethnic Division: Newars, Indians, Tibetans, Gurungs, Magaars, Tamangs, Bhotias, Rais, Limbus, Sherpas, and others
Religion: 90% Hindu, 5% Buddhist, 3% Muslim and Christian
Tourist Season: October through December
Peak Tourist Season: October through December

service to some areas, and small plane charters are available.

Health: Polio, typhus, and meningitis inoculations are suggested, and gamma globulin and malaria suppressants are recommended. Water is not potable; therefore, drink bottled or boiled water.

Shopping: Common items include handicraft jewelry, jewel boxes, wood carvings, brass vessels, prayer wheels, wool blankets, and woven shawls and rugs.

CULTURAL CAPSULE

The Nepalese are descendants of migrants from India, Tibet, and central Asia. Nearly 50 percent are Indo-Aryans. These people reside in the Ganges Basin plain and trace their ancestors to the Brahman and Chetre caste groups from India. People of Indo-Aryan and/or Mongoloid descent live in the hill region. Religion is important, and Nepal is the only official Hindu state in the world (88 percent of the population). Hinduism has been influenced by the large Buddhist minority. The Hindu temples and Buddhist shrines are mutually respected, and Buddhist and Hindu festivals are occasions for common worship and celebration. In addition, Nepal has small Muslim and Christian minorities. Certain animistic practices of old indigenous religions also exist. Nepali is the official language, although a dozen different languages and about 30 major dialects are spoken throughout the country. English is understood in government and business. Hindi is spoken by about 90 percent of the population.

Cultural Hints:
- The palms in prayer position in front of the chin and a slight bow is a traditional greeting.
- Namaste is a greeting and goodbye.
- Use a person's title in greetings.
- Do not touch another person's hair or shoulders.
- Men do not touch women.
- Do not point the bottom of your foot at another person.
- Do not touch another person with the foot.
- Beckon by waving all fingers.
- Do not whistle or wink.
- Pass objects with right hand.
- Eating and food:
  Use the right hand to eat.
  When drinking water from a communal container, the lips do not touch the rim.
  Typical food includes rice, lentil soup, vegetable curry, goat, chicken, water buffalo, fruits, and vegetables. Many people are vegetarians.

Physical Characteristics

Nepal consists of Tarai, the flat river plain of the Ganges, in the south, a central hill region, and the rugged Himalayas in the north. The climate varies from cool summers and severe winters in the north to subtropical summers and mild winters in the south.

Tourism Characteristics

Nepal, the "rooftop of the world," is most famous as the jumping-off place for climbers in the Himalayas, including Mt. Everest. The country has only been open to tourism for some 30 years. Unlike its neighbors, the Hindus and Buddhists of Nepal have lived for nearly 2,000 years in peaceful coexistence. Ashok, Nepal, was the birthplace of Buddha. Ashok is an important religious attraction. Although it is a small country, Nepal contains the greatest range of altitudes in the world, from almost sea-level tropical jungle to the rugged relief of Mt. Everest, over 29,000 feet above sea level.

Nepal is "the" place for trekkers in the world, bringing visitors from a wide variety of places. Pokhara, about 100 miles west of Kathmandu, is the starting point for treks toward the Himalayas. Tourism is the only real earner of foreign exchange, helping Nepal to finance its imports. The most important country for tourists is India, accounting for 31 percent of visitors. The close proximity and huge population base are important factors in this number. Indian-owned travel companies that deal with tourism to Nepal handle 70 to 80 percent of the tourist business to Nepal.

The European market (40 percent) is diverse, lacking the high percentage of visitors from the United Kingdom that is found in India or Pakistan. The major purpose of visiting is pleasure (almost 75 percent), with 14 percent for trekking and mountaineering. The remaining reasons for travel—business, official, and visiting friends and relatives—account for only slightly over 10 percent of the visitors. The opening of the border between Nepal and Tibet in 1985 has had a positive influence on tourism. Tour operators in Kathmandu have established tours from three to fifteen days to Lhasa, the capital and holy city of Tibet. However, they are either expensive or difficult for budget travelers who must travel by truck to Lhasa over rugged mountain roads (International Tourism Reports, 1997).

Tourist Destinations and Attractions

The two major areas of tourism in Nepal are the Kathmandu Valley and Terai, in the southern lowland, where the famous Tiger Tops for viewing wildlife was established in 1965. The three important cities in Kathmandu Valley—Kathmandu, Patan, and Bhadgaon—are also the areas with the greatest concentration of accommodations. Kathmandu, the gateway to the Himalayas and trekking, focuses on Durbar Square with its many-tiered temples, winding streets, and brick buildings that look somewhat like medieval Europe. The most important temples are Maju Deval with its nine-stage platform that has some erotic carvings, the Shiva-Parvati Temple, the Krishna Temple, and the golden-pagoda-style Taleju Temple. The market area behind Durbar Square has the Kasthmandap, an intricate wooden temple. The Swayambhunath Temple, famous for the monkeys that live there, is on Swayambhu hill. Flights over Mt. Everest and the rest of the Himalayan Range are offered. Mosaics and all of the local crafts are available in Kathmandu.

Patan, the second largest city, is over 2,000 years old and has museums, temples, monuments, courtyards, elaborately carved wooden structures, and prayer wheels. It is also the home of some of the best South Asian handicrafts. Patan's attractions include the famous Krishna Mandir, which was influenced by Indian styles and has a tall pillar on which sits the mythical bird-man Garuda with folded hands; King Yoganarendra Malla's tall column; several Shiva temples with erotic carvings; the Bhimsen Temple; the Hiranya Varma Mahavihara or "Golden Temple"; and the Tibetan refugee center of Jawlakhel.

Bhadgaon, at the east end of the Kathmandu Valley, has numerous shrines and artistic designs expressed in its elaborately carved palace and temples. Bhadgaon is reported to be the oldest town in the Kathmandu Valley. Attractions include an art gallery containing rare paintings and manuscripts from medieval Nepal; a Golden Gate; a 55-window palace; a bell of barking dogs; an exact replica of the Pashupatinath Temple with erotic carvings; the five-story Nyatapola Temple; and the Bhairabnath Temple.

The holiest temple in Nepal is Pashupati, en route to Bodhnath. The temple is located on the banks of the holy Bagmati River and as at the Ganges, cremations occur frequently. At Bodhnath, one of the biggest Buddhist *stupas* in the world (with four eyes) is an important attraction.

The second major destination center, Tiger Tops, is in the jungles of the Terai Valley, which is an extension of the Ganges River Plain. Tiger Tops, which is closed during the monsoon season, offers the full range of wildlife viewing.

Pakistan

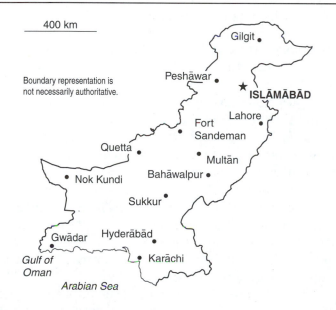

400 km

Boundary representation is not necessarily authoritative.

Gilgit
Peshāwar
★ ISLĀMĀBĀD
Lahore
Fort Sandeman
Quetta
Multān
Bahāwalpur
Nok Kundi
Sukkur
Gwādar
Hyderābād
Karāchi
Gulf of Oman
Arabian Sea

Capital: Islamabad
Government: Parliamentary
Size: 339,732 square miles (about one and one-half times the size of Texas)
Language: Urdu and English
Ethnic Division: Punjabi, Sindhi, Pushtun, Baluch
Religion: 97% Muslim, 3% Christian, Hindu and other
Tourist Season: September through March
Peak Tourist Season: November through January
Currency: Rupees

 ## TRAVEL TIPS

Entry: A visa is required. Proof of sufficient funds and an onward or round-trip ticket is required.
Transportation: International connections are made to Karachi from New York, Europe, and other Asian countries. There are good internal air and rail networks. Within cities, buses, minibuses, and motorized rickshaws are available.
Travel Caution: Travel in rural areas, particularly in Sindh Province, is not recommended. Rallies, demonstrations, and processions that are anti-American or anti-Western in nature occur in many cities periodically.
Shopping: Common items include local jade and other gemstones and native handicrafts.

CULTURAL CAPSULE

The people of Pakistan are divided into four major ethnic groups: the Punjabi (65 percent), Sindhi (12 percent), Baluchi (9 percent), and Pashtuns (8 percent). A fifth group is the Muhajir, composed of immigrants from India and their descendants. Pakistan is an Islamic republic, and their laws are based on the Koran. Ninety-seven percent of the people are Muslims (77 percent Sunni and 20 percent Shiite). Fatalism is common in the rural areas.

The two official languages are English and Urdu. The government is gradually replacing English with Urdu. Languages reflect ethnic background, with Punjabi spoken by 65 percent of the population. Eleven percent speak Sindhi, and the remaining 24 percent are other languages, such as Saraiki, Baluchi, and Brahui. Urdu, Punjabi, Pushtu, and Baluchi are of the Indo-European language group, while Brahui is believed to have a Dravidian origin.

Cultural Hints:

- A gentle handshake is a common greeting.
- Men refrain from touching or shaking hands with a Pakistani woman unless she extends her hand.
- Use title and last name when addressing someone.
- It is customary to offer coffee, tea, or other refreshments. It is impolite to reject such offers.
- Women are often kept separated in social situations.
- Do not point your foot or the bottom of your shoe at another person.
- Pass items with right hand or both hands, not the left.
- Women should dress and act modestly in all settings.
- Ask permission to photograph Pakistani women.
- Avoid touching and eye contact with the opposite gender.
- The closed fist is an obscene gesture.
- Remove shoes before entering a mosque.
- Public buses are crowded with much touching, shoving, and pushing.
- Eating and food:
  Eat food with the right hand.
  When using utensils, use the fork in the left hand to push food into the spoon.
  Men and women often eat in separate areas.
  Typical food is an unleavened bread (chapati or roti), buttermilk, yogurt, rice, vegetables, and meat, but not pork. Pakistani food is generally hot and spicy, using curry as a common spice.

Physical Characteristics

The terrain in the east is the flat Indus plain. The north and northwest are mountainous. The Baluchistan Plateau is in the west. The climate is mostly hot, dry desert. It is temperate in the northwest and arctic in the north.

Tourism Characteristics

A distant second to India in total numbers of visitors, Pakistan receives almost half of its visitors from European countries, especially the United Kingdom. Like India, it has strong ties to the United Kingdom, which accounts for over 34 percent of the international visitors. Historically travel to visit friends and family has been the major purpose of travel, but just over 40 percent of total visits are for this reason today. The average length of stay of 27 days, one of the longest in the world, is another factor indicating the importance of family ties for visitors.

Travel to Pakistan has been impacted by unrest at home and the perception of many residents of the Western industrialized countries that India offers a better set of tourist attractions than Pakistan. Another negative factor is associated with the autocratic nature of the government based on Islamic law. As in the rest of South Asia, the monsoon season affects the tourist season. The most-favored season is from September through March. The two major tourist centers are Karachi and Lahore.

Tourist Destinations and Attractions

Karachi, the former capital and still the largest city, is the center of the country's commerce and industry, largely related to its port characteristics. Although it is not an outstanding or unique city, Karachi does have interesting bazaars, gardens, a zoo, and a national museum. The principle attractions of Karachi are the Mausoleum of Quaid-i-Azam, the founder of the nation; the Defense Housing Society Mosque; Frere Hall in the Jinnah Gardens; and the National Museum. The ancient towns of the Chaukundi Tombs, Thatta, and Moenjo are near Karachi. A number of resorts are found on the tiny island of South Manora and at Hawke's Bay. Tatta, 65 miles southeast of Karachi, was the home of a number of dynasties. The mosque begun by Emperor Shah Jahan, the builder of the Taj Mahal, is the most notable Mogul architecture remaining.

Lahore, the second largest city of Pakistan, is in a picturesque region and is the educational and cultural center of the country. The Shalimar Gardens, built in 1637, are Pakistan's greatest attraction. Called the city of gardens, Lahore has Indo-Muslim architecture and the Badshai Mosque, Emperor Jehangir's Mausoleum, and the Great Mughal with its famous Hall of Mirrors. The Badshai Mosque is one of the world's largest mosques. Shah Jahan, who built the Taj Mahal, also built in Lahore one of the first mausoleums of the East for his father, the Emperor Janagir. The red sandstone tomb sits above the banks of the Ravi River, surrounded by the Dilkusha Garden.

Northwest of Lahore is Taxila, which at one time was the principal center of Buddhist learning and culture. A number of ruins of old cities and the monasteries at Mohra Moradu and Jaulian are the best preserved of their kind in Pakistan. The Zoroastrian Temple is impressive because of its architecture.

Moenjo-Daro (Mound of the Dead) is located some 400 miles north of Karachi and is one of the most impressive ancient sites in the world. This large urban complex included a sophisticated system of waste disposal and drains for fresh water. Other impressive features are the Great Bath, the Great Granary, and a citadel with walls up to 45 feet thick.

To the north are cities less developed for tourism, including Rawalpindi, the capital until Islamabad was completed; Islamabad, the capital of Pakistan;

and Peshawar, gateway to excursions into the mountain valleys and the Khyber Pass. Rawalpindi is near a number of mountain resorts. Islamabad, a relatively new city, is an administrative center for Pakistan and is an interesting example of a planned city. Peshawar is the terminal point for trips into the Khyber Pass. The Khyber Pass is 33 miles in length and has a rich history, as Greek, Tartar, and Mongol conquerors passed through it. Peshawar is known for its bazaars, the most famous of which is the Quissi Khawani Bazaar. The Bijori Gate Bazaar was the meeting place for caravans from many places. In the last decades, the Peshawar region has become home to over a million residents of Afghanistan who fled the war in that country.

Sri Lanka

Capital: Colombo
Government: Republic
Size: 24,962 square miles (half the size of North Carolina)
Language: Sinhala and Tamil, English common
Ethnic Division: 74% Sinhalese, 18% Tamil, 7% Moor, 1% Burgher, Malay, and Veddha
Religion: 69% Buddhist, 15% Hindu, 8% Christian, 8% Muslim
Tourist Season: November through March
Peak Tourist Season: December through March
Currency: Rupee

TRAVEL TIPS

Entry: Visas are not required for stays up to 6 months. Proof of sufficient funds and onward or return transportation are required.
Transportation: International connections are through India and Southeast Asia. The island has good rail or bus transportation on the islands.
Health: Malaria suppressants are advisable. Water is not safe and foods should be peeled or cooked before eating.
Travel Caution: Ongoing civil war is related to violence in Sri Lanka, and visitors should check with the Department of State before departure.
Shopping: Common items include rubies, sapphires, amethysts, opals, hand-dyed batik, and tailormade clothing.

CULTURAL CAPSULE

The two largest population groups are Sinhalese—comprising 75 percent of the population and concentrated in the densely populated southwest—and Tamils—comprising about 12 percent. A third smaller group is the Indian Tamils, whose ancestors were brought from India during the British colonial era to work on tea plantations. Moors comprise 7 percent of the population, and Malays, Burghers, and Veddahs make up the other 1 percent. The Burghers are descendants of Dutch colonists, and the Veddahs are a remnant of the island's original inhabitants. Sinhala, an Indo-European language, is the native tongue of the Sinhalese. Tamils and most Muslims speak Tamil, part of the South Indian Dravidian linguistic group. Use of English is common but declining. Both Sinhala and Tamil are official languages. Most Sinhalese are Buddhist (Theravada Buddhism), and most Tamils are Hindu. Most of the Muslims are Sunnis. Sizable minorities of both Sinhalese and Tamils are Christians, mostly Roman Catholic.

Cultural Hints:
- While a handshake is a common form of greeting, differences exist between ethnic groups.
- A traditional greeting is to place palms as in prayer under the chin and bow the head slightly.
- Use titles when addressing people.
- Pass objects with your right hand or both hands.
- Do not touch a person's head.
- Do not show or point foot at a person or object.
- Women are forbidden to touch a Buddhist monk.
- Nodding the head up and down means no.
- Shaking the head back and forth means yes.
- Remove your shoes and hat when entering a mosque.
- Never touch, sit, or lean on any image of Budda.
- Eating and food:
  Eat with the right hand.
  Typical foods are rice, curries, peas, beans, pulses, and tea. Sri Lankans consume little meat, and the Muslims do not eat pork.

Physical Characteristics

Sri Lanka is mostly low flat-to-rolling plains with mountains in the south central interior. The climate is tropical with monsoons from December to March and June to October.

Tourism Characteristics

Sri Lanka (formerly Ceylon) is an island paradise. Lying off the southern tip of India, Sri Lanka is smaller than Ireland or Tasmania. Tourism to Sri Lanka has been hurt by the continued Tamil guerrilla fighting since 1983 in the northern and eastern provinces.

The peak tourist season is November to April, reflecting both the monsoon season and the high number of tourists from Europe who desire a warm climate during the European winter. Nearly 63 percent of the visitors are from Europe. Nearly 23 percent of all visitors are from Germany, most participating in budget tour arrangements. The average length of stay is nine days.

Ten percent of the international tourists are from India, primarily because of duty-free shopping in Sri Lanka.

Tourist Destinations and Attractions

The major historical sites are Kandy, Anuradhapura, Polonnaruwa, and Sigiriya. Anuradhapura, 128 miles from Colombo, the capital, is the historical cultural capital of the Sinhalese kings and the religious center. Kandy, the former capital of Kandyan kings, is the home of scholars, writers, artists, and musicians. Temples and a Kandyan palace dot the landscape. Principle attractions in Kandy are the Temple of Tooth, Kandy Lake, the Royal Botanical Gardens, the University of Ceylon, and the Kandy Museum.

Polonnaruwa, 134 miles from Colombo, another capital city (built in A.D. 1100), is the home of the Jewel of Sri Lanka, the Lankatilaka, a colossal standing figure of Buddha. The ruins of King Parakramabahu's Royal Palace, the Royal Audience Hall, the Royal Bath, the circular Vatadage with its Buddhas facing four entrances, the Trivanka Image

House and the 55-foot-high Lankatitaka Vihara, and an unusual eleven-foot-high statue of King Parakramabahu I are impressive attractions. Sigiriya has impressive cave paintings that are outstanding in quality near the top of a 400-foot-high rock fortress.

Colombo, the present capital, is a pretty city with a British heritage seen in its Victorian homes and administration buildings. The National Museum contains treasures and artifacts from all over the island. A number of other attractions are the Cinnamon Gardens, an exclusive residential area; the Bandaranaike Memorial International Conference Hall, the beautiful Vihara Maha Devi Park, the elegant Town Hall, and a few Buddhist temples.

The beaches of Sri Lanka are outstanding, but the continued fighting between Sinhalese and Tamils has limited access to them. The interior includes the national parks of Wilpattu, Ruhunu, and Gal Oya, which have lush vegetation and wild-game preserves.

SOUTHEAST ASIA

Tourism has not affected all of Southeast Asia evenly, Table 14–3. Vietnam, Laos, and Cambodia have had political problems that greatly hinder tourism, but as a region Southeast Asia has received far more tourists than South Asia. A major characteristic of the region is the unifying element of the tropical climate. A major tourism characteristic is that much of the travel is intraregional. The largest segment of visitors to Southeast Asia is from other nations of Southeast Asia, with the exception of the Philippines, which draws strongly from East Asia and the United States, Table 14–4.

Travel from industrialized countries includes both destination and *circular tours*. Circular tours visit a number of countries as part of a tour of the Pacific region. Both Thailand and Singapore benefit from major international transit traffic. Since visitors are passing through, they will stay and sightsee or

Table 14–3 International Tourism to Southeast Asia

Country	Number of Visitors (thousands)		1996 Receipts (millions of US $)	1996 Average Expenses per Visit
	1986	1996		
Cambodia	20	260	118	454
Indonesia	823	5,034	6,087	1,209
Malaysia	3,217	7,138	3,926	150
Philippines	764	2,049	2,790	1,361
Singapore	2,902	6,608	7,916	1,198
Thailand	2,813	7,192	8,491	1,181

Source: *Yearbook of Tourism Statistics*. Madrid: World Tourism Organization, 1997.

purchase goods. This is illustrated in the relative low length of stay of 3.5 days for Singapore and 5.9 days for Thailand.

Sex tourism to Southeast Asia, particularly Thailand and the Philippines, is a major issue of tourism to the region. Group tours are arranged for the explicit purpose of sex. Group tours for sex along with the general travel to Thailand by visitors with an interest in sex has created a high incidence of HIV and AIDS in the country. The concern by male visitors over HIV has created a demand for younger and younger girls (who presumably are not infected) to meet the sex demand. Over time this spreads the disease even more widely in the general population. Thailand has instituted an educational program that encourages condom use by prostitutes. Use increased from 20 percent in 1988 to an estimated 95 percent in 1993. Sexually transmitted disease among men dropped from 210 per 1,000 in 1988 to 45 per 1,000 in 1993.

Table 14–4 Origin of Visitors to Southeast Asia (1995 Market Share)				
Country	**United States**	**Asia/ Pacific**	**Europe**	**Others**
Indonesia	3.6	73.9	18.2	4.3
Malaysia	3.1	76.42	12.7	7.8
Philippines	19.4	54.0	12.8	13.8
Singapore	4.8	78.3	13.2	3.7
Thailand	4.1	69.7	21.7	4.5
Total for Region	5.3	72.8	16.6	5.3

Source: *Annual Statistical Report.* San Francisco: Pacific Asia Travel Association, 1995

The rapid improvement claimed by Thailand's government, if accurate, indicates how important education is in preventing disease.

Indonesia

1200 km

Strait of Malacca

Medan

North Pacific Ocean

Celebes

Borneo

Sumatra

JAKARTA

Java

Timor

New Guinea

Indian Ocean

Capital: Jakarta
Government: Independent republic
Size: 741,000 square miles (more than Alaska and California combined)
Ethnic Division: Sundanese, Madurese, Malays, Javanese
Language: Indonesian, Javanese, and other local dialects
Religion: 87% Muslim, 9% Christian, 3% Hindu and Buddhist
Tourist Season: Year-round
Peak Tourist Season: August and September
Currency: Rupiahs

 TRAVEL TIPS

Entry: A visa is not required for stays up to 2 months. Proof of onward or return transportation is required.
Transportation: International access is good to Jakarta and Bali from the United States and Pacific Asian countries. Domestic service between most cities and islands is readily available. Bus service is overcrowded. Taxis and pedicabs are the most common form of urban transportation.
Health: Tuberculosis, malaria, dengue fever, hepatitis, typhoid, and cholera protection is needed. Water and food in the international hotels are safe. Outside of hotels water is not potable and care should be taken to drink boiled or bottled water.
Shopping: Common items include Indonesian crafts of batik, silver work, wood carvings, palm-leaf fans, shadow puppets, dolls, leather goods, bone figurines, and Chinese ceramics, wayang puppets, and antique batiks.

CULTURAL CAPSULE

Indonesia includes numerous related but distinct cultural and linguistic groups, mainly of Malay origin. The Javanese (Malayan) account for 45 percent; the Sundanese, 14 percent; the Madurese, 7.5 percent; and the Coastal Malays, 7.5 percent. The remaining 26 percent belong to various smaller groups. Indonesian, the national language, is a form of Malay that has spread throughout the archipelago and has become the language of all written communication, education, government, and business. English is the most widely spoken foreign language. There are approximately 300 other languages spoken in the country. About 87 percent of the population is Muslim, 9 percent is Christian (mostly Protestant), and 3 percent is Hindu. A few people still practice animistic religions.

Cultural Hints:
- A handshake and a slight bow of the head is a common greeting.
- Use of a person's title is important.
- Men rarely touch women in public except to shake hands.
- Yawning in public is impolite.
- Remove sunglasses when speaking to someone or entering a home.
- Beckon someone with the palm down and wave the fingers.
- Do not put your hands in your pockets when conversing with another.
- Use the thumb to point.
- On buses give up seats to women and elderly.
- In Bali do not photograph people washing and bathing nude or topless.
- Eating and food:
  Eating while walking on the street is inappropriate.
  Eat only with your right hand.
  Keep both hands on the table.
  In crowded restaurants others will ask to sit with you.
  To summon a waiter, raise your hand.
  To ask for the bill make a writing motion with both hands.
  When finished eating, leave a little food on your plate.
  Tips are usually included in the bill.
  Cover the mouth if using a toothpick.
  Typical foods include rice, vegetables, fish, hot sauces, tea, fruits, beef, buffalo, chilies, and coconut milk.
  Muslims do not eat pork.

Physical Characteristics

Indonesia is an *archipelago* of more than 1,355 islands extending some 3,000 miles. It is mountainous and volcanic. The climate is hot and humid all year, with some contrast in temperature between the mountain areas and the coastal lowlands.

Tourism Characteristics

The island of Bali, probably the most recognizable name relating to tourism in the Pacific, is in Indonesia. Indonesia had over 5 million visitors in 1996. The three most important generating countries, all Pacific countries: Singapore (25 percent), Japan (11.9 percent), and Malaysia (9 percent), account for nearly 46 percent of all visitors to Indonesia. Europe has been a strong market, accounting for 18 percent of visitors. Tourists come from various European countries, with the United Kingdom, Germany, Italy, and France the major market nations.

Most of the recent growth has come from Australia. Most Australian and other visitors are attracted by the island of Bali, which receives over 27 percent of all visitors to Indonesia and an estimated 60 percent of all leisure arrivals. Australia and the United States leveled off in number of visitors to Indonesia in the 1990s, with a market share in 1994 of 4.2 percent. Japan, on the other hand, continues to send more tourists to Indonesia each year, nearly doubling in number from 1990 to 1994. This is due in part to Indonesia's increased efforts to lure tourists from the entire East Asia market. For example, Indonesia has increased both advertising and flight capabilities in Korea, contributing to more Korean business investment. Since Korea and Taiwan are strong trading partners, this results in Taiwan being another East Asia market with tremendous potential for Indonesia. Monthly fluctuations in arrivals to Indonesia are small, suggesting there is no real tourist season as the climate does not change noticeably from one season to another.

There is still considerable potential for increasing tourism to Indonesia. Indonesia has not grown as rapidly as most of the other tourist nations of Southeast Asia. The country suffers from inadequate overseas promotion and the need for improved flight connectivity and frequency. The government has liberalized the process to obtain a license to build a hotel. Bali was opened to foreign airlines, and visa requirements have been dropped for more than twenty countries.

Tourist Destinations and Attractions

The major destinations include the following:

Bali. Bali is considered one of the most exotic, romantic islands in the world. It is frequently referred to as the "island of the gods" and has numerous festivals. Bali is a lush, exotic, and extremely colorful island that has attracted visitors for centuries. Religion and art are the central elements of the rich Balinese culture. With some 20,000 temples, there are almost daily temple festivals celebrated on the islands. Religion and temples are very important in the life of the Balinese. A temple is a place for communicating with the divine spirits through offerings and prayers. Temple festivals include purification by the sprinkling of holy water, bringing baskets of food and flowers for offerings. Music, dances, food, flowers, and fruits are all part of the rituals to please the gods and to placate evil spirits.

Figure 14–6 Human taxi on Bali

Women and children wearing their colorful costumes are accompanied by men bearing bountiful offerings on their heads for the temple deities. Bali is also famous for its shops, galleries, and artists who produce stone and wood carvings, highly ornamental gold and silver jewelry, traditional paintings, and woven handlooms. Most visitors fly into Denpasar and stay at one of the many beach resorts. The Bali Museum has an excellent presentation on native Balinese arts and crafts.

North Sumatra. An ancient culture dating back to prehistoric periods is the basis for this province's culture and tradition. The tourist sites include Hilisamatano, a village on the island of Nias with ancient traditional houses; Sipisopiso Waterfall; Pematang Purba, a 200-year-old village that is famous for the houses of its tribal chiefs; Lake Toba, one of the largest and highest inland lakes in the world; the island of Samosir in the middle of Lake Toba; Bawomataluo Village, which is 400 meters above sea level and accessible by 480 stone steps; and the great mosque.

West Sumatra. The home of the matrilineal Minangkabau people is a region of spectacular natural beauty. The name Minangkabau means triumphant buffalo. Throughout its highland terrain, there are lakes and deep canyons such as the magnificent Sianok Canyons. Among the high mountains and picturesque valleys are the remnants of the old Minangkabau Kingdom of Pagaruyung with art centers for silver, hand weaving, embroidery, and woodcarving.

Java and Jakarta. The island of Java and its capital city of Jakarta illustrate the nation's historic, cultural, political, and economic character. Jakarta's origin was the small, early sixteenth-century harbor town of Sunda Kelapa, renamed Jayakarta on June 22, 1527. The Dutch East Indies Company captured the town and destroyed it in 1619, changed its name to Batavia, and used it as a base for the expansion of their colonies in the East Indies. Shortly after the outbreak of World War II, Batavia fell to the Japanese, who changed the name to Jakarta as a gesture aimed at winning the sympathy of the Indonesians. The name was retained after Indonesia achieved national independence. Jakarta is a colorful city. In the early 1970s restoration began on the oldest section of Jakarta, known as Old Batavia. The old Portuguese Church and warehouse have been rehabilitated into living museums. The old Supreme Court building is now a museum of fine arts. The old Town Hall has become the Jakarta Museum, displaying rare items, such as Indonesia's old historical documents and Dutch-period furniture. One of the most interesting tourist attractions is the "Beautiful Indonesia in Miniature Park" called Taman Mini. Built to portray the variety of cultures found within the many islands contained in the Republic of Indonesia, it is an open-air museum exhibiting the many architectural styles, arts, and traditions of all 27 provinces. The Amsterdam Gate, of white-washed brick, Dutch architecture, and other reminders of the Dutch are evident along the remaining canals in the older section of the city.

Near Jakarta are Bogar, which has an outstanding botanical garden, and Puntjab, a resort town. West Java is dotted with rice granaries and with tea, rubber, and quinine plantations. It has several natural reserves; one of them, Ujung Kulon, is the home of the nearly extinct one-horn Java rhino. Pulau Dua, an-

Figure 14-7 Hotel in Bali

Indonesia: The Spirit of Torajaland

by Julie Skurdenis

The day before our arrival on the island of Sulawesi, one of the lecturers aboard our expedition vessel, *World Discoverer*, called Torajaland one of the truly magical places in this world. I'd heard these words applied to so many other places before that I was skeptical.

My skepticism evaporated swiftly after we docked at the small port of Palopo and began our ascent toward Torajaland deep in the interior of central Sulawesi.

The highway wound precipitously along the mountainside with vistas of cloud-covered peaks above and green-clad valleys below.

One final mountain pass brought us into Torajaland where rice paddies terraced the steep hillsides—rivaling in beauty those we had seen just a few days earlier on Bali—and where water buffalo placidly grazed amid a landscape of palm trees and rugged mountains.

We had entered Indonesia's Shangri-la.

One of Indonesia's 14,000

Torajaland is located on the island of Sulawesi, one of Indonesia's almost 14,000 islands and certainly one of its largest.

Torajaland's intense physical beauty is enhanced by its unique architecture. Traditional houses (tongkanan) and rice barns (alang) raised on wooden poles thrust steeply pitched prow-shaped roofs skyward.

Wooden panels of both houses and barns often are decorated with intricate geometrical and animal-motif designs.

Preparation for Death

For the upper strata of Torajans, as important as the way they live is the way they die. It is said that Torajan lives are simply a preparation for death.

Funerals are elaborate, lasting for days, with hundreds participating. Buffalo and pigs are slaughtered by the dozens. Often, the deceased will lie unburied for months, sometimes years, until enough money is accumulated for the funeral ceremonies.

At the funeral, there is prolonged feasting to celebrate the soul's release. The body then is buried within a cave or vault hewn out of the mountainside.

A wooden effigy of the dead, called a tau, is erected nearby to represent the soul. For village chiefs, an enormous boulder is erected in addition to the tau.

Torajaland Villages

Rantepao Our touring began in Rantepao, a good base from which to visit the villages nearby, some so close you can walk to them.

Rantepao is a busy little town with a number of souvenir shops selling wood carvings and intricately woven fabrics called ikats along its main street.

The town really springs to life once a week on market day when everything from plastic bottles and sneakers to betel nuts and batiks are sold just outside town.

The highlight of the market is the water buffalo—dozens of these immense, sleek creatures are placidly contemplating the action or being fed grass by their proud owners.

Water buffalo are a status symbol among Torajans and a superior specimen can fetch thousands of dollars.

Nanggala Nine miles east of Rantepao, Nanggala provided us with an instant introduction to the distinctive Torajan style of architecture. Opposite the traditional tongkanan were ranged fourteen alang, each intricately decorated and painted in red, black, yellow, and white.

Interspersed among the profusion of abstract geometric designs were stylized heads of buffalo, concentric circles, roosters and, surprisingly, detailed scenes from everyday Torajan life: buffalo in combat interlocking horns, children leading buffalo by ropes, and people being transported in trucks.

Two of the village tongkanan held "sick" people. (Torajans refer to the dead who have not yet been accorded funeral ceremonies as "sick.") We were

continues

continued

told one of the two had been "sick" almost 10 years, the other for two. The family still was gathering enough money to bury these two in appropriate style.

Nearby, hundreds of fruit bats—considered good luck—dozed the day away in a bamboo grove.

Ketekesu The village of Ketekesu, three miles southeast of Rantepao, contained another superb collection of houses and barns, some with buffalo horns affixed to their supporting front poles. One with 21 horns indicated the wealth of its owner.

A few minutes' walk beyond the village led to the limestone hill where carved wooden coffins had been inserted in crevices of the rock face.

Many of the coffins had rotted away, with ancestral skulls and bones tumbling out in disarray. We were told that one of the coffins, carved to resemble a twin-peak Torajan house, was over 900 years old.

Londa At Londa, five miles south of Rantepao, a number of coffins still rested on wooden brackets inserted into the rock, accompanied by well-dressed tau taus on a covered wooden balcony.

Guides with kerosene lamps lit our way into one of the caves dotting the hillside; we stumbled in the semidark among coffins overflowing with bones.

Someone had thoughtfully placed an offering of cigarettes in front of one of the ancestral skulls in case it needed a smoke in the afterlife.

Lemo Lemo, seven miles south of Rantepao, contains Torajaland's most spectacular collection of tau taus.

Set in niches carved into the steep rock face, dozens of these clad effigies stare fixedly across the rice paddies below them, their arms outstretched.

Scattered among them are wooden doors leading into family funeral vaults, each crammed full of bones.

Siguntu Spectacular as are the Torajan houses and cliff graves, it was the afternoon we spent walking among the rice terraces near Siguntu that most captured the spirit of Torajaland for me.

As we hiked along dirt roads and along narrow levees dividing the rice fields, we passed enormous guest houses in Torajan style dotting the hillside, mementos of a wealthy man's funeral ceremony.

We saw water buffalo grazing knee-deep among rice plants, villagers clad in colorful sarongs, a clearing dotted with 8-foot-tall megaliths each commemorating a deceased chieftain, and a dilapidated suspension bridge precariously strung across a tumbling rock-strewn stream that was more of an adventure to cross than I bargained for!

Source: International Travel News.
January 1992; pp. 71–73.

---

other reserve, is a stopping place for many migrating birds. Bandung, the capital of West Java, provides a panorama of mountains and the active volcano crater of Mt. Tangkubanperahu. Bandunk is an educational center. Unique to the area are the music, which is played on bamboo instruments, and the costumed wooden puppets (Wayang Golek).

Central Java has an interesting landscape with a number of excellent temples, Figure 14–8. The most famous temple is the Borobudur, which was built in the eighth century. It is basically a giant Buddhist stupa containing nearly 400 meditation Buddhas. Its site is a quiet and beautiful hill overlooking lush green rice fields outside Jogjakarta. Jogjakarta, the former capital, also contains ruins of the old Water Palace and the Kraton, the palace city of the sultans. Also featured in Jogjakarta is the finest Indonesian batik, as well as silverware and leather goods.

East Java has a number of attractions, including sanctuaries and temples of architectural splendors that provide images of past empires. Each village,

Figure 14–8 Kudus Mosque, Central Java, Indonesia

town, or city has its own unique historical relics and legends. East Java is a tropical jungle with many volcanoes. Surabaya, the provincial capital, and the Singosari Temple are particularly noteworthy. The district also offers visitors mountain resorts that are famous for their magnificent scenery.

Sulawesi. Sulawesi has been a tourism development area. It has some excellent beaches and *coral*

reefs. The Spanish and Portuguese influence is evident. South Sulawesi offers a panorama of nature's wonders. Tana Toraja, the land of the Torajans, is known for the grand and unique burial ceremonies and cliffs with their hanging graves. The most important festival is the "Feast of the Dead," but it is limited to only a very few visitors.

Malaysia

500 km

Capital: Kuala Lumpur
Government: Federation of Malaysia
Size: 128,430 square miles (slightly larger than New Mexico)
Language: Malay, English, Chinese
Ethnic Division: 59% Malay, 32% Chinese, 9% Indian
Religion: Muslim, Buddhist, Christian, Tribal
Tourist Season: May to December
Peak Tourist Season: May to December
Currency: Layaysian ringgit

CULTURAL CAPSULE

Malaysia's population is comprised of many ethnic groups; the Malays are a slight majority. The Malays are indigenous and, by constitutional definition, all Muslim. Nearly one-third of Malaysia's people are Chinese. They are mainly urban residents engaged in trade, business, and finance. The majority are Buddhists, Taoists, or Christians. Malaysians of Indian descent represent about 8 percent of the population. About 85 percent of the Indian population are Tamils. They are divided among Hindus, Buddhists, and Muslims. They are in the professions, agriculture, and service trades. Non-Malay indigenous groups, such as the Sea Dayaks, Land Dayaks, Kadazans, Kenyahs, Melanaus, and Muruts, are mainly farmers, civil servants, or fishermen. About 85 percent of Malaysia's population speak Malay, the national language. English is widely used in government and business. The ethnic Chinese also speak one of the various Chinese dialects. Tamil is spoken by the Indians. On the island of Borneo, in Sabah and Sarawak, numerous tribal languages are common.

Cultural Hints:
- A handshake is a common greeting.
- Show respect for elderly people.
- Among the Malays and Indians avoid touching a person's head.
- Do not show the sole of the shoe or point with the foot.
- A person standing with hands on hips indicates anger.
- Smacking the closed fist in the palm of the other hand is a rude gesture.
- Give and receive gifts with both hands.
- Cover your mouth when yawning.
- Remove your shoes before entering mosques.
- Malayans do not form a line for public buses.
- Eating and food:
  Malays and Indians eat with hands and spoons. Chinese eat with chopsticks and spoons.
  Eat with your right hand only.
  To call a waiter just raise your hand.
  A service charge is usually included in the bill.
  Waving chopsticks in the air is bad manners.
  Typical foods include rice, fish, and spiced foods such as hot peppers, vegetables, and fruits.

 ## TRAVEL TIPS

Entry: Visas are not required for stays up to 3 months.
Transportation: Direct air service to Kuala Lumpur is available to most major countries of Europe, the Middle East, and North America. Daily train service connects Kuala Lumpur with Penang, Singapore, and Bangkok. There is a well-developed national highway system. Taxis are the best form of transportation in the cities.
Health: Cholera and malaria are the two diseases with which travelers should be concerned. Tap water in major cities is considered safe to drink.
Shopping: Common items include batik sarongs, silver and gold brocade, and silver and locally manufactured pewter.

Physical Characteristics

Malaysia is a mountainous and hilly country with coastal plains on each side. The climate is tropical with heavy monsoon rain from October to February.

Tourism Characteristics

Malaysia has the second largest percentage of visitors of all Southeast Asia countries, Table 14–3. However, its location between Thailand and Singapore results in 70 percent of its visitors coming from these countries, making it one of the strongest regional destinations in Southeast Asia, Table 14–4. This regional bias is also expressed in the short length of stay of 4.6 days, which is only surpassed by Singapore. Malaysia has some excellent resorts, largely responding to the newly industrialized countries of Southeast Asia with their growing middle-class populations. Japan is the largest generator of visitors (15.4 percent) to Malaysia. The European nations contribute 6 percent, with the United Kingdom, with some 2.2 percent, having the greatest share among European nations. The United States accounts for only 1.3 percent of the visitors. To attract American tourists, the government launched a $1.6 million campaign in Southern California and designated 1994 as Visit Malaysia Year.

Figure 14–9 Palace in Kuala Kangsar, Malaysia

Tourist Destinations and Attractions

The major destinations are Kuala Lumpur, the capital; Penang, one of the oldest trading centers in the East; and the major resorts (with legal gambling) located on the beaches and in the hills. Kuala Lumpur combines narrow streets and a maze of ancient buildings with modern steel and glass structures (the recently completed twin towers of the national petroleum company are the tallest buildings in the world) to offer a wide variety of attractions. It grew from a wild tin-mining town to a thriving capital city in 100 years. It has not discarded its past colonial British heritage. The National Mosque is near the railway station, distinctive because of its 225-foot-high minaret. The Pusat Islam Center houses an Islamic exhibition hall displaying relics from Muslim civilization, such as pottery, coins, calligraphy, weapons, navigational instruments, and various Islamic manuscripts. The influences of Hinduism are also observable. One of the busiest and most colorful parts of the city is Chinatown in Petaling Street. With open markets selling textiles, herbs, household goods, fruit, flowers, cakes, and vegetables, it is a major attraction. Nearby are the Batu caves,

which contain a Hindu shrine, Templar Park, and the National Zoo.

Penang, just across the border south of Thailand, is a free port with white sandy beaches. The town of Penang, George Town, has temples, colonial architectural relics, and good tourist accommodations. The Snake Temple is probably the only one of its kind in the world. The snakes coil around objects on the altar and throughout the temple. The island is considered another tropical paradise with its lush foliage of giant palms and luxuriant ferns, flowering trees and shrubs, colorful gardens, fruit orchards, rich rice paddies, and coconut groves. It has one of the most beautiful shorelines in the country. The clear, blue waters of the Straits of Malacca allow good visibility for diving and underwater viewing.

One hundred miles south of Kuala Lumpur, Malacca is one of the oldest towns in the country. Malacca has a long history as a trading center for ships from India, Arabia, China, and Europe. It was coloniized by the Portuguese, Dutch, and British. The old fortress on a small hill; the Portuguese Catholic Church, Christ Church; Stadhuys; and Malacca Museum add to the attractions at Malacca, and many

Figure 14–10 Malacca, Malaysia

provide good examples of Dutch architecture. Mini-Malaysia reflects a cultural heritage emphasizing the unique traditional architecture of various Malay states. There are 13 Malay traditional houses of various designs, each containing works of art and crafts unique to each state. The coastal areas have beach resorts and offer an excellent variety of water sports. The east coast includes beaches, fishing villages, batik, and turtle watching. Kota Bharu, Kuala Trengganu, and Rantau Abang are popular towns along the east coast that have a number of handicraft materials and access to good water activities. At Rantau Abang in September, some 1,500 female giant sea turtles migrate to the coast in order to lay their eggs.

Visitors to East Malaysia ride longboats through the Borneo jungles and visit the Iban people in their longhouses situated on the banks of the river. Some can frolic with the baby orangutans in the tropical forests of the state of Sarawak in East Malaysia. The Sarawak Museum in Kuching, the capital of the state of Sarawak, is one of the finest in Asia. It houses a number of artifacts from the many ethnic groups of Borneo. The Tua Pek Kong Temple, Fort Margherita (now a police museum), and Istana (Palace) are additional sites in and around Kuching.

Philippines

500 km

Aparri
Luzon
Baguio
Quezon
Philippine
Sea
South
China
Sea
MANILA ★
Mindoro
Legaspi
Samar
Panay
Cebu
Palawan
Negros
Sulu Sea
Davao
Zamboanga
Mindanao
Celebes Sea

Capital: Manila (de facto), Quezon City (official)
Government: Republic
Size: 115,831 square miles (slightly larger than Nevada)
Language: Filipino, English
Ethnic Division: 91.5% Christian Malay, 4% Muslim Malay, 1.5% Chinese, 3% other
Religion: 83% Roman Catholic, 9% Protestant, 5% Muslim, 3% Buddhist and other
Tourist Season: December through March
Peak Tourist Season: December through February
Currency: Pesos

TRAVEL TIPS

Entry: A visa is not required for stays up to 21 days. Proof of onward or return transportation is required.
Transportation: There is good international access to Manila from North America and Asian countries. Philippine Airlines has scheduled flights to major cities and other important destinations throughout the country. Long-distance buses serve all parts of the country. Public transportation is by Jeepneys and motorized tricycles. Ferries are used for inter-island travel. A Jeepney is a highly decorated type of minibus built on the frame of old United States military jeeps. They travel on relatively fixed routes and stop when waved at from the sidewalk. When a passenger wishes to get out, he or she taps or pounds on the roof.
Health: Water is safe in Manila; however, untreated or unboiled water should not be drunk outside the city. Eat only fruits and vegetables that can be peeled or properly cleaned with safe water. Sanitation is not always good, and dysentery is common.
Shopping: Common items include handbags, abacca or rafia rugs, shoes, pearl and coral jewelry, embroidered shirts, wooden handicrafts, brassware, and pineapple fiber textiles.

CULTURAL CAPSULE

The majority of Philippine people are of Malay descent who migrated to the islands long before the Christian era. The most significant ethnic minority group is the Chinese, who have played an important role in commerce since the ninth century. As a result of intermarriage, many Filipinos have some Chinese and Spanish ancestry. Americans and Spaniards constitute the next largest minorities in the country. The remainder includes a number of different ethnic groups such as Negritos, who inhabit the uplands of the islands around the Sulu Sea, and the Igorot and Ifugao, who inhabit the mountains of northern Luzon. Over 90 percent of the people are Christian (predominantly Roman Catholic). They were converted during the nearly 400 years of Spanish and American rule. The major non-Hispanic groups are the Muslim population, concentrated in the Sulu Archipelago and western Mindanao, and the mountain groups of northern Luzon.

About 87 native languages and dialects are spoken, all belonging to the Malay-Polynesian linguistic family. The three principal indigenous languages are Cebuano, spoken in the Visayas; Tagalog, predominant in the area around Manila; and Ilocano, spoken in northern Luzon. Since 1939, in an effort to develop national unity, the government has promoted the use of the national language, Filipino, which is based on Tagalog. English is the most important non-native language and is used as a second language by almost half of the population. Spanish is spoken by few Filipinos, and its use is decreasing.

Cultural Hints:
- A handshake is a common greeting.
- Staring is rude.
- Respect is shown for elders.
- Over-imbibing alcohol is considered rude.
- Ask permission to take photographs of people.
- To beckon someone extend the arm, palm down, and wave the fingers.
- To beckon with the index finger is insulting.
- Filipinos seldom observe lines.
- Filipinos will recognize most popular American gestures.
- Eating and food:
  Keep your hands above the table.
  A 15 percent tip is customary.
  Leave a little food on plate when finished.
  Typical foods include rice, fish, vegetable, pork, garlic, stew of chicken, milk, seafood, and a drink of sweetened beans.

Physical Characteristics

The Philippines are mountainous islands with narrow-to-extensive coastal lowlands. The climate is tropical marine with monsoons from December to May and July to October.

Tourism Characteristics

Travel to the Philippines decreased in the 1980s, but began increasing in the 1990s. Tourism to the Philippines is the most diverse of all Southeast Asian countries. It has the lowest regional numbers of visitors, with only 5.3 percent coming from other Southeast Asian countries. The major generators of tourism to the Philippines in 1994 were the United States (19.7 percent) and Japan (17.6 percent) (Pacific Asia Travel Association, 1995). The high United States percentage reflects the long historical linkage between the two countries and the many Filipinos living in the United States today. Nearly 8 percent of all visitors are classified as overseas Filipinos, of whom almost 55 percent are from North America. The Philippines was the site of large United States military bases until recently, which also influences travel from the United States. Not only do many visitors come from the United States, but they stay longer, averaging 11.5 days per visit. The major purpose of visiting is listed as "holiday," accounting for over 68 percent of the visitors. A majority of those visiting are repeat visitors, with North America having the highest percentage of repeat visitors (64) compared to an average of 51 percent for all tourists. The government is striving to increase tourism from East Asian countries. Taiwan, Korea, Hong Kong, China, and Japan account for 40 percent of its visitors.

Tourist Destinations and Attractions

The major destinations centers are in Manila and Luzon Island. Manila is situated on a large bay on Luzon Island and is the site of the official capital (Quezon City), relics of the Spanish colonial era in Fort Santiago, and the reconstructed Cathedral of San Augustine. The Spanish colonizers moved the capital from Cebu to Manila in 1571, beginning the Walled City as the seat of both church and state. Manila has attractive parks, impressive modern buildings, and a cultural center. The Spanish colonial architecture with iron grillwork and balconies is evident throughout the city. Of special note for Americans are Manila's island fortress, Corregidor, site of General MacArthur's wartime headquarters and a famous World War II battle site, and the American Memorial Cemetery. The Church of St. Augustine is the oldest church in the city.

The Philippines offers good shopping both in modern stores and the bazaar-type markets throughout the country. The Nayong Filipino (Philippine Village) has scaled-down replicas of Bicol's Mayon Volcano, the Banaue Rice Terraces, the Chocolate Hills of Bohol, and Magellan's Cross of Cebu. Also, there are clusters of houses and their architecture reflective of six of the thirteen regions in the country to form a miniature village.

The Pagsanjan River on Luzon has one of Asia's lushest jungles and rapids and waterfalls of great beauty. Just south of the town of Pagsanjan is one of the most beautiful falls in the island. Other attractions on Luzon include Lake Taal, with a unique double volcano, and the eighteenth-century bamboo organ at Las Pinas. The beach resort of Baguio is considered one of the great resorts of the world.

Cebu City in the province of Cebu, the second international gateway to the country after Manila, is referred to as the "Queen City of the South." Cebu Province is composed of 167 islands with a variety of resorts. In addition to good diving and other water sports, its historical attractions include Magellan's Cross, planted by the Portuguese explorer Ferdinand Magellan to mark the spot where the first Filipinos were baptized, and the Basilica Minore del Santo Nino, which houses the oldest religious relic in the Philippines, the statue of the Sto. Nino (Child Jesus).

Mindanao Island is an exotic island where wild carabao are found. Zamboanga, one of Mindanao's cities, has rolling surf, palm-fringed beaches, natural swimming pools, and lovely orchids. Zamboanga is noted for its beautiful hanging gardens and parks along with the minarets and domes of its mosques. People of the Moros tribe perform their ceremonial dances in the Muslim village and mosque at Taluksangay on Mindanao. Unfortunately, the rebellion of the Muslims on the island makes it unsafe for visitors.

Singapore

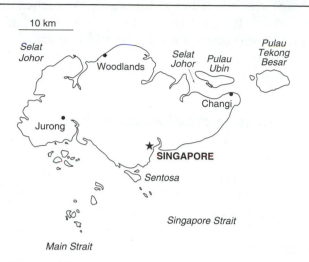

Capital: Singapore
Government: Republic within Commonwealth
Size: 223 square miles (about three times the size of Washington, DC)
Language: Chinese, Malay, Tamil, English
Ethnic Division: 76.4% Chinese, 14.9% Malay, 6.4% Indian, 2.3% other
Religion: Buddhist, Muslim, Christian, Hindu, Sikh, Taoist, Confucianism
Tourist Season: Year-round
Peak Tourist Season: None
Currency: Singapore dollars

TRAVEL TIPS

Entry: A visa is not required for stays up to 2 weeks. Proof of onward or return transportation is required.
Transportation: International access to Singapore is excellent with direct flights from North America and other Pacific Asia countries. Singapore has excellent rail linkage to Malaysia and Thailand. Public transportation is by subway and bus.
Health: No vaccinations are needed to visit unless entering from a country that has yellow fever. The water is safe to drink.
Caution: Singapore has strict enforcement of littering, jaywalking, and drug possession.
Shopping: Common items include goods from many countries as Singapore is a free port. There are many Chinese goods, handicrafts, and Thai silk. Gold and silver are also popular items.

CULTURAL CAPSULE

Singapore is one of the most densely populated countries in the world. It has a varied linguistic, cultural, and religious heritage. More than 76 percent of the population are Chinese. Fifteen percent are Malay, and a little over 6 percent

are Indian. Malay, Chinese, English, and Tamil are all official languages. English is widely used in professions, businesses, and schools. The Chinese speak a number of Chinese dialects, such as Hokkein, Chaozhou, and Cantonese. Singapore has religious freedom. Almost all Malays are Muslim; other Singaporeans are Hindus, Sikhs, Taoists, Buddhists, Confucianists, and Christians. The Christians are generally either Chinese or European.

Singapore has created a very strict society. As indicated they have very strong littering, jaywalking, and drug possession laws. They also have strong laws related to quality of goods sold in stores. If a visitor feels a purchase is defective or of poor quality and the store personnel do not correct the problem, they can be prosecuted.

Cultural Hints:
- A handshake is the most common form of greeting.
- Shoes are removed before entering a mosque.
- Visitors are expected to be punctual.
- Do not use the left hand when eating with a Malay or an Indian.
- Touching another person's head is impolite.
- Do not point the bottom of your foot at a person.
- The OK sign is considered rude.
- Do not point with finger.
- Eating and food:
  Some foods are eaten with a spoon, some with the hands.
  As service charge is included in bill, tips are not necessary.
  Typical foods include rice, fish, seafood, peanut sauce, Indian curries, Chinese dishes, and fruits.

Physical Characteristics

Singapore is a small island city-state. The climate is tropical, hot, and humid year-round.

Tourism Characteristics

Singapore benefits from its central location in Southeast Asia and its history of being the crossroads of shipping routes between the Indian and Pacific oceans. As an administrative center and military base for the British, it was well on its way to becoming an important international commercial center before World War II. Since World War II, Singapore has emerged as an important industrial producer and commercial center for the entire region. Singapore's important position in Southeast Asia reflects its situational relationship, which offsets its small size. Like Hong Kong, Singapore is a duty-free port; consequently shopping is central to the tourism industry. Visitors have the highest daily per capita expenditure in the region.

Figure 14–11 Singapore skyline

Tourists to Singapore reflect a regional market. Asian visitors accounted for over 76 percent of all arrivals in 1996. Growth in tourism has continued even with the imposition of an exit tax by Thailand and Indonesia on their citizens. Outside of the Southeast Asian region, Japan contributes the most visitors to Singapore. A significant amount of this travel is for business, as the Japanese have invested heavily in Singapore. Outside of Asia, Australia, New Zealand, the United Kingdom, and the United States send the largest number of tourists to Singapore—Australia and New Zealand because of their proximity, the United Kingdom because of historical ties, and the United States, whose travelers use it as a gateway or crossroads to Southeast Asia. A high percentage of visitors visit Singapore as part of a larger tour, as

reflected in the low average length of visit, 3.3 days. Singapore is committed to providing a good experience for visitors. It has a very strict "anti-cheaters" law, which literally forces shop owners and merchants to sell quality goods. Should a visitor buy a defective item, he or she can go directly to the store or shop and get a refund or a replacement.

Tourist Destinations and Attractions

Singapore's first and foremost tourist attraction is the duty-free shopping. Chinatown offers all the usual Chinese sights, sounds, smells, shops, food, folk medicines, and handicrafts. The architecture of Singapore illustrates its varied population, with Malay Chinese, Indian, and Hindu temples, as well as Islamic mosques and Western churches and architecture.

Some attractions in addition to the shopping are excellent zoological and botanical gardens; Jung Bird Park, with a variety of tropical Asian birds; Haw Par Villa (Tiger Balm Gardens), which houses a priceless collection of jade; Arab Street; and Chinatown. A major attraction is the 20-acre Asian Village consisting of three villages representing Southeast Asia, South Asia, and North Asia. It showcases Asian lifestyles, food, entertainment, handicrafts, and architecture. In the Underwater World Singapore, Asia's largest tropical oceanarium with more than 2,300 fish, you can wander along the bottom of the ocean in a 273-foot clear acrylic tube.

Thailand

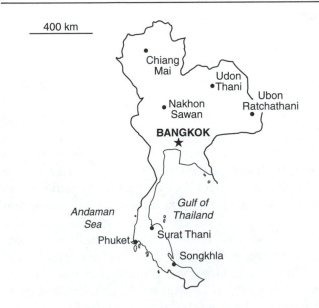

Capital: Bangkok
Government: Constitutional Monarchy
Size: 198,115 square miles (slightly larger than California)
Language: Thai, English
Ethnic Division: 75% Thai, 14% Chinese, 11% other
Religion: 95.5% Buddhist, 4% Muslim, 0.5% other
Tourist Season: Year-round
Peak Tourist Season: December
Currency: Baht

 TRAVEL TIPS

Entry: A visa is not required for stays up to 15 days. Proof of onward or return transportation is required. Customs prohibits the export of religious images. A Thai government permit is required to take antiques out of the country.
Transportation: Excellent international access is available by direct flights to Bangkok from North America, Asia, and Europe. Major cities within Thailand are served by air and train. Transportation in Bangkok is by bus, taxi, rental cars,

and samior. Local transportation in small towns is by pedicab.

Health: For travel in rural areas vaccinations are needed for typhoid, cholera, rabies, and hepatitis. Malaria suppressants are advised. Avoid tap water, raw milk, ice cream, uncooked meats, and unwashed fruits and vegetables.

Caution: Visitors are sometimes victimized by individuals offering to be guides who take tourists to gemstone dealers where the dealer will overcharge for poor-quality stones.

Shopping: Common items include Thai silk and cotton, jewelry, silver, gold lacquerware, bronze ware, Celadon pottery, teak carvings, and rattan and bamboo furniture.

Tips are not necessary, but some give a small amount (5 percent).

Typical foods include rice, spicy dishes of meat, vegetables, fish, eggs, and fruits. Curries and pepper sauces are popular.

CULTURAL CAPSULE

Thailand's population is relatively homogeneous. More than 85 percent of the people speak a dialect of Thai and share a common culture. It is divided into Central Thai (36 percent), Thai-Lao (32 percent), Northern Thai (8 percent), and Southern Thai (8 percent). The largest minorities are the Chinese (12 percent) and the Malay-speaking Muslims in the south (3 percent). Other groups include the Khmer, the Mon, and the Vietnamese. Thai is the official language and is used in schools, but each region has its own language, such as Khmer, Mon, Miao, Malay, and others. English is spoken by the educated. Theravada Buddhism is the religion of more than 90 percent of the Thai. Traditionally, all young men were expected to become Buddhist monks for at least three months to study Buddhist principles. The practice is not strictly enforced today. About 4 percent of the population is Muslim, and there are a small number of Christians. Spirit worship and animism are important in Thai religious life.

Cultural Hints:
- Place the palms of the hands together, with fingers extended at chest level, and bow slightly to greet others. This is also used to say thank you, goodby, or I am sorry.
- Remove shoes before entering a home.
- Do not step on the doorsill when entering a dwelling. Thais believe a deity resides in the doorsill.
- Avoid touching the top of another person's head.
- Do not point or show the bottom of the foot to another person.
- Do not pat another person on the shoulder.
- Avoid loud talking and demonstrative gestures.
- Do not point with your finger. Use your chin or incline your head.
- Do not cross your legs when sitting.
- Women must never touch a Buddhist monk or offer to shake hands.
- To beckon another person, hold palm down and wave fingers.
- Do not eat or pass objects with the left hand.
- Remove your shoes before entering a mosque.
- Do not defile, stand, or sit on a religious monument.
- Eating and food:
  Use the fork (left hand) to push food onto the spoon.
  Bones are placed on the plate.
  When finished eating, place utensils together on the plate.

Physical Characteristics

Gently rolling hills and plains with a southern plateau. The low coastal plain is marshy with many lagoons. The climate is tropical, hot, and humid in the south and semiarid in the north.

Tourism Characteristics

Like Singapore, Thailand is a crossroads for travel between Europe and Asia, and for some Europeans to the South Pacific. Visitors to Thailand stay longer than in Singapore, indicating the greater diversity of attractions that Thailand offers compared to Singapore. Like Singapore, however, Thailand receives most of its visitors from Asia, approximately 67 percent, with nearly 25 percent being from the other Southeast Asian countries. Thailand's neighbor, Malaysia, with 14.6 percent of the total visitors, is the most dominant market area. Outside of Southeast Asia, Japan, the United States, and Germany are the most important individual countries (Pacific Asia Travel Association, 1994). Japanese tourists include a large percentage of business travelers, often combining business with entertainment unavailable in Japan or coming specifically on package tours for such entertainment. For visitors from the United States, Germany, and other European countries, Bangkok provides an attractive option on circular tours because of its unique and diverse cultural attractions.

Tourist Destinations and Attractions

Bangkok, the capital, has an impressive and fascinating life along its canals, with shops, teak houses on stilts, temples, and snake farms. Like many nations of the world where a large proportion of the population is engaged in agriculture, Thailand has periodic markets where fresh produce is sold. Thailand's markets are unique because they are floating. The floating markets, such as the Damnoen Saduak, Figure 14–12, reflect the traditional importance of the canals and streams found in the delta of the Menam River of Thailand. Wearing enormous straw hats, men, and women bring their products to the market in long, narrow boats piled high with rice, fruits, and vegetables, dried beef and fish, flowers, and other goods and buy and sell from the water.

Figure 14–12 Floating market at Damnoen Saduak, Thailand

Within Bangkok, the Royal Grand Palace, which was the home for the king of Siam, is one of the wonders of the world. On the grounds of the palace is Wat Phra Kaeo, the chapel of the Emerald Buddha, one of the most impressive attractions in Asia. Outside of Bangkok is the "ancient city," a large outdoor museum containing 65 of Thailand's most beautiful and impressive temples and reconstructed historical monuments and the Thai Cultural Center (Rose Garden). Throughout the country, there are ornate temples and charming people. A final attraction is the

Kwai River, made famous by the film depicting Japanese efforts to make American and British prisoners of war in World War II build a railroad bridge. Nakhon Pathom, some 40 miles west of Bangkok, is the site of the 380-foot Phra Pathom Chedi, the world's tallest Buddhist monument. Ayutthay, some 40 miles upstream from Bangkok, was the Siamese capital from 1350 to 1767. It has some magnificent ruins of medieval splendor. Nearby is the Bang Pain Palace, the summer residence of early Bangkok monarchs. Phetchaburi, some 80 miles southwest of Bangkok, is the site of Buddha-filled caves, historic temples and palaces, and Kaeng Krachan.

In northern Thailand along the Burma and Laos border, there are forested mountains and fertile river valleys. This area is part of the fabled Golden Triangle and was the cradle of Thai civilization. Major places of interest are Sukhothal, where massive stone Buddhas sit within the old city walls; Si Satchanalai; Lampang, a Thai provincial capital where horse-drawn carriages are still in use; Doi Inthanon National Park, which covers Thailand's highest mountain and includes beautiful waterfalls; and Chiang Rai, the heart of the Golden Triangle.

Pattaya Beach is one of the best-known seaside resort areas in Asia. It offers excellent swimming, snorkeling, and sailing. Also along the coast are a number of fishing villages with bays and superb beaches.

Indochina—Vietnam, Cambodia, and Laos

200 km

- Phôngsali
- Louang Namtha
- Louangphrabang
- Xiangkhoang
VIENTIANE ★
- Ban Napè
- Savannakhét
- Saravan
- Pakxé

Laos

TRAVEL TIPS

Entry: *Vietnam*—A visa is required and must be obtained in a country with a Vietnamese embassy. *Laos*—A visa is required. Proof of sufficient funds for stay and onward or return transportation required. *Cambodia*—A visa is required. It must be obtained in a country with Cambodian consulate or embassy.

Transportation: International access to all three countries is generally through Bangkok.

Health: Cholera and malaria protection is needed. Tap water is not potable. Care should be taken by eating fruits and vegetables that can be peeled or cooked.

Caution: Many areas of Cambodia are considered unsafe to travel and may be restricted.

CULTURAL CAPSULE

Cambodia: The largest ethnic group is the Khmer (over 70 percent of the population). Next is the Sino-Khmer (mixed Chinese and Khmer), which accounts for about 10 percent of the population. The Chams (5 percent) are descendants of the Champa Kingdom, which was centered in present-day Vietnam and contained people of Malaysian origin. There are a number of Vietnamese and Chinese in Cambodia. The Khmer language comes from an older language called Paali, which developed as a successor to Indian Sanskrit. Thai and Lao share common words with Khmer. French is used to communicate in business and among government officials. Cambodians are Theravada Buddhists. The Cham minority are Islam.

Laos: About half of the people are ethnic Lao, who live in the lowland regions. The Lao descended from the Thai people who migrated southward from China in the thirteenth century. Mountain tribes of Sino-Tibetan (Hmong, Yao, Aka, and Lahu) and Thai ethnolinguistic heritage are found in Northern Laos. In the central and southern mountains, Mon Khmer tribes predominate. Some Vietnamese and Chinese minorities remain in cities. The predominant religion is Theravada Buddhism. Animism is common among the mountain tribes. The official and dominant language is Lao, a tonal language of the Thai linguistic group. French is understood by older people who worked in government and commerce.

Vietnam: Ethnic Vietnamese constitute almost 90 percent of the population. Originating in what is now southern China and northern Vietnam, the Vietnamese people pushed southward beginning in 939 A.D. to occupy the entire eastern seacoast of the Indochinese Peninsula. Various ethnic groups make up the remainder of the population. Chinese is the largest group, found mostly in cities. The second largest minority is the southern Montagnards (mountain people), comprising two main ethnolinguistic groups—Malayo-Polynesian and Khmer. About 30 groups of various cultures and dialects are spread over the highland territory. The third largest minority is the Khmer Krom (Cambodians), numbering about 600,000, who are concentrated in southern provinces near the Cambodian border and at the mouth of the Mekong River. Buddhism is the most common religion (55 percent), followed by Taoist (12 percent) and Roman Catholic (7 percent). Some of the minorities are animists. Vietnamese is the official language. There are a number of accents in the various regions of the country. Most officials understand English.

Physical Characteristics

The three countries are hilly and mountainous except Vietnam, which has the low, flat delta of the Mekong River in the south. The climate is tropical, hot, and humid with monsoonal rains from May to September.

Tourism Characteristics and Tourist Destinations

These three countries of Southeast Asia have experienced extensive conflict and military occupation. Tourism to the three is growing slowly, except for Cambodia. Vietnam is now welcoming tourists. Nearly 1.5 million visitors arrived in Vietnam in 1996. Half were from Southeast Asia, 30 percent from

Country	Capital	Language	Currrency	Square Miles and State Comparison
Cambodia	Phnom Penh	Khmer	Riel	69,898 (Arkansas)
Laos	Vientiane	Laotian, French	Liberation kip	91,429 (Utah)
Vietnam	Hanoi	Vietnamese, French	Dong	120,000 (New Mexico)

Europe, and 10 percent from North America. In an effort to increase its tourism trade it has encouraged foreign investment, and by the end of 1992 there were a reported 47 hotel projects underway. In addition, major hotel chains such as Holiday Inn, Peninsula, Shangri-la, and Ramada are exploring opportunities. Most foreign ventures are from Hong Kong.

Vietnam veterans and other interested travelers are beginning to slowly trickle in to observe and see the places of interest such as Ho Chi Minh City (Saigon), Cu Chi Tunnels, Mekong, Danang, and Non Nuoc Beach (China Beach). Hue, an ancient royal capital, is about a three-hour drive from Danang. The Citadel of Hue is being restored with the help of UNESCO. The Citadel comprises the Defensive Wall, the Royal Wall, and the Forbidden Purple City. In Hue also are found the seven Royal Tombs. The Cu Chi Tunnels offer a view of the war. A glass box containing a model of the former war zone, complete with light bulbs to indicate the areas of action, acts as an introduction. Visitors are then led through narrow and dark burrows to obtain a feel of life during the war. Hanoi, the capital, was a picturesque city combining the modern French-built sectors with the Vietnamese character. Two historical monuments, the Single Pillar Pagoda and the Great Buddha Pagoda, are important attractions.

Tourism to Laos has been crippled because of political instability associated with the Vietnam War. Data on tourism is difficult to obtain and unclear. The World Tourism Organization indicates that from 1986 to 1990 there were 25,000 international arrivals every year. Tourism is beginning to grow, fluctuating between 100,000 and 150,000 annually since 1994. Laos has a smaller number of visitors from the West than either Cambodia or Vietnam. Laos opened to international tourism in early 1989, and most tours are handled by the state-run Lao Tourism organization. There are two or three private agencies operating in Vientiane. Accommodations are limited as there are only two first-class hotels in Laos, in Vientiane and Luang Prabang.

The two major attractions in Laos are Luang Prabang, the royal capital with its Royal Palace, and Vientiane, the modern capital, on the Mekong River. Vientiane has many temples, of which the Luang Temple is the most important as it is said to contain Buddha's breastbone.

Cambodia 260,000 visitors in 1996. China is the reported major source (11.8 percent), followed by France (10 percent), Japan (7 percent), and the United States (8 percent). The remainder are largely inter-regional arrivals. The future of tourism is still uncertain as the likelihood of a permanent peace is still in doubt. Cambodia is trying to implement a comprehensive plan for the tourism industry. The plan includes renovation and construction of airports, hotels, entertainment facilities, and other segments of the tourism infrastructure. It is designed to preserve Cambodia's cultural and environmental assets while encouraging sustainable tourism growth.

Cambodia's capital, Phnom Penh, is the center of any potential tourism. Much has changed because of the conflict and repeated changes in policy. The Angkor Wat Ruins are the best-known tourist attraction in all of Indochina. Angkor Wat, located in central Cambodia, was the capital city of the old Khmer Empire and a number of architecturally important ruins still remain. Anghor Wat was the masterpiece of the Khmers, built between 1130 and 1160. The five cone-shaped towers rise from the jungle like little volcanoes. Jungle vines are mixed among spectacular ruins, adding a sense of greatness.

Hue, the old imperial city, has important attractions, such as the Imperial Palace, the Gold Water Bridge, and the River of Perfumes, much of which was destroyed by war.

THAILAND

DAY 1   BANGKOK

One of the most beautiful *wats* (Thai for ancient temple), and also one of Thailand's most famous, is Wat Phrakaeo. It is found in the compound of the Royal Palace, which used to be the seat of the court of old Siam. Surrounded by high walls and a huge double gate, the palace was originally built by the first king, King Rama I, in the year 1782. The Wat Phrakaeo is also known as the Temple of the Emerald Buddha and was formerly used as the royal chapel. The Royal Collection of Weapons and Coin Pavilion are also found here in the compound. The buildings of the palace are a mixture of architectural types, including almost everything from Thai to Victorian. The chapel itself has a tall, golden, three-tiered roof. The Emerald Buddha is seated on a very high altar, and the many murals found in the chapel depict Buddha's earthly life. There are many beautifully decorated buildings to be seen inside the compound. Wat Po's main attraction is its 160-foot Reclining Buddha, which symbolizes the passing of the Lord Buddha from this life to Nirvana. This temple is the oldest and largest in Bangkok. It is divided into two sections; one houses the monks, and the other contains various religious buildings. The temple compound is surrounded by a massive wall that has sixteen gates. Wat Po was a favorite of Bangkok's first four kings, and they all did their part in adding to its treasures. There are four large chedis or spires found on the grounds, which are memorials to these kings. Sometimes known as Thailand's first university, Wat Po contains objects placed as a way of helping people acquire knowledge. On the walls of an open pavilion, there are plaques that prescribe treatments for different sicknesses. Also housed in the chapel are murals in some of the finest Thai tradition that show many facets of the Thais' daily life.

Just outside of the Wat Po compound is the Giant Swing, which is one of Bangkok's calling cards. In ancient times, there was a swinging ceremony that was a Brahministic ritual, in honor of one of their gods, but that has long since been forgotten. The swing itself consists of gigantic, red-colored teak poles, with a beautifully carved beam connecting the two.

Facing the Giant Swing is Wat Suthat, which is said to be Bangkok's tallest. It is noted for its gigantic and outstanding bot (chapel). A huge gallery of gilded Buddha images is found inside. The main Buddha image, which used to stand in Sukhothai, was brought to Bangkok by King Rama I because he was so impressed by its size and beauty. The building that houses these images contains some beautifully carved doors. King Rama had the carving tools thrown into the river after the doors were completed, so that the fine carving could not be duplicated. There are beautiful murals in the chapel that King Rama III had painted, and the courtyard is filled with bronze horses and stone pagodas.

DAY 2   BANGKOK

The Buddhaisawan Chapel was built by the second king as his private place of worship. It houses fascinating murals, depicting the life of Buddha and the famous Phra Buddha Sihing, a bronze image greatly revered by the Thais.

In the middle of the very average surroundings of the Wat Trimitir, there is an open pavilion that holds one of Thailand's most prized possessions, the enormous, solid Gold Buddha. It is said that this huge image is made of 5.5 tons of the very precious metal. It also has a very interesting story behind it. The image was originally cased in plaster and housed in a semi-ruined temple by the river. When the image was being moved from the old temple by a crane, it was dropped and part of the plaster broke off, revealing its true nature.

Sitting on the banks of the Chao Phraya River, the Temple of the Dawn is very conspicuous with its five tall spires. The tallest of the spires, which is 260 feet high, is completely covered with pieces of broken, multicolored Chinese porcelain. The tall spire has a steep staircase that can be climbed to give a great view of the compound and of the river. Inside of the chapel, guarded by two giant masked gods, are many very intricately done murals. The Royal Barges are on the side of the temple that faces the river. These beautifully carved boats were used by the kings on their trips to the northern cities. The king sat high on his throne on the biggest barge among the dozens of other barges with their brilliantly dressed oarsmen that followed.

Once upon a time, the National Museum was the palace of the "second king," who had the job of a deputy. Built in 1782, the museum contains a wonderful collection of prehistoric items, along with a selection of all major art forms and styles from the many periods of Thai history. Possibly the largest museum in Southeast Asia, it is strongly geared toward religious exhibits with comparative items from other countries and cultures in Asia. Classical music and dance performances are held in the museum garden.

continues

continued

DAY 3 — BANGKOK

The Ratchdamnoen Stadium is where Thai boxing matches are held. The Thais' style of boxing is nowhere near the Western style of boxing. The bouts are fought over five rounds and begin with a prayer and a solo ceremonial dance in which one fighter tries to prove to the other that he is the more powerful one. The fighting itself is a combination of ballet, gymnastics, and mayhem, in which almost anything goes. Accompanied by a four-piece orchestra, the opponents show off their talents in a very stylized form. The fighters are allowed to use their feet, elbows, legs, knees, and shoulders. The bare feet are the favorite form of attack. With these things in mind, the sport has been nicknamed "the race of eight arms."

No trip to Bangkok would be complete without at least a half-day to browse through its many markets. There are many beautiful things to buy here. After mastering the streets, bargaining is a must. Some of the items that Thailand is well-known for are its uniquely handcrafted bronze ware, tailoring (like you would expect to find in Hong Kong), carved teak wood, the ancient art of Thai Celadon pottery, and the best-known of all Thailand's products—Thai silk, which is found in many beautiful colors and patterns.

DAY 4 — NAKHON PATHOM

Just west of Bangkok, out of the "big city" atmosphere, through scenes of flat countryside is the town of Nakhon Pathom. From just outside of this town, the Phra Pathom Chedi rises up and towers over the surrounding countryside. Standing over 127 meters high, it is the tallest Buddhist monument in the world. Set in a huge square park, the massive monument sits upon a circular terrace, with many examples of trees that are said to be connected with Buddha's life.

A visit to the Rose Garden is a definite must and is a beautiful change from all of the buildings that fill the towns of Thailand. Many local plants and all types of roses fill this large area kept only for the beauty of the flora found here.

In the days of canal travel, a royal visit from Bangkok to Nakhon Pathom was more than a day's journey so various residences were built here. The Sanam Chand Palace is one of those residences. It was built in a very unusual Thai interpretation of the English Tudor. In front of the Palace stands a statue of Yaleh, the pet dog of King Rama VI. The fierce pet, which was disliked by the court, was poisoned by the king's attendants. Even as a statue, Yaleh looks terrifying.

DAY 5 — AYUTTHAYA

North of the capital through the fertile Menam lowlands is Thailand's "rice bowl." Dams and canals are all over the countryside of this wide, fertile plain. Just past these plains lies Ayutthaya, the old capital of the Kingdom of Siam. The huge area, in which many ruins of temples and palaces are spread, gives a good impression of how great this capital was.

Chandrakasem Palace was known as the Palace of the Front, and originally was constructed outside the city walls. Built near the junction of the old rivers, it had an important defensive position. The palace now houses a museum and looks out onto the noisiest part of town. King Monkut had a tower built on the palace grounds for celestial observation and also a jetty.

Wat Phanan Choeng was built 26 years prior to the town of Ayutthaya in which it sits. The building houses a huge sitting Buddha that is so tall it seems to be holding up the ceiling. This was a favorite place for the Chinese traders to pray before setting out on their long journeys. It has an unmistakable Chinese atmosphere.

Wang Luang, the old royal palace, was completely flattened by the Burmese and the bricks were later moved to Bangkok to rebuild the capital. Now only scattered foundations are found among the trees to mark the palace site. Close by stands the royal temple, Wat Phra Sri Sanphet. The gold-leafed Buddha, Phra Sri Sanphet, that the temple was named after was irreparably damaged by the Burmese. Today the three central chedis (pagodas) have been restored and stand among the ruins.

DAY 6 — AYUTTHAYA

With its huge elephant gates, the completely restored Wat Phra Ram is an impressive sight. On the grounds of the temple, there is a gallery of mythical sunbirds and statues of Buddha. The spires of Wat Phra Ram shimmer and are reflected in the pool that almost completely surrounds the temple.

The summer palace, Ba Pa In, was built in the seventeenth century on the banks of the Chao Phraya River. The king that had it built showed his taste for European architecture. Amid beautiful gardens are two Greek-style buildings and a small Gothic church. In the middle of the lake on the grounds is an exquisite orange, green, and gold pavilion. There is also a small museum on the grounds that displays ceramics and antiques belonging to past royal families.

continues

continued

Across the lake from Wat Phra Ram, two of Ayutthaya's finest temples stand side by side. As a memorial to his brothers, the seventh king had the Wat Raj Burana built. It contains many beautiful images and items of royal jewelry. The two chedis of the temple contain the ashes of the two brothers. Across the road are the ruins of Wat Kahathat. It was built originally to a height of 46 meters. This building was not destroyed, it collapsed because it was so ancient. A number of valuable Buddhas were discovered where they had been buried to save them from the savage Burmese soldiers.

The Phu Kao Thong Temple, better known as the Golden Mount Chedi, towers over the flat countryside in the north of Ayutthaya. Built by the Burmese after their conquest in 1549, it was later rebuilt by the Siamese in their own style. To mark the 2,500 years of Buddhism, a 2,500-gram gold ball was mounted on top of the spire in 1956.

DAY 7   LOPBURI

The journey to Lopburi is through still more of the fertile "rice bowl" of Thailand. The hills of the Korat Plateau appear on the horizon, which gives a different look than the flatness of the Central Plains before this point. Lop Buri was the summer capital of Siam, and many artifacts from the Neolithic and Stone Ages that have been found in this area give us an idea of how old the city really is. The last scenes of King Narai's life were played out in the Suttha Sawan Pavilion. During his last days, the King was attended to by the only ten royal pages who had remained faithful to him. Realizing that those who had rebelled against him would probably kill his loyal pages, the King called in a Buddhist abbot to ordain the pages as monks. The robe of Buddhism would keep them safe. In return, he gave the pavilion to the Buddhist monks as a temple.

The grounds of the Lop Buri Palace are surrounded by massive walls that still enclose the major part of the modern town. The inside of the walls are covered with hundreds of leaf-shaped prints in which small lamps were lit for special occasions.

King Kongkut built the Phiman Kongkut Pavilion in the nineteenth century. It is a three-story colonial mansion, with very thick walls and high ceilings. This is how they kept cool during the hot season. The mansion actually is quite small, but is very lovely. It houses a fine arts museum that displays bronze works, Chinese porcelain, coin, Buddhist fans, and shadow-play puppets.

Another building on the complex that used to accommodate the court ladies, their children, and servants, now houses the Farmer's Museum. Here the traditional tools of Thai agriculture are displayed.

Two important relics of the Khmer (Cambodian) and Pre-Khmer periods are also found in Lopburi. The Phra Prang Sam Yod, or Sacred Three Spires, is a thirteenth-century laterite-block shrine. It has beautiful stone carvings on the towers and the door columns are fascinating. The second is the Phrang Khaek, or Hindu Spire, which is found in the center of town. Also of three laterite spires, it was built sometime in the eleventh century.

REVIEW QUESTIONS

1. What are the three major religions of South Asia?
2. What is the most important climatic feature of South Asia? Why?
3. What are the four major problems found in Southeast Asia? Why?
4. Which country in South Asia has the most well-developed tourist industry? Why?
5. What are the six major tourist regions of India?
6. Which country in Southeast Asia receives the largest number of visitors? Why?
7. What accounts for the fact that the United States provides so many tourists to the Philippines?
8. What accounts for a strong tourist trade to Singapore?

GEOGRAPHY AND TOURISM IN

Australia, New Zealand, and the Islands of the South Pacific

CHAPTER 15

MAJOR GEOGRAPHIC CHARACTERISTICS

- The South Pacific region consists of three island groups: Melanesia, Micronesia, and Polynesia; and Australia and New Zealand.
- The islands of the Pacific can be divided into the high volcanic islands and the low coral islands.
- The Pacific region covers the largest area of any world travel region, yet has a very small land area.
- Australia and New Zealand have strong economic and cultural ties to Europe.
- The economies of Australia and New Zealand rely heavily upon agriculture and natural resources.

MAJOR TOURISM CHARACTERISTICS

- The area is remote from the population and industrial centers of the world.
- The Pacific Islands are perceived as both culturally and physically exotic.
- Australia and New Zealand have some of the longest lengths of stay for visitors.
- Tourism to Australia and New Zealand is highly associated with their cultural linkage to Europe and North America.
- The growth in numbers of Japanese tourists to the area reflects honeymooners, office ladies, and visits to World War II sites.

MAJOR TOURIST DESTINATIONS

Tahiti
Fiji
Guam
Saipan
Auckland, New Zealand
Rotorua, New Zealand
Christchurch, New Zealand
Southern Alps
Queenlands and Milford Sound
Southeast coastal area between Sydney and Melbourne
Coastal areas of Queensland (Great Barrier Reef)
Alice Springs, Australia

KEY TERMS AND WORDS

Aiga	Matai
Archipelago	Melanesia
Chinese	Micronesia
Commonwealth	Oceania
Continental Islands	Office Ladies (OL)
Coral Atolls	Orographic Precipitation
Coral Reef	Pidgin
Euronesians	Polynesia
Great Barrier Reef	Southern Alps
Great Dividing Range	Tropical Rain Forest
Indian	Volcanic Islands
Isolation	

INTRODUCTION

The South Pacific is one of the fastest growing areas for tourist arrivals. However, it must be kept in mind that the numbers are relatively small. The islands of the Pacific (other than Hawaii, which is part of North America because of political ties),

Australia, and New Zealand are isolated due to their long distances from the rest of the world, Figure 15–1. The Pacific Islands are further handicapped because their isolation is compounded by their small size. Their small size hinders development of major manufacturing, resources, and agricultural commodities to justify more transportation

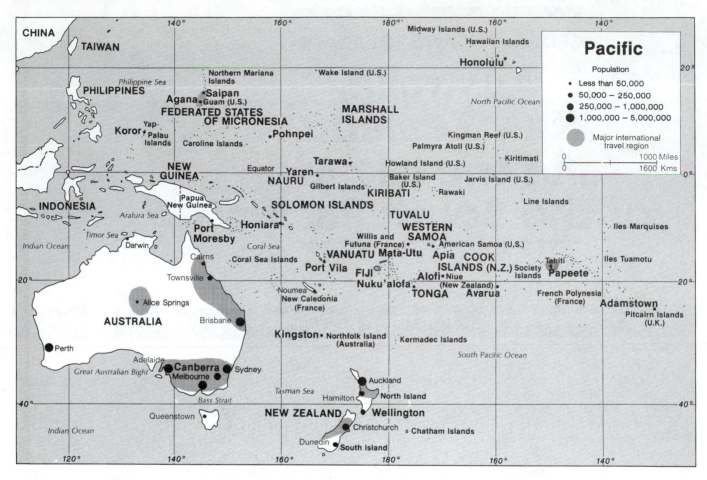

Figure 15–1 South Pacific

links with the rest of the world, which would be helpful in increasing development of tourism.

Australia and New Zealand have benefitted from their larger size and close cultural and economic ties to Europe and North America. While isolated from their European cultural hearth, the first European settlers developed towns, governments, and societal values reflecting their European origins. Both Australia's and New Zealand's earliest European inhabitants were English, and they consciously devel-

		POPULATION CHARACTERISTICS, 1997				
Country	**Population (millions)**	**Annual Growth Rate (percent)**	**Time to Double Pop. (years)**	**Per Capita GNP**	**Life Expectancy (years)**	**Percent Urban**
Australia	18.5	0.7	100	18,720	78	85
Fed. States of Micronesia	0.1	2.2	31	N/A	66	26
Fiji	0.8	1.8	38	2,440	63	39
French Polynesia	0.2	2.0	35	N/A	70	57
Guam	0.2	2.4	29	N/A	74	38
New Caledonia	0.2	1.7	40	N/A	72	70
New Zealand	3.6	0.8	86	14,340	76	85
Papua New Guinea	4.4	2.3	30	1,160	56	15
Solomon Islands	0.4	3.4	20	910	70	13
Vanuatu	0.2	2.9	24	1,200	63	18
Western Samoa	0.2	2.3	30	1,120	65	21

oped societies that replicated their perception of their homeland. Both nations have highly developed economies that have all the characteristics of developed nations. They have high literacy levels, high incomes, large amounts of leisure time, and the individualism and materialism found in other regions of the industrialized world.

Australia and New Zealand are different in physical geography, with one large and the other small, one mineral-rich and the other with few mineral resources, one an island nation and the other occupying a continent, and one reliant upon agricultural exports almost exclusively and the other reliant upon both mineral and agricultural exports.

THE SOUTH PACIFIC ISLANDS AND THEIR PHYSICAL CHARACTERISTICS

The islands of the South Pacific region (often referred to as *Oceania*) can be divided into three island groups: *Melanesia*, *Micronesia*, and *Polynesia*. Melanesia is closest to the Southeast Asian *archipelago*, and the islands are larger and have a tropical climate similar to that of the Southeast Asian mainland and the Indonesian archipelago. Melanesia extends from the Southeast Asian mainland to Australia and consists of a number of large islands, the largest being New Guinea. The size of the islands in Melanesia has led some geographers to refer to them as *continental islands*, to distinguish them from the much smaller islands of Micronesia and Polynesia. The mountains of the large islands of Melanesia are extremely rugged, with plateaus and precipitous interior valleys. The lower and coastal areas are divided by rivers with alternating swampy areas and coastal plains.

Micronesia is a complex of a few high mountainous volcanic islands and many tiny *coral atolls*. Atolls consist of a coral island or islands with a *coral reef* surrounding a lagoon. Coral atolls are low, and many rise only a few feet above the high-tide level. *Volcanic islands*, such as Guam, can reach elevations of over 2,600 feet (800 meters). The low atolls have a shortage of fresh water, which restricts tourism. The higher volcanic islands receive more precipitation, especially on their higher slopes.

Polynesia covers the largest area of the South Pacific, but its total land area is extremely small. Physically, this region includes both low coral atolls and volcanic islands. Many of these high volcanic islands have steep cliffs and mountain ranges divided by deep valleys. As air masses cross these mountains, cooling associated with higher elevations results in condensation, clouds, and precipitation in a process known as *orographic precipitation*. The heavy precipitation provides a source of fresh water. In some cases the volcanic islands are surrounded by fringing reefs that provide good fishing. While atolls are found throughout the Pacific, most of Micronesia is atolls. The atolls are extremely vulnerable to severe weather disturbances such as typhoons, unusually high seas, or droughts.

With the exception of Easter Island and New Zealand, the climate of the islands of the South Pacific is *tropical rain forest* with year-round precipitation and warm-to-hot temperatures with seasonal winds to temper the high humidity. Most of the islands in the South Pacific have a uniformly warm year-round temperature, ranging from nighttime lows near 68 degrees Fahrenheit to highs in the mid to high 80s. On the windward side of the high islands and on atolls, the warm temperatures and high humidity are offset by the cooling of the trade winds. On the leeward side and in the interior of the mountainous islands, humidity can make it very uncomfortable. In the highlands of the Melanesian Islands, particularly New Guinea, it can be quite cool, with very rare frost.

While there are no real seasonal changes as in the mid-latitudes, the year can be divided into rainy and dry seasons, especially in the savanna climate. North of the equator, the heaviest rainfall occurs from June to October, and south of the equator, from November to March. In the westernmost Pacific, monsoon winds produce heavy seasonal rains in the western Carolinas, New Guinea, and the Solomon Islands of Melanesia.

The most severe storms in the Pacific are cyclonic storms known as typhoons (hurricanes). They begin in the east and move westward. They can occur at any time of the year, but they are most frequent during the rainy season and cause great destruction and often denude and reshape the configuration of entire atolls.

The coral atolls, volcanic islands, and tropical climate combine to create a setting perceived as exotic by residents of the industrialized nations.

PHYSICAL CHARACTERISTICS OF AUSTRALIA AND NEW ZEALAND

Australia

Most of Australia has an arid (desert or steppe) climate, which limits agricultural activities and settlement, but its large landmass includes five general climatic regions.

The eastern coastal area from Brisbane south to Melbourne has abundant precipitation year-round. The climatic types range from humid subtropical in the Brisbane area, which is a major tourist region similar to Miami, to the marine west coast in the south around Melbourne and Canberra, where the tourist season is shorter. The major highland of Australia, the *Great Dividing Range*, extends along this eastern coast in a belt 100 to 250 miles wide. These rugged but low mountains rarely exceed 3,000 feet in elevation. The highest point, Mount Kosciusko, is at only 7,316 feet, which is also the highest elevation in Australia. It is in this region that the film *Man from Snowy River* was filmed, which increased international tourism interest. It is the eastern and southeastern portions of Australia that are the centers of population for Australia. The two largest cities alone, Sydney and Melbourne, account for 40 percent of the total population of the nation.

The southwestern and southern parts of Australia have a Mediterranean-type climate characterized by hot, dry summers and mild, moist winters, similar to that of Southern California. Since it is in the Southern Hemisphere, the summer dry season is from October to April and the winter wet season is from June to September. This area of Australia is an important producer of grapes and other crops typical of the Mediterranean climates of Southern Europe and Southern California. The combination of summer drought and the region's remoteness from population centers has limited the development of truck farming on a scale similar to that found in Southern California and Southern Europe. The northern coastal regions of Australia have a savanna climate with rainy summers and dry winters. Precipitation exceeds 20 inches throughout most of this northern region, but a dry season and high temperatures handicap agriculture. The northeast region does have the internationally known *Great Barrier Reef*, which has led to the development of one of the better tourist regions of Australia.

The majority of Australia is arid and semiarid. The central portion receives less than 10 inches of rainfall per year and is surrounded by a steppe land that receives 10 to 20 inches. This great, dry interior is referred to by Australians as the Outback and covers more than one-half of the total continent.

New Zealand

New Zealand consists of two large and a number of small islands. North Island contains the majority of the 3.6 million residents of New Zealand, while the larger South Island and the small islands have fewer people. The population is centered on the Canterbury Plain of the east central portion of South Island and the coastal plains and the lower slopes of the uplands of North Island. New Zealand's landforms are dominated by high mountain ranges, particularly the *Southern Alps* of South Island, which reach 12,349 feet at Mt. Cook. The mountainous nature of New Zealand provides for an extensive park system in the Southern Alps and the major tourist attraction of its highest peak, Mt. Cook. With active glaciation and many waterfalls, cirques, matterhorns, and fjords along the southwest coast, it is an area of outstanding scenic beauty.

The climate of New Zealand is a marine west-coast climate, and half of the nation is suitable for intensive grazing. The production of wool and mutton for export to Europe has been the major economic activity from the time of the first European settlements. The island character of New Zealand influences the climate. Although New Zealand lies in latitudes similar to those between San Luis Obispo, California, and the mouth of the Columbia River, its climate is cooler and more moderate because of the surrounding water. Precipitation is well distributed seasonally and varies from more than 120 inches annually along the southwest coast to less than 30 inches on the east-coast lowlands.

Tourism

As indicated, tourism to this region experienced a rapid rate of growth, Table 15–1. However, this rate is misleading since it occurred from a relatively small base that makes small numerical increases result in a large percentage increase. The increase in tourists to the islands of the South and Central Pacific, from 682,629 tourists in 1975 to 2,125,300 in 1993 creates an annual average growth rate of more than 17 percent. The change in Australia/New Zealand from 1.3 million in 1980 to nearly 5.7 million in 1996 represents a growth of over 9 percent per year. While the percentages demonstrate a rapid growth *rate*, this rate will probably slow as the numbers of tourists reach the level that tourism development in the South Pacific islands can support.

The area can be characterized by its isolation, great distances from the major tourist-generating countries of the world, poor airline connections to most of the islands, the low level of both economic and tourism development, and the intervening opportunities of tropical environments closer to the major industrialized countries of North America and West-

Table 15–1   International Tourism to the South Pacific

Country	Number of Visitors (thousands)		1996 Receipts (millions of US $)	1996 Average Expenses per Visit (US $)
	1984	**1996**		
American Samoa	30	18	10	555
Australia	1,429	4,167	8,690	2,085
Cook Islands	31	49	45	918
Fiji	258	325	321	987
Guam	262	1,363	1,415	1,038
New Caledonia	59	91	107	1,176
New Zealand	734	1,529	2,444	1,598
Northern Marianas	163	729	670	919
Papua New Guinea	32	43	62	1,442
Solomon Islands	10	14	6	429
Tahiti (French Polynesia)	122	164	275	1,677
Tonga	16	25	13	520
Vanuatu	18	45	60	1,333
Western Samoa	47	50	23	460

Source: *Yearbook of Tourism Statistics.* Madrid: World Tourism Organization, 1997.

ern Europe. Tourism to the region reflects the combination of distance and cultural linkages with former colonial ties. Tourists will go to the closest place for a tropical experience unless long distances are overcome by cultural linkages between a specific area and its former colonial master. This is reflected in the region of origin of visitors. Most of the visitors are from the more adjacent Pacific region, which in-

Table 15–2   Origin of Visitors to the South Pacific (1995 Market Share)

Country	United States	Asia/Pacific	Europe	Other
American Samoa	48.1	44.9	5.1	1.9
Australia	8.2	67.6	19.9	4.3
Cook Islands	10.8	38.4	38.4	12.4
Fiji	12.5	66.4	17.4	3.7
Guam	4.1	93.7	N/A	2.2
New Caledonia	1.0	62.4	30.8	5.8
New Zealand	10.8	64.5	18.1	6.6
Northern Marianas	14.6	85.0	0.3	0.1
Papua New Guinea	11.5	70.6	15.5	2.4
Solomon Islands	7.9	78.0	12.8	1.3
Tahiti	28.9	21.6	43.1	6.4
Tonga	19.6	61.2	17.6	1.6
Vanuatu	2.6	89.6	5.4	2.4
Western Samoa	9.2	78.2	10.2	2.4
Total for Region	9.2	71.9	14.9	4.0

Source: *Annual Statistical Report.* Pacific Asia Travel Association, 1995.

cludes Asia and Southeast Asia. The three major origin countries of Oceania are the industrialized countries of Australia, New Zealand, and Japan, Table 15–2.

South Pacific

Tourism Characteristics

The perception of the South Pacific by the residents of the industrialized world is of islands that are of extraordinary and exotic natural beauty with mountains and South Sea vegetation interspersed along the beaches and lagoons. These tropical islands have a pleasant climate, beautiful sunsets, good beaches, and friendly citizens. Europeans also perceive the region as having a variety of South Pacific cultures with many native arts and crafts that are very beautiful and interesting. The perceived characteristics are particularly true for the South Pacific islands. Tourism is viewed by many of the Pacific Island states as an opportunity to reduce their dependency on uncertain aid income. It is estimated that for every 13 international tourists who visit the islands, one full-time tourist job is generated. This would mean that the 2 million visitors to the islands would generate 150,000 jobs or approximately 12 percent of the region's total employment.

The three major origins of tourism to the Pacific Islands are the United States, Japan, and Australia and New Zealand. The Japanese dominate the trade to Guam, Northern Marianas, and New Caledonia; Australia and New Zealand dominate tourism to Fiji, Papua New Guinea, and the Cook Islands. Tahiti receives the largest number of their visitors from the United States, which accounts for 28.2

percent of the total visitors. The percentage of visitors from the United States has declined in the 1990s, largely because of an increased use of more efficient airplanes allowing non-stop flights to Australia and New Zealand from the United States. The second largest group of visitors to Tahiti is from France (24 percent), reflecting its former colonial linkage.

Other than the direct linkages from a few islands, such as Guam, Fiji, and Tahiti, there are poor international connections and even less inter-island transportation. Fewer ships call at most of the islands of the Pacific today than did fifty years ago. Combined with the lack of transportation service is the poor tourist infrastructure. The small size of the islands also provides a less diverse resource base to attract international tourists. The high degree of dependency upon sun-sea-sand created by the tropical environment leaves the region vulnerable to competitive locations that have the same tropical environment but are closer to the major tourist-generating countries of North America and Western Europe.

The average length of stay is relatively long for the islands, with the exception of Guam. The majority of tourists to Guam come from Japan for either a honeymoon or the short traditional vacations taken by the Japanese. The longer length of stay in the rest of the region indicates that most of the islands are major destinations rather than part of a group of islands visited like the Caribbean. A growing trend in the Pacific is the travel in and throughout the region by the Japanese for the purpose of visiting places where either they or relatives were involved in World War II.

Polynesia

Country	Capital	Status	Area in Square Miles	Currency
American Samoa	Pago Pago	Unincorporated United States Territory	76	U.S. $
Cook Islands	Avarua	Self-governing	93	N.Z. $
French Polynesia	Papeete	Territory of France	1,545	C.F.P.
Pitcairn	Adamstown	Dependent of Britain	1.7	N.Z. $
Tonga	Nuku'alofa	Constitutional Monarchy	260	T.P.
Tuvalu	Funafuti	Independent State	10	AS. $
Wallis and Futuna	Mata Utu	Territory of France	48	C.F.P.
Western Samoa	Apia	Independent State	1,141	W.S.T.

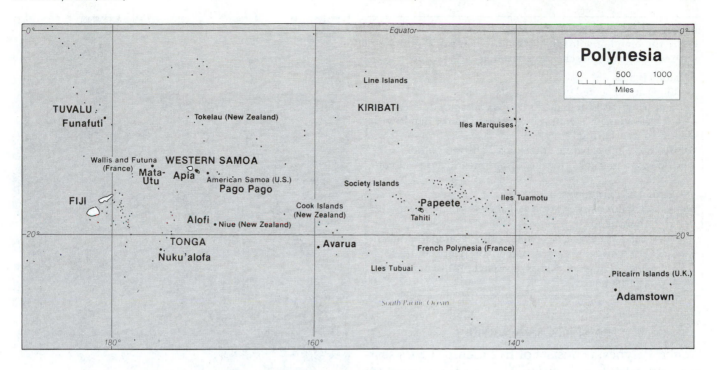

French Polynesia (Tahiti)

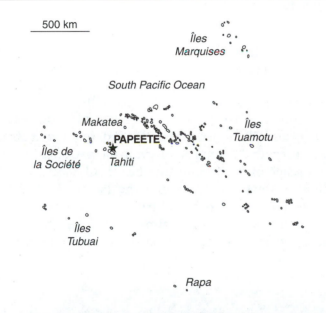

500 km

Îles
Marquises

South Pacific Ocean

Makatea
PAPEETE   Îles
Îles de   Tuamotu
la Société   Tahiti

Îles
Tubuai

Rapa

 ## TRAVEL TIPS

Entry: A visa is not required, but a passport is.

Transportation: International connections are excellent from North America, Australia, New Zealand, and Southeast Asia. Some carriers between North America and Australia and New Zealand stop in Papeete. However, with the introduction of more long-haul aircraft, some carriers are beginning to bypass Tahiti on their way from the West Coast to Australia and New Zealand. Transportation between islands is by air and ship. Local transportation is by "le truck," which carries people throughout Tahiti on a regular schedule.

Shopping: Common items include French perfumes, lingerie, and bathing suits. Tahitian items include tiki effigies and fabrics.

CULTURAL CAPSULE

While the majority of the population is Polynesian (78 percent), there is considerable mixing with *Chinese* or European. About 10 percent of the population is French, and another 12 percent is Chinese. French is the official language and is taught in the schools. Tahitian is a regional language for the Society Islands and is the language for the majority of the people as it is the language spoken in the home. The Chinese speak either the Hakka dialect of Chinese or French. English is understood in tourist areas. Each of the island groups in French Polynesia has its own language. Missionaries brought Christianity in the eighteenth century and currently almost 55 percent are Protestant (Evangelical Church), 30 percent are Roman Catholic, and the other 16 percent are divided between a number of religions including Judaism and Buddhism.

The population of French Polynesia is approximately 200,000 people. Over half (120,000) live on the island of Tahiti in the Society Islands. The capital, Papeete, is the largest city, with over 80,000 people living in the urbanized area. The balance of the population is scattered over five archipelagos that comprise French Polynesia. The Society Islands, the Tuamotu Islands, and the Marquesas Islands are the largest of these. Tahiti, Papeete, and the Society Islands in general are the major tourism destinations. The visitors enjoy the blend of volcanic peaks and lush tropical forests, with white, sandy beaches surrounding each island.

Cultural Hints:

- Tips are expected on the islands.
- Pointing with the index finger is considered rude.
- A handshake is a common greeting. (Shake hands with all in a gathering.)
- Remove shoes before entering a Tahitian home.
- To stop "le truck" (local transportation), hold out your hand.
- Food and eating:
  Wash hands before eating as Tahitians usually eat with their hands.
  Typical food consists of fish, other seafood, chicken, pork, sweet potatoes, breadfruit, fruits, and vegetables. There is a strong French influence in the tourist facilities.

Physical Characteristics

French Polynesia consists of five archipelagoes scattered over 1.5 square miles. Most of the islands are extinct volcanoes with high mountainous formations and deep, well-watered valleys. The islands are surrounded by coral reefs forming sheltered lagoons. The Tuamotu archipelago consists of mostly low, flat atolls. The Tuamotu island groups are not important for tourism. The climate is tropical, but moderate. While the rain falls throughout the year, the rainy season is between November and March.

Tourism Characteristics

French Polynesia has benefitted from its location as a stopover between North America and Australia and New Zealand. However, as indicated, more flights are now going directly between the two regions. While worldwide arrivals have increased, arrivals from North America have declined. Consequently, the Tahiti Tourist Promotion Board has begun a campaign on the West Coast of the United States designed to increase interest in Tahiti.

Tourism Destinations and Attractions

French Polynesia is made up of exotic mountain islands with deep valleys, sandy beaches, and beautiful lagoons. Its capital is on the island of Tahiti in Papeete. The island is highly dependent upon tourism and an annual subsidy from France. Most of the jobs are generated by tourism. Many consider the islands of French Polynesia to be the "Pearl of the Pacific." There are six major islands for tourism in the group: Tahiti, Moorea, Bora Bora, Raiatea, Tahaa, and Huahine. Tahiti and its capital, Papeete, attract the largest number of tourists. Many of the island's sandy beaches consist of broad ex-

Figure 15–2 Tahitian demonstration of coconut extraction

panses of black sand. The island is ringed by a road passing picturesque clusters of native straw- or tin-roofed huts. The interior is a mountain of sheer cliffs, verdant valleys, and plunging waterfalls.

Moorea, a short 90-minute ferry ride from Papeete, is less developed and less populated than Tahiti. It represents the remains of a volcano and offers a lush landscape of mountains and beautiful beaches with many resorts spread around the island. Bora Bora, about 140 miles from Tahiti, is ringed with atolls, turquoise waters, and palm-studded beaches. The flora and fauna of the ocean are spectacular. Bora Bora

Figure 15–3 Tahitian beach hotel

is one of the most picturesque islands of the Pacific. James Michener described it as the most beautiful island in the world. Raiatea, a tall volcanic island of some 6,500 inhabitants, and Tahaa are even less developed than Moorea and they are an underwater delight for fishing and photography. The islands'

mountains and lagoons are most picturesque and further development will likely continue. Huahine, the most isolated and least developed island, is beginning to attract visitors and development. In addition to the volcanic mountains and lagoons, there are many archaeological relics on the islands.

American and Western Samoa

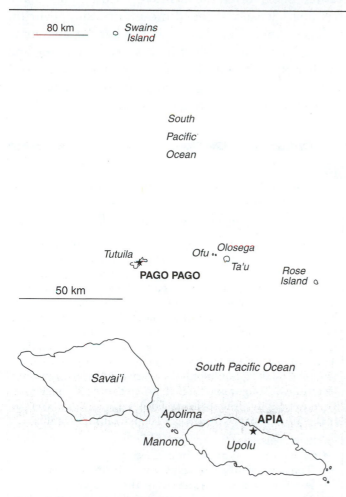

South Pacific Ocean

South Pacific Ocean

CULTURAL CAPSULE

Over 2,000 years ago, waves of Polynesians migrated from Southeast Asia to the Samoan Islands. Samoans are the second largest Polynesian group, after the Maoris of New Zealand, and speak a Polynesian dialect. The majority of the people are ethnic Samoan, of Polynesian descent (90 percent). About 7 percent are *Euronesians*, or people of mixed European and Polynesian descents. Two percent are Caucasian and 2 percent Tongan.

Samoans have tended to retain their traditional ways despite exposure to European influences. Most Samoans live within the traditional social system based on the *aiga*, or extended family group, headed by a *matai*, or chief.

Both nations of Samoa speak Samoan, a language related to Hawaiian and other Polynesian languages. In American Samoa, English is the second official language. Nearly all of the people are Christian, with the Congregational Church representing about half of the population. Forty percent are divided between Roman Catholics and Methodists.

Cultural Hints:
- Greetings are usually formal and effusive.
- A handshake is an acceptable greeting.
- When visiting a home, wait for an invitation to enter from the host and remove shoes.
- Accepting and giving gifts is common when visiting.
- To beckon another person hold the palm face down and wave all fingers.
- Pointing with the index finger is impolite.
- Swaying from side to side indicates contempt or anger.
- Eating and foods:
  Do not eat while walking in the roads and streets.
  Samoan foods are eaten with the fingers.
  Take a small amount of all food offered.
  When offered Kava (the national drink) spill a few drops before drinking.
  Typical foods are bananas, breadfruit, pineapples, papayas, coconuts, copra, yams, taro, pork, chicken, and fish.

 TRAVEL TIPS

Entry: A visa is not required for stays up to 30 days. Proof of onward or return transportation is required.
Transportation: International connections are available (usually weekly) with New Zealand, Tonga, Cook Islands, Fiji, and Vanuatu. Within the countries there is daily air and ferry service. Public transportation is available by bus, taxi, and rental car.
Health: Visitors to Western Samoa should not drink tap water. In American Samoa water is generally safe to drink.
Shopping: Common items include local handwoven tapa cloth, lava-lavas and traditional men's and women's costumes, shells, *laufala* mats and carvings, baskets, bags, and teak bowls.

Physical Characteristics

The island groups of American and Western Samoa are volcanic, providing mountain ranges with some small coral atolls in American Samoa. The climate is pleasant because of trade winds, and has frequent rains falling mostly between December and March.

Tourism Characteristics

Western Samoa receives nearly three times the number of visitors as American Samoa—50,000 to 18,000. The origin of the visitors is different as Western Samoa's market is more regional, while the visitors from the United States dominate travel to American Samoa. The United States accounts for 55.6 percent of the visitors to American Samoa, while the largest percentage of visitors to Western Samoa is from American Samoa, accounting for 36.8 percent of its visitors. Australia and New Zealand generate over 20 percent of the visitors to each of the countries.

Tourism Destinations and Attractions

American and Western Samoa are both Polynesian and are reported to have some of the world's friendliest people. Periodic markets with colorful Samoan handicraft add to the sun-sea-sand attraction. Like the French Polynesia Islands, the natural sights are spectacular. Tourism is centered around the capitals, Pago Pago on American Samoa and Apia on Western Samoa.

Pago Pago is located on a scenic harbor and is the center for exploring the island of Tutuila. This island has lush, densely wooded mountains and beautiful villages. Apia offers both a beach setting and some architecture indicative of its history. The home and tomb of Robert Louis Stevenson are here. Excursions from Apia take visitors through picturesque Samoan villages, delightful beaches, and scenic waterfalls.

Tonga

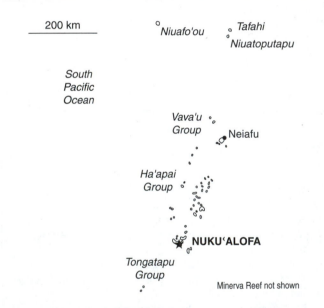

CULTURAL CAPSULE

Nearly two-thirds of the population live on its main island, Tongatapu. Tongans, a Polynesian group with a very small mixture of Melanesian, represent more than 98 percent of the people. The rest are European, mixed European, and other Pacific Islanders. Everyday life is heavily influenced by Polynesian traditions and especially by the Christian faith. For example, all commerce and entertainment activities cease from midnight Saturday until midnight Sunday. The two major religions are the Free Wesleyan (Methodist) Church and the Church of Jesus Christ of Latter-day Saints (Mormons). Tongan and English are both official languages. Government documents are in both languages, but Tongan is the most common language of daily communication.

Cultural Hints:
- A handshake is a common greeting.
- Tongans usually call people by their first names.
- A raised eyebrow means yes or that you agree.
- Do not use hand motions to call anyone other than children.
- A downward wave of the arm means come here.
- Eating and food:
  It is not customary to leave a tip for service.
  Eating and drinking while standing is not appropriate.
  Typical foods include yams, taro leaves, sweet potatoes, cassava, fish, fruits, and pork.

TRAVEL TIPS

Entry: A visa is not required for stays up to 30 days, but a passport is. Proof of onward or return transportation is required.
Transportation: Four international airlines link Tonga with Fiji, New Zealand, and Western Samoa. Public buses and taxis serve the island of Tongatapu but are limited on the other islands. Ferries travel between the island groups.
Health: Tonga is free from most tropical diseases, and drinking water is safe in the capital and in tourist resorts.
Shopping: Common items include woven mats, shells and bamboo curtains, stuffed-animal toys, shell jewelry, slippers, grass skirts, woven hats, tapa cloth, wooden carvings, and other native goods.

Physical Characteristics

Tonga consists of about 150 islands, but only 45 are inhabited. The islands are a combination of extinct volcanoes and raised coral. The climate varies from the cooler, drier southern islands to the wetter, hot, and hurricane-prone northern islands.

Tourism Characteristics, Destinations, and Attractions

Tonga receives from 20,000 to 25,000 visitors per year. Its visitors' market is relatively dispersed, with 21.5 percent from the United States, 44 percent from Australia and New Zealand, and 20 percent from Europe. The proximity of Australia and New Zealand is an important factor in the large percentage of visitors from those two countries. There is a significant Tongan population in the United States that helps account for the strong percentage of visitors from the United States.

As in Samoa, the residents are extremely friendly. Unlike Tahiti, the islands are mostly coral atolls with only a few of volcanic origin. Tonga is still ruled by a native form of government of kings and queens. Of the three major groups, Tonga has the smallest tourism trade. The main island of Tongatapu is the tourist center. However, there are a number of attractions, including a Victorian white-framed royal palace and chapel in Nuku'alofa, famous blow holes at Houma, and scenic areas, such as Hufangalupe with its huge natural coral bridge under which sea water churns, towering cliffs overlooking the sea, and a beautiful beach at the bottom of a steep downhill trail. The ancient remains of the Haamonga trilithon enabled the early people to identify the seasons. It consists of two 40-ton upright coral stones topped by a horizontal connecting stone. The Port of Refuge in the Vava'u Islands is one of the most picturesque harbors in the Pacific.

Cook Islands

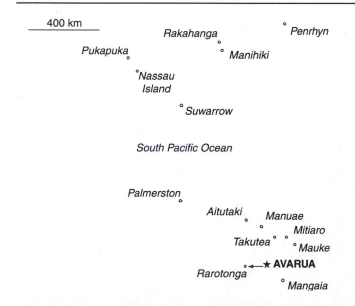

CULTURAL CAPSULE

The population is 82 percent Polynesian, 7.7 percent mixed Polynesian and European, and 7.7 percent Polynesian and other. The majority of the people belong to the Christian Church. English is the official language, and Maori is spoken widely.

Physical Characteristics

The Cook Islands incorporate a variety of geographic settings. The northern atolls are submerged volcanic peaks covered with coral and the steep, raised volcanic peaks of Rarotonga with its narrow, fringing reef. The islands of the northern group, including Manuae and Takutea, are coral atolls, while the remaining six islands of the southern group are mountainous. The climate is warm and humid from December to March. It is milder from April to November.

Tourism Characteristics, Destinations, and Attractions

Only the Cook Islands of the remaining Polynesian islands have any tourist industry of consequence and even then it is small, attracting most of its visitors from Australia and New Zealand (35 percent of visitors). Visitors from the United States and Europe have increased in numbers in the 1990s. As of 1997, only four of the fifteen islands had any kind of tourist facilities. Accommodations are somewhat limited, but locations are increasing. Currently, there are 885 rooms in all hotels, motels, guesthouses, and hostels combined. Like the rest of Polynesia, the Cook Islands are known for their volcanic mountains, beautiful beaches, and crystal-clear lagoons. Tourism centers around the capital, Rarotonga, with a slow-paced, Polynesian, friendly tourist industry. The coral reef and lagoons are centers of interest for snorkeling and scuba diving. The history of the islands can be observed in the historical road of Ara Metua and stone seats near the road. Cook Islands' Christian Church and the Mission House, which is a restored church museum, add to the historical understanding of the Cook Islands.

Other Polynesian Islands

The other Polynesian Islands of Pitcairn, Tuvalu, and Wallis and Futuna have little tourism. They have poor communication and transportation facilities.

Melanesia

Country	Capital	Status	Area in Square Miles	Currency
Fiji	Suva	Independent State	7,055	Fiji $
New Caledonia	Noumea	Territory of France	7,476	C.F.P.
Papua New Guinea	Port Moresby	Independent State	178,258	K.
Solomon Islands	Honiara	Independent State	11,496	S.
Vanuatu	Port-Vila	Independent Republic	4,587	N.F.H.

Of the Melanesian Islands only Fiji, New Caledonia, and the Solomon Islands have a significant number of visitors.

It is a region that has not developed economically and has poor visitor access. Other specific island nations are more exotic in the minds of travellers.

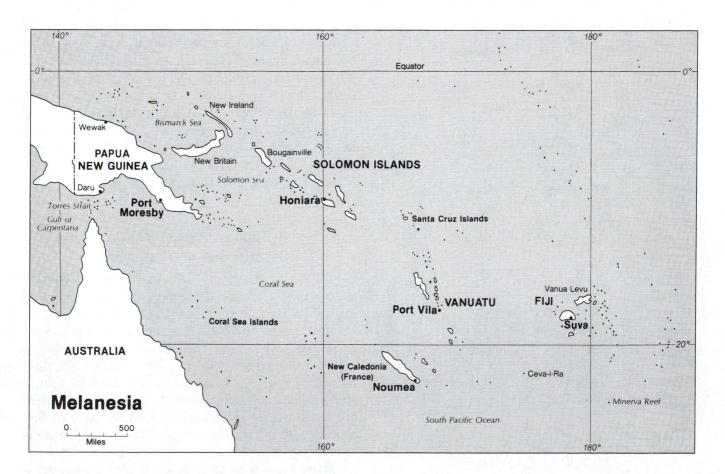

Fiji

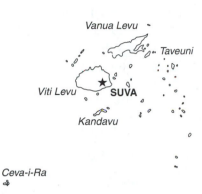

200 km   ⚜ *Rotuma*

South Pacific Ocean

Vanua Levu

Taveuni

Viti Levu ★ **SUVA**

Kandavu

Ceva-i-Ra

✴ TRAVEL TIPS

Entry: A visa is not required for stays up to 4 months. Proof of sufficient funds and onward transportation is required.
Transportation: International connections are good between Fiji and New Zealand, Australia, North and South America, and a number of other Pacific Islands. Fiji has been a stop for some airlines on travel between North America and Australia and New Zealand. Air transportation is available for service between major centers of Fiji. Public transportation is by an open-air bus.
Health: Fiji is free from most tropical diseases, and drinking water is safe in cities and major tourist centers.
Shopping: Common items include tortoiseshell jewelry, Indian silk saris, and an array of spices.

CULTURAL CAPSULE

Indigenous Fijians are a mixture of Polynesian and Melanesian, resulting from the original migrations to the South Pacific many centuries ago. The *Indian* population has grown rapidly since being brought in from India between 1879 and 1916 to work in the sugarcane fields. The rest of the population includes Pacific Islanders, Chinese, Europeans, and other ethnic groups. Fijians are Christian, 78 percent of them Methodist. Roman Catholics account for about 8.5 percent. Indians are either Hindu or Muslim, and the Chinese are either Christian or Buddhist. The Fijians are generous, friendly, and easygoing. They are relaxed and casual. Ethnic tension does exist between Fijians and the Indians. English is the official language. Bauan, a Fijian dialect, is spoken by most indigenous Fijians. Hindustani, a dialect of Hindi, is spoken by many Indians.

Cultural Hints:
- A handshake is a common greeting with visitors.
- Remove shoes when entering a home.
- Eye contact is important when talking with someone.

- To beckon someone hold palm down and wave the fingers.
- It is impolite to touch a Fijian's head.
- Eating and food:
  Tips are not expected, but will be accepted.
  Visitors should accept food that is offered them.
  Typical foods include seafood, coconut milk, chicken, pork, tapioca, and Indian cuisine. Foods are rarely deep fried.

Physical Characteristics

Fiji is composed of some 320 islands of varying size. The larger islands and tourist centers of Viti Levu and Vanua Levu are volcanic mountains offering scenic views of old volcanic landscapes. The climate is tropical with December to April being humid and hot. Destructive hurricanes occur in this period from time to time.

Tourism Characteristics

Fiji vies with Tahiti for the largest tourist industry of the South Pacific Islands. Its location close to Australia and New Zealand provides it with an excellent market, with the two countries accounting for nearly 44 percent of Fiji's visitors. In addition, it is somewhat of a crossroads for visits to other islands of the Pacific. It is a major stopover for airlines from North America to Australia and New Zealand.

Fiji has had some political conflict between the Indians and the Fijians that hurt tourism for a while in the late 1980s. However, the tourism arrivals are again beginning to increase yearly, reaching approximately 325,000 in 1996. The United States accounts for 14.2 percent of the visitors, a decrease from 18 percent in 1986. The change in aircrafts allowing

Figure 15–4 Ceremony in Fijian Cultural Center

Figure 15–5   Sacred temple, Fijian Cultural Center

non-stop trips between the United States and Australia and New Zealand is an important factor in this decline. Most of the American market is comprised of travelers to Australia and New Zealand stopping off en route or returning from these two destinations. Its attractions are similar to other Pacific Islands. It offers sandy coral and volcanic islands. The high number of Asians provides a unique cuisine that combines Chinese and Indian cooking. Tourism is centered in Suva, the capital and point of origin for trips to other Pacific Islands, and the west coast of Fiji, with its excellent water and beaches. A number of cruises depart from Suva to the surrounding islands. There are a number of resorts and two major cultural centers to entertain visitors, figures 15–4 and 15–5. The nightlife is lively and the tropical climate is moderate most of the year.

New Caledonia

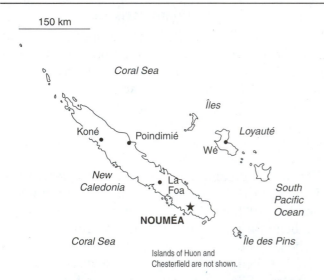

Islands of Huon and Chesterfield are not shown.

Cultural Characteristics

New Caledonia is an overseas territory of France. The ethnic character is 42.5 percent Melanesian, 37.1 percent European, and 8.5 percent Wallisian, with small groups of Polynesian, Indonesian, Vietnamese, and others. The official language is French. There are approximately 28 Melanesian-Polynesian dialects spoken. Sixty percent are Roman Catholic, and 30 percent are Protestant.

Physical Destinations and Characteristics

New Caledonia is a mountainous island with coastal plains. The climate is tropical, with the wet season from December to March. The eastern side is a lush green landscape and the western side an arid coastal plain.

Tourism Characteristics, Destinations, and Attractions

New Caledonia's tourism suffered from political unrest in the 1980s. Tourism declined to only about 60,000 visitors annually, which was only one-half of its peak visitor year in the past. However, like Fiji's tourism, it is again increasing, with 85,000 visitors annually in the 1990s. The two major contributors of tourists to New Caledonia are Japan (27.8 percent) and France (24.9 percent). The United States accounts for only 1.0 percent of the tourists (Pacific Asia Travel Association, 1995). Because of political ties with France, New Caledonia has enjoyed good airline connections to the West. The French flavor is abundant in New Caledonia. Noumea, the capital, is considered the "Paris" of the South Pacific, although in spite of containing one-half of the total population of the nation, it is still a small city. Its streets, nightlife, and foods provide a French flavor set in a South Pacific physical and cultural environment of native handicrafts and art. New Caledonia is surrounded by the second largest coral reef in the world, providing clear blue, fish-filled waters for fishing, swimming, snorkeling, and sailing.

Vanuatu

Cultural Characteristics

The population is 94 percent indigenous Melanesian. Christianity is very important, and the majority are Protestant, belonging to the Anglican Church. A local *pidgin*, Bislama, is the national language. (Pidgin is a language that is simplified and modified through contact with other languages.) English and French are also official languages.

Physical Characteristics

The Vanuatu Islands are rocky and mountainous with only limited plains. The climate can be cool May to September, while in the southern hemisphere summer from December to April, there are frequent heavy storms.

Tourism Characteristics, Destinations, and Attractions

Vanuatu (formerly New Hebrides) and the Solomon Islands have a small regionalized tourist trade.

Vanuatu had only 45,000 tourists in 1996, but this represented a 33 percent increase over 1990. Most of the tourists are from Australia and New Zealand and other South Pacific countries (87 percent). About 20 percent of visitors to Vanuatu are from other South Pacific countries (World Tourism Organization, 1997). There is presently little prospect for the islands being "discovered" because of their isolated location and lack of tourist infrastructure. If development occurs, it has some excellent attractions. The mixture of French and British institutions and some water sports and scenic volcanoes could provide the base for a tourism industry. It has been suggested that bungee jumping is based on the age-old ritual practiced by "land divers" of Vanuatu's Pentecost Island. Villagers collect vines and wind them into long cords, climb high wooden towers, tighten the vines around their ankles, and jump. This practice was adapted on the South Island of New Zealand to become "bungee jumping."

Solomon Islands

Cultural Characteristics

The Solomon Islands are a parliamentary democracy within the British Commonwealth. (A *commonwealth* is a voluntary association of countries.) The population is overwhelmingly Melanesian (93.3 percent), but there are some Polynesians (4 percent) and Micronesians (1.5 percent). In addition, there are small numbers of Europeans and Chinese. Most people reside in widely dispersed settlements along the coasts.

Most Solomon Islanders are Christian, with the Anglican, Roman Catholic, South Seas Evangelical, and Seventh-Day Adventists faiths predominating. Most Solomon Islanders maintain their traditional social structure, which is rooted in family and village life.

Physical Characteristics

The major islands of the Solomons are rugged and mountainous. Many of the outer islands of the group are coral atolls and raised coral reefs. The climate is tropical, with the most comfortable time between May and October when southeast trade winds occur.

Tourism Characteristics, Destinations, and Attractions

The Solomons receive only a few tourists each year. Since 1995, they have averaged 10,000 visitors per year. Most of their visitors are from Australia and New Zealand, with the United States accounting for about 8 percent of the total visitors. The major interests for most are the World War II sites. For example, at Guadalcanal one of the fiercest battles of the war occurred. There are war relics and major battle sites.

Papua New Guinea

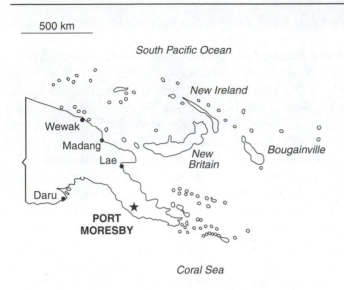

Physical Characteristics

Papua New Guinea has one of the most impressive mountain systems in the world. Parts of the lowland areas are swampy. Other than the Port Moresby area, which is in a rain shadow, the climate is hot and humid. The driest season is between May and October. The monsoon season is between December and March.

Tourism Characteristics, Destinations, and Attractions

Papua New Guinea has a small tourist industry, attracting some 43,000 visitors to the island in 1996. About 48 percent of all visitors are from Australia and New Zealand, with the United States accounting for 10.5 percent of the total visitors. While the country has had visitors for much of the 1900s, the government began to see in the 1980s that tourism might be a significant element in the future.

Papua New Guinea offers vast contrasts in climate, scenery, and terrain. Festivals have become a major attraction. Some of the most popular are at Goroka, Eastern Highlands, and Mountain Hagen. They rotate location from year to year with dancing, feasts, and group singing. World War II cemeteries at Bomana, Lae, and Bita Paka are impressive and serve as reminders of the war. Located along a beach, Port Moresby, the capital, has a colorful market, a town museum, and a nearby stilt village of Hanuobaba. The Rouna Falls and Louki Gorge are nearby. Goroka is the gateway to the highlands for views of scenic tropical forests, sunken gardens, rivers, and native villages with their thatched-roof stilt houses and group singing.

Cultural Characteristics

The indigenous population of Papua New Guinea is extremely heterogeneous. It has several thousand separate communities, most with only a few hundred people. Divided by language, customs, and tradition, some of these communities have engaged in tribal warfare with their neighbors for centuries. Melanesian Pidgin (based on English) and, in Papua, Motu serve as lingua francas. Pidgin has tended to supplant Motu. English is spoken by educated people and in Milne Bay Province. Almost two-thirds of the population is nominally Christian. The two major Christian faiths are Roman Catholic and Lutheran.

The people feel a strong attachment to the land. Most Papua New Guineans still adhere strongly to the traditional social structure, with its roots in family and village life.

Micronesia

Country	Capital	Status	Area in Square Miles	Currency
Guam	Agana	Unincorporated U.S. Territory	21	U.S. $
Kiribati	Tarawa	Independent Republic	378	Aus. $
Kosrae	Kosrae	Federated States of Micronesia	42	U.S. $
Mariana Islands	Saipan	In Association with the U.S.	182	U.S. $
Nauru	Yaren	Independent Republic	8.5	Aus. $
Ponape	Kolonia	Federated States of Micronesia	145	U.S. $
Truk	Moen	Federated States of Micronesia	45.5	U.S. $

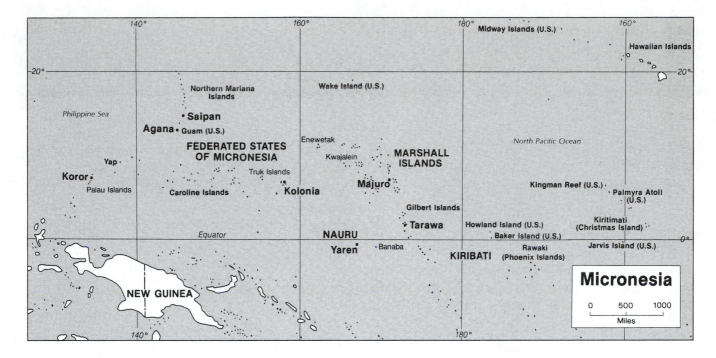

Micronesia, or "little islands," is a group of coral atolls and volcanic islands scattered across the western Pacific. Of the main island groups, the Carolina Islands, the Gilbert Islands, Northern Mariana and Guam, the Marshall Islands, and Nauru, only the Northern Marianas and Guam have a significant tourist industry. Both are commonwealths of the United States, thus enjoying the resources of development from an industrialized country. The bulk of their tourists are from Japan, with Guam receiving nearly 71 percent and Northern Marianas receiving 65 percent of their respective visitors from Japan. Of the Pacific Islands, Guam has the best tourist facilities, with more hotel beds available than any other island, while the Northern Marianas rank fourth in availability of hotel beds in the islands of the Pacific. Both spend more money advertising their islands than any other Pacific islands.

Guam is somewhat special, as it is an important destination for Japanese honeymoons. It has large, well-designed hotels, and its attractions include beautiful beaches that are ideal for water sports such as skindiving and snorkeling on the coral reefs surrounding the island. It has some remarkable rock formations and a spectacular cliff. The Northern Marianas, in addition to their close proximity to Japan, were important during World War II, and there is significant travel for the purpose of visiting war sites and identifying places where relatives died.

Other Pacific Islands

There are a number of Pacific islands not discussed in this book. They have little tourism or facilities to support tourism. Easter Island, however, deserves some mention. Its location and ties to Chile cause some books to list Easter Island as part of South America. It has a small tourist industry, attracted primarily to the giant stone statues carved by early inhabitants of the island.

New Zealand

Physical Characteristics

The islands are predominantly mountainous with some large coastal plains. The climate is temperate, with both sharp regional and altitudinal contrasts.

Tourism Characteristics

Although New Zealand is remote from the leading world population centers, tourism is one of its fastest-growing industries. In 1992 it surpassed the mil-

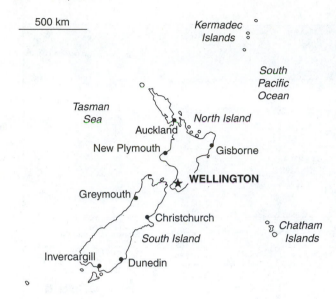

500 km

Kermadec
Islands

South
Pacific
Ocean

Tasman
Sea

North Island
Auckland

New Plymouth

Gisborne

★ WELLINGTON

Greymouth

Christchurch

Chatham
Islands

South Island

Invercargill

Dunedin

Capital: Wellington
Government: Independent State within the British Commonwealth
Size: 103,515 square miles (same as Colorado)
Language: English
Ethnic Division: 88% European, 8.9% Maori, 2.9% Pacific Islander
Religion: 77% Christian, 23% none or unspecified
Tourist Season: Year-round
Peak Tourist Seasons: November and December
Currency: New Zealand dollar

CULTURAL CAPSULE

The majority of the people are of British ancestry. The British and other Europeans comprise about 88 percent of the population. Nine percent are Maori (Polynesian). Close to 3 percent are other Polynesians, mostly from Tonga, Samoa, and the Cook Islands. Auckland has the largest urban Polynesian population in the world. Most of the people live on the North Island. English and Maori are official languages, but almost all Maoris speak English. The population is 81 percent Christian, with the Anglican Church the largest. Other Christian faiths include Presbyterians, Roman Catholics, and Methodists, but about 1 percent of the people are Hindu or Buddhist.

In 1840, the United Kingdom annexed New Zealand and, through the Treaty of Waitangi signed that year with Maori tribes, established British sovereignty. Early European settlers were attracted to New Zealand for lumbering, seal hunting, and whaling.

Cultural Hints:
- A firm handshake with good eye contact is the common greeting.
- After greeting, first names are used frequently.
- Loud speech and excessively demonstrative behavior are inappropriate.
- Cover the mouth when yawning.
- Chewing gum or using a toothpick in public is offensive.
- Eating and food:
  Hands should be kept above the table.
  Ice is not served with drinks. Water is served only on request.
  Tipping is not expected.
  Typical foods are traditionally British, consisting of meat (beef, pork, mutton), potatoes, seafood, vegetables, fruits, sausage, cheese, and ice cream.

lion mark for annual visitors. The government actively promotes tourism, with offices in many of the industrialized nations of the world. North Island and South Island, the major populated areas, are the focus of tourism.

New Zealand's strong ties with the United Kingdom since the early 1800s resulted in colonization by British settlers. This strong tie is expressed in the high numbers of visitors from the United Kingdom arriving for the purpose of visiting friends and relatives, Table 15–3. Nearly one-fourth (23 percent) of all visitors come to New Zealand for this reason.

The average length of stay is long, 21 days, reflecting the long distances as well as the high percentage of people visiting friends and relatives. Arrivals are highest in the summer months (October to April), but those traveling to visit friends and relatives prefer December and January during the holiday period.

The major markets, Table 15–4, are Australia, both because of proximity and cultural linkages; the United States, with about 80 percent from the state of California, where promotional activities are concentrated; the United Kingdom; and Japan. Australia is the most important market for New Zealand, accounting for approximately 30 percent of its visitors.

However, there has been a decline since 1977, when the percentage of visitors from Australia was a little over 55 percent. This reflects the growing interest in New Zealand by tourists from other population and industrial centers of the world. During the 1980s and

Table 15–3 Purposes of Visits to New Zealand (in percentages)

Purpose	1980	1985	1994
Holiday	59.6	57.3	57.9
Visiting Friends and Relatives	21.6	21.4	22.5
Business	10.5	11.4	10.0
Other	13.3	8.9	9.6
Total	100	100	100

Source: *New Zealand Yearbook 1992.* Wellington: Department Statistics.

1990s, growth rates for visitors from Japan and the United States were significantly higher (68 and 43 percent respectively) than from Australia, which had only a 20 percent increase (*New Zealand Official Yearbook, 1995*).

Both Japanese and United States travelers represent larger potential markets than does Australia. The growing Japanese market is a combination of honeymooners and single, female office workers, who are referred to as *office ladies*. Both come in tour groups. The honeymooners tend to prefer a highly organized tour, while the office ladies desire to be slightly more flexible. Both groups stay the shortest period of time (seven days), reflecting one week off from work.

Travelers from the United States stay longer, averaging seventeen days. The primary reason for United States visits to New Zealand is reported to be vacation. Visitors from the United States are more independent than the Japanese, using both tours and fly-drive programs, which are increasingly popular. Visitors from the United Kingdom increased in the 1980s and 1990s, with 50 percent of those arriving coming for the purpose of visiting friends and relatives (*New Zealand Official Yearbook, 1995*). Increased numbers of tourists from the populated, industrial countries of the United States, Japan, and

Table 15–4 International Tourism to New Zealand (in thousands of arrivals)

Country	1982	1987	1995
Australia	214.4	294.6	402.6
Canada	16.6	35.6	29.1
Germany	9.0	16.4	54.9
Japan	25.6	76.2	151.5
United States	73.8	180.4	152.2
Netherlands	5.2	6.3	13.3
Singapore	4.5	14.9	21.3
United Kingdom	N/A	N/A	122.3
Others	86.4	158.9	461.6
Total	472.6	844.3	1,408.8

Source: *Annual Statistical Report.* Pacific Asia Travel Association, 1995

the United Kingdom reflect in part an increased promotional campaign and the adoption of larger aircraft that make travel more comfortable.

The future of tourism to New Zealand is bright as long as the general world economy is strong. The government has increased its promotional budget significantly and has overseas offices in London, Frankfurt, Singapore, Tokyo, Osaka, Vancouver, San Francisco, Los Angeles, New York, Sydney, Perth, Adelaide, and Brisbane. The efforts of the New Zealand Tourist Publicity Department have diversified and broadened the visitor base to New Zealand and improved its image as a destination, accounting for the growing numbers visiting on vacations. The government Development Finance Corporation (DFC), set up to support high-risk ventures, has provided substantial funds to the tourism industry. Tourism follows manufacturing as the second largest sector for investment by the DFC.

Air New Zealand, formerly a state-owned airline, has been sold to a consortium of investors including Qantas, American Airlines, Japan Airlines, and various New Zealand investors. Domestic tourism has been declining, in part due to the stagnant economy plus the large outflow of travel to overseas destinations. A problem has been that many places are closed on Saturday afternoon and Sunday, decreasing the opportunity for day trips for recreation and shopping.

Tourist Destinations and Attractions

There are a wide variety of attractions on New Zealand's two main islands. New Zealand has encouraged ecotourism both for preservation and as a major source of attractiveness for visitors. Also, throughout the country the Maori culture is a major tourist attraction and is well presented for the visitor. The major museum, which is at Auckland, emphasizes Maori history and culture; Rotorua, one of the major destination areas, has a fortified Maori village with displays and a small museum. Hotels throughout the country offer Maori music and dancing.

New Zealand has a diverse, scenic physical environment, from subtropical beaches in the north through the North Island's volcanic and thermal belt, to the impressive Southern Alps and fjords of the South Island. Four major tourism regions can be identified in New Zealand. Auckland is the first region. It is the largest city and has the major international airport for New Zealand. Auckland is built on two hills with two harbors and is surrounded by forests that provide scenic drives through the city and its nearby environs. Auckland has the world's first walk-

Figure 15–6 Agradome, New Zealand

through aquarium. Parnell Village, a delightful collection of restored colonial-style shops, the Victoria Street Market, and various craft markets are all popular shopping attractions for visitors.

To the north of Auckland are the Bay Islands, a subtropical area that is a center for waterspouts. The Bay Islands Maritime and Historic Park administers a number of scenic, historic, and recreational reserves. Across the waters of the bay is Russell, the first capital of New Zealand. It is a charming Victorian town with a preserved waterfront where nineteenth-century buildings have been maintained. In the north of New Zealand, Ninety Mile Beach to Cape Reinga is an area of South Pacific beach with incredible coastal scenery and beautiful sandy beaches. South of Auckland is the village of Waitomo, known for its caves, particularly the Glow Worm Grotto, which is one of the most spectacular cave experiences in the world.

Rotorua on North Island is the largest tourist attraction in New Zealand, attracting approximately 60 percent of all holiday visitors to the country. It is the center of the Maori culture and has a model village, museum, and shop selling Maori handicrafts.

Programs that emphasize the history and music of the Maori are presented daily. Rotorua is a large thermal area, much like Yellowstone Park in the United States, with geysers, boiling mud, hot springs, and steam geysers. A number of other tourist attractions have been developed in the area, such as the sheep demonstration farm, which provides visitors with examples of the various breeds of sheep and their habitats, sheep dogs at work, and shearing demonstrations, Figure 15–6. North of Rotorua is Tauranga on the Bay of Plenty. Tauranga's attractions include a number of pleasant gardens, a historic village, mineral pools, a kiwi-fruit winery, a mission house, and an exotic bird garden.

Wellington, the capital, and its harbor serve as the major link to the South Island. Its attractive harbor, wooden houses, and the surrounding forested hillsides add to unusual museum and botanical gardens to provide an interesting attraction. Within easy driving of Wellington are the mountains and lakes of the North Island. About 130 miles to the north of Wellington, just past Lake Taupo (which is close to Rotorua, New Zealand's largest lake) is Petone, a restored village displaying early settlement in New

Zealand. Lake Taupo is the geographical center of the North Island and is the largest lake in New Zealand. It is extremely popular for trout fishing, and there is no closed fishing season, allowing fishermen to try their luck year-round. Huka Falls, Aratiatia Rapids, Cherry Island, Honey Center, and Acacia Bay Deer Park and Rabbit Ranch are other popular attractions in the Taupo area.

Christchurch on the South Island is considered the most English city outside of England. It is a garden city and has an international airport. Christchurch's similarity to England includes a Gothic cathedral built in the nineteenth century, a stream through town called the Avon, a beach called New Brighton, and a university named Canterbury. Queensland, on the edge of Lake Wakatipu, and the nearby old gold-mining town of Arrowtown are the second most-visited areas in New Zealand. Queensland's year-round appeal includes summer activities associated with the lake and the rugged Remarkable Mountains surrounding the city and lake for winter skiing. Near Queenstown is the historic and picturesque settlement of Arrowtown, where many of the original gold-rush buildings remain.

The southern Alps centered on Mt. Cook, the highest mountain in Australia and New Zealand, offer spectacular alpine scenery, Figure 15–7. Fjordland National Park, with its Norwegian-like fjords, forests, and lakes, is easily accessible. Milford Sound is the favorite destination to enjoy the fjords. The southern lake district, which provides the entrance to Milford Sound, is varied and beautiful. Lake Te Anau is one of the best freshwater fishing areas in the world. From Lake Te Anau to Fjordland, a visitor will

Figure 15–7 Ski planes on Mount Cook

pass through the spectacular forest of Eglinton and Hollyford valleys, past Lakes Gunn and Fergus and Mount Christina through a long man-made tunnel (Homer Tunnel) to a road that drops down through the Cleddau Valley, crossing some 80 bridges with outstanding vistas along the route.

Dunedin is called the "Edinburgh of the South," with such Scottish names as Glenfalloch Gardens, Larnach's Castle, Macadrew's Bay, and Princes Street and a statue of Robert Burns. Dunedin is a city of architectural eye-catchers where spires, turrets, towers, and gables adorn the roofs of many of the gracious stone buildings. Not far from and just north of Dunedin, near the fishing village of Moerake, are the intriguing Moeraki boulders—huge, strange spherically shaped rocks that weigh several tons and are up to 6 yards in circumference.

Australia

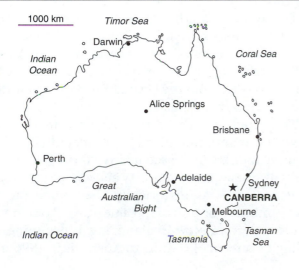

Capital: Canberra
Government: Democratic, federal-state system
Size: 2.9 million square miles (slightly smaller than United States)
Language: English, Native
Ethnic Division: 95% European, 4% Asian, 1% Aboriginal
Religion: 26% Anglican, 26% Roman Catholic
Tourist Season: Year-round
Peak Tourist Season: December
Currency: Australian dollar

TRAVEL TIPS

Entry: Visa is required. Proof of onward or round-trip ticket is required. There is an airport departure tax collected.
Transportation: Excellent international connections exist between Australia and North America, New Zealand, South America, Europe, and other Pacific Asian countries. Internal transportation is excellent by air, rail, and bus. Cities have excellent public transportation.
Health: Australia has no health problems, and no special health precautions are necessary.
Shopping: Common items include opals and gems, sheepskin hats and coats, toy koalas, and boomerangs made by Aborigines.

Physical Characteristics

Most of Australia is a low irregular plateau. The center is generally flat, barren, and arid. The southeastern quarter of the country is a fertile plain. The mountains lie roughly parallel to the east coast, in the center of the continent, and in western Australia.

Australia lies within the zones of prevailing westerly winds and the southeast trades, which provide plentiful rainfall on the coast but a very dry interior. Parts of the north are tropical with high annual rainfall.

Tourism Characteristics

Like New Zealand, Australia has had rapid growth in both tourism numbers and diversity. Australia benefitted from the international yachting competition called the America's Cup held there in 1986, a strong overseas tourism promotion, decreased airfares, the devaluation of the Australian dollar by 30 percent in 1985–1986, and internationally acclaimed Australian films. The "Crocodile Dundee" films have been a promotional boom for Australia. Australia's bicentennial celebration (1988) also focused attention on the country.

Australia is a large country, nearly as large as the United States. It consists of a federation of six states and two territories with dependencies, including Christmas Island, Cocos (Keeling) Islands, Heard and MacDonald Islands, Lord Howe Islands, Macquarie Island, and Norfolk Island. The federal government has long recognized the importance of tourism and early established the Australian Tourist Commission (ATC). The ATC is responsible for coordinating the planning and development of the travel and tourist industry in both the public and private sectors. It has

CULTURAL CAPSULE

Captain Cook claimed Australia for the United Kingdom in 1770. At that time the native population numbered some 300,000 in as many as 500 tribes speaking many different languages. Today the aboriginal population numbers about 230,000 representing about 1.4 percent of the population. Today 95 percent of the people are Caucasian. Sixty percent of them are of Anglo-Celtic heritage. The Asian population represents about 4 percent of the population. In addition the cultural mosaic is enriched by people of Vietnamese, Polynesian, Polish, Lithuanian, Latvia, Italian, Greek, German, French, Estonian, Dutch, and Cambodian ancestry.

Today, tribal aboriginals lead a settled but traditional life in remote areas of northern, central, and western Australia. English is the national language. Only about 50 Aboriginal languages have survived.

Approximately 76 percent are Christians, divided among the Anglicans (24 percent), the Catholics (26 percent), and other denominations. Religion does not play a strong role in Australian life.

Cultural Hints:
- A warm, friendly handshake is a common greeting.
- Exchanging of business cards is common.
- Winking at women is considered inappropriate.
- Cover the mouth when yawning.
- The thumbs-up gesture is considered rude.
- The V with the index and middle finger and palm facing in is vulgar.
- Respect for queues or lines is important.
- Common North American gestures are understood.
- Eating and food:
   In homes a guest receives a plate with food already served on it.
   To beckon the waiter a polite hand wave is used.
   Ask for water if desired.
   The entree is an appetizer rather than a main dish.
   Tipping is common (15 percent).
   Typical foods are fish, mutton, beef, seafood, vegetables, and fruits.

overseas offices in London, Frankfurt, New York, Los Angeles, Tokyo, Singapore, and Wellington.

The average length of stay of visitors is 23 days, largely due to its remoteness from major population and industrial centers of the world. Visiting friends and relatives accounts for nearly 27 percent of all visitors, mostly from the United Kingdom, New Zealand, Oceania, and Canada.

The rapid growth of the Japanese market has moved Japan into first place in number of visitors as Japanese tourists increased nearly 900 percent in the 1980s. Because of its proximity and common culture, New Zealand was historically the source for the largest number of tourists, Table 15–5. Tourism remains high from New Zealand, but is declining, totalling 14 percent of visitors to Australia in 1996. The

Table 15–5 International Tourism To Australia (in thousands of arrivals)

Country	1980	1987	1995
Canada	28.5	52.7	58.4
Germany	35.0	53.3	124.2
Japan	18.8	215.6	782.7
New Zealand	307.1	427.3	538.4
United Kingdom	131.5	198.9	365.3
United States	114.4	309.5	304.9
Other European countries	112.3	198.8	251.5
Other Asian Countries	73.3	113.6	1,087.2
All Others	73.3	113.6	213.2
Totals	904.6	1,784.0	3,725.8

Source: Annual Statistical Report. Pacific Asia Travel Association, 1995.

Figure 15–8 Opera House, Sydney, Australia

decline in percentage from New Zealand is offset by an increase from Asian nations such as Japan, Singapore, Malaysia, and Hong Kong, Europe (other than the United Kingdom), and the United States.

Tourist Destinations and Attractions

The major regions visited by tourists to Australia are shown in Table 15–6.

Sydney and Melbourne, the two largest cities, have international airports and account for 55 percent of all arrivals in the country.

The seasonal shift from the Northern Hemisphere's winter to the Southern Hemisphere's summer is a major attraction. Australia has a variety and diversity of attractions resulting from its size and history. Nature has provided some unique animals, which make the zoos and botanical gardens of Australia most interesting, showing kangaroos, koalas, emus, and platypuses.

Table 15–6 Regions of International Tourist Nights, 1993

Region	Percentage of Tourist Nights in Australia
New South Wales	33
Queensland	26
Victoria	16
Western Australia	12
South Australia	5
Northern Territory	4
Tasmania	2
Australian Capital Territory	2

Source: Bureau of Tourism Research. *International Visitors Survey.* 1993

The southeast of Australia, represented by Sydney and Melbourne, are the two poles of attraction for tourists. Sydney, Australia's oldest city, is attractive, in some ways resembling London, but on a smaller scale. Its Opera House, Figure 15–8, adorns many calendars and pictures promoting Australia. Many of the historical sites have been renovated and redeveloped into excellent tourist markets, such as the Rocks. The Jenolan caves, with ancient aboriginal paintings, and a number of game park reserves are a short distance from Sydney and Melbourne.

Australia's second largest city, and the capital of Victoria, is the original capital, Melbourne. It has stately homes and major sights such as the Victoria Cultural Center, the War Memorial Shrine, Botanical Gardens, and a variety of neighborhoods along the rivers cutting through the city. Many think it is Australia's most beautiful city. Short trips from Melbourne take visitors to old gold-rush towns and Phillip Island, home of penguins and seals.

Between Sydney and Melbourne is Canberra, the capital of Australia. It is a modern planned city focusing on Australia's House of Parliament. Canberra is coiled around a man-made lake and has more than twelve million trees and shrubs lining the avenues, circles, and crescents.

An hour's plane ride south of Melbourne is Hobard, the capital of the island state of Tasmania. Hobard has old, narrow, winding, hilly streets. Tasmania itself is a land of plateaus and precipitous mountains set in a green meadow landscape. It is a treasury of outdoor activities. One can fish for trout in beautiful inland lakes and rivers or for huge bluefin tuna offshore; take a bushwalk in wild and wonderful country, some of which is still unexplored; shoot the

Through Visitors' Eyes

Down Under!

Located almost exactly in the geographical center of Australia, the town of Alice Springs has a population of some 24,000 and is an oasis in the predominantly desertlike land surrounding it on all sides.

Settled in the mid-1860s as a telegraph station along the only route between North and South Australia, it became Alice Springs almost by default: a nearby waterhole was named for Lady Alice Todd, wife of the telegraph superintendent. The waterhole is still there and so are examples of the original structures close by, but times have brought tremendous change to this part of Central Australia.

Today, modern hotels are replacing the rickety old buildings, the unpaved streets when I first visited years ago are now paved, the tourism industry is booming, and oil has even been discovered about 140 miles west of the town.

One out of every four people in Central Australia is an Aborigine descendant of the original Black inhabitants of the area, and these people now are successfully developing their own arts and crafts industry.

Besides paying a visit to the site of the original village and the aforementioned waterhole, I took this opportunity to watch a broadcast from the local "school of the air," where educators reach children in remote areas by radio to conduct classes.

Other attractions here include a base for the Royal Flying Doctor Service, a camel farm where you actually can ride one of these "ships of the desert," and Anzac Hill, where you get a superb sunrise or sunset view of Alice Springs and the surrounding hills.

Alice Springs seems to give me the "mood" of this part of Australia—a speck of civilization in the center of more than one million square miles of harsh, unforgiving land known as the Outback.

Special events have been devised by the townsfolk to keep your interest, including the now famous Henley-on-Todd Regatta on a dry riverbed. In this one, competitors stand within a bottomless boat and hold up the hull as they run against other such "vessels." There are camel races, beer festivals, rodeos, balloon flights, and Aboriginal bush dances—something for one and all.

Oh yes, if all this fails, there are some good shops in the downtown area!

But for me, the great attraction of this entire area lies about 275 miles southwest of Alice Springs: it's the gigantic mountain of stone known as Ayers Rock, which rises suddenly from the desert floor like some monolithic tumor.

As tall as the Empire State Building and some five miles in circumference, this geological wonder is sacred to the Aborigine and has been the focus of awe and attention since its discovery. At sunrise or sunset, visitors stand or sit and watch it change color with the first or last light of day ... and more than 185,000 folks did just that last year!

Up until 1946, only 24 hardy climbers had managed to scale this monolith to the top ... and nineteen have died since in similar tries. Today thanks to heavy chain-rope attached to the smooth surface in places, the climb is less formidable but still quite difficult, with many having to be rescued or assisted to safety....

Several miles from famous Ayers Rock in the Australian Outback, a new resort area has sprung up to accommodate the thousands of visitors who come to the center of this country to view—and perhaps climb—this giant mountain of stone.

Yulara Resort, an oasis of comfort in this harsh land, has several hotels and campgrounds plus most of the modern-day amenities to make a stopover quite comfortable. I recently stayed at the Four Seasons Hotel, which can match most Stateside accommodations for the above, although the staff left something to be desired in the way of service and friendliness.

No matter, I was here to see and climb Ayers Rock and to view the magnificent Olgas, a nearby clump of smooth-topped redrock mountains that somehow seemed to resemble a large herd of elephants in retreat. Both of these incredible sights are a must for any visitor to Australia and somehow manage to put such a gigantic and contrasting land into proper perspective. It is as if they have been set

continues

continued

here to remind us that nature—not man—is in control of this area of the world....

In Aboriginal lore, Ayers Rock is named Uluru and carries a heavy spiritual as well as physical impact.

Bus tours to Ayers Rock and the Olgas are available at any of the hotels in Yulara and offer several different possibilities, including a descriptive tour of some of the caves in this mountain of stone plus the accompanying Aboriginal folklore. You also may get a closer look at the Olgas by hiking down Mt. Olga Gorge, a fascinating cleft through towering borders of red-colored mountains of rock.

Whatever you do, take at least a day or more to explore this part of Australia as fully as you can. It will provide memories that will endure long after you have returned home.

The Down Under wonder is a fascinating destination, from its sunny beaches and the Great Barrier Reef to tropical rainforests, strange animals, and the desolate Outback. You really do owe it to yourself to savor the experience of a visit.

For me, it's like a step back in time to the frontier days of America. With all the comforts of the present day. Truly, this is a land of great adventure—one of the last frontiers.

Source: Carter Clements, "Dead Center Down Under." Sacramento, *California International Travel News*, Feb. 1987, pp. 46–47.

---

whitewater rapids in a canoe; or brave Tasmania's challenging peaks and ski.

Queensland has Australia's greatest attraction, the Great Barrier Reef, stretching for 1,200 miles along the eastern coast. A series of islands and cities provide excellent access to the spectacular underwater views of the Great Barrier Reef. The Great Barrier Reef is made up of some 2,500 individual coral reefs ranging in size from less than two acres to 100 square kilometers. There is a rich and diverse ecosystem along the reef, containing more than 300 species of hard corals and 1,500 species of fish. It is also rich in birdlife. In 1975, the Great Barrier Reef Marine Park was created to protect the future of the park while providing for local and tourist use.

Located on the east coast just south of Brisbane, with easy access to the population centers of Sydney and Brisbane, Queensland has the greatest tourist development in such towns as the Gold Coast and the Sunshine Coast. It is comparable to the coastal resort developments in Spain and could be similar to Waikiki Beach in Hawaii. The Gold Coast is a strip of white sandy beach nineteen miles long and has a number of major attractions such as Dreamworld and Sea World. Surfer's Paradise is a must for those who want to challenge the waves. To the north, Cairns has a tropical environment, and the government has established an international airport in order to draw more visitors to the region.

South of Alice Springs in the Northern Territory is the memorable Ayers Rock, Figure 15–9, which is part of Uluru National Park. Uluru National Park includes both Ayers Rock and Mount Olga. They are famous peaks of an otherwise buried mountain range and dominate an open landscape of sandplains, dunes, and Mulga woodland. Both are colorful and impressive formations that, together with the surrounding country, have always held great significance for Aborigines. The rock is a sacred mountain for the Aborigines. It has been given back to the Aborigines, but is leased to the park service for maintenance. In addition to the area's natural beauty, visitors can see sites, rock formations, and paintings that form an important part of Central Australian Aboriginal mythology. Alice Springs is an oasis in the remote Outback, accounting for the low number of tourists to the Northern Territory.

Darwin, the Northern Territory capital, is the base for either short or extended tours into Kakadu National Park, a vast wilderness east of Darwin that abounds with wildlife and Aboriginal rock paintings unique to Australia.

Adelaide, the capital of South Australia, is the center of the country's wine-making industry due to its Mediterranean climate. Adelaide is near numerous nature reserves and opal mines, which provide nice day trips from the city. Adelaide has wide European-style boulevards, magnificent green parklands, and a number of interesting buildings such as the Parliament House, Constitution Museum, and Government House.

Perth in Western Australia has become well known because of the America's Cup. Its climate

Figure 15–9   Ayers Rock, Australia

is similar to that of Southern California, and it is the center of agriculture, mining, and industry for Western Australia. Perth is a delightful city for strolling and people watching. London Court, a sixteenth-century Tudor-style arcade, is a reminder of England. The Western Australia Museum includes a fine Aboriginal gallery as well as vintage cars, World War II memorabilia, meteorites, and the skeleton of a huge blue whale. While it offers a far better climate, water sports, and a large wildlife reserve within the city limits, its distance from population centers and major international airports handicap its tourist industry.

POLYNESIA

DAY 1 LOS ANGELES–SUVA

Depart Los Angeles for a South Pacific Odyssey.

DAY 2 SUVA

Arrive in Suva, the capital of the Fiji Islands. The evening can be spent at the nightclubs such as the Golden Dragon, Lucky Eddie's, and Rockefeller's, dancing the night away.

DAY 3 SUVA

This morning we will see the South Sea port at Viti Le'vui, Suva. Fast-cruising liners lie alongside trading schooners busy unloading bananas and other products. This port is very fast-paced and interesting to observe. This afternoon, we will visit the Fijian Cultural Center, after which you can spend the remainder of the day swimming, sunbathing, and scuba diving on the beach, with the temperature in the low 80s. The beaches are like a tropical paradise. The palms, reefs, sand, lagoons, quiet surf, and friendly people make up the relaxing atmosphere. After getting plenty of sun, we are off to shop in Suva's largest department stores. In the evening, we will be entertained while we watch a unique Fijian Indian religious firewalking activity held in the temples. Then we will attend a luau and enjoy delicious food and entertainment. Before retiring for the evening, a walk along the beach listening to flower-covered islanders strum their guitars and sing songs of the islands will end a memorable day.

DAY 4 SUVA–VANUA–LEVU– TAVENUI

Visit Vanua Levu. This is the second largest of the Fijian Islands, a 45-minute flight from Suva. We will indulge in water sports, including spear and big game fishing, visit sugarcane and copra plantations, and enjoy a tropical feast. Southeast of Vanua Levu is the beautiful island of Taveuni. We will sightsee and admire its volcanic cones and tropical plantations and fruits. West of both Viti Levu and Vanau Levu there are more volcanic islands, with many beaches containing beautiful rare shells. This evening we will attend a folk singing and dancing program.

DAY 5 TAHITI

We will fly to Tahiti. Tahiti is the main island in French Polynesia and the site of Papeete, the administrative capital and largest city. Papeete is a sandy banana-palm town. It's what a tropical town should look like. In the afternoon, we will visit such sites as the Tiare Hotel, where Lovaina was an "uncrowned queen"; Motu Uta, the tiny island in the lagoon where the old kings held their revel; vanilla plantations; and the Chinese shrine and village. The late afternoon can be spent on the coral-free sea beach, Arue. This is an undeveloped Waikiki-type beach. There is no coral on the smooth sand floor, and the waves come in at high tide in low swells. Later in the evening, around midnight, Papeete comes alive; for the adventuresome a trip to Lafayette, where the dancing is wild, will be in order.

DAY 6 TAHITI–MOOREA

A day free to visit Moorea. This volcanic island has spectacular peaks and the famous double bays—Cook's and Opanohou. Moorea is the closest island to Tahiti and easy to reach by ferry or plane. It is easy to rent a motor bike or a small jeep and ride around the island. You will observe the lush mountain valleys, coffee plantations, and pineapple fields. The Tahitian village portrays the life and customs of the people. Stops along the road to snorkel and swim in the clear multicolored lagoons combine with shopping to make the day most enjoyable.

DAY 7 TAHITI–BORA BORA

On to Bora Bora. This high volcanic island is surrounded by a calm turquoise lagoon. Scattered along the reef are small, sandy islets in which we can comb the beaches. The small villages along the road that encircle the island are ideal for a jeep tour. Late in the afternoon, we will visit the lagoonarium and take a coral-watching trip in a glass-bottomed boat.

DAY 8 BORA BORA–UNITED STATES

Return home to the states, after an enjoyable vacation in the Pacific islands.

REVIEW QUESTIONS

1. Describe the three major cultural groups of the Pacific Islands.
2. Why is tourism to the Pacific relatively small?
3. On which island groups in the South Pacific is tourism the most developed? How do you explain this?
4. On which island groups in the South Pacific is tourism the least developed? Why?
5. Describe the physical characteristics of the two different types of islands in the South Pacific.
6. Where are the four major market regions of visitors to Australia? Why?
7. What are the major categories of visitors to the South Pacific from Japan?
8. Where are the major population centers of Australia? Why?
9. Discuss the Aborigines of Australia and the Maoris of New Zealand and their importance to the tourist industry of their respective countries.
10. What impact have the Chinese and Indians had on the islands of the Pacific?

GEOGRAPHY AND TOURISM
Internet Travel Resources

General Information

Embassy Information	http://www.embassy.org/embassies/eep-1000.html Links to press and culture, education, commerce and trade, consular, travel and tourism, and employment
Embassies in Washington, D.C.	http://www.embassy.org/embassies/eep-1100.html Lists all embassies in Washington, D.C., with addresses
United States State Department Travel Warnings and Consular Information	http://www.stolaf.edu/network/travel-advisories.html Lists current travel warnings with links to Center for Disease Control, World Tourist, World-Wide Travel Mall, CIA Publications (World Fact Book), World Flags, Stanford Travel Medicine Service
Currency Exchange	http://cnnfn.com/markets/currencies.html http://www.dynamid-llc.com/demos/currency.cgi Allows you to put in United States dollars and calculates the exchange http://www.ino.com/cgi_bin/qw?exch=forex Global foreign exchange http://www.webcom.com/one/world Foreign currency exchange rates, hotels, tips, and planning for travelers, visas, tourism offices, worldwide ATM locations
International Driving Permits	http://www.driving-permit.com/ http://www.europebycar.com/EAApermits.html Application for translation of permit
Visas	http://www.webcom.com/one/world Foreign currency exchange rates, hotels, tips, and planning for travelers, visas, tourism offices, worldwide ATM locations http://www.visaservices.com/visa-info.html Information on Australian visas, Canadian passports, Russian visas, Malaysia, Republic of Niger, Philippines http://nearnet.gnn.com/gnn/metal/travel/res/visa.html GNN TCInternet Resources: Visas, Passports, and Entry requirements; Links to embassy page, foreign entry requirements, HIV testing requirements, apply for your United States passport, the Office of Overseas Citizens Services

General Tourism

Virtual Tourist	http://www.vtourist.com/vt/
City.Net	http://www.city.net
	Comprehensive guide to communities around the world updated daily for information on travel, entertainment, and local business plus government and community services.
World Travel Resource Registry	http://worldhotel.com/
	Lists cruise, consolidated, air, cars, trains, airlines, hotel specials, supplier specials, local excursions, tour operators, destination information, maps, agent referral, ASTA, Mesigure Group, business travelers, Airline Res Systems, weather, currency rates, register unlisted hotels, interesting travel sites
Worldwide Brochures	http://www.wwb.com
	Travel brochure directory listing more than 10,000 travel maps, guides, and brochures
Travel and Leisure	http://pathfinder.com/Travel/TL
	Listing weather guides, travel offices, best deals
	http://travelsearch.com
Yahoo subdirectory with travel information	http://www.yahoo.com/Recreation/Travel
TravelFile	http://www.travelfile.com/
	A series of searchable directories containing over 100,000 files of information on travel suppliers, tourism offices, attractions, and events for destinations worldwide
Airline Tickets Wholesale	http://www.traveldiscounts.com/
	Money-saving tips
ATR Travel Resource	http://www.inetbiz.com/atrtravl/home.html
	Currently under construction but will offer a complete guide to travel accommodations including bed & breakfasts, hotels, motels, condos, inns, and resorts
State and Regional Travel Bureaus	http://travelsearch.com/tourism.htm
Yahoo subdirectory	http://www.yahoo.com/Regional/Countries/Russia/Travel
	Links to Russia
Travelnet	http://www.traveler.net
MapQuest	http://www.mapquest.com
Intellicast	http://www.intellicast.com
Hotels and Travel on the net	http://www.hotelstravel.com/
Internet Guide to Bed and Breakfasts	http://www.uiltranet.com/inns/
A tour of the United States Tourism Site on Web	http://www.visitcenter.com/
State-specific information	http://www.yahoo.com/recreation/travel/regional/ U_S_States/State_name
	Two-word state names must have an underline between words
State and Regional Bureaus in the United States	http://travelsearch.com/tourism.htm
These sites are accessed through http://www.astor.ru/links.html	http://www.a1co.com
	Find 13 specialized travel-related Internet directories and search engines
	http://www.ukshops.co.uk:8000/thedoor/subjects/Travel_Tourism_and_Regional_Information/ ghindex.html
	The European Directory links to European travel-related servers classified by countries
	http://www.mckinley.com/browse_bd.cgi?Travel
	Travel and Tourism page on the Magellan Internet Guide. Lots of travel links classified into several dozen sections
	http://thehugelist.com/travel.shtml
	Travel resources section of "The Huge List." Contains links to Web sites of travel agencies, airlines, regional information, sites, etc.

	http://www.stratpub.com/shoewww.html
	Contains links to hundreds of travel-related servers all over the world. Links are classified into various sections such as accessories, accommodations, cities, countries, organizations, publications, sights to see, tours, transportation, etc.
	http://www.travelhub.com
	Contains links to searchable databases of travel resources on the Internet, travel-related conferences, mailing lists, etc.
Miscellaneous	http://www.yahoo.com/business_and_economy/companies/travel/membership_clubs/elite_traveller/
	This address gives you access to sites for promotions on all aspects of travel and entertainment, savings on accommodations, airfares, cruises, and car rental. It also gives you access to Team Elite Travel while providing you with hotel and airline reservations, car rentals to cruiseships.

Rental Car

Major United States Cities	http://www.bnm.com/rcar.htm
United States, Canada, Caribbean, Greece	http://www.acerentacar.com/
Italy/Worldwide	http://www.dollaroexpress.it/
	Rent a car without a driver
Israel	http://www.eldan.co.il/
Europe	http://www.europcar.it/
Europe, Hawaii, Australia, New Zealand, South Africa	http://www.holauto.com/holiday
Queensland, Australia	http://www.squirrel.com.au/roadsters
Asia, India, Indonesia, Korea, Philippines, Malaysia, Singapore, Thailand	http://www.singapore.com/companies/hertz
Alamo, Rent-a-Car, Avis, Eurodollar, Hertz worldwide	http://www.hk.linkage.net/markets/abt/others/car-hire.html

Hotels

Hotel Express International	http://www.cc.utah.edu/~dmd4244/traveldirect.html
	Hotel accommodations, car rentals, cruises, international and domestic airfare discounts, European Travel, vacation packages
Various	Airfare programs, auto rental in Europe, train travel in Europe: Channel Tunnel, Eurostart, London/Paris and London/Brussels

Countries and Regions

For all countries (select any country and receive travel info)	http://www.yahoo.com/Recreation/Travel/Regional/Countries

North America

Note: A general site address for most states is: http://www.yahoo.com/recreation/travel/regional/U_S_States/State_name (two-word state names must have an underline between words.)

Alabama	http://touristguide.com/b&b/bbhome.html
	http://www.bcvb.org/
	http://www.gulfshores.com/
Alaska	http://www.travelsource.com/rafting/adventurealaska.html
	http://www.alaskainfo.org/
	http://www.alaska.net/~denst1/DST.home.html
	http://www.alaska.net/~guidesak/
	http://www.gorp.com/akdisc.htm
Arizona	http://www.amdest.com/
	http://www.thecanyon.com/
	http://www.thetraveller.com/thetraveller/travellerframes.html
	http://www.arizonaguide.com/
	http://www.imsystem.com/arb/index.htm

Arkansas	http://www.state.ar.us
California	http://www.inetbiz.com/atrtravl/home.html
	http://www.research.digital.com/SRC/virtual-tourist/California.html
	http://travelsearch.com/ca.htm
	http://gocalif.ca.gov:8000/
Canada	http://www.cs.cmu.edu/Web/Unofficial/Canadiana/README.html
	http://www.alloutdoors.com/allcanada/
	http://www.yahoo.com/Regional/Countries/Canada/Travel
	http://www.yahoo.com/Regional/Countries/Canada/
	http://info.ic.gc.ca/Tourism/index-e.html
	http://ncf.carleton.ca/freeport/government/federal/passport/menu
	http://www.inovatect.com/bb/
	Bed and Breakfasts in Canada, United States, and Hawaii
Colorado	http://www.cdiguide.com/CO/coguide.html/
	http://www.databahn.net/bbia (by city)
	http://www.toski.com/
	http://www.netway.net/cofactbook/leisure.html
Connecticut	http://ctguide.atlantic.com/vacguide
	gopher://gopher.uconn.edu/11/connmenu/vacguide
Delaware	http://www.dmv.com/business/southdel/
	http://www.beach-net.com/
Florida	http://www.florida.com/florida.htm
	http://www.florida.com/
	http://florida.com/attractions/
Georgia	http://www.gomm.com/
	http://www.cdiguide.com/GA/gaguide.html
Hawaii	gopher://gopher.hawaii.edu/11/Town
	http://www.yahoo.com/Recreation/travel/regional/U_S_States/Hawaii/
Idaho	http://www.state.id.us/
Illinois	http://www.enjoyillinois.com/scripts/home.4ge
Indiana	http://www.yahoo.com/Regional/U_S_States/Indiana/Travel/
Iowa	http://www.okoboji.com/
	http://www.netins.net/showcase/villages/
	http://www.jeonet.com/amanas/
Kansas	http://www.yahoo.com/Regional/U_S_States/Kansas
Kentucky	http://www.nkycvb.com/
	http://.www.state.ky.us/tour/tour.htm
Louisiana	http://www.yahoo.com/Recreation/Travel/Regional/U_S_States/Louisiana
Maine	http://www.maineguide.com/travel/travel.html
	http://www.state.me.us/decd/tour/
	http://www.sourcemaine.com/TravelMaine/
Maryland	http://www.beach-net.com/
	http://www.covesoft.com/Eastern
Massachusetts	http://www.masstourist.com/
	http://www.magnet.state.ma.us/travel/travel.html
	http://ftp.std.com/NE/masstravel.html
Michigan	http://www.yahoo.com/Regional/U_S_States/Michigan/Travel/
Minnesota	http://www.wcco.com/travel/
Mississippi	http://www.southernnet.com/vicksburg/cvb
	http://www.gulf-coast.com/
Missouri	http://www.bransonshuttle.com/
	http://www.gxl.com/~mapmen/
Montana	http://www.marsweb.com/tourmontana/index.htm
	http://www.mcn.net/~glenarrow/glenaro1.htm
Nebraska	http://www.lincoln.org/cvb/

	http://www.ded.state.ne.us/tourism.html
Nevada	http://www.liberty.com/home/global/tforum.htm
	http://www.travelnevada.com/
New Hampshire	http://www.visitnh.gov/
	http://www.ramjack.com/intouch/
	http://newww.com/
	http://ftp.std.com/NE/nh.html
New Jersey	http://www.yahoo.com/Regional/U_S_States/New_Jersey
New Mexico	http://www.nets.com/newmextourism/
	http://www.viva.com/
New York	http://www.Fingerlakes.com/welcome.html
	http://www1.mhv.net/~intercity/hvmonth.htm
	http://www.ithaca.ny.us/Commerce/
	http://iloveny.state.ny.us/
North Carolina	http://www.hickory.nc.us/ncnetworks/clt-intr.html
	http://www.atomic.net/~awb/vnc.htm
North Dakota	http://usacitylink.com//nd.html
Ohio	http://go-explore.com/Ohio
	http://www.tw-rec-resorts.com/
	http://www.travel.state.oh.us/
Oklahoma	http://www.oktour.com/
Oregon	http://sharplink.com/touristinfo/
	http://www.teleport.com/~coastal/
	http://www.orst.edu/~glasers/travel.htm
Pennsylvania	http://gettysburg.welcome.com/
	http://www.libertynet.org/phila-visitor
Rhode Island	http://www.ids.net/ri/ritour.html
	http://www.ultranet.com/block-island/
South Carolina	http://www.sccsi.com/sc/
	http://www.palmetto.com/Charleston/
South Dakota	http://www.state.sd.us/state/executive/tourism/tourism.html
	http://www.state.sd.us/state/executive/tourism/grptour/grptour.htm
Tennessee	http://www.smoky-mtns.com/
Texas	http://travel.org/texas.html
	http://www.whitehawk.com/vacation/tx
	http://www.yahoo.com/Regional/U_S_States/Texas/Travel
Utah	http://www.awbeck.com/utah/main.html
	http://www.infowest.com
Vermont	http://www.pbpub.com/
Virginia	http://www.virginia.org/cgi-bin/visitva/tourism/welcome
	http://www.vawine.com/
	http://www.history.org/twentieth_century/index.html
Washington	http://www.nwdestinations.com/
	http://www.metropo.com/seattle/seattle.html
	http://www.travel-in-wa.com/
	http://www.tourism.wa.gov/
West Virginia	http://wvweb.com/www/wheeling.html
	http://www.uconnect.com/mbc_cvb/
Wisconsin	http://badger.state.wi.us/agencies/tourism
	http://www.wistravel.com/index2.html
Wyoming	http://www.yahoo.com/Recreation/Travel/Regional/U_S_States/Wyoming

Note: A general site address for most countries worldwide is: http://www.lonelyplanet.com/dest/dest.htm

CENTRAL AMERICA

Belize	http://www.belize.com/
Central America	http://www.greenarrow.com/welcome.htm
Costa Rica	http://www.costa-rica.com/Costa
Mexico	http://www.wotw.com/wow/mexico/mexico.html
Nicaragua	http://www.lonelyplanet.com/dest/cam/nic.htm
Panama	http://www.iaehv.nl/users/grimaldo/panama.html

CARIBBEAN

Anguilla	http://galaxy.cau/edu/Anguilla/anguilla.html
Antigua and Barbuda	http://www.interlog.com/~observer/antigua/hcontents.html
Aruba	http://www.olmco.com/aruba/
Barbados	http://www.caribsurf.com/barbados/bar_home.html
Bequia Island	http://www.freenet.hamilton.on.ca/~aa462/bequia.html
Bermuda	http://microstate.com/bermuda/
Bonaire	http://www.interknowledge.com/bonaire/index.html
Caribbean	http://www.freenet.hamilton.on.ca/~aa462/carib.html
	http://www.inetspecialists.com/cbmall/
	Weather information, travel information
Cayman Islands	http://www.wweb.com/cayman
Dominican Republic	http://www.qqq.com/dominican/index.html
Grenada	http://watt.seas.virginia.edu/~krfzw/grenada.html
Haiti	http://www.primenet.com/~rafreid
Jamaica	http://www.webcom.com/~travel/jam1html
Netherlands Antilles	http://www.antilnet.com/
St. Maarten	http://199.170.0.111/
St. Vincent	http://www.ualberta.ca/~amitchel/stvg.html
The Bahamas	http://www.bahamas-mon.com/
Turks and Caicos	http://www.fortmyers.com/caicos.htm
United States Virgin Islands	http://www.usvi.net/

SOUTH AMERICA

Argentina	http://www.lonelyplanet.com/dest/sam/argie.htm
Bolivia	http://www.lonelyplanet.com/dest/sam/bolivia.htm
Brazil	http://darkwing.uoregon.edu/~sergio/brasil.html
Chile	http://www.lonelyplanet.com.au/dest/sam/chile.htm
Colombia	http://www.univalle.edu.co/~servinfo/colombia.sp.html
Ecuador	http://homepage.seas.upenn.edu/~leer/ecuador
French Guiana	http://www.lonelyplanet.com.au/dest/sam/fgu.htm
Latin America	http://lanic.utexas.edu/
Peru	http://www.rcp.net.pe/index-ing.html (Spanish only)
Suriname	http://www.surinam.net
Uruguay	http://bilbo.edu.uy/uruguay.htm
Venezuela	http://venezuela.mit.edu/embassy/informac/index.html

WESTERN EUROPE

Austria	http://austria-info.at/
Belgium	http://www.plug-in.be/plugin/

Europe (in general)	ftp://rtfm.mit.edu/pub/usenet-by-hierarchy/rec/travel/
	http://www.iol.ie/~discover/europe.htm
	Information and travel planning aids, i.e., European rail schedules, subway navigator, money FAQ, airlines, health information, CIA factbook, Europay (European Debit Card, Eurocheque, Euro ATM cards), current weather, currency rates, city.net
	http://www.iol.ie/~discover/europe4.html
	European Tourist Information Center by country
France	http://www.france.com/fracescape/top.html
Germany	http://www.webfoot.com/travel/guides/germany/germany.html
Iceland	http://www.primenet.com/~peetah/iceland/IsMenu.html
Ireland	http://ireland.iol.ie/~discover/
	Interactive travel guide to Ireland
	http://www.bess.tcd.ie/ireland.html
Luxembourg	http://rzstud1.uni-karlsruhe.de/~ujiw/lx.html
Monaco	http://www.monaco.mc/
Netherlands	http://www.nbt.nl/holland/home.htm
Scotland	http://www.geo.ed.ac.uk/home/scotland/scotland.html
Switzerland	http://www.swissinfo.ch/swissinfo/general.html
United Kingdom	http://www.neosoft.com/~dlgates/uk/ukgeneral.html?travel_k

NORTHERN EUROPE

Denmark	http://www.sima.dk/denmark/
Finland	http://www.travel.fi/
Norway	http://www.intech.no/travel/travel1.html
Sweden	http://www.it-kompetens.se/swedish/sverunt.html

SOUTHERN EUROPE

Andorra	http://www.xmission.com/~dderhak/andorra.htm
Cyprus	http://force.stwing.upenn.edu:8001/~durduran/cyprus.shtml
Greece	http://www.cis.ohio-state.edu/hypertext/faq/usenet/greek-faq/tourism/faq.html
Italy	http://www.webfoot.com/travel/guides/italy/italy.html
Spain	http://www.docuweb.ca/SiSpan/

CENTRAL EUROPE AND THE BALKAN STATES

Albania	http://www.ios.com/~ulpiana/Albanian/index.html
Bulgaria	http://www.cs.columbia.edu/~radev/cgi-bin/logfaq.cgi
Croatia	http://tjev.tel.etf.hr/hrvatska/HR.html
Czech Republic	http://www.muselik.com/czech/frame.html
Hungary	http://www.hungary.com/tourinform/
Macedonia	http://asudesign.eas.asu.edu/places/Macedonia/republic/
Poland	http://ciesin.ci.uw.edu.pl/poland/orbis/poland.htm
Romania	http://www.qqq.com/romania/
Slovakia	http://savba.savba.sk/logos/list-e.html
Slovenia	http://www.ijs.si/slo/resources/

RUSSIA, THE BALTIC STATES, AND THE FORMER SOVIET UNION

Russia	http://www.mar.com/racc/info/russian_visa.html
	Visas; lists fees and limitations with information links to trans-Siberian railway, airport transfers, and sightseeing.
	http://www.astor.ru/
	Association of Travel Organizations of Russia
	http://www.concourse.net/bus/wnights/
	White Nights Travel

	http://www.ru/travel/
	List of several traveler information sites
Armenia	http://wotan.wiwi.hu-berlin.de/~houssik/armenia.html
Belarus	http://freedom.ncsa.uiuc.ed/~zelenko/belarus/Belarus.html
Estonia	http://www.ciesin.ee/ESTCG/
Latvia	http://latvia.vernet.iv/travel/
Lithuania	http://neris.mii.it/
	http://www.ktl.mii.lt/visitors
Russia and the Ukraine	http://www.lonelyplanet.com/dest/eur/rus.htm

MIDDLE EAST

Iran	http://tehran.stanford.edu/
Israel	http://dapsas.weizmann.ac.il/bcd/bcd_parent/tour/tour.html
Jerusalem	http://www.huji.ac.il/jeru/jerusalem.html
Jordan	http://www.mit.edu:8001/activities/jordanians/jordan/
Middle East	http://www.iii.com/~hajeri/arab.html
Syria	http://www.umich.edu/~kazamaza/syria.html
Turkey	http://web.syr.edu/~obalsoy/Turkije

NORTH AFRICA

Afghanistan	http://www.gl.umbc.edu/~hqurba1
Algeria	http://www.ift.ulaval.ca/~lechilli/algeria.html
Angola	http://www.umich.edu/~jasse/angola/angola.html
Cameroon	http://scitsc.wlv.ac.uk/~cm9032/cameroon.html
Egypt	http://www.channel1.com/users/mansoorm/index.html
Eritrea	http://www.cs.indiana.edu/hyplan/dmulholl/eritrea/eritrea.html
Ghana	http://www.uta.fi/~csfraw/ghana.html
Kenya	http://seclab.scucdavis.edu/~wee/east-africa.html
Madagascar	http://www.cable.com/madagas/madagas.htm
Morocco	http://www.ift.ulaval.ca/~asma-net/
Seychelles	http://interhealth.com/seychelles/
South Africa	http://orca.astro.washington.edu/silber/africa.html
Zimbabwe	http://wn.apc.org/mediatech/VRZ10001.HTM

EAST ASIA

Asia	http://emailhost.ait.ac.th/Asia/asia.html
China	http://solar.rtd.utk.edu/~china/china.html
Hong Kong	http://www.cuhk.hk/hk/scenery.htm
Japan	http://www.jnto.go.jp/
Korea	http://korea.com/korea/korea.htm
Taiwan	http://www.iipl.com.sg/tai/text/tourist.htm

SOUTH AND SOUTHEAST ASIA

Bangladesh	http://www.servtech.com/public/outcast/tour/
Bhutan	http://www.solutions.mb.ca/rec-travel/asia/bhutan/bhutan.html
Burma	http://www.lonelyplanet.com.au/dest/sea/myan.htm
Cambodia	http://www.lonelyplanet.com.au/dest/sea/camb.htm
India	http://www.webcom.com/~prakash/Tourism/TOURISM.HTML
Indonesia	http://www.iipl.com.sg/ino/text/tourist.htm
Laos	http://www.lonelyplanet.com.au/dest/sea/laos.htm
Malaysia	http://www.jaring.my/msia/tourism/tourism.html
Nepal	http://www.cen.uiuc.edu/~rshresth/Nepal.html
Pakistan	http://exit109.com/~fazia/Pakistan.html

Philippines	http://www.mit.edu:8001/people/mandm/rp.html
Singapore	http://sunsite.nus.sg/SEAlinks/singapore-info.html
Thailand	http://emailhost.ait.ac.th/Asia/infoth.html
Vietnam	http://maingate.net:80/vn/index.html

AUSTRALIA, NEW ZEALAND, AND THE PACIFIC ISLANDS

Australia	http://www.telstra.com.au/meta/australia.html#tourtrav
	http://www.immi.gov.au/983i(b).htm#Tourism
	http://www.ozemail.com/au~portdoug/pdvb.html
	http://www.ozemail.com/au~portdoug/pdvbl.html Australian department of Immigration - Visa Applications; Car and 4WD rentals; Visitor Information; Tours and Cruises; Australian Tourist Commission
	http://www.bom.gov.au/ Climate information: Climate averages, seasonal outlook
	http://www.wps.com.au/travel/travhome.htm Australasian Travel and Tourism Service with general information, weather, rail schedules, attractions. Passport, buses, taxis, hotels, travel tips, maps, restaurants, entertainment
Brunei	http://www.iipl.com.sg/bru/test/tourist.htm
Fiji	http://kula.usp.ac.fj/fiji/
Guam	http://ns.gov.gu/
Marshall Islands	http://www.clark.net/pub/llaack/rmi/
Micronesia	http://darkwing.uoregon.edu/~robertsr/micro.htm
New Zealand	http://www.icair.iac.org.nz/nz/tourism/index.html
	http://www.interact.co.nz/interact Best Travel itinerary of New Zealand for several different types of excursions.
Papua New Guinea	http://www.tbc.gov.bc.ca/cwgames/country/Papua/papua.html
Pitcairn Island	http://wavefront.wavefront.com/~pjlareau/pitc1.html
Vanuatu	http://www.clark.net/pub/kiaman/vanuatu.html
Western Samoa	http://www.intergroup.com/interwerb/samoa

Appendix B

GEOGRAPHY AND TOURISM
Tourism Offices and Organizations

UNITED STATES TOURISM OFFICES (by individual state)

Alabama Bureau of Tourism & Travel
401 Adams Ave.
Montgomery, AL 36103-4309
800-252-2262

Alaska State Division of Tourism
P.O. Box 11081
Juneau, AK 99811-0801
907-465-2010

Arizona Office of Tourism
1100 W. Washington St.
Phoenix, AZ 85007
602-542-8687

Arkansas Dept. of Parks & Tourism
1 Capitol Mall
Little Rock, AR 72201
800-628-8725

California Office of Tourism
801 K St., Ste. 1600
Sacramento, CA 95814
916-322-3402

Colorado Tourism Board
1625 Broadway, Suite 1700
Denver, CO 80202
303-592-5510

Connecticut Dept. of Economic Development
Tourism Division
865 Brook St.
Rocky Hill, CT 06067-3405
800-CT-BOUND

Delaware Tourism Office
P.O. Box 1401
99 Kings Highway
Dover, DE 19903
800-441-8846

Florida Dept. of Commerce
Division of Tourism
126 W. Van Buren St.
Tallahassee, FL 32399-2000
904-487-1462

Georgia Dept. of Industry
Trade & Tourism
P.O. Box 1776
285 Peachtree Center Ave.
Atlanta, GA 30303
404-656-3590

Hawaii Visitors Bureau
Waikiki Business Plaza
2270 Kalakaua Ave., Suite 801
Honolulu, HI 96815
808-923-1811

Idaho Division of Travel Promotion
700 W. State St.
Boise, ID 83720
800-635-7820

Illinois Bureau of Tourism
State of Illinois Center
100 West Randolph St., Ste. 3-400
Chicago, IL 60601
312-814-4732

Indiana Department of Commerce
Tourism Development Div.
1 North Capitol
Indianapolis, IN 46204-2288
317-232-8860

Iowa Division of Tourism
200 E. Grand Ave.
Des Moines, IA 52244
800-451-2625

Kansas Travel & Tourism
700 SW Harrison St., Ste. 1300
Topeka, KS 66603-3755
913-296-2009

Kentucky Dept. of Travel Development
Capital Plaza Tower, 22nd Fl.
500 Mero St.
Frankfort, KY 40601-1968
502-564-4930

Louisiana Office of Tourism
Box 94291
Baton Rouge, LA 70804-9291
800-227-4386

Maine Office of Tourism
State House Station 59
Augusta, ME 04333
800-533-9595

Maryland Office of Tourism Development
217 E. Redwood St., 9th Floor
Baltimore, MD 21202
301-333-6643

Massachusetts Office of Travel and Tourism
100 Cambridge St.
Boston, MA 02202
617-727-3201 Ext 208

Travel Bureau of Michigan
Dept. of Commerce
333 S. Capitol Ave.
Lansing, Ml 48909
800-543-2-YES

Minnesota Office of Tourism
375 Jackson St.
250 Skyway Level
St. Paul, MN 55101
800-657-3700

Mississippi Division of Tourism
P.O. Box 849
Jackson, MS 39205
800-647-2290

Missouri Division of Tourism
Truman State Office Bldg.
P.O. Box 1055
Jefferson City, MO 65102
314-751-4133

Montana Promotion Division
1424 Ninth Ave.
Helena, MT 59620
800-548-3390

Nebraska Division of Travel and Tourism
P.O. Box 94666
Lincoln, NE 68509
800-228-4307

Nevada Commission of Tourism
5151 S. Carson St.
Carson City, NV 89710
800-237-0774

New Hampshire Office of Travel and Tourism
P.O. Box 856
Concord, NH 03302-0856
603-271-2343

New Jersey Division of Travel and Tourism
CN 826
Trenton, NJ 08625-0826
800-JERSEY-7

New Mexico Tourism & Travel Division
1100 St. Francis Dr.
Santa Fe, NM 87503
505-827-0291

New York State Dept. of Economic Development
Division of Tourism
1515 Broadway
New York, NY 10036
212-827-6279

North Carolina Division of Travel and Tourism
430 North Salisbury St.
Raleigh, NC 27611
800-VISIT-NC

North Dakota Tourism
Liberty Memorial Building
Bismark, ND 58505-0825
800-435-5663

Ohio Division of Travel and Tourism
P.O. Box 1001
Columbus, OH 43266-0101
800-BUCKEYE

Oklahoma Tourism and Recreation Department
Marketing Services Division
500 Will Rogers Building
Oklahoma City, OK 73105
800-652-6552

Oregon Tourism Division
777 Summer St. N. E.
Salem, OR 97310
503-373-1270

Pennsylvania Travel Council
902 N. Second St.
Harrisburg, PA 17102
717-232-8880

Rhode Island Tourism Division
7 Jackson Walkway
Providence, RI 02903
401-277-2601

South Carolina Dept. of Parks, Recreation and Tourism
1205 Pendleton St.
Columbia, SC 29201
803-734-0122

South Dakota Dept. of Tourism
711 E. Wall Ave
Pierre, SD 57501-3369
800-952-3625

Tennessee Dept. of Tourist Development
P.O. Box 23170

Nashville, TN 37202-3170
615-741-2159

Texas Tourism Division
125 E. 11th St.
Austin, TX 78701
512-463-8601

Utah Travel Council
Council Hall, Capitol Hill
Salt Lake City, UT 84114
801-538-1030

Vermont Travel Division
134 State St.
Montpelier, VT 05602
802-828-3236

Virginia Division of Tourism
1021 East Cary St., 14th Fl.
Richmond, VA 23219
804-786-2051

Washington State Tourism Division
P.O. Box 42513
Olympia, WA 98504-2513
800-544-1800

West Virginia Tourism Division
Capital Complex, Bldg. 17
Charleston, WV 25305
800-CALL-WVA

Wisconsin Division of Tourism Development
P.O. Box 7970
Madison, WI 53707
800-432-TRIP

Wyoming Travel Commission
1-25 at College Drive
Cheyenne, WY 82002
800-225-5996

CANADIAN TOURISM OFFICES

Alberta Dept. of Tourism
10025 Jasper Ave., 15th Floor
Edmonton, AB T5J 3Z3
800-661-8888

Tourism British Columbia
865 Hornby St.
Vancouver, BC V6Z 2G3
800-663-6000

Travel Manitoba
155 Carlton St., 7th Floor
Winnipeg, MN R3C 3H8
800-665-0040, ext. 20

New Brunswick Tourism, Recreation & Heritage
P.O. Box 12345
Fredricton, NB E3B 5C3
800-561-0123

Newfoundland and Labrador Dept. of Tourism
P.O. Box 8700
St. John's, NF AIC 5R8
800-563-6353

Northwest Territories
Laing Bldg
Yellowknife, NWT XIA 2L9
800-661-0788

Nova Scotia Tourism
5151 Terminal Rd.
Halifax, NS B3J2R5
800-341-6096

Ontario Ministry of Tourism & Recreation
77 Floor St. W., 9th Floor
Toronto, ON, Canada M7A 2R9
800-268-3735

Prince Edward Island Dept. of Tourism & Parks
P.O. Box 2000, Charlottetown
PEI CIA 7N8
902-368-5500

Tourisme Québec
Boite Postale 125
Montréal, PQ H4Z 1C3
800-443-7000

Tourism Saskatchewan
1919 Saskatchewan Dr., 5th Fl.
Regina, SK S4P 3V7
800-667-7191

Tourism Yukon
P.O. Box 2703
Whitehorse, YK Y1A 2C6
403-667-5340

CENTRAL AMERICA AND THE CARIBBEAN

Belize
Belize Tourist Board
415 Seventh Ave., 15 Penn Plaza
New York, NY 10001

Belize Tourist Board
83 N. Front St.
Belize City, Belize

Costa Rica
Costa Rica National Tourism Bureau
1101 Brickell Ave., BIV Tower, Ste. 801
Miami, FL 33126020

Instituto Costarricense de Turismo
P.O. Box 777–1000
San Jose, Costa Rica

El Salvador
Consulate General
300 Biscayne Blvd. Way, Ste. 1020
Miami, FL 33131

Instituto Salvadoreno de Tourismo
Calle Rubén Dario #619
San Salvador, El Salvador

Guatemala
Guatemala Consulate
1138 Wilshire Blvd.
Los Angeles, CA 90017

Guatemala Tourist Commission
Seventh Ave., 1–7 Centro
Cívico, Guatemala City

Honduras
Honduras Tourist Office
11436 Fremont Ave., Ste. 107
South Pasadena, CA 91030

Instituto Hondureno De Turismo
Apdo. Postal 154-C
Republic of Honduras

Mexico
Mexican Government Tourist Office
405 Park Ave., Ste. 1002
New York, NY 10022

Mexican Ministry of Tourism
Presidente Masaryk #172
11587 Mexico D.F

Nicaragua
Nicaraguan Embassy
1627 New Hampshire Ave. N.W.
Washington, DC 20009

Institute Nicaraguense de Turismo
2nd Ave. S. between 8th & 11th Sts.
Managua, Nicaragua

Panama
Panama Consulate
Dallas, TX 75248

Instituto Panameño de Turismo
P.O. Box 4421
Panama 5, Rep. of Panama

Anguilla
Anguilla Dept. of Tourism
c/o Medhurst & Associates Inc.
271 Main St.
Northport, NY 11768

Anguilla Department of Tourism
Anguilla, WI

Antigua and Barbuda
Antigua Dept. of Tourism and Trade
6105th Ave., Ste. 311
New York, NY 10020

Antigua Dept. of Tourism and Trade
Box 363
St. John's, Antigua

Aruba
Aruba Tourist Authority
2344 Salzedo St.
Coral Gables, FL 33134–5033

Aruba Tourist Authority
L.G. Smith Blvd., #172
Oranjestad, Aruba

Bahamas
Tourist Information Office
150 E. 52nd St.
New York, NY 10022 Bahamas

Ministry of Tourism
P.O. Box N3701
Nassau, Bahamas

Barbados
Barbados Board of Tourism
800 2nd Ave.
New York, NY 10017

Barbados Board of Tourism
P.O. Box 242
Bridgetown, Barbados

Bermuda
Bermuda Dept. of Tourism
310 Madison Ave., Ste. 201
New York, NY 10017

Tourist Information Office
43 Church Street
Hamilton HM BX-Bermuda

Bonaire
Bonaire Government Tourist Bureau
201 1/2 E. 29th St.
New York, NY 10016

Bonaire Govt. Tourist
Kaya Simon Bolivar #12
Kralendjik, Bonaire

British Virgin Islands
Tourist Board
370 Lexington Ave.
New York, NY 10017

British Virgin Islands Tourist Board
Box 134 Road Town
Tortola, B.V.I.

Cayman Islands
Cayman Islands Dept. of Tourism
420 Lexington Ave.
New York, NY 10170

Department of Tourism
Box 67
George Town, Grand Cayman

Cuba
Cuban Interests Section
2630 16th St. NW
Washington, DC 20009

Cuban Tourist Board
Calle 23, No. 156 Vedado
Ababa, 4 Cuba

Curacao
Curacao Tourist Board
400 Madison Ave.
New York, NY 10017

Curacao Tourist Board
Exec. Office, Pietermaai No. 19
Willemstad, Curacao

Dominica
Caribbean Tourism Assoc.
20 E. 46th St.
New York, NY 10017

Dominica Tourist Board
P.O. Box 293
Roseau, Dominica

Dominican Republic
Dominican Tourist Info. Center
1 Times Square Plaza, 11th Fl.
New York, NY 10020

Ministry of Tourism
Box 497
Santo Domingo, Dominican Republic

Grenada
Grenada Tourist Info. Office
820 Second Ave.
New York, NY 10017

Grenada Tourist Board
P.O. Box 293
St. George's, Grenada

Guadeloupe
French West Indies Tourist Board
610 Fifth Ave.
New York, NY 10020

Office du Tourisme
5 Square de Ia Banque
B.R 10991
Pointe-a-Pitre, Guadeloupe

Haiti
Haiti Consulate
217 Madison Ave.
New York, NY 10016

Haiti National Office of Tourism
Ave. Marie-Jeanne
Port-au-Prince, Haiti

Jamaica
Jamaica Tourist Board
801 Second Ave
New York, NY 10017

Jamaica Tourist Board
21 Dominica
Kingston, Jamaica

Martinique
French West Indies Tourist Board
610 Fifth Ave.
New York, NY 10020

Office du Tourisme
Blvd. Alfassa, B.P. 520
Fort-de-France, Martinique

Montserrat
Caribbean Tourism Association
20 E. 46th St.
New York, NY 10017

Montserrat Tourist Office
P.O. Box 7
Plymouth, Montserrat

Netherlands Antilles
Caribbean Tourism Assoc.
20 E. 46th St.
New York, NY 10017

Puerto Rico
Puerto Rico Tourism Co.
575 Fifth Ave., 23rd Fl.
New York, NY 10017

Puerto Rico Tourism Co.
Box 4435, Old San Juan
San Juan, PR 00905

St. Eustatius-Saba
St. Saba Tourist Bureau
Four W. 58th St.
New York, NY 10019

St. Saba Tourist Bureau
Saba, Netherlands

St. Kitts-Nevis
St. Kitts-Nevis Dept. of Tourism
414 E. 75th St.
New York, NY 10021

Tourist Board
Box 132
Basseterre, St. Kitts

Saint Lucia
St. Lucia Tourist Board
820 Second Ave., 9th Fl.
New York, NY 10017

St. Lucia Tourist Board
P.O. Box 221
Castries, St. Lucia

St. Maarten (Dutch)
St. Maarten Tourist Bureau
275 Seventh Ave., 19th Fl.
New York, NY 10001

Tourist Information Bur.
Phillipsburg, St. Maarten

St. Vincent and the Grenadines
St. Vincent Tourist Information Office
801 Second Ave., 21st Fl.
New York, NY 10017

St. Vincent & the Grenadines
Dept. of Tourism
P.O. Box 834
Kingston, St. Vincent

Trinidad and Tobago
Trinidad and Tobago Tourist Dev.
25 W. 43rd St., Ste. 1508
New York, NY 10036

Trinidad and Tobago Tourist Board
134 Frederick St.
Port-of-Spain, Trinidad

Turks and Caicos Islands
Turks & Caicos Tourist Board
P.O. Box 594033
Miami, FL 33159

Ministry of Tourism
Grand Turk, Turks & Caicos

U.S. Virgin Islands
U.S. Virgin Islands Tourist
Information Office
1270 Ave. of the Americas
New York, NY 10020

U.S. Virgin Island Dept. of Commerce
P.O. Box 6400
St. Thomas, USVI

SOUTH AMERICA

Argentina
Argentina Tourist Information
330 W. 58th St.
New York, NY 10019

Dirección Nacional de Túrismo
Suipacha 111, 21st Floor
Buenos Aires, Argentina 1368

Bolivia
Bolivian Consulate General
211 E. 43rd St.
New York, NY 10017

Bolivian Tourist Institute
P.O. Box 1868
La Paz, Bolivia

Chile
Chilean National Tourist Board
630 Fifth Ave.
New York, NY 10020

Servicio National de Túrismo
P.O. Box 14082
Catedral 1165
Santiago, Chile

Colombia
Colombian Consulate
10 E. 46th St.
New York, NY 10017

Corporación National de Túrismo
28 #13-A-15 Calle
Bogotá, Colombia

Ecuador
Ecuatoriana Airlines
590 5th Ave., 10 Fl.
New York, NY 10036

Corporación Nacional de Túrismo
Victoria y Roca Quito
Quito, Ecuador

Paraguay
Paraguay Embassy
2400 Massachusetts Ave. N.W.
Washington, DC 20008

Director General de Túrismo
Ministerio de Industria y Túrismo
Asunción, Paraguay

Perú
FOPTUR Commercial Office
100 Brickell Ave., Ste. 600
Miami, FL 33131

Fondo de Promoción Turística
Av. República de Panama
Lima, Perú

Suriname
Embassy of the Republic of Surinam
4301 Connecticut Ave., N.W., Ste. 108
Washington, DC 20008

Suriname Tourist Board
Waterkant 8, P.O. Box 656
Paramaribo, Suriname

Uruguay
Uruguayan Tourist Bureau
Doral Inn Hotel
747 Third Ave., 21st Fl.
New York, NY 10017

Dirección Nacional de Túrismo
Avenida Agraciado 1409
Montevideo, Uruguay

Venezuela
Venezuelan Tourism Association
P.O. Box 3010
Sausalito, CA 94966

WESTERN EUROPE

Austria
Tourist Information Office
500 Fifth Ave.
New York, NY 10110

Belgium
Belgian National Tourist Office
745 Fifth Ave.
New York, NY 10151

Commissariaat-Generaal voor Toerisme
Rue Marché aux Herbes, 61
Brussels, Belgium B-1000

France
French Government Tourist Office
610 Fifth Ave.
New York, NY 10020

Ministere du Temps Libre
Div. Direction du Tourisme
8 Avenue de l'Opéra
75001 Paris, France

Germany
German National Tourist Office
122 East 42nd St., 52nd Fl.
New York, NY 10168–0072

Deutsche Zentrale fuer Tourismus
Beethovenstrasse 69
6000 Frankfurt/Main
Federal Republic of Germany

Ireland
Irish Tourist Board
757 Third Ave.
New York, NY 10017

Bord Failte Eireann
Baggot St. Bridge
Dublin, Ireland

Luxembourg
Luxembourg National Tourist Office
801 Second Ave., 13th Fl.
New York, NY 10017

Office National du Tourisme
77, rue d'Anvers
Luxembourg, Luxembourg

Netherlands
Netherlands Board of Tourism
355 Lexington Ave., 21st Fl.
New York, NY 10017

Switzerland
Swiss National Tourist Office
608 Fifth Ave.
New York, NY 10020

Schweizerisch Verkehrszentrale
Bellariastrasse 38
Zurich, Switzerland

United Kingdom
British Tourist Authority
551 Fifth Ave.
New York, NY 10019–4001

British Tourist Authority
Thames Tower Authority
London, England W69 El

NORTHERN EUROPE

Denmark
Danish Tourist Board
655 Third Ave.
New York, NY 10017

Danish Tourist Board
Vesterbrogade 6D
1620 Copenhagen V., Denmark

Finland
Finnish Tourist Board
655 Third Ave.
New York, NY 10017

Finnish Tourist Board
Helsinki 10, Finland

Iceland
Iceland Tourist Board
655 Third Ave.
New York, NY 10017

Iceland Tourist Board
Laugavegi 3
Reykjavik, Iceland

Norway
Norwegian Information Service
825 Third Ave.
New York, NY 10017

Norwegian Tourist Board
Vestganeplassen 1
Oslo 1, Norway

Sweden
Scandinavian Tourist Board
655 Third Ave.
New York, NY 10017

Swedish Tourist Board
Kungstradgarden
Box 7473
S-10392 Stockholm, Sweden

SOUTHERN EUROPE

Greece
Greek National Tourist Organization
645 Fifth Ave.
New York, NY 10022

Greek National Tourist Organization
2 Amerikis St.
Athens, Greece

Italy
Italian Govt. Travel Office
630 Fifth Ave.
New York, NY 10111

Ente Nazionale ltaliano
per iI Turismo
Via Marghera 2
Rome, Italy

Malta
Embassy of Malta
2017 Connecticut Ave.
Washington, DC 20008

Malta National Tourist Office
280, Republic St. Valletta
Valletta, Malta

Portugal
Portuguese National Tourist Office
590 Fifth Ave.
New York, NY 10036

Directorate Gen. of Tourism
86, Av. Antonio Augusto de Aguiar
Lisbon, Portugal

Spain
Spanish National Tourist Office
665 Fifth Ave.
New York, NY 10022

Director Gen. de Promocion
del Turismo
Maria del Molina, 50
Madrid, Spain

CENTRAL EUROPE AND THE BALKAN STATES

Bulgaria
Balkan Holidays USA Limited
41 E. 42nd St.
Suite 606
New York, NY 10017

Balkan Holidays
1 Sveta Nedelia Sq
Sofia, Bulgaria

The Czech Republic & Slovakia
CEDOK, Czechoslovak Travel Bureau
10 E. 40th St.
New York, NY 10016

Hungary
IBUSZ Hungarian Travel Co.
1 Parker Plaza
Suite 1104
Fort Lee, NJ 07024

IBUSZ Tourist Office
Felszabadulas, Ter 5
Budapest, Hungary 1364

Poland
Orbis Polish Travel Bureau
342 Madison Ave.
Suite 1512
New York, NY 10137

Orbis
2 Stawki St.
Warsaw, Poland 00–193

Romania
Rumanian National Tourist Office
573 Third Ave.
New York, NY 10016

Ministry of Trade and Tourism
17 Apolodor St.
Sector 5
Bucharest, Romania

RUSSIA AND THE COUNTRIES OF THE FORMER SOVIET UNION

Armenia
Embassy of Armenia
122 C Street, N.W., Suite 360
Washington, DC 20001, U.S.A.

Azerbaijan
Permanent Mission of Azerbaijan to the United
   Nations
136 East 67th Street
New York, NY 10021

Belarus
Embassy of the Republic of Belarus
Suite 619, 1511 K St. NW
Washington, DC 20005

Kazakhstan
Permanent Mission of Kazakhstan to the United
   Nations
136 East 67th Street
New York, NY 10021

Turkmenistan
Embassy of Turkmenistan
Ulitsa Askakova 22
Moscow, Russia

Ukraine
Embassy of Ukraine
Chancery: 2001- L Street NW., Suite 200
Washington, DC 20036

Russia
Embassy of the Russian Federation
Chancery: 1125 - 16th St. NW.
Washington, DC 20036

Estonia
Embassy of Estonia
Chancery (temporary): 9 Rockefeller Plaza
Suite 1421
New York, N.Y. 10020

Latvia
Embassy of Latvia
Chancery, 4325 - 17th St. NW.
Washington, DC 20011

Lithuania
Embassy of the Republic of Lithuania
Chancery, 2622 - 16th St. NW.
Washington, DC 20009

Moldova
Permanent Mission of Moldova to the United
  Nations
573–577 Third Avenue
New York, NY 10016

Tajikistan
Embassy of Tajikistan
Skatertny Pereulok 19
Moscow, Russia

Kyrgyzstan
Permanent Mission of Kyrgyzstan to the United
  Nations
136 East 67th Street
New York, NY 10021

Uzbekistan
Permanent Mission of Uzbekistan to the United
  Nations
122 West 27th Street, 8th Floor
New York, NY 10001

Georgia
Russian Embassy
1125 - 16th St. NW.
Washington, DC 20036

Intourist
630 Fifth Ave, Suite 868
New York, NY 10111

Intourist-Holding
16 Marx Ave.
Moscow, USSR 103009

MIDDLE EAST AND NORTH AFRICA

Bahrain
Embassy
3502 International Dr., NW
Washington, DC 20008

Embassy
Shaikh lsa Rd., Box 26431
Manama, Bahrain

Iraq
Permanent Mission to the UN
14 E. 79th St.
New York, NY 10021

Ministry of Culture and lnfo.
Summer Resorts and Tourism Service
Baghdad, Iraq

Israel
Israel Ministry of Tourism
350 Fifth Ave.
New York, NY 10188

Israel Ministry of Tourism
24 King George St.
Jerusalem, Israel

Jordan
Alia, Royal Jordanian Airlines
535 Fifth Ave., 5th Fl.
New York, NY 10017

Ministry of Tourism and Antiquiti
P.O. Box 224
Amman, Jordan

Kuwait
Embassy
2940 Tiden St. NW
Washington, DC 20008

Ministry of Information
P.O. Box 193
Safat, Kuwait

Lebanon
Embassy
2560 28th St., NW
Washington, DC 20008

Brd. of Foreign Economic Rel.
Tourism Section
P.O. Box 5344
Beirut, Lebanon

Oman
Embassy
2342 Massachusetts Ave., NW
Washington, DC 20008

Embassy
Box 50202
Muscat, Oman

Qatar
Embassy
600 New Hampshire Ave., NW
Ste. 1180
Washington, DC 20037

Embassy
Fariq Bin Omran, Box 2399
Doha, Qatar

Saudi Arabia
Embassy
601 New Hampshire Ave., NW
Washington, DC 20037

Arab Tourism Union
Box 2354
Amman, Jordan

Syria
Embassy
2215 Wyoming Ave., NW
Washington, DC 20008

Ministry of Tourism
Abu Firas al-Hamadani St.
Damascus, Syria

Turkey
Turkish Culture and
Information Office
821 U.N. Plaza
New York, NY 10017

Ministry of Culture and Tourism
Ankara, Turkey

United Arab Emirates
Embassy
600 New Hampshire Ave.
Suite 740
Washington, DC 20037

Embassy
Al-Sudan St., Box 4009
Abu Dhabi, United Arab Emirates

Yemen Arab Republic
Embassy
600 New Hampshire Ave., NW
Ste. 840
Washington, DC 20037

Yemen Arab Republic-General
Tourism Corporation
P.O. Box 129
Sana's, Yemen

Algeria
Embassy
2118 Kalorama Rd., NW
Washington, DC 20008

Egypt
Egyptian Tourist Authority
630 Fifth Ave.
New York, NY 10111

Egyptian Tourist Information
Sadly St.
Cairo, Egypt

Libya
Permanent Mission to the UN
309 E. 48th St.
New York, NY 10017

Embassy
Shari Mohammad Thabit, Box 289
Tripoli, Libya

Morocco
Moroccan National Tourist Office
20 E. 46th St.
New York, NY 10017

Moroccan Tourist Board
22 Avenue D'Alger, P.O. Box 19
Rabat, Morocco

Sudan
Embassy
2210 Massachusetts Ave., NW
Washington, DC 20008

Sudanese Tourist Corporation
D.R. of Sudan, Box 2424
Khartoum, Sudan

Tunisia
Embassy
Tourist Section
1515 Massachusetts Ave., NW
Washington, DC 20005

Tunisian Nat'l Tourist Office
1 Avenue Mohamed V.
Tunis, Tunisia

SUBSAHARAN AFRICA

Benin
Embassy
2737 Cathedral Ave., NW
Washington, DC 20008

Botswana
Embassy
4301 Connecticut Ave., NW
Ste. 404
Washington, DC 20008

Burkina Faso
Africa Travel Association
347 5th Ave., Ste. #610
New York, NY 10016

Embassy (US)
Boite Postale 35
Ouagadougou, Burkina Faso

Burundi
Embassy
2233 Wisconsin Ave., NW
Ste. 212
Washington, DC 20007

Cameroon
Africa Travel Association
347 5th Ave., Ste #610
New York, NY 10016

General Delegation for Tourism
Public Relation Service
Yaounde, Cameroon

Cape Verde
Embassy
3415 Massachusetts Ave., NW
Washington, DC 20007

Central African Republic
Embassy
1618 22nd St., NW
Washington, DC 20008

Chad
Embassy
2002 R St., NW
Washington, DC 20009

Comoros
Embassy (US)
Government Liaison Office
Boite Postale 1318/1319
Moroni, Comoros

Congo
Embassy
4891 Colorado Ave.
Washington, DC 20011

Cote D'Ivoire
Embassy (US)
5 Rue Jesse Owens
01 Boite Postale 1712
Abidjan, Cote D'lvoire

Djibouti
Permanent Mission to the UN
866 UN Plaza, Ste. 4011
New York, NY 10017

Equatorial Guinea
Embassy
801 Second Ave., Rm. 1403
New York, NY 10017

EthiopIa
Embassy
2134 Kalorama Rd., NW
Washington, DC 20008

Gabon
Gabon Tourist Information Office
347 5th Ave., Ste. 810
New York, NY 10016

Gambia
Permanent Mission to the UN
19 E. 47th St.
New York, NY 10017

Ghana
Ghana Embassy
3512 International Dr., NW
Washington, DC 20008

Guinea
Embassy
2112 LeRoy Pl., NW
Washington, DC 20008

Guinea-Bissau
Permanent Mission to the UN
211 E. 43d St., Ste. 604
New York, NY 10017

Kenya
Kenya Tourist Office
424 Madison Ave.
New York, NY 10017

Lesotho
Embassy, Tourist Board
1601 Connecticut Ave., NW
Ste. 300
Washington, DC 20009

Liberia
Embassy
5201 16th St., NW
Washington, DC 20011

Madagascar
Embassy
2374 Massachusetts Ave., NW
Washington, DC 20008

Malawi
Embassy
Bristol House
1400 20th St., NW
Washington, DC 20036

Mali
Embassy
2130 R St., NW
Washington, DC 20008

Mauritania
Embassy
2129 LeRoy Pl., NW
Washington, DC 20008

Mauritius
Mauritius Tourist Info. Service
15 Penn Plaza
415 Seventh Ave.
New York, NY 10001

Mozambique
Embassy
1990 M St., NW
Washington, DC 20036

Namibia
Embassy
P. O. Box 34728
Washington, DC 20043

Niger
Embassy
2204 R St., NW
Washington, DC 20008

Nigeria
Embassy
2201 M St., NW
Washington, DC 20037

Tanzania
Tanzania Tourist Office
205 E. 42nd St.
13th Fl., Rm. 1300
New York, NY 10017

Togo
Togo Information Service
1706 R St., NW
Washington, DC 20009

Uganda
Uganda Tourist Information
5909 16th St., NW
Washington, DC 20011

Zaire
Embassy
1800 New Hampshire Ave., NW
Washington, DC 20009

Zambia
Embassy
2419 Massachusetts Ave., NW
Washington, DC 20008

Zimbabwe
Embassy
2852 McGill Terrace, NW
Washington, DC 20008

Rwanda
Embassy
1714 New Hampshire Ave.

Washington, DC 20009

Sao Tome and Principe
Sao Tome and Principe Permanent Mission to
    the UN
801 Second Ave., Ste. 1504
New York, NY 10017

Senegal
Embassy
2112 Wyoming Ave., NW
Washington, DC 20008

Seychelles
Seychelles Tourist Board
820 Second Ave., Ste. 1900F
New York, NY 10017

Sierra Leone
Embassy
1701 19th St., NW
Washington, DC 20009

Somalia
Embassy
600 New Hampshire Ave., NW
Ste. 710
Washington, DC 20037

South Africa
South African Tourist Board
747 Third Ave.
New York, NY 10017

Swaziland
Embassy
4301 Connecticut Ave., NW
Washington, DC 20008

EAST ASIA

China
China National Tourist Office
60 E. 42nd St.
New York, NY 10165

National Tourism Administration
No. 9A Jian Guo Men Ave.
Beijing, China

Hong Kong
Hong Kong Tourist Assoc.
590 Fifth Ave.
New York, NY 10036

Hong Kong Tourist Assoc.
35th Fl, Jardin House
1 Connaught Place, Central
Hong Kong

Japan
Japan National Tourist Organization
630 Fifth Ave.
New York, NY 10111

Japan National Tourist Organization
10–1 Yurakucho, 2-chome
Chiyoda-Ku
Tokyo, 100 Japan

Korea, South
Korea Nat'l Tourism Corp.
460 Park Ave.
New York, NY 10022

Korea Nat'l Tourism Corp.
10 Ta-Don, Chung-ku
Chumgmuro Chung-Ku
Seoul, Korea

Macau
Macau Tourist Information Bureau
70 A Greenwich Ave., Ste. 316
New York, NY 10011

Department of Tourism
1 Travessa do Paiva
Macau

Taiwan
Taiwan Visitors Assoc.
One World Trade Center
Suite 7953
New York, NY 10048

Tourism Bureau
280 Chung Hsaio E. Rd., 9th Fl.
Taipei 105, Taiwan

SOUTH AND SOUTHEAST ASIA

Bangladesh
Bangladesh Embassy
3431 Massachusetts Ave., NW
Washington, DC 20007

Bangladesh Parjatan Corp
Islam Chambers
T25-A Motijheel
Dacca 2, Bangladesh

India
Gov't. of India Tourist Office
30 Rockefeller Plaza
New York, NY 10112

Dept. of Tourism
New Delhi, India

Nepal
Embassy of Nepal
2131 Leroy Pl., NW
Washington, DC 20008

Dept. of Tourism Office of the Director General
Kathmandu, Nepal

Pakistan
Embassy of Pakistan
2315 Massachusetts Ave., NW
Washington, DC 20008

Pakistan Tourism Development Corp.
Hotel Metropole, Club Rd.
Karachi, Pakistan

Sri Lanka
Sri Lanka Tourist Board
North American Office
630 Third Ave., 20 Fl.
New York, NY 10017

Ceylon Tourist Board
228 Havelock Rd.
Colombo 5, Sri Lanka

Indonesia
Information Section
41 E. 42nd St., Ste. 621
New York, NY 10017

Tourist Information Office
Jalan Kramat Raya 81
Jakarta, Indonesia

Malaysia
Malaysian Tourist Info. Ctr.
818 West 7th St., Ste. 804
Los Angeles, CA 90017

Tourist Development Corp.
P.O. Box 10328
50710 Kuala Lumpur
Kuala Lumpur, Malaysia

Philippines
Philippine Ministry of Tourism
556 Fifth Ave.
New York, NY 10036

Ministry of Tourism
Agrifina Circle, Rizal Park
Manila, Philippines

Singapore
Singapore Tourist Promotion Board
590 5th Ave., 12 Fl.
New York, NY 10036

Tourist Promotion Board
250 N. Bridge Rd.
Singapore-0617

Thailand
Tourism Authority of Thailand
5 World Trade Ctr., Ste. 3443
New York, NY 10048

Tourism Authority of Thailand
4 Ratchadamnoen Nok Ave.
Bangkok, Thailand

ISLANDS OF THE SOUTH PACIFIC

Australia
Australian Tourist Commission
489 Fifth Ave.
New York, NY 10017

Fiji
Fiji Visitors' Bureau
5777 W. Century Blvd., Ste. 220
Los Angeles, CA 90045

Fiji Visitors' Bureau
G.P.O.92
Suva, Fiji Islands

French Polynesia (Tahiti)
Tahiti Tourist Promotion Board
300 N. Continental Blvd., Ste. 180
El Segundo, CA 90245

Guam
Guam Visitors' Bureau
425 Madison Ave., 14th FL.
New York, NY 10017

Guam Visitors' Bureau
P.O. Box 3520
1220 Pie San Vitores Rd.
Tamuning, Guam 96911

New Caledonia
New Caledonia Gov't Tourist Office
P.O. Box 688
39–41 Rue de Verdun-Immeuble Manhattan
Noumea, New Caledonia

New Zealand
New Zealand Gov't Tourist Office
432 Park Ave. S., Ste. 1206
New York, NY 10016

New Zealand Tourism Board
P.O. Box 95
Wellington, New Zealand

Papua New Guinea
Embassy
1615 New Hampshire Ave., N. W.
Washington, DC 20009

Tourist Information Office
P.O. Box 773
Port Moresby, Papua New Guinea

GEOGRAPHY AND TOURISM
Glossary

ABC Islands The Netherlands Antilles Islands of Aruba, Bonaire, and Curacao.

Absolute Location The position or place of a point on the surface of the earth expressed in degrees, minutes, and seconds of latitude and longitude.

Accessibility The ease by which interchange or travel can occur between two places or people.

Acropolis The upper fortified part or citadel of the ancient Greek city of Athens.

Adriatic Of or pertaining to the Adriatic Sea or to the people inhabiting its islands and its coast. The Adriatic Sea is an arm of the Mediterranean, 500 miles long and up to 140 miles wide, between Italy and Croatia.

Affluence A high level of income (wealth).

African Pertaining to Africa, its people, or its language; a person born in Africa.

African Riviera The coastal area of the Ivory Coast between Abidjan and Sassandra of beautiful beaches, plantations, casinos, and picturesque fishing villages.

Afrikaaners An Afrikaan-speaking descendant of the early Dutch settlers to South Africa.

Aiga The extended family groups in traditional Samoan cultures.

Alemannic A High-German dialect spoken in Alsace, parts of southern Germany, and Switzerland.

Alhambra Moorish palace in Granada built on the hill overlooking the city. It has imposing towers and halls, rooms decorated with lacy carvings, colored tiles, and gold mosaics, and courtyards with fountains, hidden gardens, and hedges.

Alluvial Deposits of mud, silt, and sand by rivers and streams. Alluvial plains adjoin many larger rivers. Alluvial deltas mark the mouths of rivers, such as the Mississippi. Alluvial fans mark the outlet of canyons of streams.

Alps An alpine chain of high, rugged mountains in central Europe.

Altitudinal Zonation Vertical regions of South and Middle America. Each zone has a different physical, environmental, and population characteristic.

Amazon A river of South America that originates in the Peruvian Andes and flows north then east through northern Brazil to the Atlantic Ocean.

Amazon Basin The lowland, tropical rain forest area of the Amazon River drainage region in South America.

AMTRAK Name used by the National Railroad Passenger Corporation (a semipublic corporation formed by the Rail Passenger Service Act of 1970 and charged with managing and rejuvenating United States intercity passenger railroad service).

Ancient Cities Cities that developed early in the history of humankind.

Andalusia A region of southern Spain comprising the provinces of Almeria, Granada, Jaen, Malaga, Cadiz, Cordoba, Huelva, and Seville. Strongly influenced by the Moors of Northern Africa.

Andes A 4,000-mile-long mountain system stretching the length of western South America from Venezuela to Tierra del Fuego.

Anglican A member of the Church of England or any church related to it.

Anthropology The study of the origins (including the physical, social, and cultural development and behavior) of humankind.

Arabian Plateau Plateau in the Arabian Peninsula.

Arawaks Indian people living in parts of Guyana, Suriname, and French Guyana; the language spoken by these Indians.

Archaeological The study of material evidences of human life and culture in past ages.

Archipelago A group or chain of islands in close proximity to one another.

Arid China The dry western and north western regions of China.

Asia The largest of the continents, it occupies the eastern portion of the Eurasian landmass and adjacent islands.

Ashkenazim Jews from Western and Central Europe.

Atacama Arid desert of Chile between the Pacific Ocean and the Andes Mountains. One of the driest deserts in the world.

Atolls Coral islands that are low and have an open lagoon surrounded by a reef.

Austro-Hungarian Empire A former dual monarchy of central Europe, formed by the union of Austria, Bohemia, Hungary, and parts of Poland.

Baksheesh A tip in Arab countries.

Balance of Payments Statement of international monetary transactions; the amount of money leaving a country for goods and services, as opposed to that spent to purchase goods and services within a country.

Balkan Peninsula A peninsula in southeastern Europe including the countries of Greece, Albania, Yugoslavia, and Bulgaria.

Barrios Low-income neighborhoods in Middle and South America.

Basques A people of obscure racial and linguistic origin who retained autonomy until the nineteenth century. Concentrated in Northwestern Spain and Southern France (around the Pyrenees Mountains).

Bazaar An Arabic market usually consisting of a street or streets lined with shops and stalls.

Bedouin Nomadic group in the Middle East and North Africa.

Biomass The amount of vegetative (organic) matter in an ecosystem in a designated surface area.

Boers Descendants of Dutch colonists in South Africa.

Bord Failte Eireann Irish National Tourist Board.

Border Towns Towns and cities along borders between two countries that receive large numbers of day visitors.

Buddha A representation of Gautama Buddha who was the originator of Buddhism.

Buddhism A religion found today in Southeast Asia, China, Japan, and Korea; an attempt to reform the Hindu belief system. Buddhism maintains that the path of salvation is based on four truths. These truths are: first, recognition that life is full of suffering; second, awareness that desire is the cause of suffering; third, that happiness and satisfaction (the end of suffering) come from overcoming desires; and fourth, that proper conduct, including honesty, forgiveness, compassion, and consideration, is the means of overcoming cravings and desire.

Caldera A large crater formed by volcanic explosion or by collapse of a volcanic cone.

Caliph The leader, both religious and secular, of a Moslem state.

Calypso Music of the West Indies centered in Trinidad. Uses improvised lyrics on topical or humorous subjects.

Canadian Shield The low, crystalline rock shield that extends over half of Canada, from Labrador southwest around Hudson Bay and northwest to the Arctic Ocean.

Capital A town or city that is the official seat of government in a state, nation, or other political entity.

Capital Transfers A part of the balance of payments in which money is transferred from one country to another in the form of foreign aid or some kind of cash grant.

Caravanserai Inn for travelers and traders along the Silk Road and other routes of Central Asia.

Caribbean An area of the Atlantic Ocean bordered by North America, Central America, and South America; characterized by its warm climate and beaches; a major tourism area.

Caribbean Tourism Organization A Caribbean organization consisting of eighteen countries that provides statistics and deals with common tourism problems of the region.

Caribs Original inhabitants of the Lesser Antilles and northern South America.

Carrying Capacity The number of animals, crops, or people an area can support on a continual basis without degrading the environment. The carrying capacity varies with technology, land-use techniques, and geographic characteristics.

Casbah The old native quarter consisting of housing, the citadel, and the palace, in Arabic cities of North Africa.

Castellano A regional dialect of Catalonia in northwestern Spain.

Castle A stronghold or a fortified medieval town.

Cataracts A series of large waterfalls.

Cathedral Cities Cities in which a dominant characteristic of the landscape is the cathedral.

Cathedrals Large, impressive churches that contain the official throne of the bishop.

Catholic A member of any Catholic Church, particularly Roman Catholic.

Catholic Inquisition The medieval effort of the Catholic Church to combat heresy.

Caucasians A division of humanity comprising the major ethnic groups of Europe, North Africa, and Southwest Asia.

CEDOK The official tourism organization of the Czech Republic and Slovakia.

Celt An ancient people of western and central Europe, including the Britons and the Gauls.

Celtic A subfamily of the Indo-European family of languages.

Central America Consists of all the countries south of the Mexican border to the northern border of Colombia.

Central Location Places that are located central to their market.

Central Place A community that possesses a certain measure of centrality and forms the urban focus for a particular region.

Central Planning Planning and economic development that are controlled by the central government.

Chateau A French castle or manor house.

Chinese A native of China, a person of Chinese ancestry, or a group of Sino-Tibetan languages and dialects spoken in East Asia.

Christian Those who follow the teachings of Jesus Christ.

Christianity The Christian religion, based on the teachings of Jesus.

Cinder Cone The cone formed in the center of a volcano.

Circular Tours Tours that visit a number of places between the origin and return point in a circular manner.

Cirque A steep hollow occurring at the upper end of mountain valleys. Formed by glaciation.

Civil War A war between two factions or regions of one country.

Climate Generalized statement of the prevailing weather conditions at a given place, based upon statistics of a long period of record and including average values, departures from those averages, and the probabilities associated with those departures.

Colonial Of or relating to being controlled by a European or other foreign power. Individuals in the controlled countries may be called colonials.

Colonial Territories Territories controlled by a foreign power.

Common Market Name given to a group of fifteen European countries (as of 1996) that belong to a supranational association to promote their economic interests. The official name is the European Union (EU).

Commonwealth Formerly the Commonwealth of England, today it refers to independent countries that were once colonies of England and are now part of a political community. Major member countries include the United Kingdom, Australia, New Zealand, India, and Canada.

Commonwealth of Independent States The newly independent republics of the former Soviet Union except Estonia, Latvia, and Lithuania.

Communism The economic system whereby all factors of production are owned by the state in the name of the workers. Private ownership is nonexistent and competition is unacceptable. Individuals perform for the benefit of society rather than the individual.

Compatriots A fellow countryman. China considers Chinese overseas residents of Hong Kong, Taiwan, and Macau as compatriots.

Complementarity Production of goods or services by two or more places in a mutually beneficial fashion.

Coniferous A cone-bearing evergreen tree with needle leaves, straight trunks, and short branches.

Continent One of the major landmasses of the world; Africa, Antarctica, Asia, Australia, Europe, North America, and South America.

Continental Europe The countries of Europe that are on the continent.

Continental Islands The large islands of the Pacific stretching from the Southeast Asian mainland to Australia.

Continentality A characteristic of climate in large landmasses where the land heats and cools quickly, creating large daily and yearly changes in temperature.

Copper Belt The area of Zambia and Zaire that has a large concentration of copper.

Coptic The Christian Church of Egypt.

Coral Atoll A coral island or islands with a reef surrounding a lagoon.

Coral Reef A marine ridge or mound consisting of compacted coral.

Creole Persons born of European descent in the West Indies or Spanish America. The French patois is spoken by these people.

Crown Colony Colony of Great Britain.

Cruise Ships Luxury passenger ships in which the purpose is vacation and recreation in a given region of the world.

Cultural Centers Cultural attractions that display and maintain important cultural artifacts and ways of life.

Cultural Geography The study of peoples and their works, the site, situation, and specific time.

Cultural Hearth A region of origin for a group of people.

Cultural Links Ties and interactions between two cultures.

Currents The patterns or movements of air and water in a constant direction.

Czar The emperor in the former Russian Empire.

Daibutsu Great Buddha. A huge 700-year-old bronze image of Buddha.

Danube The major river of southeastern Europe.

Deccan Plateau A triangular plateau extending over most of peninsular India.

Deciduous A tree that loses its leaves at the beginning of winter or the start of the dry season.

Delta A flat, fertile lowland created by a river as it deposits its load of soil near the mouth when the water slows.

Demilitarized Zone An area wherein military control forces, weapons, and installations may not be established.

Demokratization The movement to democracy in the former Soviet Union.

Desert A region that is barren or partially barren and receives little or no rainfall.

Desert Pavement A relatively smooth area in a desert region with pebbles closely packed together to create a hard surface.

Developing The economic development of a country associated with industrialization and an improved standard of living for its people.

Double-cropping The planting, cultivation, and harvesting of two crops successively within a single year on the same farmland.

Druids A priestly caste of ancient Gaul and Britain that performs incantations and enchantments.

Druze A member of a religious sect in Syria and Lebanon whose primarily Muslim religion contains some elements of Christianity.

Eastern Orthodox Division of Catholicism derived from the church of the Byzantine Empire that acknowledges the primacy of the patriarch of Constantinople.

Economic The production, development, and management of material wealth of a country, household, or business enterprise.

Economic Colonialism The control of a less industrialized economy or businesses by companies in an industrialized country.

Ecotourism Tourism that is based on interest in nature and the environment.

Edo The early name of Tokyo during the Shogunate government in the 1600s.

English Channel A portion of the Atlantic Ocean between England and France, connected with the North Sea by the Strait of Dover.

Environment The total circumstances surrounding an organism or group of organisms, including physical, cultural, and social surroundings.

EU European Union. (*See* Common Market.)

Euronesians Persons of mixed European and Polynesian ancestry.

European Cities The major cities of Europe.

European Plain Low, flat, fertile area of Western Europe.

Excursionist A temporary visitor staying less than 24 hours in a country.

Fall Line The point in rivers on the coastal plain at which waterfalls occur, thus limiting navigation up stream. Cities and industrial centers are often located at the fall line.

Far East An area commonly including the Koreas, Japan, China, and the islands belonging to them. Sometimes used to refer to all of Asia east of Afghanistan.

Fens A low-lying, marshy land.

Fjord Narrow, steep-sided, elongated, and coastal valley deepened by glacier ice that has since melted away, allowing the sea to create an inlet. Found especially along the coasts of Norway, Alaska, and New Zealand where they are important tourist attractions.

Flood Plain The level, low valley floor bordering a river.

Folk Culture The way of life of a traditional society.

FONATUR Mexican State planning office; Fondo Nacional De Fomento al Turismo.

Forbidden City Palace of the former emperors of China in Beijing.

Friday Mosque Islamic mosques in which Friday prayers are held.

Gaelic The language of the Gaels. The Celtic language of the Irish and the Scottish Highlanders.

Game Reserve Area set aside by government legislation to protect and manage the habitat of wild animals. While preservation is a major goal, controlled accessibility by visitors for viewing, photographing, and in some cases hunting is also desired.

Game Viewing The national parks of Africa provide an opportunity for visitors to watch animals in a natural setting.

Gaming Official name for gambling entertainment, especially in the United States.

Gauchos An Argentine cowboy in the Pampas region.

Geographic Location Where something is permanently located; an area on a map.

Geography The study of the earth as the home of mankind.

Geomancy The belief that the earth has a spirit and can influence human activities.

Ghetto A section or quarter of a European city to which Jews were restricted. Also used to refer to slum areas of American cities or any poor section of a city whose population is dominated by a distinct ethnic group.

Ginza Major shopping street in Tokyo.

Glacial Drift Glacial deposits on the earth's surface.

Glacial Features Landscape features resulting from glaciation.

Glaciation An area which at one time was covered by glaciers.

Glacier-burst The breaking opening of glaciers.

Global Interdependence The dependency of countries and regions of the world upon each other for production of goods.

Glockenspiel Clock and tower in German-speaking countries.

Golden Triangle The area of India encompassing Delhi, Agra, and Jaipur; a major tourism region in India.

Gothic The architectural, painting, cultural, and literary style prevalent in Western Europe from the twelfth through the fifteenth centuries.

Grand Tour Itinerary of extended duration or relative luxury. Started in the eighteenth century for the sons of wealthy Western Europeans who traveled for some 3 years. Major destination was Florence, Italy.

Great Barrier Reef The extensive coral reef off the northeast coast of Australia.

Great Dividing Range The major mountain range of Australia located in the southeast of the continent.

Great Trek The Dutch, who settled South Africa, became in conflict with British. The Dutch, as a group, moved to the interior of South Africa.

Great Wall The Great Wall of China was completed about 200 B.C. It was built to protect China's eastern farmers from the pastoral herders of the Asian interior.

Greco-Roman Pertaining to the culture of both Greece and Rome.

Greek Islands The islands of the Aegean Sea and Mediterranean that are culturally and politically Greek.

Gulf Stream A warm ocean current of the North Atlantic issuing from the Gulf of Mexico and flowing east through the Straits of Florida, then northeast along the southeastern coast of the United States, then east to the North Atlantic current.

Hacienda A term referring to large estates in Latin America, commonly used in Mexico.

Hajj The pilgrimage to Mecca. The Islamic religion includes the belief that each believer should ideally make the pilgrimage at least once in his or her lifetime.

Hall of Fame Museum that honors outstanding individuals in a particular sport or endeavor.

Han The ethnic group referred to as Chinese.

Hanging Valley The valley of a tributary that enters a main river valley from a considerable height above the bed of the latter, and so forms rapids or waterfalls.

Hanseatic League A mercantile association of towns formed to control trading throughout Europe in the Middle Ages.

Health Resort Complex of facilities and natural features used by tourists interested in health-giving qualities, such as mineral waters, sun, air, exercise, and expert health personnel.

Hemisphere The northern or southern half of the earth as divided by the equator; the eastern or western half as divided by the Prime Meridian.

Hidden Economy The trading, bartering, buying, and selling of goods without a record for government accountability.

Himalayas A high mountain range in south central Asia.

Hinduism The religion of the majority of the population of India.

Historical Houses Houses preserved for historical purposes, frequently important for tourism.

HIV Human immunodeficiency virus. The virus associated with AIDS.

Holiday A day established by law or custom on which ordinary work is suspended; outside the United States, a vacation or time away from work.

Holy Week The week before Easter in Christianity.

Horn of Africa The area of Ethiopia and Somalia that extends out into the Indian Ocean.

Humid China The hot, humid area of eastern China.

Hurricanes Tropical cyclonic winds in excess of 75 miles per hour.

IATA (*See* International Air Transportation Association.)

Iberian Peninsula A 230,000-square-mile peninsula in Europe occupied by Spain and Portugal.

Ibero-European European people of the Iberian Peninsula or the influence of this region.

Impact Envisioned or actual consequences (negative or positive) of a decision. The impact may be economic, sociocultural, political, environmental, or other; direct or indirect; intended or not; favorable or unfavorable.

Indian Indigenous populations of North and South America.

Indian Markets Markets in Latin American countries with Indian populations. Usually held once a week, the market allows Indians to exchange, sell, and buy goods and products.

Industrial A highly developed industry.

Industrial Revolution The Industrial Revolution involved the substitution of machine power for muscle power sources, allowing production increases and creating a growth in demand for resources.

Industry A business employing labor, as the tourist industry.

Infrastructure Investments, such as utilities (water, sewer, electricity), transport (roads, harbors, airports), site development, health care, and schools.

Insularity An island or, by extension, being isolated like an island.

Interaction The relationship between places in terms of tourism, trade, etc., that creates joint action.

International Air Transportation Association (IATA) World association of international airlines. It promotes a unified system on international routes by setting fares, rates, safety standards, and the appointment of travel agents to sell international tickets.

International Date Line The line where the date changes by exactly one day as it is crossed. It is approximately 180 degrees West or East.

International Travel Itinerary involving the crossing of the border between countries, usually requiring some degree of formal permission or recognition.

Intervening Opportunities The substitution of a desired destination for a location similar but closer in time and cost.

INTOURIST The privatized travel agency of Russia and countries that were formerly part of the Soviet Union.

Invisible Exports Tourism, banking or other services that do not result in the export of goods.

Invisible Trade The flow of invisible exports and imports out of and into a country.

Iron Gate Gorges created by rock masses between the Hungarian Plain and the Wallachian Plain of the Danube River.

Islam Religion founded by the prophet Mohammed (Muhammad) in Saudi Arabia around 624 A.D. Islam is the name of the religion and means submission to the will of one God (Allah). Muslim or Moslem refers to a member, one who submits himself or herself to the will of Allah.

Islamic The Moslem religion.

Islamic Cities Cities that have developed according to Islamic beliefs and are in the Islamic cultural region.

Islamic Fundamentalism The movement among some Islamic faithful to return to more conservative Muslim beliefs, practices, and social-political systems.

Islamic Law Some countries of the Islamic World base their political and legal systems on the Koran, the holy book of Islam.

Islamic World The countries of North Africa, the Middle East, and South and Southeast Asia where the great majority of the people are Muslims.

Island A landmass that is smaller than a continent and surrounded by water.

Isolation The condition of being geographically cut off or far removed from mainstreams of thought and action. It also denotes a lack of receptivity to outside influences, caused at least partially by inaccessibility.

Jainism A branch of Hinduism that denies the existence of a perfect or supreme being.

Japan Alps The central mountain region of Japan.

Jet Age The era since the development and use of the jet engine.

Jewish Characteristic of the Jews, their religion, or their customs.

Jungle An area of dense vegetation and trees, normally referring to tropical like conditions.

Karst Topography A limestone region of hills, gullies, and valleys in which most or all of the drainage is by underground channels, the surface being dry and barren.

Kimono A long, loose, widesleeved Japanese robe, worn with a broad sash.

Koran The book of sacred writings of the Prophet Muhammad.

Kremlin The old walled fortress from which the czars ruled the Russian Empire. Now home to the government of Russia, it is also an important tourist attraction.

Lake A large inland body of fresh or salt water.

Lake Kinnereth Name given to the Sea of Galilee by the Israelis.

Landforms The configuration of the land surface into distinctive forms, such as hills, valleys, and plateaus.

Language Any method of communicating ideas by a system of symbolic sounds, or the corresponding written symbols where a written form of the language exists.

Latitude Angular distance north or south of the equator, measured in degrees, minutes, and seconds.

Leeward The side of an island or mountain that is opposite to the side that receives the prevailing winds.

Legal Systems A system of law.

Leisure Freedom from time-consuming duties, responsibilities, or activities; free time.

Lifestyle A person's way of life as indicated by the daily or regular activities of the person in clothing, food, drink, leisure, opinions, occupation, work, friendships, and the like. Lifestyle factors are a major influence on a person's tourism behavior and preferences.

Lingua Franca Refers to use of a second language spoken and understood by many peoples to overcome diversity of language in an area.

Location Where something is found.

Loch A lake, fjord, or arm of the sea in Scotland.

Loess Fertile soil created of fine dust deposited by wind.

Longitude Distance east or west of the meridian of Greenwich, measured in degrees, minutes, and seconds.

Lutheran A branch of Protestantism started by Martin Luther, common in Northern Europe and areas settled by migrants from this area.

Madrassa Islamic school or seminary training young men.

Maquiladoras Industrial plants established along the Mexican–United States border given special import and export considerations.

Maritime A climate characterized by moderate temperature, medium to high rainfall, and generally high humidity. Usually found along coasts.

Maritime Influence Of or relating to the influence of the ocean on countries with a maritime location.

Massif Central Plateau region of southeastern France.

Masurian Lake District Lake region in Poland.

Matai Chief of Samoan traditional society.

Matrilineal A society in which ancestry is traced through the female line.

Mayan World Circuit The countries of Mexico, Belize, Guatemala, Honduras, and El Salvador have begun joint marketing of the Mayan ruins in Middle America.

Mecca The most sacred city in Islam. Muslims face Mecca for daily prayers and make pilgrimages to the city.

Medieval (Middle Ages) Period of time in history from 700 A.D. to 1500 A.D.

Medina The site of the Prophet Muhammad's tomb in eastern Saudi Arabia.

Mediterranean The Mediterranean Sea, the region surrounding the sea, or the climatic type found in the area characterized by hot, dry summers and mild, warm winters that are excellent for coastal tourism.

Melanesians A cultural group of people who have very dark skins and dark hair.

Memorial An object or event designed to commemorate a person or event.

Meridians Great circles passing around the poles at right angles to the equator.

Mesa Central The southern half of the plateau region of Mexico containing the valleys of Mexico, Huamantla, Puebla, Toluca, Morelia, and Guadalajara.

Mesa del Norte The northern half of the Mexican plateau.

Mestizo An individual in Latin America whose parentage and lineage are composed of both European and Indian descent.

Mezzogiorno The southern part of Italy. An area economically behind northern Italy.

Micronesians Inhabitants of a small island group in the Pacific north of Melanesia and east of the Philippines.

Middle America The region from the northern Mexican border to the southern Panamanian border.

Middle Class People who occupy a social or economic position between the laboring class and those who are wealthy in terms of land or money.

Middle East The area in Asia and Africa between and including Morocco in the west, Pakistan in the east, Turkey in the north, and the Arabian Peninsula in the south.

Midnight Sun At high latitudes around midsummer the sun does not sink below the horizon and so may be seen at midnight.

Ming Tombs The burial tombs of the rulers during the Ming Dynasty (1364–1644).

Mobility The ability to travel easily and quickly.

Monsoon Technically refers to a seasonal reversal of winds, but it also brings heavy precipitation.

Moonscape A view or picture of the surface of the moon or, by extension, any desolate landscape.

Moors A Muslim people living mainly in northern Africa who invaded Spain in ancient times.

Mosque A Muslim house of worship.

Mt. Fuji The highest peak in Japan (12,388 ft), it is considered a sacred mountain. It is 70 miles west southwest of Tokyo.

Mt. Kenya The highest mountain in Kenya (17,058 feet).

Mt. Kilimanjaro Highest mountain in Africa (19,340 feet).

Mountains A mass of land considerably higher than its surroundings, and of greater altitude than a hill.

Muslim (Moslem) A follower of Islam.

Nation Refers to a group of people with a distinct culture that may or may not coincide with political boundaries.

National Museum A museum that contains several artifacts and documents of national interest, or a museum designated as the official repository of such items.

National Park Area designated by the federal government for public education and enjoyment. In some cases, such areas must be limited in access to preserve their unique qualities. Areas so designated are unique by reason of history, geological formations, or ecological resources.

National Trust An organization in Great Britain dedicated to the preservation of historical sites.

Nation-state A country whose population possesses a substantial degree of cultural homogeneity and unity. A political unit wherein the territorial state coincides with the area settled by a certain national group or people.

Nile A river in East and North Africa and the longest on the continent (3,405 miles).

North Atlantic Drift The relatively warm currents of the Atlantic resulting from the Gulf Stream.

Nucleated Settlements A closely packed settlement, village, or hamlet sharply demarcated from adjoining farmlands.

Oasis A fertile green spot in a desert created by a spring, well, or other local water source.

Oceania The islands of the South Pacific.

Office Ladies Japanese women who are single and work in offices.

Old Quarter The old part of a town, which characterizes the history of a town.

Orient The countries of the Asian continent, excluding Russia and the former states of the Soviet Union.

Orographic Precipitation Precipitation caused by an air mass being forced to cross a physical barrier, such as a mountain range.

Ottoman Referring to the empire centered on Turkey, 1299 to 1923 A.D.

Ottoman Empire The Turkish Empire from 1299 to 1919 in southwestern Asia, northeastern Africa, and southeastern Europe. The capital was Constantinople. Also known as the Turkish Empire.

Outback The arid interior of Australia.

Overseas Chinese Chinese who live outside of China.

Package Tour Any prearranged (usually prepaid) journey to one or more destinations and returning to the point of departure. Includes transportation, accommodations, meals, sightseeing, and other components of travel.

Pagan One who is not a member of an organized religion.

Pagoda A religious building of the Orient, such as an ornate Hindu temple or many-storied Buddhist tower.

Pampas The plains of South America extending for nearly 1,000 miles from the lower Parana River to south central Argentina. It is an important livestock-raising area.

Parallels Parallels of latitude are lines drawn round the earth parallel to the equator and may thus be described as approximate circles with the two poles as centers. The circles become smaller with increasing proximity to the poles.

Party Customer or group of customers to be serviced in the same way; members of the same tour group.

Patagonia Region in South America south of the Limay and Rio Negro rivers to the Strait of Magellan. It is barren tableland between the Andes and the Atlantic Ocean.

Patrilineal A society in which ancestry is traced through the male line.

Peninsula A long, narrow projection of land into water.

Peninsular Having the characteristics of a peninsula, as Europe is peninsular.

Perception The view or understanding of a place or people.

Perestroika Russian term meaning restructuring. One of the key ideas of the late 1980s that helped lead to the breakup of the Soviet Union.

Permafrost Permanently frozen water in the soil and bedrock, as much as 1,000 feet in depth, producing the effect of completely frozen ground. Generally found in high latitudes, it can thaw near the surface during the brief summer season.

Phoenician An inhabitant of ancient Phoenicia.

Pidgin A simplified language used to communicate in areas with numerous distinct languages.

Piedmont Hilly, rolling land, lying at the foot of a mountain range and forming a transition between mountain and plain.

Pilgrimage Travel to and for the purpose of visiting a location regarded as sacred by the traveler.

Pinyin Created by China's communist government to simplify the written form of the Chinese language throughout China.

Place Any specific site that can be recognized, as a town, house, etc.

Plateau Upland surface, more or less flat and horizontal, upheld by resistant beds of sedimentary rock or lava flows and bounded by a steep cliff.

Playa Lakes Shallow lakes in flat-bottomed desert basins. They are generally dry or small during the driest season, but expand or fill when it rains.

PLO Palestine Liberation Organization, founded in 1962 by displaced Arabs from Israel.

Po Valley The agricultural and industrial heartland of Northern Italy.

Polder Land adjacent to shore reclaimed from the sea by constructing dikes and pumping out the water.

Pollution Foreign matter placed into nature by human activity.

Polynesia An area east of Micronesia and Melanesia. It forms a triangle stretching from the Hawaiian Islands to Chile's Easter Island to New Zealand.

Population The total number of inhabitants of a particular race, group, or class in a specified area.

Population Density The number of people in a given area, usually a square mile or kilometer.

Port A place where goods are brought into and out of a country.

Poverty The condition of being poor. The lack of means to provide basic necessities of living.

Preexisting Forms The character of an area (physically and culturally) before changed as a result of tourism.

Prime Meridian Reference to meridian of zero longitude; normally accepted as the Greenwich Meridian.

Privatization The process of changing ownership of property from state ownership to private ownership.

Province A territory governed as an administrative or political unit or a country or empire.

Punic Of or relating to ancient Carthage.

Pyramid An ancient, massive monument with a broad base tapering to a point above. Found especially in Egypt and Mexico.

Qanat A gravity-fed underground irrigation tunnel in the Middle East.

Qing Zang The Tibetan Plateau.

Queues A term used in Britain, New Zealand, and Australia for a line of people waiting to purchase some service or product.

Racism The belief that one's own racial group is superior to others.

Rain Forest An area of dense broadleaf vegetation that receives heavy rainfall year-round.

Rainshadow Areas with low rainfall because they are on the leeward side of mountain ranges, which trap the moisture in air masses.

Region A specified area characterized by a common element; an area having naturally or arbitrarily assigned boundaries.

Relative Location Refers to location of a place or region with respect to other places or regions. Used interchangeably with situation.

Republic A political order that is not a monarchy.

Resort Geographic or business area offering a variety of facilities, services, and activities for the accommodation, use, and enjoyment of visitors.

Rift Valley Trench-like valley with steep, parallel sides; association with crustal spreading; East Africa's Rift Valley is the most famous.

Ring of Fire Volcanic mountain region encircling the Pacific Ocean.

River Valleys Valleys that have formed as a result of the rivers.

Riverine Located on or adjacent to a river.

Riverine Basins Basins formed as a result of rivers.

Riverine Population Concentrations The population clusters found in the river basins of the world.

Riviera A narrow coastal strip that is a famous resort area and extends along the Mediterranean Coast from Italy to France and includes the towns of Monte Carlo, Nice, and Cannes.

Roman Era A time period in history associated with the Roman Empire.

Romance Languages Languages that have developed from Vulgar Latin. The principal languages are French, Italian, Portuguese, Rumanian, and Spanish.

Royalty A person of royal lineage.

Safari Lodges Lodges built in game parks and reserves from which visitors travel to view game.

Sagas Poetry recounting the legends and beliefs of the pre-Christian Nordic-Germanic people who settled in Iceland.

Sahara The large desert of North Africa.

Sahel Semiarid zone across most of Africa between the southern margins of the arid Sahara and the moister savanna and forest zone to the south.

St. Lawrence Major river between United States and Canada.

Sami Native people of the Arctic regions of Scandinavia. Sometimes referred to as Lapps.

Sanctuaries A reserve area in which animals or birds are protected from hunting or other molestations.

Savanna The tropical regions of the world that have climates with seasonal wet and dry periods, or the grassland with scattered trees and bushes that characterizes this climate.

Scandinavia Geographically, it refers to the northwest European countries of Norway, Sweden, Denmark, and Iceland. Finland is often included, although it is not technically part of Scandinavia.

Sensible Temperature The temperature as "sensed" (felt) by the body. Ninety degrees with high humidity feels hotter than 90 degrees with low humidity.

Sephardim One of the two main divisions of Jews. A Spanish or Portuguese Jew or one of his descendants.

Serengeti A national park in Tanzania known for its abundant wildlife.

Sex Tourism Tourism in which prostitution, pornography, and related activities are important attractions.

Shatterbelt Region located between stronger countries (or cultural-political forces) that is recurrently invaded and/or fragmented by aggressive neighbors.

Shiite An Islamic minority concentrated in Iran and Syria. They believe the leader of Islam should be a direct descendent of Muhammad.

Shinto The aboriginal religion of Japan, marked by the veneration of nature spirits and of ancestors.

Shrine A sacred place.

Siberia A large region in Russia extending from the Ural Mountains to the Pacific Ocean.

Sikh Member of a religion concentrated in the Punjab region of northwest India. Members are characterized by the common surname Singh, and males wear long hair, a full beard, a turban, and a dagger.

Sikhism A religious group that developed on the interface between Islam and Hinduism in India.

Site The internal locational attributes of a place, including its local spatial organization and physical setting.

Situation The external locational attributes of a place; its relative location with reference to other places.

Skane A region in southern Sweden. A popular tourist destination region.

Slavic A group of languages or peoples living in Eastern Europe.

Social and Cultural The way of life of a group of people.

Socialism A variety of political and economic theories and systems of social organization based on collective or governmental ownership and distribution of goods.

South Asia The countries of Asia south of the Himalayas.

Southeast Asia The countries of Asia east of Myanmar to China and southeast to Papua New Guinea.

Southern Alps Chain of high, scenic mountains in New Zealand.

Soviet Russian term meaning a council.

Spa (*See* Health Resort.)

Spatial Interaction Interaction that occurs between two regions or places, such as trade or tourism.

State The formal name for the political units we commonly call countries.

Steppe Plains land forms with vegetation class consisting of short grasses sparsely distributed in clumps and bunches and some shrubs, widespread in areas of semiarid climate in continental interiors of North America and Eurasia; also called short-grass prairie.

Stupa A dome-shaped Buddhist shrine, often with a cupola on top.

Submergent Coast Coastal areas that have sunk.

Submergent Landforms Land areas that have sunk along coastal areas or river mouths, causing permanent flooding.

Subtropical Warm, humid areas on the eastern coasts of continents.

Sunni (Sunnite) The major religious division of Islam found in North Africa, Pakistan, and Indonesia.

Sun-Sea-Sand Coastal areas that have plentiful sun and sand are major attractors of tourists.

Suq (Souk) Market areas in Arabic towns filled with shops and eating establishments.

Swahili An African Bantu language of eastern and central Africa. It is widely used as a lingua franca.

Symbiotic Mutually beneficial relationships in which both parties in a relationship are better off than they would be if they were operating alone.

Taj Mahal The famed tomb in Agra, India, built between 1630 and 1652 by the emperor Shah Jahan for his second wife.

Taxes A contribution or levy for support of a government, or the fee charged members of an organization to support it.

Temple A sacred place of worship.

Territory An area of land; a district or region.

Tiananmen Square The major central square in Beijing, China. Around the square are the Forbidden City, Mao Zedong's mausoleum, and the People's Hall.

Tierra Caliente The hot coastal lowlands and piedmont (usually below 2,500 feet in elevation) in the Andes Mountains of Latin America.

Tierra Fría The cool upland elevations (usually above 6,000 feet) in the Andes Mountains of Latin America.

Tierra Templada The temperate middle elevations (usually between 2,500 and 6,000 feet) in the Andes Mountains of Latin America.

Time Zones The 24 longitudinal divisions of the earth's surface in which a standard time is kept. Each zone is 15 degrees of longitude in width, with local variations.

Tourist Any person traveling outside his or her normal commuting radius for the purpose of pleasure. A tourist is a person who has traveled away from home, is visiting other locations, and does not plan to relocate or stay away from home permanently.

Tourist Patrol Green patrol cars in Mexico that offer assistance to motorists in trouble.

Trade Unions A labor-specific union limited to people of that specific trade.

Transferability The level of ease or difficulty with which one can move from one place to another.

Transit Cities Cities where transit tourism is important. They are cities in which visitors change types of transportation or major directions when traveling.

Transportation The process of carrying passengers, goods, material, or the like.

Tribalism The practice of tribal religion.

Tropical A hot and humid area.

Tropical Rain Forest Vegetation of dense forest areas in the tropics.

Trust Territories A trust territory is a former colonial holding assigned by the United Nations to one of the industrialized nations for development assistance.

Trustee A person holding legal title to a property.

Tundra A zone between the northern limit of trees and the polar region in North America, Europe, and Asia. Tundra areas have only one summer month with an average temperature above freezing; their vegetation is composed of grasses, sedges, lichens, and shrubs.

Turkic A region or subdivision of the Middle Eastern area.

Tyrol A mountain region in Austria east of Salzburg.

Urban Pertaining to a city; city life.

Village Small town.

Visigoths Members of the western Goths that invaded the Roman Empire in the fourth century A.D. and settled in France and Spain, establishing a monarchy that lasted until the early eighth century A.D.

Volcanic Islands Islands that are volcanic in nature.

Vulcanism Volcanic activity or force. The movement of magma from the interior of the Earth to or near the surface.

Wafaku The traditional Japanese clothing of a long robe with sleeves, wrapped with a special sash.

Wat A Buddhist monastery and temple.

Wealth An abundance or large quantity of a valued resource or material possessions.

Welfare Health, happiness, and general well-being; relief work.

Welfare State A country that provides a general social service coverage for their citizens in education, health, and unemployment benefits.

Westerlies The prevailing winds at the middle latitudes flowing from the west to the east.

Western Culture Characteristics typical of the western hemisphere.

White Gold The idea that a white beach or excellent white snow is as valuable as gold for tourists.

Wilderness An unsettled, uncultivated area left in its natural condition.

Windward Area or side of a mountain, island, or other location that receives the prevailing winds directly.

World War II A war fought from 1939 to 1945 in which the United Kingdom, France, the Soviet Union, the United States, and other allies defeated Germany, Italy, and Japan.

Xerophytic A plant living in a region where little moisture is available. Its roots are long or enlarged, leaves are small and thick or lacking, as in cactus plants. The plant stores water for extremely long periods of time.

Yurt A circular, domed, portable tent used in Mongolia and by Mongols of Siberia.

GEOGRAPHY AND TOURISM
Bibliography

Chapter 1

Briassoulis, Helen, and van der Straaten, Jan. *Tourism and the Environment: Regional, Economic, and Policy Issues.* Boston: Kluwer Academic Publishers, 1992.

De Blij, Harm J., and Muller, Peter O. *Geography: Regions and Concepts, Eighth Edition.* New York: John Wiley & Sons, 1990.

Deneen, Sally. "Marketing Mother Nature." *Hotel & Motel Management,* Vol. 208 (1993): 25.

Fisher, James S. *Geography and Development: A World Regional Approach.* New York: Macmillan, 1992.

Getz, Donald. *Festivals, Special Events, and Tourism.* New York: Van Nostrand Reinhold, 1991.

Jackson, Richard H., and Hudman, Lloyd E. *World Regional Geography: Issues for Today, Third Edition.* New York: John Wiley & Sons, 1989.

Parker Pen Company. *Do's and Taboos around the World.* Elmsford, N. Y.: Benjamin, 1985.

Prentice, Richard. *Tourism and Heritage Attractions.* New York: Routledge, 1993.

Rogers, Alisdair. *Peoples and Cultures.* New York: Oxford University Press, 1992.

Smith, Valene L. *Hosts and Guests: The Anthropology of Tourism.* Philadelphia: University of Pennsylvania Press, 1989.

Chapter 2

Amory, Cleveland. *The Last Resorts.* Baton Rouge: Greenwood Press, 1952.

Ashman, Mike. "The Island Lifestyle: An Endangered Species." Paper read at Pacific Area Travel Association Workshop, April 1976, Kona, Hawaii.

Casson, Lionell. *Travel in the Ancient World.* London: George Allen & Unwin Ltd., 1974.

Fairburn, A.N. "The Grand Tour." *The Geographic Magazine,* Vol. 24 (1951): 118–27.

Feifer, Maxine. *Tourism in History: From Imperial Rome to the Present.* New York: Stein and Day, 1986.

Feldman, Joan. "The Jet Was the Catalyst for Prolonged Travel Boom." *Travel Weekly,* May 31, 1986: 124–28.

Franklin, John Hope. *A Southern Odyssey.* Baton Rouge: Louisiana State University Press, 1976.

Hudman, Lloyd E. "Inside the Packages." *The Sunday Times* (London), August 6, 1972.

Mathieson, Alister, and Wall, Geoffrey. *Tourism: Economic, Physical and Social Impacts.* London & New York: Longman, 1986.

Sinclair, M. Thea, and Stabler, Mike. *The Tourism Industry: An International Analysis.* Wallingford, Oxon, UK: C. A. B. International, 1991.

Smith, Valene L. *Hosts and Guests: The Anthropology of Tourism.* Philadelphia: University of Pennsylvania Press, 1989.

Waters, Somerset R. *The Travel Industry World Yearbook: The Big Picture 1995.* New York: Child & Waters, 1996.

Williams, J.E., and Zelinsky, W. "On Some Patterns of International Tourism Flows." *Economic Geography,* October 1970: 549–67.

World Tourism Organization. *Yearbook of Tourism Statistics.* Madrid: World Tourism Organization, 1997.

Chapter 3

"Canada." *International Tourism Reports.* London: The Economist, No. 1, 1996.

Canada. Greenville: Michelin, 1992.

Canadian Travel Survey: Canadians Traveling in Canada 1984. Ottawa: Statistics Canada, 1985.

Gatty, Bob. "Inbound Travel May Brighten Gloomy Economy." *Hotel & Motel Management,* Vol. 207 (1992): 14.

Jones, Oscar, and Jones, Joy. *Hippocrene U.S.A. Guide to Historic Hispanic America.* New York: Hippocrene Books, 1993.

Mobile Travel Guide. Englewood Cliffs, N.J.: Prentice Hall, 1996. (Series includes California and the West; Great Lakes; Middle Atlantic; Southeast; Southwest and South Central; Northwest and Great Plains; Northeast; and Frequent Traveler's Guide to Major Cities.)

1996 Road Atlas. Chicago: Rand McNally, 1996.

"*National Parks: Managing Paradise.*" *Economist,* Vol. 326 (1993): 31.

Tourism Tomorrow: Towards a Canadian Tourism Strategy. Ottawa: Minister of State (Tourism), undated.

Thum, Marcella. *Hippocrene U.S.A. Guide to Black America.* New York: Hippocrene Books, 1991.

Touriscope: 1995 International Travel. Ottawa: Ministers of Supply and Services Canada, Nov. 1995.

Tourism and Recreation: A Statistical Digest. Ottawa: Statistics Canada, 1986.

Tourism's Top Twenty: Fast Facts on Travel and Tourism. Washington, D.C.: U.S. Travel Data Center, 1992.

"United States." *International Tourism Reports.* London: The Economist, No. 3, 1991.

U.S. Data Travel Center. 1995 *National Travel Survey.* Washington, D.C.: U.S. Data Travel Center, 1994.

U.S. Data Travel Center *1986 National Travel Survey.* Washington, D.C.: U.S. Data Travel Center, 1987.

Waters, Somerset R. The *Travel Industry World Yearbook: The Big Picture 1996.* New York: Child & Waters, 1994.

World Tourism Organization. *Yearbook of Tourism Statistics.* Madrid: World Tourism Organization, 1997.

Chapter 4

"The Bahamas." *International Tourism Reports.* London: The Economist Publications Limited, No. 4, 1990.

"Cuba." *International Tourism Reports.* London: The Economist Publications Limited, No. 1, 1991.

"Dominican Republic." *International Tourism Reports.* The Economist Publications Limited, No. 1, 1990.

Farquharson, Mary. "Ecotourism: A Dream Diluted." *Business Mexico,* Vol. 2 (Jun. 1992): 8–11.

Hasek, Glenn. "Mexico Is Banking on Megaresorts." *Hotel & Motel Management,* Vol. 208 (Mar. 1993): 3.

"Jamaica." *International Tourism Reports.* London: The Economist Publications Limited, No. 3, 1988.

Jesitus, John. "New Caribbean Hot Spots Due to Emerge." *Hotel & Motel Management,* Vol. 207 (May 1992): 15–16.

Rowe, Megan. "Caribbean Tourism Hurting." *Lodging Hospitality,* Vol. 49 (Jan. 1993): 21.

"Travel & Leisure." *World Travel Overview 1987/1988.* New York: American Express Publishing Company, 1988.

"Trinidad and Tobago." *International Tourism Reports.* London: The Economist Publications Limited, No. 1, 1988.

Waters, Sommerset. *Travel Industry World Yearbook: The Big Picture.* New York: Child and Waters, 1996.

Wolff, Carlo, "Checking into Cuba." *Lodging Hospitality,* Vol. 48 (May 1992): 34–44.

World Travel Organization. *Yearbook of Tourism Statistics.* Madrid: World Tourism Organization, 1997.

Chapter 5

"Argentina." *International Tourism Reports.* London: The Economist Publications Limited, No. 4, 1987.

"Bolivia." *International Tourism Reports.* London: The Economist, No. 4, 1987.

The Cambridge Encyclopedia of Latin America and the Caribbean. Cambridge: Cambridge University Press, 1992.

Crowther, Geoff. *South America on a Shoestring.* Hawthorn, Australia: Lonely Planet Publications, 1990.

The Cultural Guide of Bolivia. La Paz, Bolivia: Fondación Cultural Quipus, 1990.

Devine, Elizabeth. *The Travelers' Guide to Latin American Customs and Manners.* New York: St. Martin's Press, 1988.

"Ecuador." *International Tourism Reports.* London: The Economist Publications Limited, No. 2, 1992.

Fodor's South America. New York: Fodor, 1993.

Handbook of Latin America. Gainesville: University of Florida Press, 1935–1993.

"Perú." *International Tourism Reports.* London: The Economist, No. 2, 1988.

Tips for Travelers to Central and South America. Washington D.C.: U.S. Department of State, 1989.

World Tourism Organization. *Yearbook of Tourism Statistics.* Madrid: World Tourism Organization, 1997.

Chapter 6

"Austria." *International Tourism Reports.* London: The Economist Publications Limited, No. 2, 1993.

"Belgium." *International Tourism Reports.* London: The Economist Publications Limited, No. 1, 1988.

"England and Wales." *International Tourism Reports.* London: The Economist Publications Limited, No. 2, 1986.

"France." *International Tourism Reports.* London: The Economist Publications Limited, No. 4, 1991.

Frommer's Europe '93 on $45 a Day. New York: Prentice Hall Traveler, 1993.

Let's Go: Europe. New York: St. Martin's Press, 1996.

Ludolph, Josephine. "The EC's Accomplishments in and Prospects for a Single Market in Services." *Business America,* Vol. 114 (May 1993): 6–10.

"Luxembourg." *International Tourism Reports.* London: The Economist Publications Limited, No. 3, 1993.

"Netherlands." *International Tourism Reports.* London: The Economist Publications Limited, No. 2, 1988.

"Scotland." *International Tourism Reports.* London: *The Economist,* 1994.

Tourism Policy and International Tourism in OECD Member Countries. Paris: Organization for Economic Co-Operation and Development, 1992.

Turpin, Kathryn S., and Saltzman, Marvin L. *Eurail Guide.* Malibu: Eurail Guide Annual, 1992.

"United Kingdom." *International Tourism Reports.* London: The Economist Publications Limited, No. 3, 1991.

"Germany." *International Tourism Reports.* London: The Economist Publications Limited, No. 2, 1994.

Western Europe on a Shoestring. Berkeley: Lonely Planet, 1993.

World Tourism Organization. *Yearbook of Tourism Statistics.* Madrid: World Tourism Organization, 1997.

Chapter 7

Fodor's Scandinavia 1993. New York: Fodor's Travel Publications, 1993.

"Scandinavia." *International Tourism Reports.* London: The Economist Publications Limited, No. 1, 1986.

Scandinavian & Baltic Europe on a Shoestring. Berkeley: Lonely Planet Publications, 1993.

Yearbook of Tourism Statistics. Madrid: World Tourism Organization, 1997.

Chapter 8

Anderson, James M. *Spain, 1001 Sights: An Archaeological and Historical Guide.* Calgary: University of Calgary Press, 1991.

Casas, Penelope. *Discovering Spain.* New York: Knopf, 1992.

"Cyprus." *International Tourism Reports.* London: The Economist Publications Limited, No. 24, 1992.

"Greece." *International Tourism Reports.* London: The Economist Publications Limited, No. 3, 1990.

Hudson, Kenneth. *The Cambridge Guide to the Museums of Europe.* New York: Cambridge University Press, 1991.

"Italy." *International Tourism Reports.* London: The Economist Publications Limited, No. 2, 1990.

Italy. Greenville, SC: Michelin Travel Publications, 1990.

Let's Go: The Budget Guide to Europe. New York: St. Martin's Press, 1993.

Mediterranean Europe on a Shoestring. Berkeley: Lonely Planet Publications, 1993.

"Portugal." *International Tourism Reports.* London: The Economist Publications Limited, No. 1, 1993.

"Spain." *International Tourism Reports.* London: The Economist Publications Limited, No. 4, 1990.

Trekking in Greece. Berkeley: Lonely Planet Publications, 1993.

Yearbook of Tourism Statistics. Madrid: World Tourism Organization, 1997.

Chapter 9

"Bulgaria." *International Tourism Reports.* London: The Economist Publications Limited, No. 2, 1993.

Fodor's Eastern Europe '93. New York, Fodor, 1993.

Insight Guides: Czechoslovakia. Boston: Houghton Mifflin, 1993.

Levine, Leonard. *Maverick Guide to Prague.* St. Gretna: Pelican Publishing Co., 1993.

"Poland." *International Tourism Reports.* London: The Economist Publications Limited, No. 1, 1992.

Senior, Robert. *The World Travel Market.* New York: Facts on File, 1982.

Stanley, David. *Eastern Europe on a Shoestring.* Berkeley: Lonely Planet, 1991.

Yearbook of Tourism Statistics. Madrid: World Tourism Organization, 1997.

"Yugoslavia." *International Tourism Reports.* London: No. 4,1988.

Chapter 10

Insight Guide: Russia. New York: Houghton Mifflin, 1993.

Jackson, Richard H., and Hudman, Lloyd E. *World Regional Geography: Issues for Today.* New York: John Wiley & Sons, 1990.

Khodorkov, L. R., and Avdania, N. V. "Geography of Foreign Tourism in the USSR." *Geography and Recreation.* Moscow: 23d International Geographical Congress, 1976.

"Russia." *International Tourism Reports.* London: The Economist Publications Limited, No. 3, 1997.

Smirnov, V. I. "The Present State and Prospects of Development of Tourism and Excursions in the USSR." *Geography of Tourism and Recreation.* Moscow: 23d International Geographical Congress, 1976.

"USSR." *International Tourism Reports.* London: The Economist Publications Limited, No. 1, 1992.

World Tourism Organization. *Yearbook of Tourism Statistics.* Madrid: The World Tourism Organization, 1997.

Chapter 11

"Egypt." *International Tourism Reports.* London: The Economist Publications Limited, No. 1, 1991.

Fodor's Jordan and the Holy Land. New York: Fodor's Travel Publications, 1989.

Hansen, Kathy. *Egypt Handbook.* Chico: Moon Publications, 1993.

"Jordan." *International Tourism Reports.* London: The Economist Publications Limited, No. 3, 1992.

Ministry of Tourism. *Tourism and Hotel Services Statistics Quarterly.* Tel Aviv: Government Publishing House, No. 4, January 1987.

"Morocco." *International Tourism Reports.* London: The Economist Publications Limited, No. 3, 1993.

Parnes, Sharone. "Israel Sets Sights on U.S. Tourists." *Advertising Age,* Vol. 63 (1992): 3-4.

Tilbury, Neil. *Israel: A Travel Survival Kit.* Berkeley: Lonely Planet Publications, *1992.*

Ritter, Wigano. "Recreation and Tourism in the Islamic Countries." *Ekistics,* Vol. 40 (July 1975): 56-59.

"Tunisia." *International Tourism Reports.* London: The Economist Publications Limited, No. 4, 1988.

Wayne, Scott. *Adventuring in North Africa: The Sierra Club Travel Guide to Morocco, Algeria, Tunisia, and the Maltese Islands.* San Francisco: Sierra Club Books, 1991.

World Tourism Organization. *Yearbook of Tourism Statistics.* Madrid: World Tourism Organization, *1997.*

Chapter 12

Bechky, Allen. *Adventuring in East Africa.* San Francisco: Sierra Club Books, 1990.

Crowther, Geoff. *Africa on a Shoestring.* Berkeley: Lonely Planet Publications, 1989.

Dieke, Peter. "Tourism in the Gambia: Some Issues in Development Policy." *World Development*, Vol. 21 (1993): 77–89.

"The Gambia." *International Tourism Reports*. London: The Economist Publications Limited, No. 3, 1990.

Insight Guides: Namibia. Boston: Houghton Mifflin, 1993.

"Seychelles." *International Tourism Reports*. London: The Economist Publications Limited, No. 43, 1992.

Trillo, Richard. *The Real Guide. Kenya.* New York: Prentice Hall, 1989.

World Travel Organization, *Yearbook of Tourism Statistics.* Madrid: World Travel Organization, 1997.

"Zimbabwe." *International Tourism Reports*. London: The Economist Publications Limited, No. 3, 1992.

Chapter 13

Annual Statistical Report, 1987. Pacific Asia Travel Association, 1990.

"China." *International Tourism Reports*. London: The Economist Publications Limited, No. 3, 1990.

Cummings, Joe. *China.* Berkeley: Lonely Planet Publications, 1991.

Chon, Kye-Sung, and Hyun-Ju Shin. "Korea's Hotel and Tourism Industry." *Cornell H. R. A. Quarterly*, Vol. 31 (1) (1990): 69–73.

"Hong Kong." *International Tourism Reports*. London: The Economist Publications Limited, No. 1, 1992.

Hong Kong Travel Trade Manual 1988. Hong Kong: Hong Kong Tourist Association, 1988.

Kinoshita, June, and Palevsky, Nicholas. *Gateway to Japan.* New York: Kodansha America, 1992.

Korea: The Best Kept Secret in Asia. Seoul: Korea National Tourism Corporation, 1986.

Lianhua, Zhang. *Continue to Improve and Develop the Work of China International Travel Service.* Beijing: China International Travel Service, 1983.

Nilsen, Robert. *South Korea Handbook.* Chico, Calif.: Moon Publications, 1988.

Rapoport, Roger, and Wiles, Burl. *2 to 22 Days in Asia: The Itinerary Planner.* New York: John Muir Publications, 1993.

"South Korea." *International Tourism Reports*. London: The Economist Publications Limited, No. 2, 1990.

"Taiwan." *International Tourism Reports*. London: The Economist Publications Limited, No. 2, 1986.

Travel Manual: Japan 1988-89. Tokyo: Japan National Tourist Organization, 1988.

Yearbook of Tourism Statistics. Madrid: World Tourism Organization, 1997.

Yu, Lawrence. "Emerging Markets for China's Tourism Industry." *Journal of Travel Research*, Vol. 31 (1) (1992): 10–13.

Chapter 14

Armington, Stan. *Trekking in the Nepal Himalay.* Berkeley: Lonely Planet, 1991.

Caplen, Brian. "Indonesia: Planners Work on Green Gold." *Asian Business*, Vol. 29 (1993): 22–23.

Dalton, Bill. *Indonesia Handbook.* Chico, Calif.: Moon Publications, 1991.

"India." *International Tourism Reports*. London: The Economist, No. 2, 1991.

"Maldives." *International Tourism Reports*. London: The Economist Publications Limited, No. 2, 1987.

"Nepal and Bhutan." *International Tourism Reports*. London: The Economist Publications Limited, No. 1, 1991.

Pacific Asia Travel Association PATA Annual Statistical Report 1991. San Francisco: Pacific Asia Travel Association, 1992.

Richardson, Derk. *2 to 22 Days in Thailand: The Itinerary Planner.* Sante Fe: John Muir Publications, 1993.

"Singapore." *International Tourism Reports*. London: The Economist Publications Limited, No. 4, 1986.

Sesser, Stan. *The Lands of Charm and Cruelty.* New York: Random House, 1993.

Spitzer, Dan. *Fielding's Budget Asia, Southeast Asia, and the Far East.* New York: Fielding Travel Books, 1990.

Tsui, John F. "Vietnam: The Last Tourism Frontier." *World Development*, Vol. 49 (1993): 24.

"Thailand." *International Tourism Reports*. London: The Economist Publications Limited, No. 3, 1988.

Wheeler, Tony. *Bali & Lombok, A Travel Survival Kit.* Berkeley: Lonely Planet, 1992.

World Tourism Organization. *Yearbook of Tourism Statistics.* Madrid: World Tourism Organization, 1997.

Chapter 15

"Australia." *International Tourism Reports.* London: The Economist Publications Limited, No. 4, 1990.

Bone, Robert W., and Voltz, Keven. *Maverick Guide to Australia.* St. Gretna, La.: Pelican, 1993.

Carter, John. *Pacific Islands Yearbook: Fourteenth Edition.* New York: Pacific Publications, 1981.

"Fiji." *International Tourism Reports.* London: The Economist Publications Limited, No. 2, 1988.

Jarrett, Ian. "Scramble for Tourists." *Asian Business,* Vol. 29 (1993): 61-62.

Kay, Robert F. *Tahiti and French Polynesia Travel Survival Kit.* Berkeley: Lonely Planet, 1993.

"New Zealand." *International Tourism Reports.* London: The Economist Publications Limited, No. 2, 1990.

New Zealand Official Yearbook, 1992. Wellington: Department of Statistics, 1992.

Pacific Asia Travel Association. *Annual Statistical Report, 1990.* San Francisco: Pacific Asia Travel Association, 1990.

Wheeler, Tony. *Islands of Australia's Great Barrier Reef.* Berkeley: Lonely Planet, 1993.

Wigglesworth, Zeke and Joan. *Fielding's New Zealand.* New York: Fielding, 1993.

White, Kenneth. "Comparative Tourism Development in Asia and the Pacific." *Journal of Travel Research,* Vol. 31 (1992): 14–23.

World Tourism Organization. *Yearbook of Statistics.* Madrid: World Tourism Organization, 1997.

Index

Bold page numbers indicate a reference in a chart or table or other extra-text source

338.4   Hudman, Lloyd E.
Hud
          Geography of travel &
          tourism.

DATE			